Sixties British Pop, Outside In

Sixties British Pop, Outside In

Volume 1: Downtown, 1956–1965

GORDON ROSS THOMPSON

OXFORD
UNIVERSITY PRESS

OXFORD
UNIVERSITY PRESS

Oxford University Press is a department of the University of Oxford. It furthers
the University's objective of excellence in research, scholarship, and education
by publishing worldwide. Oxford is a registered trade mark of Oxford University
Press in the UK and certain other countries.

Published in the United States of America by Oxford University Press
198 Madison Avenue, New York, NY 10016, United States of America.

© Oxford University Press 2024

All rights reserved. No part of this publication may be reproduced, stored in
a retrieval system, or transmitted, in any form or by any means, without the
prior permission in writing of Oxford University Press, or as expressly permitted
by law, by license, or under terms agreed with the appropriate reproduction
rights organization. Inquiries concerning reproduction outside the scope of the
above should be sent to the Rights Department, Oxford University Press, at the
address above.

You must not circulate this work in any other form
and you must impose this same condition on any acquirer.

Library of Congress Cataloging-in-Publication Data
Names: Thompson, Gordon, 1949– author.
Title: Sixties British pop, outside in / Gordon Ross Thompson.
Description: New York, NY : Oxford University Press, 2024. |
Includes bibliographical references and index.
Identifiers: LCCN 2024015134 (print) | LCCN 2024015135 (ebook) |
ISBN 9780190672348 (hardback ; volume 1) | ISBN 9780190672386 (hardback ; volume 2) |
ISBN 9780190672355 (paperback ; volume 1) | ISBN 9780190672393 (paperback ; volume 2) |
ISBN 9780190672362 (volume 1) | ISBN 9780190672409 (volume 2) |
ISBN 9780190672379 (epub ; volume 1) | ISBN 9780190672416 (epub ; volume 2) |
ISBN 9780197638248
Subjects: LCSH: Popular music—Great Britain—1961–1970—History and criticism.
Classification: LCC ML3492 .T565 2024 (print) | LCC ML3492 (ebook) |
DDC 781.640941/09046—dc23/eng/20240403
LC record available at https://lccn.loc.gov/2024015134
LC ebook record available at https://lccn.loc.gov/2024015135

DOI: 10.1093/oso/9780190672348.001.0001

Paperback printed by Marquis Book Printing, Canada
Hardback printed by Bridgeport National Bindery, Inc., United States of America

For Jane, Katie, Annie, & Meg

Contents

Preface: Outside In ix

Introduction: The Music between Us 1

PART I BEFORE THE FLOOD, 1950–1962

1. Common Roots 17
2. First Responders 31
3. Channeling English Pop 44
4. Behind the Stars 60
5. Beatle Beginnings 72

PART II A DOOR OPENS, 1963

6. The Beatles: Outside In 89
7. Northwest Passage 103
8. Capital Connections 115
9. Where Stones Roll 129

PART III FRONTIERS, 1964

10. Consuming the Beatles 143
11. Northern Waves 156
12. Middle English 171
13. An Independents Movement 185

PART IV THE FEMININE MUSIQUE

14. The Problem That Has No Name 201
15. Women: The Next Wave 223

PART V TRANSITIONS, 1964–1965

16. Scenes	245
17. Down the Road a Piece	263
18. Meet the Rolling Stones	283
19. Modifications	296
20. Uncommon Folk	309
Epilogue	323
Volume 1 Discography	331
Volume 1 Media Sources	409
Volume 1 References	425
Song Index	443
Subject Index	449

Preface: Outside In

I failed to appreciate what I was starting when I first proposed teaching a course on sixties British pop. In Skidmore College's Music Department, I taught courses on music and culture, and on the musics of South Asia, and as the director of the Asian Regional Studies Program I advised students preparing to study in Japan, China, or India. With those qualifications, the College invited me to advise our students in the UK, where I would also be required teach a course tailored to that location. The associate dean suggested a course on London as a center of intercultural exchange. I chose to focus on sixties British pop.

As a Canadian musician living across from Detroit in the sixties, I had been interested in British pop and had collected records, read interviews, and played in bands that had selectively covered this music, but my knowledge was predictably uneven. In preparation for the course, I began building an online chronology around record releases and performance dates, spent innumerable hours reading publications such as the *New Musical Express* on microfilm, and compared what I found with contemporary social, political, and economic events. I wanted to show these musicians and their music in their cultural context.

I spent my five-month stint at Regents College, London, in January 1996 collecting books and recordings to prepare for classes. Fan-oriented material and biographies were plentiful and could be entertaining, but verifiable, well-researched, and objective sources were thin on the ground. Mark Lewisohn's publications on the Beatles offered one way to organize the chaos, but my objective was to help students (and myself) understand the broader cultural environment. My research orientation favors listening to individuals and contextualizing their memories, and, although attempts to contact the "stars" often proved futile, others were happy to share their stories.

Since that semester, I have continued to interview musicians, songwriters, music directors, producers, and engineers. Supplementing those conversations, writers in the *New Musical Express, Melody Maker, Disc, Record Retailer and Music Industry News*, and other contemporary publications have provided a sense of how the culture understood itself. My first book, *Please Please Me: Sixties British Pop, Inside Out* (2008) derives from that research and offers an introduction to this music culture. This book expands on that work.

Outside Looking In

Some readers may come to this book expecting a history of British pop. If so, you will not be completely disappointed; but my approach is informed by ethnography and its goals of achieving an "understanding of local knowledge, values, and practices from the 'native's point of view'" (Howell 2018). Ethnographic analysis is "inductive and builds upon the perspectives of the people studied" by focusing on the "beliefs, values, rituals, customs, and behaviors of individuals interacting within socioeconomic, religious, political, and geographic environments" (American Anthropological Association 4 June 2004). In addition to observations and interviews, ethnographers analyze texts and audio-visual materials while considering the ethical implications of their work. I take the same approach, intending neither to praise nor to denigrate. My goal is to contextualize the era to show the relationships between the currents of sixties British pop and how they reflected the evolving world of postwar UK society. This approach, however, is not without its pitfalls.

The stories participants tell have inherent biases, and their reconstructions can contradict each other and material evidence. In the sixties, when press agents looked for ways to gain coverage for their clients, reality and fiction often blurred, and when individuals now recall events, stories blur. One individual assured me that what they were telling me was the real story, not a Rashōmon world of conflicting accounts. Of course, in the film *Rashōmon* (1950) we do learn what happened, but only by piecing together different versions to understand their perspectives.

Popular culture provides an active forum in which sectors of a society can challenge, confirm, or reject core social values while entertaining new ideas. Culture is always in flux, but mass media gives commerce a greater role in a conversation traditionally dominated by religion and government. That environment, while requiring a degree of predictability, also finds individuals searching for ideas and technologies that give them advantages. That interplay between stasis and volatility also underlies popular music culture.

An Ethnomusicology of Sixties British Pop

Ethnomusicology embraces and respects the breadth of humanity's capacity to communicate through sound. Its interest in understanding what that says about us has routinely clashed with the ethnocentricity inherent in programs designed to preserve the preferential status of musics and musicians associated with elite White traditions.[1] In addition to its disdain for non-Western culture,

---

[1] For example, when I was an adjunct professor early in my career, a chair called me into his office and warned me against being a cultural fifth columnist (a seditionist) in the department.

the academic music establishment also fears popular music as a threat to the privileges it has enjoyed. Thus, both ethnomusicology and sixties British pop stand apart from the core of the Western academic music canon.

Ethnomusicology can generate numerous questions applicable here. For example, who was involved in the creation of a performance and/or recording and what did they contribute? What were their backgrounds? What were their models and how did they learn them? Second, who were the intended and eventual audiences? What roles did performances and recordings play in connecting musicians and audiences? What were the intrasocial relationships between performers and between performers and their audiences? Third, what were the material and performative symbolic elements? What did music mean to musicians and their audiences? Fourth, where did music performance and listening occur? How did these contexts shape the creation, experience, and interpretation of music? Fifth, how did this music reflect core English/British values? What appealed to youth culture and did this contribute to changes in English/British behavior? How did the technology of this culture shape music-making? And finally, who were the mediators (the curators) between the creators and the consumers? How did they shape the creative and the experiential processes? Obviously, this work cannot address everything, but these questions have shaped my approach.

Acknowledgments

You would not be reading this book had not Skidmore College sent me to live and teach in London in 1996, 2007, and 2016 and provided several grants to fund research trips and to cover photo permissions. The courses, lectures, papers, and publications I developed from those residencies and the questions that my students and others have asked inform my approach. Special thanks go to Joe Klockowski for permission to use his cover image of four musicians, which he designed as a student for Skidmore College's annual Beatlemore Skidmania concerts.

My research has benefited from interviews and conversations with many individuals, including Malcolm Addey, Eric Allen, Sterling Ball, James Baring, Stan Barrett, Andy Bennett, Dave Berry, Charles Blackwell, Vic Briggs, Joe Brown, Joel Brown, John Carter, Clem Cattini, John Clarke, Bill Covington, Bryan Daly, Roger Dean, Tim Dove, Dawn Eden, Bob Efford, Danny Fields, Matthew Fisher, Vic Flick, Herbie Flowers, Mo Foster, Graham Gouldman, Bobby Graham, Arthur Greenslade, Bill Harry, John Hawken, Les Hurdle, Nazir Jairazbhoy, Viram Jasani, Nita Katz, Jody Klein, Peter Knight, Jr., Derek Lawrence, Spencer Leigh, Carlo Little, Dave Maswick, Joe Moretti, David Morgan, Mitch Murray, Tony Newman, Margo Quantrell, Jon Ramsey, Les Reed, Jon Renbourn,

Steve Rowland, John Schroeder, Ken Scott, Arthur Sharp, Norman Smith, Geoff Stephens, Jim Sullivan, Shel Talmy, Ronnie Verrell, John Warburg, Pip Wedge, John Weider, Allan Weighell, Michael Weighell, Andy White, Chris Wright, and others. Thanks also to Llora Jean Miller, who, as my student assistant, transcribed many of the interviews.

I would be remiss if I did not also acknowledge the music journalists from whose work I have drawn: Keith Altham, Derek Boltwood, Maureen Cleave, Ray Coleman, Louise Criscione, Bob Dawbarn, Richard Green, David Griffiths, June Harris, Tom Hibbert, Dawn James, Peter Jones, Norman Jopling, William Mann, Barry Miles, Chris Roberts, Alan Smith, Penny Valentine, Alan Walsh, Chris Welch, Jan Wenner, and the anonymous contributors to the trade papers. Their contemporary reviews and interviews provide us with insights into how artists and the trade thought about pop music, albeit while navigating the flotsam and jetsam provided by publicity agents. I have also benefited from the more recent insightful work of Spencer Leigh, Johnny Black, Peter Frame, and Johnny Rogan.

Many thanks to John Anzalone, Margaret Sarkissian, Paul McGrath, and the anonymous readers who read and commented on drafts. Thanks also to Suzanne Ryan, Norman Hirschy, Egle Zigaite, and Gwen Colvin at Oxford University Press, who have shepherded this project through its various stages. In addition, I am indebted to Roger Dopson for plying me with recordings and publications over the years. Finally, my wife, Jane Thibodeau Thompson, read multiple drafts and offered sanguine advice during this project's long gestation. Kudos to you.

Dear Reader: When I began this project, Suzanne Ryan advised me to write in a way that appealed both to academics and to the general reader by telling stories. This "academic trade" path requires presenting material in a way that meets the critical standards of scholarship, that is written in language understandable to laypeople, and that introduces new ideas or approaches to both audiences.

One of my models, Kate Fox's *Watching the English* (2004/2014), balances research with accessibility, albeit with some controversy. Although acknowledging that her approach was outside the conventions of the discipline, David Mills in *Anthropology Today* (April 2006) suggests that her book represents "public anthropology," while Keith Hart (June 2006) describes it as "popular anthropology." One of my goals is to apply ethnomusicological approaches in similar ways that both inform and remain accessible. For academics, I attempt to show how sixties British pop reflected contemporary cultural trends.

For the faithful and obsessive fans of this music and for those just learning about it: this book is not a comprehensive survey. Most overviews of this music fragment the culture into discrete, detailed stories that highlight individual musicians or groups. This book contains many such stories. My goal, however, is to select stories that highlight the *culture* that produced these musicians and recordings, as it evolved from peripheral imitation to innovative international prominence.

Introduction: The Music between Us

Everything felt new: new sounds, new clothing, new hair styles, new feelings, new attitudes. The attraction of sixties British pop lay in its eagerness to seize the present before it escaped into predictability.[1] Best of all, that newness frightened adults.

British pop artists flooded international markets in the mid-1960s, supported by a network of producers, engineers, music directors, arrangers, songwriters, publishers, broadcasters, managers, agents, journalists, and session and stage musicians. A transatlantic wave of postwar births generated adolescent audiences eager to embrace this music as representative of the changes under way in their everyday life. Together, they transformed London from a pop-music outpost in the grip of economic stagnation into a trendsetting cosmopolitan hub.

London's role as a postcolonial capital brought together musical, timbral, and textual ideas from around the world, which British musicians reimagined in the context of midcentury tectonic shifts in technology, demography, economics, and politics. Underlying this cultural integration, Britain's and particularly England's deep-seated attitudes regarding humor, class, gender, ethnicity, age, fairness, shaped the recordings, the music, and audience reactions. Inherent in this process, Britain's urban and suburban, public and private places and spaces—its pubs, clubs, dance halls, concert halls, and studios—served as the sonic and social vessels forming this musical environment.

Numerous publications atomize this scene into individual detailed biographical and institutional vignettes. These two volumes attempt to place these many stories on a single evolving stage to show how this culture adapted to the realities of the postwar world. Three major vectors apply: demographics (age, gender, ethnicity, class, etc.), culture (English-British culture, transatlantic culture, technology, etc.), and location (space and place).

---

[1] I use the term "pop" to describe all "commercial popular music" intended to be both "accessible" and "tuneful" (*The Oxford Dictionary of English*, 2010).

Sixties British Pop, Outside In. Gordon Ross Thompson, Oxford University Press. © Oxford University Press 2024.
DOI: 10.1093/oso/9780190672348.003.0001

Britain in the 1960s

Arthur Marwick in his seminal work *The Sixties: Cultural Revolution in Britain, France, Italy, and the United States* (1998) demarcates the period as beginning around 1958 and extending to 1974, dividing it into the periods 1958–1963 ("First Stirrings"), 1964–1969 (the "High Sixties"), and 1969–1974 ("Catching Up") (1998, 7). Dominic Sandbrook gives a more limited definition of the sixties describing the period in two volumes: *Never Had It So Good* (2005) encompasses 1956–1964 and *White Heat* examines 1964–1970 (2006). And Virginia Nicholson adheres strictly to the years 1960–1969 in her stinging *How Was It for You: Women, Sex, Love and Power in the 1960s* (2019).

Marwick, Nicholson, and other historians characterize the sixties as an era of change. Even Dominic Sandbrook (2005, xxiv–xxv), who emphasizes continuity with adjacent decades, observes that individuals *believe* that they experienced significant change. For this current study, the years 1956–1970—beginning with the Suez Canal Crisis and the rise of rock 'n' roll and ending with the Labour Party's electoral defeat and the dissolution of the Beatles—serve as benchmarks. Reflecting cultural trends, volume 1 covers the years 1958–1965; volume 2 covers 1964–1970.

The Contexts

At the close of the nineteenth century, Britannia ruled the waves, the sun never set on her empire, and her factories hummed productively. These halcyon years, however, depended on the subjugation of peoples and the exploitation of colonial resources, as well as often dangerous and demeaning working conditions at home. By the middle of the twentieth century, a global financial depression and two world wars had fundamentally undermined Britain's economy and its international status.[2] What Germany's Luftwaffe and rockets had not lain to waste, postwar economic shortages had set to rot as successive British governments struggled to balance budgets and to rebuild the nation. In the meanwhile, like Rome to Athens, the US economy superseded Britain to dominate global markets with its exports of cars, films, food, and, of course, pop music.

One of the most powerful weapons in the American arsenal did not rest on the nose of a missile but instead in its role as the world's financier. Perhaps most prominently, the framers of the European Recovery Plan (1948–1952) (the

---

[2] Britain had borrowed heavily to sustain its war effort in the 1940s, finally closing its debts at the end of 2006 with "payments of $83.25m (£42.5m) to the US and US$22.7m (£11.6m) to Canada" that were "the last of 50 instalments since 1950" (BBC News, 29 December 2006).

"Marshall Plan") recognized the lessons of World War I by underwriting the reconstruction of Western Europe both to discourage fascism and to establish a bulwark against the Soviet Union's political and military ambitions. Britain received about a quarter of these funds, with the rest divided among France, West Germany, Italy, the Netherlands, and others.[3]

The Empire Strikes Back. With the decline of Britain's international power came the dissolution of her empire. Civil servants and members of security forces who had spent their lives in British outposts now returned to a mother country that their children had never known. Others headed to Canada or Australia, joined by British emigrants escaping bomb-devastated cities. Indeed, so many emigrated from Britain in the latter half of the twentieth century that more individuals left the UK than arrived (Sandbrook 2005, 308).

At the end of the 1940s and during the 1950s in response to this exodus, Britain invited Commonwealth immigrants to help rebuild the nation. As incentive, Clement Attlee's Labour government passed the *British Nationality Act of 1948* to allow citizens of the Commonwealth and British colonies the right to UK citizenship. Britain's role in international commodities exchange and manufacturing had already created pockets of ethnic diversity in every major British city, as had her pivotal role in the slave trade up until the early nineteenth century. The postwar arrival of tens of thousands of Commonwealth citizens from South Asia, Africa, and the Caribbean, however, began to challenge the conceit of a predominantly White Britain.

Landlords such as Peter Rachman profited by renting to these immigrants, crowding them into neighborhoods such as Notting Hill and Brixton in London and Toxteth in Liverpool. Eventually, these communities established conduits for the music they preferred, which also attracted White youth who sought the excitement of these neighborhoods. Others, however, reacted violently.

With a downturn in the economy in August 1958, violence erupted in the Saint Ann's district of Nottingham in the British Midlands. Simmering community tensions broke into violence when West Indians responded to racist taunts from groups of jeering Whites (see Pressly 2007). A week later, a second wave of riots broke out in the Notting Hill district of London (see Travis 2002). In both cases, working-class "Teddy Boys" played a prominent role in confrontations with Caribbean immigrants.

Members of Oswald Mosley's Union Movement, the successor to his British Union of Fascists, incited the Teds—who were too young to have served in the war but old enough to have experienced its violence—by stoking fears of

---

[3] The American-based International Monetary Fund and World Bank (both established in 1945) also sought to stabilize economies through loans and subsidies. Britain was both a member of these organizations and a significant beneficiary.

miscegenation and lost jobs (see Olden 2008). Waves of xenophobic agitation eventually led Harold Macmillan's Conservative government to pass the Commonwealth Immigration Act of 1962 to restrict immigration.

Nevertheless, many members of the generation born in the postwar years embraced ethnic and cultural diversity. As the sixties dawned, confidence gradually returned to Britain and these youth began transforming clubs, church halls, and dance halls into their spaces.

Globalization and the British "Invasion"

Although jazz had long been part of America's rising cultural hegemony, the 1950s brought rock 'n' roll, thrilling British teens even as it frightened their parents, guardians, and institutional custodians. In the vanguard of this attack, Bill Haley's "Rock around the Clock" topped British charts at the beginning of 1956, and when a film of the same name played in cinemas later that year, youth danced in the aisles and ripped seats. His records returned to British charts at the beginning of 1957 as he commenced his first UK tour. By then, however, Americans Little Richard, Guy Mitchell, the Platters, Fats Domino, Johnny Ray, and, of course, Elvis Presley were also competing in that market.

British musicians attempted to duplicate the confidence and exuberance they heard in American recordings, but their earliest attempts usually paled in comparison to the originals. Eventually, however, they created hybrids that paid homage to their sources while reflecting the contexts in which they performed. By the mid-1960s, American adolescents proved as discerning consumers of the British "invasion" as their UK counterparts had been of American blues, rhythm and blues (R&B), rock 'n' roll, jazz, and pop.

Invasions. One of the most common American-centric clichés of twentieth-century music, the notion of a "British Invasion" in pop music derives from the success of recordings by the Beatles and other British performers. These may have elicited surprise in the United States (if not the UK), but their arrival in America had precedents in Sony transistor radios from Japan, Volkswagen Beetles from West Germany, and film and theater from Britain. Rapid technological developments in recording, broadcasting, and playback as well as in transportation helped change the way the world engaged with music (see Thompson 2008).

The roots of American surprise at the success of British pop lay in arrogance. American popular music, piggybacking on American political, economic, and military power, had grown ubiquitous in Western listening habits. As Britain saw its status decline as a world power, American popular culture grew to be a major influence on everyday British life. In addition to Hollywood films and television shows, rock 'n' roll in the mid-1950s confirmed America's ascendance as Britain struggled to offer a competitive response.

As the 1960s unfolded, however, musicians around the world developed their own versions of American pop with occasional success in the postwar world's largest and most lucrative market. Bert Kaempfert's "Wonderland by Night" ("Wunderland bei Nacht") from West Germany proved an American hit in 1960, as did Kyu Sakamoto's "Sukiyaki" (originally "Ue o Muite Arukō," "I Look Up as I Walk") from Japan in 1963. Nevertheless, just as George Bernard Shaw joked about the Americans and the British being one people separated by a shared language, UK artists possessed a distinct linguistic advantage in the US market.

The Bulge. The audiences for sixties British pop entered the postwar world in three phases: the prewar years (roughly the 1930s), the war years (1939-1945), and the postwar years (1945 to the early 1950s). Sometimes referred to in the UK as the "Bulge," births peaked in 1946 and 1947 while the parallel American "Baby Boom"—reflecting more robust economic circumstances—continued until 1964.[4] Contributing to this rise in birthrates, medical advances (e.g., antibiotics) improved infant mortality rates and ensured that more children reached adulthood.[5]

The generation that would reimagine Britain's role in the world was shaped by an academic system intended to perpetuate class. For the financially and socially privileged, the option of elite public schools (e.g., Eton College) offered a path to universities, board rooms, and ministerial posts. A test at the end of primary school divided other students among three other educational destinations. For the academically successful, grammar schools with their curricula rooted in classical studies could lead to social and financial advancement. For most of the working class, however, secondary modern and technical schools focused on skills that the government deemed best to benefit the economy. All could leave school at age fifteen, and many did.

The key roles played in the ecology of sixties British pop broadly but not exclusively fall into three overlapping role categories: curators, creators, and consumers. Curators included producers, music directors, promoters, publishers, journalists, broadcasters, and those who determined what music consumers got to hear and to purchase. They tended to have been born during the prewar years (1920s and 1930s) and had middle-class affiliations, but that pattern began to change over the decade. The creators—musicians and songwriters, but also recording engineers—were the interpreters of cultural trends, listening

---

[4] The term "Bulge Generation" appears in this book to distinguish the British postwar generation from American "Baby Boomers." The two populations have different demographic profiles. See Jackson 1998.

[5] Access to birth-control pills, although introduced in the 1960s, had only a modest effect on population growth in the early part of the decade.

to, responding to, and realizing the sounds that form the subject of this study. The popular press emphasized those artists with a median age weighted toward wartime births and with working-class backgrounds, but in a competitive environment, age and class mattered less than success. Last but crucial, all were consumers of popular culture, with the tastes of the Bulge generation taking on an increasingly important role in what paths creators and curators took.

Many of the most prominent musicians of the first wave of British pop were born during the war (e.g., John Lennon, 1940) with their producers often a generation or more older (e.g., George Martin, 1926). That accident of birth placed these performers at an age young enough to share an affinity with their Bulge Generation listeners but old enough to have the knowledge and experience necessary to create the music.[6] In contrast, the producers (known as artist-and-repertoire managers in the early sixties) controlled the recording process and generally held different priorities and musical aesthetics.

The White Heat of Technology

Developments emerging before, during, and after World War II transformed the creation, recording, reproduction, and consumption of popular music. For musicians, electromagnetic technologies contributed pickups and amplifiers that allowed what had been largely acoustic performances (enjoyed by only small audiences) to expand first into clubs and then into dance halls. Replacing dance bands dominated by trumpets, saxophones, and trombones, amplification enabled bands with guitars to project a sound that signified all that was modern and young.

In a parallel development, studios abandoned lathes and hot wax for magnetic tape and recorder technologies that Germans had developed during the war and that Americans and others improved and manufactured.[7] This medium not only allowed an enhanced audio response range but also empowered producers to edit recordings together to create composite performances. Equally important, tape equipment would empower small studios to compete with major facilities like the EMI Recording Studios in London's Abbey Road.

For the consumer, polyvinylchloride (PVC) replaced shellac as the preferred material for discs, with the Americans standardizing the formats: the $33^1/_3$-rpm

---

[6] Publicists also often distributed information that claimed the performers were younger than they were.
[7] Although EMI had developed one of the first condenser microphones in the 1930s, German Neumann and Sennheiser microphones and American Ampex and Swiss Nagra and Studer tape decks dominated the market.

12" LP and the 45-rpm 7" single.[8] Not only did vinyl discs have less surface noise than shellac but also "microgroove" technology allowed longer play times on the turntables, while amplifiers and built-in speakers were manufactured in response to the demand. Perhaps most significant, the recorded object itself emerged as an independent artistic medium. (See Thompson 2008, 35–38.)

The Transatlantic Community. A few weeks after the launch of the telecommunications satellite Telstar, President John F. Kennedy (23 July 1962) expressed the hope that this technology would bring the world closer together. In the months following that transatlantic video transmission, however, he would use the medium to address the Cuban missile crisis, and broadcasters would use it to cover his funeral. Five years later, they experimented with the idea of a worldwide video transmission during the *Our World* broadcast, with different countries selecting material they thought best represented them. (Great Britain chose the Beatles.)

The inauguration of intercontinental flight strategically shortened the time it took to travel between locations, especially when commercial transatlantic jets came into service in 1958.[9] This freedom to travel contributed to intercultural contact, with a corresponding broadening interest in and understanding of the role culture plays in how we view the world. As musicians traveled around the globe, new markets for their music and for their recordings opened. This spread of regional cultures into global markets accelerated in the 1960s, and where some in Britain had complained about an invasion of American artists in the 1950s, some in the United States would come to complain about a British Invasion in the 1960s. A few recognized that an interconnected globalized music and recording industry constituted the new normal.

Places I'll Remember

If music be the food of love, then it also carries information about personal and group identity that is communicated wherever musicians perform it, audiences listen to it, and the media discuss it. Place and space are important influences on our reactions to music. In the UK, London has served as the nation's preeminent place for concerts, recording, broadcasting, and publications, with Manchester, Liverpool, and Birmingham in prominent supporting roles. Even when British

---

[8] The British also favored the EP version of the 45 rpm disc, which took advantage of the longer playing times by including either more than one recording per side or longer recordings than 78 rpm shellac discs.

[9] London's Heathrow Airport opened for commercial air travel on 17 May 1946. The first transatlantic commercial jet passenger flight occurred on 4 October 1958 when BOAC commenced flights between London and New York.

musicians honed skills and repertoire in suburban or provincial venues, financial and artistic recognition drew them into these urban environments.

Being English. The notion of being British has its roots in the move to unify the nations of England, Scotland, Wales, and Ireland through the Acts of Union (1707), a political move that nevertheless cemented English hegemony. Similarly, sixties British pop broadly implied a national identity but emphasized Englishness, given the origins of the musicians and their audiences, and the headquarters of record companies and their studios, and the media.

In Kate Fox's ethnography of English behavior, *Watching the English*, "The Core" represents the fundamental problem of "social chronic inhibitions and handicaps" that she describes as "Social Dis-ease" (2014, 548). In this construction, the English exhibit a "general inability to engage in a direct and straightforward fashion with other human beings," which offers one explanation for the importance of pop music in adolescent life (549). All social settings carry rules about how to interact, with the English often focused on class. Listening to music in private diminishes social contact. Concerts, however, offer contexts in which individuals can test expectations.

Fox attributes the flourishing of English music-oriented subcultures that began in the 1950s to youth searching for a "sense of identity and a means of annoying their parents" (2014, 397). She observes that music provided opportunities for "periods of 'natural' remission from our dis-ease in private and among intimates" (549). Performances in the 1960s, however, offered opportunities for individuals—both audiences and performers—to behave in ways that defied conventional social norms.

City Sounds. English sociologist, disc jockey, and music critic Charlie Gillett asserted in *The Sound of the City* (1983, viii) that rock 'n' roll represented the "first form of popular culture to celebrate without reservation characteristics of city life that had been among the most criticized . . . the strident, repetitive sounds . . . reproduced as melody and rhythm." Gillett reasoned that cities shape popular culture through the empowerment of "audiences or creators" to "determine the content of a popular art communicated through the mass media" (viii).

Donald Nonini (2014) suggests a variety of avenues for exploring how cities inform the human experience: spatiality, community, markets, buildings, class, gender, sexualities, ethnicity, extralegality, governance, and cosmopolitanism. Drawing on this and other research, these concepts can help illuminate observed urban musical life to describe interactions between performers and audiences (Low 1999, 5). In particular, the spaces of music performance and audition shape our experience.

The act of listening to music, whether privately or socially, involves the creation of psychological spaces interlinked with consciousness of our external reality. For example, we encounter musical time differently than clock time when listening and performing, whether in private or in public. This alternative experience of time occurs in our immediate visceral response to a groove, particularly when we engage physically with the music. Moreover, individuals who are corporally and mentally involved in the creation of music experience time differently from passive listeners. Physical environment plays an important role in that engagement.

Upstairs, Downstairs

The 1970s television drama *Upstairs, Downstairs* portrays the intermingled lives of two groups of people residing and working at No. 165 Eaton Place, an elegant townhouse located in the elite London district of Belgravia during the first decades of the twentieth century. Living upstairs on the house's middle floors, an affluent London family—headed by Richard Bellamy, MP, and Lady Marjorie Bellamy—react to contemporary events such as women's suffrage, World War I, the Great Depression, and other social, economic, and political events slowly eroding their privilege. Downstairs, Mr. Angus Hudson oversees the staff, which includes the irrepressible cook Mrs. Kate Bridges, parlormaid Rose Buck, and others, who respectfully toil in an environment that both gives their lives meaning and inherently diminishes their personal value.

The quasi-fictional 1820s five-story townhouse—with ten bedrooms, two drawing rooms, a dining room, a library, a morning room, and a nursery along with servants' quarters in the attic and in the basement, not to mention the mews stabling five horses and two carriages—illustrates a socioarchitectural arrangement echoed in other London buildings. In the drama and the period represented, the family and their guests access the townhouse through its grand front door, while tradesmen and staff enter through separate doors to the basement or the mews.

The vertical architectural and social aspects of this structure can be understood to have functional justifications, but they also reinforce social hierarchy. Indeed, this physical articulation of social rank reflects deep preoccupations with class in Britain that have found innumerable manifestations. Unsurprisingly, the organization of London performance spaces in the 1960s also reflected this combination of functional organization and interpersonal distance.

Spatializing

Setha Low describes spatializing as "studying culture and political economy through the lens of space and place" (2014, 22), particularly for the purposes of "uncovering material and representational injustice and forms of social exclusion" and to "locate, both physically and conceptually, social relations and social practice in social space" (1999, 111). Some researchers (e.g., Bourdieu 1977) have described social spaces in binary terms such as exterior–interior, privileged–common, public–private, masculine–feminine, hot–cold, light–dark, and dry–wet.

Low offers another dialogic analytical element: spaces are both socially produced and socially constructed. The social production of space includes the "social, economic, ideological, and technological" factors that go into the "historical emergence and political and economic formation of urban space." Low's idea of the social construction of space implies that the "phenomenological and symbolic experience of space" is "mediated by social processes such as exchange, conflict, and control." The former underlies the design and the building of physical structures, while the latter describes spaces through "people's social exchanges, memories, images, and daily use" (1999, 111).

Low contributes one more variable to these modes of analysis: embodied space. As individuals interact with physical structures, they react with "feelings, thoughts, preferences, and intentions, as well as out-of-awareness cultural beliefs and practices" that consequently give space "meaning" and "form" (2014, 35). Although Low's work largely focuses on open spaces such as parks and markets, it can also be understood as operational in interior contexts such as clubs, concert venues, and recording studios.

London Studio Architecture. Henri Lefebvre observed that "space and its arrangement and allocation are assumed to be transparent . . . but . . . never are" (Low 2014, 34). Or, as Sherlock Holmes observes in *The Boscombe Valley Mystery*, "there is nothing more deceptive than an obvious fact."

Magnetic-tape technology allowed entrepreneurs to adapt existing spaces into recording studios. For example, an eighteenth-century French chapel in Marylebone became Olympic Studios in 1958. And when that neighborhood and building were scheduled for demolition at the end of the 1960s, Olympic Sound Studios relocated to a 1906 Edwardian music-hall theater (Byfield Hall) in Barnes on the other side of the Thames. The most important London recording facility of the era, however, sits in the quiet residential district of Saint John's Wood behind the 1840s Georgian townhouse at No. 3 Abbey Road, a complex with its own upstairs and downstairs.

The Gramophone Company initially opened this purpose-built structure in 1930, which was soon renamed EMI Recording Studios after a corporate merger. EMI inaugurated its cavernous (5,434 square feet) art-deco Studio One a year later (12 November 1931) by having the London Symphony Orchestra perform music by Sir Edward Elgar with the composer present, Sir Adrian Boult conducting, and George Bernard Shaw and others in attendance. A year later

(1932) the rather more utilitarian Studio Two, under half the size (2,305 square feet), opened down the hall and perpendicular to Studio One (Massey 2015).

Form and Function. The social production of these spaces involved architects, company executives, and others (e.g., financial backers) who collaborated in decisions that determined the location, size, shape, and configuration of both the external and internal aspects of the complex. With the opening of EMI Recording Studios, however, technologists and musicians socially reconstructed and modified the internal spaces through the kinds of equipment that they developed and installed, through their modifications to the interiors, and through the music they performed.

Three broad categories of mostly White male specialists dominated 1960s London studio culture: the artists who created content, the technologists who controlled the recording process, and the producers whose oversight came with their roles as representatives of and intermediaries with record companies. As technologists responded to the transition from mechanically transcribing sounds to manipulating electronic signals, production teams modified the recording studio spaces to address their acoustic aesthetics. Engineers needed to monitor and work with the electromagnetic sound objects they created, while musicians played with the acoustic qualities of the studio space.

In 1960s London, a class-informed hierarchical social structure underlay the relationships between these participants. Artist-and-repertoire *managers* oversaw "*control* rooms" and "*balance* engineers" who selected microphones and worked at mixing boards, and who instructed "tape ops" on when and how to start and to stop equipment. Larger studios often also employed "technical engineers" who designed, adapted, and maintained this equipment and other outboard devices (e.g., compressors), as well as the facilities. Finally, the "studio floor" had its hierarchy of music directors, conductors, arrangers, and various statuses of musicians who labored to create material that engineers could manipulate and producers and corporations could sell.

Spatializing EMI. The architectural layout of the EMI Recording Studios in Saint John's Wood reflects both its intended socially produced purposes and the socially constructed ranks of the participants. In Studio One—a cathedral to Western classical music—the initial layout included an elevated stage with the control room on the studio floor. Built at the beginning of the era of electrical recording, a tiered performance platform situated the orchestra in front of a microphone connected to a lathe that cut variegated grooves in wax.

Eventually, they eliminated the tiers, placing both the orchestra and the control room below the conductor so that when Sir Edward Elgar, Sir Adrian Boult, Sir Thomas Beecham, Sir Malcolm Sargent, etc. stood on the podium, their physical situation not only allowed them to see the orchestra but also reflected their social status. That is, lest there be any doubt as to who was in command, with knights of the realm conducting, the control room waited for its cue too.

Studio Two. Such was *not* the case with Studio Two, where most of EMI's pop music was recorded and where the control room sits one story above the performance floor of the two-story (24 feet), shoebox-shaped space. Looking down on the studio floor allows those in the control room to observe the placement of musicians and microphones, but the arrangement also reflects the inherent social hierarchy of pop music recording sessions. Other architectural features of Studio Two also separate those working upstairs and downstairs.

Musicians passed the control-room door when entering Studio One but accessed Studio Two through doors immediately *below* its control room. Moreover, performing in Studio Two meant seeing the control room window only after you had entered and when someone (usually the balance engineer) told you where to position yourself. Moreover, with overhead lights reflecting off the control room window, the producer and the balance engineer could see musicians entering and could instruct them, while performers sometimes could only hear instructions through the intercom or headsets.

As with the physical relationship between the studio floor and the control room, access to the building and its spaces also reflected both operational and social realities. Most converted recording spaces in London, such as Decca in West Hampstead, had one principal entrance, often convenient for administrators but difficult for musicians carrying instruments; however, the purpose-built EMI Recording Studios had two entrances.

The front door to the original 1840s house—the entrance one sees from the street—sits at the top of a short set of stairs and opens to a space where the studio administration had offices and where staff clocked in for their shifts. Recording stars also made their entrances and exits via this door, sometimes for photographers and fans. Most working musicians, however, arrived by entering a door at the bottom of a ramp on the left side of the building. If you were unloading amplifiers or drum kits, access to studios from the ramp door made sense, but the workman's entrance also implied social status.

Overseeing Production

Philosophers Jeremy Bentham and Michel Foucault both saw architecture as articulating social position, with the latter submitting that spatial organization locks both the observer and the observed in a mutually dependent relationship (2014, 329). In the *Upstairs, Downstairs* recording-studio metaphor, the placement of both the control rooms and musician access are significant, as are the ways individuals reacted to these spaces. Singer Marianne Faithfull remembers that Olympic Studios in Carton Street had a "control room . . . far above the studio" that was full of men "like gods looking down on us . . . the workers toiling in the factory while the fat cats directed operations from on high" (2000, 22). Other London studios such as Decca, Lansdowne, IBC, and Trident paralleled this arrangement.

To be a musician performing in EMI Studio Two meant needing an invitation to climb the stairs to the control room. Session guitarist Vic Flick (best known for playing the James Bond theme) noted that producers at EMI sometimes invited musicians into the control room, but "only . . . for specific listening reasons" and that the "novelty soon wore off" for them (interview 29 October 2018). Appropriately, the control room's limited size could only accommodate a few individuals, which further emphasized the exclusiveness of the space. Paul McCartney recalled a similar but different experience when the Beatles first arrived in EMI's Studio Two. "We weren't allowed [into the control room] through there, the staircase' . . . That was for the grown-ups and we had to come in this entrance . . . which was the tradesmen's entrance" (Beatles 2000, 93). Like workmen, they "were there at 10:00, ready to work at 10:30 sharp, expected to have done two songs by 1:30" (75). Access to the control room came only on invitation. "If we'd done a particularly good take they might say, 'Would you like to listen to it in the control room?' We'd think, 'What, us? Up those stairs, in heaven?'" (75).

A veteran EMI balance engineer insisted to me that no one thought about hierarchy in the recording studio, even as he dismissed the opinions of musicians whom he asserted knew little about what went on in the control room. He also maintained that in the early to mid-1960s, every employee at EMI wore a suit and that studio technicians wore lab coats only to keep their suits clean while setting up microphones and coiling cables. It was a very practical consideration, he assured me. Reflecting on the studio having been purpose-built that way, however, the engineer did ponder why the control room was on the second floor given that the stairs were a "bloody nuisance."

Embodied Space, Relationships, and Memory. The sociomusical ecology of British recording studios in the 1960s offers numerous illustrations of how we function in the spaces within places that cultures create. Engineer Geoff Emerick (with Massey 2006, 135) writes that producer George Martin liked "being looked up to, so he never sat in a normal chair." And Martin (with Hornsby 1979, 132) recalled that when musicians auditioned songs for him, he liked to "perch" himself on a "high stool." The social arrangement did not escape Paul McCartney, who has observed: "it was Us and Them. They had white shirts and ties in the control room, they were grown-ups" (The Beatles 2000, 93). His language is instructive.

Current research has some of the earliest evolutionary parts of our brain relate to memory and are built from grid cells and place cells that help us to remember where to locate food and safety. In terms of verticality, research also confirms a relationship between physical height and career success (e.g., Judge and Cable 2004) and between elevation and our experience of social status (Holmgren, Isager, and Schubert 2018). Our access to and experience of places carries deep significance, with the architectural design of EMI's studios evoking both the assumption of authority associated with vertical placement and privilege based on path of access.

Spatializing also raises broader questions. How does the architecture of musical spaces shape the creation and the consumption of music in venues like basement clubs or dance pavilions? How is the internal embodied listening experience shaped by architectural space? What are the roles of gender and ethnicity in the embodied musical experience of space? Perhaps space is the final frontier.

PART I
BEFORE THE FLOOD, 1950–1962

1
Common Roots

When the postwar global popular-culture conduit opened, a convergence of history, media, and market found Britain linked with the world's most avid consumers. British musicians, producers, and journalists routinely measured success by American reaction.

In the genesis of this relationship, immigrants from England, Scotland, Ireland, and Wales, as well as other parts of Europe, brought their songs and dance tunes to North America and began trading and adapting them in the New World's ethnic stew. Perhaps the earliest and most influential English musician and songwriter to tour the United States arrived in the first half of the nineteenth century. Living in upstate New York, Henry Russell accompanied himself on piano and sang about contemporary social issues. His performances and songs served as inspirations for American musicians like Stephen Foster and the Hutchinson Family, helping to lay the foundations of popular music in the United States.

Reciprocally, British audiences—already familiar with staged forms such as pantomime with its double entendres, elaborate costumes and makeup, and reversals in gender roles—took an interest in American minstrel shows. The success of the British and American economies of the seventeenth and eighteenth centuries depended on African slaves, but freedom was not all they took from their captives. White performers in blackface were a familiar feature of rural England through Morris dancers, but minstrel shows depicting Blacks as lazy and stupid reflected America's and Britain's conjoined history of racism.[1]

In the early twentieth century, a different version of American culture arrived when military bands introduced Europeans to ragtime, jazz, and New York's growing Tin Pan Alley song catalogue. Midcentury, the American influence on Britain's popular culture only accelerated when World War II troops and materials poured into her ports and US performers entertained Allied troops. Brits took to this music while at the same time fostering their own popular music culture.

---

[1] *The Black and White Minstrel Show*, which ran on BBC television for 20 years beginning in 1958 and featured White performers in blackface, shows the lasting significance of this genre in British musical life.

Sixties British Pop, Outside In. Gordon Ross Thompson, Oxford University Press. © Oxford University Press 2024.
DOI: 10.1093/oso/9780190672348.003.0002

Music Hall

British popular music is a rich bed of rural and regional traditions springing from all corners of the Isles and from different socioeconomic backgrounds. When the Industrial Revolution drew rural workers to cities, they brought their regional musical cultures to Britain's cosmopolitan centers. Where they gathered for drink, food, and song, taverns and other establishments grew into theaters. Initially maligned by genteel patrons, these dedicated entertainment spaces proved resilient. In the mid–nineteenth century, as the British middle classes took to musical theater/operetta (e.g., Gilbert and Sullivan's *The Mikado*) and parlor song (e.g., Sullivan's "The Lost Chord"), performers like George Leybourne filled halls singing "The Flying Trapeze" and "Champagne Charlie."

In the late nineteenth and early twentieth centuries, a British parallel to American vaudeville flourished in London and other major cities. Perhaps modeled after the upper-class "catch clubs" of the mid-seventeenth to late eighteenth centuries, houses with working-class clientele arose that offered their own distinctive entertainments. By the 1830s and 1840s, London taverns with music licenses provided environments where audiences could both listen to and engage in song.

These all-male song-and-supper clubs (e.g., the Coal Hole in London's Covent Garden) developed their own musical culture, with the proprietors acting as hosts and interlocutors between the audience and the performers (Lamb 2001). As urban centers expanded, the clubs grew with them, competing for the most popular entertainers, some of whom capitalized on their fame by appearing at more than one venue in an evening.

The first use of the term "music hall" appears in 1848 with the Surrey Music Hall, followed a year later when Charles Morton established the Canterbury Arms with capacity for about 700 people and a platform for performing (Lamb 2001). Morton would soon open perhaps the best known of the halls, the Oxford,[2] where the repertoire included ballads, popular songs, "nigger minstrel" acts, selections from popular operas, and comic bits/monologues. Competition for audiences raised the profiles of performers as halls resorted to increasingly elaborate architecture, for example balconies that mirrored the social stratification of the clientele.

Eventually, a gentrification of this entertainment led to syndicated "variety houses" early in the twentieth century that attracted middle-class audiences. The "Great War," however, shifted the national mood, and music halls fell into a slow decline, unable to compete with the new technologies of the cinema, recordings,

---

[2] The Dominion Theatre would later be located at this same intersection of Oxford Street and Tottenham Court Road where Bill Haley and His Comets made their London debut.

and radio. Adapting to these new media, performers such as Stanley Holloway, Gracie Fields, and George Formby had to find ways to reinvent themselves.

Lancashire Lad

If British pop groups had a prototype, it might have been George Formby. Near the height of the music hall's popularity in the early twentieth century, George Booth adopted the stage surname Formby to reference the coastal town north of Liverpool, his Lancashire roots, and his stage character. A highly successful music-hall singer and comedian, George Formby played on the regional comedic stereotype of the northern country fool.

When Booth/Formby died, his eldest son, George, recreated some of his father's music and routines and performed initially as George Hoy (his mother's maiden name) before assuming his father's stage name. As George Formby, he established his own stage identity when he incorporated a ukulele (or banjo uke) into his act, singing material that varied from the sentimental to the bawdy with an unpolished delivery that endeared him to audiences. And when he married dancer Beryl Ingham, her personal management and coaching proved invaluable.

In 1932, with a global economic depression in full swing, Formby auditioned for a film role as that medium grew in popularity and as music halls declined. His comedic roles as an honest working-class underdog triumphing over often middle-class cads appealed to audiences, but his film roles also symbiotically fed his recording career. Bringing the music hall to the cinema, his humorous film songs taunted censors with double entendres. Unsurprisingly, one of his most popular songs, "With My Little Ukulele in My Hand" featured phallic puns that the BBC banned. His signature tune, however, took the voice of a hapless window cleaner.

A Nosey Parker. In his 1936 film *Keep Your Seats, Please*, Formby's character attempts to find precious gems hidden in a chair sold at an estate sale. "When I'm Cleaning Windows" features wordplay from the perspective of the voyeur as he observes "honeymooning couples," a "chamber maid," a man drinking his bath, and a "famous talky queen" who looks "more like eighty than eighteen" when seen in proximity. The song had such lasting appeal that he rerecorded it in 1950, adding a band backing him to satisfy postwar tastes. All his recordings feature his slightly nasal delivery and northern English accent, while his rapidly strummed ukulele solo rejects virtuosity for enthusiasm.

Formby's popularity before and during World War II earned him an Order of the British Empire (OBE) from King George VI and even the Order of Lenin from Stalin for his service entertaining troops. Health problems and changes in taste, however, doomed a comeback in the 1950s as British audiences fled film theaters for a new technology. The broadcast of Elizabeth II's coronation in June 1953 served as encouragement for a national surge in television purchases even though programming remained in development.

The preface to John Osborne's play *The Entertainer* (1957) laments the decline of variety performers like Formby, noting that a "significant part of England" was dying with the tradition. Formby's failing health prevented him from participating in a stage show based on his catalogue that might have marked a new phase in his career. At his death in March 1961, Formby left an imprint on those who grew up watching his films and listening to his records, and for whom he represented something very English.

Trad, Dad

In the postwar era, some British jazz musicians (e.g., tenor saxophonist Ronnie Scott) embraced modern, esoteric, and technically challenging styles like bebop performed by virtuosi like Charlie Parker. However, much more accessible repertoire from the twenties and thirties associated with the Mississippi River Valley from New Orleans to Chicago represented authentic American culture to aficionados. In the United States and the UK, revivalist jazz gained advocates dedicated to resurrecting a music they understood as traditional, if not also associated with a nostalgia for a simpler prenuclear world.

They celebrated American musicians who were now in their fifties, sixties, or older and who found themselves caught between an inclination to create new music (or no music at all) and an audience invested in them as ambassadors from the past. Bandleader Chris Barber notes that the British press began shortening the word "traditional" to "trad" to describe the music, simply because journalists liked to "refer to things in words of one syllable" (Leigh and Firminger 1996, 122). In the late fifties, trad jazz appealed to audiences of college students and a wide swath of White youth who were attracted by its accessible rhythms and its mix of blues and simple melodies.

British promoters responded by sponsoring visas for Americans such as Louis Armstrong, even though the British Musicians' Union often resisted the idea of them bringing accompanists.[3] These original artists, however, often wanted to record new material, updating the style for modern and often foreign audiences, as when Sidney Bechet (then in his late fifties) released "Petite Fleur" (1954) in France.

---

[3] British and American musician unions refused to recognize singers as musicians and instead classified them as actors, allowing them to perform, but only with British "musician" accompanists.

In the familiar pattern of White musicians covering music by Black musicians for White audiences, British trad musicians also had success in the American market. Monty Sunshine with Chris Barber's Jazz Band, for example, covered "Petite Fleur" (1959) and reached #5 in the United States. But not all British trad found success by covering American artists. Kenny Ball interpreted a Russian song as "Midnight in Moscow" (1962) and nearly topped American charts with the BBC providing domestic promotion.

The Best of Everything

When the BBC formed, its founders had something different in mind from America's competitive commercial radio licenses. In 1922, several fledgling British telecommunications companies amalgamated to form the monopolistic British Broadcasting Company as an extension of the Royal Mail under general manager John Reith. By 1926, over 2 million subscribers had purchased radio licenses to pay for the programming and for the privilege of receiving a broadcast, a number that continued to grow over the following decades (Briggs 1961, 18).

In May 1926, the nine-day General Strike suspended newspaper publishing, leaving the BBC as the only public source of information, a situation the government of the Conservative prime minister, Stanley Baldwin (and Winston Churchill, chancellor of the exchequer, in particular) sought to work to their advantage. A Royal Charter the next year (1 January 1927) established the British Broadcasting Corporation, taking the potential for political control of the broadcaster away from Parliament and placing it under the Crown. Parliament would continue to hold the purse strings, but Director-General Reith, soon to be knighted, chaired the BBC Board and religiously maintained the Corporation's independence (Briggs 1961, 18).

Before 1967, the BBC operated three domestic services: the Home Service (regional programming), the Light Programme (popular entertainment), and the Third Programme (the heart of their mission). The Corporation prioritized the broadcast of plays, symphonies, and debates between scholars and politicians on the Third Programme, while pursuing the education of the population with programs on subjects like farming and housekeeping on the Home Service. The very title of the "Light" Programme inferred the inferiority of a service that provided game and variety shows, with a window for popular music. The Musicians' Union lobbied heavily for live music in these broadcasts, making the Corporation the largest employer of musicians in the country (see Witts 2012).

Reith advocated for the "best of everything to the greatest number of homes," an approach deeply rooted in his Scottish Presbyterian middle-class roots (BBC,

The BBC Story: 1920s n.d.). As ownership of radio sets expanded and listener demographics grew more diverse, however, lower middle-class and working-class families came to dominate the audience. BBC producers responded by looking for programming that met their standards but also passed as popular content. With the continued parental and conservative approach to programming that had earned it the nickname Auntie Beeb, the BBC began scheduling British trad jazz on the Light Programme.

The Guv'nor. If one figure in this era held an unquestionable reputation as an unflinching and dogmatic advocate for revivalist jazz, it would be Ken Colyer. Known as the Guv'nor for his intensity and repertoire knowledge, Colyer brought an authenticity that originated both in his experiences playing in bands in New Orleans and in the letters he wrote from abroad to the readers of the *New Musical Express* describing his encounters. Supporting his authenticity, his resume included time spent in an American jail, perhaps after running afoul of segregation laws but more likely because the Immigration and Naturalization Service insisted on a visa.

Colyer's ensembles built their audiences performing in British clubs, coffee houses, and universities, as well as marching in New Orleans–style parades to support the Campaign for Nuclear Disarmament. Although he never had a hit record, the BBC Light Programme booked him for appearances on the influential *Jazz Club*. For example, with a repertoire carefully cultivated by Colyer, his Jazzmen chose "The Sheik of Araby" for a performance on *Jazz Club* in April 1953. The tune had been a favorite of New Orleans musicians who, consistent with their milieu, never questioned the sexist and ethnic stereotypes of its lyrics.[4] Indeed, for both Americans and Brits, the song represented an opportunity for parody (for example, Fats Waller's 1939 interpretation). Not everyone, however, was content with being authentic.

Stanger on a Strange Shore

Mr. Acker Bilk and His Paramount Jazz Band found commercial success in a bit of excess. Although he first gained notoriety playing in Ken Colyer's band, Bilk's popularity grew dramatically under the guidance of press agent Peter Leslie, who encouraged him and his band to wear bowler hats and striped Edwardian waistcoats. To feed this vintage image, their publicity often consisted of an

---

[4] The original 1921 version piggybacked on the success of the film *The Sheik* and references a scene where Rudolph Valentino (as the Sheik) rapes Agnes Ayres (as Lady Diana Mayo).

"elephantine pastiche of Victorian advertising prose, larded with unbearable puns" (Melly 1970, 61). The costume, however, proved perfect for the emerging medium of television and contrasted with Colyer's no-frills approach. Although Bilk's costume and eclectic repertoire put him at odds with purists, trad ensembles like the Temperance Seven expanded on the cliché with their comic interpretations of Edwardian style.

As the fifties gave way to the sixties, promoters looked for ways to remain relevant as other forms of music occupied the minds and hearts of British youth. Indeed, Bilk's most successful recording had little to do with trad. He had originally composed and named the lilting "Jenny" for his daughter, but in 1961, when the producers of a children's television program thought his recording appropriate for its theme, he reconsidered the title. The clarinet solo accompanied by an orchestra sounds quite unlike trad, but the exposure helped to make "Stranger on the Shore" an international hit.

Part of the appeal of the trad repertoire for young audiences, however, came from irreverent Dixieland standards like "Sister Kate." Originally written by bandleader Armand Piron and recorded by Ladd's Black Aces (1922),[5] "Sister Kate" proved popular with many artists, including Anna Jones, with Fats Waller, who recorded one of the most notable versions in 1923. For British trad musicians, the song offered a touch of music-hall naughtiness. In an April 1960 broadcast of *Jazz Club*, Bilk's band included a performance of the song with drummer Ron McKay imitating Louis Armstrong's raspy voice. The original text takes the perspective of a woman who wonders how she might become as popular as her sister, and McKay maintains this perspective but also alters the lyrics, presumably to navigate around BBC censors looking for sexual allusions and drug references. The line "shake it like jelly on a plate" might have raised a censor's eyebrow, but "I get my stuff about as high as a kite, you know I do it for you every night" did not make the cut.

Trad, however, relied on ethnic stereotypes consistent with minstrel shows and an underlying assumption that Black American culture offered something more licentious than White English culture. As British youth grew into adolescence, that projection served as a rationale for testing British behavioral standards regarding sex and drugs. Trad, thus, served as a medium in which young British musicians and their audiences could begin to challenge the societal strictures they associated with adults and authority figures.

---

[5] Although Piron copyrighted the song, Louis Armstrong and others contested the authorship. Piron maintained that the song predated them all.

Don't You Rock Me, Daddy-o

While dealing with Britain's postwar recovery, trad fans and musicians exploring Americana discovered recordings made during the late 1920s and the economic depression of the early 1930s. One musical niche of this era featured eclectic instrumentations such as a washboard, a jug, a kazoo or tissue-covered comb, a washtub bass, and even a suitcase played with whisk brooms, which appealed to beginning musicians with very few financial options. Those playing banjos and guitars seemed like pros. American bands from the Great Depression, such as the Mound City Blue Blowers (who described themselves as playing "novelty jazz"), took popular tunes and gave them makeovers. Some called their performances "jug band music" or the ensembles "spasm bands." At least one source referred to it as "skiffle."

In their passion for Americana, Ken Colyer's band probably first introduced this music to Britain between trad sets to keep patrons entertained and to stretch out performances. Chris Barber acknowledges that he "didn't coin the word 'skiffle,' but we were the ones who put it onto that kind of music." Crediting the 1929 Paramount disc *Hometown Skiffle*, Barber "thought 'skiffle' was a nice, jolly name . . . that people wouldn't have heard already" (Leigh 1992).

On that disc, Alex Hill hosts a sampler that claims to feature guitarists Blind Lemon Jefferson and Blind Blake,[6] pianists Charlie Spand and Will Ezell, the Hokum Boys, and banjoist Papa Charlie Jackson playing as though at a rent party. Hill's verbal patter and the music resonated with trad's intoxication with an exotic Black American world so different from postwar Britain and yet familiar.

Up to London. Many extended British families had some member who owned a piano in their front room; if not, then guitars offered a cheaper musical alternative. Importantly for sixties British pop, skiffle interested teens in learning how to play the guitar. As the music's popularity spread in the midfifties, skiffle bands and clubs appeared in every major city.

In their search, skiffle fans perused a range of different preelectric American guitarist-singers, including Robert Johnson, Huddie Ledbetter, and even Woody Guthrie. With little information available, these musicians occupied places in fan imaginations, if not in their disc collections. Prominent in defining how the UK understood American roots music, Big Bill Broonzy visited several times in the 1950s, introducing audiences to the musical world he had inhabited. In the United States, he had played an important role in the postwar folk revival, especially as an early proponent of Black Americana at universities, clubs, camps, and concert halls. Now he took the music across the Atlantic.

---

[6] The label lists Jefferson as playing, but Jefferson had died a few years earlier. Blake probably plays a passage meant to imitate Jefferson.

London musicians like Chris Barber became part-time impresarios when they invited Broonzy and similar artists to perform, encountering resistance from a surprising institution. Unions on both sides of the Atlantic (the American Federation of Musicians and, in the UK, the Musicians' Union) enforced a reciprocal quota system balancing the number of performers that entered each country.

Nevertheless, by the end of the 1950s, London had a sizable audience for these American folk musicians. Guitarist Jim Sullivan recalled as a teen going "up to London [from Hounslow] to what eventually became the Skiffle Cellar" when it was "a folk club and guys like Sonny Terry and Brownie McGhee, Ramblin' Jack Elliott . . . used to play there." By that time, however, Britain already had its own "King of Skiffle" (interview 22 January 2001).

The Gamblin' Man

Tony Donegan was in his midteens when he bought his first guitar. His incentive to play came from the revivalist jazz he heard on the BBC and, later, the recordings he heard when visiting the American Embassy's cultural offices. With some practice, he got his first gigs with local dance bands (Leigh 1992), and by the early 1950s, this aficionado of American folk music had dropped his given name to become Lonnie Donegan after one of his favorite musicians, Lonnie Johnson (Frame 2007, 56–57).

The Americans who most influenced him were guitar-playing singers, but revivalist jazz bands had work and preferred banjos, so he learned to play that instrument well enough to audition successfully for Chris Barber's Jazz Band. In 1954, Decca's Hugh Mendl brought Barber's band into the studio with a £35 budget to produce an album capitalizing on the popularity of trad, but he ran into a problem. "It was apparent the Chris Barber Band did not have a very big repertoire. . . . Everybody felt they ought to go home but there was too much money involved" (Mendl in Bragg 2004). Donegan, however, had come prepared to play skiffle and had brought his guitar as well as his banjo.

Donegan's sets during Barber's trad programs had been popular, and now two of his numbers helped to fill out the album. When Decca released the disc *New Orleans Joys* (December 1954), it included the guitarist performing "John Henry" and "Rock Island Line" with accompaniment by Chris Barber (bass) and Beryl Bryden (washboard) as "Lonnie Donegan's Skiffle Group." The liner notes credit the inclusion of these tunes to a "newly awakened interest in the true Negro 'race' music" that Barber and Donegan had been "fostering for some years" and that now "opens up a whole new field of traditional jazz." Of the two songs, "Rock Island Line" would eventually launch skiffle as a national juvenile obsession.

Rock Island. Donegan bases his "Rock Island Line" performance closely on Huddie Ledbetter's 1953 recording, which tells the story of a train engineer signaling to a "depot agent" that his cargo consists of livestock.[7] Once the agent has expedited the train's passage, the engineer laughs that he has fooled the agent and that he's really carrying "pig iron." Ledbetter symbolizes the engineer's comments by imitating the train's two-note whistle and by playing with the rhythm of the words. At that point, Ledbetter doubles the strumming pattern to suggest the accelerating train and sings the chorus championing the Rock Island Line as "the road to ride."

Humor—one of Kate Fox's reflexive English behaviors (2014, 100)—offers one possible explanation why Ledbetter's recording attracted Donegan's attention and why it caught the imaginations of young listeners in British cities. In addition to the story of the engineer fooling the depot agent, Ledbetter and Donegan insert short rhyming couplets such as "A, B, C, double X, Y, Z; cat's in the cupboard but you don't see me," drawing on a nursery rhyme to joke about the deception.[8] Donegan was so taken by this convention that he built it into future recordings. What the British singer does not copy is Ledbetter's low raspy voice. While Donegan does affect an awkward American accent, he sings with a decidedly nasal delivery that codes the performance as Euro-American rather than Black-American.

The Gap. Barber's *New Orleans Joys* sold modestly well in Britain, but very few adolescent consumers purchased LPs, and as the band moved on to other material, the disc slid out of the charts. By late 1955, however, American Bill Haley's "Rock around the Clock" topped the British charts, and Decca released "Rock Island Line" as a single, albeit on a 78 rpm disc. Responses came quickly. Donegan's disc not only became a hit in the UK but also found a spot in *Billboard*'s top-ten on the other side of the Atlantic.

American success brought an invitation to tour the United States. The American Federation of Musicians, however, blocked Donegan from bringing a band, so promoters in each city provided accompanists. When he appeared at the venerable Fox Theater in Detroit (21 June 1956), Johnny Burnette and the Rock 'n Roll Trio backed him, putting the "rock" into the "Rock Island Line." Donegan's response to what he heard when he returned to the UK positioned skiffle as a transitional vehicle to British rock 'n' roll.

Having reaped a £3 10s session fee from Decca for "Rock Island Line," Donegan signed a contract with Pye Records where artist-and-repertoire manager Denis Preston with balance engineer Joe Meek tackled the problem of how

---

[7] Ledbetter originally recorded his performance in 1942, but Folkways did not release it until 1953. Donegan structures his performance so similarly to Ledbetter's recording that where the original clocks in at 2:28 in duration, Donegan's lasts 2:27.

[8] For example, Donegan pronounces *z* as an American "zee" rather than as a British "zed."

to record amplified music. After several modestly successful acoustic releases (including "Don't You Rock Me, Daddy-o"), Donegan selected "Cumberland Gap," an Appalachian tune recorded by Woody Guthrie and Cisco Houston (1952) that echoed the feel of "Rock Island Line." Donegan, however, updated his version. Having Nick Nicholls on drums was consistent with trad-band practice; however, Denny Wright's electric guitar solo shifted the feel. While the recording may not offer the most polished performance, Wright captures some of the excitement of contemporary American guitarists, and the disc topped British charts.[9]

Donegan's success inspired thousands of adolescents to try their hand at skiffle. "We were always a very professional group but the songs were so simple that this encouraged the kids," Donegan noted. "Any kid could knock them out with three chords on a guitar and someone could bang a suitcase for drums" (Leigh 1992). Kids did pay attention.

Puttin' on the Style

Popular music in the late 1950s reacted to two important emerging vectors: the demographics of the postwar generation and television. Donegan continued to draw on Americana for his repertoire; however, he also increased the broad humor by adding slapstick for the television cameras. Appearing on ATV's popular *Val Parnell's Sunday Night at the London Palladium* (12 May 1957), Donegan debuted two new songs. For "Puttin' on the Style" (the A-side of the release), he mugs for the camera while playing a banjo à la George Formby and having the drummer play a tambourine, the lyrics mocking teens (and a preacher) as superficial.

Aware of his audience, Donegan also raided the competing skiffle group Les Hobeaux to replace Denny Wright with Les Bennetts on guitar, a younger musician with more of a sense of rock 'n' roll. They followed up "Puttin' on the Style" on the program by plugging in Bennetts's electric guitar and setting up a drum kit. Their version of "Gamblin' Man"[10] captures some of the energy of "Cumberland Gap," but Donegan was transitioning. "Puttin' on the Style," with its amalgam of skiffle, humor, and social commentary, topped British charts in late June 1957, just before Elvis Presley's "All Shook Up" occupied that position for almost two months. Donegan was retreating to the music hall, while Britain was turning to rock 'n' roll.

---

[9] Wright possibly heard guitarists Danny Cedrone, on the recording of Bill Haley's "Rock around the Clock," and Franny Beecher, when Haley and His Comets began their tour of Britain two weeks before Donegan recorded "Cumberland Gap."

[10] Donegan released "Gamblin' Man," originally "Roving Gambler" (traditional), as the B-side to "Puttin' on the Style."

Shortly before Christmas 1958, Donegan recorded "Does Your Chewing Gum Lose Its Flavour (on the Bedpost Overnight)?" in a performance at the New Theatre Oxford. The lyrics of this novelty tune from the 1920s appealed both to parents and to tweens too young to be openly interested in sex. Again, eschewing the guitar for the banjo, Donegan rattles off lines that detail the imagined problems encountered by a gum chewer, interspersed with short jokes. Donegan no longer feigns American pronunciations and instead sings with a clear English accent on a disc that reached #3 on UK charts and #5 in the United States.

When British listeners heard Donegan's "My Old Man's a Dustman (Ballad of a Refuse Disposal Officer)" (March 1960), many identified the song with working-class Liverpool. The disc topped British charts in the spring of 1960 and peaked at #5 in the United States, demonstrating an early American interest in things English, albeit as a novelty. Donegan, however, was becoming an adult act, appearing on variety television with comedians and movie stars, and not on teen-oriented shows.

We Just Didn't Know How to Do It. As a cultural artifact, skiffle reflected some of the era's modestly shifting social arrangements, including a subtle undermining of gender stereotype. Males populated most skiffle groups, with women (if included at all) relegated to singing or playing the washboard or the tea-chest bass with little obvious sense of irony. Nancy Whiskey and the Chas McDevitt Skiffle Group, however, proved a notable exception. With Whiskey singing and playing guitar on their cover of Elizabeth Cotten's "Freight Train" (1958), their recording not only put them in the top five on British charts but also earned them an appearance on the *Ed Sullivan Show* (30 June 1957) in the United States.[11]

Skiffle, however, proved a fad, bursting into the British consciousness in the mid-1950s but fading as Western youth culture embraced other styles of American pop and notably rock 'n' roll. The musically conservative bandleader Jack Payne emphasized the transitional relationship between skiffle and rock 'n' roll, noting that their audiences significantly overlapped and that the styles held musical traits in common (Payne 1957, 5). While Payne held both skiffle and rock 'n' roll in low esteem, his explanation for why British teens embraced this bit of Americana rang true.

Skiffle, however, represented only one of the American musical styles discovered by revivalists. Chris Barber admitted that by the early 1960s they sometimes had other kinds of music in mind. "We've been accused of going on a Muddy Waters kick since we heard his band in the flesh on our trip to the States. . . . Yet back in the days when Lonnie Donegan played with us, we were trying to create a Muddy sound in some of the skiffle numbers. We just didn't know how to do it" (Tony Brown 1961, 3).

---

[11] They appeared on the same program as the Everly Brothers.

COMMON ROOTS 29

Fig. 1.1 George Formby, in *Turned Out Nice Again*, 1941.

Fig. 1.2 Acker Bilk, *Creole Jazz*, 1961.

Fig. 1.3 Lonnie Donegan, *Putting on the Donegan*, 15 June 1961.

2
First Responders

In many 1950s adult minds, rock 'n' roll represented danger. In the United States, its rise coincided with the civil rights movement and *Brown v. Board of Education* (1954), which fed the willingness of many youth to question adult authority. In the UK, rock 'n' roll challenged convention and history. Arriving from America first on recordings, then on film, and finally in person, this music psychologically created spaces in which youth culture could confront the status quo.

When films like *The Girl Can't Help It* (1957) played on screens in Britain, youth danced in the aisles. When Bill Haley (1957), Buddy Holly (1958), Jerry Lee Lewis (1958), Gene Vincent (1959), the Everly Brothers (1960), Eddie Cochrane (1960), and Little Richard (1962) arrived, rock invaded Britain. Rock culture implicitly defied adult expectations.[1] Why conform when rebelling felt right? Moreover, freedom in London during the 1950s had a district.

Walking through Soho in London's West End in this era, one encountered the sex and film industries as well as coffeehouses, clubs, pubs, and restaurants. For minors in search of music, excitement, and each other in 1953, London's first Gaggia espresso machine at the Moka Bar in Frith Street paved the way for other coffee bars to spread across the district (Green, 9 March 2017). Several of these venues featured music, with the 2i's in Old Compton Street justifiably claiming to be the home of British rock 'n' roll.[2]

Drummer Carlo Little described the 2i's (named for brothers and original owners Fred and Sam Irani) in the late 1950s as

> a coffee bar upstairs with a basement what held about fifty people ... and that was really pushin' it. A very small place underneath with a tiny little stage.... [The room was] very small, you know, maybe 25 foot by 10 foot by 12 foot. [The stage] took about a fifth of the room up. ... At least 20% of the room was the band.
>
> You got about fifty people in there and it was hot.... It was just concrete walls [but the sound was] great! Bounced all the way around. But the crowd helped soak it up....

---

[1] I use the term "rock" as a generic term for musics associated with and derived from rock 'n' roll.
[2] Although many sources use an uppercase *I* when spelling the coffee bar's name, the business address used the lower case.

The upstairs was just a coffee bar with chairs and . . . one of those little jukeboxes on the wall, like you put your money in . . . and selected your stuff.

That was quite a popular place in the fifties and the early sixties. (Interview 30 March 2000)

This music carried an American brashness that attracted some and frightened other British listeners. Like the frothy coffee, rock 'n' roll offered an exotic, imported commodity onto which musicians and audiences could project their own meanings. Listening to recordings on Radio Luxembourg or by ordering discs from the United States,[3] British youth could hear music that was excluded from BBC playlists. In response, a corps of British performers endeavored to make their own versions of this music.

Early British Rock 'n' Roll

Melody Maker—a paper best known to fifties British musicians as a jazz publication—warned its readers of a musical invasion: "Club, Disc Boom as Rock-and-Roll Craze Spreads" (14 July 1956). Venues for this new music were opening nationally, it proclaimed, as sales of rock 'n' roll records rose, potentially threatening the livelihoods of jazz musicians. Moreover, American musicians posed a recurring source of concern for them, especially servicemen stationed in the UK. For example, *Melody Maker* reported that the Musicians' Union had lodged a protest about Americans from the Sculthorpe airbase playing "Hillbilly music" on Tuesdays and rock 'n' roll on Thursdays for free at a pub in King's Lynn (about a hundred miles northeast of London) ("Storm over USAF Men in 'No Fee' Band, 'Matter of Principle,' Say MU Members" 29 September 1956).[4]

Some British musicians reacted to the "craze" by adapting what they knew to what they heard. Trad musicians like Donegan tried to capture some of the excitement of rock 'n' roll by changing the ways they presented skiffle. The first British musicians to call what they did "rock 'n' roll," however, came from modern jazz backgrounds. They knew something was happening. They just were not sure what it was.

---

[3] Radio Luxembourg had offices in London through which they arranged broadcasts intended for British audiences.

[4] Leigh and Firminger (1996) refer to this era's music as Britpop.

Teach You to Rock

The summer of 1956 proved important in British popular music. Among the events that season, *Melody Maker* announced that Tony Crombie and His Rockets would be switching to rock 'n' roll ("Crombie Forms Rock-and-Roll Unit" 4 August 1956). The modern-jazz drummer had put together "a band with a similar line-up to Bill Haley's" but better, in his opinion: "a swinging jazz band with a good singer [Cliff Lawrence] . . . playing with a rock 'n' roll beat" (Leigh and Firminger 1996, 17). *Melody Maker*'s review of their Portsmouth show painted the audience as "sober and sedate, older folk smiling faintly, the younger element contented, perhaps even sated" ("Crombie Rocks" 15 September 1956).

EMI producer Norrie Paramor recorded Tony Crombie and His Rockets covering Freddie Bell and the Bell Boys' "Teach You to Rock" (October 1956) a song they had learned by watching the film *Rock around the Clock*.[5] The performance closely copies the original, with the distinction that they replaced Bell's trumpet with electric guitar, bringing the sound closer to Bill Haley's Comets. Not for the last time, a British cover compared favorably with its American original.

Crombie's band quickly composed and recorded similar material that repeated the musical formula of "Teach You to Rock" by recontextualizing the material as English, for example "Brighton Rock" (1957) for the British film *Rock You Sinners* (1957). With the emergence of Elvis Presley, however, British teens sought authenticity, especially as "The King" (Presley) only performed in the United States. As good as Crombie's band was, he came from their parents' generation, and would-be managers began lurking around London's coffee bars looking for someone more convincing.[6]

Other bands also soon formed, including the Rockin' Horses and Art Baxter and His Rock and Roll Sinners, ("New Rockin' Horses Band Gets Rolling" 13 October 1956), but Crombie's ensemble gained the most notice. Jeff Kruger, the agent for these bands (and who would later be an owner of the Flamingo Club), told Bob Dawbarn of *Melody Maker*: "since you were last here three months ago, the income of this office has trebled—and it's all due to Rock 'n' Roll." Kruger complained that even though Tony Crombie's Rockets had already earned £20,000, the media were boycotting the genre. "The BBC and ITV can't see further than the ends of their noses. Rock 'n' Roll has an enormous following here, but neither will give it a showing. . . . They and the cinema managers

---

[5] Crombie's Rockets released their version of "Teach You to Rock" as a disc in the UK before the Freddie Bell and the Bellboys disc.

[6] Over the next year, Crombie sought out young musicians interested in exploring this new musical style, including Terence "Jet" Harris, for whom he bought one of the first electric bass guitars in Britain (Laing, 21 March 2011).

who are scared of the name are not giving the music a fair deal" (Dawbarn 8 December 1956).

A Kid from Bermondsey

Tommy Hicks and his friends "always used to wonder what people got up to north of the Thames—but we were frightened to go out of Bermondsey," presuming that "people like us weren't allowed in the West End" (Frame 2007, 140). Like many South East London working-class youths in the late forties and early fifties, Hicks left school at fifteen to find employment, in his case on transatlantic passenger ships. What he heard in American ports—especially country and rockabilly—resonated with him. He learned enough guitar to entertain crew members and passengers with his small repertoire of comic skits, music hall numbers, and increasingly American country-tinged songs.

Back in the UK, he formed a duo with Canadian Jack Fallon to play US bases during layovers,[7] billing themselves as the Sons of the Saddle and himself as "Chick Hicks, all the way from the Grand Old Oprey." As his stagecraft developed, he made the rounds of coffee bars in parts of London where he had once feared to tread, playing his covers of Hank Williams and a few of the rock tunes he had learned (Dopson 1990).

In 1956, while Premier Nikita Khrushchev warned the world that the Soviet Union could deliver hydrogen bombs on intercontinental missiles and President Dwight Eisenhower forced Britain and France to abandon their invasion of the Sinai Peninsula, the 19-year-old Hicks initiated his career as a comedian working in a trio with Lionel Bart and Mike Pratt. Calling themselves the "Cavemen," they parodied emerging rock 'n' roll artists in a skit they called "Rock with the Caveman." Hicks later described it as "a joke, a spoof, the sort of thing Monty Python might have done, or the Two Ronnies" (Leigh and Firminger 1996, 18). Their song references Piltdown Man and the British Museum, recontextualizing American rock 'n' roll as English, which in 1956 was itself humorous and English.

A Star Is Born. A couple of Soho businessmen saw potential in Hicks as a solo artist and arranged for him to sit in at the 2i's with the Vipers Skiffle Group for a photo shoot. New Zealand photographer John Kennedy, however, saw a star through his lens and plotted to introduce his discovery to the world. In this venture, the kid from Bermondsey proved a willing collaborator.

Kennedy and his protégée began their campaign with the idea of creating a new stage persona. Richard Maxwell, one of the most successful British crooners of the mid-1950s, had taken the name "Dickie Valentine." Kennedy and Hicks

---

[7] Fallon became an artist agent and later played violin for the Beatles on "Don't Pass Me By."

wanted something more virile and settled on the Hicks family name Stil, changing it to Steel, adding an "e" later for good measure.

Having created Tommy Steele, they constructed a trope: a talented working-class lad discovered at the 2i's and swept into the spotlight by fate and middle-class management. Kennedy, however, was well aware that many British adults associated rock 'n' roll with adolescent defiance and violence. Anticipating this reaction, he looked for ways to give the music a new and nonthreatening face that was Tommy Steele's.

In a mutually beneficial fabrication, Kennedy staged a photo op for a newspaper with Steele performing before young, dancing, well-dressed women (in reality, models). The captions intimated that they were in a middle-class home in the proper London borough of Wandsworth. When the photos appeared in *The People* (Sunday, 16 September 1956), they came with the headline "Rock and Roll Has Got the Debs Too" (Frame 2007, 144).

Steele soon found himself at the exclusive Stork Club in upscale Mayfair (Frame 2007, 145). The stunt and the booking had worked. All they needed was financial backing for the clothes, instruments, and publicity necessary to complete the transformation. Kennedy knew that clothier Larry Parnes held entertainment-business aspirations and persuaded him to underwrite their enterprise (Rogan 1988, 17).

Cave Rave

The newspaper publicity created a media identity, but a media identity without a successful recording proffered a short shelf life; enter the artist-and-repertoire manager Hugh Mendl, who was still looking to bring the latest music to Decca. As he had with Lonnie Donegan, Mendl proved central in transforming Steele from a local favorite into a national phenomenon. Mendl also heard potential and scheduled a September recording date, a session that Kennedy photographed and proffered to *Melody Maker* (Frame 2007, 146).[8]

Understanding that other London producers were searching for their own British versions of rock 'n' roll, Mendl (with Arthur Lilley again serving as his balance engineer as he had for Donegan) quickly recorded Steele's first single: "Rock with the Caveman" (October 1956). The session band included the respected jazz saxophonist Ronnie Scott, a practical choice, as they needed to improvise an accompaniment. Lionel Bart later admitted that he "didn't really write music" and

---

[8] A short blurb about the session appeared in the same issue as the story in which the Musicians' Union complained about American airmen playing rock 'n' roll in a pub ("Storm over USAF Men" 29 September 1956).

"didn't have any parts.... We had a tea break and the boys, being jazz musicians, improvised an instrumental, which was pretty good" (Oldham 2000, 24). Scott concurs: "there was no arrangement, no music. We had to run through it and work out something on the spot. The record has sold millions and we got £12 for the session" (Leigh and Firminger 1996, 18).

The success of the disc (#13 on *The New Musical Express*'s chart) prompted calls for a national tour and the necessity of a backing band. Drummer Leo Pollini formed the Steelmen, which included Allan Weighell (bass), who remembered that touring "didn't make any money, but we had a good time" (interview 27 March 2001).

Some concerts, particularly in the north, broke out in mini-riots as teens took the music and events as opportunities to break established theater protocols. In the south, however, *Melody Maker* ("Rock 'n' Roll [or Was It Skiffle] Comes to Town" 8 December 1956) greeted Steele's London theater debut on 3 December with contempt. "What a phenomenon Rock-'n'-Roll singer and guitarist Tommy Steele is! A phenomenon because, on Monday, in his London variety debut at Finsbury Park Empire, it seemed little short of a miracle that this 19-year-old youth could receive such a rapturous ovation for the little musical talent he displayed" (8).

Singing the Blues

In January 1957, discs by Bill Haley and His Comets, Johnny Ray, Fats Domino, and the Platters all figured prominently in UK charts. To compete, British artist-and-repertoire managers and musicians copied them. In the United States, Guy Mitchell had the most successful version of "Singing the Blues" (October 1956), topping *Billboard* in December 1956. In January 1957, although his disc did equally well in UK charts, Tommy Steele's version (November 1956) briefly replaced it.

In the fifties, television emerged as key to gaining adolescent interest, which was how the British came to know Steele. On the BBC, he performed on *The Petula Clark Show* (10 January 1957) and notably on Jack Good's *Six-Five Special* (2, 9, 16, 23, and 30 March 1957). At ATV,[9] he appeared on *Val Parnell's Sunday Night at the London Palladium* (27 January and 24 February 1957). The medium, however, also shaped his setlist.

---

[9] The Television Act 1954 allowed the creation of the commercial Independent Television network (ITV) to compete with the BBC. ITV independently franchised regional broadcasters, the three largest serving London, the Midlands, and north England.

As the decade waned, Steele waffled between pop and rock, with brief ventures into his preferred repertoire of country music. Although other artists eclipsed him on the charts, he remained popular with the earliest wave of the Bulge Generation. Perhaps more important, he served as an example for working-class males (and some females) who began to see being a pop musician as a path out of poverty.

Larry Parnes played a significant role in coaching Steele on the way he behaved on stage, encouraging him to talk with his audiences and taking notes on how they responded (Rogan 1988, 19). He consequently steered Steele's transformation into an "all-round entertainer," someone who could draw audiences to Christmas pantomimes, films, musicals, and variety.

Parnes also helped establish a British model of pop management in which a middle-class businessman recognizes and exploits the cultural and financial value of a young working-class performer. Although an outsider to the British Establishment who hid his Jewish and homosexual identity from the public, the pop and entertainment industries offered a domain where he and others could find acceptance.

A Boy from Hertfordshire

Rodger Webb (an Indian Railways catering manager), his wife, Dorothy, and their children had all been born and had spent their lives in South Asia under the British Raj. Postcolonial policies following the creation of the Republic of India in 1947, however, forced the Webb family to leave the privilege they had known for an England where they arrived as immigrants. After a life with servants, they stayed with relatives in the northern Hertfordshire suburbs of London until Webb secured work and a flat in Cheshunt.

For the children, the transition proved difficult, with their Anglo-Indian accents setting them apart from their classmates. With his dark hair, eight-year-old Harry Webb struggled at first to adjust to school, with some children identifying him ethnically as an Indian and calling him a "nigger" ("The Short, Busy Life of Cliff Richard" 12 November 1960). He strove to fit into youth culture, joining a skiffle group before forming more ambitious plans.

In March 1957, after first playing truant to secure tickets and then seeing Bill Haley and His Comets in concert, he realized: "I hated skiffle. . . . I left and the drummer left with me" (Frame 2007, 329). Webb, drummer Terry Smart, and occasionally guitarist Norman Mitham formed a band and, while playing in a local pub, attracted the attention of budding rock 'n' roll enthusiast John Foster, who arranged an audition at the "hot, sweaty, and very exciting" 2i's. There, Ian Samwell (about to be demobilized from National Service) joined them as lead guitar (Cliff Richard in Leigh and Firminger 1996, 39). As their local popularity grew, a promoter suggested that their singer needed an appropriate stage name. Thus, Harry Webb became Cliff Richard and the band was named the Drifters.

As promotion, Foster offered the band's services as preshow entertainment for a talent contest at the Gaumont Theatre in the West London suburb of Shepherd's Bush. Cliff Richard remembered: "we wanted to top the bill," and when "there was a lot of screaming for us . . . we invited ourselves back a month later at the same price—nothing" (Leigh and Firminger 1996, 39). Circus agent George Ganjou also lent a hand,[10] encouraging them to make a demo recording that he could shop to record companies (Frame 2007, 333). The offices above the HMV store in Oxford Street cut demo discs from a tape.

Real Country Music

At EMI's Manchester Square offices, Ganjou met with Columbia's Norrie Paramor, who had exhausted Tony Crombie's attempts at ad hoc rock (Tony James, 6 May 2005). The producer found the covers by Cliff Richard and the Drifters of American artists like Jerry Lee Lewis strong enough to sign the now seventeen-year-old and his mates. Recording in EMI's Studio Two, Richard chose a cover of "Schoolboy Crush" by American country artist Bobby Helms as their debut, hiring backing singers and musicians for the July 1958 recording session.

As was common practice, the B-side of the disc went to a song whose royalties could benefit the recording manager, a promising songwriter, or perhaps the artists themselves.[11] They chose "Move It!," something that Ian Samwell had written celebrating youthful defiance and that many (e.g., Frame 1993, 2) describe as Britain's first true rock 'n' roll recording.

Building on a Chuck Berry–influenced three-chord model, Samwell had attempted to make this song "as American as possible" (Johnny Black, September 2008). The opening words echo the beginning of "Teach You to Rock,"[12] while the chorus challenges the notion that rock 'n' roll is a passing fad, asserting that "ballads and calypso" have nothing on "real country music." As important, Richard's vocal delivery imbues the words with just the right degree of sultry arrogance to perturb adults and tempt adolescents. The distinguishing feature that separates it from recordings like "Teach You to Rock" and "Rock with the

---

[10] Samwell claims that he visited Ganjou at his 26 Albemarle Street offices and invited him to hear the band (Frame 2007, 332).

[11] If the A-side sold, so did the B-side, with royalties going to both the songwriter and the publisher.

[12] Samwell suggests that the opening might have been inspired by Eddie Cochran's "C'mon Everybody," but that recording did not find release until the fall of 1958 (Johnny Black September 2008).

Cave Man," however, lies in the groove. Rather than the triplet swing of those performances, "Move It!" rocks with duple eighths.

With studio novices Terry Smart on drums and Ian Samwell on guitar, Paramor insisted on adding veteran sessioneers Ernie Shear (electric guitar) and Frank Clarke (acoustic bass) to give the Drifters both an edge and depth that the band's equipment, if not their experience, lacked. Paramor advised Samwell that the session musician had "a much better sound. Let him play it" (Foster 2000, 158). Nevertheless, Samwell's opening guitar riff (played by Shear) sets the atmosphere, captured by twenty-four-year-old engineer Malcolm Addey working his first solo session at the desk (Thompson 2008, 112–114).

The Drifter. In anticipation of the Columbia release of "Schoolboy Crush" (with "Move It!" on the obverse) (August 1958), Franklyn Boyd started plugging the disc. Boyd, who worked for the British publisher of "Schoolboy Crush," began knocking on doors, which led him to Jack Good, the producer of the television show *Oh Boy!* Good had successfully launched the popular *Six-Five Special* for the BBC but had left when they pushed him to make the show more adult friendly. Moving to ITV, he planned to feature rock 'n' roll on his new show, with British rocker Marty Wilde hosting guests, including Americans.

Good rolled his eyes at "School Boy Crush": "a real drippy song, and I hate drippy songs" (Good in Leigh and Firminger 1996, 39). "Move It!" however, stopped him in his tracks. When he played it for Wilde, the musician thought the recording "very good, but it has to be some American, we can't make records like that." Good responded: "It's a boy from Hertfordshire" (39). The recording proved that the British not only could perform convincing rock 'n' roll but could also compose it.

While the Drifters (with Samwell now on bass reinforced by guitarist Ken Pavey) backed Richard for gigs around London, Paramor, Richard, Foster, and Richard's father, Rodger, had reached the conclusion that the singer needed a better band. Guitarists Brian Rankin and Bruce Cripps had originally traveled to London from Newcastle to compete in a skiffle contest, lingering in the hope of finding something more permanent. At the 2i's, they did odd jobs and occasionally played, which was how they met John Foster on his mission to find Richard's new band. Foster had hoped to secure guitarist-singer Tony Sheridan, but Rankin impressed him enough to be invited to be a Drifter along with his friend Cripps, replacing Norman Mitham and Ken Pavey.

Rehearsing as the Drifters in Hertfordshire in October, Rankin and Cripps followed the example of Cliff Richard and adopted new names, becoming Hank Marvin and Bruce Welch. They also argued that they needed a solid bass player and drummer, recommending two former members of the Vipers: Terrence "Jet" Harris (bass) and Tony Meehan (drums). With the original band members replaced, Samwell unexpectedly found himself promoted to explore his potential as a songwriter and producer.

Mean, Moody, and Magnificent

Richard and the Drifters' appearances on *Oh Boy!* in the fall of 1958 helped "Move It!" rise to #2 on *New Musical Express*'s charts and catapulted them into the national spotlight. In Cliff Richard, Jack Good had someone with star potential he believed he could mold. Richard admits that at first, he was a "carbon copy of Elvis. All I had was a leg, a guitar, and a lip." Good, however, wanted something more English, instructing the singer to shorten his sideburns and not to smile to become "mean, moody, and magnificent" (Leigh and Firminger 1996, 39).

Lionel Bart's success with Tommy Steele had landed him the opportunity to write music for *Serious Charge* (1959), a film about teen sex and blackmail (Stafford and Stafford 2011). For one of the roles, he and Terence Young (who would direct the first James Bond films) wanted a performer who would look good on screen and pass as a teen. In 1959, at age 19, Richard clearly fit the role.

Bart's "Living Doll" objectifies a woman as a "crying, talking, sleeping, walking living doll" whom he threatens to lock in a trunk to keep her away from other men. Bart originally wrote it as an up-tempo swing number, which Richard mimes in the film while improbably reclining in a coffee-bar chair as the music emanates from a juke box.[13] Although Young and Bart were specific about the soundtrack recording, Paramor and the band had other ideas for the single (Ewbank and Hildred 2010, 146–147). Bruce Welch suggested they try a slower tempo, giving it what he thought of as a relaxed country feel (Vallance 1999).

Hank Marvin establishes his distinctive guitar sound and playing style in this recording, but perhaps the most remarkable aspect of it lies in the electric bass. Harris plays a short solo introduction with a pick on his imported American Fender bass, producing a sound that shouted "modern" in 1959. This slower version of "Living Doll" (July 1959) became Richard and the Drifters' first UK #1.

Shadows. With British success and a lack of interest on the part of EMI's American subsidiary, Capitol, Norrie Paramor searched for a different US distributor and settled on Atlantic. The American singing group the Drifters (featuring Clyde McPhatter), however, also released their records through Atlantic, so Richard's band searched for a new name. Harris suggested "the Shadows," and their next release in early October, "Travellin' Light" (October 1959), was the first disc under this new name.

---

[13] Notably, women sitting at the table with him enact a form of "hand jive" that Jack Good had been promoting on *Oh Boy!*, showing an early crossover between film and television.

With an expanding audience, Norrie Paramor recommended to Richard and his father that they needed an industry insider as manager and suggested publisher Franklyn Boyd. In this arrangement, Boyd took over bookings, and Foster became the road manager, an arrangement that only lasted about a year, at which point Richard canceled concert dates, complaining of exhaustion. His parents, having observed how performers on *Oh Boy!* handled bookings, turned to Tito Burns, a once successful singer who had gradually moved into the role of agent (Fordham 2 September 2010). This arrangement, too, however, was short-lived as Richard pursued a strategy of self-management, setting an example for others once they had achieved similar success.

Expresso Bongo

The next phase in the transformation of Harry Webb came less than two years after the debut of "Move it!" with a film role. *Expresso Bongo* (1959) relates the story of struggling musician-agent Johnny Jackson (Lawrence Harvey) in search of a young talent whom he can manage to his financial benefit. Richard plays the charismatic but deceptively naïve Bert Rudge whom Jackson discovers in a coffee bar (modeled after the 2i's) and whom he promotes through a recording contract and a new name: Bongo Herbert. Like Richard, however, Rudge eventually replaces his manager to take control of his own career.[14]

Just after his twenty-second birthday in 1962, Richard made his American debut on *The Ed Sullivan Show* with an elaborate dance production of "The Young Ones" (January 1962) from his film of the same name. Frustrated, he never came close to the success he had in the UK, which he blamed on record companies that failed to promote him.

Instead, he broadened his British and Commonwealth audiences, observing that consumers were "still into ballads, and I went very heavily into ballads" (Savage February 1995b). Although moving into "variety," he retained rock 'n' roll interests. Nevertheless, he knew "deep down . . . that the mums and dads had the money. 'Living Doll' got me a mum and dad audience," and film appearances "moved me very solidly into it" (Savage February 1995a).

Richard would continue to balance his film, recording, and live performance careers, releasing discs in every decade up to the 1990s. Jack Good, however, lamented: "my God, I spent all these hours making him mean and magnificent, and he throws it all away with one bloody song ["Living Doll"]. I love Cliff but he should have stayed moody" (Leigh and Firminger 1996, 41).

---

[14] The film features music composed for Richard and the Shadows with "A Voice in the Wilderness" reaching #2 on British charts.

Fig. 2.1 Tommy Steele, in "Teenage Party" (promotional film), 1957.

Fig. 2.2 Cliff Richard and the Shadows: Bruce Welch, Cliff Richard, Tony Meehan (obscured), Jet Harris, Hank Marvin, in *The Young Ones*, 1961. Alamy/Reportage/archival

3
Channeling English Pop

Households across the UK in the fifties made space for a new piece of furniture intended to draw the family not only into the front room but also into the modern world. The television joined the radiogram[1] in delivering information and entertainment molded to suit the limitations and possibilities of the equipment and the medium.[2] Ownership of these media devices both symbolized a family's socioeconomic status and aspirations and provided them with a window onto cultural changes under way nationally and internationally. Programming, thus, conveyed attitudes about class, gender, ethnicity, and other parameters of Britain's evolving identity.

The Tele. After suspending their initial television broadcasts during the war, the BBC resumed programming in June 1946 for around 25,000 relatively affluent London homes. By the coronation of Elizabeth II in 1953, that number had grown to 3 million across most of the nation. In these broadcasts, the BBC applied the same unchallenged paternalistic programming to television that they had to radio. The Television Act 1954, however, created a separate, independent, and commercial network regulated by a board to ensure that good taste prevailed. After commencing broadcasts on 22 September 1955, ITV was drawing over 70 percent of the nation's viewers by 1957, with programming directed at a broad audience and emphazing the identities of its on-air personalities (see Sandbrook 2005, 383).

Our identities are dynamic and shift with time and context reflecting how others respond to our physical self (age, health, appearance, etc.) and cultural qualities (language, education, wealth, etc.). We associate ourselves with those whom we see as our peers—or at least with those whom we would like to imagine as our peers—through multiple parameters.[3] In that process, the media (particularly television, film, and recordings) and urban centers play powerful roles.

The Cosmopolitan Canopy. When Tommy Hicks from Bermondsey in southeast London and Harry Webb from Cheshunt in northern metropolitan London became Tommy Steele and Cliff Richard in Soho, they demonstrated the way

---

[1] British English for a combination radio/record player (gramophone).
[2] Combined radio and television licenses grew in the UK from 764,000 in 1951 to more than 10 million in 1960 (Sandbrook 2005, 384).
[3] This approach is based on John Turner's ideas about the relationship between the individual and society (see Haslam et al. 2012).

cities provide contexts in which individuals can reinvent themselves. Whether arriving from abroad or from the suburbs, urban settings provide a degree of anonymity that allows individuals to reinvent themselves as they move from one new context to another. Soho especially offered a "cosmopolitan canopy" under which different ethnicities, classes, genders, and their agendas mingled, and where performers could adopt new personas appropriate to the spaces where they appeared (Nonini 2014.)

Steele and Richard, however, represent only the most successful British pop artists navigating the urban and adolescent landscapes of late 1950s London. In both cases, while concert appearances dominated their finances, British media and especially television figured prominently in their success. A web of symbiotic relationships involving live performance, record production and marketing, and radio, television, and film underlay the fabric of postwar British popular music. Musicians, managers, producers, publishers, and songwriters in the sixties encountered rapid, diverse, and continual changes in aesthetic tastes as Britain's youth became teenagers and struggled to establish their own identities.

The Good Parnes and the Wilde Brown Fury

In a pas de deux of convenience, Larry Parnes and Jack Good danced the most powerful unofficial symbiotic partnership of late 1950s British pop. Parnes's success managing Tommy Steele had empowered his own reinvention from Oxford Street clothing merchant to Britain's premier talent scout through the curation of singers such as Vince Eager, Dickie Pride, Duffy Power, and Johnny Gentle. The press compared Parnes to a "stud farmer" with a "stable of stars" and described him as transforming common coffee-bar singers into celebrities through "extensive grooming": haircuts, skin treatments, and tailored clothing, but most of all his lectures on how to behave with the public. His success encouraged others; however, with little guidance, the career of at least one musician demonstrated the way sudden elevation to stardom could be disastrous. Singer Terry Dene (managed by one of the owners of the 2i's) had early success with Jack Good until a series of escapades landed him in court and his career in a downward spiral (Rogan 1988, 27).

Good's groundbreaking television productions *Six-Five Special* (BBC, 1957–1958), *Oh Boy!* (ITV, 1958–1959), *Boy Meets Girls* (ITV, 1959–1960), and *Wham!!* (ITV, 1960) featured a quick succession of music performances with novel camera placements. In an era when the popular British soap opera *Coronation Street* elevated the lives of common people doing everyday things, Good and Parnes transformed the boys next door into pop icons. Their unofficial partnership channeled contemporary cultural trends by imagining British pop in the image of a young, working-class, sexually potent male.

Although television censors preferred family-friendly performers, Good understood that youth and especially young women wanted more than middle-aged crooners. His television shows established a model that would be imitated by *Ready Steady Go!* (ITV, 1963–1966) and other British and American popular music programs for the next decade. In 1958, as he prepared to leave the BBC's *Six-Five Special* over artistic differences and to begin planning new shows at ITV, Good turned to Parnes for content. London's premier pop Svengali did not disappoint.

Reg from Greenwich

Before he was Marty Wilde, Reg Smith had left school at 15 to work as a messenger at a commodity firm but spent his nights in Soho making music (Frame 2007, 273; David Parker February 2014). In his hometown of Greenwich, a local record merchant had introduced him to the music of some of Elvis's forebears, including Willie Mae Thornton, Muddy Waters, and Howlin' Wolf (271). And when Smith saw the film *Blackboard Jungle* (1955), he knew he "was going to be a singer. There wasn't much doubt of that" (Wilde in Savage February 1995a).

Initially under the stage name "Reg Patterson," he alternated between the Blue Angel (Mayfair) and el Condor Club (Soho) where he earned £1 a night plus a bowl of spaghetti before catching the last train back to Greenwich (Frame 2007, 271–272). The Condor was where Lionel Bart watched the 19-year-old wow the room, and Smith's door was where Larry Parnes soon arrived after hearing Bart's description. Wasting no time, the Svengali came bearing a contract with the singer's name already inscribed (Rogan 1988, 21).

The construction of a new identity for Parnes's new client began with a name change, a combination of working-class humility inspired by the film *Marty* and the excitement the manager saw in Smith's performances. Henceforth, Reg Smith would be Marty Wilde. That established, they descended into the den of London's burgeoning rock 'n' roll scene in search of musicians to become the Wildcats. Jim Sullivan remembered that "the rockers, you know, the hardened rockers used to go down the 2i's 'cause you could have a play down there." In that cramped basement, Sullivan received an invitation to be a Wildcat, with the stipulation "you got to get your hair dyed blonde" (interview 22 January 2001).

To Philips Records producer Johnny Franz, Wilde represented a convincing Elvis-like British vehicle for covering American hits, especially if Parnes could arrange television appearances. To Jack Good, Marty Wilde offered a more authentic rock 'n' roll artist than Tommy Steele, and Good scheduled him for episodes of the *Six-Five Special*. Live performances on these shows and later Good productions helped bring Wilde's interpretations of American hits into Britain's top ten, including covers of Jody Reynolds's "Endless Sleep" (June 1958), Ritchie Valens's "Donna" (March 1959), Dion and the Belmonts' "A Teenager in Love" (June 1959), and Phil Phillips and the Twilights' "Sea of Love" (September 1959).

The Bad Boy. During this run, however, the Good-Parnes relationship grew complicated when Cliff Richard became the television producer's new star. Wilde had featured in summer pilots for Good's new ITV show *Oh Boy!* (meant to compete with *Six-Five Special*, which continued at the BBC); however, when the show went on the air in September 1958, Richard occupied center stage. Parnes felt Good had betrayed a gentleman's agreement and in October pulled Wilde from the series, in the process alienating both the singer and the television producer (Rogan 1988, 22). The music press buzzed about the split between the two youth moguls, but Good and Parnes needed each other's talents too much to remain at odds. Wilde returned to *Oh Boy!* in February 1959, and when Good launched *Boy Meets Girls* that September, Parnes's client had a prime spot.

An ongoing challenge for the British popular music and recording industries in this era lay in the lack of good original material. With Ian Samwell still working on another hit, Good contracted American songwriters Mort Shuman and Doc Pomus to write new material for British artists, producing "It's Been Nice" for Wilde. The song and its performance rocked; however, Britain preferred Wilde's self-penned song on the flip side. "Bad Boy" (December 1959) pits young love against adult control, with Wilde singing quietly and close to the microphone to create an atmosphere of intimacy. Significantly, for both "It's Been Nice" and "Bad Boy," the Wildcats demonstrated their growing effectiveness as British interpreters of American rock 'n' roll, country, and pop and American timbral aesthetics. Unfortunately, the musicians also found themselves confined by old-school production aesthetics.

Jim Sullivan recalled that he had brought an "echo unit like Cliff Gallup and James Burton" to the session to give the recording a "rockabilly" feel only to have Franz veto the effect. The guitarist had also turned up his amplifier, so it had "a bit of bite. . . . It was a really good crunch." Franz, nevertheless, told him to "turn the amp right down so it was all totally clean. Totally soulless and if you listen to the album [*Wilde about Marty*], that's how we did the whole album. I nearly cried when I heard the sound back" (interview 22 January 2001).

By 1961, however, Good was ready to leave British television, and Marty Wilde was ready to make the leap from rocker to stage star, landing a lead role in the London production of *Bye Bye Birdie*. He seemed perfectly cast for a story loosely based around the rise of Elvis Presley, but the camera would not embrace him the way that it did Cliff Richard. Nevertheless, his career arc and that of others resonated with the optimism of postwar Britain and the conceit of a young working-class male gaining financial rewards through the beneficence of a middle-class manager.

Ron from the Dingle

If Jack Good and Larry Parnes were looking for an authentic working-class male icon who could sing for the microphone and look good for the camera, they found him in Ronald Wycherley. Growing up in the Dingle, one of Liverpool's most economically challenged neighborhoods, Wycherley had developed rheumatic fever as a child. Confined at home, his parents tried piano lessons to ameliorate his recovery; however, buying him a guitar proved better medicine.

Like many other working-class Liverpool lads, Wycherley left school at 15. By day, he worked the Merseyside docks on the crew of the tugboat *Formby*. By night, he and his friends performed in pubs and clubs, engaging in Scouse word play and naming themselves the Formby Sniffle Gloup (Bell 2014). Skiffle, however, only occupied his attention until rock 'n' roll arrived.

With his good looks, musical abilities, and a decent version of Elvis's hip swivel, locals loved him. Moreover, perhaps inspired by Buddy Holly, who toured the UK in March 1958, Wycherley began writing his own songs, recording demos at a local studio, and sending them to Larry Parnes for Marty Wilde. It was Wycherley's mother, however, who gained an invitation for the 18-year-old to meet the manager when the Parnes's "Extravaganza" tour played the Essoldo Theatre across the Mersey River from Liverpool (1 October 1958).

Parnes was impressed even before Wycherley took out his guitar. Standing in the wings, the manager asked the singer-songwriter if he had "the guts" to go on stage (Frame 2007, 381). Wycherley took the challenge, to the delight of the audience, creating one of the great stories of British rock 'n' roll. He joined the tour the next morning on its way to London to continue his grooming.

The Sound of Fury. As with "Marty Wilde," Parnes created a stage identity for his new client, combining a familiar and friendly first name with something implying excitement. The first proved easy by namechecking the popular band leader Billy Cotton. For a last name, however, Parnes wanted to emphasize his client's working-class roots and to build on his personal story. He found his inspiration in *Sea Fury* (August 1958), a recent film about a crewman working on a tugboat (Frame 2007, 382). Although Wycherley had his own opinions about a stage name, Parnes was ahead of him, and the morning papers announced the arrival of "Billy Fury."

In late 1958, although Johnny Franz declined to record Fury, Dick Rowe at Decca heard potential in the Liverpudlian singer-songwriter and encouraged Hugh Mendl to sign him. The agreement ultimately included granting Fury some artistic control, with Mendl assigning Frank Lee as recording manager. As the Good-Parnes dispute subsided, Harry Robinson agreed to serve as music director, drawing on musicians from Lord Rockingham's XI, the house band for *Oh Boy!* (Frame 2007, 383 and Rogan 1988, 24–25).

Among the tunes Wycherley had originally proffered to Larry Parnes, one emerged as Billy Fury's first single. Released in mid-January 1959, "Maybe Tomorrow" was the first of several British hits that Fury penned and recorded, including "Margo" (May 1959), "Collette" (January 1960), and "That's Love" (May 1960). Even more unusual for the time, his first album, *The Sound of Fury* (May 1960), consisted entirely of his own material in an era when most songs were written by somebody other than the singer.[4]

Fury's television persona grew through his role as a coffee-bar musician in the teleplay *Strictly for the Sparrows* (October 1958), which prepared him for Jack Good's *Oh Boy!* and *Boy Meets Girls* and the BBC's *Six-Five Special* and *Drumbeat*. Like Marty Wilde, however, Fury never made a convincing leap to film, remaining a club and cabaret artist who occasionally released recordings. Nevertheless, his English combination of Elvis Presley and Buddy Holly inspired others, especially in his native Liverpool.

A Boy from Plaistow

In contrast to carefully coiffed singers anchored to a microphone lest they move out of the camera closeup, constraining Joe Brown proved difficult. Grooming would neither soften his London cockney accent nor slick back his shock of bushy blond hair. With a guitar strapped around his neck and a smirk on his face, he emerged as Britain's first unmitigated English country artist.

When he was a boy, the Browns lived upstairs over a pub run by his uncle in Plaistow, East London, where his mother served as "housekeeper-barmaid" and where another family often busked for tips and drinks playing the accordion, piano, and guitar. Their patriarch was "a gypsy kind of character [who] would make a living by picking up bits of old brass and lead, old scrap metal, and stuff" and reselling it (Brown interview 8 July 2001). He also sold Brown's mother a guitar and taught her son the basics of chording and soloing, albeit with an unconventional tuning.

When skiffle swept Britain, Brown found himself ahead of most guitarists and ready for rock 'n' roll, quickly progressing to play ballrooms, holiday camps, and clubs. In 1959, Larry Parnes hired him to sit in with a band that was backing

---

[4] One of Fury's most successful recordings came in 1961 with a cover of Carole King and Gerry Goffin's "Halfway to Paradise."

some of the manager's artists auditioning for *Boy Meets Girls*. Although disinterested in the singers, Jack Good inquired about the blond guitarist. Without missing a beat, Parnes claimed proprietorship, which, although not the case at that moment, soon would be.

Working on Good's shows, Brown backed Billy Fury, featured on *The Sound of Fury*, and, with the television producer's encouragement, began to sing. The 18-year-old, however, proved Parnes's match by rejecting the initial contract offer. "He was very good about it. He went and saw my mum and all that.... I said if he gets me mum out of the pub and that, and gives us a decent place to live, I'd sign it. But, the most important [is] my motorcar: I can't afford the payments on it. And he said, 'I'll take that over, tomorrow'" (interview 8 July 2001).[5]

A Picture. Brown would meet and play with several American performers on the show, but one above all others influenced British rock 'n' roll guitarists. In addition to his music, Eddie Cochran gave them advice about playing, including replacing the top strings with a lighter gauge to allow them to bend notes. "Eddie was great, because there were only a few of us guitar players around, like Jim Sullivan and Colin Green and all that. We all used to get together with Eddie. I mean he was a good, good player and he showed us all that, which we thought, 'Oh Christ, this is easy now'" (interview 8 July 2001).

Brown's second act of defiance came when he refused to take a stage name. Parnes "wanted to call me Elmer Twitch. That wouldn't pass . . ." (interview 8 July 2001). Joe Brown would steadfastly remain Joe Brown in name and person. Embracing his working-class background, they named his band the Bruvvers, a term referencing labor-union membership with a colloquial cockney consonant switch on "brothers."

By the spring of 1962, however, most of his discs—with the exception of cockney comedy tunes like "Jellied Eels" and "I'm Henery the Eighth I Am"—were fairing poorly. With Ray Horricks producing at Decca and Brown's English humor in mind, Bruvvers Peter Oakman and John Beveridge wrote "A Picture of You," a country-flavored song with lyrics that pine for a lost love, who turns out to be only someone whom the singer has surreptitiously photographed. In May 1962, "A Picture of You" initiated a string of successes, including "It Only Took a Minute" (November 1962) and "That's What Love Will Do" (February 1963).

Like Steele and Richard, the singer-guitarist appeared in films such as *What a Crazy World* (1963) and *Three Hats for Lisa* (1966), on stage in *Charlie Girl* (1965–1968), and on television programs such as on *The Billy Cotton Band Show*.[6] Although Brown would be Larry Parnes's last major artist, others were eager to have their images on home screens.

---

[5] Two years later, the dealership reclaimed the car after Parnes failed to make the payments.
[6] The BBC, however, banned "Little Ukulele" (October 1964), his version of George Formby's "With My Little Ukulele in My Hand."

Telly Stars

The growing availability of televisions in the UK had significant implications for British society. For example, working-class men were less likely to go to their local pub in the evening, instead staying home to watch the telly (Sandbrook 2005, 384). In response, broadcasters scheduled programs based on whom they thought was in the front room: housewives during the day, families in the early evening, and married couples at night.

Jack Good designed shows to appeal to the recent phenomena of teenagers living at home with a disposable income in their pocket, no families to maintain, and a hunger for pop music. They watched in the early evening before heading out to the cinema, a club, and/or a dance hall, and television programming primed their tastes.

In numerous variations during the late 1950s and 1960s, others imitated the narrative about a young working-class musician spotted by a sharp-eyed manager who grooms and transforms his or her charge. They also noted the role television played in the promotion of artists with the right face, voice, song, arrangement, production, and promotion. For the adolescents who watched these television shows, however, performative identities offered ideas on how males and females should look, sound, and behave.

Terry from Acton

Eve Taylor's family roots in the music hall shaped her approach to artist management. The so-called Queen Bee of Show Business was managing John Barry and his band when Barry recommended another client for her roster (Altham 16 July 1965). At 15 and working as an assistant film editor, Terry Nelhams from Acton, West London, was singing with the skiffle group Worried Men in the 2i's when Jack Good descended the stairs, dressed in an "American baseball jacket" and looking "down through his glasses [with] his head raked back" (Frame 2007, 282). The band impressed the producer enough that when the BBC broadcast a live edition of the *Six-Five Special* from the 2i's (16 November 1957), the Worried Men opened and closed the show.

After a return performance (4 January 1958), Good encouraged Nelhams to "leave the group and go solo," which was when Eve Taylor began molding him to be an actor (Leigh and Firminger 1996, 32; Altham 16 July 1965). The manager initially saw a "dying duck in a thunderstorm . . . [dressed] in a blue pullover and blue jeans worn white at the knees." The television producer, however, saw "Britain's singing James Dean." Teaming him with former Viper Freddy Lloyd as "Teddy and Freddy," Good put them on his new show, *Oh Boy!* (14 March 1959) (Faith in Frame 2007, 283). And when that failed, Good had another idea.

The creation of Adam Faith offers an example of television's role in presenting gender in late 1950s teen singers. Nelhams's version of his renaming references Jack Good's home, where a baby had just arrived and where the singer found a "book of kids' names": "Adam" came from the boys' section and "Faith," from the girls' (Leigh and Firminger 1996, 96).[7] Adam Faith—the good-looking, well-dressed, and manicured young man—offers an example of the "pretty boy" figure in pop. His combination of male and female identities offered a British version of Americans like Bobby Rydell: a nonthreatening, telegenic presence that could be the boy next door . . . only safer.

Taylor arranged for an appearance on ATV's documentary series *Keeping in Step* (2 April 1958) to introduce Adam Faith to Britain, but other connections put him in the charts.[8] Having worked with Faith on *Oh Boy!*, John Barry—now the music director for the BBC's *Drumbeat*—recommended Faith as a recurring guest beginning on its 4 April 1959 episode.[9]

What You Want. Television not only brought singers into millions of British homes for teens but also provided a window on pop culture for the music industry, which was how songwriter Johnny Worth came to see Faith as a vehicle for one of his songs (Frame 2007, 415–416). To budding British songwriters of the era like Geoff Stephens, Worth was "brilliant . . . he wrote great pop songs! That man was Britain's first real pop songwriter to challenge the Americans . . . strictly pop, but very, very on the mark" (Stephens interview 2 March 2001). Worth had written "What Do You Want?" with rocker Johnny Kidd in mind and had asked Barry's pianist, Les Reed, to record a demo for him. When Kidd rejected the song, however, Worth, Barry, and Reed reimagined it for Faith, who also added his own touch.

With Buddy Holly's recent posthumous hit "It Doesn't Matter Anymore" (January 1959) serving as a model, Reed and Barry added a pizzicato string accompaniment reminiscent of the American's recording. Faith credits fellow *Drumbeat* regular Roy Young with coaching his interpretation of "What Do You Want?" and specifically in his quasi-American pronunciation of the word "baby" as "bay-beh" (Leigh and Firminger 1996, 96). In the studio, the John Barry Seven with orchestral musicians provide the backing overseen by artist-and-repertoire manager John Burgess and balance engineer Malcolm Addey in EMI's Studio Two.

---

[7] Peter Frame (2007, 283) suggests that the names came from friends of the singer: Adam Fremantle and Nicholas Faith.

[8] Barry became best known for his film compositions, including scores first for several James Bond films and Oscars for others later.

[9] *Drumbeat* aired on Saturday evenings.

In anticipation of Parlophone releasing the disc in late October 1959, Jack Good booked Faith for an appearance on his latest show, *Boy Meets Girls* (14 November 1959). The song, the performance, the recording, and the promotion all helped the disc to top British charts the first week of December, where it became a British pop benchmark.[10] Faith topped British charts again with another John Worth tune, "Poor Me" (January 1960), followed by the top-five hits "Someone Else's Baby" (April 1960) and "The First Time" (September 1963).

Holloway Road

The major British record companies EMI, Decca, Pye, and Philips had the advantages of owning purpose-built recording studios and pressing plants, not to mention distribution arrangements that enabled de facto domestic control of the disc industry. In the 1950s, however, the industry shifted. Instead of lathes cutting into warm wax discs, iron-oxide tape slid over electromagnetic heads as independent recording studios opened across London.

One of the earliest independent facilities, Denis Preston's Lansdowne Studios (1957) near Holland Park had Joe Meek not only designing the room and mixing board but also serving as its chief engineer (Massey 2015, 99). Preston knew Meek from IBC Recording Studios,[11] and from his reputation engineering several significant releases of the era, including Lonnie Donegan's "Cumberland Gap" and Humphrey Lyttelton's "Bad Penny Blues." In 1960, however, the laissez-faire owner/producer and the obsessive-compulsive engineer came to their inevitable dénouement. Meek moved to Holloway Road in North London to open RGM Sound,[12] where his limited resources meant relying on creativity and ingenuity as his principal resources to liberate him from corporate protocol. That proved to be the case when Robert Stigwood brought John Leyton to Meek and Holloway Road.

Remember Me. Leyton, who had acted in the short-lived television series *Biggles* (1961) and already had a fan club, looked to add "singer" to his portfolio by having Meek record his covers of "Tell Laura I Love Her" (August 1960) and "The Girl on the Floor Above" (October 1960) (Young 29 December 2013). Although neither disc charted, Stigwood was able to book his client for the new weekly ITV department-store drama *Harpers West One*. Leyton would appear as rock 'n' roll star Johnny Saint Cyr singing his latest release to fans in the store's record department. They prepared to record a disc quickly and have it pressed,

---

[10] This would be Parlophone's first No. 1 pop disc.
[11] IBC had originally opened in the 1930s but only became a full-time music production facility in 1962 (Massey 2015, 88-98).
[12] The initials stand for Joe Meek's birth name, Robert George Meek.

ready to coincide with Leyton's television appearance on 24 July 1961. All they needed was a song.

Meek headed to Denmark Street and publishers Southern Music, where Geoff Goddard had a song that he believed Buddy Holly had inspired, if not had dictated from beyond the grave (Repsch 2000, 117). "Johnny Remember Me" plays on themes established in "Tell Laura I Love Her," articulated as though part of *Wuthering Heights*, with the singer hearing a lost love's ghostly voice in the wind calling him. To achieve that effect, music director Charles Blackwell brought in singer Lissa Gray to help create the impression of an "eerie choir" with Meek adding layers of reverberation.

The television tie-in helped the recording to top British charts in August 1961 (replacing Helen Shapiro's "You Don't Know") and was followed by "Wild Wind" (September 1961). Stigwood and Leyton's interests, however, lay in his film career playing working-class English soldiers in *The Great Escape* (1963), *Guns at Batasi* (1964), and *Von Ryan's Express* (1965). Moreover, the terrain was shifting under British pop in the early 1960s as a succession of British pop artists entered the market, including a young girl.

Queen for Tonight

Perhaps the most successful British pop singer of 1961, Helen Shapiro challenged the male-star trope that had dominated both Jack Good's programming and Larry Parnes's casting. Growing up in working-class East London, the granddaughter of Jewish Russian immigrants, her parents enrolled her for singing lessons at the Maurice Burman School of Modern Pop Singing in Marylebone. Burman had figured in ITV's *Find the Singer* series, a talent contest looking for Britain's next big star. Shapiro's parents believed that "people were discovered" at his school, and her dad shelled out "25 shillings every Saturday, which was something he could ill afford" (Shapiro in Leigh and Firminger 1996, 99).

When Burman invited Columbia's Norrie Paramor to listen to his students, the producer sent his assistant. After listening to several of the students, the 24-year-old John Schroeder took notice when the 13-year-old sang. What he heard sounded "so professional." What he heard was a contralto "voice that was totally incomparable, so deep and rich in tone and so full of emotion" (Schroeder 2009, 58). When he played her tape for Paramor, however, the producer misread her gender: "HE is good, isn't he?" (Schroeder 2016, 39).

At first, Paramor thought he had found an answer to America's Brenda Lee, but identifying appropriate material that balanced puberty and innocence and that sounded suitable for a not-quite-14-year-old with a deep voice to sing would prove difficult. Ultimately, he turned to the person at EMI who knew Shapiro's voice best; John Schroeder, however, had never really written a song.

An Ordinary Girl at School. Developing a melody that he thought would fit her range, Schroeder turned to freelance journalist Mike Hawker, who had recently joined EMI's promotion department and who was boarding with him.[13] Hawker recognized that their challenge lay partly in how to present Shapiro's combination of youth, gender, innocence, and puberty and came up with the idea for "Don't Treat Me Like a Child." Shapiro later reasoned that "girls who are that age think they're terribly grown up but adults still treat you like 14-year-olds. . . . People still tell me, I wanted to be like you, which was the secret—to identify with the ordinary girl at school" (Aston 1994). Paramor began planning a release date with one remaining decision: her name.

British women singers often adopted monikers that their managers and producers thought sounded appropriate (e.g., Anne Shelton née Patricia Sibley); however, renaming the 14-year-old Shapiro presented a different quandary. In the 1950s, Alma Cogan (who had also been a student at Maurice Burman's school) had changed her name from Alma Cohen to mask her Jewish identity. Other important performers in this era, such as saxophonist Ronnie Scott (née Ronald Schatt) and drummer Tony Crombie (née Anthony Kronenberg), had also masked their ethnicity in response to British anti-Semitism. A decade later, you still "didn't keep a Jewish name" because it meant receiving hate mail (Shapiro in Leigh and Firminger 1996, 96). Although Paramor felt uncomfortable with the name Shapiro, he believed it would stand out, telling her she could keep her name because "it sounds Italian" (Schroeder 2016, 43).[14]

"Don't Treat Me Like a Child" (February 1961) climbed to #3 and stayed in British charts for 20 weeks, despite the absence of a television booking. For her follow-up "You Don't Know" (June 1961), appearances first on ITV's *Thank Your Lucky Stars* (17 June 1961) and then on the BBC's *Juke Box Jury* (5 August 1961) helped that disc to top British charts for three weeks and to stay commercially relevant for 23 weeks.

Look at Life. With this success, the Rank Organisation approached Paramor about a film describing the creation of her next recording. *Look at Life* offered a series of 10-minute shorts that ran before feature presentations in theaters, with Shapiro's episode covering the creation of a song, rehearsals, and the recording of her presumed soon-to-be hit disc. Although Schroeder struggled to come up with a musical idea, a short walk home from the pub provided inspiration. And when Hawker heard the tune, his expectations of seeing his girlfriend provided

---

[13] Hawker would soon leave EMI to work for Larry Parnes.
[14] Another factor, however, might be the success of the film *Exodus*, which depicted the plight of Jewish refugees attempting to migrate to Palestine and which United Artists released at the end of 1960.

the necessary verbal inspiration for "Walking Back to Happiness" (September 1961). Like a trained actor, the not-yet-15-year-old Shapiro delivers emotions ranging from the regret of leaving a lover to the anticipated joys of returning.

A few days after the July recording date, everyone returned to EMI's Studio Two, where they recreated the session for Rank's film crew, including a fictionalized version of Schroeder introducing the song to Paramor and Shapiro. Columbia then held release of the recording until 22 September 1961 to allow for film editing and duplication so that a coordinated release of the disc and the documentary would achieve maximum results. Once again, Shapiro's recording topped British charts and remained there for three weeks, firmly establishing her as a star and Schroeder as a production savant.

Shapiro continued to have hits with John Barry's "Tell Me What He Said" (February 1962) and Schroeder and Hawker's "Little Miss Lonely" (July 1962) after Schroeder had moved on to become a producer at Pye's Piccadilly Records, but the musical tide was changing. "Let's Talk about Love" (April 1962), "Keep Away from Other Girls" (October 1962), and "Queen for Tonight" (January 1963) failed to make the UK's top twenty as youth culture focused on electric guitars and keyboards.

Fig. 3.1 Billy Fury, 1961.

Fig. 3.2 Adam Faith, April 1960.

Fig. 3.3 Johnny Leyton, *The John Leyton Touch*, 1961.

Fig. 3.4 Joe Brown, on *Pops and Lenny*, 1962.

Fig. 3.5 Maurice Burman, Helen Shapiro, Norrie Paramor, John Schroeder, at EMI Recording Studios, 1961. Pictorial Press Ltd/Alamy Stock Photo

4
Behind the Stars

Although the emergence of nuclear energy informed the postwar years politically, militarily, and economically, electromagnetism shaped everyday musical reality. The same technology that underlay the introduction of iron-oxide tape in the recording industry also allowed the development of electric guitars, microphones, amplifiers, and other devices. And, although one of the most important means of consuming music still relied on a stylus careening down the grooves of a disc, each year saw consumers gaining access to higher fidelity electronic playback systems.

Bands featuring electric instruments offer one of the signature features of 1960s British pop: self-contained male-dominated cliques experimenting with sounds and solving musical problems collectively. They always stood behind the featured singer literally and figuratively, as the Wildcats did for Marty Wilde, the Drifters for Cliff Richard, and the Bruvvers for Joe Brown. "It was always Joe Brown and *His* Bruvvers," remembered drummer Bobby Graham. "The Bruvvers were always pushed into the background whenever there were newspaper articles or photographs" (interview 14 March 2001).

Managers and producers, of course, had practical reasons to promote a singer whom they could groom and who had the possibility of a long career on stage and/or in film. Producers could replace band members in the studio, managers could relegate them to sleeping on the tour bus, and artists could drop the band altogether if they felt challenged. Moreover, most female fans in this era came to see the singer, not the band.

American bands, however, were establishing collective stage identities, attracting fans, and, consequently, making their own recordings. For example, Buddy Holly had played as a member of the Crickets on their seminal "That'll Be the Day" (May 1957) before emerging as the headliner. Moreover, the beginnings of California surf music in 1961 featured bands like the Beach Boys. British music culture would be quick to follow suit, adding some of the working-class egalitarian aesthetics of the trad band and/or the skiffle group.

Demographically, as the peak of Britain's postwar births reached puberty in 1960, many males began imagining themselves on stage as objects of the female gaze. While most men and women may have paid admission to watch the singer, many soon came to watch the band, appraising instruments and technique while imagining their own invasions of the performance space.

Transformers

British popular culture has a rich history of alternative identities, in not only the theater proper but in traditions such as the Christmas pantomime. Indeed, British pop musicians like Tommy Steele and Marty Wilde often engaged in these annual winter theatrical events, costumed to be part of fairy tales for this very English entertainment. This role-playing allows participants to adopt behaviors that would normally be unacceptable (e.g., cross-dressing) and to behave in ways proscribed in everyday life.

With the growing number of British pop bands in the late 1950s and early 1960s, some performers looked for ways beyond musicianship to distinguish themselves from the competition. For example, when going to see Nero and the Gladiators, one could expect to encounter fictional representatives of the Roman Empire playing electric guitars. Two bands in particular, however, proved important for their costuming and stage presentations, for the music they created, and for the musicians who passed through their ranks.

Fred from Willesden

Frederick Heath, like so many other performers in this era, started as a skiffle musician in Willesden, North London, playing tunes made popular by Lonnie Donegan, mixing his repertoire with whatever audiences requested. With the success of artists like Cliff Richard, Marty Wilde, and Billy Fury, Heath's skiffle groups segued into a series of rock bands. At night, Heath built a community of fans in and around the northwest London suburbs of Willesden and Wandsworth, from workingmen's clubs to dance halls, while by day the singer painted houses. Following the familiar model, middle-class entrepreneur Guy Robinson convinced Peter Sullivan at EMI's HMV label to offer a recording test that led to a contract (Barrett 2006).

With Sullivan and engineer Malcolm Addey in Studio Two's control room, Freddie Heath and His Rock 'n' Roll Combo recorded the singer's composition "Please Don't Touch." Although being in EMI was new to the musicians, the real surprise came when Heath saw that the session had been registered as "Johnny Kidd and the Pirates." When Heath asked "Who the hell is that?" Sullivan and Robinson informed him that this would be his and the band's new professional name (Barrett 2006).

Articulating a theme to which Heath would return several times in other songs, "Please Don't Touch" reworks the psychophysical elements of Jerry Lee Lewis's "Whole Lot of Shakin' Going On" (1957). The tremulous refrain "Please don't touch, I shake so much" and the chorus's "gonna spend my life shakin'" like a leaf" managed to convey sexual arousal without running afoul of BBC censors. A month later "Please Don't Touch" (May 1959) reached a respectable #25 on British charts.

Heath/Kidd and Robinson (no doubt with input from Sullivan) also concluded that the Pirates needed reorganization, keeping guitarist Alan Caddy but bringing in Brian Gregg (bass) and Clem Cattini (drums). As a quartet, they would firmly establish themselves as Pirates over the next two years. "We played this place . . . every Saturday night and we used to have 1,500 to 2,000 people there," Cattini remembered. "We all became like friends. When it was your birthday, they all bought you presents." Moreover, "people went to see a rock and roll show" in which Kidd began to develop a "very macho" stage persona that appealed to "both sexes" (22 January 2001). Their reputation around London and their sound also gained the notice of Jack Good, who put them on two episodes of *Wham!!*

Shakin'. This configuration of the Pirates proved its potential in one of their first discs. Despite the relative hastiness of its composition and recording, "Shakin' All Over" (June 1960) joins "Move It!" as a benchmark of British rock 'n' roll. The simple lyrics expand on Kidd's favorite theme of "shaking," now with added "quivers" and "tremors" thrown in for good measure. Brian Gregg recalls that "on the day before the session, we went to the Freight Train coffee bar . . . in Soho, went downstairs, sat on some Coke crates and wrote 'Shakin' All Over' in six minutes or so. We recorded the song live—first take" (Barrett 2006). To round out the band and to get the sound they wanted, however, they added a fifth player just for the session.

Scottish guitarist Joe Moretti already had a reputation among British rockers for his guitar solo on Vince Taylor's "Brand New Cadillac" (April 1959) during which the singer calls him "Scotty." Moretti remembers sitting "in the restaurant in Old Compton Street called the Golden Egg [when] Clem [Cattini] came in with Johnny Kidd, Brian Gregg, and Alan Caddy" to ask him to play on their recording session. In rehearsal, he created the iconic introduction that repeats throughout the song, basing it on "a sort of mix from 'Move It!' and Duane Eddy" (interview 17 July 2003). He also improvised slides played with a cigarette lighter that punctuate the alternating refrain/chorus structure of the song.

With the disc's success, Kidd gradually commenced a stage transformation, beginning with his trademark patch, which he initially wore to correct weak eye muscles. The Cattini-Gregg-Caddy version of the Pirates originally dressed in suits, albeit with American cowboy boots, the front line kicking in time with the music. Kidd, however, also began to plan a more elaborate theatrical presentation that included a mural he unfurled behind the band depicting sails and rigging. Although Caddy, Cattini, and Gregg jumped ship, Kidd began elaborating on his costume, adding swords and pistols as he veered away from Gene Vincent as a performance model and more toward Errol Flynn's Captain Blood. Though dramatic, Kidd's theatrics had real competition from a performer of a different sort.

David from Kilburn

Perhaps one of the most remarkable personalities of 1960s British rock 'n' roll, David Sutch possessed ingenuity albeit without much musical finesse. Indeed, he was more often noted in his lifetime for his political misadventures leading the anarchistic Official Monster Raving Loony Party than for his music.

Denying that he copied Screaming Jay Hawkins, Screaming Lord Sutch nevertheless employed some of the same theatrical devices as that American icon (Leigh and Firminger 1996, 52). Both artists parodied the B-picture horror films of the era, with Sutch long holding a "fascination with horror and the macabre." Going to the cinema, however, he became "more intrigued by the special effects" than the plots (Sutch with Chippindale 1991, 20).

From the beginning, costuming played an important role, and when Sutch auditioned at the 2i's, he found a way to separate himself from other performers—all of whom he saw as Elvis impersonators. With buffalo horns attached to a motorcycle helmet and his long hair hanging out, he wore a leopard-skin coat he had borrowed from his aunt. His band became the Raving Savages (or just the Savages). And they stood out.

Just Chaos. Their shows typically began with an announced introduction, but when the curtains opened, the stage would be empty. From the back of the hall, dressed like "Tarzan," members of the band rushed through the audience, leapt on stage, and broke into the groove for Little Richard's "Lucille." After a while, however, the piano would intone Chopin's "Funeral March" (Sonata no. 2 in B♭ Minor). This cued a group of men dressed as monks to file into the hall carrying a coffin with Sutch inside. Once placed on stage, he would begin screaming and groaning before bursting out as the band played his signature tune, "'Til the Following Night."

His costume often included prosthetic rubber hands and heavy theatrical makeup, in which he would chase mostly women around the hall before spitting out a "mouthful of green gunge." Drummer Carlo Little remembered that "we had fires going on stage, coffins, and all hell would break loose. You know, curtains would be ripped down and the stage would be like a shambles. But the kids loved it.... It was just chaos."

And sometimes, Little noted, the props could be a problem:

> so, we had a biscuit tin, you know, a foot square biscuit tin filled with paper and petrol. And when you took the lid off, the fumes were quite strong and it

was always the piano player's job to light that fire on the first beat of the bar of the guitar solo.... And many a time he put too much petrol in and it would really go up with a six-foot flame. And if it was a low ceiling, like with bits of stuff hanging down—sometimes these clubs would have a little decoration hanging down, especially if it was near Christmas ... you know, that papier mâché stuff—it would go straight away.... We just carried on. We just pulled it down from the ceiling, stamped on it, poured the watering can on it, and carried on.... Every song had something about it. (Interview 4 April 2000)

Sutch's limited vocal skills meant difficulty finding a label willing to record him, but in 1961 Joe Meek took on the challenge of creating an appropriate aural landscape. HMV would lease their recording of "'Til the Following Night" (December 1961), which begins with the "Funeral March" accompanied by the sounds of a squeaking coffin lid and howling winds. Over this sonic tableau, Sutch begins screaming, culminating with the band breaking into the music for "Lucille," which he overlays with his tale of life in a graveyard with cats, bats, zombies, and skeletons.

While the music is far from special, the recording does capture some of the enthusiasm British musicians had for American culture in this era, as well as a penchant for theatrics presaging 1970s glam rock. As challenged as he was as a singer, Sutch's band nevertheless offered a training ground for some of the era's most remarkable musicians, all of whom carried some of their experiences as Savages with them.

Stepping Forward

The dance bands of the 1930s and 1940s, performing instrumentals and backing singers, derived from the same lineage as blues, country, and rock 'n' roll groups. American guitar-based ensembles like those backing Elvis Presley and Muddy Waters offered new versions of those models and something British musicians could imitate ... if they could obtain the equipment. Due in part to tariffs meant to address Britain's ongoing economic challenges, the cost of American instruments such as Fenders, Gibsons, and Ludwigs was prohibitive. Instead, British musicians often turned to European makes such as German Hofners and Czechoslovakian Futuramas or to English manufacturers like Dallas and Premier. (See Babiuk 2015; Babiuk and Prevost 2013.)

On stage, musicians sometimes staked out territory like homesteaders in a land rush. Often, the piano and drums spatially anchored the ensemble with other instruments positioned around and among them. Stage space in clubs such as the 2i's, however, could be tight: drummers often found themselves wedged between amplifiers and the back wall while guitarists struggled to find footing that kept them from falling into the audience. Performance spaces also often had other challenges. Pianists commonly had to contend with out-of-tune house instruments or, in the case of electronic keyboards, stairways that presented formidable obstacle courses. As groups moved from clubs into dance halls, they often encountered larger stages that articulated their underlying social and musical structure: guitars moved to the front with the singer, while the keyboard, bass, and drums had their backs.

A raised platform, however, not only afforded audiences a view of performers but also performers a view of their audience: were they dancing or reacting and, if so, to what and how? When not accompanying singers, instrumental dance-oriented compositions dominated early backing-band repertoires, often with titles and themes referencing people and places.

Rockingham

When Jack Good planned *Oh Boy!* to counter what he saw as the staid variety show format that the BBC had in mind for *Six-Five Special*, he needed a band that could play all the emerging styles. He relied on Harry Robinson to recruit the best musicians available for the new sound who, after listening to the top American records of the time, formed an ensemble that could play that music live on television (Leigh and Firminger 1996, 39). As in New York, Detroit, and Los Angeles, many of these musicians would be devotees of straight-ahead and modern jazz with the ability to read music and to improvise.

Good called the show's band Lord Rockingham's XI, positioning them along the viewer's right side of the stage (stage left) facing the center, where featured singers would stand. Center and front on the lower level of the band, four saxophonists crouched behind their stands with two (sometimes three) guitars above and behind them and the bass, drums, and piano above and to their right.

Prowling the keys of her white padded Hammond B3 organ and downstage from the saxophones (partially obscuring them), Cherry Wainer occupied the visual and musical core of the band—one of the few women instrumentalists actively performing in this scene. She sat closest to the audience, often with the drum kit and percussion raised and directly behind her, while resident vocal groups stood upstage on risers.

The band had to be able to back both crooners and rockers, so flexibility was important. Robinson not only pulled the musical program together each week but also oversaw the arrangements and rehearsed the house singers (the Dallas Boys, the Vernons Girls, and Neville Taylor and the Cutters). Performances by self-contained groups such as the John Barry Seven with their own arrangements only added to the production challenges of a show that usually went out live in London from the Hackney Empire theater each week after rehearsals in a separate Islington facility. This meant that everything moved every week.

Aboot This Hoose. Lord Rockingham's XI also occasionally recorded instrumentals separately, beginning with "Fried Onions" (May 1958) and "Hoots Mon" (September 1958), the latter topping British charts that December. Given Good's intention to present rock and pop as good clean fun, "Hoots Mon" carried elements of humor, albeit as English stereotypes of Scotland. Robinson (himself Scottish) arranged the traditional tune "A Hundred Pipers" with a rock groove, and he yells the phrase "Hoots mon, there's a moose loose aboot this hoose" during breaks.[1]

The band's success, however, also led to problems when Good and Robinson found themselves on opposite sides of a lawsuit over ownership of the name "Lord Rockingham's XI." The band's discs bore the title "Jack Good Presents Lord Rockingham's XI"; but with Robinson as the driving force behind the band, the question arose as to what exactly the name of the band was and, more important, who owned it. Although Good won the case, he and Robinson would work together again even if the blush was off the rose.

Moving Shadows

As Cliff Richard's backing band, the Shadows earned a substantial fan base of their own, with Hank Marvin, Bruce Welch, Jet Harris, and Tony Meehan often appearing as extras in the singer's films. Each member established a separate identity, with Marvin (his horn-rimmed glasses reminiscent of Buddy Holly) proving one of the most influential pop guitarists in Britain and Europe during the late 1950s and early 1960s. His clean tone and mix of American jazz, country, and pop styles influenced many guitarists, aided immeasurably by the Fender Stratocaster that Cliff Richard purchased for him directly from the United States (Foster 2000, 163).[2] He was also one of the first British pop guitarists to use new electronics in the form of an Italian-made Meazzi Echomatic echo unit played through British-made Vox Amplifiers.

Part of the band's identity derived from its modest choreographed stage movements of simple synchronized steps inspired by watching films like *The Girl Can't Help It*. The American band the Treniers had impressed Welch and Marvin

---

[1] "There's a mouse loose about this house."
[2] The British government lifted import restrictions in 1959.

during a London performance with the idea that they "must do something like that because it looks interesting" (Welch in Leigh and Firminger 1996, 38).[3]

Spatially in concerts, the Shadows would play a short set before Richard's appearance, aligning themselves with Marvin stage left, Harris in the middle front, Welch stage right, and Meehan behind them with amplifiers lined up often in front of him. When Richard emerged from the wings, he moved in front of Harris, with Marvin and Welch sometimes shifting forward on either side of him to sing harmonies before retreating to their set positions: sociomusical hierarchy on display.

Travelogues. As Richard's popularity in the UK grew, the band attempted to establish themselves as a parallel and independent vocal-and-instrumental ensemble. Bruce Welch sang lead on Ian Samwell's "Feelin' Fine" (February 1959),[4] and in June they featured Harris's electric bass on his composition "Jet Black." When those releases failed, they made one more unsuccessful attempt at singing harmonies on Marvin and Welch's "Saturday Dance" (December 1959).

Amid recording and promoting Cliff Richard's "Please Don't Tease" in the summer of 1960, the Shadows had their first hit. They had been impressed by the Jerry Lordan composition "Apache" (July 1960) that guitarist Bert Weedon had recorded and that Top Rank Records was about to release. Inviting the composer to the studio, the band and Norrie Paramor gave over the last forty minutes of their three-hour session to Lordan's impression of an American western soundtrack (Geddes 1999). With Cliff Richard imitating the music of Native Americans by playing repeated sixteenth notes on a tacked drum, Marvin's guitar echoes the theme of the television show *Bonanza*.[5]

The Shadows' recording of "Apache" topped British charts in August 1960 and was the first of several UK instrumental hits for the "Shads."[6] Many of these tunes were meant to suggest exotic places in an era of espionage and the beginnings of commercial jet travel. "Man of Mystery" (November 1960), "F.B.I." (February 1961), "Frightened City" (May 1961), "Kon Tiki" (August 1961), "Wonderful Land" (February 1962), and "Dance On!" (December 1962) offered fictional audio travelogues.

Perhaps the most successful evocation of the era's embrace of adventure, however, came from a group of studio musicians in a flat over a leather-goods store in Islington.

---

[3] The Treniers performed on the same program as Jerry Lee Lewis during his ill-fated and short-lived 1958 UK tour. Welch and Marvin would have seen the choreographies of both the Treniers in *Don't Knock the Rock* and Freddie Bell and the Bellboys in *Rock around the Clock*.
[4] Originally released as the Drifters, Columbia DB 4263, February 1959.
[5] *Bonanza* had debuted in the United States the previous year and in the UK in May.
[6] At this writing, the song still shows up in commercials.

Telstars

The Tornados offered an instrumental alternative to the Shadows, with fewer hits and a shorter existence but a much broader audience. Alan Caddy (lead guitar) and Clem Cattini (drums) had left the Pirates to join George Bellamy (rhythm guitar), Heinz Burt (bass guitar), and Roger LaVern (keyboards) as Joe Meek's most recent house musicians. At RGM Sound, they backed John Leyton and other Meek clients before becoming Billy Fury's road band in early 1962, a year marked by another significant event.

On 10 July 1962, NASA placed Telstar 1 into a stationary earth orbit, launching the beginning of the modern era of telecommunications and inspiring Meek—a science fiction enthusiast—to express his excitement through music. Unfortunately, Meek's musicianship had limitations. "All we had was a melody on a tape, with him singing over a backing track that had nothing to do with the melody," remembered Cattini (interview 22 January 2001).

After choosing chords to accompany the melody, they explored rhythms that would be suitable for a composition about a satellite. The groove established by Cattini eschews the standard backbeat that accompanied most performances in this era in favor of a continuous roll with brushes on his snare drum that propels the performance forward. Adding to the otherworldly soundscape, Meek recorded LaVern playing piano at a slower tape speed so that in playback his sped-up arpeggios glide like a harp. He also double-tracked Caddy's guitar solos,[7] giving them a surreal, wavering effect.

Technological Transformations. Perhaps the most distinctive instrumental sound on the recording, however, came when Geoff Goddard overdubbed the melody on a new keyboard. The Clavioline's electronically synthesized sounds had already appeared on American Del Shannon's "Runaway" (February 1961).[8] Goddard now used the instrument to symbolize the promise of international communication and the possibilities of space exploration.

Another remarkable aspect came from Meek's experiments in musique concrète: the electronic and magnetic manipulation of sounds. The recording begins and ends with a roar suggesting a rocket launch and a satellite being hurled into space. Meek had been playing for years with taped sounds to simulate his imagined worlds of the future, and "Telstar" (August 1962) gave him the perfect opportunity to introduce others to his dreams.[9]

---

[7] Double-tracking involved overdubbing the same material so that two versions of the same musical line double the original. In this case, Caddy played the same guitar solo twice to create the effect of two guitars playing together.

[8] Studio photos suggest that Meek may have been using a German variation of the Selmer Clavioline.

[9] One session musician has suggested that Meek recorded the sound of a toilet flushing as the basis of this effect.

Unfortunately, when requests came for the Tornados to tour the United States, their manager, Larry Parnes, refused to send them unless they were backing Billy Fury, about whom the Americans cared little. Nevertheless, "Telstar" heralded globalization, sounded perfectly in tune with modernity's obsession with technology, and offers another landmark in British pop. The first week of October 1962, as the Cuban missile crisis brought the world to the brink of destruction, Britain awoke from its postwar funk: "Telstar" topped both British and American charts, the first Bond film (*Dr. No*) debuted, and Parlophone released the first Beatles single, "Love Me Do."

Fig. 4.1 Screaming Lord Sutch as Jack the Ripper, 1964.

Fig. 4.2 The Savages; left to right: Bernie Watson, Nicky Hopkins, Ricky Fenson, and Carlo Little. Photo courtesy of Giselle Rollins.

Fig. 4.3 The Shadows, 1962; left to right: Bruce Welch, Jet Harris, Tony Meehan, and Hank Marvin.

Fig. 4.4 The Tornados, 1964.

5
Beatle Beginnings

Fans and scholars have extensively chronicled the daily lives of the Beatles, their concert appearances, their music, and their studio work through a multitude of books, websites, and publications. Mark Lewisohn, both by himself (1988, 1992, and 2013) and with others (e.g., Schreuders, Lewisohn, and Smith 1994), has provided a wealth of information. Not to be outdone, the Beatles (2000) have attempted to control how the world perceives the band and their music, through interviews, by creating their own documentaries and publications, and by issuing new mixes and masters of their catalogue.

Most of these publications have the goal of celebrating the originality of the Beatles' songwriting, recording, performances, and audience reception, an approach resembling a Seder question: How is this band unlike all other bands? John Lennon, however, in *Rolling Stone* (Wenner 21 January 1971) later suggested that they were "just a band that made it very, very big, that's all." Despite his penchant for dramatic overstatement (or perhaps understatement here), Lennon implies that he thought of the Beatles as typical of pop in this era.

Evaluating the Beatles' importance should involve understanding how they responded to their environment. Rather than unique and different, they remained extraordinarily good at reflecting culture: a mirror to the world around them. In particular, they reflected English culture adapting to the sixties.

Liverpool

In Fox's observations about English behavior, she notes the connection between class and accent, and how some British cities have developed their own versions of what she calls "multicultural London English" (2014, 105). Given the cosmopolitan nature of pop culture and Liverpool's history as a port city and its own identifiable accent, the Beatles articulated a Scouse[1] version of an emerging multicultural English pop.

Situated on the northwest coast of England, Liverpool offers a suitable postwar Dickensian setting for pop-music hero mythology. Ravaged by World

---

[1] "Scouse" derives from the name of a type of stew but has come to refer to the peculiaritries of working-class Liverpudlian speech.

War II Luftwaffe air raids and hobbled by economic stagnation and obsolescent technology, the city's social cohesion deteriorated as chronic unemployment and crime rose.[2] Nevertheless, residents persevered with a fatalistic sense of humor and a reliance on family and friends for collective solutions to daily problems. Unions represented one manifestation of this bonding strategy, but working-class families had long survived by sharing limited resources.

As one of Britain's principal ports, Liverpool's ethnically diverse population derived in part from the city's prominent role in the transatlantic slave trade and later the cotton that arrived from South Asia and the American South for processing in Manchester's mills. In the nineteenth century, the fledgling United States of America set up its first British consulate in Liverpool, and during the American Civil War the Confederate States of America continued to sail ships into the city's docks. By the twentieth century, locals often called those who worked the ship lines "Cunard Yanks" for the American goods and culture they brought home with them.

The Manchester-Liverpool metropolitan area represents a counterbalance to the cultural hegemony of London. Sometimes referred to as "Manpool," the two cities—an hour apart by train or car and linked since the end of the nineteenth century by a canal—have functioned as the historic heart of the UK's industrial and shipping economies. In the postwar years, however, these cities saw a decline in international trade due to import restrictions and strikes that neither saved jobs nor substantially raised wages. This version of northern English culture shaped the Beatles.

The Nucleus

The combination of the complementary but contrasting talents of John Lennon and Paul McCartney would help to upend popular music not just in Britain but in the Western world. As boys they came from different social and familial backgrounds even though they lived in adjacent neighborhoods. As teens, however, they discovered that each represented something the other admired.

Born in 1940, John Lennon belonged to the first generation to avoid military duty in the National Service, which had historically served to force young British men into conformity. Abandoned by his father, Alfred, surrendered by his mother, Julia, and embraced by his Aunt Mimi (Stanley), John Lennon came from a family that occupied the precarious borderland between middle-class pretension and working-class ambition. He grew up in the comfortable southern

---

[2] This association resonated in the BBC television police drama *Z Cars,* set in the Liverpool-Merseyside region.

Liverpool suburb of Woolton behind leaded, stained-glass windows in his Aunt Mimi's semidetached house, where she did her best to instill proper values in her nephew. His mother, Julia, lived with her common-law husband a 10-minute bike ride away on the other side of a golf course in Allerton and in a different social reality. She took the role of the affectionate, spoiling aunt who taught him songs and encouraged his passion for music, much to her sister's dismay.

Twenty months younger, Paul McCartney lived in council housing that had become available to his nurse-midwife mother, Mary Mohin McCartney, and that was coincidentally a 15-minute walk from Julia Stanley's home. His father, James (Jim) McCartney, was a self-taught pianist who had led a dance band in the 1920s but now worked in the cotton trade. With a piano in the front room, Paul McCartney's parents encouraged his musical ambitions, at first buying him a trumpet, until the teen successfully argued that a guitar would allow him to sing while he played. In 1956, however, when Mary McCartney died of complications from breast cancer, her 14-year-old son turned to music for solace, which opened the path to meeting Lennon.

American Invasion. The 15 February 1957 issue of the *New Musical Express* (10) declared "The American Invasion Is On!" and Lennon and McCartney, like many young British musicians of the late 1950s, found themselves captured. As children, they had sung church hymns, songs taught in school, and music-hall ditties. Cunard Yanks, however, had also introduced them to country artists like Hank Williams and to emerging American rock 'n' roll musicians. Thus, 16-year-old Lennon—inspired by films like *Rock around the Clock*—obtained a guitar, learned a few chords, and organized his school friends into a skiffle group (Lewisohn 2013, 102).

The Quarry Men (named after the Quarry Bank School, which they attended) played one of their first gigs on a truck bed outside Saint Peter's Parish Church in Woolton on 6 July 1957. A photo shows a defiant Lennon in a plaid shirt, his hair falling across his forehead, and, without his glasses, straining to focus on the photographer. A crowd of teens gathers around them, including a friend who had brought McCartney. Impressed, the two future collaborators met afterward in the church hall, where they shared musical ideas. A week later, McCartney received an invitation to join the group.

As a teen, Lennon gained admission to the Liverpool College of Art, where he proved a disinterested student who would eventually be expelled. Across the way, McCartney attended the Liverpool Institute Grammar School, where he showed promise for university entrance and perhaps a teaching career.

McCartney proved no less ambitious than Lennon and, in February 1958, encouraged his friend George Harrison to show up at a Quarry Men performance. Harrison and McCartney had met on the bus while traveling to the Liverpool Institute, where they were both students. Harrison's father, Harold, had worked on the White Star Line, but with a layoff, a marriage with Louise French, and a growing family, he became a bus driver and an active member of his union. In 1943, when George was born, the family lived in a central Liverpool council house with neither indoor plumbing nor central heating other than a coal fire. Although a move to Speke near Liverpool's airport brought a significant improvement to the Harrisons' situation, the area proved violent and George retreated his room to indulge in his interests, particularly his love of the guitar, which was how he became friends with McCartney. A short audition on the upper deck of a bus gained Lennon's approval, and Harrison too became a Quarry Man.

Rock the Casbah

In the spring and summer of 1958, around the time that the soon-to-be Billy Fury visited recordist Percy Phillips to tape songs he hoped would impress Larry Parnes, Lennon (17), McCartney (15), and Harrison (15), along with a drummer and pianist, boarded a bus into town to visit the same studio. In addition to a close cover of Buddy Holly's song "That'll Be the Day," they proffered McCartney's song "In Spite of All the Danger,"[3] with Lennon singing lead. The song draws on the same catalogue of pop clichés that Fury had applied to "Maybe Tomorrow," but there would be no television appearance or national tour for the Quarry Men.

The death of Lennon's mother a few weeks later, after being hit crossing the road, put their collective energies on hold as the 17-year-old sank into a period of despair and self-destruction. Harrison began playing with others, but when those musicians backed out of a late August engagement on the opening night of the Casbah Coffee Club, he called his friends from the Quarry Men. Such youth clubs had sprung up across the country in the second half of the 1950s as the Bulge Generation began reaching puberty. The small basement venue under Mona Best's house in West Derby in the Eastern suburbs of Liverpool now came to serve as their rehearsal space and musical home while they began building an audience.

In the fall of 1959, the trio renamed themselves Johnny and the Moondogs and entered a talent contest run by Canadian expatriate Carroll Levis. They survived the initial Liverpool rounds with a guitar-less Lennon flanked by Harrison and McCartney to compete in the Manchester finale, where they managed to still be standing by the last round. Unfortunately, with no money and the last train to

---

[3] The song is credited as McCartney-Harrison, probably due to Harrison's solo.

Merseyside soon departing, they made a strategic retreat, undefeated and ready for another adventure.

Beatles. Like many young British groups at the turn of the decade, Johnny and the Moondogs lacked two important musical essentials: drums and an electric bass. Not only were these instruments expensive but getting the drums from one place to another could present substantial problems without a vehicle, and these teens clearly lacked finances. Lennon's art-school friend Stu Sutcliffe, however, had recently won prize money for one of his paintings, and Lennon and McCartney convinced him that rather than buying brushes, canvases, and paint he could be a British rock 'n' roll version of James Dean. All he had to do was apply the prize money toward an electric bass guitar and learn a few notes (Lewisohn 2013, 275). Although not much of a musician, Sutcliffe would bring more to this group than his bass and his movie-star looks. He and Lennon played with variations on both the name of Buddy Holly's band (the Crickets) and the English terminology for what they played ("beat" music). Together, they arrived at the name, the "Beatles."

With a bass player, a name, and their ambitions reignited, they could not have missed a factor that had contributed to every other recent success story: a manager. Allan Williams, the owner of the Jacaranda, a coffeehouse where they sometimes loitered, seemed the most likely, albeit perhaps reluctant, candidate. He began by booking them for a variety of questionable gigs, and when Larry Parnes and Billy Fury came to town looking for a band, Williams included them on the audition list. A photo from the day shows Lennon asking Fury for his autograph, but accompany him they would not.

Parnes, nevertheless, thought them good enough to back fellow Liverpudlian Johnny Gentle on what proved to be a tough northern tour. Scotland offered a test that they were lucky to survive after an auto accident put a recruited drummer briefly in hospital. Nevertheless, they remained optimistic, toying with stage names as they waited for their next opportunity to be professionals. It would mean crossing the North Sea.

Club Life

Hamburg flourished in the postwar years when the Marshall Plan pumped economic development into Western Europe through her docks. Unsurprisingly, the Saint Pauli quarter's clientele of sailors, gangsters, businessmen, and sex tourists exceeded Soho with its music venues, bars, and prostitution.

With a growing roster of Liverpool groups looking for work, Williams traveled to Hamburg to introduce his clients as economic alternatives to the American originals. Despite an initial unsuccessful meeting there, Williams again met

Bruno Koschmider at the 2i's in Soho, where the German club owner had come looking for bands. They struck a deal, and soon Liverpool musicians were playing in Koschmider's clubs. In this context, Williams prepared to send the Beatles, if they could procure a drummer. Shortly before their departure, they recruited Pete Best, the owner of a new drum kit and the son of the Casbah's Mona Best.

In August 1960, the Beatles began their next transformation, first at Koschmider's Indra club and then, after a neighbor's complaints about the noise, his Kaiserkeller, a larger club where they shared the stage with strippers. Competing with other bands on the Reeperbahn for audiences demanded that the Beatles quickly expand their repertoire, improve as musicians, and become tighter as an ensemble as they logged hundreds of hours on stage and in rehearsal. Their housing in bare bunks in an unheated storage room at the back of a cinema often left them tired, cold, and hungry on stage, prompting Koschmider to shout "Mach Schau!" ("Make a show") while a sympathetic employee plied them with amphetamines.[4]

Joseph Campbell in *The Hero with a Thousand Faces* (1949) makes the case that myths follow a common story structure (a monomyth) in which a journey transforms a protagonist, often with help from allies. Hamburg transformed the Beatles from enthusiastic amateurs into hardened professionals who confronted and overcame their fears about being successful performers. They offered an English version of American rock and pop for mostly German audiences (many of whom spoke English) by honing the core musical elements.

Saint Pauli and the Reeperbahn

Under the cosmopolitan canopy of the Saint Pauli quarter, its main thoroughfare, the Reeperbahn, offered Klaus Voormann and fellow middle-class art students a place where they could hear and see an English version of American rock 'n' roll. Some described themselves as existentialists ("exis") and brought a style into these clubs that challenged the Liverpudlians' vision of manhood. The preference for monochrome suede, corduroy, and velvet (reflecting their relative affluence) worn over black turtlenecks drew glances even on the Reeperbahn (Clayson 1997). Significantly, Voormann's girlfriend, photographer Astrid Kirchherr, began influencing Sutcliffe's choices in clothing and hair style, which bandmates would eventually follow.

In November 1960, when Bruno Koschmider discovered that a competitor had promised the Beatles better accommodations and pay, he immediately had

---

[4] Both sides of World War II had provided amphetamines to service personnel to push their endurance. In the postwar years, these drugs continued to figure in European life.

the 17-year-old Harrison arrested for being underaged and out after curfew. Soon after, Hamburg police took McCartney and Best into custody for mischief and deported them, leaving Lennon to travel home alone. The exception would be Sutcliffe, who remained with Kirchherr in Hamburg, where he planned to return to art school to study with Eduardo Paolozzi.

Toward the end of this stay in Hamburg, McCartney had tormented Sutcliffe about the quality of his playing. Now back in Liverpool with rehearsals at the Casbah and upcoming gigs, they needed a bass player and settled on a friend of Pete Best who was home from school for the winter break. At a performance in the north Liverpool suburb of Litherland (27 December 1960), locals hardly recognized the tight and raucous group on stage, some thinking they were German. As 1961 dawned and their temporary member returned to school, McCartney now found himself taking the role of bass player, even though he would have to improvise an instrument.

Top Ten. Toward the end of March, now that Harrison was safely 18, they returned to Hamburg to play at the Top Ten Club, alternating with and sometimes backing Tony Sheridan, who had been a regular on Jack Good's *Oh Boy!* It was in this context that German bandleader and producer Bert Kämpfert signed Sheridan to a recording contract; the singer-guitarist in turn asked the Beatles to accompany him. Their studio session would be in a high school auditorium.

Given the current fad of updating older tunes for contemporary audiences that pervaded early 1960s pop recordings, the West German producer instructed them to prepare a rocked-up version of "My Bonnie." Polydor released the disc in West Germany under the name "Tony Sheridan and the Beat Brothers," which generated a minor German hit (October 1961). Because the performance was in English and by Sheridan,[5] Polydor also later released it in the British market (January 1962), where a Liverpool merchant heard about the disc.

The Cavern

In the fall of 1961, the Beatles were in a critical phase. As adults, they continued to play local venues, particularly at the Cavern Club, where they drew a devoted audience much younger than them.[6] Fans filled cobblestoned Mathew Street and descended the club's circular stairwell to its rancid subterranean arched chambers during lunch breaks and at night. Success in Liverpool and Hamburg

---

[5] Two introductions to the recording exist, one in German and the other in English.
[6] Lennon had reached the age of majority, able to sign contracts and to vote; by this age, most Liverpool males had married and started a family.

encouraged the band, but they had hit a wall until Brian Epstein's polished shoes descended the stairs.

Brian Epstein had endured his own share of trials. His time in elite schools had proved less than successful, he had been discharged from the army for insubordination, and he had been forced to leave the Royal Academy of Dramatic Arts after being entrapped for allegedly importuning an undercover policeman in a public toilet. When his family opened North End Music Stores in central Liverpool in 1958, however, Epstein and his brother made NEMS *the* place to look for discs in Liverpool. In part to promote that business, he began writing a record review column for *Mersey Beat*, a local music magazine that also carried articles on and popularity polls for local beat groups.

A photo of the Beatles, clad in black leather, as the most popular beat group in Liverpool (not to mention friends of the paper's publisher), appeared prominently in *Mersey Beat*. Epstein, whose sexual encounters with working-class men sometimes put him in danger, could not have missed it. A habitué of opera and symphony concerts, his venture into the Cavern Club in November 1961 brought him uncomfortably onto the home turf of his pop-entused store customers, some of whom were the band.

The Beatles' performance and audience reaction electrified Epstein, and he began concocting a plan to manage them. To the Beatles, he certainly seemed more respectable than Allan Williams (with whom they had severed relations earlier in the year); moreover, he promised higher pay, more and better bookings in Liverpool and beyond, AND a record contract. He also, however, had conditions about the "right clothes and not smoking, eating, or chewing during their performance," including a "proper programme, playing" their "best numbers each time" (Davies 2006, 174–175). They accepted his offer, but his task would not be easy.

As the most important disc retailer in Liverpool, he wrote to EMI and to Decca extending an invitation to audition the band. The former turned him down outright. Decca, however, sent Mike Smith to the Cavern, where they impressed him enough to earn a recording test in London on 1 January 1962.

London

Paul McCartney remembers being asked "Where are you from?" When he replied, "Liverpool" he was told, "You'll never do anything from there. Too far away. You'll have to be in London before you can do it. Nobody's done it from Liverpool" (Davies 2006, 175).

With Britain's major record companies, newspapers, and broadcasters all headquartered in the capital, any hope for national success had to include contacts there. Getting recently promoted Mike Smith from Decca to take the train up to hear the Beatles at the Cavern Club had provided an opening. The physical and social structures of record corporations, however, had the implicit intention of articulating power to intimidate novices like the Beatles so that they would be compliant.

The Tests

When the Beatles arrived in London on New Year's Eve, the city ready to party and, with their hotel close to the University of London, the perennial night owls explored the town. Unsurprisingly, the Decca audition the next morning proved ill-fated, beginning with Epstein being the only one to show up on time and feeling slighted. The first setback came when engineers dismissed the band's instruments and amplifiers as unprofessional, insisting that Lennon, McCartney, and Harrison use the studio's equipment.

Epstein had advised the Beatles to prepare some of their own compositions (e.g., "Like Dreamers Do"), Motown covers (e.g., "Money"), show tunes (e.g., "Till There Was You"), and even a rocked-up version of a trad favorite ("The Sheik of Araby"). At the end of the audition, Smith offered his noncommittal compliments, and the Liverpudlians returned home anticipating good news. Smith, however, auditioned two groups that day—first the Beatles and then Brian Poole and the Tremeloes. Recording director Dick Rowe felt that his new producer could only add one new group, forcing Smith to decide between the band from London and the one from Liverpool. When Epstein learned of the rejection the next month, he returned to London to protest.

Folklore has Rowe informing Epstein: "groups of guitars are on the way out. . . . You really should stick to selling records in Liverpool"—advice the Beatles manager did not heed (Miles 1997, 89). Discouraged after unsuccessful inquiries at other labels, he headed to HMV's store on Oxford Street to transfer the Decca audition tape to a disc. That was when the engineer copying the tape suggested that EMI might be interested in publishing Lennon and McCartney's songs and sent Epstein upstairs to see Sid Colman of EMI's publishers, Ardmore and Beechwood. Colman was indeed interested, but Epstein insisted on a recording contract, leading to a call to the director of EMI's Parlophone, George Martin.

Parlophone. Martin offers an example of the complexity of English social status. Although his carpenter father could only afford the most basic urban lodgings, his mother had arranged for introductory piano lessons and made sure her son attended and graduated from grammar school. The boy had shown that he not only possessed a musical ear but also could teach himself basic theory and harmony.

After serving in the Royal Navy, he applied for and received at the end of the war an educational stipend to enroll at the Guildhall School of Music and Drama to study composition, arranging, conducting, theory, piano, and oboe. He impressed a professor there, who recommended him as an assistant to the director of Parlophone Records, where, in 1955, EMI appointed Martin (29) the youngest director of an EMI label. He would sign Adam Faith as well as the Vipers but by 1962, the music world was changing, which was when he took a chance on Epstein's group.

On Wednesday 6 June 1962, the Beatles arrived at the EMI Recording Studios in Abbey Road through the side door at the bottom of a ramp that they recognized as a tradesmen's entrance. They knew they had gained the audition because of Sid Colman's interest in Lennon and McCartney's songs, but Martin was doubtful about them as a band. Based on the material they offered that day, balance engineer Norman Smith remembered: "we saw no potential of their songwriting abilities." They did, however, impress the crew with their presence and humor, leading Smith to suggest to Martin: "I think we should sign them."[7]

Starr Time. Martin would agree to record them, but both he and the band had reservations about Pete Best, who had helped the band get to Hamburg but whose musicianship now hobbled them. And then there was his appearance. Back in Hamburg, when Sutcliffe had adopted the exi look, Lennon, McCartney, and Harrison had followed by adopting the schoolboy haircut. Best, however, had remained unchanged and he simply no longer fit. With the future at stake, they replaced Best with the best-known drummer in Liverpool.

They had known Ringo Starr (born Richard Starkey) since their skiffle days and had become friends in Hamburg, where their bands had sometimes alternated sets. Like schoolmate Billy Fury, Starr's origins in Liverpool's congested and impoverished Dingle district had contributed to sickness as a child, with music as one of his joys. As a teen, his reputation as a drummer in Liverpool was solid, and he had adopted the stage name "Ringo Starr" for its American country sound. He had already subbed when Pete Best called in sick and, in August 1962, when the Beatles asked him to join, he proved willing to change his hair style and his life.

---

[7] Smith also told Mark Lewisohn (2013, 617) that the managing director of EMI's records division, L. G. Wood, had "virtually ordered [Martin] to record the Beatles" to show his disapproval of the producer's demands for better remuneration and his ongoing affair with his secretary. The decision to award a contract, however, was probably both more complicated than can be explained by a single factor.

Love Me Do

A recording test at a major British studio in the early 1960s offered a production team a chance to hear what artists sounded like on tape, the parallel to a screen test. Norman Smith remembered that on 6 June the Beatles had "tiny . . . Vox amplifiers . . . stuck on chairs for the test, and . . . when I opened up the microphone, all I got was just extraneous noises, they were that bad" (interview 17 October 2001). As had happened at Decca, he and another engineer improvised a cleaner sound from studio equipment—particularly for McCartney's bass. There were problems, but something had caught the ears of Smith and assistant producer Ron Richards, and they called George Martin from the canteen (Lewisohn 2013, 243).

McCartney has described "Love Me Do" as a "completely co-written" form of "the blues," having composed the "main structure . . . when he was sixteen, or even earlier" and Lennon having "something to do with the middle" (Miles 1997, 36–37). Whatever its origins, "Love Me Do" qualifies lyrically and musically as one of the simplest entries in the Beatles' catalogue. With only 17 discrete words and only two chords for most of the song, "Love Me Do" lacks a distinct melody and relies on harmonies. Lennon noted that it had started as a "slower number like [Billy Fury's] 'Halfway to Paradise,' you know, Dum-di-di-di-Dum; but George Martin . . . suggested we do it faster" (Roberts 9 February 1963). This early arrangement, however, also made an uneasy rhythmic shift from triple and duple (swing versus "straight") during the second chorus, where Pete Best's tempo wobbled significantly on 6 June.

Perhaps with Bruce Channel's hit "Hey! Baby" (December 1961) in mind, Martin asked, "Can anyone play harmonica?" (Miles 1997, 91).[8] Having Lennon play a solo during the second chorus, however, had consequences for McCartney, who now had to cover the lower vocal by dropping from his part to sing the hook solo.[9] "I was very nervous," he recalled. "George Martin started arranging it on the spot. It was very nerve-wracking" (Dowlding 1989, 31). The producer, however, now had an idea of their potential and scheduled a return session in September.

Round Two. When they arrived with Ringo Starr on 4 September, the Beatles followed the same overall musical arrangement for "Love Me Do" with the exception that they now omitted the meter change during the second-chorus harmonica solo. As important, McCartney brought a new custom-built amplifier and speaker cabinet that allowed his bass to punch through the mix with Starr

---

[8] Channel began a UK tour on 5 June 1962.
[9] Lewisohn (2013, 1194) asserts that Lennon had already incorporated the harmonica into their performance of the song before they arrived at EMI.

following him closely. Faster than the test, this version ends almost 15 seconds earlier. Moreover, as part of their studio education and unlike the 6 June recording, which had them performing live in studio, Martin introduced the Beatles to superimposition. They first recorded the instrumental backing and then, playing it back, added vocals and handclaps.

Martin, however, had also insisted that they learn a new song and believed (correctly) that "How Do You Do It?," written by Mitch Murray, could be a hit. They dutifully albeit perhaps dispassionately prepared that song for their next session. The final decision about the release, however, rested with neither Martin nor the Beatles: as an independent songwriter, Murray had the final say.[10] He and his publisher, Dick James, had gone to Martin in the hope that Adam Faith would record the song and had deep reservations about an unknown group from Liverpool. After hearing the Beatles' performance, Murray declined Martin's request to release their recording and later wondered whether the Beatles might have "deliberately screwed it up" so as to record their own song (interview 7 April 2001). When the band showed up for their third visit, they brought "P.S. I Love You" and "Please Please Me," and Ron Richards, whom Martin had deputized to run this session, also scheduled another take of "Love Me Do." George Martin, however, wanted insurance that the session would go smoothly.

White Time. Ringo Starr's playing had been an improvement over Pete Best's, but with session time adding up, Martin instructed Richards to hire a session musician. The Beatles arrived unaware that Andy White (of Jack Good's Firing Squad and Billy Fury's sessions) would be drumming. When Starr walked into Studio Two that Monday, he "saw a drum kit that wasn't mine, and a drummer that, most definitely, wasn't me! It was terrible" (Womack 2017, 49).

"Please Please Me" needed more work, but "P.S. I Love You" rolls along smoothly, with White's Latin-influenced rhythm grooving along with Ringo's maracas. Tackling "Love Me Do" at the end of the session, this recording offers the steadiest and fastest tempo of the three versions, McCartney and White tightly linking their parts to provide a punch to the groove that Starr's backbeat tambourine only deepens. Lennon's harmonica solo, however, is noticeably sloppier than the 4 September performance. Perhaps for that reason or simply to build the band's confidence, Martin chose to release Starr's version of "Love Me Do" with "P.S. I Love You" on the B-side (5 October 1962).

---

[10] McCartney has recently claimed that the Beatles turned down the song.

Meet the Media

As the peak of the British Bulge turned 15 in 1962 (and many left school), the model for how music was chosen for the teen market began to capsize. The adults in control of the industry—producers, corporate executives, and disc jockeys—had assumed that they knew what teens wanted; however, as Gillett has observed, adolescents began to take control (1983, viii). The Beatles arrived on the charts at this tipping point when young consumers nationally began to overpower corporate condescension.[11]

A week before the disc's release, EMI posted perhaps the first national advertisement for "Love Me Do" in *Record Retailer and Music Industry News* (27 September 1962, 2), accompanied by four headshots by photographer Dezo Hoffmann. In the same issue on the "Plug Page," EMI announced "Love Me Do" along with eight other recordings (23). A week later, the same paper briefly reviewed "Love Me Do," mentioning the band's popularity in Liverpool and describing this recording as "the strongest outsider of the week" ("Your Review Guide to the New Discs" 4 October 1962, 6). An accompanying press release (ghostwritten by Tony Barrow) presciently bore the title "Introducing . . . the Beatles" (29). Publishers often pushed recordings of their songs, and in the 11 October 1962 issue of *Record Retailer*, store owners read in Robbie Lowman's "Alley-gations" column that Ardmore and Beechwood were promoting "Sherry" by the Four Seasons. "Love Me Do" appears much farther down the list.

Although disc retailers would have seen this advertising, most British teens did not read industry news. In the national popular press, *Disc* ("New to You" 6 October 1962, 8) was the first to carry a review of "Love Me Do," comparing the Beatles to the Everly Brothers, with a brief introduction to the band on the same page. No mention of the disc, however, would appear in the *New Musical Express* until Alan Smith (26 October 1962) made a connection between the Beatles and Billy Fury. Meanwhile, "Love Me Do" crept into *Record Retailer*'s "Britain's Top 50" at number 49, representing a remarkable feat for a first release, let alone one from Liverpool.[12]

Recognition. Despite tepid coverage in the London press, disc sales continued to grow, probably driven by the band's fan base in the Manchester-Liverpool region. In *Record Retailer*, the disc reached #17 at the end of December, #21 in

---

[11] *Record Retailer* ("Marked Rise in October Sales" 10 January 1963, 5) would note that October 1962 had seen a 17 percent increase over the same month in 1961.

[12] *Record Retailer* prided itself on having its finger on the pulse of record merchandising by polling its readership: Britain's retail disc merchants. *Record Retailer* ("Chart Error on Elvis Disc" 25 January 1962) noted with some satisfaction that when a flu swept through Decca's manufacturing plant, disrupting their ability to press records, both *Melody Maker* and the *Daily Mail* published charts showing Elvis Presley's newest recording ("Rock-a-Hula Baby") suddenly holding the #20 position, despite the lack of any discs to sell.

Melody Maker the first week of January, and no higher than #24 in a December issue of *Disc*. Television appearances on Granada Television's northern UK program *People and Places* in October and November helped build sales in that region. Moreover, the band's performance schedule for October 1962 shows numerous trips on the two-lane highway between Liverpool and Manchester. The resulting sales caught London's attention.

Tony Barrow identifies a significant media moment for the Beatles in London. On 16 November he attended a taping for *The Friday Spectacular*, a radio program that EMI recorded in London to be broadcast on Radio Luxembourg. When host Muriel Young began announcing the given names of the band,

> before she could reach Ringo the audience shrieked its approval and rushed forward to the tiny stage. I read a great deal into this. With "Love Me Do," a debut single, in the shops for only a month and no stage dates in the capital to back it up, all these London kids had bothered to find out the group's first names (Barrow 2005, 28).

Fig. 5.1 The Beatles performing in the Cavern Club, 1962. *People and Places*, 17 October 1962.

PART II
A DOOR OPENS, 1963

6
The Beatles
Outside In

The world survived the fall of 1962 . . . barely. On the one hand, Martin Luther King, Jr., received the Nobel Peace Prize in Stockholm, Pope John XXIII convened the twenty-first Ecumenical Council in Rome, and Cliff Richard and Helen Shapiro appeared on the *Ed Sullivan Show* in New York. On the other hand, the Soviets and the Americans threatened mutual nuclear annihilation. The superpowers backed down over missiles in Cuba, but the psychological impact on adolescents lingered: the adults had nearly ended humanity. The following year would further undermine confidence in the Establishment.

Although the Education Act 1944 had attempted to address class discrimination by opening avenues for working-class students to attend grammar schools, historic institutional and familial prejudices and privileges persisted. Moreover, deeply ingrained attitudes about class and gender continued to shape career options. Compounding the problem of how to address educational inequities, the arrival of the Bulge Generation prompted educators to establish tracks to sort the population across the available faculty and facility resources. The "eleven-plus" tests (taken around the age of 11) largely divined which children attended grammar schools, secondary modern schools, or technical schools. That determination figured prominently in who ultimately gained entrance to universities and polytechnics and who worked in offices, shops, and factories (Sandbrook 2005, 420).

Agency. As the peak of the Bulge Generation turned 16 in 1963, it began to sense its power. Adolescents vastly outnumbered adults in performance venues and, sensing their advantage, felt able to express themselves (see Millard 2012, 132). Women, who had systemically found themselves denied a say in their lives, found they could express themselves emotionally. Initially interpreted as a sound of submission, screaming expressed both intense sexual desire and empowerment. Their numbers and confidence now began to claim public spaces, and some, with modest improvements in birth control,[1] took an active role in

---

[1] The rollout of oral contraception in the UK was slow and initially limited to married women, with working-class women having the least access. Although an echo boom in births came as the Bulge Generation turned 17 in 1964, it was smaller than it might have been.

articulating their gender and sexuality. In particular, a cohort began to avoid immediately becoming mothers and to earn enough to become independent (see Nicholson 2019, 77).

In this environment, adolescents began to sense that they had the freedom to choose how they wanted to be identified. Innovative fabrics in new colors allowed designers to replace the drab offerings of the immediate postwar years for both women and men. No less important, music defined youth and demarcated the spaces they occupied.

The Beatles emerged into this world neither as an inevitability nor as a total fluke but as a screen onto which adolescents could project their independence from adults. With schoolboy haircuts and infectious irreverence, they symbolized a synthesis of the irresponsibility of childhood and the freedom of adulthood, an amalgam that echoed in their music.

As the band responded to audiences in every club and dance hall they played in Hamburg, Liverpool, and Manchester, they planned their next recording session. They knew they were tapping into the excitement. The question was how.

Departures

Building an audience means identifying who and where they are, knowing what they want, and finding the best ways to connect with them. National newspapers like the *Daily Mirror* carried articles about pop musicians, but only about the best-known performers like Cliff Richard, unless someone like Screaming Lord Sutch found an outrageous stunt to attract attention. Popular music papers like the *New Musical Express* and *Melody Maker* initially focused on people in the music industry as their audience but began to attract a growing popular readership. Filling the gap, small local papers like Bill Harry's *Mersey Beat* catered to select audiences, while national magazines like *Boyfriend* (launched in 1959) targeted adolescent females with information about fashion, relationships, and pop culture (Savage 5 September 2009).

With Jack Good's departure from UK television, British pop music fans were left with limited viewing options. Programs intended for children offered some opportunities to see performers, summarizing corporate attitudes to programming for teens in this era. On the radio, the BBC's Light Programme offered a limited number of shows, like *Saturday Club,* that played records, interviewed musicians, and often included taped live performances.

For the Beatles, getting both television and radio airtime in the south proved difficult for a variety of reasons, including condescension about anything from outside metropolitan London. Among the shows booking them were *Tuesday*

Rendezvous, an ITV children's program, and *The Talent Spot* on BBC radio.[2] Photos in teen magazines like *Boyfriend*, however, helped to introduce them to readers in southern England who began to wonder who these northerners were. The Beatles' appearance defied contemporary conventions, and their stripped-down music and cheeky interactions with adult program hosts defied the polish so many artists affected. They were outsiders breaking into the south's cultural hegemony with American music.

Pleasing Them

Lennon remembered beginning "Please Please Me" in the upstairs bedroom at his aunt's house in Woolton with Roy Orbison's ballad "Only the Lonely" on his mind (Sheff 1981, 150). From Orbison, he had also absorbed the idea of musical architecture: the manipulation of a melody's internal space to build and to crest emotionally. For lyrics, he reached into the 1930s American songbook for a pun from Bing Crosby's "Please."[3]

When the band arranged the song, they drew on ideas from rock 'n' roll, rhythm and blues, and rockabilly. As they had with "Love Me Do," the Everly Brothers inspired the harmonies, this time with "Cathy's Clown" serving as a model where Lennon sings a descending line against a top note held by McCartney. When they reach the refrain, however, they change direction, with Lennon calling out "Come on" and the others responding, each time at a higher pitch so that everything climaxes at a melodic peak to reinforce the song's title.

When they had first played the song for George Martin in September, he had recommended that, for audiences to associate this recording with "Love Me Do," the band should again feature Lennon's harmonica. And he suggested that, as in that first recording, they speed up the performance. By the time they returned to EMI on 26 November 1962, they had been rehearsing and revising the song for several months. When they finished, Martin opened the intercom to inform them, "Gentlemen, you've just made your first number-one record" (Martin with Hornsby 1979, 130). The next day, Brian Epstein was in Denmark Street looking for a new publisher.

Thank Your Lucky Stars. Ardmore and Beechwood had played a critical role in helping the manager make good on his promise to secure a recording contract, but the promotion of "Love Me Do" had revealed Sid Colman to be

---

[2] Before the Beatles had any chance of appearing on BBC radio or television, the corporation required an audition to determine whether they would offer a contract and, if so, at what rate of remuneration. On 23 November 1962, they had a successful 10-minute audition in London, but not through Epstein or EMI: a fan had submitted the request (Lewisohn 1992, 83–84).

[3] Heard in the films *The Big Broadcast* (1932) and *Please* (1933) (Sheff 1981, 150).

preoccupied with other artists. With a copy of the Beatles' new recording in hand, Epstein entered the red sandstone edifice at the corner of Denmark Street and Charing Cross Road to meet Dick James. James had attained fleeting celebrity with Martin's recording of him singing the theme to the television show *The Adventures of Robin Hood*. The hits, however, had ended, and he had opened his own publishing company to represent young songwriters like Mitch Murray.

Martin had let James know that Epstein wanted a national television appearance for his band, and consequently the publisher had a plan (Bramwell with Kingsland 2005, 86). While Epstein watched, James "called up his old friend Philip Jones," a producer of *Thank Your Lucky Stars*. Putting the phone to the speaker and dropping the needle, he had played "about eight bars of the song when Philip said, 'OK, that'll do, they're on the show'" (Southall with Perry 2006, 13). They set the Beatles' appearance for Saturday, 19 January 1963.

James convinced Keith Fordyce at the *New Musical Express* (located at the other end of the block on Denmark Street) to include the release in his weekly "Singles Review" (11 January 1963). The critic did not disappoint. Although dismissing the hyperbole of an ad that had declared "Please Please Me" to be the "record of the year," Fordyce nevertheless praises the disc, concluding that he cannot "think of any other group currently recording in this style" (11 January 1963, 4). The UK, however, was focused on other events.

First, union disputes concerning workers' overtime at power plants meant rolling blackouts. Second, Britain was enduring one of its coldest winters in memory, leaving families huddled around their home fires. And finally, Hugh Gaitskell, longtime leader of the Labour Party, died on Saturday, 18 January. Thus, the next day when the power returned, families gathered around their televisions to catch the ITV news brief at 5:45, followed by *Thank Your Lucky Stars*, where they saw four young musicians with distinct haircuts and rakish suits miming to "Please Please Me."

January 1963's charts were dominated by Cliff Richard's "Bachelor Boy" (written by Richard and Bruce Welch) and "The Next Time," from his album *Summer Holiday*; the Shadows' "Dance On!"; and ex-Shadows Tony Meehan and Jet Harris's "Diamonds"; as well as the Tornados' "Globetrotter" and Elvis Presley's "Return to Sender." "Please Please Me" broke into this crowded field, peaking in March at #2 in *Record Retailer* and #1 in the *New Musical Express*.

A Style of Their Own

Shortly before the Beatles joined the Helen Shapiro tour, Maureen Cleave in *The Evening Standard* (2 February 1963) described the band as "scruffy, but scruffy on purpose." The day before that, poet Adrian Mitchell had introduced them in the *Daily Mail* as part of a wave of Liverpudlian content that included Alun Owen's plays, new releases by the Vernons Girls, and the television crime drama *Z Cars*. A week before these articles, Patrick Doncaster in the *Daily Mirror* (24 January 1963) had already advised readers to "Watch the Beatles" as performers who had a "style of their own."

Touring Britain in buses during the winter meant treacherous highways, greasy food at roadside cafés, and exposure to every cold, flu, and other respiratory ailment circulating among musicians and support staff.[4] As "Please Please Me" passed Shapiro's "Queen for Tonight" (January 1963) in the charts, George Martin sought to capitalize on the media attention. Thus, the Beatles briefly left the Shapiro tour near Newcastle-on-Tyne to drive 275 miles south on two-lane highways to EMI's Recording Studios.

Martin organized an album session that would include covers as well as original compositions from their setlist, including a song they had written for Shapiro, "Misery." They spent the day recording until illness and exhaustion had so thoroughly undermined Lennon's voice that only his exuberance triumphed over pain in his performance of the Isley Brothers' "Twist and Shout." With "Please Please Me" topping NME's charts, Parlophone announced the release of the album, which would bear the same name. Landing on store shelves Friday 22 March 1963,[5] that album similarly topped the charts by the end of the month.

Northern Songs. As Dick James heard Lennon and McCartney growing as writers, he made a calculated proposition. Neither Epstein nor Lennon or McCartney understood that publishing meant more than simply printing sheet music. "John and I didn't know you could own songs. We thought they just sort of existed in the air . . . we couldn't see how it was possible to have a copyright in it. And therefore, with great glee, publishers saw us coming" (McCartney in Southall with Perry 2006, 17).

Publishing generated royalties from the record company that sold the disc that contained the song, from broadcasters who played the recording, and from theaters where the song was performed. For every commercial use of a song written by one of the Beatles, the Performing Right Society collected fees and paid them to Ardmore and Beechwood or to Dick James Music. Both publishers then wrote checks to Brian Epstein's NEMS Enterprises, which distributed a percentage to Lennon and McCartney. At every step in the process, however, someone took a fee.[6]

On 22 February 1963, as "Please Please Me" approached the top of the British charts, Lennon, McCartney, Epstein, and James took the unusual step of setting

---

[4] In March, the Beatles briefly performed as a trio due to Lennon being too sick to perform.
[5] In the early sixties, British corporations released singles, EPs, and albums on Fridays.
[6] For example, Phonographic Performance Limited (PPL) collected fees both for record companies to share with the performers and for itself.

up Northern Songs, a separate publishing company for the songwriters' prospective catalogue. James had a controlling percentage of the company (51 percent), with Lennon and McCartney each holding 20 percent and Brian Epstein's NEMS the remaining 9 percent.[7] Before this arrangement, they had received only royalties as songwriters. Now they received a share of the publishing too. Before any of those allotments were made, however, Dick James Music took a 10 percent administrative fee, so that Epstein and the songwriters took home 49 percent of 90 percent (44.1 percent).

Lennon and McCartney already had an agreement with Epstein to write songs, but a company of which they were part owners that was dedicated to their music was innovative in 1963. Not for the last time, they established a precedent on which others built.

From Us

Whether gangsters in Hamburg's Saint Pauli Quarter or young adults in Liverpool's Cavern Club, the Beatles had learned how to connect person-to-person with their audiences. In 1963, however, their fanbase began to be dominated by members of the "tween scene" and specifically 11– to 13–year-old females who might have only seen them on television (Lowe 2004).

Music can allow individuals to "identify with groups of their choosing and to escape the bonds of tradition provided by parents, schools, and other governmental apparatuses" (Rice 2007, 31). Fans who associated with the Beatles built multilayered and textured identities: independent acts of volition that helped to define them as individuals. As winter gave way to spring 1963, British fascination with the Beatles grew at each performance (27 shows in March alone) and with each radio and television appearance.

Pronouns. Three months had separated "Love Me Do" from "Please Please Me," and three more months meant anticipation for their next release in April. In the northern cold of 28 February 1963, as their cramped bus barreled from York to Shrewsbury on the Shapiro tour's final zigzag retreat toward London, Lennon and McCartney huddled to create something they could record at their next EMI session.

Lennon describes the evening as just "fooling around on guitar" and not taking themselves very seriously, but, in this semichaotic environment and with others half-watching, the songwriters began "From Me to You." The idea for the refrain probably came from the readers' letters section ("From You to Us") of *The New Musical Express*. The idiomatic letter salutation "with love from me to you"

---

[7] James shared this percentage with his partner, Charles Silver.

became the hook that would trigger responses, repeating the letter-song model they had used in "P.S., I Love You." With the line "I've got everything that you want," the rest of the song unfolded (Beatles 2000, 94).

McCartney, however, remembers a more intentional approach to songwriting that drew on personal pronouns to connect with listeners, under the presumption that fans interpreted lyrics personally. "There was a little trick we developed early on and got bored with later, which was to put 'I,' 'Me,' or 'You' in it, so it was very direct and personal: 'Love Me Do'; 'Please Please Me'; 'From Me to You'—we got two of them in there" (McCartney in Miles 1997, 148–149). The song also quotes the "ooo" from the Isley Brothers' "Twist and Shout." Audiences always screamed at performances when the band shook their heads as they sang this interjection. Inserting it into "From Me to You" allowed them to continue the conceit.

When the Beatles joined their next tour, however—this time supporting Americans Tommy Roe and Chris Montez—they left EMI's studios without completing "From Me to You." Contending with an incomplete recording and a band that would be unavailable soon for retakes, George Martin resorted to a technique he had applied to comedy and classical projects: he physically cut and spliced the recording tape to select parts of different takes and then edited them together to create a single virtual but complete performance.[8] His editing proved successful. By May, not only did *Please Please Me* top British album charts but "From Me to You" (April 1963) did the same for singles.

Pop Go the Beatles

In 1963, the Beatles' success depended significantly on their access to the media and on their adroitness (and luck) in articulating and managing their collective aural and visual image (Frontani 2007). For their audiences, they created polysemic symbols mediated by Brian Epstein and his NEMS employees, by George Martin and his production team, and most of all by themselves.

In addition to the BBC glove puppet show *Pops and Lenny* (16 May), they made return appearances on ITV's *Thank Your Lucky Stars* (23 February, 20 April, and 18 May), as well as on summer versions of that show (29 June and 24 August). Radio appearances also multiplied quickly, beginning with the *Saturday Club* (26 January, 16 March, and 25 May), which proved so popular that the BBC Light Programme created *Pop Go the Beatles,* which ran for four episodes beginning

---

[8] Editing in 1963 called for considerable self-confidence, as you mentally mapped out which parts of which takes went together just before you put brass scissors and adhesive tape to magnetic tape.

in late April, followed by eleven more episodes that summer (see Lewisohn 1992, 110–113).

Dick James secured another important media opportunity on the popular weekly BBC television program *Juke Box Jury*, where panelists rated selected discs (see Bramwell with Kingsland 2005, 115). These guests normally couched their comments in polite generalities, but when John Lennon participated and dismissed all the recordings, including Elvis Presley's "Devil in Disguise," he pried open an emerging cultural divide.[9]

Lennon articulated the arrival of Bulge Generation adolescents looking for their own music. Lush string arrangements and deeply earnest vocal deliveries lacked the kinds of authenticity demanded by those who went to dance halls and clubs where rock 'n' roll and rhythm-and-blues dominated. The popularity of beat music reflected an aesthetic that relished the essential and the visceral in popular music, and although older styles persisted, teens demanded this more modern sound.

They Love You

On Monday, 1 July 1963, a small crowd of teens, who had learned that the Beatles would be recording their next single, milled about outside EMI's recording studios. Inside, George Martin and Norman Smith went about capturing what they could of a song that Lennon and McCartney had concocted in a Newcastle hotel room a week earlier. The Liverpudlians may have been inspired by "Forget Him," a song by British songwriter and recording manager Tony Hatch (under the pseudonym Mark Anthony) and recorded by American star Bobby Rydell in London. That song's conversation about a third person appealed to McCartney, who has described "She Loves You" as an "answering" song (see Everett 2001, 174).

Lennon and McCartney build on ideas they had explored in "From Me to You," including both an emphasis on pronouns and the incorporation of the Isley Brothers' "ooo." The choice of the response "yeah, yeah, yeah," however, carried an ideological message for fans. When the two songwriters stopped in Liverpool the day after writing it in Newcastle, they played their new creation for McCartney's father. Although liking the song, he complained about the distinctly American flavor of the language, instead preferring "yes, yes, yes," which his son described as a "middle-class" response (Miles 1997, 150).

---

[9] Lennon: "I wasn't knocking Presley. All I did was voice the opinion of many other Presley followers who think that his discs of late are ordinary!" (Badman 2000, 61).

In a context where the Beatles' primary audience sought to distinguish themselves from their parents' generation, this simple use of language proved a subtle and effective social marker. "Yeah, yeah, yeah" evoked both rebellion and the innocence of teen infatuation that their parents might protest but could not ban, especially coming as it did in the context of lyrics. They could correct their children's speech, but the words to a song offered a poetic exception (Thompson 2008, 202–203).

At the end of that session, the band sped away to record another episode of *Pop Go the Beatles* and to continue concertizing, again leaving Martin and Smith with a spool of takes, none of which was individually suitable for release. The producer and engineer once more set about selecting the best parts to capture some of the excitement of the day,[10] splicing together a complete performance that had never happened. As in April, fan anticipation for the release of a Beatles single built advance sales that ensured a quick rise to the top of the British charts. "She Loves You" (August 1963), however, would tip the scales.

Beatlemania

The cultural environment in which the Beatles rose to popularity roiled with controversy, as the Conservative government of Harold Macmillan lost public confidence, especially in terms of national security. While Western powers militarily, economically, and politically stood nose-to-nose with the Soviet bloc, Britain's domestic counterintelligence Security Agency (MI5) and its Secret Intelligence Service (MI6) increasingly appeared to be dysfunctional, James Bond notwithstanding.[11] On 23 January 1963, as renewed suspicion grew, MI6 agent Kim Philby vanished from Beirut, where he had been posing as a journalist, only to reappear in Moscow, where the Soviets later confirmed his role as a mole.

Against this backdrop, John Profumo, secretary of state for war (and member of the Privy Council), came under criticism for having an extramarital affair with model Christine Keeler, who was simultaneously in a relationship with a Soviet naval attaché and intelligence officer. Profumo denied accusations of damaging national security but eventually resigned after admitting that he had misled Parliament. As a scapegoat, police arrested well-connected osteopath Stephen Ward—who had facilitated Profumo and Keeler's liaisons—and charged him with "living on the earnings of prostitution" (Sandbrook 2005, 675). He died of a drug overdose three days after his guilty verdict but before his sentencing.

---

[10] Fans had briefly invaded EMI's studios, creating pandemonium for the staff.
[11] *From Russia with Love* premiered on 10 October 1963.

Harold Macmillan's government seemed to lurch from one crisis to another, while the Labour Party elected the affable northerner Harold Wilson as its leader in the wake of Hugh Gaitskell's death.[12] The year 1963 began with the embarrassment of France's President Charles de Gaulle vetoing the UK's request to join the European Economic Community. In September, after protestors attacked and burnt Britain's Jakarta embassy following the Indonesian nationalization of British companies, the Conservatives replaced Macmillan with Sir Alec Douglas-Home. To adolescent Britain, the noise at the top only confirmed their distrust of all things adult and Establishment.

Mediamania. That summer, Beatles' press officer Tony Barrow "worked the boys very hard . . . grabbing them at every opportunity and hauling them into our new office for whole days at a time to do press interviews" (2005, 40). To build relationships, he prepped them with the names of and information about journalists and involved the provincial press, knowing that most readers gravitated to their local papers rather than the national publications.

Perhaps more important, Barrow focused on the rapidly expanding "teen magazine sector," particularly *The Beatles Book*, a magazine publication that first appeared in August 1963 and built a solid and long-lasting fan base (Barrow 2005, 41). In all this marketing, the Beatles themselves were willing participants, especially McCartney, who seemed to relish the role of interacting with the press and who urged his bandmates to do the same.

The Beatles began that autumn headlining "The Great Pop Prom" at the Albert Hall,[13] but perhaps their most significant appearance came on a new ATV television program dedicated to teens. The first episode of *Ready Steady Go!* had aired in August 1963 and drew heavily on Jack Good's model of a dedicated rock and pop show for teens rather than family entertainment. Producer Elkan Allan's background in documentary film shaped the show's simple sets (often just scaffolding), camera work, and the close proximity of the audience to the performers. The program aired early on Friday evenings with the tagline "The weekend starts here!" and proved a powerful influence on music and adolescent fashion. The Beatles' appearance on 4 October 1963, however, started more than just the weekend.

On 13 October, the Beatles appeared on the important nationally broadcast ATV program *Val Parnell's Sunday Night at the London Palladium*, a variety show meant to appeal to a wide audience. Barrow (2005, 92) describes this appearance as marking the moment that national Beatlemania began. Fans congregated outside the Argyll Street entrance to the Palladium before swarming the stage door on Great Marlborough Street in hopes of seeing the Beatles leave. The next

---

[12] Wilson's Huyton riding was part of metropolitan Liverpool.
[13] The Rolling Stones served as one of their warm-up acts.

day's papers carried images of young women stifling screams and crying, and the televised news showed the band escaping out the theater's front door. The term "Beatlemania" may have first appeared in a *Daily Mail* headline on 21 October to describe the chaos when fans shut down Heathrow Airport to greet the Beatles as they returned from concerts in Sweden.

The Royal Circle

If, as some claimed, Beatlemania was a national disease, then a benefit concert at the Prince of Wales Theatre hosted by the Queen Mother threatened to eradicate it. The art deco theater, located near Leicester Square, offers a highly structured internal social space dominated by "stalls" on the ground floor below the "royal circle."

On 4 November 1963, the Beatles did not expect this audience to respond in the same way as their adolescent fans. Moreover, the concert posed a potentially disastrous public relations scenario, with members of the press anticipating that teens would disown the band as sellouts. The musicians, however, proved adept at disarming pretension with an enthusiastic performance, McCartney's corny jokes, and Lennon's irreverent request that the wealthiest patrons just rattle their jewelry as evidence of audience participation. By employing the essential English reflex of humor, they disarmed the inherent awkward class hierarchy of the context.[14]

With the Beatles. The Beatles' first album, *Please Please Me,* still sat near the top of the British LP charts, and their tour schedule ran with few breaks, but success depended on more than television appearances, radio shows, and concerts: they needed to release more recordings, especially for the Christmas market. Thus, on 18 July 1963, they began a series of visits to EMI to work on their next album, which they would name *With the Beatles.*

As with *Please Please Me*, they drew on their current repertoire, which included a stylistic range of covers, including a show tune ("Till There Was You"), a "girl group" tune ("Devil in Her Heart"), and a classic rocker ("Roll Over Beethoven"). And, reflecting wide interest in music by Detroit's Motown and Tamla artists, they also covered material by the Marvelettes, the Miracles, and Barrett Strong.

As for original material, "All My Loving," "It Won't Be Long," "Little Child," "All I've Got to Do," "Not a Second Time," and "Hold Me Tight" reveal Lennon and McCartney to be growing as songwriters. And demonstrating their growing confidence, they included "I Wanna Be Your Man," a song that Lennon and

---

[14] The Beatles also refused every subsequent annual request to play the event.

McCartney had intended for Ringo and that they had recently shared with the Rolling Stones. The reclusive George Harrison also debuted as a songwriter with the aptly titled "Don't Bother Me."

Two weeks before the release of the album, *Record Retailer* ("Beatles' New LP—Advance over 250,000" 7 November 1963, 6) noted that advance sales had "passed the quarter million mark" and that EMI's production facilities were being "stretched to the limit." Parlophone released *With the Beatles* on 22 November 1963 with Robert Freeman's black-and-white photograph of the band's four somber faces.[15] By the end of the month, the disc had topped *Record Retailer's* and *Melody Maker's* album charts, with their first album, *Please Please Me,* in second place.

English Homelife

Given their schedule, finding time to write new songs proved increasingly difficult for Lennon and McCartney. Gone were the relaxed afternoons sitting in the front room of McCartney's Frothlin Road childhood home, playing their favorite songs, while attempting to create their own variations on American classics. Although "From Me to You" had begun on a bus and "She Loves You" in a hotel room, they needed a more homelike space, something more like Frothlin Road.

Returning repeatedly to London for media access, recording, and concerts, the Liverpudlians inevitably needed to become residents of the capital. Lennon found an apartment in Kensington for his wife and child while McCartney became a lodger in the Marylebone home of his girlfriend, the actress Jane Asher. Asher's mother, Margaret, taught oboe at the Guildhall School of Music, where George Martin had been one of her students, and her music room in the family home's basement became Lennon and McCartney's new retreat.

Like the McCartney home in Liverpool, the Asher studio had a piano where the songwriters could sit together at the keyboard. McCartney noted that when "trying to write ... with a guitar," he would sometimes run into a creative impasse. Changing to the piano could open possibilities (Roberts 1 February 1964, 11). Lennon's memories of the Asher "cellar" included sitting with McCartney on the piano bench working on what would become "I Want to Hold Your Hand," a process he called "one on one, eyeball to eyeball." This quiet domestic space accelerated their songwriting. Arranging performances and creating recordings, however, required a different space.

---

[15] The photo imitates images taken by their Hamburg friend Astrid Kirchherr (who was also Stu Sutcliffe's fiancée).

Outstanding English Composers. Many pop-music consumers in this era had only small record players such as Dansette turntable-amplifier-speaker combinations.[16] The 45-rpm discs "Love Me Do," "From Me to You," and "She Loves You," came in a mono format created by George Martin and Norman Smith by mixing two recorded tracks, sometimes "bounced" between two machines. Capturing performances meant relying heavily on musicianship and careful miking to balance the original sound. Toward the end of work on *With the Beatles*, however, Martin and Smith introduced something new: a four-track recorder that facilitated adding and balancing tracks and consequently provided more time to polish performances.

For "I Want to Hold Your Hand," the studio chatter reveals a band musically directed by McCartney and socially directed by Lennon. McCartney can be heard instructing his bandmates to make a "clean start" to the recording and coaching them on how to phrase the syncopated introduction. We also hear Lennon attempting to dispel the tensions that McCartney provokes, at one point mocking him in jest and, at another, complimenting him on his bass part.

When Parlophone released "I Want to Hold Your Hand" (November 1963), the press had already surrendered to the inevitable. Perhaps the most surprising review, however, appeared in a bastion of British conservatism. William Mann, music critic at the *Times,* begins by praising Lennon and McCartney as perhaps the "outstanding English composers of 1963" (27 December 1963). And while he bemoans the general decline of "English" popular music and the rise of American influence, he nevertheless hears an "indigenous" style emerging in the music of the Beatles that he describes as "imaginative and inventive."

---

[16] The relatively recent commercial notion of "stereo" and the ability to play two separate channels remained the purview of only those who could afford the luxury.

Fig. 6.1. The Beatles: George Harrison, Ringo Starr, Paul McCartney, John Lennon, 1963. Pictorial Press Ltd/Alamy Stock Photo

7
Northwest Passage

London's Denmark Street understood that northern England had an active music life, with *Melody Maker*'s Hubert W. David declaring that "more records and sheetmusic [sic] are sold in the top half of Great Britain" than in the south. In Manchester, Liverpool, Leeds, Glasgow, and Newcastle, "you will see and hear entertainment, which would make many southerners gape with astonishment" (26 May 1956).

Manchester and Liverpool in northwest England have a long competitive history that grew more intense as Britain's economy shifted in the postwar period (Witts 2015). The two cities—center-to-center only 35 miles apart—experienced an industrial decline that served as a backdrop for plays, television dramas, and films about their inhabitants. Those depictions of poverty and crime, as well as quintessential English values, would help shape the nation's response to its musicians.

Musicians from Manpool would lead the first wave of midsixties British pop,[1] with a stripped-down guitar-driven hybrid of show tunes, country, folk, rhythm and blues, and rock 'n' roll. As they imitated American models, however, they developed a British musical equivalent. Where Southern California celebrated middle-class surf and car cultures, the northwest declared a working-class determination to survive hardship, if not to triumph against the odds.

Every time musicians set up on a stage and audiences walked in the door, they encountered an environment that shaped their behavior. Peterson and Bennett describe "situations where performers, support facilities, and fans come together to collectively create music" as "scenes" (2004, 3–12). Manpool venues like the Cavern Club, the Iron Door, the Twisted Wheel, the Oasis Club, and dozens of other pubs, clubs, and dance halls incubated scenes in which musicians and their audiences created thriving interconnected music cultures.

When northerners began to tour the country and to arrive in London, however, the new contexts changed them. Londoners in the sixties (if not still) commonly viewed the north as less sophisticated than its home-county southeastern counterpart:[2] working-class grit made acceptable with a sense of humor.

---

[1] The idea of merging Manchester's and Liverpool's infrastructures is a twenty-first-century idea. (See Groom 24 February 2014.)

[2] The home counties surround London.

As musicians from the north adapted to southern audiences and performance spaces, and to the expectations of record companies, the media, and publishers, they became cultural hybrids in an industry built on planned obsolescence.

Merseybeat

Late in the summer of 1962, while the Beatles were changing drummers, Norman Jopling rhetorically asked in the *Record Mirror* (4 August 1962) whether Liverpool was the "rockingest part of the great British Isles." His question arose after reading Bill Harry's paper *Mersey Beat*, which enumerated the top performers in the city. The summer before the release of "Love Me Do," Jopling condescendingly cited the Beatles and Ringo Starr as examples of how musicians from Merseyside were competing with the Americans for clever names. A year later, he would have a different appreciation of these musicians developing their art away from London's hegemony.

The Liverpool scene in the early mid-1960s saw possibly hundreds of groups competing for gigs (Leigh 2004b). Soon after George Martin's success with the Beatles, other producers made the pilgrimage to Merseyside in search of artists to record. Some London publications began using "Merseybeat" to refer to an imaginary musical style rather than the cultural scene invading the national consciousness.

By mid-1963, musicians associated with Liverpool and particularly with Brian Epstein appeared across the mediascape in Britain. Among the programs competing for adolescent eyes and ears, a "Merseybeat Special" episode of *Lucky Stars: Summer Spin* (29 June 1963)[3] was recorded in Birmingham and featured a disparate slate of musicians. The Beatles, Gerry and the Pacemakers, Cilla Black, the Searchers, the Vernons Girls, Billy J. Kramer with the Dakotas, the Big Three, and Lee Curtis may have had only Merseyside in common, but to a national audience these musicians suggested a northern invasion.

How You Do It

Like Billy Fury and Ringo Starr, the Marsden brothers hailed from Liverpool's Dingle district and got their start "musicking" with family and friends (Joynson 1995, 213).[4] Gerry Marsden (guitar and vocals) with older brother Freddie

---

[3] Summer title of *Thank Your Lucky Stars*.
[4] *Musicking*: Christopher Small's term for any activity involved with music from composing and performing to listening and dancing (Small 1998).

(drums), Les Chadwick (bass), and Les Maguire (piano) formed Gerry and the Pacemakers;[5] they played both the Merseyside circuit and Hamburg's clubs (Leigh 2004b). In these environments, audiences expected a band's set list to include a mix of standards, current hits, and perhaps a few novel interpretations or selections with an emphasis on familiarity. The Pacemakers built their reputation interpreting American material through Gerry Marsden's personality.

Where the Beatles took an "aggressive, surly approach," Marsden played "as though he was having the time of his life: Tommy Steele with a hard edge" (Leigh 2004b, 72).[6] "We used to do every one of the Top 20 in our show and that got us around a bit. We were one of the few groups in Liverpool that used a piano, so we could do the Jerry Lee Lewis ones and the Fats Domino ones better than most of the other bands" (Gerry Marsden in Leigh 2004b, 39).

In the beginning, Marsden's father booked their gigs (Geller 2000, 51), but when Brian Epstein took over, he arranged for concert and media appearances, raised their performance fees, and got them an EMI audition. The success of the Beatles gave George Martin and Ron Richards the inside track as London's music and recording industries turned their attention to Merseyside. The producers particularly thought that Gerry and the Pacemakers represented better interpreters of the Mitch Murray song that the Beatles had recorded unsuccessfully.[7] Indeed, the perpetually perky Gerry Marsden captured the balance of innocence, simplicity, and surprise of "How Do You Do It?" (February 1963) in ways that escaped John Lennon.

Southern Audiences. With guitar perched high on his chest, Marsden found the fulcrum point between youthful joy and George Formby's knowing wink to make "How Do You Do It?" the best-selling record in *Record Retailer*, *Melody Maker*, and the *New Musical Express* for most of April. Indeed, Gerry and the Pacemakers can boast of having had a true chart-wide number-one hit before the Beatles. That success led Murray to provide them with "I Like It," which plays on some of the same conceits as "How Do You Do It?" and produced similar results.[8]

Despite the growing success of the nation's songwriters and the creativity of production teams, British audiences still often expected covers of foreign and especially American songs. John Lennon observed that "while down South you were experimenting with new sounds, we were working out new arrangements to old ones." Moreover, the Beatles routinely had to "throw in one or two items from the hit parade" into their concerts for southern audiences (June Harris 23

---

[5] The word "pacemaker" referring to a wearable heart pulse rate regulator did not come into common usage until the mid-1960s.

[6] The two bands interlocked lunch-hour appearances at the Cavern Club, alternately playing Tuesday/Thursday one week and Monday/Wednesday/Friday the next.

[7] Richards had originally brought the Murray tune to Martin's attention.

[8] Murray had only been a professional songwriter for a year when "I Like It" dethroned "From Me to You" in June 1963 for four weeks, making him one of the hottest talents on Denmark Street.

March 1963). Agreeing, Marsden acknowledged that the Pacemakers would have to do the same, which probably contributed to the decision to record "You'll Never Walk Alone" (October 1963).

Rock groups in this era often included show tunes or Tin Pan Alley standards in their set lists, and Marsden had heard Tony Sheridan in Hamburg performing the Rodgers and Hammerstein song from the musical and film *Carousel* (1956) (Leigh 3 January 2021). The Pacemaker version of "You'll Never Walk Alone" starts with the stripped-down band and articulates a sentiment that resonated with working-class audiences.[9] Midway through the recording, George Martin adds strings that add emotional intensity to the performance but also distance the band from its roots. With their first three releases topping British charts, however, Gerry and the Pacemakers seemed unstoppable as 1963 came to a close.

A Very Good-Looking Boy

Sitting beside Merseyside's dockyards, the borough of Bootle suffered heavy German bombing in World War II, but postwar development brought council housing for the working poor, including for Bill Ashton, who left school at 15 to work for British Railways (Geller 2000, 53; Schaffner 1982b). Like many young musicians in this era, he took easily to skiffle before making the transition to pop and rock 'n' roll, eventually becoming a solo singer when someone stole his guitar. Reflecting British youth's obsession with American culture, one of his bandmates suggested a stage identity. Billy "Kramer" namechecked Elvis Presley's pianist, Floyd Cramer, although they altered it because they "thought that spelling it with a K made it sound more masculine" (Leigh 2004b, 83).

After seeing Kramer perform in a *Mersey Beat* concert,[10] Brian Epstein bought out his contract (£50) and began transforming the 19-year-old whom the manager called the "best looking singer in the world" (Rogan 1988, 114). Kramer was also impressed. "Let's face it, if you are just a working-class kid from Liverpool and you become associated with somebody who speaks well and wears Savile Row clothes and Turnbull & Asser ties and handmade shirts, it's a bit intimidating" (Kramer in Geller 2000, 55–56). As Parnes had with Billy Fury, Epstein took Kramer to London for transformation, replacing the singer's gold lamé jackets with black mohair suits (Geller 2000, 54). In the process, Epstein created an imagined working-class version of himself: identifiably virile and

---

[9] "You'll Never Walk Alone" became a football anthem for the Liverpool FC, whose fans began singing the song at games shortly after the release of the Pacemakers' version. The song's title now appears above one of the gates to Liverpool's stadium.
[10] Possibly "Operation Big Beat IV" on 3 August 1962.

masculine but middle class with hints of a gay or gender-neutral sexuality that could appeal to both females and males.

In addition to Epstein's coaching in how to behave on (and off) stage, Kramer took advice from John Lennon, who recommended adding the middle initial *J* to make his name sound more American (Leigh 2004b, 83). Finally, they replaced his Liverpool band with a group from Manchester whose name also referenced America. With Epstein's growing reputation and the encouragement of Lennon and McCartney, Billy J. Kramer with the Dakotas were soon headed to the Star-Club in Hamburg for three weeks of musical bootcamp before recording auditions in London (Joynson 1995, 314).

The Secret. Cajoled by Brian Epstein, George Martin concurred that Kramer was a "very good-looking boy" but concluded that the manager's newest client did not possess "the greatest voice in the world" (Martin with Hornsby 1979, 134). He resolved the problem with a technical solution: he would double-track Kramer's voice, laying two vocal performances on top of each other to hopefully cancel out pitch problems. Strategic mixing would cover the rest, the Dakotas would provide the backing (with overdubbing by Martin), and Lennon and McCartney would provide the material.

In March 1963, Billy J. Kramer with the Dakotas arrived at EMI to record a song that had begun with a memory of Lennon's mother singing "Wishing Well" from Disney's animated film *Snow White and the Seven Dwarfs* (1937). Its opening lyrics—"Want to know a secret? Promise not to tell?"—had provided the verbal germ that grew into "Do You Want to Know a Secret" (April 1963).[11] Kramer's disc soon joined those of the Beatles and Gerry and the Pacemakers, topping the *Melody Maker* and *New Musical Express* charts at the end of May and launching the singer's career, while also reinforcing Lennon's and McCartney's reputations as Britain's premier songwriters, Martin's status as London's hottest producer, and Epstein's apparent knack for identifying talent.

Kramer released two more Lennon-McCartney compositions before the year was out: "Bad to Me" (July 1963) and "I'll Keep You Satisfied" (November 1963), both of which proved hits. Epstein and Martin seemed to know a secret. Others wondered if they could too.

The Search

Having a brother in the Merchant Navy proved an advantage when John McNally became the recipient of a guitar and a stack of records from the United States.

---

[11] Although George Harrison had sung "Do You Want to Know a Secret" on their album *Please Please Me*, they had not released it as a single.

Practice and a good ear helped him develop as a musician, but playing with like-minded Merseysiders proved transformative. In this environment, McNally and Mike Pender began trading guitar licks and ideas on how to escape Liverpool (Norris 2000; Leigh 2004b, 31). Pender had been taken with Buddy Holly and his music, especially after the American had played at Liverpool's Philharmonic Hall (20 March 1958). After that, he felt that "everything I learned, everything I played, was based on Holly" (Pender in Leigh 2004b, 32). When Pender and McNally added Tony Jackson (bass) and Chris Curtis (drums) as singers, the four built arrangements around vocal harmonies and interlocked guitars. They named themselves after the Hollywood western *The Searchers* (1956).[12]

Successful bands had managers, and Brian Epstein had briefly considered an earlier version of the group until witnessing a drunken and chaotic performance at the Cavern Club (Norris 2000). The proprietor of the Iron Door Club booked their gigs, but Chris Curtis took the initiative to shape the band and its music, Pender describing him as their "driving force." The ambitious drummer's securing of a residency at Hamburg's Star-Club provided the context for the next phase of their personal and musical transformation (Barnard 2015; Clayson 1997).

London learned about them when Breakaway singer and Liverpudlian Margo Quantrell mentioned the band to Pye producer Tony Hatch. After listening to a tape, Hatch traveled to Liverpool to hear them for himself at the Iron Door (Leigh 18 August 2003). That visit generated a recording contract and the expectation that they would bring rehearsed material to London.

The intense competition between Merseyside groups in the early sixties meant continually updating repertoire and finding unique ways to perform it. As with other British groups, the Searchers' repertoire drew heavily on American material obtained by scouring record store bins for songs they could cover, which was how Curtis found in Hamburg a copy of "Sweets for My Sweet" performed (July 1961) by the Drifters.[13]

Blanco It Up. Curtis explained that when the Searchers adapted the music of Black America, they would take an arrangement and "Blanco it up," that is, alter it to match their musical resources if not make it more palatable to White British audiences (Leigh 2004b, 75). Jackson's nasal lead on "Sweets for My Sweet" (June 1963) and the smooth backing vocals signal the Whiteness of the Searchers' version. The sped-up groove and electric guitars that replace the piano and Latin percussion of the laid-back original confirm the recontextualization.

---

[12] The film included a quote that had inspired Buddy Holly to write "That'll Be the Day" (Leigh 2004b, 34).

[13] The American originals, not the proto-Shadows.

When John Lennon described "Sweets for My Sweet" as the best recent release out of Liverpool, the sudden swell of attention forced the Searchers to buy out their Star-Club contract to return to London (Norris 2000). A little over a month after its release, the disc occupied the top of British charts (Leigh 2004b, 134). The sudden success, nevertheless, revealed musicians unsure of themselves. Jackson complained that the band was "still using our original battered guitars stuck together with tape" while McNally was "frightened to get new [instruments] in case it spoils the sound" (Dawbarn 10 August 1963, 6).

After the quickly recorded album *Meet the Searchers* (August 1963) and EP *Ain't Gonna Kiss Ya* (September 1963), Hatch proffered a song he had written, albeit under the pseudonym Fred Nightingale. "Sugar and Spice" (October 1963) combines musical ideas from Tommy Roe's "Sheila" and Buddy Holly's "Peggy Sue" while lyrically referencing "Sweets for My Sweet." The arrangement again features guitars and vocal harmonies and placed another disc in Britain's charts that further confirmed Merseyside's significance. It also intensified the search for new songs.

Like other British musicians in the first half of the sixties, the Searchers looked for material that distinguished them from others, which for them lay in their eclectic choices in American pop. Their first album, *Meet the Searchers,* includes covers of tunes as diverse as the Isley Brothers' "Twist and Shout," the Crystals' "Da Doo Ron Ron," and Pete Seeger's "Where Have All the Flowers Gone." The next year saw them expand on this strategy.

Manchester

The success of Liverpudlian performers spurred London producers to search for other hidden gems they could bring into the studio. With Merseyside already covered, the next most obvious place to look was Manchester, Britain's second largest population center and Liverpool's conjoined but competitive sibling. The foundation of Manchester's success had been the cotton and weaving industries that flourished during the eighteenth century when canals connected her mills to coal from the north and allowed access to the Atlantic Ocean in the west. As the British Empire disintegrated and as India and the United States developed their own textile industries, however, Manchester's cotton-based economy collapsed.

The city mounted a comeback in the postwar years, rebuilding and attracting new industries, including media (Granada Television) and education (Alan Turing worked on computing at Manchester University). This concentration of broadcasting and education challenged the hegemony of London in the UK. Indeed, the increasing importance of television in promoting musicians and their music positioned Manchester to play an important role in the rise of British pop.

The Fool

In *Watching the English*, Kate Fox describes humor as a primary reflex behavior permeating "every aspect of English life and culture" (2014, 79). In that frame of reference, Mancunian Freddie Garrity made drollery central to his performances. One of the oldest musicians in his cohort, the diminutive, bespectacled Garrity had played with a variety of skiffle and rock 'n' roll groups before forming Freddie and the Dreamers (Joynson 1995, 198; Leigh 2004a). Where others emoted at the microphone, Freddy and friends mocked the sincerity and choreographies of groups like Cliff Richard and the Shadows, performing silly synchronized dances behind Garrity's often awkward theatrical gags.

The Dreamers' local success attracted the attention of local entertainment entrepreneur Danny Betesh, an accountant who had purchased a dance hall in Macclesfield about 20 miles south of Manchester. When he brought performers to town, he also booked local talent, and that business grew into Kennedy Street Enterprises, the most important agency in Manchester and the northwest. Garrity, however, would be one of only a few artists Betesh managed directly (Tims 1964, 4).

Making a Song of It. Aware of George Martin's and Ron Richards's successes in Liverpool, EMI's John Burgess auditioned Garrity and the Dreamers and chose "If You Gotta Make a Fool of Somebody" (April 1963) for them to record. The waltz had been an American R&B hit in 1962 for James Ray with a bluesy harmonica and a nostalgic brass band. The American's performance emphasizes pathos, reinforced by a tempo that suggests a bittersweet memory. Garrity on the other hand emphasizes the fool part of the lyrics. The Dreamers' version speeds up the song like a fairground ride, with Garrity almost shouting the lyrics and clownishly rushing the word "somebody."

In an appearance on *Thank Your Lucky Stars* (1 June 1963), the band members spin in unison as Garrity mocks being heartbroken, intermittently running in place. While John Profumo was admitting to Parliament that he had "misled the House" about his affair with Christine Keeler and the *News of the World* was running an exposé on her, Garrity's buffoonish comedy distracted audiences enough to break into Britain's top five.

Perhaps the recent rise of British songwriting led Garrity to attempt to do the same, beginning with the words "I'm telling you now" sung to a wide upward leap reminiscent of "How Do You Do It?" That, however, was as far as he got, and Betesh soon asked Mitch Murray to meet with Garrity to finish the effort. Murray "went away and made a song of it," recording a demo for Freddie and friends to learn.[14]

---

[14] Betesh demanded 80 percent of the royalties for the song, to which the songwriter made an inverse counteroffer. They settled on 50 percent/50 percent.

Once more, they rehearsed goofy choreography for a recording that this time was punctuated by Garrity's cackling laughter. Although "I'm Telling You Now" (August 1963) competed with Billy J. Kramer's "Bad to Me" and the Beatles' "She Loves You," it still managed to reach into the top five in British charts. Murray's follow-up "You Were Made for Me" (November 1963) did the same, this time emoted by the singer kneeling à la Al Jolson in *The Jazz Singer*.

At the core of Fox's analysis of English humor sits the notion that one should never take one's self too seriously. She characterizes it as respecting the "Importance of Not Being Earnest" (2014, 79–84). The arts, of course, provide contexts in which that rule does not apply. Audiences routinely expect performers to take their roles seriously, whether in a theater production or a concert. We do not anticipate Hamlet winking at us or Gerry Marsden pulling a face while singing "You'll Never Walk Alone." In 1963, however, Freddy and the Dreamers mocked earnest pop performance. The strategy worked... for a while.

Just Like Holly

As the Beatles and Lennon and McCartney were to Liverpool, so the Hollies and Allan Clarke and Graham Nash were to Manchester. The Mancunian band's tight harmonies, prominent guitars, and solid drum-bass foundation gave them a quintessential 1963 beat-group sound, but while they were popular at home, it was in Liverpool that someone from London took notice.

Clarke and Nash grew up in the Manchester suburb of Salford and discovered their shared love of music when as classmates they improvised harmonies while they sang the Lord's Prayer at school one morning (Nash 2013, 16). At the Salford Lads Club, they sang in a minstrel group until rock 'n' roll, teenage hormones, and guitars came into their lives (Barnard 2014). When a concert by Bill Haley and His Comets in Manchester's Odeon Cinema (13 February 1957) was announced, Nash's school principal beat him for skipping class to buy tickets, but the die had been cast. By the time the Everly Brothers played the Free Trade Hall (22 April 1960), Nash and Clarke were already appearing before audiences, having memorized the Tennessee duo's songs and harmonies.[15] Paying gigs were important in a working-class environment, and their families wondered whether playing music would put food on the table, but by Christmas 1962, Nash and Clarke had already formed a band and named it after a seasonal decoration and a recently deceased American rocker (Nash 2013, 24–25).

Through the Door. Like Liverpool bands, Manchester's Hollies felt that people in the south treated them like "peasants" and that "everybody south of

---

[15] Clarke and Nash met the Everly Brothers after the show in Manchester.

Birmingham was posher than we were.... When the Beatles opened that door," however, "we all wanted to run screaming through it" (Nash 2013, 55). After the Hollies made their Cavern Club debut at the "Rhythm and Blues Marathon" (3 February 1963), Ron Richards introduced himself and told the band he was interested (Nash 2013, 55–56). With Gerry and the Pacemakers already on his calendar, he now proposed a recording test for the Hollies.[16] In anticipation, the band decided to quit their day jobs, but their lead guitarist chose to stay in Manchester. They soon recruited Tony Hicks both to play guitar and to provide a third vocal harmony.

As with many other beat groups, the Hollies' repertoire drew heavily on American rhythm-and-blues adapted in ways that matched their resources and resonated with their audiences in northwestern England. For example, where the Coasters' "(Ain't That) Just Like Me" (March 1957) features saxophone chords over a deep drum-bass groove and open voices, the Hollies' version (May 1963) features bright choppy electric guitars and double-tracked slightly nasal vocals.

Although the disc received little media coverage, it sold enough to a make respectable #25 on *Record Retailer*'s charts and led Richards to choose the Coasters "Searchin'" (March 1957) as the Hollies' follow-up (August 1963). This time, an appearance on *Thank Your Lucky Stars* (7 September) helped their disc sales, but, as with the Beatles, ambition led to a further change in personnel.

Don Rathbone and his father's van had been an integral part of their enterprise, but the band lacked confidence in the drummer. In what must have been an uncomfortable conversation, Rathbone became their road manager, and one of Manchester's best drummers, Bobby Elliott, replaced him. With Elliott and bassist Eric Haydock now locking down the fundamentals, their anglicization of Maurice and the Zodiacs' "Stay"—supported by appearances on *Ready Steady Go!* (29 November), *Thank Your Lucky Stars* (28 December), and the BBC's new program *Top of the Pops* (1, 7, and 15 January 1964)—broke them into Britain's top 10.

The northwest had invaded London but not without a southern response.

---

[16] Rather than the EMI Recording Studios in Saint John's Wood, Nash (2013, 57) remembers them auditioning at the De Lane Lea Studios.

Fig. 7.1 Gerry Marsden, on *Ready, Steady, Go!*, 1963.

Fig. 7.2 Freddie and the Dreamers; left to right: Derek Quinn, Peter Birrell, Freddie Garrity, Bernie Dwyer (obscured), Roy Crewdson, on *The Ed Sullivan Show*, 25 April 1965.

8
Capital Connections

As those in the peak of the British Bulge turned sixteen in 1963, they formed a complex culture increasingly self-aware of its economic and political importance. When these youth sought symbolic representations of themselves, not only as a generation separate from their parents but also as the bearers of a new worldview, they often turned to music, musicians, and musical spaces and places to articulate their identities.

Recordings by "older" solo White male singers still had success: 28-year-old Elvis Presley's "(You're the) Devil in Disguise" (June 1963) and 25-year-old Frank Ifield's "Wayward Wind" (January 1963) both topped British charts that year. Younger White English male vocal-instrumental groups, however, released discs that occupied the top of *Record Retailer*'s charts almost 90 percent of the time. Starting in April, however, around 63 percent of the performers at the top were from England's northwest.

Adaptations. Cliff Richard responded to the cultural shift by returning to his rock-band roots after the orchestral accompaniments of "Summer Holiday" (February 1963) and "It's All in the Game" (August 1963). Richard and the Shadows introduced an electric 12-string guitar to brighten their sound on "Don't Talk to Him" (November 1963), a move that took them almost to the top of British charts during the chaos of Beatlemania.[1] Their next success came with "I'm the Lonely One" (January 1964), written by 28-year-old Gordon Mills in response to the music of the beat boom.[2]

Johnny Kidd had also attempted to update his sound by recording Mills's "I'll Never Get Over You" (June 1963) and "Hungry for Love" (November 1963) but by the fall of 1963, he was in his late twenties, five years older than Cliff Richard and John Lennon, and half a generation away from the emerging market. Even with producer Peter Sullivan double-tracking Kidd's voice, audiences still associated him with the era of the *Six-Five Special*.

Notwithstanding the success of Merseyside groups, their chart domination proved temporary. Many British towns and cities can boast historical, economic,

---

[1] The Shadows had a relationship with the British manufacturer Burns Guitars in 1963, which led to Hank Marvin playing their "Double Six" electric 12-string guitar on this track. George Harrison of the Beatles obtained an American Rickenbacker 360-12 electric 12-string guitar during their visit to the United States in February 1964.

[2] Like Harry Webb/Cliff Richard, Mills was born in India.

Sixties British Pop, Outside In. Gordon Ross Thompson, Oxford University Press. © Oxford University Press 2024.
DOI: 10.1093/oso/9780190672348.003.0009

political, military, and artistic importance, but London occupies the national crossroads. As the seat of the central government, its concentrations of population, wealth, and privilege have always attracted artists, and no art reflected culture quite as effectively in this era as popular music.

The best London musicians had privileged connections to a network of producers, promoters, publishers, songwriters, and media figures that gave them advantages over performers from the provinces. In and around the capital, dance halls contributed to the generation of new forms of British pop while clubs sprang up to incubate the growing interest in American blues.

Now That I Can Dance

Dance halls played an important role in English social life for most of the twentieth century, providing formalized contexts in which men and women—especially from the working and lower-middle classes—could meet and court (see Nott 2015).[3] The large open spaces of these purpose-built or modified dance halls allowed a postwar sociopolitical aesthetic to question England's deep-seated class divisions. Mecca Dance Ltd.'s codirector, for example, asserted that they treated all their patrons equally, with "no class distinction whatsoever," albeit knowing who their clientele was (Nott 2015, 224). In the postwar years, however, the ballroom dancing that had characterized earlier decades gave way to "solo dancing" that allowed individuals more freedom of self-expression (Nott 2015, 97).

Dancing creates an internal psychological space while defining a personal space within a social space, movement mapping personal and social territorial boundaries in shared territory. The popularity of dance halls in the first half of the century generated crowded floors where couples could explore personal compatibility while engaging in ritualized gestures. In these contexts, individuals could physically express themselves while engaging in the implicit sexuality of dance. Moreover, dance mitigated some of the emotional isolation that has historically characterized English behavior by structuring microclimates where participants agreed to a relaxation of normative social rules (Fox 2014, 130 and 381).

In the postwar years, dance and its gendered behaviors adapted to a reality in which women began to question culturally prescribed passivity. Their mothers had worked in factories during and after the war, tasted the freedom their meager wages afforded them, and passed that model on to their daughters. Where playing rock 'n' roll allowed men to express sexual desire, dance did the same for women, empowering them to make personal albeit limited decisions.

---

[3] Dancing for homosexuals took place in clandestine private clubs.

On stage, musicians responded to changing social climates, to the spaces where they played, and to the technologies of creation and dissemination. Small groups of musicians with electronic instruments replaced dance orchestras of violins, trumpets, trombones, and saxophones,[4] and these musicians competed for gigs with repertoires that they hoped would keep dancers on the floor.

Do You Love Me?

Shortly after the Beatles left their 1962 New Year's Day audition at Decca, Brian Poole and the Tremeloes arrived fresh after a short drive from East London.[5] Poole, Alan Blakley, and Alan Howard had been schoolmates in Barking, rehearsing after school in a classroom and over Blakley's father's greengrocer shop. Adding drummer Dave Munden and guitarist Rick West, and with Poole donning horn-rimmed glasses to cover Buddy Holly hits, they honed their skills playing schools, social clubs, and dance halls around Barking and Dagenham.

Their local success helped them get gigs at American air bases and at a Butlins summer camp, but they needed someone who could help them secure a recording contract and media appearances. Peter Walsh had grown up near Manchester and had been a concert promoter in Dublin before managing the Brook Brothers, who were Everly imitators (see Rogan 1988). Promoting that duo had brought him into contact with London's recording, media, and music industries, which was how he had met Dick Rowe, who had recorded the Brook Brothers' first discs, and Jimmy Grant, a producer for the BBC Light Programme's *Saturday Club*.

The band's home-counties popularity helped secure an appearance on the nationally broadcast *Saturday Club* (30 September 1961), even though they had yet to record a disc (Joynson 1995, 421). A Decca recording test came at the end of the year after Poole and East London resident Mike Smith met through their optician (Rogan 1988, 84). Reflecting on the New Year's Day session, Poole surmised that Decca "wanted a front singer . . . [and believed that] we were doing a type of music that was about to be popular" (Rogan 1988, 84).[6]

They Were All Dancing to Us. The band developed their style and repertoire playing dance halls where "nobody sat down," Poole asserted; "they were all up dancing to us" (Howells 2014). Their Decca releases reflect that background, albeit with limited initial success. Poole and the Tremeloes' first release, "Twist Little Sister" (April 1962)—written by John Beveridge and Peter Oakman of Joe

---

[4] Changes in licensing laws facilitated the arrival of disc jockeys (Nott 2015, 96).
[5] Earlier in their career, they also spelled their name "Tremolos" and "Tremilos" but settled on "Tremeloes" after a newspaper's misspelling.
[6] That Smith's boss, Dick Rowe, already knew Peter Walsh probably also helped.

Brown's Bruvvers—failed to chart, despite promotion on *Thank Your Lucky Stars* (19 May 1962) and *Saturday Club* (16 June 1962). The same was true of their next three releases: "Blue" (September 1962), "A Very Good Year for Girls" (January 1963), and the self-penned "Keep on Dancing" (March 1963). Nevertheless, Decca renewed their contract, while using them to back Tommy Steele and visiting Americans Gary U.S. Bonds and Johnny Burnette before they scored their own hit.

Poole and the Tremeloes claim not to have heard the Beatles' version before releasing "Twist and Shout" (June 1963; Rogan 1988, 85), which reached the top five on British charts. By the third week of July, however, the Beatles' *Twist and Shout* EP was outselling the Tremeloes' single. In search of a follow-up, the Tremeloes covered the Contours' "Do You Love Me" (September 1963),[7] which both closely matches the musical structure of "Twist and Shout" and reiterates their focus on dance.

They promoted their version of "Do You Love Me" (September 1963) with another appearance on *Thank Your Lucky Stars* (13 September), but more significantly, they would be among the first guests on ITV's *Ready Steady Go!* (9 August and 11 October 1963). The appearances significantly contributed to the success of the recording, which topped British charts in October 1963. Brian Poole and the Tremeloes, however, had to contend with the same problem many other British acts had: where would they find the next song? Touring with Roy Orbison that fall led them to cover his "Candy Man" (January 1964), which also reached into the top 10, but they had competition on London's dance circuit.

Glad All Over

Bands can be like work crews, each member contributing a specific skill that allows the ensemble to collectively accomplish a task, whether it be keeping dancers on the floor, accompanying singers, or making demos. Many musicians from upper working-class and lower middle-class backgrounds treated what they did as work with implicit expectations for remuneration. Indeed, one of most successful London groups of this era illustrates this transactional aspect of musical labor.

Dave Clark left school at 15 to work as a film extra at North London's Elstree Studios, including "fighting on horseback, sword fights, explosions, car crashes. It was all fun. You were young, confident, if you wanted to do something, you'd do it" (Clark in McCormick 2015). Among the things he wanted to do was play drums in a band, so he placed ads in *Melody Maker* for musicians (Gary James

---

[7] Originally recorded by the Contours (October 1963).

1994). From the beginning, his name appeared prominently both on his bass drum and on the enterprise.

Most important among those Clark recruited, singer and keyboardist Mike Smith had studied his way through the Royal Conservatory piano grades until Elvis Presley's "Heartbreak Hotel" changed his mind (Leigh 2008). An early adopter of the Vox Continental electronic organ, his musicianship drove the band, and his bluesy, raspy voice distinguished them from the competition. That said, he seldom asserted himself in anything but the music. "I was doing something that I enjoyed," he recalled. "My ego's never been that big, and maybe I lost out because of it" (Leigh 2008). Apropos of that attitude, their first release, "That's What I Said" (June 1962), was their only disc under the name "The Dave Clark Five Featuring Mike Smith."

With Smith as the band's musical heart, the Dave Clark Five built their reputation in Mecca's southern England ballrooms, with the Tottenham Royal serving as their home base. What set them apart from many other bands of the era was Clark's business orientation. He took the role of manager, paying salaries and controlling their image, even if they sometimes resembled "the younger members of a yacht club with their blazers, tab-collared shirts, and white trousers" (Leigh 2013). The Harold Davison Agency booked most of their gigs, including making demos in Denmark Street. Mitch Murray, for one, "used to pay them £12 for the whole group, for the whole evening ... [and paid] [Regent Sound] studios about the same ... [to] do two or three titles."

Our Group Plays for Dancing. Work on demos provided valuable experience, however, and, with Joe Meek as a model, Clark took an active role writing material, producing the band's recordings, and leasing them. And, although he "never professed to be a great drummer," he felt he could make good records with the right engineer and musicians (McCormick 2015).[8] He learned about production from their initial albeit unsuccessful releases with Piccadilly records, including "what the top rate was for an independent" producer. When that lease agreement ran out, he approached EMI and "asked for three times that, thinking that it left you room for maneuver" (Gary James 1994). Perhaps knowing Piccadilly and about the band's home counties reputation, and not having to pay for studio time, EMI surprised Clark by agreeing to the rate.

Clark booked Lansdowne Studios in West London with Meek's protégé Adrian Kerridge as engineer, on whom he relied so much that the production of these early discs carries the credit "Adrian Clark." Their cover of "Do You Love Me" (September 1963) showcases the sound Clark and Kerridge were developing. And while Mike Smith's powerful vocal and the band's thunderous recorded

---

[8] Clark used session musicians Bobby Graham (drums), Eric Ford (bass), and Vic Flick (guitar) on some sessions.

sound briefly challenged the Tremeloes' disc, the DC5 release arrived too late to compete successfully. It did, however, attract attention.

Clark and Smith wrote their follow-up, beginning with the hook "Glad All Over"[9] and built the song and arrangement on the band's Mecca dance circuit experience and particularly on Clark's penchant for four-on-the-floor drumming.[10] Perhaps the most distinguishing quality of the recording, however, comes where Kerridge and Clark double-track both the vocals and the drums, placing the latter forward in the mix.

As 1963 wound down and with the Beatles' "I Want to Hold Your Hand" and other Merseybeat recordings on the radio, "Glad All Over" (November 1963) entered British charts. Emphasizing their work ethic, Clark told David Griffiths at *Record Mirror* that "our group plays for dancing and that's a lot harder than being a stage act doing a quarter of an hour a night" (14 December 1963). By January 1964, however, "Glad All Over" topped *Record Retailer*'s singles, and the DC5 too became a stage act.

Blue Britain

Fox observes that the English form clubs and societies as "facilitators to help us engage socially with our fellow humans [and] to overcome our social dis-ease." Members might enjoy cultivating knowledge of a subject, but "the real purpose of all these clubs is the social contact and social bonding that we desperately need, but cannot admit to needing" (2014, 366).

Given the parallel English preoccupation with class, knowledge of a club's subject matter also helps to establish relative rank. Members (formally or otherwise) research history, collect objects, and become familiar with the discourse around a topic, not only to confirm membership but also to fix their hierarchical social position vis-à-vis others in the club. In the 1960s, British music clubs—both as social and physical constructs—were homes to performers and aficionados exploring a variety of different genres. Such was the British blues scene, which first found local and then translocal audiences.

Blues Exotique. In the 1940s (or possibly earlier), British record collectors and musicians became fascinated with American blues, and their fixation only grew during and after the war with the spread of American influence. Everything about the form seemed so utterly un-English: the earthiness of the performers,

---

[9] Inspired by Carl Perkins's "Glad All Over" (December 1957).
[10] Playing and accenting all four beats of a measure.

the naked emotions, and the often-outright sexuality of the lyrics. Just listening to the music suggested indiscretion.[11]

Some cognoscenti treated this music with the romantic intensity of nineteenth-century orientalists, as when English historian Paul Oliver went hunting for the blues near an American military base. "We stayed behind the hedge, getting cold. I was getting impatient too, when suddenly the air seemed split by the most eerie sounds. The two men were singing, swooping, undulating, unintelligible words; and the back of my neck tingled" (Shapiro 1996, 57).

Shaping their approach, their primary sources in the beginning were recordings made in the 1920s and 1930s, some by commercial companies and others by documentarians such as John Lomax and his son Alan, including recordings of figures like Huddie Ledbetter and Muddy Waters. Alan Lomax—strategically escaping McCarthy-era America—resided in London during the 1950s, where his obsession with establishing a geocultural map of definable musical styles and his distaste for the commodification of music helped inform the way the British/English folk music establishment approached the blues. (See Lomax 1968.) The consequence would be the formation of another bond in the symbiotic British-American music-cultural relationship.

The British fascination with this American form produced numerous books and pamphlets as well as heated arguments about the genre's origins and substyles. They also sometimes lamented that contemporary American Blacks had abandoned this music for more urbane forms. The obsessions of British advocates, however, helped to resurrect the careers of many musicians and to bring some forms of the blues back from obscurity.

Recreating the Blues. As Paul Oliver and others collected records, interviewed musicians, and published columns, pamphlets, and books, promoters arranged for their musical icons to perform in the UK. British blues fans enthusiastically but sometimes condescendingly discussed the authenticity of these musicians and their performances, despite how nebulous that concept proved to be. Moreover, the irony of Black musicians altering their performances to appeal to the expectations of foreign White audiences (who knew the music primarily through recordings made decades in the past) seems to have escaped the attention of many fans.

With an idealized past in mind, British blues enthusiasts in the 1950s privileged acoustic performances as heard on recordings by musicians like Blind Lemon Jefferson and Robert Johnson. This aesthetic consequently shaped the decisions of promoters who brought artists like Bill Broonzy across the Atlantic for concerts. In the UK, "audiences, promoters, and often bandleaders" expected

---

[11] See Schwartz 2007 for a detailed history of the British fascination with and cultivation of the blues.

visiting American blues musicians "to deliver . . . in a 'down-home, Uncle Tom' style" (Scott 2012).

The blues, like most of America, however, had long since gone electric. British audiences tolerated a microphone capturing the sound of a singer accompanying themselves on an acoustic guitar, but ideologues interpreted performances with electric guitars and drums as abominations, as when Rosetta Tharpe plugged in her white Gibson Les Paul Custom during a tour of British concert halls.

Concert halls—architectural symbols of privilege—were designed to reverberate acoustic performances by musicians elevated on stages intended both to foreground them and to create a discrete distance between the observed and the observers. Audiences in such venues were unused to blues musicians with amplifiers. Moreover, formal spaces that physically separated performers from audiences created settings alien to American blues performance practice.

In 1958, when Chris Barber brought Muddy Waters and pianist Otis Spann to London's Saint Pancras Town Hall, some audience members reacted negatively to the amplified sound, while the context alienated the performers. After the concert, however, electric blues advocates Alexis Korner and Cyril Davies invited the Chicago duo to their Thursday night Soho club to perform in a context that they believed better suited the music. Their hunch proved correct.

Blue London

Korner and Davies made for unlikely collaborators, as their social and aesthetic differences reflected some of the core contradictions of the burgeoning British blues scene. Korner's Jewish middle-class family had arrived in London from Europe and North Africa just before the war, and after attending private schools, he could have taken employment in the family business. Instead, he chose a musician's life and to be an occasional broadcaster and journalist who worked out of his Bayswater flat. Cyril Davies on the other hand could be an intimidating working-class phenomenon who ran an auto body shop in East London, pounding metal by day and bending notes by night (Scott 2012).

Korner was an enthusiastic advocate both for electric blues and for other musicians. Mick Jagger, however, thought him not "much of a vocalist" who sometimes sang with a "very upper class English accent" (Frame 1997, 27). Chris Barber similarly noted that the musician had trouble simultaneously singing and playing guitar and occasionally came in at the wrong time (Pidgeon 2009).[12] In

---

[12] Korner described his own playing style in this era as having a "dual function": to provide a "blues groundwork for other people to blow over" and "to direct the band in musical terms." "I played atmosphere rather than solos," he explained and admitted that he had never been a good improviser (Pidgeon 1971).

contrast, Davies brought a natural musicality to his performances, his personal experiences with poverty and violence adding to the intensity and perceived authenticity of his performances.

The two met in 1955 when Korner played guitar in Chris Barber's band and Davies was recruited for a skiffle set, where his renditions of Huddie Ledbetter and, more important, his harmonica chops—if not his passion—impressed even the most critical British blues connoisseurs. When Davies set up the "London Skiffle Centre" (or "London Skiffle Club") Thursday nights on the first floor of the Roundhouse pub in Soho, he and Korner often played as a duo. By 1956, however, Davies told Korner, "I'm fed up with all this skiffle rubbish, I want to open a blues club, will you run it for me?" (Shapiro 1996, 56).

Blues, Inc. Although Thursday night audiences for the "London Blues and Barrelhouse Club" above the same pub were initially small, they grew as musicians found a place to experiment. And sometimes American artists showed them how it was done, as in 1958 when Korner and Davies brought Waters and Spann to the upstairs venue. Impressed by the Americans, Korner and Davies bought their own amplifiers to better imitate their Chicago mentors. Unsurprisingly, the pub terminated their lease.

On 19 January 1962, Mr. Acker Bilk needed an opening act, and the Korner-Davies collective of musicians got the call to bring their "Blues Incorporated"[13] experiment to Croydon Civic Hall. The success of that gig encouraged them, sending Davies and Korner to West London to start the once-weekly "Ealing Rhythm and Blues Club." From its opening on Saturday, 17 March 1962, a legion of young musicians from all over London and beyond passed through the Ealing Broadway Underground station, crossed the road, descended a narrow set of stairs between buildings, and entered a door underneath a tea shop to listen to and/or sit in with Blues Incorporated.

Chris Barber came too and, seeing the crowds, invited Davies and Korner to bring their musical collective to Thursday nights to a bastion of London jazz: the Marquee Club (Pidgeon 2009).[14]

Against Trad

As the experts argued about the blues, British musicians learned to play them. In Korner's conception of their enterprise, Blues Incorporated offered a context in which musicians applied the skills they already knew while internalizing what

---

[13] Perhaps referencing the film *Crime Inc.* (1945).
[14] The economic significance of the Thursday night slot lay in the paychecks that generally arrived on Fridays, which meant that the night before was when patrons were least likely to have extra cash for admission.

they heard on records. "Most of the people in the first band had played trad jazz at one time or another," he remembered, and Blues Incorporated was "basically a reaction against trad" (Pidgeon 2009). The media reacted too.

News of the young crowds gathering in Ealing and Soho attracted the attention of Jack Good, who, sensing a trend, set up an album recording session. Blues Incorporated's *R&B from the Marquee* (November 1962) features Cyril Davies and "Long John" Baldry singing blues standards and the band playing Alexis Korner instrumentals (e.g., "Down Town").[15] Although the album was recorded in Decca's West Hampstead studios, the growing reputation of the Marquee and the excitement of that environment proved too attractive for Good to ignore.

Built for Comfort. Their rendition of Willie Dixon's "Built for Comfort" (1959),[16] with Baldry singing, betrays the default orientation of the band as they layer melodies like a trad performance rather than highlighting a soloist. Other tracks, however, suggest the emergence of a British rhythm and blues, as when Davies and crew adapt Muddy Waters's "I'm Your Hoochie Cooche Man" (1954).[17] Although the bandleader closely mimics Waters's delivery and verbal syntax (e.g., "pretty womens"), his harmonica extemporizations and the band's reworking of the accompaniment illustrate how comfortable these British musicians were beginning to feel with American models.

An invitation to appear on the BBC Light Programme's *Jazz Club* (12 July 1962) represented a major recognition of Davies, Korner, and Blues Incorporated. The budget for their national broadcast debut, however, limited them to six instrumentalists plus a singer. With Korner (guitar), Davies (harmonica), Charlie Watts (drums), Dave Stevens (piano), Jack Bruce (bass), and Dick Heckstall-Smith (saxophone), they initially intended Art Wood to sing but ultimately excluded him from the broadcast. Two other current singers—Mick Jagger and John Baldry—and members of the Blues Incorporated family covered their regular Thursday night engagement at the Marquee Club. That gig would prove to be more significant, as Jagger's group named themselves after Muddy Waters's song "Rollin' Stone" (1950).

---

[15] Regulars Keith Scott (piano), Spike Heatley (acoustic bass), Graham Burbidge (drums), and Dick Heckstall-Smith (tenor sax) played the session, but they also included Teddy Wadmore (electric bass) and Big Jim Sullivan (guitar).

[16] Sung by John Baldry; the original album release excluded this track.

[17] The *R&B from the Marquee* album copied the spelling of this tune from Muddy Waters's original recording as "Hoochie Cooche" rather than "Hoochie Coochie," which is how it appeared on later recordings, including subsequent reissues of this album.

At the Marquee

In the fall of 1962, Davies left Korner to form his own band with members of Screaming Lord Sutch's Savages, who had abandoned their eccentric singer over a pay dispute. Some of them had been already sitting in with Blues Incorporated, so bassist Rick Brown recruited bandmates Carlo Little (drums), Nicky Hopkins (piano), and Bernie Watson (guitar) to become Cyril Davies' Rhythm and Blues All-Stars.[18] At the Marquee, owner Harold Pendleton installed Davies's band on Thursday nights;[19] they drew crowds of mostly young Whites to the former ballroom below an Oxford Street cinema. Inside, the circus-tent décor transported audiences to a world apart from the department stores of London's busiest commercial thoroughfare.

As he did at his autobody shop, Davies insisted on complete control over the band, paying them wages they interpreted as reducing them to employees. Selecting musicians who had been playing rock 'n' roll, moreover, led to tensions with the bandleader. Seeing other Blues Incorporated spin-offs include rock 'n' roll in their sets, the All-Stars lobbied to mix some Chuck Berry into their repertoire. Davies, however, "wouldn't let us play anything like that," Carlo Little remembered. "Cyril was a purist [and] it had to be all the old Chicago type blues" (interview 30 March 2000).

Country Line Special. In February 1963, as "Please Please Me" was climbing British charts, Davies and crew descended into Pye's studios to capture some of their Marquee energy. Pye's "head of A&R," Alan Freeman, had approached young producer Peter Knight, Jr., and asked, "'Pete, I've got this band, Cyril Davies and His Rhythm and Blues All-Stars. . . . Can you meet with the manager and him and do a couple of sessions?'" Knight noted that "once we got the sound set up," they recorded "Country Line Special" (April 1963) in a "maximum of two takes" (Knight interview 26 August 2005). This performance reflects the synergy of rock and blues that would influence a generation of British musicians.

Backing Davies's harmonica, Bernie Watson's distorted guitar welds the arrangement together, particularly during his solo, where he bends and slurs the notes in a way that led another young guitarist to take notice. "Bernie Watson was the first guy I ever saw bending notes and the first I ever saw playing a twin-cutaway Gibson semi-acoustic," Eric Clapton remembered. "He always sat down with his back to the audience; never stood up . . . a very mysterious man" (Frame 1997, 27). Watson's guitar, Rick Brown's electric bass, and Carlo Little's drumming

---

[18] Rick Brown was also known as Ricky Fenson.
[19] Harold Pendleton (Chris Barber's manager and partner) not only owned the Marquee but also published *Jazz News,* whose editor, John Martin, became Davies's manager.

establish a one-chord groove down which the metaphoric train rumbles while Nicky Hopkins vamps on electric piano.

Although the disc failed to sell in any great numbers, Davies and His Rhythm and Blues All-Stars appeared on television and toured, building audiences in and around London and the UK. As they promoted the single, however, the bandleader grew short-tempered and frustrated, stomping his feet and slapping at cymbals as he attempted to articulate what he wanted (Scott 2012). By the fall, everyone noticed the difficulty in his breathing and his increased alcohol consumption. By January 1964, the 31-year-old musician was dead.

At the Flamingo

Tucked into a basement at the Chinatown end of Wardour Street in Soho, the Flamingo Club's weekend all-night sessions attracted an unusual audience. A mix of Caribbean, African, and European immigrants, Black and White US servicemen, and curious Brits came for the multiethnic environment, the sex, the drugs, and the music. Most notoriously, perhaps, singer Aloysius "Lucky" Gordon and promoter Johnny Edgecombe got into a knife-fight over showgirl Christine Keeler. Other patrons, however, brought recordings for house musicians like Georgie Fame to hear.

Fame—the son of a dance-band musician—had started out as Clive Powell, singing in church on Sundays and learning to play proper piano in the family's front room in Leigh (between Liverpool and Manchester). The family radio, however, picked up the American Forces Network, from nearby bases in Wales, playing recordings by Jerry Lee Lewis, Fats Domino, and Little Richard, all of whose music Powell could imitate when he joined local bands (Soul and Jazz and Funk, 2015).

As a teen on holiday in North Wales, friends cajoled him into taking the stage at a Butlin's camp, leading to an invitation to join the band on piano and, at the end of the season, to relocate to London. In 1960, Larry Parnes first picked him to back Gene Vincent and Eddie Cochran on their ill-fated tour and then renamed Powell "Georgie Fame" to lead Billy Fury's band, the Blue Flames.[20]

The Blue Flames, however, grew disinterested in Fury's pop-rock as they listened to American jazz-flavored rhythm and blues. "We were fed up with the British rock thing," Fame remembered. We "had been listening to Ray Charles, Louis Prima, and King Pleasure, and we wanted to do some of that" (Frame 1997, 25). After concert dates in Paris in 1961 and while on tour in England,

---

[20] The April 1960 car crash on this tour killed Cochran and severely injured Vincent and other passengers.

the Svengali abruptly replaced them with the Tornados, leaving the Blue Flames stranded at a Lincolnshire train station with no return fare.

Return to Soho. Not long afterward in February 1962, however, the Flamingo Club's Rik Gunnell hired the Blue Flames to fill a Monday night spot, eventually making them the de facto house band and assuming duties as their manager (Welch 3 August 1974). Gunnell had positioned the club to respond to the growing diversity of London's population and the city's role as a cosmopolitan portal between Europe and America. The Blue Flames' music did the same.

Peter Frame describes Fame and the Blue Flames' contribution to British music as their development of "Flamingo R&B," a jazzier alternative to "Marquee R&B" (1997, 25). Impressed by American organists like Jimmy Smith, Fame obtained a Hammond organ (at considerable expense) in order to exploit its inherent power to fill the dance club. The Blue Flames' sound, moreover, defied the aesthetics of the beat boom by emphasizing the combined punch of horn section and organ, despite the great guitarists that passed through their ranks, including Joe Moretti, John McLaughlin, and Colin Green. By 1963, they were well known in London for their Motown and Jamaican-ska setlists, and when Ghanaian conga player Speedy Acquaye joined them, they were introduced to West African jazz.

In 1963, Gunnell signed Fame and the Blue Flames with Columbia, where former Shadow Ian Samwell produced their live album *Rhythm and Blues from the Flamingo* (January 1964), drawing obvious comparisons to Blues Incorporated's *R&B from the Marquee* (November 1962).[21] Columbia would also release one of the album's tracks, "Do the Dog" (January 1963), a cover of Rufus Thomas's "The Dog" (1962), as a single. Fame, however, lacks the American's comic delivery, while the Blue Flames' performance misses the tightness of Thomas's Memphis horn section. Like Cyril Davies's "Country Line Special," only a select few bought "Do the Dog."

Meanwhile, back at the Marquee, a Blues Incorporated spinoff was hybridizing pop, blues, rock 'n' roll, and rhythm and blues in ways that would prove quite successful.

---

[21] Strategically the releases differ in that the live Fame recording includes some of the band's banter and the sound of the crowd, while Korner and Davies recorded at Decca. The albums did share something, however: Big Jim Sullivan plays on both recordings.

Fig. 8.1 The Dave Clark Five; left to right: Lenny Davidson, Mike Smih, Rick Huxley, Dave Clark, Denis Payton (British Pathé, 1963).

Fig. 8.2 Cyril Davies and the Rhythm and His Blues All Stars; left to right: Rick (Fenson) Brown, Carlo Little, Cyril Davies, John Baldry, and Bernie Watson with the Velvettes; left to right: Mamsie (Mumsie) Mthombeni, Patience Gcwabe, Hazel Futa. Photo courtesy of Todd Allen.

9
Where Stones Roll

In early 1963, 15-year-old John Pidgeon and a friend with access to his family's car drove from London to Windsor to hear Cyril Davies and His Rhythm and Blues All Stars playing Leo's Jazz Club in a British legion hall. Although he perceived Davies as "a balding, badly-dressed man, who looks middle-aged," the performance warranted the 4-shilling ticket, the 2 half crowns Pidgeon's mother had given him for petrol,[1] and a return trip the next week. Walking back to the car after that second visit, however, he heard music down a side street and saw "dancers silhouetted in the open windows of an upstairs room attached to the back of what [was] plainly more pub than hotel" (Pidgeon 2009).

Decorated with fishing nets hanging from the ceiling, the Ricky-Tick Club that night had a slightly raised corner stage from which the Rollin' Stones provided a soundscape that gave dancers an excuse to shake the building.[2] This "studently" crowd included "snappy dressers" who were "younger and hipper, and the girls prettier, than at Leo's" (Pidgeon 2009). Moreover, a young woman in black with short hair caught Pidgeon's attention, and the music and the room provided a context in which they could acknowledge each other through dance, defying the norms of social distance invoked in everyday English life. The juxtaposition of the 30-year-old Davies with Mick Jagger, 10 years his junior and far more in tune with the adolescent crowd, describes some of the generational tension between the blues-purist crowd and the emergence of a rock 'n' roll oriented audience.

Davies and Alexis Korner played to blues devotees in pursuit of authenticity. The Rollin' Stones, however, tapped into the music's inherent hormonal appeal and its importance to the adolescent quest for independence. Their approach to this music reflected the seismic shift under way as the Bulge Generation began to assert its own Britain.

---

[1] A crown was worth 5 shillings ("bobs") with 20 shillings to a pound. A shilling had the value of 12 pence; thus, a half crown was worth 2 shillings and 6 pence. The British government decimalized the currency in 1971.

[2] *Rollin'* was spelled with an apostrophe early in their career.

In Dartford

In 1943, 18 miles downriver from London Bridge, the historic town of Dartford in Kent might have seemed an unlikely birthplace for two musicians who would so effectively offend the British Establishment. As boys during Britain's postwar housing shortage, Michael Jagger and Keith Richards lived only about a block apart, went to the same primary school, and, although not friends, knew each other. Economics and class would separate them. Music would bring them together.

Michael "Mick" Jagger's athletic middle-class father, Joe, had followed his father into teaching and hoped his son would do the same. Michael's mother, Eva, was born in Australia, where her father, a boat-builder, had emigrated. When that marriage had failed, Eva's mother had returned with Eva and her siblings to the stability of Dartford (Norman 2012, 16). Eva had been a hairdresser before marrying up into a family where the social insecurity of class-revealing shibboleths was always a possibility.[3]

In contrast, Keith Richards's father was a foreman at a General Electric factory, which occupied much of his time and energy. When Keith was nine, they relocated to a semidetached house in a sprawling development "across the tracks." As with many such postwar housing estates, the planners had ignored basic historic social nexuses such as local pubs, stores, churches, and other places where residents could form communities (Kynaston 2013, 20). The Richards's new neighborhood—with its lack of parental supervision and roving gangs of adolescent males—proved an example of just such dysfunction and lay the foundations of his interactions with the world (Richards with Fox 2010, 35).

Family Values. Music played important roles in the lives of both families. The Jaggers entertained each other with music, and Michael enjoyed singing at home, at school, and in a church choir. Like many young Britons, he became fascinated with America, learning how to imitate accents, picking up clichés and phrases from imported television shows and films, and rehearsing them for his school friends. As adolescence set in, Little Richard, Jerry Lee Lewis, Buddy Holly, Fats Domino, and Chuck Berry contributed to his repertoire, despite his father's dismissal of the music.

Richards's mother shaped his aesthetics by finding BBC programming featuring "Ella Fitzgerald, Sarah Vaughn, Big Bill Broonzy, [and] Louis Armstrong," which steered his listening tastes "to the black side of town" (Richards with Fox 2010, 56–57). Like many young British musicians, Little Richard's "Long Tall Sally" and Elvis Presley's "Heartbreak Hotel" formed Richards's earliest memories of rock 'n' roll (58).

---

[3] Fox describes various ways the English reveal their class prejudices (2014, 472–473).

His maternal grandfather had led a dance band in the prewar years and encouraged his grandson's interest in music by sometimes taking him into instrument shops in London. At home, he sat a guitar on top of his upright piano just out of the boy's reach but eventually let him play it. And when his parents failed to qualify for the credit necessary to buy Keith his own guitar, his grandfather came to the rescue.

Shaping the development of Jagger and Richards as individuals, school placement tests confirmed English presumptions about social class, the role of teachers, and the purposes of education. Jagger's aspirational family kept him focused on his studies so that he attended grammar school and did well enough on his exams to gain admission into accounting at the London School of Economics. The same system but different family priorities channeled Richards into a technical school, which eventually expelled him, leading to his transfer to nearby Sidcup Art College. Although his program emphasized the graphic arts, a more accurate description might say that he studied guitar with other enthusiasts who made the "john" (toilet) a space where they played and traded songs and techniques (Richards with Fox 2010, 69).

East of Ealing

On a Tuesday morning (25 October 1961), Richards stood on a platform waiting for the train to Sidcup when another ticket holder caught his attention. In most versions of this story, Mick Jagger clenches precious discs in his arms, their covers advertising an interest in American blues. In a letter Richards wrote to his aunt five months later, he mentions his and Jagger's common love of the music of Jimmy Reed, Muddy Waters, Howlin' Wolf, John Lee Hooker, and "all the Chicago bluesmen real lowdown stuff, marvelous. Bo Diddley he's another great" (Richards with Fox 2010, 78). With a common passion, they drove to Manchester the next year for the American Folk Blues Festival.

The social company that his former primary schoolmate kept similarly impressed Richards, as for example when they visited a friend who lived in a "massive detached" house where they were served by a butler (Richards with Fox 2010, 78). Jagger had also been to see Buddy Holly, had a collection of relatively rare recordings, and had access to a car, all things that were out of the guitarist's economic league. Nevertheless, their shared musical interests overrode prevailing class barriers, and with Jagger singing, Richards playing guitar, and friend Dick Taylor on bass, they began imitating what they heard on recordings.

Workers and Art Students. In March 1962, an announcement in *Melody Maker* for the Ealing Rhythm and Blues Club jumped out at them, and the 18-year-olds eagerly made the trip from Dartford to West London (over an hour away by car) where Cyril Davies and Alexis Korner held court. As they compared their attempts with what they heard from the stage, they worked up the nerve to perform some of the music they had been rehearsing. Ealing thus served a function other than just providing a venue where musicians could play and celebrate this music: it provided a context in which musicians, fans, and cognoscenti could share their English interpretations of a distinctly American phenomenon.

Situated under a sidewalk with thick glass tiles overhead, Jagger remembered the stage as "so wet that Cyril had to put a horrible sheet, revoltingly dirty, over the bandstand, so that the condensation didn't drip directly on you. It just dripped through the sheet." Richards remembered the crowd as "workers and art students" whose long hair got them rejected by dance hall proprietors (Wyman with Havers 2002, 32).

Among Jagger's and Richards's favorite artists recording for Chess Records (the label that released Muddy Waters and Howlin' Wolf), Chuck Berry particularly satisfied their thirst for all things American. Cyril Davies, however, reasonably argued that Berry's music fell into the category of rock 'n' roll, rather than blues or rhythm and blues, and rejected it. Ultimately, however, the musicians drawn to the Ealing Rhythm and Blues Club to play all of this music left it to others (often nonmusicians) to argue about genres and their stylistic characteristics.

The musicians who congregated at the club came from all over the country, including singers Eric Burdon from Newcastle and Paul Pond (later Paul Jones) from Oxford, as well as a guitarist from Cheltenham who called himself Elmo Lewis. Lewis turned out to be an alias for Brian Jones whose slide guitar work impressed almost everyone in the house, including the two kids from Dartford who struck up a conversation with him.

Bricklayers

In the spring of 1962, Brian Jones recruited Richards and Jagger and their friend Dick Taylor to form a rhythm-and-blues band and placed an ad in *Jazz News* inviting other interested musicians to meet at the Bricklayers Arms in Soho. When the Dartford trio climbed the stairs to the room on the first floor of the pub, they encountered pianist Ian Stewart, who seemed to be running the auditions. Over that evening and subsequent ones, the makings of a band emerged with Jagger singing, Jones and Richards playing guitar, Taylor on bass, and Stewart rounding out their sound on piano.

In Ealing, Korner and Davies gave their qualified approval of the young band's blues and rhythm-and-blues interpretations, while continuing to question the inclusion of Chuck Berry's music. Moreover, with an impending appearance by

Blues Incorporated on the BBC's *Jazz Club*, Korner delegated Jagger and company to fill their regular Thursday night Marquee Club engagement.

The Bricklayers Arms crew began planning their setlist, with Jones suggesting that they call the *Jazz News* to say they would be playing and to add their performance to the concert calendar. When an editor asked for the name of the band, the question apparently caught Jagger, Richards, and Jones by surprise. If they were not Blues Incorporated, who were they? While working on their set list, they turned to the first thing they saw, a song on the first side of *The Best of Muddy Waters*. "Rollin' Stones," Jones informed the paper, and to reassure the jazz publication that they were legitimate, Jagger added, "I hope they don't think we're a rock 'n' roll outfit" (Paytress 2003, 16; Richards with Fox 2010, 97).

The Rollin' Stones' Marquee debut (12 July 1962) probably had its rough moments, but the experience invigorated them. Working with drummer Mick Avory, they covered blues standards by Robert Johnson ("I Believe I'll Dust My Broom"), Muddy Waters ("I Want You to Love Me"), Jay McShann ("Confessin' the Blues"), and others. In the middle of their performance, however, Keith Richards insisted on inserting Chuck Berry's "Back in the USA." Club owner Harold Pendleton, of course, knew rock 'n' roll when he heard it, but the Rollin' Stones had glimpsed the future and liked it. Despite his reservations, Pendleton would bring them back in September.

102 Edith Grove

In August, Jagger and Jones moved to near World's End in Chelsea, with Richards joining them at their first-floor crash pad in Edith Grove. The location may have shortened Jagger's travel time to the London School of Economics, but the ability to pay rent and eat meant survival through a combination of luck, charity, intimidation, and theft.

The flat, nevertheless, provided a space where Richards and Jones could spend long hours listening to records and playing guitars while Jagger was at school. As they listened to discs in the growing dark that fall and worked out complementary guitar parts, the band's musical and social core gelled. Not everyone shared their commitment, however, or their tolerance for squalid living conditions. By December 1962, Dick Taylor had departed, and they recruited different drummers and bassists to fill out the band.[4]

Bill Wyman was six years older than Jagger and Richards, was supporting a family with a day job, and his hairstyle, clothing, and tastes seemed a generation

---

[4] They briefly recruited Carlo Little and Ricky Brown from Screaming Lord Sutch's Savages before they joined Cyril Davies.

removed from the others. Nevertheless, he owned a Vox AC30 amplifier that Richards and Jones coveted and had solid professional experience having accompanied Dickie Pride for Larry Parnes. He joined as an outsider, leaving another band because he thought that the Rollin' Stones were a "better bet" (Wyman with Havers 2002, 41).

As for a drummer, a string of musicians passed the band up until Blues Incorporated's Charlie Watts gave them a try. In contrast with Jagger, Richards, and Jones, his musical aspirations lay in jazz; moreover, the graphic designer had stature on the scene that demanded a proper fee for his services. As the band's fortunes improved in early 1963, Watts too saw possibilities in the Rollin' Stones.

The Crawdaddy. Gigs at the Flamingo, the Marquee, and other clubs and dance halls in and around London had begun to provide just enough income to persevere, especially after securing a regular stint with jazz filmmaker Giorgio Gomelsky at the Crawdaddy Club across the Thames in Richmond on Sunday nights. They impressed Gomelsky enough that he took on unofficial management duties, and when he happened to meet the Beatles one Sunday at a television studio in nearby Teddington, he invited them to stop by the Crawdaddy on their way back to London.

Having just released "From Me to You," the "four-headed monster" arrived quietly, dressed in long dark leather coats, and stood in the shadows as the crowd gradually began to realize who had arrived. Eventually Bill Wyman too recognized what was happening and muttered, "Shit, that's the Beatles" (Paytress 2003, 26). The Liverpudlians, however, liked what they heard and gave the Rollin' Stones tickets to the Beatles' first big London Concert at the Royal Albert Hall. As Brian Jones helped load the Beatles' equipment into a van after that show, some fans mistook him for the Liverpudlians. The experience left him wanting fame too. All they needed was someone to take them to the next level.

Commodifying the Stones

Cities provide places and spaces for the sale of goods and services, and no city in Europe could quite compare to London in these enterprises. In the postwar years, a commodification of the arts formed a highly visible part of London's economy as entrepreneurs explored how to take advantage of existing laws and business models to exploit the emerging market that was the Bulge Generation. Larry Parnes and Jack Good had demonstrated that a combination of artist image and media exposure could sell tickets and discs, and Brian Epstein had improved on their strategy. The commodification of the Rollin' Stones took this model one step further by playing on the growing generational divide between adults and teens, and the media's appetite for scandal.

The Roar of the Whole World

London's music industry had several preferred watering holes in the early 1960s, one of which was the De Hems, just outside the gates to Chinatown. There, while promoting a client story to Peter Jones of the *Record Mirror*, Andrew Loog Oldham learned that the paper would be publishing a review of a local band, even though they had yet to release a disc. Norman Jopling's article raved about the Rollin' Stones and how he believed they represented the next big thing in music (Oldham 2000, 183).

Oldham had arrived in this world as the consequence of a liaison between an American airman who had died in the war and a British nurse. She, like Jagger's mother, had been born in Australia before emigrating to Britain when her parents' marriage failed. A Jew living in postwar London, his mother worked to remain independent while receiving the beneficence of an investment banker/lover who supported her and her child, including with school tuition. As a teen, popular culture and especially music attracted Oldham, who began venturing into Soho and once escaped his boarding school two hours outside London to join the audience of Jack Good's *Oh Boy!* (Oldham 2000, 37).

After leaving school, Oldham first dressed windows by day for fashion designer Mary Quant and worked behind the counter of the Flamingo at night. He and friend Pete Meaden formed a public relations company and reconnoitered Soho clubs for clients, one of whom was Don Arden. That contract to promote a UK tour by Little Richard and Sam Cooke, however, ended unceremoniously after Oldham's press release suggested that audiences would be ripping up their theater seats.

More successfully, Oldham served as singer Mark Wynter's publicist, which took him to Birmingham for a January 1963 taping of *Thank Your Lucky Stars*, where the Beatles were making their national debut. Wasting no time, Oldham approached manager Brian Epstein about becoming a publicist for NEMS Enterprises and was soon walking the Beatles around London to meet journalists. In February on the Helen Shapiro tour, he experienced the growing chaos as the band played on the small stage of the Granada Cinema in Bedford, where the "kids broke *all* the backstage windows." He described the sound of the ecstatic adolescents as the "roar of the whole world" (Oldham 2000, 182).

Incredible Bullshitter, Fantastic Hustler. The Sunday after Peter Jones had told him about the Rollin' Stones, Oldham surveyed the band at the Crawdaddy and sensed what he had felt in Bedford. As a minor, he lacked legal status to sign contracts and proffered a comanagement proposal to Brian Epstein. When that was rejected, Oldham turned to Eric Easton, with whom he shared office space, who had an agent's license and, as an adult, could sign contracts. Oldham, however, had one more goal: he saw himself as both manager and producer.

Impressed by what Phil Spector and Joe Meek had been able to achieve, the 19-year-old sought control, not just of the performers but also of their recordings. Easton agreed to help and to act as a comanager, should the band accept them. He was also willing to supply limited funds that allowed Oldham to pursue his self-confident belief that he could produce.

The next Sunday (28 April 1963), Oldham and Easton approached the Rollin' Stones at the Crawdaddy and expressed interest in being their managers. Giorgio Gomelsky, who was in Switzerland attending his father's funeral, had never insisted on a contract, so the two would-be Svengalis had a narrow window to sign the band before he returned and Jopling's story ran. Keith Richards, while skeptical about Oldham, remembered thinking him both an "incredible bullshitter" and a "fantastic hustler," figuring that he would make something happen (Oldham 2000, 196). Days later, the two middle-class members of the band, Brian Jones and Mick Jagger, sat in Eric Easton's office with Oldham to discuss a contract. They apparently never gave Gomelsky a second thought.

As with Epstein and the Beatles, the conversation with Jones and Jagger included a recording contract, but they had yet another previous entanglement to sever. They had made (and Brian Jones had signed) an agreement with IBC Studios allowing engineer Glyn Johns to make and to lease their recordings. With little time to spare, they concocted a deception. Approaching George Clouston, one of the owners of IBC, Brian Jones spun a story about disbanding the Rollin' Stones to form a better group. Clouston listened as Jones explained how his parents would cover the recording costs and buy the band out of their contract . . . for £90. Money in IBC's pocket won the day, and Glyn Johns would have to wait to work on a release by Jagger and his group.

Come On

About a week later, the Rolling Stones (having dropped the apostrophe) arrived at Olympic Studios in Marylebone for a three-hour recording session. Jagger showed up, schoolbooks under his arm, ready to record Chuck Berry's "Come On," along with Muddy Waters's "I Want to Be Loved," the Clovers' "Love Potion No. 9," and Bo Diddley's "Pretty Thing." Richards describes the choice of "Come On"—with Berry's complaints about a car that will not run and a relationship that will not start—as a deliberate "commercial pitch," "something that would make a mark." He also admits that in this era he "loved pop music" and that "Come On" was "just a way to get in" the charts with a "very Beatle-ized" version (Richards with Fox 2010, 129–130).

For self-proclaimed purists of the Chess canon, the Rolling Stones' version of the song differs in several ways from Berry's original, including a faster tempo and replacing the word "jerk" with "guy" in one phrase. More important, the new version drops the calypso feel of the original in favor of a strong rock 'n' roll backbeat as well as replacing the saxophone of the original with a harmonica. Finally, the Stones insert a key change in the middle of the recording to bring the music up a step, a standard pop device meant to invoke excitement.

Olympic engineer Roger Savage ran the mostly live studio session. With only £40 to cover their three-hour slot, Oldham used the time to record (including double-tracking Jagger's voice), not realizing that balancing the final version was also necessary. In the end, Oldham told Savage he would pick the tapes up in the morning, leaving the engineer to create a very rough, muddy, and hurried mix.

Oldham did, however, make one significant production decision: he cut the microphone going to Ian Stewart's piano. He had concluded, almost from the first day, not only that six band members were one too many but also that Stewart—with his short hair—simply did not look the part. Oldham gave Brian Jones the task of demoting the pianist to road manager and session musician (who nevertheless sometimes still performed with them on stage).

Compromises

As George Harrison and Dick Rowe sat together as "Lancashire and Cheshire Beat Group Contest" judges in Liverpool's Philharmonic Hall, a lull in the proceedings allowed a quick verbal exchange. Joking about how the Decca producer had rejected the Beatles in January 1962, Harrison told Rowe about a band he had seen at the Crawdaddy Club. Before the program had ended, Rowe was on his way back to London and to Richmond to hear the Rolling Stones. The buzz from Norman Jopling's review meant that record companies were interested, and Rowe was eager not to add to his reputation as the man who also turned down the Rolling Stones. Although poorly recorded, Rowe leased Oldham's tape, and Decca would issue "Come On" (June 1963). An appearance on *Thank Your Lucky Stars* (13 July) a month later helped bring "Come On" into the charts.

To promote the record, the fashion-conscious Oldham insisted on aesthetic accommodations by a band that had been accustomed to dressing casually for young rhythm-and-blues fans in smoky subterranean clubs that disdained anything smacking of professionalism. Oldham and Easton, however, had ideas about how to make the Rolling Stones the greatest commodity since sliced bread. Following standards of the day, Oldham put them into matching houndstooth suits with velvet collars, and Easton began booking them for gigs outside London, including engagements such as a debutante ball in a resort town on the southern coast of England.

Making the Rolling Stones a recording success, however, proved more difficult than Oldham had originally anticipated; in particular, he worried about material for the follow-up release. He had thought "If You Gotta Make a Fool of Somebody" a great song, but Freddie and the Dreamers had already released it. The Rolling Stones instead recorded a version of Jerry Leiber and Mike Stoller's "Poison Ivy" at Decca Studios. The song itself carries some of the humor of "Come On," and the recording clearly represents them as playing well together. Moreover, this time the engineer paid more attention to balancing the sound. The band, however, apparently felt uncomfortable with both the song and the recording (perhaps because they sounded like just another beat group), and as much as Decca pushed to release the disc, the Rolling Stones rejected it—one of their first acts of defiance.

I Wanna Be Your Band

With "She Loves You" about to top British charts and Beatlemania building, John Lennon and Paul McCartney had just received a songwriting award and were leaving the ceremony when they saw Oldham (their former publicist) out for a walk in the proper Saint James district of central London. Invited into their cab, the fledgling manager and producer suggested that they attend a Rolling Stones rehearsal currently in progress. On the way, he related his and his clients' frustration at finding a song to record as a follow-up to "Come On." Lennon and McCartney offered that they might have something appropriate (Miles 1998, 81). At the rehearsal in the empty subterranean confines of Ken Colyer's Studio 51, the two songwriters played through bits of an unfinished "I Wanna Be Your Man" for the approving band.

The songwriters may have originally had drummer Ringo Starr in mind for "I Wanna Be Your Man," as its simple melody, limited range, and minimal lyrics suited his skills.[5] The Stones' interpretation, however, conveys bluesy sexual provocation with a hint of violence supplied by Brian Jones's slide guitar. In the fall of 1963, anything in the UK connected to the Beatles was gold, and with advance publicity around Lennon and McCartney having written the song, the Stones' recording (November 1963) climbed into *Record Retailer*'s top 10, and the Rolling Stones hit the road.

Absolutely Disgusting. Joining their first package tour with Little Richard, the Everly Brothers, and Bo Diddley (with members of the band backing him), the Rolling Stones began to adapt their performances to the new contexts they

---

[5] Released on *With the Beatles* (22 November 1963), Starr's version—informed by public perception of his personality—renders the song's lyrics playful and nonthreatening.

encountered.[6] Brightly lit stages with wings and curtains and theaters with high ceilings and fixed seats shaped how they interacted both with each other and with their audiences, especially as they watched how the Americans worked a house. Little Richard knew how to play a room, taking advantage of the possibilities of theatrical lighting and of unusual entrances and exits. For their part, Mick Jagger proved a no-slouch student as he amped up his performance persona while Keith Richards began to explore his stage space in a half-crouch.

As the tour went from venue to venue, the audiences began to scream louder and louder for the Rolling Stones as they worked through a short set that commonly ended with the Chuck Berry tune that John Pidgeon had heard them playing at the Ricky-Tick, "Bye Bye Johnny." Keith Richards observed that the shows were "winding tighter and tighter, until one day you get out there halfway through the first number and the whole stage is full of chicks screaming, 'Nyeehhh'" (Greenfield 1971). These audiences, however, extended beyond theaters.

Although Brian Epstein had had the authority of age and social class to shape the Beatles' stage image, Oldham, not quite a social peer of Jagger and Jones, was younger than any of the Rolling Stones. Consequently, he often had to submit to the band's passive-aggressive resistance to his ideas. They soon abandoned the houndstooth jackets he had selected and temporarily replaced them with matching leather waistcoats before abandoning the idea of a matching uniform altogether and strategically any appearance of being "professionals."

Over the course of 1963, the Stones (as people had already begun to abbreviate their name) began their love affair with the camera through appearances on *Ready Steady Go!* (23 August, 22 November, and 27 December) and *Thank Your Lucky Stars* (14 September and 23 November). Adolescents, eager for personal independence, loved what they saw, especially when their parents expressed outrage at the band's visual iconography, including but not limited to Jagger's camera mugging. "It is disgraceful that long-haired louts such as these should be allowed to appear on television. Their appearance was absolutely disgusting," wrote one viewer after the band's July debut on *Thank Your Lucky Stars* (Paytress 2003, 33). More was to come.

Professional Amateurs

The original contexts in which the Rolling Stones developed as musicians (e.g., the Ealing Rhythm and Blues Club) focused them on audiences with narrow tastes in repertoire, styles, and performers. Bands like the Beatles, in contrast, had started out playing dance halls, where they had needed to cover a wide variety of musical styles. Moreover, whereas the Beatles and others had labored

---

[6] The tour also included British singer Mickie Most.

for years playing in every type of venue from strip clubs to theaters and from Liverpool to Hamburg, with all the musical and cultural compromises those contexts demanded, the Rolling Stones ascended relatively quickly and, consequently, brought with them the arrogance and benign ignorance of beginners.

In 1963, Jagger described the Stones as "professional amateurs" who "still have the enthusiasm to treat the business as an enjoyable pastime," as though musicians who made music their career no longer enjoyed what they did (Paytress 2003, 34). A similar attitude had prevailed in sports, where those who proudly proclaimed themselves as amateurs disdained cricket and football athletes who played for salaries (see Kynaston 2013, 223–224). Jagger's comments smack of middle-class ignorance of working-class economic constraints: he performs not because he needs to earn an income but because he feels like it, as though that renders his actions and art purer than the lives and work of those who rely on performing for their livelihood.

Furthermore, the band's internal social tensions contributed to its dynamics, with the posturing and emoting middle-class Jagger strutting out front and working-class Wyman and Watts laboring dispassionately at the back of the stage. Moreover, as Wyman and Watts maintained day jobs to support themselves (and in Wyman's case his family), class condescension informed the group's everyday interactions, particularly when Jones mocked Wyman and Watts. And then there was the growing tension between Jones (who presented himself as the leader of the band and demanded a hidden extra payment from Oldham and Easton) and the Dartford lads Jagger and Richards.

Fig. 9.1. The Rolling Stones, at the Glasgow Odeon, 17 October 1963.
Tracksimages.com/Alamy Stock Photo

PART III
FRONTIERS, 1964

10
Consuming the Beatles

> America was not even a possibility for anybody before the Beatles.
> As a place to practice your business, it wasn't even a consideration.
> Before the Beatles, what were the possibilities?
> —Andrew Oldham

Ian MacDonald characterizes the sense of cultural change that many British experienced in the 1960s as an "inner one of feeling and assumption: a revolution in the head."[1] He also speculates that the decade "inaugurated a post-religious age" that functioned "mostly below the level of the rational mind in an emotional/physical dimension of personal appetite and private insecurity" (1998, 24). In this psychological revolution, the revelations of science both undermined confidence in authority (particularly religious and political authority) and generated technologies that transformed everyday life. This "cocktail of scientific innovations . . . TV, satellite communications, affordable private transport, amplified music, chemical contraception, LSD, and the nuclear bomb . . . produced a restless sense of urgency headily combined with unprecedented opportunities for individual freedom" (27).

Mark Donnelly in his study of 1960s Britain prioritizes the establishment of a "modern consumer economy" and a "preoccupation with personal autonomy" as defining characteristics of the decade (2005, xiv). The gradual recovery of the British postwar economy combined with programs designed to create housing and rebuild urban centers contributed to an environment in which identity was "best expressed via personal consumption of material goods" (2). In Donnelly's estimation, acquisition offered a way to symbolically represent both individual uniqueness and group identifications. Consumers looked for purchases that linked them to prosperity, and nothing said prosperity quite like access to the world.

Economically, the transatlantic conduit that the World War II Allies had established to transport war materials and personnel now delivered US manufactured farm and industrial machinery eastward to Europe and returned with goods (and revenue) with which Americans reified their new-found global superpower

---

[1] The epigraph to this chapter is from Andrew Loog Oldham, quoted in Kamp 2002.

Sixties British Pop, Outside In. Gordon Ross Thompson, Oxford University Press. © Oxford University Press 2024.
DOI: 10.1093/oso/9780190672348.003.0011

status. The rise of commercial air travel brought cultures into contact more frequently than ever, especially as the wealthiest individuals (the "jet set") exercised their ability to purchase flights to destinations both near and far, domestic and international.

A recovering Europe under the Marshall Plan brought multiple nations into competition for the attention of cash-flush American consumers. In Britain's immediate postwar years, automobile exports formed one of the economy's most important sources of foreign currency, but the British also applied a cultural advantage. With international markets opening and tourism growing, Britain began fine-tuning a commodified version of its culture.

An Aura of Unacceptability. As the Boomer and Bulge Generations came into full-fledged adolescence, the consumption of pop music emerged as a preferred symbol of personal identification. Purchasing records, magazines with stories and photos, and/or other music-related merchandise, as well as buying tickets to performances and listening to the radio or watching television, offered ways to express one's personal identity. To own a recording said (a) I have the resources to buy this object, (b) I have access to the equipment needed to play it, and (c) I think that this performer and/or their music says something about who I think I am.

In response, magazines, concerts, and fan paraphernalia reflected personal identification, especially when youth mounted these trophies on bedroom walls and shelves. Finally, fashion provided yet another way to declare allegiance to one social or musical group or another. Into this world, the Beatles opened an American door for other British musicians and with them British culture in general.

The *Science News Letter* (1964, 141) quotes an unidentified psychologist who asserts that the Beatles carried an "aura of unacceptability to the adult world" that made them appealing to adolescents. The article rationalizes that the band played "right to the young people's needs" during a "strenuous period of emotional and physical growth." Although the gist of the article was that the marketing of the Beatles took advantage of children who were already vulnerable to influence, another interpretation might suggest that these British performers responded to the fundamental adolescent developmental and psychological needs of their audiences.

In many ways, the Beatles, their images, their performances, their music, and their recordings became so highly sought after and consequently valuable that they created their own economy. They had accessed a communications portal to a transatlantic bank account. A flow of American culture—from films and television shows to music—had already been inundating the world. In the 1960s, however, the world began accessing that portal to America. When that stream became a flood, Americans called the arrival of the Beatles and other performers the "British Invasion" and found themselves on the receiving end of a global conduit they had helped to create.

Pop Globalization

A tipping point in the global commodification of British culture came in the fall of 1963 when fans crowded Heathrow Airport on a Thursday Halloween to greet the Beatles returning from a Swedish tour. Unable to exit his plane, the American Ed Sullivan wondered who could strand him and Britain's new prime minister, Alec Douglas-Home, on the tarmac (Miles 1998, 83). He soon learned the cause. A week later, Brian Epstein sat in an office in New York negotiating appearances for his protégées on *The Ed Sullivan Show* at Studio 50 on Broadway.

The venerable American news anchor Walter Cronkite remembered first hearing about the Beatles in the fall of 1963 from UK correspondents who sent film clips of the band that briefly appeared on in mid-November. A few days later, however, "President Kennedy was assassinated in Dallas," and for "the next few weeks, the President's death dominated the news" (Cronkite in Spizer 2003, iv).

Kennedy's assassination had a significant impact on the psyche of the nation and the Western world. Television brought the unfolding tragedy directly into American homes: the grieving widow, the casket lying in state, the Washington funeral procession, the saluting son. Not until 7 December did CBS feel comfortable running other feature stories, by which time, audiences yearned for something uplifting (see Spizer 2003, iv).

Earlier in the year, despite success in Britain, EMI's American subsidiary, Capitol, had repeatedly declined George Martin's entreaties to release the Beatles' discs in the United States. Capitol, who had begun releasing discs by the Beach Boys, believed that they knew the American market and the American market would not be interested in the Beatles. That decision forced Parlophone to lease Beatles recordings to smaller independent American labels, like Vee-Jay (*Introducing the Beatles*), that had limited promotional resources (Spizer 2003, 73).

In November, however, when Capitol turned down "I Want to Hold Your Hand," Brian Epstein contacted Capitol's president directly. With appearances scheduled for *The Ed Sullivan Show* and the American press interested in Beatlemania, Epstein convinced Alan Livingston to override production staff decisions, to release the record, and to spend an unprecedented $40,000 on promotion (Spizer 2003, 73). American teens, however, were ahead of them.

Breakthrough. On 17 December 1963, radio station WWDC in Washington, DC, invited one of their listeners to introduce a recording she had heard about on the news and that she had requested the radio station play. Soon, other listeners were calling the station, asking to hear the disc again. Quickly, WWDC and stations in Chicago and Saint Louis placed the recording (or taped copies of it) into their rotations. Its hand forced, Capitol canceled its planned mid-January release of "I Want to Hold Your Hand" in anticipation of the Sullivan appearances and issued the disc on 26 December 1963, a day when most music stations were playing a summary of the year's top hits (Spizer 2003, 82–83).

Several factors contributed to the success of the Beatles and their recordings in the United States, where Baby Boomers held deep anxieties about their world. A year after the Cuban missile crisis, when students had received instructions on how to survive a nuclear bomb, the assassination of President Kennedy filled their television screens. Nevertheless, the American economy continued to expand, and the rise of consumerism encouraged the purchase of discs, especially as home audio equipment—record players and radios—improved in quality, became more affordable, and soon occupied prized places in homes.

The Beatles and their exuberance provided an emotional outlet for adolescents' apprehensions. Recordings allowed them to create their own internal worlds, define their social spaces, and develop bonds with their peers. Friends listened to the recordings and discussed instruments and how they might be played, the quality of voices, the meanings of lyrics, and sundry other sonic, sartorial, and social details, if not the minutiae of album covers and disc labels.

A Really Big Show

In the middle of January, the Beatles and Brian Epstein tackled the historically English-resistant French market with a two-week Parisian residency at the Olympia Theatre. While press officers Tony Barrow and Brian Sommerville attempted to interest the French media, unexpected equipment malfunctions and largely adult audiences tamped some of the excitement. In the former case, George Harrison suspected equipment sabotage. In the latter, Ray Coleman's review claimed that it was "the men who screamed, rather than the girls" (25 January 1964, 9). Nevertheless, between shows, the band learned that "I Want to Hold Your Hand" had leapt to the top of American charts. Three weeks later, the Beatles boarded a Pan Am flight to New York's recently renamed John F. Kennedy Airport.

Capitol's marketing office in Manhattan had responded to Alan Livingston's directive with a slogan that echoed the Revolutionary War cry "The British are coming." Small ads declaring that "The Beatles Are Coming" appeared in magazines and on flyers, especially in the New York area. Some local radio stations even began a countdown to the band's arrival on Friday, 7 February 1964, when 3,000-plus anxious teens invaded the airport. In a crowded JFK lounge, the band playfully parried insipid questions from condescending middle-aged male newshounds who clearly had underestimated and misunderstood what was happening (Spizer 2003, 4).

New York, New York. New York City in the sixties ruled unchallenged as the media capital of the United States, with the three major networks broadcasting national news and entertainment programming from Manhattan. In the competition for Sunday night viewers, Ed Sullivan prided himself on securing the most popular international performers of the day, believing that many Americans were interested in the world beyond their borders. The Beatles perfectly fit that programming model.

Their debut came on Sunday, 9 February 1964, at 8:00 PM Eastern Standard Time, when an estimated 73.7 million Americans watched the Beatles open and close the show. Adolescents anticipated the event by positioning the family in front of the television and ensuring that the CBS eye logo appeared on the screen. As Sullivan started his introduction and the audience erupted with screams, North America experienced one of those singular events in media history when a significant portion of the population temporarily stopped to watch.

With Vee-Jay and other labels already distributing Beatles discs, Capitol began an extended legal fight to secure the leasing rights they had once refused. The company began by cherry-picking parts of the albums *Please Please Me* and *With the Beatles* to create the American album *Meet the Beatles*. Moreover, before disassembling British albums that had originally each featured 14 tracks to create American albums that generally included 12 or fewer, staff engineers culturally adapted the recordings by remixing the sound to match American audio aesthetics (e.g., adding reverberation).[2] When demand grew, Capitol drew on the remaining album tracks and other Beatles recordings (e.g., EPs) to construct new albums (e.g., *The Beatles' Second Album*), which conveniently also maximized their revenue.

Buy Me Love

During the Beatles' claustrophobic January stay in Paris, Paul McCartney had begun working on the bluesy but exuberant "Can't Buy Me Love."[3] Partly as a matter of convenience in consideration of their busy tour schedule, George Martin had arranged for the Beatles to record "Komm, Gib Mir Deine Hand" and

---

[2] One reason for the repackaging was that the US and the UK credited album copyright differently.
[3] McCartney, reflecting on how success had privileged them in hedonistic ways, later suggested that a better title might have been "Can Buy Me Love" (Miles 1997, 162).

"Sie Liebt Dich" (March 1964), German versions of "She Loves You" and "I Want to Hold Your Hand," at EMI's Pathé Marconi Studios while in Paris.[4]

After the Beatles had very reluctantly but quickly completed that task, they had filled the remaining studio time by working on McCartney's song, routining[5] the arrangement, finding a suitable key, and honing the details. With the basic backing for "Can't Buy Me Love" completed, they had something they could resume once they returned from the United States the next month. The American experience, however, would carry its own consequences for the recording.

Rickenbacker had noticed pictures of Lennon playing a repainted and modified version of one of their guitars and had quickly set up a display room at the Savoy-Plaza Hotel for the Beatles to inspect. Looking over the gear, Lennon thought that Harrison (who was sick in his room) would like the Rickenbacker 360-12, the company's new electric 12-string guitar and brought the complimentary instrument back to his bandmate. The guitarists would have already known about the British-made Burns Double Six that Bruce Welch had played on Cliff Richard's "Don't Talk to Him," but the American-made instrument carried more prestige, if not a distinctive sound.

A big part of their spring 1964 schedule would be their first film, which meant writing and recording new material for the soundtrack, including Paul McCartney's Paris song. George Martin had already dubbed a piano part to add texture, and they now began adding McCartney's vocals and planning Harrison's guitar inserts. Brandishing the Rickenbacker 360-12, Harrison applied its distinctive jangly sound to the chords that stab away during the song's chorus and that would become a defining aspect of their sound for the rest of the year.

£3,000,000. Two weeks before the disc's release, EMI confirmed that "Can't Buy Me Love" had already earned silver status in the UK with presales of over a half million and more orders arriving daily. They anticipated advance sales of over a million before the release date of Friday, 20 March 1964, which would match what "I Want to Hold Your Hand" had achieved and would earn the disc gold status ("Beatles' Next: Half Million Already" 5 March 1964, 31). A week later, advance sales topped 865,000 ("Beatles Single—865,000" 12 March 1964, 1).

By 2 April 1964, Beatles LPs held down the top two sales positions in the UK; the one, three, five, and six positions in EP sales; and the top position for singles, with "I Want to Hold Your Hand" still hanging in the charts at number 42. Perhaps more amazing, in America's *Billboard* charts, the Beatles held the top five positions for singles, with two other recordings in the top 50. By the end of April, their publisher, Dick James, had moved from his cozy quarters off Denmark Street to rather more posh premises in New Oxford Street. Meanwhile, EMI

---

[4] EMI believed that German audiences would only buy discs in their own language.
[5] To routine a performance is to set and rerehearse its arrangement.

informed investors that the company would be earning "not less than £8 million during the current financial year—a dramatic £3,000,000 more than in the past 12 months" (*Record Retailer*, 30 April 1964, 20).

Beatles for Sale

As had been demonstrated by Elvis Presley, pop culture can sell more than records and tickets. As the Beatles juggernaut gathered momentum, they had only a vague awareness of their cultural wake and of their merchandise potential. For example, a Bethnal Green (East London) factory was producing "several thousand" Beatle wigs each week, while others identified their products as connected to the "Beetles" (Norman 2003, 231). Oblivious, Epstein initially saw merchandise as promotion, not a source of profit, and inspected each product so that official goods met his standards.[6]

By late 1963, Epstein realized that merchandise sales had grown too large and too fast for him to control, so he handed the issue over to his solicitor, David Jacobs, who in turn approached Chelsea Set regular Nicky Byrne about licensing. When Jacobs drew up the agreement forming companies to handle merchandise and NEMS, Byrne brazenly asked for and received 90 percent of the profits, and Jacobs and Epstein agreed! The manager and his lawyer, not fully fathoming the value (both monetary and cultural) of this business, rationalized that 10 percent was better than the nothing they were currently getting (Norman 2003, 234).

When Byrne formed Stramsact in the UK with a subsidiary, Seltaeb ("Beatles" spelled backward) to cover American rights, the Beatles and NEMS lost millions of pounds and dollars on the sale of Beatles-inspired goods from the aforementioned wigs to lunch boxes, clothing, and publications. Merchandise, however, was not the only way to make money off the Beatles.

A Hard Day's Night

In the early London autumn of 1963, George Ornstein of United Artists watched as stories about Beatlemania made the front pages of every major British newspaper. Ornstein and another American expatriate, producer Walter Shenson, anticipating a quick exploitation of a potentially short-lived phenomenon, contacted Brian Epstein to propose a film. For his part, the manager, eager to gain American exposure for the Beatles, saw the proposal not only as an expansion of the band's career but also as another gateway to America. After discussions about

---

[6] He also refused direct endorsements by the Beatles lest doing so diminish their status as artists.

the Beatles' interests and preferences, Shenson recommended another American associate as the director.

Richard Lester's catalogue included the short absurdist comedy *The Running Jumping and Standing Still Film* (1959) as well as *The Mouse on the Moon* (1963), both of which featured Beatles favorites Peter Sellers and Spike Milligan. He had also directed Helen Shapiro and others in *It's Trad, Dad!* (1962), which reassured Epstein, Shenson, and United Artists that he could handle the Beatles. With a limited budget (£150,000), they planned a pseudodocumentary describing a day in the life of the Beatles in a money-saving black-and-white cinéma vérité style. All they needed was a script.

Prisoners of Their Success. In November 1963, a week after returning from Sweden and having their fans close Heathrow Airport, the Beatles headed out again, this time for Ireland with screenwriter Alun Owen in tow. Owen, who had grown up in Liverpool, had written the teledrama *No Trams to Lime Street* about sailors on leave in Merseyside, which the Beatles had seen and had appreciated.

Watching the band in Dublin, Owen quickly settled on a story, telling Lester and Shenson, "I've got it—they're prisoners of their success. They go from the airport to the hotel to the theater or stadium or concert hall, back to the hotel, back to the airport. In any city it's always the same" (Yule 1994, 6). The film would be about the Beatles' reacting to their fame in different spaces.

Lester had to work with musicians who knew little about acting and would need to make a limited budget and dramatic naïveté a virtue, but he also embraced the chaos and exuberance of Beatlemania. Rather than treat the musicians and their fans with condescension the way many in the British establishment did, he celebrated their dynamism. Fortunately, the Beatles proved naturals in this format.

Toward the end of the filming in April 1964, Shenson approached the Beatles for title suggestions and a title song. Ringo Starr inadvertently resolved the first with one of his malapropisms. "I used to, while I was saying one thing, have another thing come into my brain and move down fast," Starr recalled. "Once when we were working all day and then into the night, I came out thinking it was still day and said, 'It's been a hard day,' and looked round and noticing it was dark, '. . . 's night!'" (Beatles 2000, 130). Shenson and Lester liked it and, with the film title now *A Hard Day's Night*, all they needed was a song.

The "next morning [Lennon] brought in the song" (Sheff 1981, 174–175). For "A Hard Day's Night," Lennon adopts the form of a work song in which a singer weighs the exhaustion of labor against the anticipation of love.[7] Knowing that the song/recording "would open both the film and the soundtrack LP . . . we wanted a particularly strong and effective beginning," recalled George Martin (Lewisohn

---

[7] In some ways, the song is the antithesis of "Can't Buy Me Love."

1988, 43). To that end, they devised the iconic opening chord with its added tones and dissonances begging for resolution and immediately establishing anticipation.

Objectification. In America, this United Artists recording pulled crossmarket audiences into theaters as the film helped define the Beatles as a brand while creating a cinematic version that substituted for a live concert experience. Alun Owen's brief experience with them and the physical limitations of the medium meant that he reduced their personalities to what he saw as their quintessential qualities. Starr would be the funny one; Harrison the quiet one; McCartney the cute one; and Lennon the sarcastic rebel.

The Beatles, for their part, failed to fully appreciate their insidious loss of agency in letting others define them. They continued to make music and to take advantage of the extravagances that their fame afforded them, but these same forces began to pull them away from what had originally brought them together. The Beatles had become willing victims of their own success, if not also complicit in their own commodification.

The Summer of '64

When Parlophone released the single "A Hard Day's Night" as well as the album of the same name (July 1964),[8] both discs shot immediately to the top of Britain's charts. An EMI representative waxed ecstatic: "the single has sold 600,000 . . . the film soundtrack LP a quarter of a million," and in "America, we expect two million sales with the album" (Coleman 18 July 1964, 1). In the United States, however, United Artists rather than Capitol owned the rights to the soundtrack, which contained eight Beatles recordings from the film and four pieces arranged for studio musicians by George Martin.

Not wanting to miss the July media frenzy, Capitol released both the title track and selected items from the film as singles: "I'll Cry Instead" with "I'm Happy Just to Dance with You" and "And I Love Her" with "If I Fell." Capitol also created another composite album. *Something New* (which was only partly that) included material from the soundtrack, the *Long Tall Sally* EP, and the German version of "I Want to Hold Your Hand." Moreover, as United Artists and Capitol Records flooded the North American market with Beatles recordings, labels in other countries joined the global feeding frenzy. All that was missing was a world tour to promote sales.

Around the World. The Beatles were far from the first UK act to venture beyond Britain's shores. Cliff Richard and the Shadows had taken to the American

---

[8] Although United Artists released the album in the US, Parlophone held the rights in the UK.

road in 1960, followed by performances in South Africa, New Zealand, Sweden, Norway, Australia, and France, as well as returning to the United States again. And only months before the Beatles, Andrew Oldham had sent the Rolling Stones on a furtive American tour, with mixed results (see Hutton 1964, 8–9). Seeking to avoid that kind of fiasco, Brian Epstein and Tony Barrow opened a "Press and Public Relations" office in New York to anticipate and respond to possible negative media reaction ("Epstein Opens Press Office in New York" 11 June 1964, 4).

For the summer of 1964, Epstein scheduled two major concert tours, the first visiting Denmark, the Netherlands, Hong Kong, Australia, and New Zealand and the second North America, in addition to UK dates. As the Liverpudlians packed their bags, however, an unexpected complication arose. The day before their European leg was to begin and during a photo shoot, tonsillitis and pharyngitis caught up with Ringo Starr, hospitalizing him. George Harrison wanted to stop the tour, but Brian Epstein overruled him, arguing that the stakes were too high and the scope of the business plans too complicated to abdicate.

To deputize for Starr, Epstein and George Martin drafted Jimmy Nicol—a drummer who had recently recorded with another Epstein artist, Tommy Quickly, and had played on an album of Beatles covers. So on the afternoon of the day Starr went into hospital at University College, London, and the day before they were to depart, Nicol rehearsed with the Beatles at EMI. Ringo rejoined them in Australia, but this episode revealed an underlying problem: they were still working-class musicians following middle-class orders. They had yet to realize their collective authority.

Eight Days a Week

The success of the Beatles in the United States was not an isolated phenomenon but part of a broader American embrace of the world's cultures and in particular English-British culture. Ed Sullivan had been in London in search of British entertainers for his program, which included cast members from the musical *Oliver!* who also made their American television debut that February night. Likewise, United Artists heavily promoted the James Bond franchise in the United States with *Dr. No* (1962), *From Russia with Love* (1963–1964), and *Goldfinger* (1964). Thus, the American version of Beatlemania came nested in the broader cultural commodification of Britain.

Alignments of demographics, technology, and economics had created Beatlemania. Now a cycle of creation, recording, and promotion generated singles, EPs, and albums that responded to consumer demand. In that context, during the fall of 1964, the Beatles and Brian Epstein began talks with George Ornstein and Walter Shenson about a second film that they tentatively called *Eight Arms to Hold You*. That inspired McCartney to write "Eight Days a Week" for a release they would eventually call *Help!*; both titles describe the lives of the Beatles in this period.

In the middle of October 1964, for the first time in two years, no Beatles single appeared in either the *Record Retailer*'s "Britain's Top 50" or in America's *Billboard* singles charts. As British blues and rhythm-and-blues artists began scoring transatlantic hits, journalists asked if the Beatles had peaked. With only a short break after returning from America and as they continued touring the UK, they snatched available studio time to make a single and a UK album for a Christmas release.

Unsurprisingly, their music reflects some of the effect the business of being the Beatles were having on them. On *Beatles for Sale* (December 1964) they draw on their rockabilly and rock 'n' roll inspirations, as well as revealing their growing interest in the music of Bob Dylan. Lennon's tunes in particular (notably "I'm a Loser," "Baby's in Black," and "I Don't Want to Spoil the Party") suggest stress and insecurity.

Collaborative Creativity

Both sides of their next single—Lennon's "I Feel Fine" and McCartney's "She's a Woman" (November 1964)—rework the core three-chord harmonic, melodic, and textual conceits of the blues. The songs and recordings also illustrate some of their internal creative process as an ensemble.

Textually, McCartney's "She's a Woman" continues the transactional theme of "Can't Buy Me Love," with the object of his affections providing love rather than material "presents." Musically, the arrangement's syncopated accompaniment (perhaps reflecting the ska that was invading British dance halls) relies on Lennon's increasingly dissonant backbeat chords behind McCartney's bluesy vocals.[9] Lennon, however, got the A-side.

For the text of "I Feel Fine," Lennon invokes routine transactional blues themes in terms both personal ("Baby says she's mine") and material ("Baby buys me rings"). The music similarly begins as a variation on a motif used by Ray Charles as the opening to "What'd I Say" (July 1959) as reconfigured by Bobby Parker for "Watch Your Step" (July 1961) with a dash of Roy Orbison's "Oh, Pretty Woman" (August 1964). Lennon knew these recordings well and mined this riff cluster to create something new.

---

[9] Harrison dubbed his solo the next day.

When he arrived at the session, he told Ringo Starr, "I've written this song, but it's lousy" (Beatles 2000, 160). Nevertheless, as the band harmonized the vocals and fell into the groove, the music and performance coalesced. The recording's most memorable moment, however, occurs in its first seconds.

The Accident. At some point during rehearsal, an unexpected howl filled Studio 2. The official story has Lennon leaning his guitar against his amplifier without setting the rig to standby. The mistake created a feedback loop where the guitar's pickup and the amplifier began to continuously recycle the frequencies of the open strings. They eventually realized that the Vox AC-100 amplifiers,[10] specifically built for them to play large concert venues, were too powerful for the comparatively intimate contexts of Abbey Road. Absentmindedly propping his acoustic Gibson against the cabinet, Lennon triggered an accident waiting to happen.

The distinctive sound at the beginning of "I Feel Fine," nevertheless, does not originate with Lennon leaning his guitar against his amplifier but with McCartney plucking the open A on his bass with an octave harmonic and allowing it to feed back. That sound sets Lennon's open A string vibrating sympathetically and available to feedback. The effect appears on the very first take, indicating that they had discovered the sound in rehearsal and played with the duration of the note. Other guitarists of the era employed feedback as a part of their technical repertoire—individuals interacting alone with their equipment (e.g., Jeff Beck). Lennon and McCartney, however, approached feedback in "I Feel Fine" as a team.

Like many other British performers in the midsixties, the Beatles created material and performances as a social unit while relying on their production team to help realize their ideas as recordings. Indeed, much of their creativity in this era came when these northerners shared in the creation of material, collectively contributing ideas and modifying them. Socially conditioned, they approached music-making interdependently. Just as their families had survived the war and postwar years through communal sharing, the Beatles generated music through a process of collaboration for their collective good.

---

[10] McCartney had a slightly different but equally powerful Vox amplifier.

Fig. 10.1 *A Hard Day's Night* (1964).

Fig. 10.2 *A Hard Day's Night* (1964).

11
Northern Waves

The Beatles' quick February 1964 return to the UK after appearances on *The Ed Sullivan Show*, at Carnegie Hall in New York, and at the Coliseum in Washington, DC,[1] left a sudden cultural vacuum. American teens demanded more "Fab Four," so in the band's absence, disc jockeys, television programmers, and concert promoters filled the gap. Young men who played guitar and had long schoolboy haircuts formed the core visual stereotype, with some Americans using the word "Beatle" as a generic term for any young British male. Peter Asher remarked: "people would actually come up to you and say, 'Are you a Beatle?'" (Kamp 2002).

British pop presented as a Whiter version of America, an amalgam of pop styles repackaged as something both foreign and familiar. Although British musicians drew on the rock 'n' roll and rockabilly of White America (e.g., Carl Perkins), they also benefited from the same prejudices that deprivileged Black America. Anglophilia—no matter how unable Americans were at distinguishing one English accent from another—and the perception of urbanity masked the appropriation.

Adolescent Empowerment. As the leading edge of the postwar generation entered their later teen years, their priorities adjusted to their growing awareness of both the world and the degree of their responsibilities in it. Adolescents consumed pop music, pop art, and pop literature voraciously, embracing representations that reflected their ambitions and discarded the obsolete or irrelevant. They bought new identities.

Just as in Britain, American print publishers seized the opportunity to provide teens with promotional interviews and photos of their favorite performers. In addition to mainstream publications like *Life* and the *Saturday Evening Post*, magazines like *Tiger Beat* and *Datebook* offered stories about the latest British musicians. Concurrently, nationally broadcast American television shows like *Shindig!* (ABC) and *Hullabaloo* (NBC) framed performers (British and American) in a teen-friendly format. Of course, not all musicians achieved transatlantic resonance in this "British Invasion," but many contributed to this quickly changing music market.

---

[1] CBS filmed the Washington, DC, performance and leased it to the National General Corporation to be telecast in film theaters across the US and Canada in March 1964.

Ed Sullivan's international approach to television programming had positioned him to exploit the demand for British pop artists. Agents working for him in London simply looked at the current British charts, and while the artists they chose might not have produced the same viewing numbers as the Beatles, they satisfied the immediate demand. In this environment, many in the first wave of British performers that America encountered on many Sunday nights came from northern England.

Merseyside

If 1963 repositioned Liverpool from cultural backwater to a national obsession, then 1964 pushed it onto an international stage. At first, Gerry and the Pacemakers, the Searchers, Billy J. Kramer with the Dakotas, Cilla Black, and others went from playing the Cavern and the Iron Door to theater stages on package tours across the UK. As the attention of foreign audiences soon followed, however, domestic consumer appetite continued to shift, leaving Merseyside performers struggling to remain relevant.

Their most immediate challenge involved repertoire, whether in finding American recordings to cover, in relying on British songwriters like Mitch Murray, or in attempting to compose new material themselves that reflected performer strengths and kept pace with audience expectations. Being from Liverpool attracted record companies, but musicians needed both airplay and visual media (magazines and television) to sell discs and concert tickets. Over the course of the year, hairstyles shifted from adult combed-back coiffures to boyish bangs and bobs, and from singers with bands to bands with singers. Some musicians, however, fell into the transition gap, neither new nor old, fashionable or passé.

The Big Three possessed proven advantages in 1963: Brian Epstein managed them, they were from Liverpool, and they were talented. Their hastily recorded Decca cover of Richie Barrett's "Some Other Guy" (March 1963) reached *Record Retailer*'s top 30, and their follow-up, Mitch Murray's "By the Way" (June 1963), did even better. Nevertheless, even after an appearance on *Ready Steady Go!* (1 November 1963), the hits and the novelty of a three-piece rock band were gone by the time Ed Sullivan's scouts came looking. Those who did make the transatlantic trip, however, prolonged their fade from fame.

Gerry Cross the Mersey

Gerry and the Pacemakers had once been Merseyside equals to the Beatles, with whom they had shared club and dance hall stages in Liverpool and Hamburg.

Those experiences had sharpened their musical intuition and contributed to their local popularity, as did Gerry Marsden's adult-friendly appearance and toothy smile. Broader success, however, had meant appealing to more anonymous and heterogeneous audiences. In London, their initial triumphs had come with Mitch Murray songs followed by Rodgers and Hammerstein's "You'll Never Walk Alone," repertoire far from their Liverpool reputation for covering American rock 'n' roll.

Despite that success, Gerry Marsden could not have helped observing that his friends Lennon and McCartney earned royalties when they recorded their own material. His initial recorded songwriting attempts came in collaboration with bassist Les Chadwick as B-sides that echo Mitch Murray's early writing style. With those models in mind, he was the sole author of their next A-side, "I'm the One" (January 1964), which reached #2 on British charts in February 1964. Their first big American hit, however, came as a group effort.

The Sun Never Sets. "Don't Let the Sun Catch You Crying" (April 1964) draws on the same theme of emotional support heard in "You'll Never Walk Alone" and plays to both Marsden's vocal strengths and his perceived personality.[2] He again sings with a small orchestra (arranged and conducted by George Martin)[3] and resists the temptation to croon melodramatically, coming across as unaffected and honest, even when he reaches into his higher tessitura during the middle-eight.[4] "Don't Let the Sun Catch You Crying" was a top-10 hit in the UK and placed in the American top-five in the summer of 1964, bolstered by appearances in May on *The Ed Sullivan Show*.

Their follow-up single, "It's Gonna Be Alright" by Marsden (August 1964), returned to their earlier beat style but stalled in the middle of the charts, particularly in the United States, where "How Do You Do It"? (US June 1964) and "I Like It" (US September 1964) were rereleased and climbed into *Billboard*'s top 20 over a year after their original releases.

To exploit this sudden fame, Gerry and the Pacemakers participated in the creation of the pseudobiographical film *Ferry Cross the Mersey* (January 1965). The story takes Marsden and the band back to Liverpool, now a nostalgic place where they had attended art school and had played in competitions. In the same stylistic vein as "Don't Let the Sun Catch You Crying," the song "Ferry Cross the Mersey" (December 1964) longs for the innocence of 1963. By 1965, however, that world had begun to feel like a distant memory.

---

[2] The first artist to record the song was Louise Cordet for Decca (February 1964), with Tony Meehan arranging and producing it as an up-tempo beat ballad.

[3] The songwriting credits on Cordet's release list Marsden, Chadwick, and Les Maguire as the songwriters, while the Pacemakers' version credits only Marsden. Subsequent releases credit Gerry Marsden, Freddie Marsden, Les Chadwick, and Les Maguire.

[4] British pop musicians often referred to the contrasting B section or chorus of a song as the "middle eight," referring to the number of measures it might or might not last.

From a Window

Like the Pacemakers, Billy J. Kramer with the Dakotas had benefited from their associations with the Beatles and Brian Epstein, especially when they had tapped into Lennon and McCartney's song catalogue. Kramer's performances of Lennon's songs in particular (with George Martin's production) had brought him repeated success in 1963: "Do You Want to Know a Secret," "Bad to Me," and "I'll Keep You Satisfied" all made Britain's top five. In the fall of 1963, when few US consumers even knew about the Beatles, Brian Epstein brought the conservatively groomed Kramer to the United States, where manger and client met Ed Sullivan. By the summer of 1964, Epstein and Sullivan felt that American audiences were ready for Kramer with the Dakotas, and vice versa.

Perhaps under the influence of Lennon, Kramer rejected McCartney's "A World without Love" and turned instead to a song by John McFarland and American expatriate Mort Shuman (Southall with Perry 2006, 22).[5] The distinctly American flavor of "Little Children" (February 1964) features a number of phrases that would have been unusual in the UK (e.g., "going steady") with some outright Americanisms and pronunciations (e.g., "I'll give you candy and a quarter, if you're quiet like you oughta"). A month after its release, "Little Children" sat atop British charts, and with an appearance scheduled for Ed Sullivan's show (7 June), Imperial Records reissued the disc in the United States to see it climb onto *Billboard*'s top 10.[6]

Although Beatlemania and a demand for recordings by British artists swept America in July 1964, Kramer's return to the Lennon-McCartney catalogue with "From a Window" (July 1964), while doing well in the UK (#10 on *Record Retailer*'s charts), failed to chart in the United States. Touring North America in the fall of 1964 helped, but his version of Burt Bacharach and Hal David's "Trains and Boats and Planes" (May 1965), while making #12 in *Record Retailer*, only reached #47 in *Billboard* in the United States.[7] With his fame in decline and gazing out a theater dressing-room window at a street devoid of fans, he turned to a journalist and asked, "Do you think I'm finished as a top star?" (Dawn James March 1965).

---

[5] Everett (2001, 168) suggests that the song Kramer declined was McCartney's "One and One Is Two," but it may be that he declined both that song and "World without Love."

[6] As with the other artists produced by George Martin in 1963, success in the UK did not automatically convince EMI's subsidiary Capitol to release their discs in the US.

[7] Bacharach recorded his own version, which reached #4 on *Record Retailer*'s charts.

Needles and Pins

By the end of 1963, the Searchers had scored a UK number one with "Sugar and Spice," and both their EP (*Sweets for My Sweet*) and their album (*Sugar and Spice*) had been selling well. For a follow-up, they turned to "Needles and Pins" (April 1963), a cover of Jackie DeShannon's original recording that had featured Jack Nitzsche's layered arrangement of jangling acoustic guitars, bass, drums, piano, organ, and chorus for a song he had written with Sonny Bono.[8]

In London, producer Tony Hatch and the Searchers make a virtue of economic necessity in their imitation of the emerging Los Angeles folk-rock sound. They quicken the tempo and drop the key while the guitars preserve and highlight the prominent harmonic suspensions of the original. The sparseness and close miking of Hatch's production, unlike producer Dick Glasser's rich soundscape for DeShannon, relies solely on voices, guitars, and drums,[9] and reflects the sonic aesthetics of midsixties British rock. Deciding which Searcher would sing "Needles and Pins," however, presented another issue.

"When we first tried it out, we each sang it on our own," drummer Chris Curtis explained. "It's amazing how different the four versions were" (Dawbarn 1 February 1964, 9). Although Tony Jackson had originally joined the band as its singer and had been featured on their first hits, Curtis favored Mike Pender, who closely copies DeShannon's singing, including her tendency to add a vowel to the ends of phrases (e.g., "needles and pins-a"). Three weeks after Pye released the Searchers' "Needles and Pins" (January 1964), the disc had quickly entered NME's top five and by the end of the month was outselling all other records. In the United States it entered *Billboard*'s top 20 in April, supported by the band making a quick trip to New York for an appearance on *The Ed Sullivan Show* (5 April 1964).

A Beat Group. With the rise of bands like the Rolling Stones in London, Ray Coleman at *Melody Maker* (29 February 1964) asked whether the Searchers intended to become a rhythm-and-blues group. De facto music director Curtis had chosen the Orlons' "Don't Throw Your Love Away" (November 1963) to cover as their next single but insisted: "we don't call ourselves an R&B group. We play some R&B, some rock. In other words, we're a beat group!" Nevertheless, despite that assertion, changes were under way.

For the Orlons' release, songwriters Bill Jackson and Jim Wisner had created a sophisticated arrangement that the British again simplify. The Searchers had probably been attracted by the harmonic suspensions of the original, which

---

[8] They had heard DeShannon's disc on Radio Luxembourg but had also seen Cliff Bennett and the Rebel Rousers performing it in Hamburg.

[9] The close miking also captures a squeaky bass-drum pedal.

would have provided continuity with their previous release. Mike Pender once more sings lead, and "Don't Throw Your Love Away" (April 1964) found success in both the UK and US charts. Internal tensions, however, were undermining them musically.

Curtis claims never to have liked Tony Jackson, complaining that "if I'd had the nous,[10] I would have had someone else in the first place." At the root of their antagonism, Jackson challenged Curtis's musical decisions, to which the drummer often responded by walking away and warning his bandmate that any further complaining and he was out (Leigh 2004b, 143). Unsurprisingly, after their next release, "Some Day We're Gonna Love Again" (July 1964), Jackson quit.

With Frank Allen arriving on bass, the Searchers returned to Jackie DeShannon's catalogue and her self-written "When You Walk in the Room" (November 1963) for a performance and recording that reflects Southern California's emerging hybrid of folk, rock, and pop.[11] Glasser's production and Nitzsche's arrangement feature an electric 12-string guitar and an introduction that foreshadows that of the Byrds' "Eight Miles High." Nevertheless, in the world of American pop, where the industry discouraged women from taking active writing and performing roles, disc jockeys played the Searchers' simpler version (September 1964).

At the end of the year, the Searchers turned to another song by an American woman: Malvina Reynolds's antinuclear lament "What Have They Done to the Rain" (November 1964). Their folkish cover (Curtis plays bongos) did less well than their versions of DeShannon's songs but kept them in the charts. Ironically, the most successful Searcher disc in the United States that year came when Kapp reissued a Tony Jackson cut from their first album after it had gained traction with some American disc jockeys: Leiber and Stoller's "Love Potion No. 9" (October 1964).[12]

Mancunian Attractions

In the winter of 1965, the British-American pop pas de deux intensified as agents and industry savants searched for the next big thing. Unlike their Liverpudlian neighbors, however, most in the northern English music scene failed to earn invitations to appear on American television. An unlikely exception proved to be the Danny Betesh–managed Freddie and the Dreamers, whose recordings had been British hits in 1963 and who now represented a quaint past. Garrity had

---

[10] British colloquial term for "common sense."
[11] Initial pressings listed her as "Jack DeShannon."
[12] Released in the US as "Love Potion Number Nine."

attempted an image change away from slapstick comedy with a melancholy cover of the Four Tunes' (1954) "I Understand" (October 1964); however, the singer was approaching 30 and his career was on a slide into obscurity when Jack Good called.

Good had taken his ideas for pop-music television to the United States to produce *Shindig!* for ABC, which was where Garrity and the Dreamers made a series of appearances (27 January, 24 February, and 28 April 1965) as well as on NBC's imitation of that show, *Hullabaloo* (16 February and 4 May 1965) and, of course, *The Ed Sullivan Show* (25 April 1965). Capitol's original American release of "I'm Telling You Now" (October 1963) had gained little traction, but with the new media exposure, a rerelease of that disc (March 1965) topped American charts (April 1965). Three months later and almost two years after its British debut and after an initial release on Capitol, "You Were Made for Me" (March 1965) reached #21 on *Billboard*. Nevertheless, despite a brief round of interest by American preteens in "Do the Freddie" (April 1965), the Boomers, like their Bulge counterparts, moved on to more serious fare.

Meanwhile, other musicians associated with the southern counties of northern England continued to adapt their music and performances to expand their importance on the British and European scenes, if not also to attract the interest of some American listeners.

Staying Alive

After nationally broadcast appearances on *Ready Steady Go!*, *Thank Your Lucky Stars*, and *Top of the Pops*, the Hollies and their cover of Doris Troy's "Just One Look" (February 1964) reached the top five in British charts. A spot on a national tour headlined by the Dave Clark Five allowed them to further expand and to deepen that audience. Interband rivalry was normally cordial in the UK, but even modest class differences and regional stereotypes run deep. In this case, the DC5 came across to the others as arrogant and controlling. Graham Nash of the Hollies remembered: "we fuckin' hated the Dave Clark Five! They were just awful to us. They were snotty and they couldn't play for shit. I mean, if you're great, maybe you have the right to be a little stuck-up, but if you're not great, fuck you and your attitude" (Kamp 2002).

Despite that experience, success led to an invitation to the Hollies to perform on the annual *New Musical Express* Winners Concert (26 April 1964) in the cavernous Wembley Pool, in northwest London. Appearing along with the Beatles and Cliff Richard confirmed their status as members of Britain's pop elite and attracted the attention of songwriters. Among the first to offer material, American Mort Shuman and Englishman Clive Westlake tailored "Here

I Go Again" (May 1964) to highlight Allan Clarke and Graham Nash's distinctive vocal harmonies. The tight performance and recording helped the disc to reach #4 on British charts but still only garnered modest attention in the United States.

Looking both to capture some royalties and to generate more material suited to their performance strengths, Allan Clarke, Tony Hicks, and Nash also began writing. "We're Through" (September 1964) reached into *Record Retailer*'s top 10 and opened a path they would follow in the future. Their first number one, however, came from an American, Clint Ballard, Jr., whose "I'm Alive" (May 1965) follows the classic "climber" form in which the melody crests on the song's title. Once again, however, the disc failed to break them into the United States, and an American tour evaporated (Altham 2 July 1965).

Funnier Than It Would Seem

Less than 40 miles east of Manchester, Sheffield nevertheless lies on the other side of the Pennines, the range of hills running from Scotland into England and dividing the island into east and west. Despite that geophysical separation, Sheffield musicians have often gravitated to Manchester, which was how one of the most theatrically innovative musician-performers of the midsixties came to have Danny Betesh as his agent.

Dave Grundy grew up in a musical family; his father, who had been a semi-professional jazz drummer, often read sections of *Melody Maker* to his son and took him to see touring American jazz musicians. The teenager largely skipped skiffle for rock 'n' roll, first playing drums with a guitarist in a duo that gradually grew into a group celebrating Chuck Berry and his songs about cruising in automobiles. Thus, when Grundy became the singer in 1960, he adopted the stage name Dave Berry, and his band became the Cruisers.

With the success of the Beatles, Berry remembers, "record companies went scouring the country," particularly the north, looking for gold (interview 24 March 2004). Among those scouts, Decca's Mike Smith trekked to the town of Doncaster, east of Sheffield, to see and hear Berry and the Cruisers. Smith clearly heard and saw possibilities, but Berry's first three Decca releases would be covers, each a different slice of American popular music. Chuck Berry's "Memphis, Tennessee" (September 1963), Elvis's "My Baby Left Me" (January 1963), and the Shirelles' "Baby It's You" (April 1964) all charted but did so in a wave of British artists doing similar material. Adapting, Smith and Berry began plotting a more distinctive niche.

The Crying Game. In the sixties, producers like Smith commonly chose possible songs to record before discussing them with clients like Berry. Thus, in June 1964, when the singer took the train south to London and Decca's headquarters, he did so to routine Reg Guest's arrangement of Geoff Stephens's "The Crying Game."[13] Smith felt that Stephens's unusual ballad about lost love called for something special and asked Guest to score strings as backing. After listening to the recording, however, Smith decided that a core ensemble of guitars, piano, bass, and drums best captured the ethereal atmosphere of the song and the performance, particularly with Jim Sullivan on guitar.

Sullivan demonstrated why he was one of the most requested session guitarists in London by deftly weaving a virtuosic line around Berry's breathy leaping vocal. Meant for a pedal steel guitar and anticipating later technologies, his DeArmond foot pedal controlled both volume by pressing or releasing it and tone by swiveling it.[14] The crying sound Sullivan produced would influence scores of guitarists, and "The Crying Game" (July 1964) reached #5 on *Record Retailer*'s charts, supported by Berry's appearances on *Top of the Pops* (12 and 19 August and 2 September) and *Thank Your Lucky Stars* (22 August). The sound, however, was not be the only remarkable feature to emerge from these performances.

After watching Gene Vincent's "static approach ... where [he had a] microphone ... on the stand that would be outstretched like an extra leg," Berry developed his own idiosyncratic performance style (Berry interview 24 March 2004). Gingerly holding the microphone in his hands while moving slowly, deliberately, and dramatically, he accentuated these moves by dressing in black so that only his hands and his face stood out as he wrapped the stage curtain around him, augmented by a lighting specialist who focused a bright white spot on him.

In keeping with Kate Fox's observation that the English never want to appear too earnest, Berry offers that this dramatic presentation "was always supposed to be more tongue-in-cheek and funnier than it would seem" (interview 24 March 2004). Nevertheless, his stage presence anticipated performers like David Bowie.

Northeastern Escape

On beyond Liverpool, Manchester, and Sheffield, in the River Tyne's historic coal country (Tyneside) and on northeast England's coastal plain, the city of Newcastle upon Tyne suffered many of the same indignities as other northern industrial cities. The Great Depression and wartime bombing had crippled the region's economy, and in the postwar years, as coal pits and shipbuilding yards struggled, unemployment represented a norm. For those who held jobs, working

---

[13] See Thompson 2008, 175–178.
[14] Sullivan had first heard the effect on the Chet Atkins recording "Boo Boo Stick Beat" and solicited a friend to bring him one from the US. "There were lots of musicians playing on the boats, going on the trips over to New York," the guitarist remembered. "They'd go into Manny's and bring whatever we wanted back" (interview 24 January 2001).

conditions could be brutal, with industrial accidents devastating lives that relied on community ties for survival.[15] Unions gave a voice to those in industries large enough to support them, but many labored in small establishments where safety oversight was minimal.

Like the Scousers of Merseyside, the Geordies of Newcastle have celebrated their distinctive dialect and local customs and have resented the perceived privileges of England's southerners. As print and increasingly electronic media brought news of the world into their homes, many working-class Tynesiders also saw parallels between their lives and the systemic suppression of Black Americans. In particular, the civil rights struggle in the United States held special significance for young Geordie musicians, who responded to the lyrics and the music of blues and rhythm-and-blues artists. To escape the poverty, violence, and limited options of northeast England, one group of musicians found a path to the outside world through songs about America's dark corners.

Geordie Accent

In Newcastle, young musicians interested in blues and rock 'n' roll from across the city found each other in clubs, pubs, and dance and church halls where the music, lubricated by hormones and alcohol, drew enthusiastic teens eager to forget Tyneside. The realities of northeastern working-class life soon closed in on most of them, but music lured a select few looking for a way out.

Eric Burdon grew up in East Newcastle, where his electrician father earned enough as an independent contractor to stay off the factory floor and to buy one of the first televisions in their neighborhood. In art school, the teen joined a trad band and became a singer, which was where he encountered trumpeter and drummer John Steel, who remembered that his fellow student "couldn't play trombone to save his life" (White 2011). Rock 'n' roll and blues soon captivated Burdon, bringing him onto a scene where Alan Price was also active.

After an industrial explosion killed Price's father and the factory resisted paying compensation, his mother worked to give her grammar-school son piano lessons (Welch 23 March 1974). With a good ear, he was soon playing piano and guitar in different bands while working in a tax office by day. By the early 1960s, he had recruited Bryan "Chas" Chandler, a shipyard worker and a bassist, to form the Alan Price Trio.

A'Gogo. Price and Burdon first encountered each other in local talent contests, where Burdon was offering his blues renditions and Price was channeling Jerry

---

[15] The march known as the Jarrow Crusade/March (1936) offers an example of how workers responded to southern indifference to Tyneside's economic problems.

Lee Lewis. To Burdon, however, Price was an outsider and "not a native son" of Newcastle because he been born a dozen miles away in the port of Sunderland and had gone to school in Jarrow, across the Tyne River (Burdon with Craig 2001, 10). Their differences, though small, set them at odds from the beginning, with social microaggressions further driving a wedge between them. Nevertheless, Burdon and Price needed each other's skills, and with Steel and Chandler, the Alan Price Rhythm and Blues Combo became the house band at the Club A'Gogo.[16] They needed a guitarist, however.

With his father having abandoned the family and his mother having passed away, teen Hilton Valentine found work in a furniture factory. Economically resourceful, he learned guitar by convincing friends to pay him to take lessons ("2 shillings and sixpence" each), after which he then taught them.[17] By the time he was 20, he was eager to quit the factory and become a professional musician, which was what happened when he joined Price and Burdon at the Club A'Gogo (Gary James 2005; Roger Smith 2011 and 2012).

On the Origin of Animals. Watching from the wings, London native Mike Jeffery, the son of postal workers, had served two tours in the British army before establishing himself in Newcastle by managing a series of clubs. Musically nondenominational, he changed bands as audience tastes moved from jazz to rhythm and blues, for which the Alan Price Rhythm and Blues Combo had the required skills (Hamilton 2010). When visiting American blues artists such as John Lee Hooker and Sonny Boy Williamson toured the northeast, Price's band accompanied them, as well as playing with tours like the Everly Brothers when they came to town, often ending up at the Club A'Gogo. And when the band opened for the Graham Bond Organisation, Bond recommended a name change to help break into the London circuit (White 2011).

With Epstein-like promises of steady work and a recording contract, Jeffery dubbed them the "Animals" (Roger Smith 2011 and 2012; White 2011).[18] In London, he met with agents and other club managers, including Ronan O'Rahilly (The Scene) and Giorgio Gomelsky (The Crawdaddy Club), who booked the Animals for gigs. Pursuant to his promise of a recording contract, he met with a fledgling independent producer, Peter Hayes, who had already heard the band in Newcastle back in October 1963 when he had been a supporting act on an Everly Brothers' tour.

---

[16] Advertising restrictions sometimes reduced their name to "the Alan Price Combo."
[17] That arrangement ended once he found a self-instructional book that promised "1,000 chords for half a crown," an investment that allowed him to move from skiffle to rock 'n' roll (Guerra n.d.; Hoffmann 2011).
[18] Burdon claims that the name change was his suggestion and referred to the nickname of a gang member and patron at the Club A'Gogo (Gary James 2010).

The Rising House Band

The son of a regimental sergeant major, Hayes had grown up in Aldershot—the "home of the British army"—about 40 miles southwest of metropolitan London. Unconvinced that school had much to teach him, he left and "just didn't show up for the last six months" (Tobler and Grundy 1982, 125). Exempted from military service by a factory foot injury, he became a habitué of the 2i's, where he and a friend formed a singing duo called the Most Brothers, for which Hayes became Mickie Most. When the duo dissolved in December 1958, he moved to South Africa to start a career recording and producing his own records before returning to London in 1962 to form Mickie Most and the Gear. In that incarnation, he was on tour with Bo Diddley, the Everly Brothers, and the Rolling Stones when, after a concert in Newcastle (18 October 1963), he heard the house band at the Club A'Gogo.

London presented opportunities for independent producers with their ears to the ground, as recording studios multiplied in response to the world taking notice of British pop. Thus, when Jeffery approached him about the Animals, Most set up a recording session for late February 1964 in the subterranean De Lane Lea Studios opposite the Holborn tube station.[19] He also had specific ideas about what they should record. British artists had long scoured American charts for records they could cover as closely as possible. Mickie Most, however, looked more creatively into Americana and asked the Animals to listen to Bob Dylan's first album and to reimagine what they heard. Perhaps the Animals could rock some folk.

Rocked Folk. Released in March 1962, Dylan's eponymous LP contained a mix of songs currently popular on the American folk circuit as well as his original tunes. The disc had already generated a hit with "Blowin' in the Wind" (June 1963) for Peter, Paul, and Mary, and Mickie Most could not have missed the disc when he flew to New York in search of material. John Steel notes that the "only reason we did 'Baby Let Me Take You Home' as our first single" was because Most suggested that they adapt it (White 2011). Their adaptations include an anglicization of the song's title, "Baby Let Me Follow You Down," the replacement of the spoken introduction with a Hilton Valentine guitar solo, the insertion of a Burdon monologue in the middle, and a faux gospel ending.[20] When Columbia released "Baby Let Me Take You Home" (March 1964), appearances on *Ready, Steady, Go!* (20 March) and *Thank Your Lucky Stars* (4 April) as well as a national

---

[19] Most asserted that he paid for the session. "I'll bring you down to London and I'll pay for the recording session, and if you don't like it, then that's it—you've got nothing to lose" (Tobler and Grundy 1982, 126).

[20] In addition, Burdon references the Rolling Stones' recent recording of Lennon and McCartney's "I Wanna Be Your Man."

tour supporting Chuck Berry and Carl Perkins helped the disc climb to #21 on *Record Retailer*'s chart.

For a follow-up, they took a train after a performance in Liverpool and stopped on their way to Southampton in London, where Most drove them to De Lane Lea for an 8:00 AM session (Buskin 2003). He had given them another song to develop, indeed the very next song from the same Dylan album. For the bluesy "The House of the Rising Sun" (June 1964), Hilton Valentine again provides the introduction, with Price building the arrangement by gradually adding the distinctive sound of his electronic Vox Continental. After a quick sound check, they recorded it in one take, "straight to mono" (Buskin 2003). By 8:15 AM and take 2, Most had the recording he wanted, and they spent the rest of the session working on an album he anticipated would be their next step.

The recording of "The House of the Rising Sun," however, lasted four and a half minutes in an era when broadcast practice expected recordings to be no longer than three minutes.[21] Nevertheless, the relatively new format of the vinyl microgroove 45-rpm disc had extended the possible duration of a recording to a little over seven minutes, much longer than the older shellac 78 rpm discs. Leasing the entire recording of "The House of the Rising Sun" to Columbia, Most argued: "if it's boring then it's too long, and if it's not boring, it's got to be right" (Tobler and Grundy 1982, 127). The disc topped British charts in July, and in early September did the same in the United States. By October, the Animals were in New York and on *The Ed Sullivan Show*.

---

[21] Dylan's version lasts 5:20 minutes.

Fig. 11.1 The Searchers, on *The Ed Sullivan Show*, 5 April 1964.

Fig. 11.2 The Hollies, on *Top of the Pops*, 1964.

Fig. 11.3 The Animals, on *The Ed Sullivan Show*, 24 January 1965.

12
Middle English

In *Life, the Universe, and Everything*, Douglas Adams's protagonist, Arthur Dent, learns how to fly by allowing himself to be distracted at the last instant while throwing himself at the ground, which he consequently misses leading to the ability to self-levitate (1982, 363). Sixties British pop might be described the same way. That is, in the process of imitating Americans, British songwriters, musicians, and producers often failed to copy exactly but, by adding their own stylistic accent, created their own version.

The idea of accent can be applied to linguistic and physical behaviors that individuals consciously and unconsciously adopt as part of their identities. English southerners, for example, watched in 1963 and 1964 as one after another northern performer crashed into the pop charts and onto their television screens. Singers who had once affected American accents now sometimes wondered if they needed to sound Scouse. Furthermore, in addition to regional associations, language communicates class markers with Britain's educational institutions playing a powerful role in defining and perpetuating social behaviors.

Class Convergence. Despite characterizations of sixties Britain as an era of classlessness (Donnelly 2005, 92) or of "class convergence" (Bradley 1992, 93), middle-class performers, especially those living in and around London,[1] nevertheless held strategic advantages. Indeed, most music executives, publishers, and managers came from or associated themselves with the middle class. Their economic safety positioned them to know that success was not only possible but also optional. Paul Atkinson of the Zombies, for example, considered being a pop musician an avocation: "we weren't looking for a ticket out.... We all, individually, could have gone to university and done well" (Johansen 2001, 73).

Fox also contends that class has little to do with "income or occupation" but can be better understood through the concept of cultural and "linguistic capital" (2014, 115). Vocabulary and pronunciation mark the individual, and she cites George Bernard Shaw's declaration that "it is impossible for an Englishman to open his mouth without making some other Englishman hate him or despise him" (2014, 101). However, numerous other markers also signal class association.

---

[1] The home counties include Buckinghamshire, Hertfordshire, Essex, Berkshire, Middlesex, Surrey, Kent, and Sussex, and surround London.

Among the rituals characterizing the English middle class, for example, Fox suggests that weddings copy protocol carefully, while nevertheless illustrating how to do things distinctively (2014, 541–542). That model might also be applied to music and recordings by mid-1960s English middle-class songwriters, musicians, and producers.[2] Musical choices (songs, instrumentation, arrangements, etc.) and performative behavior (clothing, posture, social interaction, etc.) needed to adhere to music industry standards. But the English music scene also found ways to personalize performances by adding subtle accentuations that, although often innocuous and sometimes trite, were also on occasion quite successful.

Middle-Class Folk

The singing voice, a powerful way to express identity,[3] represents one of the hallmarks of British music, whether in Thomas Tallis's choral works, pornographic bawdy ballads, or the congregational hymn singing that has long served as an important part of Protestant worship, where it has informed the ears of many young musicians. Moreover, group singing has served as a unifying national musical response, as heard in the singing of "God Save the Queen" and Thomas Arne's "Rule Britannia" at the end of the annual BBC Proms. At the local level, raucous sing-alongs in pubs once offered more profane manifestations of this cultural preference that music-hall performers exploited to draw in audiences.

Singing in unison can blend voices to form a collaborative sound, suggesting a shared mission while representing a musically safe approach with two or more voices supporting each other. By extension, the interdependence of harmony singing offers a division of labor that creates a sound one individual could not achieve, while expanding the possibilities of creating something unique. Rehearsed closely blended voices singing both in unison and in harmony can also offer parallels to the middle-class wedding model: no surprises in form but with the possibility of something distinctive. Two British male singing duos of 1964 offer examples of how middle-class musicians came to their profession, how they represented the values of English culture, and how audiences understood them.

---

[2] Fox differentiates lower-middle, middle-middle, and upper-middle classes.
[3] Alan Lomax in his work on cantometrics (e.g., "Universals in Song" 1977) explored how to describe music through a variety of parameters such as vocal quality (nasality, rasp, etc.), group cohesiveness (e.g., tonal blend), organization (e.g., solo to multipart), and other parameters, and associates them with the social structures of cultures.

Swiss Cottage

Despite government attempts to standardize Britain's educational system, it still retained some of its historic quirkiness. Thus, although David Chadwick and Jeremy Clyde came from different backgrounds and parts of the country, they came together through music and institutional windows intended to reward talent.

Chadwick, the northerner son of a lumber foreman and a nurse, showed early musical promise, earning scholarships, first as a chorister at Durham Cathedral,[4] and later as a student at the Central School of Speech and Drama, Swiss Cottage, London. There he met Clyde, a southerner (grandson of Gerald Wellesley, the seventh Duke of Wellington), who had attended Eton and studied at Grenoble University, France, before entering the Central School (Dave Thompson 2000). They connected when Chadwick taught Clyde how to play "Apache" (and more) and the two began performing, in which contexts David "Chad" Chadwick became Chad Stuart.

On leaving school, Stuart worked for a music publisher, while Clyde pursued acting in Scotland, but chance and an actor's strike intervened, and the acoustic duo reconvened in London to play milquetoast folk songs in clubs and cafes. As they worked through a set at Tina's in posh Mayfair, composer and bandleader John Barry sat and listened. Although already involved in scoring films, including the recently released Bond flick *From Russia with Love*, Barry had agreed to produce singles for the independent label Ember Records.[5]

Yesterday's Gone. To Barry, the folk duo offered the prospect of a refined English version of the Everly Brothers. Among the tunes they played for him, Stuart's "Yesterday's Gone" sounded promising, and in signing the duo to Ember, the producer let the songwriter score the accompaniment. In the recording, the duo sings in soft unison, almost whispering, and blending their voices until the song's coda, when the songwriter wafts to a harmonizing part: nonthreatening yet distinctive.

Chad Stuart and Jeremy Clyde's "Yesterday's Gone" (September 1963), however, sold only modestly. In addition to the duo's select but limited fan base, Ember lacked the resources and experience to promote the disc. Disappointed after the failure of a follow-up, Barry bought out his contract. To replace him, Ember engaged recent American arrival Shel Talmy, who was having British success with the Irish trio the Bachelors (see Gordon Thompson 2008).

Talmy had moved to London from Los Angeles as a freelancer and agreed to produce the album, but Ember proved reluctant to release it. The *Daily Express* had published a photo (the idea of the duo's manager) of a nine-year-old Clyde

---

[4] Fifteen miles south of Newcastle.
[5] Owned by Jeff Kruger, the proprietor of the Flamingo Club.

dressed in velvet and standing beside his maternal grandfather at Queen Elizabeth's coronation. For Stuart, the publication of Clyde's photo meant they could never be successful in the UK: "if you're an aristocrat, in the eyes of your average working class hero, you're an 'over-privileged, pompous, little twit'" (Craig Harris 2009, 22). America, however, was enamored with British pop.

The Pittsburgh-based World Artists Records, a new independent label eager to be part of what the press was beginning to call a "British Invasion," had picked up the American distribution of "Yesterday's Gone" and began promoting it (April 1964). When WABC New York put the single into rotation, it reached into the station's top 20.[6] Encouraged by that success in the summer of Beatlemania, World Artists made plans to release the album Talmy had recorded and selected "A Summer Song" (July 1964) for release as a single. As Chad and Jeremy (rather than their full names), their album *Yesterday's Gone* (July 1964) sold well, and media exposure helped the single to reach #7 on *Billboard*'s charts that fall.

Expatriates. American television programmers, in search of Beatles-like ratings, booked the duo for several shows, beginning with the weekly variety program *The Hollywood Palace* (25 April 1964). Their continued American success with "Willow Weep for Me" (November 1964) prompted the duo to move to California, where their training as actors helped them land spots on programs such as *The Patty Duke Show* (17 February 1965). Meanwhile, in the UK, few cared.

World Artists marketed them in the United States as parent-friendly and dressed in English business attire: bowler hats, pin-striped suits, and umbrellas. The connection to the Duke of Wellington, moreover, made them even more marketable to the royalty-obsessed in the United States. In the UK, however, they remained a novelty, even after appearances on *Thank Your Lucky Stars* and hosting one episode (15 August 1964). Moreover, they were working in the shadow of a better-connected folk-pop duo.

Westminster

History abides in the shadows of Westminster Palace, on the grounds of Westminster Abbey, where the elite Westminster School for Boys put down roots in the fourteenth century. This setting proved auspicious enough for two professional-class teens to start singing together.

Peter Asher and his sister Jane had been child actors,[7] his father was a prominent psychiatrist, and his mother taught oboe at the Guildhall School of Music, where George Martin had studied with her. As a student at Westminster, Asher

---

[6] American stations often had their own disc rankings.
[7] E.g., "The Children of the Greenwood" episode of *The Adventures of Robin Hood* (2 April 1956).

was a proponent of modern jazz until another student, a year behind him, broadened his interests. Gordon Waller—another professional-class student, the Scottish-born son of a surgeon—loved the modern pop coming out of America. The schoolmates took up playing guitars and singing, sometimes as Gordon and Peter but eventually as Peter and Gordon, and continued even after Asher had gone on to study philosophy at the University of London, leaving Waller to find ways to circumvent Westminster's curfew.

Among their gigs, they scored a slot at comedian Harry Secombe's Pickwick Club, which was where EMI producer Norman Newell heard them (Leigh 22 July 2009). In 1964, Newell represented old-school music at EMI, more comfortable with musicals and opera than rock 'n' roll. In Asher and Waller's performance, however, he heard polite folk-pop: conventional yet original. Moreover, Asher's sister's boyfriend was Paul McCartney (Leigh 2004).

Jane Asher—a regular panelist on *Juke Box Jury*—had met the Beatles after their Albert Hall debut when, aged 16, she had reviewed the concert for the magazine *Radio Times*. When she and McCartney had begun seeing each other, and with the Liverpudlian needing a place to stay in London, the Asher family had offered a room in their proper Wimpole Street home. With Lennon and McCartney sometimes writing in the basement music room and McCartney debuting bits for the family, Asher and Waller had heard an unfinished song.

Lock Me Away. McCartney had started "A World without Love" years earlier, but the Beatles seemed unlikely to record it, given Lennon's blunt assessment that the lyrics were risible, particularly the opening phrase, "Please, lock me away." The song remained incomplete until McCartney, with Jane Asher taking a role in the creation of the chorus, offered it to Peter and Gordon (Peter Jones 11 April 1964). Like the songs that Stuart and Clyde recorded in this era, "A World without Love" offers sentimentality and a dreamy state of ennui.

Song and artists secured, Newell turned to Geoff Love to arrange and to direct the performance. The son of an American, Love was one of the few Black British artists working in London's music business and had a reputation for the kind of light, popular orchestral arrangements Newell preferred.[8] For Peter and Gordon, however, Love drew on his work for Jack Good's *Oh Boy!* when he had included an organ and asked for Vic Flick, the guitarist from the John Barry Seven. The basic ensemble (guitars, organ, bass, and drums) relies on an unusually heavy

---

[8] Love's biggest success came with a series of albums under the title "Manuel and His Music of the Mountains."

bass line for 1964 over a sustained but often almost inaudible organ wash with acoustic-guitar chords,[9] punctuated by Vic Flick's electric 12-string guitar riffs.[10]

Peter and Gordon's "World without Love" (February 1964) charted almost immediately and, with appearances on *Thank Your Lucky Stars* (14 March) and several trips to *Top of the Pops* (beginning 25 March), rose to the top of British charts by the third week of April. In the United States, EMI's subsidiary, Capitol, released the disc at the end of April and saw it accomplish the same on *Billboard*'s charts by the end of June.

Nobody I Know. With that success, McCartney's follow-ups "Nobody I Know" (May 1964) and "I Don't Want to See You Again" (September 1964) built on the formula. The success of Peter and Gordon drew not only on the popularity of the Beatles and the clout that major companies like EMI and Capitol had over independents like Ember and World Artists but also on the marketing of their image. Interviews with the duo (e.g., Altham 26 September 1964) and with Jane Asher (Peter Jones 11 April 1964) reference their academic backgrounds, which in Britain pegged them as solidly middle class. Like Chad and Jeremy—both playing acoustic guitars and singing, one bespectacled and the other not—they represented a subdued sexuality in comparison to the rhythm-and-blues beginning to percolate. Not all middle-class performers, however, fit so neatly into this envelope.

Polite English Rock

By the midsixties, Britain's capital had risen from its postwar malaise like a phoenix from its ashes: sooty but reborn. The world—domestic and international—began arriving, eager to partake of the urban adrenaline experience that would eventually be called "Swinging London." Success, however, required more than talent.

Working-class provincial musicians like the Beatles and the Searchers showed up needing to find housing, with instruments and equipment (sometimes homemade) damaged from constant travel. Middle-class musicians living in or near London on the other hand, in addition to easier access to the business of music, were more likely to have professional-quality keyboards, guitars, amps, and drumkits. Moreover, with knowledge and education being signature parts of their social rank, these artists brought musical symbols of their erudition into their performances.

---

[9] Harold Smart's console organ presented problems. Flick recalls that on the day of the recording, the organist "had to get some city workers digging the road up outside, to bring his organ in.... He had this great big, Wurlitzer type of organ, with two poles carried ... like an emperor's litter" (interview 15 February 2001).

[10] Flick's guitar part echoes Cliff Richard and the Shadows' "Don't Talk to Him" not only in sound but also in melodic shape.

In the capital's cultural cauldron, musical influences and alliances were in a constant state of forming, dissolving, and reforming in search of the most successful social and musical amalgams. This environment facilitated the formation of groups with members from different ethnicities, classes, regions, and even countries. Indeed, vital urban centers rely on a continual influx and admixture of ideas and personalities, even if the juxtapositions are sometimes inherently unstable. At other times, of course, socially homogeneous formations emerged from neighborhoods and localities. All, however, were drawn to London's economic flame.

Musical identity in midsixties British pop employed aural glyphs to reference cultural affiliation and aspiration. For the middle class, familiarity with classical music and jazz and/or an esoteric knowledge of Black Americana could signal to the musical establishment and to audiences the relative social rank of musicians. Refraining from appearing too earnest and/or proud of that discernment, however, meant displaying a degree of politeness.

Commonwealth Clause

Manfred Lubowitz's parents had planned for him to join the family's Johannesburg printing business, but he never felt right about "bossing around all the people who had been with the firm 20 years" (Griffiths 1964). Instead, lessons with an American expatriate jazz pianist and with an Austrian professor in music theory sent him down a different path.

As South Africa slid deeper into apartheid, Lubowitz and others with the economic resources and inclination fled. His Commonwealth passport allowed emigration to London in 1961, where this self-confident music nerd's prospects for success seemed more promising than in Johannesburg.

In this new life, he became Manfred Manne (after American drummer Shelley Manne) under which name he wrote the occasional article on theory for *Jazz News* while picking up a few private students interested in improvisation. Like many other immigrants, he sought a new identity, and becoming Manne (and then Mann) reflected not just that but also the reality of anti-Semitism in Britain, where blending into society allowed one to avoid the more routine forms of discrimination.

When playing polite dinner music proved unrewarding, Manne took a dance band gig at a seaside resort where he and percussionist Mike Hugg began planning something more interesting than foxtrots (Webber 2014). As an investment in their future, they put aside money (£325) to cover the purchase of a Vox Continental electronic organ (Griffiths 1964).

Disgruntled College Beatniks. The Mann-Hugg Blues Brothers grew into a seven-piece ensemble that included Oxford University student Paul Pond, who had adopted the stage name Paul Jones as his musical persona while singing with Blues Incorporated (Jopling 16 May 1964). Besotted with blues and rhythm-and-blues recordings, Jones had cultivated a distinct vocal delivery—tight-throated and slightly nasal with a hint of rasp—and a stage presence that balanced a slinky hip swivel while rooted to the microphone stand (an adaptation to tight stage space).

Repertoire carried ideological and social significance in the sixties, and the musical aesthetics of this group were divided between Mann the jazz devotee and Jones the advocate for rhythm-and-blues. In the divide, Hugg played peacemaker by drawing the line at rock 'n' roll, justifying the band's inclusion of rhythm-and-blues in their repertoire as "nearer to being a jazz musician than a rock musician" (Jopling 2 May 1964).

Class and power also underlay the tension between the keyboardist and the singer: Mann an immigrant from the South African Jewish merchant middle class, Jones a product of the English Protestant professional class. The internal friction would prove a continuing challenge for their manager.

When Ken Pitt approached the Mann-Hugg Blues Band at a gig in early 1963 with a management proposal, he already had trepidations. The group hardly looked like pop stars with their "Marks & Spencer black roll-neck sweaters, beards, and thick rimmed glasses" that gave them (especially Mann) the appearance of "disgruntled college beatniks." Jones, however, was "boyishly good-looking" and a quick learner: he "improved so rapidly . . . [that] each day he'd learn something new [and] he would always go out beforehand and size up a stage" (Rogan 1988, 39–42).

After Mann reached the conclusion that five in the ensemble made more economic sense than seven, Pitt demonstrated his managerial value by securing a regular night at the Marquee. The club had become a routine haunt of London's record producers in search of talent, which was how EMI's John Burgess came to hear them. His work with Adam Faith and with Freddie and the Dreamers may not have impressed the band, but a contract with a major label did.

Down the Street. Renamed to simply Manfred Mann,[11] their first recording—Mann's instrumental "Why Should We Not" (July 1963)—displays the heterodyne core of the band, with a jazz-tinged Mike Vickers saxophone solo competing with a bluesy Paul Jones on harmonica (Webber 2014). That disc failed, but their next attempt—Jones's R&B-flavored "Cock-A-Hoop" (October 1963)—reached *Record Retailer*'s top five, a spot matched by the Jones-Hugg-Mann collaboration "5-4-3-2-1" (January 1964). That disc brought the band even further into

---

[11] Burgess may have precipitated the name change.

the national spotlight when *Ready Steady Go!* adopted about 40 seconds of it as opening theme music. The group-composed "Hubble Bubble (Toil and Trouble)" (April 1964) followed a similar formula as they contemplated how to be more than a jazz, blues, and R&B band.

Jones recommended the Exciters' "Do Wah Diddy," a disc that had done modestly well in the United States but failed to chart in the UK (Swanson 2015). Manfred Mann's performance of "Doo Wah Diddy Diddy"—with timpani rolls and clean stops—was too long, and Burgess, taking out the editing scissors at 01:42, removed a section to bring the recording's duration to a radio-friendly 02:22.

The band debuted "Doo Wah Diddy Diddy" on *Ready Steady Go!* (10 July 1964), followed by appearances on *Thank Your Lucky Stars* the next day and *Top of the Pops* shortly after that, with repeated showings. A month later, the disc topped British charts, but when EMI's American subsidiary, Capitol, declined to issue it, Burgess leased it to Ascot Records, and by the third week of October 1964, that disc sat at #1 on *Billboard*'s charts. To close out the year, they followed the same strategy of drawing on the American R&B charts to find and then successfully cover the Shirelles' "Sha-La-La." Pop culture, however, was shifting rapidly. Heading into 1965, the band was already looking for a new muse.

Saint Albans Enterprise

When the Romans built a road heading north out of London, the first major town travelers encountered had already been occupied for centuries: a proper origin site for a proper English band.

Rod Argent, Paul Atkinson, and Hugh Grundy met at the venerable Saint Albans School on the grounds of the cathedral and abbey of the Church of Saint Alban, where the three gravitated to the music club on Tuesday nights (Palao 1997, 7–8). Like his father, who had played in a dance band, Argent took up the piano, at first slogging through conservatory lessons until Elvis ignited his passion for rock 'n' roll, tempered by Miles Davis and Bill Evans, who opened his ears to jazz harmonies. Atkinson's family had similarly encouraged his musical interests by buying him a violin when he was 12, only to see him trade it for a guitar so he could play with his friends. Accompanying them, Grundy began tapping on tabletops as he imitated the drummers he saw on television and heard on recordings. Meanwhile, across town at the Saint Albans Grammar School for Boys, Colin Blunstone, who had been singing since boyhood, added a guitar to his unique vocal imitation of the American sound (Palao 1997, 8).

Around 1960, the three Saint Alban School students formed a band and brought along Argent's friend Paul Arnold on bass, even though he had played very little and would have to build his own instrument (Palao 1997, 8–9). Arnold, however, also knew Blunstone, both from grammar school and summer camp, so when they needed a guitarist who could sing, Arnold had a recommendation. Rehearsals at the local Blacksmiths Arms (April 1961) brought another Arnold suggestion: why not call themselves the Zombies (Faist 2007)?

They were financially comfortable enough that band revenue could be set aside to purchase a Vox AC30 amplifier and a Hohner Pianet. An amplified electric keyboard, as it had for Manfred Mann, allowed Argent to take musical control of the band, to shape their harmonies and melody lines, and to give them a jazzier tinge.

By 1963, as the suburban kids were reaching the end of their school days, they and their families contemplated universities and careers. Under the influence of the Beatles, however, Argent convinced his family that taking a gap year to be a musician would be a good thing. Arnold on the other hand had long planned on attending medical school and recruited Chris White to replace him on bass (Faist 2007). White had attended the Saint Albans Grammar School for Boys, like Blunstone. Moreover, his father had played bass in dance bands, and his uncle, Ken Jones, had been an arranger and bandleader who owned a production company. Consequently, White also brought social capital.

She's Not There. The turning point in this musical avocation came on 10 May 1964 at Watford Town Hall, where the "Herts Beat Contest" pitted Hertfordshire bands against each other in pursuit of £250 and bragging rights. The Zombies R&B (as they were sometimes called) won each round and, in the end, the contest. Scouting for talent in the comfortable leafy suburbs, Decca's Dick Rowe proffered a recording contract for their families to peruse, who in turn contacted Chris White's uncle, Ken Jones. Through Jones's Marquis Enterprises, they negotiated a contract with Decca, set up a generous publishing agreement for Argent and White, and arranged for Jones to produce and oversee the leasing of their recordings (Johansen 2001, 72).

The next month at Decca's studios, when the assigned recording engineer overindulged at lunch and was sent home, Jones turned to second engineer/tape operator Gus Dudgeon to record the session (Palao 1997, 17). Jones and Dudgeon nevertheless captured a crisp aural image of the band, who had prepared a Rod Argent's, "She's Not There." The song plays with major and minor tonalities over a Hugh Grundy and Chris White broken-beat accompaniment. The song, Blunstone's breathy ethereal voice, and the production result in a recording that hints at a supernatural presence reminiscent of the poetry of Percy Bysshe Shelley.

When debuted on *Juke Box Jury* (25 July 1964), "She's Not There" impressed panelist George Harrison, and it soon reached into the UK's top 20 before climbing into the top five in the United States (Palao 1997, 18).[12] Although

---

[12] The Beatles would soon begin using a Hohner Pianet on their recordings.

their next release, Chris White's "Leave Me Be" (October 1964), failed to chart, Argent's "Tell Her No" (January 1965) made *Billboard*'s top 10 in the United States. That disc, however, only broke into *Record Retailer*'s top 50, partly due to the band's limited UK exposure.

Convinced that they needed someone able to get them better engagements and media presence, they switched from Marquis to Cliff Richard's former manager, Tito Burns, without fully understanding why Richard had fired him. They soon learned. Burns hired his wife as their agent, which allowed the couple to routinely scoop up around 60 percent of the band's performance income. Even when the musicians began to understand this conflict of interest, they continued to retain the Burnses in the hope that they could get them "airplay and TV" (Palao 1997, 18).

Whenever You're Ready. Like Chad and Jeremy, the Zombies found themselves in a curious position: they were more successful in the United States than the UK. Definitions of musicianship, however, determined how the American music industry treated them.

The American Federation of Musicians and the Musicians' Union (MU) in Britain had collateral policies that limited who could perform in their respective countries (Johansen 2001). The American Federation of Musicians treated Chad and Jeremy as singers, not musicians (i.e., they were not primarily instrumentalists) and allowed them to tour. In the surge of British acts looking to cross the Atlantic, however, the Zombies played instruments and were prohibited from touring the United States outside the five boroughs of New York City.

The Zombies' trip to America at the end of 1964 initially held the promise of a breakthrough, until the American Federation of Musicians limited their visas to playing "Murray the K's Xmas Show" at the Fox Theatre, Brooklyn, and an appearance on the debut episode of NBC's *Hullabaloo* (12 January 1965). Brooklyn's cold winter provided the backdrop to shows that were at once grueling and boring: short sets played between cartoons followed by waiting backstage for hours. The next year held further disappointment when Argent's "She's Coming Home" (March 1965) and "Whenever You're Ready" (September 1965) failed to chart despite their growing a fan base.

English Translation. Americans heard something in the Zombies that the British failed to perceive. John Mendelsohn in *Rolling Stone* (1969), for example, described the band's sound as distinctively "more English" than that of their British contemporaries, which he attributed largely to Argent. By way of proof, he correlated their aesthetic approach with the relative absence in their setlists of American rock 'n' roll like Chuck Berry, Buddy Holly, and others who had figured prominently in the repertoires of bands like the Beatles. Instead, standards like "Summertime" suggested associations with jazz.

When Mike Saunders (1972) later suggested that their sound had "something to do with feminism," he may have been referring to Blunstone's voice, which contrasts dramatically with stereotypical contemporary male voices like those of Tom Jones or the Walker Brothers. Saunders may have also had in mind the dominance of the keyboard rather than electric guitars or, more likely, the hints of ideational complexity and the absence of extravagant technical virtuosity.

Both American authors might have said the same for Manfred Mann, or Chad and Jeremy or Peter and Gordon for that matter. The critics' backgrounds—rooted in responding to rock 'n' roll, rhythm and blues, and blues forms and performances—clearly inform their descriptions: jazz-influenced pop meant Frank Sinatra to them rather than Thelonius Monk.

These and other observations suggest that some Americans perceived Englishness as rooted in musical and production styles that Saunders describes as "polite rock." This model poses American rock as masculine and associated with the sexual aggressiveness of blues-based forms. In contrast, Saunders perceives emergent sophisticated rock as feminine. The picture would grow even more complicated over the decade.

Fig. 12.1 Chad and Jeremy, on *American Bandstand*, 28 November 1964.

Fig. 12.2 Peter and Gordon, in *Pop Gear*, 1964.

Fig. 12.3 Zombies, on *Shindig!*, 1965.

13
An Independents Movement

When Joseph Lockwood became chair of EMI in 1954, the company had been recording music on lathes and distributing it on 78-rpm shellac discs while losing money manufacturing radios and televisions. Musically, EMI's catalogue had concentrated on orchestras and chamber music along with various mainstream British and American artists such as Eddie Calvert and Frank Sinatra, all primarily intended for domestic consumption (Martland 1997, 150). A technological revolution, however, was about to upend the business. Magnetic tape and recorders were transforming studios as consumers began searching for 45-rpm singles and 33 1/3-rpm albums pressed in vinyl, both of which were quieter, lighter, and less breakable than shellac 78s. Ten years later, EMI was recording some of the era's best-selling British pop artists and had purchased Capitol Records in North America to become part of a growing and lucrative global market.

With British artists attracting international attention in the midsixties, London's music and recording industries scrambled to provide musical and recorded content to millions of adolescents. Corporations lacked nimbleness, but corporate producers had advantages: prime access to some of the city's best studios, equipment, and staff and the resources to fund arrangers and session musicians. Corporations also had their own pressing plants and promotion and distribution systems for getting discs to market. Moreover, although corporate producers received very few direct monetary rewards if a disc sold well, they also did not risk personal loss if it flopped. A byproduct of this approach, however, was a culture comfortable with the predictable.

When Dick Rowe at Decca allegedly told Brian Epstein in 1962 that guitar groups were on the way out, Rowe may have been seeing a trend of singers accompanied by orchestras or perhaps of Phil Spector–like walls of sound. Even though Decca would sign a guitar group anyway, they did so because it seemed the safe thing to do. Corporations, nevertheless, survived or failed by how successfully they found and exploited new creative talent, and increasingly they turned to other sources to provide the content they needed.

Outside Talent. Rather than feeling threatened by the growing success of independent producers, corporations came to rely on them. Having an outsider expend the time, energy, and resources to find new artists, to oversee a recording, and often to pay for studio time all saved a corporation money. Leasing a recording allowed a corporation to decide whether to press and to distribute. If the disc sold, the company profited. If it failed, the independent and/or their backers bore the creative costs. In addition, although the independent often owned the master recording and leased it to the corporation, the consensus of the time was that discs had a relatively short shelf life and little lasting value.

Independent producers found and recorded performers and music on the creative edges of the British popular music scene. They had models in American producers like Sam Phillips, who had first recorded and distributed Elvis Presley, Carl Perkins, Jerry Lee Lewis, and others. In America, however, studios like Phillips's were scattered across the nation's urban landscapes, while Britain's independent studios were mostly located in and around London.

Around the city, unsurprisingly, studio competition intensified to find new artists to replace those who had already seen their moment of fame evaporate into the pop ether. This intense competition contributed to a gradual industry-wide upheaval, and in the mid-1960s, a multileveled musical independence movement arose to liberate creativity and upend the status quo. The heart of British pop—songwriters and musicians—began bucking a hierarchical business embedded with barriers that blocked the success of newcomers and protected the privileges of the established. Casualties, however, mounted.

Most musicians lost out in this process as they struggled to understand what was happening to them and why everyone but them seemed to be profiting from what they had created. Musicians were, however, learning from each other's mistakes.

Group Survival

The size and complexity of a city offers numerous paths for those adventurous enough to explore its possibilities. Where some resign themselves to the stability of structures intended to preserve and protect establishment order, others embrace the opportunities of chaos. In the chaos of sixties London's socioeconomic environment, individuals employed their cultural expertise to survive, if not to flourish, all the while understanding that pitfalls lurked for the naïve. One strategy involved bonding with others for security.

Self-contained groups who sang and played instruments formed the bedrock of British pop in the mid-1960s, and accessing new material was the way to stand out from the competition. For independent producers, bands offered an economic advantage: they could rehearse independently and had a core of instruments ready to back a singer or singers.

Seemingly every city, town, and village across the UK produced ambitious musicians thrilled to have audiences in the back rooms of local pubs, in church halls, in school auditoriums, and in any space where youth culture dominated. Innumerable variations on the same two instrumentations (guitar-based and keyboard-based) played the same songs much the way everyone else did. The sheer number of participants, however, guaranteed the emergence of outliers, variants that most often proved dismal but sometimes revealed fleeting gems.

Invasion Pieces

The British Invasion began almost as a whimper. The success of "Glad All Over" in January 1964, just as the Beatles were breaking in the United States, positioned the Dave Clark Five to follow in their wake and onto American televisions and record players. Clark's agent, Harold Davison, however, heard problems in the studio and asked Les Reed (who had directed sessions by Joe Brown and others) if he would advise the DC5.

Reed's arrival at Lansdowne Studios in its leafy upscale Holland Park neighborhood found Clark and engineer Adrian Kerridge working on a follow-up with an issue they seemed to have either missed or were unable or unwilling to fix. Clark and singer-keyboardist Mike Smith had written "Bits and Pieces" after hearing and watching audiences stomp during the refrain of "Glad All Over," a sound effect they planned to incorporate into this new recording. As with "Glad All Over," they used session musicians, like drummer Bobby Graham, to build a saturated backing track. Reed, however, noted that Mike Smith's Vox Continental electronic organ was "out of tune" with the other instruments. (See Thompson 2008, 151.)

Fans, however, disregarded the tuning issues, and sales put "Bits and Pieces" (February 1964) at #2 on *Record Retailer*'s chart, which drew the attention of Ed Sullivan. Clark later claimed that he had initially turned the American down for a trip to New York because he "had never heard of Ed Sullivan." Nevertheless, the offer of "airfares, hotels, and everything" proved too tempting, which led to a nearly disastrous debut watched by millions almost exactly one month (8 March) after the Beatles had first appeared (Gary James 1994).

CBS Studio 50. To replicate the sound of their disc, Clark brought a prerecorded instrumental backing track for playback during the broadcast over which they would sing. When the curtains opened, however, the tape failed. Confusion reigned as several false starts were followed by a screen blackout that left the band awkwardly and obviously miming. Some suspected sabotage, but the band returned the next week as Epic Records sequentially released "Glad All Over," "Bits and Pieces," and "Do You Love Me," each reaching *Billboard*'s top 10 that spring.

Returning to Britain, work quickly began on their next single, Smith and Clark's "Can't You See That She's Mine," which they debuted on *Ready Steady Go!* (15 May 1964) to whet consumer appetites a week before its release. But rather than promote the disc in the UK, the band headed for North America.

As one of the first British bands to tour in 1964, the American Federation of Musicians granted them permission for two weeks of concerts, including four 24-minute shows at New York's Carnegie Hall (see Wilson 1964). To coincide with the American release of the recording and the day after the Carnegie appearances, they returned to CBS Studio 50 (five blocks away) for another appearance on *The Ed Sullivan Show* (31 May 1964).

For a few months in 1964, the Dave Clark Five rivaled the Beatles in the United States, but discs by other British pop acts were also being played. The American press was already using the phrase "British Invasion" to refer to the influx of plays, actors, and directors into theaters (e.g., Gross 21 October 1959) and the sudden appearance by British artists on American record charts prompted headline-hungry journalists to reapply that epithet.

Islington, Right?

The Mildmay Tavern in Islington had been in operation since Victorian times: a pleasant neighborhood pub that by the late 1950s had seen better days. Management had been hiring bands to attract clientele, which was how the Sheratons came to be on stage when two BBC television writers came to listen (Rogan 1988, 182).[1] Ken Howard and Alan Blaikley had met at the University College School in London before moving on to complete graduate degrees.[2] Although the BBC frowned on employees moonlighting, the two friends (under the nom de plume Howard Blaikley) had been writing songs and were looking for a band to record demos.

The Sheratons had been founded by hairdresser Martin Murray with vocalist Dennis D'Ell, guitarist Alan Ward, bassist John Lantree, and his sister, drummer Ann "Honey" Lantree. Honey Lantree was Murray's coworker, but, as a drummer she attracted audiences curious to see if a woman played differently from a man (Joynson 1995, 260). For the Sheratons, the proposal to record a demo for Howard and Blaikley offered a bit of excitement: a trip to a studio and perhaps a disc to show families and friends.

The best-known studio in Islington, RGM Sound occupied the upstairs over a leather-goods store on busy Holloway Road and belonged to Joe Meek. Listening

---

[1] Sources also describe them as the Sheritons or the Sherabons.
[2] Not to be confused with Alan Blakley of the Tremeloes.

to the songs and the band, the unorthodox producer concluded not only that Howard and Blaikley's "Have I the Right?" could be a hit but also that the Sheratons could be the vehicle. As with the Tornados and others, Meek applied his usual tape techniques with almost everything double-tracked and parts recorded at different speeds. Meek may also have been paying attention to the Dave Clark Five. Apropos of "Bits and Pieces," Meek added the effect of the Sheratons stomping in the stairway outside his studio.

Honeycomb. Looking to expand their enterprise, the songwriters proposed becoming the band's managers and had Howard's father (an entertainment lawyer) draw up a contract.[3] After lease rejections at EMI and Decca, Louis Benjamin at Pye expressed interest, albeit with one change: the band's name. Sensing marketing possibilities for a group featuring hairdressers and a woman drummer, he rechristened them the "Honeycombs."[4]

"Have I the Right?" (June 1964) initially did little in the charts, until the pirate station Radio Caroline began playing the disc, which led to an appearance on *Thank Your Lucky Stars* (1 August 1964) and repeated plugs on *Top of the Pops* (12 August to 9 September). By the end of August, the disc was selling more than any other in Britain and, in September, entered *Billboard*'s top five. Despite being blocked by the American Federation of Musicians from touring the United States, they formed part of a phalanx of British artists with success on American charts.

Unfortunately, their novelty was short-lived, and although they would have other successes, the next Howard and Blaikley release, "Is It Because?" (October 1964), barely scratched into the British top 40. But they had a more immediate problem. Murray's relationship with the band in general (and in particular with Honey Lantree) had deteriorated. Before they embarked on an Asia-Australia tour, the band and its founder severed relations.

Meanwhile, success and press coverage had also attracted the attention of the BBC, which learned that "Howard Blaikley" was two of its employees. When the Corporation demanded they cease and desist this outside work, the friends responded by resigning. "Pop music was the thing that England could do," and they had ambitions (Howard in Rogan 1988, 182).

The Hard Road

In London's "stockbroker's belt," more than 20 miles southwest and a world apart from Islington, another group of young musicians joined the rock 'n' roll revolution.

---

[3] The contract was based on theatrical Equity agreements, which was "unusually geared in the artiste's favour" (Rogan 1988, 182).

[4] Perhaps also Jimmie Rodgers's "Honeycomb" (1957).

They too stood out from the legions competing for gigs and proved themselves capable of playing with the best while still falling prey to the milieu's ruthless environment.

When John Hawken's pianist mother married an executive and moved her family from Weybridge to Manchester, her son forsook Chopin for Little Richard. Several years later, on returning to Surrey, the 18-year-old "looked so frightfully square: short back and sides ... lived in a nice house. ... Totally uncool ... [and] an absolute nerd." But he knew Little Richard's "Lucille" and "hammered the shit out of the piano" to join a band (Hawken interview 5 February 2011).

On the other socioeconomic side of Weybridge, Arthur Sharp's father had died at Dunkirk, and when his mother remarried, they had moved to a council house where going to "bed hungry was the norm." She worked "for the gentry, doing anything she could: polished, cleaned, and cooked. She was in service" (interview 22 March 2011). To make ends meet, Sharp found a job selling records in a shop, listening to the music customers ordered and imitating what he heard.

By 1962, Sharp and friend Ray Phillips had taken to singing together, but they needed better backing. After discussions and a few pints in a local pub, they merged with Hawken's band. They were in their twenties but chose to call themselves the Nashville Teens, referencing the Everly Brothers' "Nashville Blues."

Honing their chops playing pubs, clubs, and dance halls, they eventually packed in their day jobs, contacted an agent, turned professional, and headed for Europe. Life on the road, however, turned out to be less than glamorous. In Köln, West Germany, for example, they played six hours a night, Monday through Friday, with short breaks each hour, plus two one-hour matinees on Saturday and a one-hour matinee on Sunday. Each hour, the floor manager called out "Pause, Jetzt!" (break, now), followed a few minutes later with "Nicht Pause! Spielen Jetzt!" (No break! Play now!) (Hawken interview 8 February 2011).

Returning to Surrey, they were performing in Kingston upon Thames at the Jazz Cellar in late 1963 when Don Arden came looking for a band to accompany American artists. With the phrase "I'll make you stars" echoing in their ears, they opened for and backed Jerry Lee Lewis (March 1964) and then Carl Perkins (May 1964) on their British tours (Hawken interview 8 February 2011). With this exposure and with adolescents excited about groups, Arden scheduled a recording session.

That's the One. Mickie Most met them at De Lane Lea Sound Studios, where they played their cover of Mose Allison's "Parchman Farm" (1959); but after working on it for over an hour, the producer asked what else they had. Sharp had heard "Tobacco Road" when a customer had ordered the album *Twelve Sides of John D. Loudermilk* (1962), and as the band played their sped-up, electrified version, the producer began "leaping up and down" and declaring "That's it! That's the one" (Hawken interview 8 February 2011).[5]

With its theme of working-class poverty, "Tobacco Road" (June 1964) saw chart success in both the UK and the United States, which led to plans for an American tour and a spot on *Murray the K's Xmas Show*. The name "Nashville Teens," however, confused some American adolescents looking for British content. Moreover, although their follow-up—a cover of Loudermilk's "Google Eye" (October 1964)—reached #10 in Britain, American teens turned up their collective noses at a song about catching and frying fish. With "Google Eye" floundering in the charts and the American Federation of Musicians blocking a tour, Arden looked to salvage his investment by arranging for a recording session in New York.

When questioned about their production agreement with Most, Arden assured them: "Mickie's good with that. No problem" (Hawken interview 8 Febraury 2011). Thus, they recorded Dennis Lambert and Lou Courtney's "Find My Way Back Home" (February 1965) with the songwriters producing. Unfortunately, Arden had misled them, and Most rescinded their contract.

Back in the UK, as they began running out of money, they asked Arden for £1,200 in back pay, delegating Hawken to travel to Soho to collect the check. The manager offered him only £120. When Hawken protested, Arden rose from his desk, put his hands around Hawken's neck, and bent him out an upper-floor window, threatening: "You're going down, John." Hawken escaped and took the £120, but the Nashville Teens were left hanging professionally (Hawken interview 8 February 2011).

Not Like Everybody Else

In the sixties, one British pop group after another entered a recording studio, went on tour, experienced brief fame, struggled financially, and ultimately found themselves discarded. Some, however, survived by finding ways to challenge the music establishment.

Sixties British pop culture attracted individuals from different classes—insiders and outsiders with old and new ideas. The music they created grew out of attempts to sound American while failing successfully through a combination of skill, timing, and serendipity. That is, the emergence of an identifiable English-British style and sound came through individuals who purposefully and/or accidentally put an idiosyncratic stamp on both the music and recordings they created. Like the subjects of Joseph Campbell's *The Hero with a Thousand Faces*

---

[5] Most recorded the Animals' "House of the Rising Sun" with its parallel themes of poverty and alcoholism around the same time.

(1968), they had companions, were inspired by figurative gods and goddesses, confronted obstacles, had guides help them obtain a boon, and returned home transformed.

In at least one example, home was the reward.

Denmark Terrace

When the BBC first began television broadcasting in 1936, it chose Alexandra Palace for its studios and antenna. From the high grounds of this "Palace of the People," visitors could see the Thames and beyond on a clear day. Nearby, in the terraced shops, pubs, and houses of Muswell Hill and Fortis Green, working-class and lower-middle-class families built a vibrant community.

In one of these homes in Denmark Terrace, the Davies family raised eight children, with the two youngest—the only boys—developing interests in music.[6] For Ray and his younger brother Dave, music in the front room played a central role in family life, singing around the piano, plucking their father's banjo, or playing the radiogram so loudly that the speaker ultimately failed (Dave Davies 1996; Ray Davies 1994).

When Ray was about to turn 13, his oldest sister, Rene, visited from Oshawa, Ontario, and brought him an acoustic guitar for "Rayday" (his birthday). Her rebelliousness inspired him, but childhood rheumatic fever had compromised her health. She was home feeling she had little time left and, that night, went out dancing and died doing what she loved (Davies 1994, 35–36).

Given the size of the Davies clan and the limited space in the two-up-two-down family home, Ray moved in with his sister Peggy and her Irish husband, Mike Picker. Picker and Davies liked listening to records together and imitated the performers they heard, particularly Hank Williams and Buddy Holly. And when Picker began classical guitar lessons, he taught his young brother-in-law how to read music and play pieces by composers like Ferdinando Carulli. One night, Davies realized that he too could write music, and although his initial songs may have been "fucking brilliantly bad," they were his (Ray Davies 1994, 71).

Fortis Green. In the fall of 1961, a teacher at William Grimshaw Secondary Modern School asked who played an instrument. When 17-year-olds Ray Davies and Peter Quaife raised their hands and identified themselves as guitarists, the teacher encouraged them to form a band. Davies brought in his younger brother Dave on guitar, while Quaife brought a drummer (see Hinman 2004, 8–9). The Ray Davies Quartet played a mix of instrumentals and pop songs, with a fellow

---

[6] Davies is pronounced "Davis."

student named Rod Stewart singing with them at least once, but he never quite fit in (Rogan 2015, 66).

Increasingly interested in American blues and rhythm-and-blues, in December 1962, after Blues Incorporated had played at his school, the Hornsey College of Arts and Crafts, Davies asked Alexis Korner for advice about being a musician. Korner suggested talking to Giorgio Gomelsky, who in turn introduced Davies to Dave Hunt, a trombonist looking for a young guitarist who could read jazz charts (Rogan 2015, 83). Playing in that band introduced Davies to Soho's music scene and London's music culture.

Back home, Ray Davies rejoined his brother, with Quaife playing bass, and as the Boll-Weevils, they explored the musics of Americana (see Hinman 2004, 11–14). As they did so, however, a multitude of culturally embedded habits shaped by their English working-class lives inevitably changed the music. The ways they cut their hair, spoke, walked, and ate and a catalogue of other micro behaviors marked them every time they ventured out of the Denmark Terrace front room and the safety of Fortis Green. Their background also marked the ways they played music.

Denmark Street

With stories routinely in the papers about stars and their managers, Messrs. Robert Wace and Grenville Collins ventured to Denmark Street in search of a band. Wace worked by day at his father's company but dreamed of being Cliff Richard. His friend Collins, a trainee broker at the London Stock Exchange, positioned himself as a manager. Their expedition into the shadows of Saint Giles in the Fields proved successful when Terry Kennedy, a former member of Terry Dene and the Dene Aces, provided a contact that led them to the Boll-Weevils.

Gigs with Wace paid decently, and in addition to the clothing Collins purchased for them (not to mention the Vox AC30 amplifier), the now renamed Ravens encountered a posh side of London they had previously only seen in the papers and in films. The arrangement, of course, was fraught with problems from the start, beginning with Wace's discomfort with performing for anyone other than London's entitled. To the lads from Fortis Green, his accent and demeanor came across as a "camp comic fusion of Buddy Holly and Noël Coward" (Rogan 2015, 102).

Abandoning a singing career and reconsidering their business plan, Wace and Collins formed Bascobel Productions to manage the Ravens. They started by arranging for a recording session at Regent Sound Studios in Denmark Street to create a demonstration disc of originals and covers. Making the rounds, they attracted the attention of a talent manager.

Larry Page the "Teenage Rage" had been a minor celebrity in the fifties, but his lingering reputation derived from publicity stunts such as dyeing his hair blue. When his performance career tanked, he found his niche in promotion, eventually establishing Denmark Productions with publisher Edward Kassner. In their mutually beneficial arrangement, Page scouted, recruited, and managed talent while promoting songs published by his partner (see Rogan 1988, 137).

Page convinced the two gentlemen managers that he could advance the careers of their clients and have Kassner publish some of Ray Davies's songs for only 10 percent of the earnings. He steered them to Shel Talmy, an American, who heard potential in their demo disc and convinced Louis Benjamin at Pye to lease six sides. Before entering the studio, however, Page made one last major change. Given the number of other bands already named the "Ravens," that Quaife and Dave Davies had the habit of dressing in black leather, and that some had begun to apply the term "kinky" to their appearance, Page changed their name to the Kinks (see Hinman 2004, 17).

On the Road

At a Chinese-restaurant New Year's Eve gig, the soon-to-be Kinks impressed promoter Arthur Howes enough for him to add them to the Dave Clark Five's spring tour. Being on the road, however, meant turning professional. Dave Davies was already experimenting with unemployment, but Peter Quaife had a day job he would have to leave. As for Ray Davies, an academic advisor at the Croydon College of Art suggested he take a six-month leave to give music a chance (Hinman 2004, 19).

In preparing for their three-hour session at Pye, the band, the producer, and the unwieldy team of Wace, Collins, Page, Kassner, and Howes weighed which songs to record. Ray Davies had prepared several of his own compositions, including "You Still Want Me." The Beatles, however, were now closing their shows with "Long Tall Sally," and Howes insisted that this song be put into the queue (Hinman 2004, 19). Unsurprisingly, the powerful agent won out, and "Long Tall Sally" became their first release.

Talmy double-tracks Ray Davies's voice and harmonica over crunchy guitars while his bandmates add harmonies and punctuate the proceedings with screams to build excitement. They also, however, slow the groove from Little Richard's original panicked dash to the swagger of his "Lucille." Release prepared, advertising planned, and tour scheduled, all they needed was a drummer.

Talmy had booked the studio services of Bobby Graham for the Pye sessions, and the Kinks now held auditions for permanent band member at the Camden Head, a pub in Islington. Mick Avory had been active in the Blues Incorporated scene and had briefly drummed with the Rolling Stones. At the audition, however, he encountered Dave Davies and Peter Quaife camping it up to see how he reacted. He nevertheless took the gig, demonstrating a sense of humor, but this would not be the last time Dave Davies taunted him.

You Still Want Us? Quartet in place, Pye released "Long Tall Sally" (7 February 1964) and placed an ad (with a photo) on the front cover of the *New Musical Express*, the same day that a video of the band performing at Liverpool's Cavern Club appeared on *Ready Steady Go!* The DC5 tour where they could promote the recording, however, would not start until the end of March, and "Long Tall Sally" quickly slipped into inconsequence.

The Kinks joined the Hollies and others in Coventry for a tour, during which the Dave Clark Five's equipment sometimes blew theater fuses. Clark suspected sabotage,[7] and on the bus after the show in Southampton (1 May 1964) he issued a warning: if he caught the responsible parties, he would take them to his room for "a punishment of the severest nature" (Ray Davies 1994, 116). The bus, of course, suppressed chuckles.

Given the lackluster response to "Long Tall Sally" and rather than return to the studio to work on a new tune and recording, Pye released "You Still Want Me" (April 1964), once again supported by a front-page ad in the *New Musical Express*. Out-of-tune guitars mar the performance, but buried behind the double-tracked vocals and tightly compressed drums, Ray Davies offers hints of his future songwriting. Despite a positive review in the *New Musical Express* and the band touring, however, very few wanted the Kinks.

Pye had now released two of the three contracted discs. Only one remained. The Kinks were running out of chances, and Ray Davies for a few moments might have pondered what art supplies he would need when he returned to school in the fall.

People Fighting for Something

In the weeks leading up to the Dave Clark Five tour, Ray Davies sat at the family piano doodling with a couple of chords he had already been playing on guitar, toying with standard blues conceits, and remembering a woman he had seen while playing with Dave Hunt's band (Myers 29 October 2014). When the Kinks next gathered, they forged it into something more rock-like before heading to Regent Sound Studios to record a demo of this unmitigated proto-punk proclamation of lust.

The Kinks put "You Really Got Me" into their set, modifying their arrangement as the tour moved from theater to theater. At one point, after a discouraging

---

[7] Graham Nash supports this thesis (2013, 75).

concert review and their subsequent demotion on the program, Arthur Howes dispatched Billy Fury's former road manager to help. Hal Carter, while offering stage presentation advice, observed that the new song needed something. He suggested adding "even just plain 'girl'" at the beginning to personalize it (Ray Davies 1994, 147).

When the Kinks proposed "You Really Got Me" as their third single and Louis Benjamin rejected it, he encountered an immovable object. Like sister Rene's insistence on dancing, if this recording represented the Kinks' last stand, it would be on Ray Davies's terms. With their management and Shel Talmy supporting him, Benjamin relented, and the Kinks returned to Pye's studio in the middle of June.

This confrontation marks a significant moment. Benjamin rightfully heard the song as unconventional, if not rude. Nevertheless, for working-class musicians to question the judgment of the Pye Records CEO represented a challenge to class authority. The confrontation was not over.

You Got Me. Listening to the recording, Talmy recalled Ray Davies having "a hissy fit and decided he had to do it faster" (interview 21 July 2003). Over the next few weeks, Davies demanded that they record it again, and Benjamin refused. Strategically, Larry Page blocked Pye's release through his and Kassner's control of the publishing rights, but Wace and Collins would have to fund a new session for a sped-up and rougher-sounding "You Really Got Me."

Rather than Pye, they booked IBC, an independent studio in the basement of a converted Marylebone house. Once again, Talmy contracted Bobby Graham to drum, this time also recruiting veteran arranger and bandleader Arthur Greenslade to play piano. Greenslade remembered contractor Charlie Katz asking him to stay after a previously scheduled session that had ended at 10:00: "at the back of these studios, there would be a little mews and there was a pub there.[8] And I can remember Bob and me self, we went out through the back door of these studios, through the garden, and into the pub. . . . We came back in about 11:30. . . . And about twelve o'clock, who should come in but the Kinks" (interview 8 January 2002).

During the intensity of the studio performance, Ray Davies yelled during his brother's solo, "willing him to do it, saying it was the last chance we had" (Schaffner 1982a, 96). Indeed, some of the most distinctive aspects of the performance lay in the simple guitar-chord voicings and the overdriven sound of the amplifier. Dave Davies recalls that he plugged his guitar into a smaller amp with a ripped cone and then "into my AC30, and it really came to life. It was the first 'effect pedal'" (Fanelli 2015). The guitarist also considers the performance as informed by "a working-class environment, people fighting for something" (Hinman 2004, 29).

---

[8] Dover Castle.

The English Message

With the British press still buzzing with stories about government ministers and their mistresses, as well as prominent judicial figures purported to be involved in sadomasochistic parties, the name "Kinks" carried provocative associations in 1964. Some of Larry Page's initial promotional photos of the band even have them carrying whips. In addition, although Wace and Collins's middle-class sensibilities had originally put the band in matching John Stephen suits, with Americans talking about a "British Invasion," the management considered a more obviously English image.

In the weeks leading up to the release of "You Really Got Me," Brian Sommerville joined the organization to provide advice on how to present the band. Sommerville had recently accompanied the Beatles to New York and provided Wace and company with ideas about how to appeal to Americans. They decided that red hunting jackets (with a bunch of lace at their chins) associated with foxhunts and landed gentry would befit a band from Fortis Green. The jackets were not only incongruous with the Kinks' background but also hot under stage lights.

They shot promotional photos around the Tower of London and in Hyde Park that would hold different meanings for British and American audiences. In an era that questioned upper-class privilege and celebrated urban working-class grit, the jackets signaled privilege and pretension in Britain. Americans saw the images as English, however, as did the British.

The weekend before the disc's release, the Kinks appeared on *Ready Steady Go!* Even more attention came on Tuesday 4 August 1964, when Pye experimented with a midweek release that caught the music papers' review cycle off guard. The BBC's answer to *Ready Steady Go!*, *Top of the Pops* featured the disc for six weeks, the last three as *the* top of the pops. By the second week of September, "You Really Got Me" occupied *Record Retailer*'s #1 position, and in November it reached #7 in the United States. The recording's impact, however, would go far beyond those rankings.

During a blind listening test for *Melody Maker*, Dave Berry described the recording as "fabulous," especially when he realized it was British. What would have impressed Ray Davies and his bandmates, however, was Berry's assessment that "this group sounds like they actually recorded what they wanted" (Hinman 2004, 31). Berry's review provided Ray Davies and the Kinks with affirmation of their relevance (see Hinman 2004, 30).

The band from north London had been outsiders grumbling about how the "Marquee musos"—the virtuosi of Soho—dismissed them musically. Every teenage musician with rock 'n' roll aspirations, however, heard something else.

Fig. 13.1 The Nashville Teens: John Hawken, John Allen, Ray Phillips, Barry Jenkins, Pete Shannon, Art Sharp, 1965. Photo courtesy of John Hawken.

Fig. 13.2 The Kinks: Peter Quaife, Mick Avory, Dave Davies, Ray Davies, in Hyde Park, London, 1965.
Pictorial Press Ltd/Alamy Stock Photo

PART IV
THE FEMININE MUSIQUE

The only way for a woman . . . to find herself, to know herself as a person, is by creative work of her own.
                                    Betty Friedan, *The Feminine Mystique*

14
The Problem That Has No Name

Near the beginning of World War II (27 January 1940), Winston Churchill emphasized the "immense importance of expanding [Britain's] labour supply [by] bringing great numbers of women into industry to replace the men taken for the armed forces" (1948, 438). He predicted that the nation would need "more than a million women" to "come boldly forward into our war industries" (439). In the postwar years, however, to open factory positions for men, successive British governments sought to reverse that pattern. Many women accepted a return to their prewar roles as mothers and homemakers. Others, however, resented the loss of the personal autonomy they had enjoyed and passed this attitude on to their daughters.

On the other side of the Atlantic, Betty Friedan in *The Feminine Mystique* (1963) documented the ways the advances women had made in the first half of the century were being systematically undermined.[1] Postwar "experts" asserted that women had been masculinized, with "enormously dangerous consequences" for the American family (Friedan 1963, 35).[2] Western civilization, they argued, had undervalued femininity by encouraging women to envy men "instead of accepting their own nature, which can find fulfillment only in sexual passivity, male domination, and nurturing maternal love" (36). Friedan described this subjugation of women as the "feminine mystique" (35) and compared American society's attitudes about women to Nazi Germany's dictate "Kinder, Küche, Kirche" (children, kitchen, church) (29).

Citing women's magazines, the popular arts, and her own experiences in publishing, Friedan observed that prewar heroines of women's fiction had been independent, mature, involved in the world, and focused on their careers. By 1949, however, "only one out of three heroines in women's magazines was a career woman—and she was shown in the act of renouncing her career" (Friedan 1963, 37). Similarly, women in films went from self-confident figures like Marlene Dietrich to sex objects like Marilyn Monroe (48). That was when some women—lamenting their isolation, belittlement, and disenfranchisement—began resisting.

---

[1] The epigraph to this chapter is from Friedan 1963, 416.
[2] The work of these postwar "experts" included, for example, Lundberg and Farnham, *Modern Woman: The Lost Sex* (1947). See also Stabile, *The Broadcast 41* (2018).

Come Outside

Contestations of the feminine mystique by second-wave feminists unfolded slowly and incompletely in sixties Britain. The control men exerted over women's repertoire, appearance, and personal agency reflected the deep conservative cultural reentrenchment under way during the postwar years. Virginia Nicholson, however, suggests that an incipient feminism was emerging. She argues that parts of British society began to "replace centuries of male domination with the gentler, more 'womanly' virtues of anti-materialism, peace, love, and spirituality" (2019, 3). The British music world, however, reflected the deep-seated patriarchal prejudices of British society.

Like the political, religious, athletic, business, manufacturing, and other institutions of the era, men controlled the music and record industries. They dominated performance on stage and in the studio, music direction as arrangers and conductors, recording as producers and engineers, and content creation as songwriters and publishers, as well as marketing, advertising, journalism, and broadcasting. Some women in sixties London did begin to make inroads, including in broadcasting (e.g., Vicki Wickham), personal management (e.g., Eve Taylor), and journalism (e.g., Penny Valentine), despite the systemic misogyny. Nevertheless, contemporary record charts illustrate the reality of a patriarchal culture.

Between 1960 and 1965, women artists occupied the top spot on *Record Retailer*'s weekly charts only 7 percent of the time, and in the years 1960, 1962, and 1963, no woman scored a number one. Culture change, however, can be heard. In the novelty recording "Come Outside" (1962), producer-songwriter Charles Blackwell has Mike Sarne, crooning with an East London accent, refer to television actor Wendy Richard as "little doll." She, however, rejects his advances, responding with sarcastic spoken Cockney put-downs and the insistence that she would rather dance with her friends.[3] The disc, which topped British charts in the summer of 1962, although satirizing working-class manners, suggests the stirrings of feminist resentment.

Singing Gender. Although print and broadcast media characterize the popular music scene of the sixties as young women screaming for men playing guitars, that image obscures a more complicated picture. At the local level, many young women were eager to join the band on stage to offer a ballad or to belt out a rocker. Each singer who stepped up to the microphone modeled her voice on the voices of others and modified those features to her own unique vocal physiology. As she adapted her performance to her contexts, audiences played a role in her decisions.[4]

---

[3] The song ends with spoken repartee in which Sarne offers "slap and tickle," which she also rejects.
[4] See Apolloni (2021) for discussion of women's vocal production in sixties British pop.

Marshall McLuhan's 1964 maxim "The medium is the message" also applies to the voice. The core cultural prejudices that held sway in sixties London shaped the ways listeners interpreted the range and quality of a disembodied voice to identify a singer's gender, age, and ethnicity. A singer's success, however, sometimes derived from defying those anticipations, as when seasoned producer Norrie Paramor, listening to John Schroeder's tape of Helen Shapiro confidently negotiating a melody, mistakenly thought she was a boy (see chapter 3).[5]

Reflecting Fox's rules for English behavior, sixties British listeners expected both male and female professional musicians to show moderation and restraint. Even when John Lennon screams on tunes like "Twist and Shout" to imply ecstatic release, he still complies with theatrical convention. Fox, however, also allows for "social micro-climates" where rules can be tested (2014, 306). Music clubs in the sixties (particularly in northern Britain) provided contexts where just such exceptions were possible and where women were allowed a chance to break conventions, albeit with limits.

The women who stepped up to the microphone in these clubs still endured the condescension of male-dominated bands, who preferred they sang ballads. And when a woman did belt out a rocker, some described her sound as a "screech," reflecting deep-seated discomfort with female assertiveness.[6] Many singers in Britain negotiated these criticisms with professional restraint, but some pushed the envelope, learning from the lessons of their predecessors.

First Wave

In the national fatigue of World War II, music steadied the national resolve. Women singers proved popular with both the armed forces and the populace as they forged a prototype that would remain important long after the war. Two artists stand out.

Born and raised in working-class East London, Vera Lynn (the "Forces' Sweetheart") began her career as a teenager singing with Bert Ambrose's ensemble. She went solo when some of his key musicians joined the Royal Air Force band (the Squadronaires) and toured bases both in the UK and Europe as well as in Egypt, India, and Burma (Laing 18 June 2020). Never presented as glamorous or sexy, her girl-next-door persona performed and read letters on her BBC broadcasts to troops.

Lynn sang in an emerging transatlantic style that upper- and middle-class English critics condemned as demoralizing and that one MP denounced as

---

[5] See Cusick (1999) for discussion of performances of sex and gender.
[6] See Warwick and Adrian (2016, 3) for comments on this aesthetic response.

"refaned Cockney." Nevertheless, her relaxed delivery, distinct from the studied sounds of trained singers, resonated with her audiences as honest and familiar, and her recordings of "We'll Meet Again" (1939) and "The White Cliffs of Dover" (1942) proved popular with the enlisted and the public alike.

With her husband as her manager (a former member of Ambrose's band), she remained popular with the war generation long after the conflict, despite the BBC deleting her "sob stuff" from its programming (Laing 18 June 2020). Illustrative of her continued importance, in November 1952, when the *New Musical Express* first published weekly charts and as the Korean War raged, she had records in the 5, 9, and 10 slots.

On Lynn's departure from Bert Ambrose's band, he found another teenager. Anne Shelton also broadcast and performed throughout the war, even the day after escaping her bombed home (Herald 31 July 1994). Like Lynn, her easy contralto and note-preparing slides in "Lilli Marlene" (May 1944) offered a reassuring nostalgic balm for war-weary psyches. A decade later, as British, French, and Israeli forces confronted Egypt over the Suez Canal (1956), her "Lay Down Your Arms" (August 1956) overcame a temporary BBC ban to reach number one.[7]

The Sound. Perhaps the most recognized British woman musician of the fifties and sixties, Julie Andrews began her career as a child entertaining troops with her parents. By 1956, she was starring in *My Fair Lady* on Broadway with the cast album triumphing on *Billboard*'s charts. In "Wouldn't It Be Loverly" from that musical, her character, working-class Cockney Eliza Doolittle, is trained to give the impression of being upper-class. To reflect that transformation, Andrews shifts her voice from a pinched nasal sound identified with working-class entertainments like the music hall to a controlled sound reminiscent of art song. That sound—a blend of common and elite, and reflective of the actor's vocal training—would later help to keep *The Sound of Music* (March 1965) in the charts for over 370 weeks, making it perhaps the most successful pop album of the decade.

All three women—Lynn, Shelton, and Andrews—embodied in their own ways the submissive, nurturing version of the feminine mystique as postwar culture relegated women to childrearing and serving husbands. By the early sixties, however, rock 'n' roll had grabbed the attention of the rising adolescent Bulge Generation, even if the deaths of Buddy Holly and Richie Valens and the arrest of Chuck Berry had temporarily stifled that movement.

After bringing 15-year-old Helen Shapiro into the studio and writing three hits for her, John Schroeder suggested that global insecurity was leading audiences

---

[7] BBC censors were concerned that the song undermined soldier morale. See Freedman (1998) for discussion of these and other British wartime artists.

back to ballads. The recently hired Pye producer asserted that girls were effective emoters,[8] "provided they get the right songs" (Wells 14 April 1962). Audiences were also looking for new variations on the trope of the musician woman.

Color Coding

As Britain waffled between conservative nostalgia for simpler times and progressive fascination with the modern, women musicians still had to work around and with the prejudices of British society. Sex, however, was not the only factor shaping musical status. With the collapse of the British Empire and the Commonwealth's policies of open immigration, ethnic stereotyping also played a role in the careers of women of color.

Trinidadian pianist Winifred Atwell had been a child prodigy playing Chopin before studying to be a pharmacist. Music, however, led her to lessons in New York and then admission to the Royal Academy of Music in London. She would always seek to be identified with European classical music, but her management saw her effortless stride-piano playing as a more lucrative option to exploit (Harris 28 November 1959). Record companies saw this too. After the death of George VI and the crowning of Elizabeth II, Atwell's "Britannia Rag" (December 1952) and "Coronation Rag" (May 1953) made *New Musical Express*'s short list, and both her "Let's Have Another Party" (November 1954) and "Poor People of Paris" (November 1956) topped those charts.

Part of her success in the nascence of broadcast television came from a willingness to mug for the camera, recreating the ambiance of a Saturday night at the local pub, albeit dressed in elegant evening attire. The British press, however, often made music secondary to discussions of her appearance, as when Alan Smith in *New Musical Express* commented on Atwell's weight (18 May 1962). Equally problematic, her marketing promoted the sound of "her other piano."

The sound of the slightly out-of-tune upright piano her marketers had purchased for her simultaneously suggested authenticity and foreignness, with hints of working-class familiarity and impropriety. This postcolonial otherness relegated Atwell to the role of a subaltern in White Britain, and her music to a feminine popular other against classical music's masculine dominance. Variations on this discrimination would also burden other British-born women of color.

Cleopatra. The father of the girl who became Cleo Laine arrived in London from Jamaica as a teen before enlisting with the British Expeditionary Force during World War I (Church 1995). When those hostilities ended, he and a farmer's

---

[8] Apropos of the time, he uses "girls" and "boys" generically to refer to females and males.

daughter began raising a family in West London while moving from one house to another. Clementine Bullock remembers her father as a "very good singer" who auditioned often but unsuccessfully (Cobb 1977) and sometimes busked outside train stations to help pay the bills during the Great Depression (Freeman 2010). While running a boardinghouse, her mother—a "real theatre mum"—arranged for singing and dancing lessons for her children (Cobb 1977). Only her eldest pursued that dream. After seeing Judy Garland and Lena Horne in films, Clementine dreamt: "one day, I'm going to do that" (Freeman 2010).

In her twenties, while in a foundering marriage, and raising a son, she auditioned for bands until John Dankworth heard her potential and began creating arrangements for her. To the Johnny Dankworth Seven, however, Clementine Bullock seemed an inappropriate name for this ambitious musician. They chose "Cleo Laine" as her stage name, referencing the Egyptian queen and perhaps the American singer Frankie Laine (Church 1995).

Her early recordings, such as her cover of Fats Waller's "Honeysuckle Rose" (May 1953), reveal a confident contralto singing with a bluesy transatlantic voice and accent. To have a hit in the pop charts, however, she would need to bring this fluency to "You'll Answer to Me" (July 1961), a close and more successful cover of American Patti Page's original.

Being a "band singer," however, was confining, as Vera Lynn and others had realized. After marrying Dankworth, she went solo, with her saxophonist husband continuing to write and arrange for her and accompany her (Cobb 1977). They became fixtures of London's jazz-blues scene, offering one model for how postwar women artists could survive an industry notorious for destroying them.

The Tomboy. Shirley Bassey describes herself growing up in Cardiff, Wales, as a "tomboy," a girl climbing trees and playing on railway sleepers (ties). The youngest of seven, she hardly knew her Nigerian father before he left, and as the "only coloured kid in the school," she learned survival in the face of institutional and communal racism (Hattenstone 2009). She also developed a voice and singing style while performing in pubs and workingmen's clubs that found a recording contract in 1956 when she was 19.

Producer Johnny Franz initially typecast the woman who would become known for powerful James Bond title tracks like "Goldfinger" (September 1964) as a calypso artist singing "The Banana Boat Song" (February 1957) and "Kiss Me, Honey Honey, Kiss Me" (1958). Bassey, however, confronted stereotypes of Blackness, Welshness, and femininity directly. An appearance on the *Six-Five Special* (15 November 1958) to promote "As I Love You" (1958) left no doubt about her identity, as that ballad and "Reach for the Stars" (July 1961) both topped British charts.

Bassey embraced the persona of a bold, sexually and musically confident woman. That role, however, also marked her as too professional, too adult, for many in the Bulge Generation. Michael Watts in *Melody Maker* (18 September 1971), although declaring himself a fan, remembered watching as she "stuck out her bottom and waggled it provocatively" on *Sunday Night at the London Palladium*. She was "that bint you were always seeing on the telly as a kid." One record company representative dubbed her "Burly Chassis" (Watts 18 September 1971).

Bassey remained sanguine and astute about her identity, noting that most of her letters were from women explaining how their husbands were infatuated with her. She also recognized that the "people who buy my records don't come to my cabarets"—that those were different audiences, each with their own priorities (Watts 18 September 1971). The feminine mystique of the petite demure blond was obviously never meant to include her, Laine, and Atwell. In response, they defied it. Of course, others seemed perfect for the role.

Gentlemen Prefer Ilford

Kathleen O'Rourke's single mother saw potential in her redheaded daughter, entering her as a toddler in talent contests and later paying for singing lessons. When Kathy left school at 15, she showed academic potential, but the opportunities in the working-class East End were limited without the right connections. Kathy, however, had beauty and talent. At the Ilford Palais de Danse, she transformed into a glamorous blond, arriving "in a tight black dress and black evening gloves" à la Marilyn Monroe in *Gentlemen Prefer Blondes* (July 1953; Laing 2011).

Leading the orchestra at the Palais, Bert Ambrose took notice of the adolescent who approached him and asked to sing. As a Jewish Polish immigrant, he had studied violin as a child and had played in London and then New York before becoming a prominent bandleader. Forty-two years older than the 16-year-old who took the stage that night, he had debuted Vera Lynn, Anne Shelton, and others as teenagers. By the mid-1950s, however, estranged from his wife and daughters in the United States and with popular culture shifting, he was looking for something new.

With Ambrose's assistance, Kathleen O'Rourke completed her transformation into Kathy Kirby (obscuring her Irish ethnicity) to sing with his band before he took over her management and became her lover. Within a few years, she had a string of hits and was one of the highest paid women in the British music industry.

She had been told early in her career that being a successful pop singer was "very hard for girls . . . unless they are ugly! The theory is that if you are all, well, glamorous, women won't like you" (Griffiths 18 March 1967). Maureen Cleave (7 September 1963), nevertheless, suggests that Kirby's fans were "mothers and fathers, sons and daughters and aunts and uncles—entire families." Her story, however, also offers a cautionary tale.

Secret Love. After Kirby's first recordings with Pye failed to impress disc jockeys, Ambrose negotiated a new contract with Decca involving artist-and-repertoire manager Peter Sullivan and arranger and music director Charles Blackwell. Sullivan had overseen Johnny Kidd's seminal "Shakin' All Over" (June 1960), Blackwell had worked with iconoclast Joe Meek, and together they brought Kirby into the British beat boom.

After the bluesy "Big Man" (October 1962) by English songwriter Clive Westlake, they reworked "Dance On" (June 1963), which had been an instrumental hit for the Shadows the previous year. That brought her into the top 20. More successfully, Blackwell radically rearranged Doris Day's "Secret Love" (October 1963), maintaining the dramatic phrases of the chorus (complete with timpani) before introducing guitars, bass, drums, and brass to transform the original wistful ballad into a saucy rocker.

Kirby's big voice and image found an audience, winning her the rank of top "British Female Singer" in *New Musical Express*'s 1963 reader's poll and a spot in the annual concert (26 April 1964). On that program, she introduced her next single, a reworking of "La Malagueña" as "You're the One" (May 1964). Video of the performance confirms a woman in complete control of her instrument, warming notes with vibrato and deftly turning ornaments as she powers over the orchestra.

Ambrose fashioned her as a British Marilyn Monroe, and she soon had her own television show, but he responded to her affair with a prominent television host by building a wall around her. To keep her under his observation, he not only rejected opportunities to expand her career but also mismanaged her finances to the point of eventually leaving her destitute. When asked about her competition, he acknowledged only two other British women. "There's Petula, of course, a wonderful artiste, but hardly anyone else," he said, before acknowledging "Dusty Springfield, always a favourite with you press boys" (Griffiths 18 March 1967).

Survivors

Throughout World War II and into the subsequent Cold War, the BBC used radio and then television not just to entertain audiences but also to establish oases of predictability. The Forces Programme (1940) and later the General Forces Programme (1944) sought to create the impression of a personal connection with performers. Embedded in the scripts and music, these broadcasts projected core English-British values, including Establishment expectations for women.

The women who performed on these programs balanced these priorities with their own need for respect as artists.

The program *Sincerely Yours—Vera Lynn* (1941–1942) offered a "letter in words and music from home, from the wives and mothers and sweethearts, signed by Vera Lynn" (BBC 27 February 1941, 7). Each episode included segments such as "News from Home," "messages from munitions girls to their husbands," and "congratulations to some new fathers in the Forces" (BBC 21 November 1942, 7). Singers like Lynn and Anne Shelton (e.g., *Anne to You*) came across as domestic nurturers, reassuring audiences of the value of the safe predictability of home life. Implicit in these broadcasts was the postwar feminine mystique that framed women in their prewar status as subservient to men. They also, however, demonstrated that women were fully capable of commanding center stage.

When the BBC resumed experimenting with television broadcasting (7 June 1946), producers built on these radio models. Thus, when the Suez Canal Crisis saw British troops deployed to Egypt, the Forces' Sweetheart returned to appear before cameras on *Vera Lynn Sings* (October 1956–January 1957). As the 1950s unfolded, however, pop culture embraced new ideals reflecting a preoccupation with building the future. In this environment, Lynn found "very few songs" that she felt were appropriate for her to sing (Robertson 21 October 2016). Other women musicians, nevertheless, found repertoire that resonated with audiences and in the process paved the way for Bulge Generation singers.

The Girl with the Giggle in Her Voice. Helen Shapiro studied singing at Maurice Burman's school knowing that another young Jewish singer had also been a student. Alma Cogan's East European refugee parents had had ambitions for their daughter, entered her in competitions, and had her audition for plays. That was how Vera Lynn came to recommend the 14-year-old for a stage show. By the late 1940s, aged 17, Cogan was singing to diners at the Cumberland Hotel, a posh setting where she competed with the clatter of cutlery by developing a stage persona that beamed positivity.

When HMV producer Wally Ridley heard her, he teamed her with arranger-conductor Frank Cordell to cover "To Be Worthy of You" (June 1952).[9] Cogan matches Cordell's big-band sound with confidence, optimism, and control that only lacked broader recognition. That came in 1953 when her giggly optimism at the Cumberland impressed one of the writers for the BBC radio comedy show *Take It from Here*. Denis Norden has asserted that no television star today is as "big as radio stars were then. We were getting audiences of 20–25 million. We discovered Alma . . . but she would have burst forth anyway" (Robertson 21 October 2016).

---

[9] First released by Frankie Laine (December 1951). Cordell championed popular culture and modernism in Britain.

Cogan's radio appearances helped promote her cover of Teresa Brewer's "Bell Bottom Blues" (March 1954), which made *New Musical Express*'s top five. A year later, her delivery and Cordell's arrangement of the DeMarco Sisters' "Dreamboat" (May 1955) made her the first British woman to have a domestic #1. Her singing style gained her the moniker "The Girl with the Giggle/Laugh in Her Voice" and her own British television shows (*Alma Cogan*, February–March 1956 and *The Alma Cogan Show*, April–May 1957).

Atypical of the era, Cogan managed herself, demanded a say in her repertoire and productions, designed her own flamboyant, voluminous, and numerous dresses and gowns, and eschewed romantic identification with a man. She was a professional at a time when women were being told their place was in the home feeding a husband, raising children, and cleaning up after them. Her careful construction of her television and stage persona and her cultivation of the press established a model that others would adapt.

Downtown

Petula Clark made her radio debut (22 November 1942) as a nine-year-old during a BBC broadcast at the Criterion Theatre in Piccadilly Circus, where she had gone hoping to send a message to an uncle serving in Iraq (Simon 2013). When an air raid interrupted the rehearsal, the producer asked if anyone would like to "say a poem or sing a song to just take the edge off the nervousness.... Nobody else offered," so Clark "stood up and sang into the microphone" (Melissa Parker 2014).

The BBC seized on the innocence of its "latest find" to boost morale, a child who learned "her songs" by "listening to the wireless" and who had rendered "Mighty Like a Rose" so compellingly (BBC 12 December 1942).[10] More radio performances led to her film debut at aged 11 in *Medal for the General* (November 1944) and a recurring role in the popular Huggetts comedies.[11] In parallel with these film appearances, she also emerged as a television pioneer.[12]

As the BBC experimented with the new medium, they filmed a 13-year-old Clark performing "Miser, Miser" and broadcast it every day except Sundays from 1946 to 1951 on a program simply called *Variety*. She soon featured in her own 15-minute time slot on Sunday afternoons (September 1946–July 1947) before hosting the occasional *Pet's Parlour* (November 1950 to July 1953). At 23, she

---

[10] "Mighty Like a Rose" was a modified version of the American pop song "Mighty Lak' a Rose," which would have taken on a new meaning in the context of the Blitz in London.

[11] For example, *Here Come the Huggetts* (November 1948) in which the 16-year-old played Pet Huggett.

[12] At the end of the war, she and Julie Andrews toured the UK together, entertaining troops.

became one of the first British women to host her own television program: *The Petula Clark Show* (January–February 1956 and December 1956–January 1957).

This exposure promoted her recordings, such as "The Little Shoemaker" (May 1954), which made *New Musical Express*'s top 10; but after a performance in Paris in 1957, she signed a contract with Disques Vogue, moved to France, married, and started a family (Melissa Parker 2014; Zekas 2005). There she had hits like "Prends Mon Coeur" (1959)—a reworking of Hank Snow's "(Now and Then There's) A Fool Such as I" and Elvis Presley's cover of it. She also continued to release discs in the UK, with "Sailor" (January 1961) topping *Record Retailer*'s charts, beating out Anne Shelton's contemporary version. Her biggest hit, however, would come when she was in her thirties.

Citysong. In 1966, the American Paul Williams in *Crawdaddy* (March 1966) described the rise of the citysong: sociological pop that celebrates the urban centers that youth were reclaiming. He credits two 1964 recordings with its rise: Martha and the Vandellas' "Dancing in the Street" and Petula Clark's "Downtown."

In October 1964, Tony Hatch was already a successful producer and songwriter (e.g., the Searchers) when he arrived in New York looking for material (Myers 12 June 2013). On his itinerary was the Brill Building, which sat at the center of the East Coast's music industry and was where some of its most prolific songwriters worked, including Barry Mann and Cynthia Weil. In their take on New York, the lyrics to "Uptown" describe downtown as an "angry land" where everyone is the subject's "boss" who treats him like a "little man." "Uptown," in contrast, is where his lover makes him feel "tall, he don't crawl . . . he's a king." Delivering that message, Phil Spector's production of the Crystals (February 1962) layers Latino ideas over orchestral pop sensibilities.

When Hatch returned to London, he brought memories of midtown Manhattan, and a few days later he was in Paris pitching ideas to Clark when one caught her attention: "if you can write a lyric as good as that melody, I'd love to sing it." "Downtown" has Times Square in mind, using American words such as "sidewalk" and "movie shows" instead of the British "pavement" and "cinemas."[13] Indeed, a Warner Brothers rep loved the "fact it was America seen through the eyes of an Englishman" (Simpson 11 October 2016).

Instead of escaping the noise and the hurry, Hatch counsels a friend to go where the lights are bright, to forget their troubles and cares, and to find someone who might help them or whom they might help escape loneliness. Indeed, the lyrics suggest that "you'll be dancing with 'em too before the night is over."[14]

---

[13] The constructs of "downtown," "midtown," and "uptown" are also characteristically American.

[14] Clark later described the song as encouraging depressed and lonely people to feel as though they were part of something social (Simpson 2016).

Key to the recording's success, Clark captures the sentiment behind the lyrics while Hatch's piano mixes with backing singers, brass, strings, and a rhythm section, all embracing the excitement. When released, "Downtown" (November 1964) reached number two in *Record Retailer* and would topped *Billboard*'s charts in the United States, making Clark the first British woman to do so as part of the so-called British Invasion.

Reinvention. The success of "Downtown" prompted Hatch to write and produce follow-ups for Clark such as "I Know a Place" (February 1965), which builds on the same sentiments and musical ideas. When these discs ushered Clark back into the pop culture mainstream, however, she needed to adapt. Some audiences already knew her and had expectations. A new audience was just getting acquainted.

Managed by her father, the diminutive (5'1") singer had grown up in front of a camera, each phase of her life finding a new construction as she matured. Her first appearance was as an innocent child in British Pathé's *Youngest Sweetheart—Petula Clark* (1945), but that was followed by an adult-ish makeover of the 13-year-old by the BBC (*Variety* 1946). Film directors first cast her as a precocious teenager and then as a vulnerable young woman before television in the fifties reinvented her again. With the dawn of the sixties, the confident multilingual pop singer, who had had hits on both sides of the English Channel, was focusing on motherhood. "Downtown," however, meant balancing societal expectations for women with pop culture stereotypes.

Other women singers from the generation born before the war reacted in their own ways to the shifts in postwar technology, demographics, and their own maturity. Some, like Vera Lynn, stayed true to their original audiences by playing cabarets, where they entertained the parents of the Bulge Generation. Others, like Kathy Kirby, found themselves navigating a market where rock 'n' roll, rhythm-and-blues, and folk were supplanting big-band jazz. For them, like Clark, finding a place in pop culture meant creating hybrid identities.

From the Middle of Nowhere

The girl who became Dusty Springfield spent her childhood during and after the war in High Wycombe, Buckinghamshire, home to the Royal Air Force and US Air Force bomber commands, where American servicemen and their music were an influence on town life. When her lower-middle-class family moved to Ealing, West London, in the early 1950s, Mary O'Brien and her brother Dion began singing and accompanying themselves on guitars for family and friends. They also, however, occasionally experienced the withering critiques of their Scots-Irish accountant father and his disparagement of their Irish Catholic mother. Oblivious of the psychological effects, he mocked the physical appearance of his nearsighted, redheaded daughter, nicknaming her "Pudge." He also, however, played piano and instilled high expectations in his family, who listened together to his eclectic record collection. In this environment, Mary and her brother learned to mimic what they heard, performing with friends at school and getting hired as a singing duo at a summer holiday camp.

In 1958, the 19-year-old Mary used those skills to join the Lana Sisters, singing the lower harmony parts and filling out their sound. Her first transformation came when she adopted the stage name Shan and abandoned her glasses, despite the way that affected getting on and off stage. She also dyed her hair blond in the conceit that they were indeed sisters. Their manager, Eve Taylor, booked them for appearances on the BBC's *Drumbeat* (9 May 1959) and other shows and for concerts with Tommy Steele, Cliff Richard, and Adam Faith, all of which built O'Brien's confidence. Nevertheless, their recordings like—"Mister Dee-Jay" (April 1959) and "(Seven Little Girls) Sitting in the Back Seat" (with Al Saxon, October 1959), covers of American releases—failed to chart, and Shan O'Brien embarked on a new incarnation.

Springfield. In 1960, Dion convinced Mary to join him and Tim Feild to become the Springfields (Welch 1999). In the late fifties and early sixties, pop folk artists like the Kingston Trio were enjoying chart success, and Johnny Franz (who had produced recordings by Anne Shelton, Winifred Atwell, and Shirley Bassey) along with arranger Ivor Raymonde thought the Springfields could create a British equivalent. The trio reworked American material (e.g., "Dear John," May 1961) and wrote their own imitations (e.g., "Breakaway," July 1961),[15] sometimes mimicking or mocking Appalachian and African accents. The brother and sister also assumed new identities, adopting the stage personas Tom and Dusty Springfield.

Just as Kathy O'Rourke (who had also dyed her red hair blonde) had become Kathy Kirby, the name Springfield obscured the O'Briens' Irish ethnicity. A new stage name, however, was only part of Dusty's ongoing transformation, in which dyeing her hair and shedding her glasses represented just the first stage. The end of rationing in the late fifties had ushered in nostalgia for elegance, including the resurrection of architecturally structured hair, a practice associated with the eighteenth century. In her transformation, Dusty Springfield's bouffant paralleled adoptions by America's first lady and by Black artists like the Crystals, the Ronettes, and Martha and the Vandellas.

Always self-conscious, Springfield initially wore wide frocks in a folky version of Alma Cogan that hid her legs: long dresses were always in her stage wardrobe. Moreover, recognizing the power of the television closeup that Cogan had

---

[15] See chapter 20.

exploited, she began to accentuate her eyes with mascara and shadow. And when she found herself without an instrument and sandwiched between two men playing guitars, she learned gestures that complemented the performance and drew audience attention.

Success eventually led the siblings to want their own careers. Tom became a producer, and after the last appearance of the Springfields on *Ready Steady Go!* (30 August 1963), producer Vicki Wickham booked Dusty as a guest host. A month later (4 October 1963), as Helen Shapiro watched from the wings and millions from home, Springfield interviewed and introduced the Beatles in their *RSG!* debut. A month after that, she premiered her first single on the same influential program.

Mimicry. Wickham did not hear Dusty Springfield's singing style as British. Instead, she described what the singer did as a "mixture of American genres from country to soul, from folk to pop." The singer herself believed that the British could "never be authentic" so that what she did was "mimicry" (Stanley 2009). In the creation of this vocal identity, she copied "every black singer" she heard. "One week I was Baby Washington, next week I was lead singer of the Shirelles" (Fong-Torres 1999). Nevertheless, as with other British musicians, what she created was an amalgam of sounds from both shores of the transatlantic postwar world.

The Springfields' producer at Philips Records, Johnny Franz, and arranger Ivor Raymonde pivoted with her new incarnation and interests. Referencing the repertoire of American girl groups and respecting Dusty's vocal strengths, Raymonde crafted a melody and arrangement that echo both the Crystals' "Da Doo Ron Ron" (April 1963) and the music coming out of Motown. For lyrics, however, he turned to Mike Hawker (who had collaborated with John Schroeder on Helen Shapiro's hits) to create "I Only Want to Be with You."[16]

Franz produced the sessions, arranged for studio time and musicians, and oversaw the recording process, which included doubletracking Springfield's vocals, referencing the sound of the Beat Boom. "I Only Want to Be with You" (November 1963) would reach into Britain's top five and into *Billboard*'s top 20 with performances on the debut program of the BBC's *Top of the Pops* (1 January 1964) and in the United States on *The Ed Sullivan Show* (10 May 1964).

Gateways. Although the music and recording industries limited the participation of women in the creative process, Springfield challenged those restrictions and consequently experienced pushback. Although Franz had given her artistic control, she sometimes exercised that right with an edge reminiscent of her father's critiques. Recording sessions could prove tense if the singer grew

---

[16] Raymonde recorded a demo of "I Only Want to Be with You" with Hawker's wife, Jean, singing. Jean Hawker was a member of the Breakaways, backup singers for both Petula Clark and Dusty Springfield. She had also inspired the lyrics for Shapiro's "Walking Back to Happiness."

unhappy with her own performance and/or those of session musicians and demanded numerous retakes.[17] Indeed, she seems never to have been happy with herself or any of her recordings. Nevertheless, she claimed that she did the "whole bloody lot" herself and never took "any credit. It wasn't fashionable for women" (Fong-Torres, 1999).

The sixties saw the beginning of a questioning of Britain's behavioral norms and laws governing sexuality and gender. Clandestine spaces like the Gateways Club in Chelsea, however, offered retreats for lesbians like Springfield, who would be one of the first pop stars to hint that her orientation might not be heterosexual (Nicholson 2019, 127). Indeed, the lyrics for many of the songs Springfield sang—"I Only Want to Be with You," "I Just Don't Know What to Do with Myself" (June 1964), "In the Middle of Nowhere" (June 1965), and "Some of Your Lovin'" (September 1965)—avoid specific mention of gender, allowing her and her audiences the freedom of interpretation.

In an era when musicians increasingly took political stands, Springfield did too, as when the South African government revoked her tour visa in late 1964 after she refused to perform for segregated audiences. She also positioned herself as an advocate for Black American artists both in the studio and in broadcasts. By the mid-1960s, however, Springfield—now in her midtwenties—faced a wave of younger women singers who brought their own experiences and attitudes to their performances and to the singles charts.

---

[17] Springfield could also reject musicians because of their appearance (see Thompson 2008, 262).

Fig. 14.1 Vera Lynn, in *We'll Meet Again*, 1943.

Fig. 14.2 Cleo Lane, 1965.

218 THE FEMININE MUSIQUE

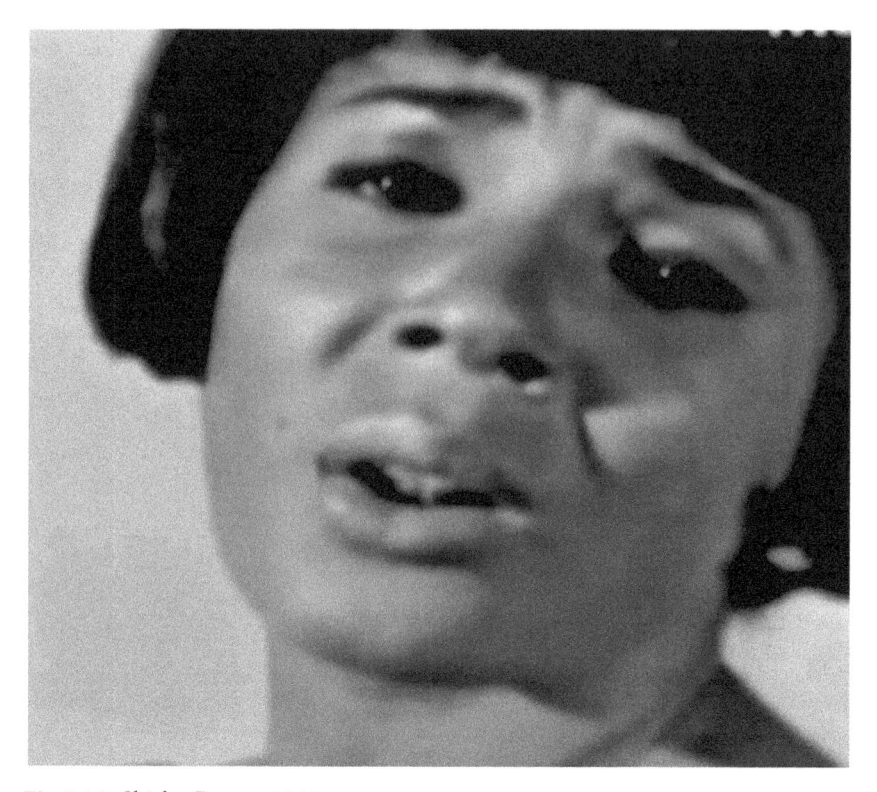

Fig. 14.3 Shirley Bassey, 1964.

THE PROBLEM THAT HAS NO NAME 219

Fig. 14.4 Kathy Kirby, 1964.

Fig. 14.5 Alma Cogan, 1963.

Fig. 14.6 Petula Clark, 1964.

Fig. 14.7 Dusty Springfield, on *Ready, Steady, Go!*, 1963.

15
Women
The Next Wave

A biochemical revolution was under way in the postwar years. In addition to the antibiotics that enhanced human survival, birth control began to allow some women to question how culture defined them. Court battles had blocked the unlinking of sexual intimacy from pregnancy, but at the end of 1961, Conservative Minister of Health Enoch Powell informed the House of Commons that married women would be able to obtain oral contraception through the National Health Service. Obstacles remained, but the "pill" helped some middle-class and upper-class women to gain a degree of control over their bodies and lives, and this access gradually spread.

Challenging domestic expectations, young women were heading into cities to find work in offices, shops, and galleries, establishing a beachhead against patriarchal authority. In this domestic rebellion, the socially empowered and potentially sexually active "dolly bird" emerged as a mascaraed saboteur. Although she still had to contend with toxic male privilege, the relative freedom of urban environments allowed her choices in hair, clothing, and behavior that defied British feminine stereotypes.

The Look. The dolly bird's enabler-in-chief emerged in the form of Mary Quant, a thirtysomething entrepreneur who almost single-handedly placed London on the sixties fashion map. She opened her first clothing factory in 1961, the same year Enoch Powell made his announcement. In the midsixties, many young women gravitated to Quant's stylish and functional designs, even if they often purchased cheaper copies. Her core aesthetic—the "Look"—emphasized simple shapes that defied adulthood by deemphasizing the bust and hips. Her designs referenced clothes worn by children such as "pinafore dresses, short skirts, knickerbockers, knee socks, and black stockings" (Sandbrook 2006, 230).[1]

Quant hoped that those wearing her clothes would say "I'm very sexy. I enjoy sex. I feel provocative, but you're going to have a job to get me. You've got to excite me and you've got to be jolly marvelous to attract me. I can't be bought, but if I want you, I'll have you" (Levy 2002, 47–48). Not everyone could afford her

---

[1] With the consequences of postwar food rationing still obvious, Quant also marketed to a population of thin women.

designs (despite her intentions for her bargain brand, the Ginger Group), but she helped shift clothing from postwar gray modesty to an unabashed modern and colorful adventure, as clothiers began using the materials postwar science was creating. Her visual collaborator, Vidal Sassoon, contributed to this redefinition of the feminine in 1964 with the "Shape," a geometric and easy-to-maintain bob that regendered beat-group hair.

From the Outside

Quant, Sassoon, and the pill may have given some women a sense of independence, but not everyone interpreted this as positive. Most of Britain lived outside London, only reading about "dolly birds" in the papers or by watching television exposés. Traditionalists interpreted women seeking personal freedom as undermining British values and formed a base that would help elect Margaret Thatcher in the seventies. Feminists like Germaine Greer (1970), however, criticized the Look as infantilizing women, presenting them as "girls" rather than as adults and as female "eunuchs" for pedophiles.

As girls born during and after the war came into adolescence, they began to contest spaces dominated by men, performers finding their places on tiny stages, and making room in the music for their voices. Those spaces—hot, smelly, and noisy backwater clubs and pubs—shaped their singing and how they presented themselves. Among their models, 15-year-old American Brenda Lee had had UK hits with "Sweet Nothin's" (January 1960)[2] and "I'm Sorry" (June 1960). Her nasal voice, confident delivery, and unglamorous appearance encouraged adolescent females that they too could capture a room's attention. British culture would attempt to define and to control these young women, but some would rebel.

Rebel. In Liverpool, Beryl Hogg was 14 when her friends pushed her onto a stage with a band, where she belted out the Shirelles' "Boys." A year later, now as Beryl Marsden, she was gigging regularly with the Undertakers and singing covers of Brenda Lee. Defying her mother, who wanted her to work in an office, Marsden saw herself as a "rebel" and believed that singing was what she was "meant to do" (Marsden, n.d.). In 1963, as the 16-year-old was preparing to head to Hamburg with Lee Curtis and the All-Stars, Brian Epstein approached her with a management offer. "He was really nice, a real gentleman, but I was planning to go off to Germany to perform at the famous Star Club" (Killelea 2014). Why would she need a manager?

To perform in the Saint Pauli quarter, however, she would need a chaperone, and the All-Stars' manager, Joe Flannery[3] (the brother of Lee Curtis) agreed to

---

[2] Released as "Sweet Nuthin's" in the UK.
[3] Flannery also worked with Brian Epstein as a booking agent.

serve in that capacity. He eventually became her manager, but he lacked Epstein's connections, influence, and instincts. He attempted to dress her in frilly frocks, but Marsden again rebelled, donning "leather jeans, straight short hair, a sloppy pullover or polo neck, and pin-toed boots. It was unstructured, young, 'beatniky,' and androgynous. And it was, of course, cool" (Nicholson 2019, 63).

Marsden recorded "I Know (You Don't Love Me No More)"/"I Only Care about You" (August 1963) at Decca with Peter Sullivan and "Who You Gonna Hurt?" (1965) at Columbia with Ivor Raymonde. Neither of these producers, however, seems to have understood the woman who was arguably the best female singer in Liverpool. Meanwhile, George Martin was reshaping another Scouse artist several years Marsden's senior who had signed with Epstein.

A Cavern Screecher

Priscilla White grew up working-class Catholic in Liverpool, singing for friends and winning talent contests. By day, she labored as a typist at a construction company. By night, she checked coats at the Cavern Club and sometimes sang with the bands (Laing 2015). Performing, however, intimidated her. During her first paid gig, she literally held her boyfriend Bobby Willis's hand while she sang, but her unpretentiousness proved endearing (Cilla Black 2003, 61). As the British beat boom began to focus on Liverpool, "Swinging Priscilla" was gaining Merseyside fans while earning an extra pound or two each week.

In the context of sixties British pop, English society expected women to conform to patriarchal expectations in the construction of their stage personas. For Cilla White, deference to men meant that when she was asked to perform in Hamburg, she had to say no: she was 19, and her father would not grant permission. As a singer, she also had to rely on male musicians and promoters who made decisions for her.

At the Beatles' urging, Brian Epstein agreed to audition her, assigning her a spot in the middle of their set at a local dance hall. She chose "Summertime," a song on their setlist that she had sung with other bands but, with no rehearsal and with "one last wicked wink . . . John set the group off playing," only to discover that the "music was not in [her] key" (Cilla Black 2003, 65). After a polite, "Thank you," the manager left, but the story was not over.

Months later, after discreetly watching her from the shadows at a club, Epstein thought her "magnificent—a slender, graceful creature with the ability to shed her mood of dignified repose if she were singing a fast number" (1998, 132). He offered the 29-year-old singer and her parents a contract, but with stipulations. The name Cilla White struck him as unacceptable. She would become Cilla

Black. She would also have to spend more time in the capital, for which her father agreed that Bobby Willis could look after her.

Defining Cilla. As with Beryl Marsden, Cilla Black's new persona represented both her transition into a professional and a way out of working-class Liverpool. Epstein thought her the "singer everyone loves and admires but whom no one envies because of her utter simplicity" (1998, 132). To the music, recording, and television industries, she offered a tabula rasa ready to be inscribed. Over the next months, she participated in the construction of a British pop icon: the vulnerable, stylish, and attractive child-woman, comfortable as an object yet ultimately subversive. Throughout, she nevertheless held her Scouse memories and identity close, even if the "Big Smoke" (an outsider's term for London) could be less than receptive and if some folks at home resented her success.

The Beatles' producer, George Martin, heard Black as "a problem child" with a "good, if thin, voice . . . a rock-and-roll screecher in the true Cavern tradition." In particular, he recoiled at her "piercing nasal sound," a vocal production that many pub singers adopted to be heard in noisy environments (Martin with Hornsby 1979, 135).[4] Along with class condescension, Martin's reaction reflected a common prejudice: men heard women who sang aggressively as threatening and abrasive, if not unsophisticated.

The producer was hesitant at first to sign her to Parlophone, but when McCartney offered "Love of the Loved," Martin relented. In reshaping the Cavern screecher into a balladeer, he began by tamping down her working-class Scouse accent, finding her pronunciations "much too Liverpudlian," even after 15 takes (Cilla Black 2003, 79). "Love of the Loved" (September 1963) may have stalled at #35 on *Record Retailer*'s charts, despite its pedigree, but her appearances on *Ready Steady Go!* (27 September 1963), *Thank Your Lucky Stars* (5 October 1963), and especially *Juke Box Jury* (2 and 23 November 1963) built an audience.

Along the way, she bonded with fellow traveler and *Ready, Steady, Go!* host Cathy McGowan, a "nineteen-year-old ex-secretary from Streatham" (south London) who "hit the modernistic, lower-middle-class, suburban button to perfection" (Nicholson 2019, 138). Both were young and Catholic, and both began to demonstrate how Bulge-generation women could manipulate the media that defined them.

Her World. That fall, when Brian Epstein returned from New York after reaching an agreement with Ed Sullivan for the Beatles' American debut, he brought a copy of Burt Bacharach and Hal David's most recent composition and production: Dionne Warwick's "Anyone Who Had a Heart" (November 1963).

---

[4] Martin does not similarly demean the voices of men like John Lennon who also sometimes sang with a nasal voice. A nasal voice, however, is also a common feature of Anglo-Irish and American traditions: for example, the sean-nós of West Ireland or the American bluegrass tradition.

Martin thought it perfect for Shirley Bassey, but Epstein persisted, and the producer brought in Johnny Pearson to orchestrate and direct the session (Martin with Hornsby 1979, 137).[5] Bacharach's asymmetrical phrases and contrasting melodies proved intimidating, but Black delivered the song with a delicate, breathy, and warm lower register that contrasted with her tense upper voice to convey the poignancy of David's lyrics. Appearances on *Thank Your Lucky Stars* (15 February) and *Top of the Pops* (six times beginning 5 February) helped Black's "Anyone Who had a Heart" (January 1964) top British charts. The search for a follow-up began immediately.

As focused as British artists and producers were on securing the best American material, the conduit for musical ideas was hardly just transatlantic. Europeans had been appropriating each other's songs and adapting them for centuries, and postwar media only sped up these exchanges. For Black, Martin selected Umberto Bindi's "Il Mio Mondo" (1963) with new lyrics by American Carl Sigman (Sigman 2015). Pearson copying the original arrangement closely and Black delivers "You're My World" (May 1964) with vulnerability and passion. When launched on *Ready Steady Go!* (1 May 1964), *Thank Your Lucky Stars* (9 May 1964), and again multiple appearances on *Top of the Pops* (beginning 13 May 1964), the disc made her the first British woman since Helen Shapiro to score back-to-back British number ones.

Success continued with Lennon and McCartney's "It's for You" (July 1964) and a cover of the Righteous Brothers' "You've Lost That Lovin' Feeling" (January 1965). Along the way, she continued to evolve from the provincial girl next door in fluffy dresses and hair into a stylish Mod dressed in the "Look" and wearing the "Shape." Her transformation from Cavern dweller into television icon was paralleled by a young Scottish musician whom London also sought to redefine.

The Mask

Marie Lawrie's father was an offal dresser at Gallowgate meat market in Glasgow who fenced stolen beef, drank heavily, and beat his wife. Despite his faults, he spent some of his ill-gotten gains on home luxuries like their radiogram and the discs his daughter demonstrated a knack for imitating. She won talent contests as a child and, with adolescence, as a diminutive singer became a staple on southern Scotland's thriving club-and-dance-hall scene. Among her influences, she remembers American servicemen calling her "Scotland's Brenda Lee" because she sang a "lot of her songs which suited my voice" (Lulu 2002, 45).

---

[5] Pearson would soon be appointed music director for the BBC's *Top of the Pops* (Leigh 22 March 2011).

Nevertheless, there was a "lot of violence" in Marie Lawrie's world, a world in which she would become responsible for the care of her siblings, if not also her parents. She recalled pretending that "nothing was wrong" as she created a "mask [to] not really let anyone in." She would be "tight lipped" and not let her "feelings show . . . even when everything was falling apart" (Devoy 28 February 2015). Music and a stage persona provided an escape from this world.

In 1963, at age 14, she was singing with the Gleneagles on Sunday nights upstairs at Glasgow's Lindella Club, where her manager brought potential clients to hear her. They included Londoner Tony Gordon, who was interested in opening a discotheque; however, hearing her led him to promote her to the Scottish press and arrange for recording auditions. In London, Ron Richards at EMI redirected Gordon to see Peter Sullivan, a former colleague now at Decca, who did offer a contract, albeit with conditions (Lulu 2002, 55–57).

Decca wanted her in London with London artist management, not with a businessman in Glasgow, but bringing an adolescent Scottish girl south presented numerous problems. To shepherd Marie Lawrie in an industry preyed on by industrial wolves, Gordon recruited his sister. In the mold of Larry Parnes and Brian Epstein, but with a motherly touch, Marion Massey was comfortably middle-class, Jewish, a mother, and lived in a large home near Holland Park. Lawrie "had a heavy cold, was pale, and was wearing three jumpers" when this "very sophisticated" woman with a "loud, commanding voice to match her big personality" first heard Lawrie at the Lindella (Judd 2008). Massey was a classically trained musician and may have cringed at the singer's loud, raspy, and nasal style, but what the voice lacked in conservatory patina, the individual radiated in energy.

Shout! Massey and Gordon set to commodifying their artist, rebranding her Lulu and her band, the Luvvers.[6] The singer remembers them choosing her new name because it was "short, cute, and sounded American," but many also saw parallels between the 5'1" singer and the mischievous cartoon character Little Lulu (Lulu 2002, 60). More changes would come. As struck as Peter Sullivan might have been with Marie Lawrie/Lulu, he was less impressed with the Luvvers as a studio band. Thus, he contracted music director Reg Guest to assemble some of London's best session musicians and focused on her audition piece, the Isley Brothers staple "Shout."

Lulu's performance explodes with energy heard in few other English-British recordings of the era. Guitarist Vic Flick remembered it as a "great session . . . that just happened . . . a really rockin', rockin' take" (interview 28 February 2001). Scottish law, however, required that wee Marie Lawrie stay in school until the end of term, at which point, Decca could release "Shout" (April 1964) and Lulu was

---

[6] "Luvvers" imitated the spelling of Joe Brown's band, the Bruvvers.

free to promote it. She was at home in Glasgow in their third floor flat watching *Ready, Steady, Go!* when John Lennon told Cathy McGowan that "Shout" was his favorite current release (Lulu 2002, 63). Back in London, Lulu lodged with Massey's mother while her manager made appointments with Vidal Sassoon followed by clothes shopping.

As the disc climbed to #7, Lulu presented a challenge for Decca. As with Helen Shapiro, the Scottish singer's youth and innocence was a fragile commodity that complicated finding a suitable follow-up. Sullivan turned to Bert Berns (who had cowritten "Twist and Shout") to write and produce her next recording. The American offered "Here Comes the Night" (November 1964), a slower and more orchestrated arrangement that showcases Lulu's vocal abilities while playing on her youth. The performance, however, bears little resemblance to the voice audiences had heard in "Shout" and barely made the top 50.[7] Lulu nevertheless built a successful Decca catalogue with "Leave a Little Love" (May 1965, #8) and "Try to Understand" (August 1965, #25), each recording proving she could do much more than shout.

Young Fry

Maureen Cleave, writing in the *Evening Standard* (4 July 1964), tells readers about two "younger fry" who are performing with "shameless wickedness in the way they prance about the stage, winking and swaying their hips and clicking their fingers." Both have hit records, are "totally un-girlish," are just over five feet tall, and have "monstrous charm." The White Scottish 15-year-old was Lulu. The Black Jamaican 16-year-old was Millie.

The daughter of a sugar-cane plantation worker, Millicent "Millie" Small at 12 had won a talent contest in Montego Bay before moving to the capital to live with an aunt. In Kingston, producer Coxsone Dodd heard parallels between Small's high, nasal voice and American R&B singer Shirley Goodman, and paired Small with Owen Gray as Owen and Millie to cover several Shirley and Lee[8] tunes for the Jamaican market (Cane-Honeysett 2010). By 1962, the 14-year-old's "We'll Meet" (1962), recorded with Roy Panton as Roy and Millie and the City Slickers (Roy Black 2013; Graves August 2016) came out just as Jamaica was gaining independence from the UK (6 August 1962). The disc was among the possessions packed by Chris Blackwell, the former aide-de-camp to the island's governor, when he relocated to Britain.

---

[7] Her recording was overshadowed the next spring by the version by Them, again with Berns producing.

[8] Shirley Goodman and Leonard Lee.

Islands. Jamaica holds a special place in the British imagination.[9] That relationship, however, is rooted in a social and cultural history of White land and slave owners and the Afro-Caribbean, South Asian, and Chinese workers who labored in colonial sugar-cane fields and bauxite mines. The end of the World War II and the devolution of the British Empire updated this story when the British government recruited Jamaicans as cheap labor to help rebuild Britain's infrastructure. When these workers arrived in the UK, they brought sustaining cultural commodities, including music, to help make life in Britain's socially cold and hostile cities more bearable.

Among the entrepreneurs looking to profit from this trade, Chris Blackwell started a company that reflected his interests in Jamaican music and the American rhythm-and-blues that had influenced it. The young White British-Jamaican jazz enthusiast had been born into a relatively wealthy island family and had briefly attended the elite Harrow School in London. Having started a business importing records from the United States into Jamaica and from Jamaica into the UK, he began recording Jamaican artists for his own label, Island Records (Majd 2009; Stratton 2010, 442).

The voice on "We'll Meet" caught the attention of Blackwell's London friends, who responded to Millie Small's "very high pitched and funny voice" and demanded that they had to "'have that record'" (Blackwell in Stratton 2010, 450). The 16-year-old arrived in the UK on 22 June 1963, after Blackwell had approached her parents with a contract, which they signed, that made him not only her manager but also her guardian (Roy Black 2013).

In London, Blackwell enrolled her in the Italia Conti Academy, a finishing school meant to enculturate her into English behavior and subordinate her Jamaican roots. Guardianship and being a young, Black, poor, immigrant woman, whose accent and voice marked her as socially inferior in England, made her vulnerable, which was underscored when Blackwell reduced her to a single name: Millie. She was, however, also stubborn, talented, and self-confident.

Lollipop. Blackwell and his partner, Harry Robinson (Jack Good's former music director) first presented Millie as a pop artist.[10] "Don't You Know" (November 1963), however, demonstrated that Robinson and Blackwell really did not know what their Jamaican expatriate clientele and a growing audience of White British consumers wanted. They next turned to 14-year-old American Barbie Gaye's "My Boy Lollypop" (January 1957), which had been popular in the New York City area and copies of which Blackwell had sold to Kingston deejays (Stratton 2010, 453).

---

[9] For example, Jamaica features prominently in the first James Bond film, *Dr. No*, released in 1962, the year the nation gained full independence.

[10] Her records on Smash in the US identified her as Millie Small.

Millie's version of "My Boy Lollipop" (February 1964) mirrors Gaye's version closely in the same key and at roughly the same tempo, with the voices and the lyrics of both versions suggesting childlike innocence. For Small's recording, however, Blackwell brought in Jamaican guitarist and arranger Ernest Ranglin to create a pop-ska version,[11] using a British R&B band with a small horn section (Stratton 2010, 445). For the ska groove, Ranglin modified the choked guitar-chord backbeat shuffle groove of Gaye's original to emphasize what Jamaicans sometimes called the "skank," the sharply articulated pickup-beat hallmark of ska.

Confident of the disc's success, Blackwell leased her recordings to Fontana, because "small labels couldn't collect that money from the stores fast enough to pay the pressing plant to make more records in order to meet the demand" (Majd 2009). His prediction proved accurate. Fontana in the UK and Smash Records in the United States both saw "My Boy Lollipop" climb to #2. Although her follow-up "Sweet William" (June 1964) and subsequent releases sold less well, she was at the vanguard of the Jamaican pop that was beginning to spread from the Caribbean expatriate community to a subsection of the British youth market and soon the world.

Presenting Millie, however, meant engaging a market that interpreted Small's high-pitched voice as foreign, childlike, and hyperfeminine. Peter Jones in the *Record Mirror* (4 April 1964), for example, described her as a "Jamaican born bombshell" and a "dark-skinned very feminine ball of fire" with "great big saucer-like brown eyes." And, if the exoticism was not obvious enough, he offers an aside that her uncle was a "witchdoctor" who practiced "Voodoo."

Role Models

The importance of television in the sixties fed on audience relatability to screen talent as adolescents built identities separate from their parents. In 1964, many of the 17-year-old women born at the peak of the Bulge Generation saw Millie (18) and Lulu (16) as defying the hegemony of Establishment culture, with Lulu asserting that television offered her an opportunity to "give my views on things" (Stephens 21 February 1964). Indeed, women used the new disruptive potential of the small screen to exploit gaps in the patriarchal edifice.

Sylvia Stephen, in the pages of *Fabulous* (21 February 1964), asked Lulu, Cilla Black, Sandie Shaw, and *Ready Steady Go!*'s Cathy McGowan whether television had anything to do with "how many girls [were] making it big in show business."

---

[11] The British press called the music "Blue Beat," but Small told Peter Jones the style was "scuff" (4 April 1964). In the US, *Billboard* (23 May 1964) refered to the music as "ska."

The journalist suggested that instead of women screaming at men in concerts, men wanted "something to look" and to "whistle at." All agreed that broadcasts were helping them to reach new audiences, but Lulu and Black sidestepped Stephen's proposition by countering that audiences were simply "tired of seeing boys all the time" (Stephens 21 February 1964).[12]

Shaw emphasized that *Ready, Steady, Go!* occupied an important place in pop culture, with McGowan agreeing. "By appearing regularly on the small screen," the presenter asserted, people "feel they know me." Both she and Cilla Black heard from women with questions about aspects of their appearance such as body shape, clothes, and makeup. McGowan offered: "fans write to ask me if I think it would be right for them to leave home" or "do I think they have the wrong figure for mod clothes" (Stephens 21 February 1964). To the Bulge Generation, McGowan and Black (both 21) represented older-sister role models, as did other women singers born during the war. The path to challenging English-British culture's stereotypes of women, however, would be uphill.

The Bridge. The music industry treated most singers as products with finite shelf lives to be exploited and discarded before their cultural expiration date. In this environment, the norm for women was to be alone in a studio of men, almost all of whom were older and had more security. Each artist in these contexts responded with psychological and musical adaptive strategies that focused on artistic creativity. Their recording careers were shaped by artist-and-repertoire managers and the corporations to whom they supplied product. These curators focused on what they thought audiences wanted by relying on intuition and experience to guide their decisions. The default was to reproduce normative gendered themes.

In the older-sister category, Jackie Trent was 24 when she cowrote "Where Are You Now" (April 1965) with her producer, paramour, and future husband, Tony Hatch. Trent's dramatic delivery and the recording's role in the ITV police drama *It's Dark Outside* helped the disc to top British charts with its theme of lost love. A different sentiment prevailed when Johnny Franz oversaw 21-year-old Julie Rogers's "The Wedding" (July 1964), an orchestral pop version of "La Novia" ("The Bride"). The new lyrics by Fred Jay remade Antonio Prieto's lament about a marriage of convenience into a saccharine celebration that rose to #1 on *Billboard*'s "Easy Listening" chart in January 1965. Neither Trent nor Rogers would be long for the charts, however. Nor would Carol Hedges, a singer with an R&B focus and bad luck.

A Long Time. Closer to the Bulge Generation, Hedges was 16 when she won a singing contest and the attention of manager Mike Sarne and producer Robert Stigwood. They renamed her Billie Davis and sent her to classes for elocution, deportment, and modeling; she then, with Charles Blackwell directing, replaced

---

[12] She appears as Sylvia Stephens in her early *Fabulous* publications and later (presumably accurately) as Sylvia Stephen.

Wendy Richard as Sarne's foil for "Will I What" (August 1962). Blackwell remembers that the recording was "a kind of introduction for her . . . to shine some publicity on her" before they released her cover of the Exciters' "Tell Him" (January 1963), which proved a top 10 hit in the UK.

Success seemed assured when her follow-up, Blackwell's "He's the One" (May 1963) was climbing the charts, only to be foiled by fate. She later recalled: "I had this car accident which put me out for a year and a half. We were coming back from a show and hit a bus." The accident "broke my jaw"; so she was unable to "do anything at all" during a critical era in British pop. While incapacitated, "the Sandie Shaws and the Cilla Blacks came along . . . and I was pushed into the background. A year is a long time, a hell of a long time" (Frith 1973). If the accident had not been bad enough, Davis's extramarital relationship with Jet Harris (formerly of the Shadows) and the tabloid coverage it generated rendered her untouchable in an era of gendered hypocrisy.

Facing double standards, women performers found themselves defined by a business inclined to validate stereotypes, including being marketed as hypersexualized and/or infantilized. Two iconic singers illustrate versions of these cultural norms.

Dagenham Dreams

Sixteen-year-old Sandra Goodrich tentatively stepped up to a microphone at the Ilford Palais. The "aspiring working class" singer was punching computer cards in Ford's Dagenham factory by day, doing some modeling on the side, and performing with bands in East London dance halls and social clubs at night. But it was the joy she clearly got from performing that led her aunt to encourage her to enter this Palais talent contest (Cooper 2013). Although she placed second, she attracted the attention of a music publisher who teamed her with a group to perform on a show at the Commodore Theatre in Hammersmith, West London. There Adam Faith saw and heard potential and recommended her to his (and Jackie Trent's) manager, Eve Taylor (Auld 2010).[13]

Taylor's cynical approach to artist management at first proved a mismatch for Goodrich's headstrong innocence, but Faith's enthusiasm for the teen's potential won a reprieve. When Tony Hatch agreed to record demos, the singer's reaction to the studio floor caught his attention: she sang better with her shoes off. Taylor's husband associated her bare feet with the beach and suggested they name her Sandie Shore, only to have his accent misheard as Shaw. Unfortunately, her demos failed to generate enthusiasm at EMI, Decca, or even Pye, where

---

[13] Faith mentored Sandie Shaw and, unknown to her at the time, also took a percentage of her earnings as a finder's fee (Auld 2010).

Hatch produced. As an alternative, Taylor and Faith proposed financing an independent production (Bret 2014, 92–93).

With Hatch behind the glass, Shaw's first release was of Dagenham singer-songwriter Chris Andrews's "As Long as You're Happy, Baby" (July 1964), but its beat-heavy groove already sounded passé and failed to sell many records. Nevertheless, Shaw's visual style and barefooted appearances on *Thank Your Lucky Stars* (18 and 24 July 1964) and *Ready Steady Go!* (24 July 1964) drew fans (Cooper 2013).

If any sixties female pop star can be said to have epitomized the Look, then Shaw's slim 5'8" stature was perfect for Quant's modern clothing. Moreover, unlike Dusty Springfield's elaborate blond bouffants, Shaw wanted "clean, shining, fresh-smelling hair" and refused to "have it stuck up with lacquer just because [of] a makeup girl, or a TV producer" (Jean-Marie 1965). Moreover, her cheekbones and chin proved perfect foils for a modified version of Sassoon's geometric Shape.

Something There. For Shaw's second release, Taylor arrived back from Los Angeles with Burt Bacharach and Hal David's "(There's) Always Something There to Remind Me," which Bacharach had produced for Lou Johnson in the United States. Given Hatch's preoccupation with Petula Clark, Taylor and Faith installed Chris Andrews as producer and contracted Les Williams to duplicate the original arrangement. The underlying groove of both the Johnson (July 1964) and Shaw (September 1964) recordings emphasizes the growing cosmopolitan interest in Latin music. Shaw's voice, which ranges from intimate to impassioned, relaxed to strained, all the while remaining completely engaged with the lyric, helped to score her first UK #1 (Bret 2014, 92–93).

With that disc's success, Andrews wrote more material drawing on jazz-flavored Latin rhythms. He did so, however, in collaboration with his client, who found ways to make the songs and recordings more effective. The partnership between the songwriter-producer and the singer increasingly allowed Shaw a say in the creation of her material, including lyrics, melody, and instrumentation, even if her contributions went uncredited. "No one wanted you to be seen to be doing anything that might be considered unsexy," she remembered; "they wanted you to do the pretty stuff." By way of justification, Taylor insisted that Shaw could not "possibly put your name on it because people will think you can't afford a producer" (Shaw 2015).

Their next release originally had "I'd Be Far Better Off without You" as the A-side, but station program directors preferred the flip, "Girl Don't Come" (November 1964) with its low-brass introduction, compelling opening ascending melody line, and, most of all, Shaw's breathy delivery. That disc was still in the charts when they focused on the brass sound that had underpinned her first two charting singles. Recruiting trumpeter Ken Woodman as music director and arranger, "I'll Stop at Nothing" (February 1965) made the top five, and the calypso-tinged "Long Live Love" (May 1965) gave them their second #1.

Despite that success, however, the reality of being a woman performer during the midsixties meant routine objectification.

The Problem. Shaw has described the sixties as "not good times to be a young woman," despite her success (Hardy 2013). In an era of "miniskirts, lightweight bras, and the Pill," men could and did sexually harass women with few legal or social consequences (Nicholson 2019, 222). When Shaw complained to her manager, she recalled, "I'm not going to work in the studio with that man . . . or I'd not use a certain photographer," the unsympathetic Taylor told the singer to "shut up if I wanted to stay in work" (Hardy 2013). Although standards were changing, Shaw realized that her manager had come from a "previous generation where it was casting couch stuff, so for her it was like, 'What's the problem?'" (Maguire 2013).

The pressure on young women performers to conform to male sexual fantasies dichotomized feminine stereotypes into the brunette girl next door (Cilla Black) and the blond sex goddess (Kathy Kirby). In this environment, Shaw felt compelled to compare herself to another contemporary pop-culture icon. In an interview with Keith Altham (19 March 1965), she offered that she had seen Brigitte Bardot in a Parisian club and the actress "looked lovely. I still wish I looked like her," and then demurred: "but I haven't got the goods." The journalist felt compelled to offer: "the goods are there—they're just put together in a different, but equally good package." A few weeks later (9 April 1965), he described another singer as a "sex-kitten."

Folky Bohemian Child-Woman

When Marianne Faithfull was a child and her parents—a former British secret agent and a Hungarian baroness—separated, her mother retreated with her child to Reading, Berkshire, and moved them into a small house with no telephone, no gramophone, no car, "no money, no nothing." Although Marianne had to enroll as a "charity boarder" at a Catholic school, the baroness nevertheless attempted to maintain dignity and instill it in her daughter (Faithfull with Dalton 2000, 9). By 1963, however, the 16-year-old was visiting London clubs like the Marquee and the Flamingo, reading Simone de Beauvoir's book *The Second Sex* (1953), and plotting her escape from Reading.

At 17, Faithfull fell in love with socially connected university student and artist John Dunbar. She was attending a party with him in March 1964 when Andrew Oldham approached Dunbar from across the room and asked if his girlfriend could act and/or sing, and if Faithfull really was her name. Her only musical experience had been in the school choir and a "little bit of folksinging in coffee bars and folk clubs." What the Rolling Stones' producer and manager saw, however, was an "angel with big tits" who could sell records (Faithfull with Dalton 2000, 15 and 21).

Brick Walls. Oldham had instructed Mick Jagger and Keith Richards to write a song with "brick walls all around it, and high windows and no sex" and offered food if they were successful. Having now found someone to perform their lament for lost innocence, all he needed was funding to record "As Tears Go By" (Faithfull with Dalton 2000, 23).[14]

Toward the end of May at Olympic Studios, Oldham and music director/arranger Mike Leander rehearsed Faithfull singing "I Don't Know How (to Tell You)," a new song by Lionel Bart that Oldham had little intention of leasing. Instead, he used it as a ruse to get Bart (now the successful playwright of *Oliver!*) to pay for an orchestra and studio time (Oldham 2000, 317). After laboring through Bart's song, they turned to "As Tears Go By," with Oldham instructing Faithfull to "sing very close to the mike." She believes that this approach changed "the spatial dimension" of the performance and helped her to "project" herself into the song (Faithfull with Dalton 2000, 24). Her fragility, vulnerability, and quivering vibrato helped the disc, released in June 1964, to slowly climb into the top 10 in the UK and the top 30 in American markets. Along the way, Oldham fashioned Faithfull into an icon of sixties English pop femininity.

Little Bird. As a follow-up, her version of Bob Dylan's "Blowin' in the Wind" (October 1964) failed to chart, but the success of "As Tears Go By" led to American Jackie DeShannon writing "Come and Stay with Me" (February 1965) for the Austro-Hungarian/English chanteuse. That disc both put Faithfull into the UK's top five and aligned her with the emerging folk-rock scene. Oldham's attention, however, had wandered, partly preoccupied by the Rolling Stones and by his new record label, Immediate. Instead, his partner, Tony Calder, took over production and chose John D. Loudermilk's song "This Little Bird" (April 1965) for her, only to discover that the Nashville Teens were also recording it with Oldham. Nevertheless, Faithfull's ability to deliver the song's fragility put her back into *Record Retailer*'s top 10. This fragility, however, had consequences.

Oldham's publicist, Andy Wickham, had introduced Faithfull as a "little seventeen-year-old blonde ... who still attends a convent in Reading ... daughter of the Baroness Erisso." His press release describes her as "lissome and lovely with long blonde hair" and "shy, wistful, and waif-like" (Faithfull with Dalton 2000, 32). The press took the pitch and ran with it. Keith Altham calls her "wistful" and having "almost waif-like appeal": a "little girl lost" (3 October 1964). Six months later, he would depict her as a combination "sex-kitten" and "society hostess" (9 April 1965). Indeed, a promotional photo from this period suggests a schoolgirl (in white knee socks) reclining suggestively in a pub booth. Television directors

---

[14] Originally called "As Time Goes By," Oldham reworked the song, including changing the title to "As Tears Go By" to avoid confusion with the anthem from the film *Casablanca* (Oldham 2000, 317; Thompson 2008, 209).

similarly framed her as a passive object displayed for examination.[15] This "eerie fusion of haughty aristocrat and folky bohemian child-woman" would haunt her (Faithfull with Dalton 2000, 32).

Like many women singers of this era, Faithfull found herself subject to patriarchal control, facilitated by her general naïveté about the commercial culture she had entered. That midsixties world reduced her to an English feminine cliché: sexy, talented, passive, delicate, and ultimately expendable. Even her now husband, John Dunbar, dismissed her success and routinely undermined her self-confidence so that she never thought she was "anything interesting" (Griffiths 8 April 1965). Evocative of Oldham's instructions to Jagger and Richards, her life had become "like having a big wall round you and you can't get out, you can't climb over it" (Stephens 12 December 1964).

Fig. 15.1. Cilla Black, on *Ready, Steady, Go!*, 1965.

---

[15] For example, as in a promotional video for *Top of the Pops* (2, 9, 16, and 24 September 1964).

238   THE FEMININE MUSIQUE

Fig. 15.2. Lulu, on *Ready, Steady, Go!*, 1965.

Fig. 15.3. Millie Small, 1964.

Fig. 15.4. Cilla Black, Petula Clark, Sandie Shaw, 1965.
PA Images/Alamy Stock Photo

Fig. 15.5. Adam Faith and Sandie Shaw, London, 1964.
Trinity Mirror/Mirrorpix/Alamy Stock Photo

242 THE FEMININE MUSIQUE

Fig. 15.6. Marianne Faithfull, on *Hullabaloo*, 1965.

PART V
TRANSITIONS, 1964-1965

16
Scenes

As the peak of the Bulge Generation turned 18 in 1965, sixties British pop verged on maturity, when curators (production crews, publishers, journalists, broadcasters, and various kinds of promoters and managers) and creators (musicians, songwriters, and other artists) minded the gap between what they heard and saw coming primarily from America and what was happening locally. From the cultural and commercial interactions between the haves and the have-nots, the young and the not quite as young, the domestic and the international, and the privileged and the unprivileged arose the interconnected consumer scenes that the press would eventually call Swinging London.

In an environment where Germany, France, Japan, and Italy were beginning to export to world markets and when the UK government battled a weakening pound, the creation of branded British goods (particularly music) became a national obsession. In this era, the UK enjoyed rising living standards from robust domestic consumption and from international markets attracted by the buzz of British pop culture. Every sound emanating from radiogram speakers and every image, color, shape, fabric, and face that appeared in magazines, on television, or in films offered opportunities for individuals to signal their allegiance with and/or differences from their parents and peers.

The profiles of these curators, creators, and consumers of sixties Britpop roughly paralleled the demographics of those born before the war, during the war, and in the postwar Bulge. And while age, ethnicity, and class differences may have separated these groups socially, their common interests and the resulting cultural symbioses drove the innovation and self-confidence that characterized the intermingled scenes overlapping in London neighborhoods like Chelsea. Performers responded by exploring a range of musical adaptations and identities for the youth of Britain and those of the interconnected cosmopolitan world to explore.

Players

In the comfortable corners of London's pop-culture scene, the "well-connected, well-educated, and reasonably affluent" Chelsea Set partied. Mary Quant described them as "painters, photographers, architects, writers, socialites, actors, conmen, superior tarts, racing drivers, gamblers, and TV producers" (Sandbrook 2006, 229).[1] And when they ventured east of Sloan Square, many headed for the cosmopolitan umbrella of central London's entertainment district. There in the streets of Mayfair and Soho they met their working-class and lower-middle-class counterparts who arrived at night on trains, buses, scooters, and, for a fortunate few, in cars from the suburbs.

Prominent among these suburban invaders, Mods (short for "modernists") imitated what they knew of urban Black American hip modernity; the initial wave embraced modern jazz before various amplified versions of blues (and, for some, Jamaican ska) captured their attention. Most contrasted with Rockers—those anachronistic leather-clad, rock-'n'-roll-loving, motorcycle-riding holdovers from the fifties. Mods took their sartorial inspiration from the Italians and the French spending significant portions of their incomes on clothes that embraced a modernist European aesthetic as modified by London tailors. Individuals adopted the look if not also the attitude of Miles Davis's New York circa 1960, applied a touch of Milan, and proclaimed themselves English in a highly personal but shared visual language.

Their range of choices reflected the balance between individual and cohort tastes, as shaped by economic necessity. Male clothing ranged from Army to Armani while women drew on a variety of Quant-inspired attires available in shops that catered specifically to them. Hebdige (1979, 52) credits Mods with inventing a "style which enabled them to negotiate smoothly between school, work, and leisure": cultural subversives in plain sight, amped on amphetamines and R&B.

The Soho Scene. With the Conservative government stimulating the economy to generate a gush of consumer buying before national elections in the fall of 1964, Mod style evolved quickly. Eric Clapton remembers Mod men at The Scene,[2] in Soho, wearing a "hybrid of American Ivy League and the Italian look... so on one day they might be wearing sweatshirts with baggy trousers and loafers, on another, maybe linen suits" (2007, 61).

The proprietor of The Scene, in Ham Yard, Ronan O'Rahilly—the son of a wealthy Irish family and an active member of the Chelsea Set—brought an ambitious if sometimes erratic worldview to his endeavors. He booked bands like the Animals, the Rolling Stones, and the Yardbirds to play in this low-ceilinged subterranean venue that John Paul Jones described as "smoky, loud, [and] very punky" (Oldham 2000, 78). Audiences accessed The Scene through doors in a

---

[1] This social scene provided the context in which Andrew Oldham (briefly Quant's assistant on King's Road at the beginning of his career) first envisioned Marianne Faithfull as his canvas.

[2] Previously known as the Piccadilly Jazz Club, where Ray Davies had played his first professional gigs.

corner nook of a space opened by a World War II bomb to dance, to listen, and to find others like themselves.

Soho, of course, already had a well-deserved reputation as the center of London's sex industry: a place where worlds tangentially intermingled and a new blues-based rock-pop hybrid found a protective harbor. All the music needed was a way to be heard beyond Soho.

Caroline and the Pirates

The major interdependent revenue streams of Britain's music economy in 1964 included live performances, recordings, film, publishing, and radio and television broadcasts. Performance venues were plentiful—from small local clubs with maybe a hundred listeners and dancers to the Empire Pool with seating for several thousand—and provided promoters, agents, and musicians with income opportunities both above and under the table. Disc sales in this era grew dramatically, with smaller companies (e.g., Island Records) nipping at the heels of the major labels (EMI, Decca, Pye, and Philips) for a piece of the domestic and international vinyl pie. And, while sheet music sales were in decline, music publishing continued to profit from the royalties generated by disc sales, as well as from films and broadcasting that responded to the expanding interest in pop music.

Radio, however, occupied a privileged place in British music culture, with the BBC's national monopoly supporting its mission to shape public taste. Its main competition had been Radio Luxembourg, which broadcast from across the English Channel and benefited from British record companies and music publishers leasing program time. The only other limited challenge came from regional American Forces Network stations until a subversive idea arrived from Scandinavia.

Australian-born Allan Crawford, the former managing director of Southern Music, had formed his own publishing company but grew frustrated trying to get the BBC to broadcast artists playing music from his catalogue (Nicol 1999). He turned to the model of Radio Nord, with which he had been associated: a studio that had been located on a ship anchored in international waters off Stockholm, whence it had broadcast over seldom-used radio wavelengths until the Swedish government shut it down. Among Crawford's ideas, he believed that if listeners heard the cover recordings he made with session musicians, they would purchase those discs instead of the originals. With the backing of investors, he could launch a British equivalent to Radio Nord, charge for advertising, and determine what it broadcast. Ronan O'Rahilly thought it a very good idea.

Greenore. With Northern Ireland sometimes visible across the Carlingford Lough, O'Rahilly's family had a ship facility at Greenore on the coast of the Republic of Ireland, and there Crawford began renovating the original Radio Nord boat with a new transmitter, generator, and radio mast. As the publisher made his plans, however, so did O'Rahilly, obtaining his own ship and outfitting it in the same yards. In this setting the Irishman gained most of the advantages, including an engineer from Radio Nord to oversee his project and, on at least one occasion, to sabotage Crawford's rig (Cawley 2014).

On 28 March 1964, O'Rahilly's Radio Caroline began broadcasting off the east coast of England near Harwich,[3] followed in early May by Crawford's Radio Atlanta anchored just north of that position.[4] Others soon joined them both on ships and on abandoned World War II gunnery platforms in the Thames Estuary. The most successful competitor was Radio London, which began broadcasting in December 1964, also off the coast of Essex.

From the beginning, these "pirates" supported themselves by selling advertising and programming slots (including religious shows) while avoiding paying royalties to record companies and publishers because they were in international waters. The British government immediately condemned the practice, declared the stations illegal, and threatened several times to shut them down; but the broadcasters persisted.

O'Rahilly's anarcho-capitalist philosophy advocated freedom from government intervention but lacked a solid plan for how to stay solvent. Informed by having managed Blues Incorporated and having been involved in Georgie Fame's recording of "Do the Dog," which the BBC had refused to air, he saw his station as a platform for music the Establishment either blocked or ignored (Midgley 2014). Although broadcasts on Radio Caroline in its early days could be described as at the "sophisticated end of the adult market," its programming set precedents (Chapman 1990, 5). In contrast to O'Rahilly's approach, Radio London built a solid advertising base, with its American owners importing jingles and incorporating playlist strategies to boost listenership (Chapman 1990, 1992).

Like contemporary urban British society, these stations and the music they played employed the possibilities of modern technology to generate excitement in new ideas.

---

[3] A number of unresolved origin claims abide as to why the station was called "Caroline," ranging from Caroline Kennedy to a girlfriend (Midgley 2014).

[4] Unfortunately for the publisher, he soon encountered financial difficulties that led to his ship coming under the control of O'Rahilly and his investors.

The Train Leaves the Station

London's blues and rhythm-and-blues fans found their club scene expanding in early 1964 from its foundations at The Marquee, The Flamingo, and The Scene in Soho, at The Crawdaddy across the river in Richmond, and at The Jazz Cellar in Kingston upon Thames, as well as at The Ricky Tick nearby in Windsor. From their humble beginnings in Ealing, performers connected to Blues Incorporated were now gaining national attention. So too were some of the American musicians they imitated.

In May 1964, Granada TV filmed the special *Blues and Gospel Train*, redecorating a Manchester railway platform to look like one in the American South,[5] except for a few hundred English adolescents watching from the physical and social other side of the tracks. The program allowed British blues devotees and others to see Muddy Waters, Sonny Terry and Brownie McGhee, Sister Rosetta Tharpe, the Rev. Gary Davis, Otis Spann, and Cousin Joe Pleasant performing on a cold Manchester spring day. That October, the American Blues Festival arrived in the UK, featuring Sonny Boy Williamson, Sunnyland Slim, Willie Dixon, Hubert Sumlin, Clifton James, Lightnin' Hopkins, Sleepy John Estes, Howlin' Wolf, and others.

In addition to acoustic performances, Muddy Waters, Sister Rosetta Tharpe, and others played electric guitars accompanied by bass, piano, and drums, the dance-centric hallmarks of modern rhythm-and-blues. This music offered British teens something their parents rejected: loud instruments played by African American musicians singing about sex, drugs, booze, and oppression. Pianist Brian Auger saw the writing on the wall and began playing R&B and pop because he "couldn't make a proper living" playing jazz around London anymore (Dawbarn 22 February 1964). Graham Bond had already made the switch.

Bond had been a sought-after saxophonist in London jazz bands before American organists Jimmy McGriff and Jimmy Smith had demonstrated how a Hammond organ could dominate a room and a band. Although the bulk and weight of the instrument created difficulties when traveling, its sound could shake brick walls while reverberating in adolescent hearts. He formed the Graham Bond Organisation with drummer Ginger Baker, bassist Jack Bruce, and initially guitarist John McLaughlin before saxophonist Dick Heckstall-Smith replaced him in early 1963. By 1964, Bond was taking his jazz-tinged R&B message to the provinces, which was where in Newcastle he encouraged the Animals to go south.

---

[5] Wilbraham Road Railway Station, Chorlton-cum-Hardy, Manchester.

An American Sound

To Animals' drummer, John Steel, The Scene was a Mod "hangout," with Ham Yard "packed with scooters, Lambrettas and Vespas all gleaming chrome, mirrors and aerials. We'd never seen anything like it because it was purely a London phenomenon at the time" (Alan White 2011). Responding to this audience, Eric Burdon and Alan Price wrote "I'm Crying" (September 1964), the core of which builds on a Mod favorite: Booker T and the MGs' "Green Onions" (May 1962). As with "The House of the Rising Sun," organ and guitar anchored the arrangement while Burdon's delivery helped sell the recording, which reached Britain's top 10 and America's top 20.

As they and other bands worked through the catalogue of this American idiom, the question arose as to whether their interpretations betrayed anything distinctively British. Eric Burdon thought not, and neither did *Melody Maker's* Bob Dawbarn (16 May 1964), who asserted that the band had "developed an American Negro sound." What exactly constituted that sound and how White British musicians could make it, however, remained undefined.

Although British musicians and audiences lacked unanimity even as to what exactly constituted R&B musically (Coleman 9 May 1964), London audiences were developing expectations. The Animals' first albums *The Animals* (September 1964 in the United States with a different version in the UK, October 1964), *The Animals on Tour* (US, February 1965), and *Animal Tracks* (with different versions again for the UK in May 1965 and for the United States in September 1965) all rely heavily on covers of Ray Charles, John Lee Hooker, and other Black American artists. As they and other British bands interpreted this American idiom with the resources at hand and with their inherent cultural biases, however, listeners on both sides of the Atlantic began to hear something new (Dawbarn 18 April 1964).

Outta This Place. When the Animals first arrived in London, their musical core derived from the sonic synergy of Alan Price's Vox Continental organ and Hilton Valentine's Gretsch Tennessean guitar. Their next single, "Don't Let Me Be Misunderstood" (January 1965), covers Nina Simone and features Burdon passionately delivering the song's plea. Again, at the center of this arrangement, the intermeshing of organ and guitar helped to create the Animals' signature sound. Over the next months, however, an internal dispute arose that would dissolve this musical collaborative.

Manager Mike Jeffery had assigned the arrangement copyright for "The House of the Rising Sun" to Price, with perhaps a tacit understanding that the organist would share the royalties with the others, a plan with fundamental flaws. Burdon (with Craig 2001, 63) asserts that Price left after "he got his first big check from worldwide royalties," but divisions had already been brewing and, in early May 1965, the organist departed to start his own band.

Through American publisher Allen Klein, Mickie Most got his hands on a demo of a song by Barry Mann and Cynthia Weil and heard a suitable vehicle for Burdon. Unlike previous Animal recordings, the organ and the guitar do not combine in "We Gotta Get Out of This Place" (July 1965); instead, Chas Chandler's bass supports the musical infrastructure of drums, guitar, and organ (now played by Dave Rowberry). Against this backing, Burdon embraces the dramatic architecture of the melody, particularly in his improvised scoops that anticipate the chorus. Moreover, the song's theme of escape from poverty to a "better life" came across as authentic from a band with demonstrable proletarian roots.

Their performances at The Scene had helped establish them with London Mods as British interpreters of American blues and rhythm-and-blues. Other clubs, however, also catered to this audience, with some musicians bringing a jazzier multicultural sophistication to their interpretations of American originals.

Flamingo R&B

If London was the crossroads of Britain's postcolonial world, then one of those roads ran through Soho, where the party was at the Flamingo. "Extremely seedy, hot, and sweaty" but with a "brilliant vibe" is how John Paul Jones remembers the club. Its survival derived from an unwritten agreement with the district's police allowing the windowless venue to serve as a meeting place for a wide range of jazz and blues devotees, American servicemen (Black and White), African and West Indian men, gangsters, hoodlums, prostitutes, and London's after-hours night scene at large. Jones characterizes the music of that era as Black R&B with some jazz played by British and American artists (Jones in Oldham 2000, 79).

In 1962, however, fights between patrons—including one altercation over showgirl Christine Keeler that contributed to the fall of the Conservative government—were drawing the unwanted attention of London's Establishment. The stories, however, also attracted a new crowd. "It got terrible and after a while, it was put off limits to the GIs," Georgie Fame recalled. "Then all the white kids who had been too scared to come before heard about it and the next week the place was packed with Mods" (Welch 3 August 1974).

Fame. Managed by Rik Gunnell, one of the proprietors of the Flamingo, Fame and the Blue Flames were the first band to perform live on *Ready Steady Go!* and were fixtures of London's Mod club life. And although Ronan O'Rahilly's attempts to get radio play for "Do the Dog" failed, the Ian Samwell–produced album *Fame at Last* (September 1964) reached #6 on *Record Retailer*'s charts, suggesting that the Blue Flames had an audience, just not one that bought 45-rpm discs.

With American Tony Palmer producing their next single, Fame and the band proposed "Yeh, Yeh"—a tune originally recorded by Cuban artist Mongo Santamaría (May 1963) and to which Jon Hendricks had added words for his vocal trio Lambert, Hendricks & Bavan (*At Newport '63*, November 1963). Blue Flames tenor saxophonist Peter Coe remembered: "we'd been playing it around the clubs, but we thrashed out a version, which we thought was suitable for a single" (Frame 1997, 25).

Fame and the Blue Flames took "Yeh, Yeh" (December 1964) at a faster tempo than both the Santamaría and the Lambert, Hendricks & Bavan versions, and stripped down the arrangement, with Fame's sustained Hammond organ replacing the piano montuno of the original.[6] Key to the recording's success, Fame's singing recontextualizes the lyrics to convey a dynamism and joy of urban youth. A month after its release, the recording not only topped British charts but also broke into *Cashbox*'s top 20 in the United States. Fame, however, had its limits.

Out of Soho. Venturing out of Soho could mean problems for a band that routinely included one or two Commonwealth musicians like Ghanaian percussionist Nii Moi "Speedy" Acquaye. And the Blue Flames, when contemplating a North American tour, encountered visa problems when US immigration found yet more reasons to block British artists. Traveling in parts of the UK, moreover, could also present issues for a multicultural ensemble.

Mod idealization of the Black American experience came in the multicultural contexts of Britain's colonial past. The arrival of laborers from Commonwealth nations beginning in the late 1940s and the 1958 riots in Nottingham and Notting Hill Gate had exposed the nation's endemic intolerance, xenophobia, and racism. Three years later, the Bradford Mecca Locarno—one of the largest dance halls in the UK—banned single Caribbean and African men from entering, ostensibly because of occasional fights but also for fears of miscegenation. This racism also shaped British politics.

In the runup to the 1964 British elections, residents of the community of Smethwick (just outside Birmingham) woke to find flyers declaring "If you want a nigger neighbour, vote Liberal or Labour" (Sandbrook 2006, 669). Despite the national success of the Labour Party in the election, the local Labour incumbent lost to the antiimmigration Conservative candidate.

---

[6] The Lambert, Hendricks & Bavan version comes from a live performance at the 1963 Newport Jazz Festival.

Back in London, rhythm-and-blues forms were inspiring some musicians to create their own variations that were almost, but not quite, entirely unlike the originals. That is, just as the music of Black American musicians reflected their lives as they migrated to the urban industrial North, adapting blues and gospel forms to create rhythm-and-blues, so too did White British musicians adapt rhythm-and-blues to reflect their world.

Set Me Free

The visual arts had shaped how Ray Davies thought about and expressed ideas about creativity. He equated color with expression in good painting. In good songwriting, sincerity made the difference, if one had the time and latitude (Ray Davies 3 October 1964). The Kinks had established their London reputation with energetic interpretations of rock 'n' roll and rhythm-and-blues standards, but success had only come when Davies found ways to internalize and recombine elements of these repertoires.

In the late summer of 1964, the band hastily completed an album of covers, Ray Davies originals, and filler material by producer Shel Talmy that was released in one version by Pye as *The Kinks* in the UK (October 1964) and in another version by Reprise as *You Really Got Me* (October 1964) in the United States. Public attention, however, had been whetted by "You Really Got Me" (August 1964) and Talmy wanted a follow-up single that was as raw and was clearly identifiable as the Kinks. In response, Ray Davies returned to the same blues-based schema.

"All Day and All of the Night" (October 1964) again features Dave Davies's distorted guitar sound, Ray Davies's snarling nasal vocals, and Talmy's tightly compressed production. The recording and performance also capture the Kinks' protopunk energy and subsequently made the UK's top five and America's top 10. That goal accomplished, Talmy agreed to release the song Ray Davies had originally offered as a follow-up.

"Tired of Waiting for You" (January 1965) stays in the same general harmonic wheelhouse but explores material that had been on the songwriter's mind for a while. The backing track came together quickly in the studio, but Davies lacked lyrics (Ray Davies 1994, 174–175). Rushed and responding to his increasingly complicated life, the 20-year-old drafted words that moved beyond adolescent lust to reflect his impending marriage and fatherhood.

The Whore. The businesses of music performance, recording, and publishing demanded more singles, and quickly. Thus, over the next year, Davies's "Everybody's Gonna Be Happy" (UK March 1965), "Set Me Free" (US and UK May 1965), "Who'll Be the Next in Line" (US July 1965), and "Till the End of the Day" (November 1965) all work from the same palette as the Kinks' first singles.

Despite chart success, the songwriter began to question himself. He felt "ashamed" of "Set Me Free," explaining that although he tried never to use familiar chord sequences, he had resorted to a harmonic cliché that others had "used in hundreds of songs," thinking that "nothing else would go in." To him, that decision signified songwriting he described as "hackmanship" and that left him feeling "like a whore" (*Melody Maker* 21 August 1965). He needed a new palette.

Davies's songwriting in 1964 and 1965 suggests an intentional primitivism: music that sounds simple (e.g., the minimalist chord choices and text of "You Really Got Me") but is reconstituted in unique ways. As Picasso had abstracted existing ideas (e.g., his series of paintings based on Velázquez's "Las Meninas"), Davies took existing musical idioms, reduced them to their essential qualities, and reassembled them, in the process subversively upending musical conventions. Nevertheless, he had reached a turning point. As the Kinks traveled the UK playing ballrooms and theaters, the songwriter found himself drawn to stories closer to home. The world around him became important, whether fishermen he heard singing in Bombay or Londoners on trains and in the street. In that mode, other influences began to subvert the conventions of R&B.

Blues Base

Although electronic keyboards like the Clavioline, the Vox Continental, the Hohner Pianet, and various models of the Hammond organ provided an important sonic signature for mid-1960s British pop, guitar virtuosi attracted audiences. The British popular music press had lionized Shadow guitarist Hank Marvin, whose association with Cliff Richard had elevated his reputation. By the mid-1960s, a wave of young White male guitarists initially influenced by Marvin began developing their own styles in the performance spaces that were springing up across the country. For them, blues-related idioms and styles encouraged explorations of the electric guitar's possibilities.

With American blues figures serving as their models, British musicians created sonic and social environments distinctly their own. Clubs like The Scene—subterranean stone boxes tightly packed with dancers and gawkers—provided spaces that shaped the sounds and experiences of the music. As guitarists amped up the loudness of their performances to explore the new interpretive possibilities of feedback, audience members physically absorbed the sound. Over the course of 1964 and 1965, a generation of British blues exponents exploited the spirit of American originals to develop a sonic echo that sounded like London.

The challenge for every young aspiring British blues musician (indeed, every musician) lay in the reality that a convincing performance relied on more than simply good copying: they needed to create something new and compelling. With American originals like Muddy Waters occasionally touring the UK, the British fascination with this music and its musicians entered a new phase and encountered an old problem: British audiences generally preferred White faces to Black, and domestic performances to foreign, no matter how much White musicians praised the originals.

Us and Them

Belfast had seen both the arrival of Scottish and English immigrants and then waves of emigrants to North America, all before becoming the capital of Northern Ireland in the early 1920s. Since then, the British province's intense religious, political, and economic animosities had played out on the city's streets between Protestants aligned with the UK and Catholics seeking unification with the Republic of Ireland. Belfast's popular music scene reflected these tensions, developing characteristics that reflected both deep-seated Anglo-Celtic traditions and modern cosmopolitan aesthetics.

Van Morrison grew up in Belfast listening to jazz and Americana discs collected by his father, a shipyard electrician and descendant of Scottish Protestants (Collis 1997, 26). As a teen, Morrison became a saxophonist in an Irish showband,[7] and when the bandleader suggested he sing, he embraced a persona that allowed him to "gyrate around the stage" and "leap down into the audience" (39).

In 1963, when that band folded after punishing tours in Scotland and West Germany, Morrison headed to London to experience its blues scene. Returning home enthused, he found kindred spirits in guitarist Billy Harrison, bassist Alan Henderson, drummer Ronnie Milling, and 15-year-old organist Eric Wrixon. Wrixon suggested they call themselves Them,[8] because "it just seemed to sound modern to have a band name without a 'the' in the front" (Wrixon in Collis 1997, 52).

With students crowding their shows at the Maritime Blues Club on Friday nights, a former Decca engineer sent a recording of the band to Dick Rowe. Summoning Them to London, Rowe produced their cover of Slim Harpo's "Don't Start Crying Now" (September 1964), but Morrison's raspy nasal voice and the

---

[7] These were bands with seven to nine members who played contemporary pop hits, usually while standing and often with synchronized moves.
[8] Named after the 1954 science fiction film *Them* (Collis 1997, 52).

band's unmemorable backing failed to impress blues fans already familiar with the Rolling Stones, the Animals, and others.

Preferring that the Irish band have management with London connections,[9] Rowe had contacted members of a prominent Decca shareholder's family. The Solomons already managed mainstream acts like the Irish pop-folk trio the Bachelors (Clayson 20 June 2011), and with Rowe's encouragement Phil Solomon added this new Ulster band as clients. Unfortunately, he booked Them into Irish pubs rather than the clubs where London's Mods were congregating, which meant no name recognition in the charts (Collis 1997, 58). Meanwhile, the band had already changed.

Don't Go. With his parents unwilling to let him turn professional, Wrixon had left to finish school, and with only sporadic and unsatisfactory gigs and after sleeping in the band's van, Milling returned home to support his family. Restructuring, Pat McAuley became the drummer, and his brother Jackie arrived from Belfast with a Farfisa electronic organ (Collis 1997, 60). Meanwhile, Phil Solomon began to secure better bookings as the band began to establish itself in London's R&B club scene.

Perhaps realizing that R&B was not his greatest strength, Rowe passed production responsibilities for their next single to American Bert Berns. Morrison proposed covering the blues standard "Baby Please Don't Go" (November 1964),[10] with Billy Harrison's slightly distorted guitar riff opening the recording over Henderson's throbbing bass. To enhance the performance, the American also contracted studio guitarist Jimmy Page, who played choked chords during verses and added a "bass part on lead,"[11] in response to Morrison's calls (Morrison in Collis 1997, 61).

On the flip side, Berns reworks Dick Rowe's initial take of Van Morrison's "Gloria" by adding a second and busier drum part played by Bobby Graham. The presence of contracted musicians, however, while improving the band's performances, also created friction. Page remembers the sessions becoming "very embarrassing" when Berns replaced band members: "there'd be times you'd be sitting there ... and wishing you weren't" (Page in Frame 1997, 31).

Evidence that London was beginning to accept the Irish band came with an invitation to appear on *Ready Steady Go!* (20 November 1964) and when the show's producers chose part of "Baby Please Don't Go" for the closing credits (December 1964). The television appearances and club gigs helped push the disc into *Record Retailer*'s top 10 and established the band in both the British blues

---

[9] They were managed by three local entrepreneurs.
[10] Originally recorded by Joe Williams' Washboard Blues Singers 1935 but also covered by John Lee Hooker, Muddy Waters, and others.
[11] Perhaps a baritone guitar.

community and the broader pop market. Moreover, the energy of their eponymous EP and LP attracted the attention of amateur musicians on both sides of the Atlantic.

As with the Kinks, recordings by Them inspired a host of teens to take up instruments to play for any audience who would listen. This music scene grew an audience eager to crown the first guitar hero of sixties British R&B.

Ain't Got You

Keith Relf remembered the blues guitar devotee from the Kingston School of Art (in the southwest of Greater London) who had attended one of his band's performances. Eric Clapton had walked up to then guitarist Paul Samwell-Smith in the Kingston Jazz Cellar and requested, "do me a favor: don't play any more solos" (Clayson 2002, 75).

Clapton had been part of the Blues Incorporated scene, sometimes climbing on stage to sing Chuck Berry tunes while in private learning to copy the guitarists he heard on blues records. A child of the war raised by his working-class grandparents (to hide their daughter's pregnancy), Clapton joined Relf (vocals and harmonica), Samwell-Smith (bass), Jim McCarty (drums), and Chris Dreja (guitar) to play as the Yardbirds.

When Andrew Oldham signed away the Rolling Stones, Giorgio Gomelsky, the promoter of the Crawdaddy Club, turned to the Yardbirds (Unterberger 2000, 126). Gomelsky, who had started the club in Richmond with a loan from Ronan O'Rahilly, had earned a reputation for discovering talent from managing the Stones. In the Yardbirds, he heard redemption.

To build their national recognition and reputation for authenticity, he booked the band to accompany Sonny Boy Williamson on his British tour. To blues devotee Clapton, the man passing as Williamson was really Rice Miller, a talented opportunist who had assumed the name of a deceased icon. To the American, the Brits were borderline incompetents, later commenting: "those English kids want to play the blues so bad—and they play the blues so bad" (Clapton 2007, 48). British audiences, however, disagreed.

Young and White. The pairing of Sonny Boy Williamson with the Yardbirds responded to fears that adolescents would not turn out to hear an old Black American unless young White English musicians were accompanying him (Schwartz 2007, 149). The tour experience, while humbling and frustrating at times, did help the Yardbirds recognize that their strengths lay in normalizing blues idioms to English contexts. And although many British performers in this milieu carefully avoided claiming that what they performed was authentic, at the same time their attempts created something new (Schwartz 2007, 142).

Gomelsky booked time at the R. G. Jones Studios in London's southwest suburbs to record the Yardbirds playing, among other things, a cover of Billy Boy Arnold's "I Wish You Would" (May 1964). Clapton (2007, 48) remembers being disappointed in the playback, thinking that even though the song was "very catchy," the Yardbirds still sounded "young and white." Columbia's release generated little acclaim, and their second single, "Good Morning Little Schoolgirl" (October 1964), barely made Britain's top 50. Those who bought the disc, however, also heard Clapton's growing expertise on the flip side in "Ain't Got You" (another Billy Boy Arnold cover).

As the Yardbirds played venues in London, Birmingham, Liverpool, and Manchester, young men began gathering on Clapton's side of the stage to watch his guitar technique. He had learned to string his guitar with a light-gauge top wire that was easier to bend but also sometimes broke. As he replaced the string while the band continued playing, this coterie often went into a slow handclap, and the regularity of this phenomenon led Gomelsky to coin the nickname "Slow Hand" for the guitarist (Clapton 2007, 49).

Although heroes to a community of blues aficionados, the Yardbirds' lack of chart success led Gomelsky to bring them a publisher's demo of "For Your Love" written by young Manchester musician Graham Gouldman. Where Gomelsky and Samwell-Smith heard the song as a way to break into the pop market, Clapton heard evidence that they had "completely sold out" (Clapton 2007, 53). When "For Your Love" (March 1965) climbed to #3 on *Record Retailer*'s chart and broke into *Billboard*'s top 10 in the United States, it catapulted the Yardbirds into pop stardom. In the background, however, Gomelsky strove to keep the band's star guitarist content with the B-side instrumental "Got to Hurry," which bore the annotation "Featuring Eric 'Slow Hand' Clapton." The guitarist resigned anyway to maintain his aesthetics.

Fig. 16.1 Rosetta Tharpe, on *Blues and Gospel Train*, May 1964.

Fig. 16.2 Georgie Fame, on *Ready, Steady, Go!*, 1964.

Fig. 16.3 The Kinks, on *Shindig!*, 1965.

Fig. 16.4 Van Morrison with Them, at New Musical Express Winner's Concert, 1965.

Fig. 16.5 The Yardbirds, on *Shindig!*, 1965.

17
Down the Road a Piece

After the Labour Party won a narrow parliamentary victory in October 1964, the new chancellor of the exchequer inherited a budget deficit of about £800 million. The Conservatives, in their attempts to maintain the illusion of Britain being an international power and to stimulate the economy, had depleted the treasury. The Exchequer now contemplated the unpleasant options of cutting public programs and raising taxes (Sandbrook 2006, 86ff).

Labour's campaign theme of modernization, with its promise of a better future through the white heat of technology, had resonated in many corners of British society. With the deficit, however, that agenda now seemed in jeopardy, with the distinct possibility of the government defaulting. Despite the dire situation, the sudden global success of British popular culture offered a hint of optimism.

As London consolidated its position, not only as a major player in the popular-music industry but also as a center of Western popular culture, an ambitious legion of artists, entrepreneurs, and charlatans descended on the city. Musicians, songwriters, graphic and clothing designers, filmmakers, poets, and others fed the world's voracious appetite for British pop culture. Youth went in search of recordings, magazines, and more by day and for music in clubs, dance halls, and theaters by night.

As the dollar had replaced the pound as the coin of international exchange, however, so too American songs and recordings had become the currency of Western pop music. Nevertheless, by internalizing the syntax of American pop, rock, and blues, British musicians, in their imitations, adapted existing ideas in response to mid-twentieth-century Britain and specifically to the aesthetics of London audiences.

Brum Blues

Although Liverpool and Manchester had led the first wave of provincial contributions to sixties British pop, Birmingham, at the center of the Midlands, is closer to the capital. The city had once been the heart of England's industrial revolution, but the Luftwaffe had destroyed significant parts of its infrastructure (Marwick 2003, 93). Postwar redevelopment then leveled many blocks, replacing nineteenth-century red-brick rowhouses with grey concrete, steel, and glass

Sixties British Pop, Outside In. Gordon Ross Thompson, Oxford University Press. © Oxford University Press 2024.
DOI: 10.1093/oso/9780190672348.003.0018

towers that, in 1964, journalist Geoffrey Moorehouse thought expressed a modernist "excitement in the air" (Sandbrook 2006, 626). As this "moving forward" destroyed neighborhoods and relocated families to suburban residential units, it also opened urban spaces to redefine.[1] Adding to the city's history of union and political activism, Caribbean, Asian, and African immigrants enhanced this already culturally and socially rich environment.

The symbiotic relationship between the two cities, less than a hundred miles apart, meant that London exercised influence in Birmingham in a way Liverpool and Manchester had resisted. This proximity also gave "Brummie" musicians easier access to London's clubs, publishers, and studios. In Birmingham's competitive environment, musicians employed several strategies for survival and success, forming and reforming musical alliances in attempts to link like-minded and complementarily skilled performers.[2] As musicians shifted between bands and listened to each other, they created their own unique amalgams of "Brum Beat."[3]

At the Golden Eagle

In 1963, 23-year-old Welsh musician Spencer Davis had already been a grammar-school head boy and had worked in London for the government before studying German at the University of Birmingham. Local audiences, however, knew him for his folk-blues performances at the Golden Eagle, an art deco pub clad in black marble in the center of town. With the trade papers trumpeting the rise of rhythm-and-blues in London, he learned about a band fronted by two brothers from Birmingham's northern suburbs, the sons of a foundry worker who was also a semiprofessional musician. Hearing them, what impressed Davis most about Muff Winwood's band was the vocal, guitar, and piano virtuosity of his 14-year-old brother, Steve, whom they sometimes had to hide in pub performances because he was clearly underage (James n.d. "Davis").

Steve Winwood had sung in his church choir before briefly studying piano at a local conservatory, where teachers had failed to understand his appreciation of both Paul Hindemith and Ray Charles. As soon as possible, he left school to join the Spencer Davis Rhythm & Blues Quartet, in which Davis played guitar and harmonica and sang while Muff Winwood switched from guitar to bass to

---

[1] The Midlands and its industrial base attracted Commonwealth immigrants, with Birmingham's West Indian population alone growing from 8,000 to 30,000 between 1953 and 1958 (Sandbrook 2006, 666).

[2] See Peter Frame's "Birmingham Beatsters" for a graphic representation of the personnel interconnections among some of these groups (Frame 1993, 14).

[3] "Brum" is a colloquial abbreviation of Birmingham derived from Brummagem or "Brummie," the dialect and accent of English associated with the city.

establish the groove with drummer Peter York. Audiences at the Golden Eagle and other Birmingham venues, however, came to hear the shy youngest member, who gradually took center stage. What the band then needed was a path to London.

Giorgio Gomelsky had first met Spencer Davis when Davis had showed up at the Crawdaddy Club in early 1964 boasting about his band and searching for bookings. The manager soon heard the group open the Rhythm and Blues Festival in Birmingham Town Hall (28 February 1964), where Sonny Boy Williamson headlined the show with the Yardbirds. Gomelsky took immediate notice of the 15-year-old Steve Winwood and approached Davis with a management contract for the band;[4] but he had competition.

Every Little Bit. Chris Blackwell had brought protégé Millie Small to Birmingham to tape an appearance on *Thank Your Lucky Stars* (broadcast 28 March 1964) when a tip sent him to the Golden Eagle to hear Spencer Davis's band and its boy wonder. When he too proposed a management contract, Davis chose Blackwell's confident English public-school demeanor over Gomelsky's "Rasputin" appearance and European hustle (James n.d. "Davis"). When Blackwell negotiated a distribution contract with Fontana Records, he also encouraged the band to shorten its name. They chose the Spencer Davis Group.[5]

Although Steve Winwood's tense nasal tenor more closely resembled White country singers, he emulated Black urban blues musicians (Johnny Black May 1997). British listeners heard him as an English Ray Charles, especially given his rendition of "Georgia on My Mind."[6] Nevertheless, he expressed embarrassment. "No matter how hard you try you can never sing the blues like a coloured person. . . . That's their life they are singing about" (Winwood in Altham 11 February 1966). He also sometimes found himself in competition with the originals.

Anticipating the Spencer Davis Group's initial Fontana release of "Dimples" (May 1964), EMI countered with John Lee Hooker's original 1956 recording to capture sales. Looking to avoid repeating that scenario, Blackwell introduced the Birmingham band to "I Can't Stand It" (October 1964) by the Jamaican trio the Soul Sisters. Even with Steve Winwood's deft guitar playing (sometimes doubled by his voice), their cover only just broke into Britain's top 50. And for their third release (February 1965), they reworked Brenda Holloway's "Every Little Bit Hurts" (March 1964), for which Winwood brought his most fragile teenage angst to the performance while playing organ over an understated backing track on

---

[4] Winwood sang and played guitar on a sped-up cover of John Lee Hooker's "Dimples."
[5] As the most senior and experienced member of the group and multilingual, Davis functioned as their spokesperson.
[6] In a precedent, a previous generation identified trumpeter and singer Nat Gonella (who also performed "Georgia on My Mind") as an English Louis Armstrong.

which he also played piano.[7] The disc failed to reach audiences, however, and sold only modestly.

At the 5th National Jazz and Blues Festival (6–8 August 1965), Winwood was invited to join other featured artists (Eric Burdon and Steampacket singers John Baldry, Julie Driscoll, and Rod Stewart) to sing with the Animals for the finale. The invitation signaled recognition of his skill and acceptance by London's blues scene. What the Spencer Davis Group needed, however, was a record that would distinguish them from everyone else.

M&B

In May 1964, Ray Thomas (harmonica and vocals) and Mike Pinder (keyboards) returned from grueling German club dates to Birmingham to face competition from a sudden abundance of young musicians. Turning to other seasoned Brum musicians, they formed a new band with Denny Laine (guitar and vocals), Graeme Edge (drums), and Clint Warwick (bass) (Frame 1993, 13). They had hoped that by naming themselves to reference a popular local English bitter (M&B Brew XI) the brewery might sponsor them. When that proposition fell flat, the M&B Five instead became the Moody Blues (Woodhouse 2015), and sponsorship came from two eager entrepreneurs.

Tony Secunda and Alex Murray (Mickie Most's former singing partner) were partners in Ridgepride, a management and production company that shared office space with Nicky Byrne's Beatles merchandising enterprise, Seltaeb. Searching for a group with potential, the Moody Blues impressed Secunda and Murray enough for them to finance new equipment and move the band to a flat in London. Secunda negotiated gigs first at the Crawdaddy and then at the Marquee, replacing Manfred Mann when they were unable to play. Murray negotiated a recording contract with his previous employer, Decca.

The group's repertoire had benefited from a record collector and fan who knew an American deejay and had R&B discs that were generally unknown in the UK. This curation introduced the Moody Blues to recordings like James Brown's "I'll Go Crazy" (January 1960), which they adapted for British contexts. And when Murray brought them to Olympic Studios for their first sessions, their cover of Bobby Parker's "Steal Your Heart Away"[8] (September 1964)—a 12/8 blues

---

[7] The mono single features the organ, but the album version has strings overdubbed. Winwood had encountered a Hammond B3 at the Place in Stoke-on-Trent (27 October 1963) and, like Graham Bond, was taken by its power and potential for R&B. See Johnny Black May 1997.

[8] The flip side "Watch Your Step" (July 1961) was covered by several British artists and served as inspiration for John Lennon's "I Feel Fine."

featuring Denny Laine on vocals—came off best.[9] Even though the disc failed to chart, the concert and club performances and an appearance on *Ready Steady Go!* (28 August 1964)[10] prepared British audiences (including pirate deejays) for their next release. For that, they turned to Bessie Banks's blues waltz "Go Now" (March 1964).

Go Now. The Moody Blues' recording of "Go Now!," like the original, features the piano and a descending stepwise bassline that at once echoes the gospel origins of the song and a common harmonic device taught in music theory classes. Denny Laine describes their version as "bopped" and "sort of gospel in our own limited way" (Woodhouse 2015). The music and Laine's delivery perhaps foretells a new strain of British pop, but the sound of the recording also struck listeners' ears as unusual.

With finances strained, Murray had begun recording "Go Now!" in the demo studio of the publisher Chappell and Co., but when that session proved unsatisfactory, he turned to a cheaper alternative (Cushman 2017, 43). Recording in a studio behind the Marquee that "hadn't been fully finished" (Pinger in Cushman 2017, 43), resulted in a tape that "sounded like it had been recorded in a public lavatory" (Murray in Bob 2009). Nevertheless, the sound and performance of "Go Now!" (November 1964) stood out and as 1965 dawned, the disc was selling well in both the UK and the United States, with assistance from a stark black-and-white promotional film of them miming to the recording.[11]

Unfortunately, their subsequent releases of "I Don't Want to Go On without You" (February 1965), "From the Bottom of My Heart" (May 1965), and "Everyday" (October 1965), as well as their album *The Magnificent Moodies* (July 1965), although charting, never quite captured the same excitement. During a year in which the band did not release a single, Laine and Warwick left. The Moody Blues would reinvent themselves, with Thomas taking up the flute, but new management, production, and repertoire would mean taking more chances.

Brum Pop

Birmingham's versions of sixties British pop perhaps first caught national attention in 1964 when the Applejacks (from the comfortable suburb of Solihull) scored a top-10 hit with Les Reed and Geoff Stephens's "Tell Me When" (February

---

[9] The flip side was an up-tempo country-flavored blues written by Laine and Pinder that initially bore the misspelled title "Loose Your Money (but Don't Loose Your Mind)." This title, perhaps indicative of the team's inexperience, if not the lack of a critically engaged editorial eye at Decca, was corrected in later reissues to "Lose Your Money (but Don't Lose Your Mind)."
[10] The *Ready Steady Go!* appearance featured the flip side, "Lose Your Money."
[11] This film influenced future music videos, notably Queen's "Bohemian Rhapsody."

1964), followed by Lennon and McCartney's "Like Dreamers Do" (June 1964). Decca had picked up the band in part because of their unique lineup, which included a woman (Megan Davies) playing bass, but also because producer Mike Smith and music director Mike Leander believed they could shape the band's sound to conform to contemporary pop tastes.

After a two-hour drive to Decca's studios in West Hampstead, they were neither the first nor the last musicians from the Midlands who had made the trek on two-lane highways only to be told what to play by a London producer. Musicians from Birmingham, however, not only contributed some of the most successful and innovative performances and recordings of the era but also played important roles in defining the sound of sixties British pop.

Singers like Steve Winwood and Denny Laine may have learned how to imitate the phrasing and ornamentation of Americans like Ray Charles and Bessie Banks, but their voices betrayed their White English backgrounds. Their counterparts in the pop mainstream, on the other hand, more easily conformed to Euro-American singing-style expectations.

English Equivalents

In 1959, budding teenage songwriters John Shakespear and Ken Hawker boarded a bus for London hoping to sell their material on Denmark Street. Several publishers rejected them, but Terry Kennedy heard possibilities, and through him they eventually secured a contract with Southern Music. When they applied for membership in the Performing Right Society,[12] however, they encountered a minor problem: someone had already registered the name John Shakespear. Kennedy thought that the names John Carter and Ken Lewis worked better anyway.

To support themselves, they broke into the London music scene as Everly Brothers soundalikes, passing a BBC audition to perform on radio programs such as *Saturday Club* and *Easybeat*. Nevertheless, songwriting remained their goal, and with a band named after their publishers, Carter-Lewis and the Southerners began learning about London's music, recording, and publishing industries by trial and error.[13] When none of their discs charted, however, the band dissolved and moved into session work, joined by another Birmingham songwriter, Perry Ford.[14]

---

[12] The Performing Right Society is a copyright protection and collection cooperative.
[13] The Southerners included 19-year-old Jimmy Page on guitar and future Pretty Thing Viv Prince on drums.
[14] Ford would play piano on the Kinks' "All Day and All of the Night."

The three often provided backing vocals, with Carter switching to a falsetto in situations that allowed them to pitch songs to producers. While working on a Herman's Hermits session, for example, they convinced Mickie Most to put their "Can't You Hear My Heart Beat" (January 1965) on a B-side, which became a hit in the United States.

Elizabethans. In the summer of 1964 as the world awoke to British pop, the group took the stage as the Ivy League, a vocal trio described in advertising as having "Hair by Phillipe" and clothes by "Alexandre of Oxford St." Recorded in the tiny Regent Sound Studios, their first release, "What More Do You Want" (September 1964), failed to chart, but as 1965 dawned, they found a sound and a style that resonated with listeners. Bob Dawbarn (6 February 1965) thought that "Funny How Love Can Be" (February 1965) sounded "Elizabethan," possibly referring to the arrangement's harmonic suspensions. Carter, however, remembered copying "Americans to try to get an English kind of equivalent" (interview 26 June 2000).

"That's Why I'm Crying" (April 1965) and "Tossing and Turning" (June 1965) kept them in the charts, with the latter squeaking into *Billboard*'s Hot 100. As they were promoting this last recording, however, touring ended abruptly when, late one night in Hertfordshire, their car went off the road. The crash threw Carter from the vehicle and put him in hospital, leading the singer-songwriter to abandon live performances for the safety of the studio. The Ivy League increasingly became a construct of convenience, with Carter writing and recording and other musicians performing on stage. Indeed, like Brian Wilson of the Beach Boys, he questioned the very notion that the musicians one saw on stage needed to be the same people you heard on a recording.

He's in Town

Hamburg had tested the mettle of many British musicians, including the Rockin' Berries, of Birmingham. When they lost several members to the Reeperbahn's excess and exhaustion, guitarist Chuck Botfield returned home to recruit Roy Austin (bass) and school friend Geoff Turton (guitar) to join him, impressionist Clive Lea, and drummer Terry Bond in the Saint Pauli quarter. As they rehearsed, the group gravitated toward vocal harmonies, especially when Turton realized that he "could sing in this falsetto," and they turned to American recordings that matched their strengths (Turton in Woodhouse 2016). Their shows came to alternate Turton's plaintive vocals with Lea's comedy routines, a juxtaposition of music and humor as English as the music hall.

Returning to Birmingham, the group staged a showcase to attract attention, which led to a proposal from Maurice King's Capable Management and a recording contract with Decca. When those discs failed to chart, John Schroeder—who had left EMI to manage Pye's Piccadilly label—came to see them at the Cadbury Club,[15] in southwest Birmingham. The producer saw the Berries' "slick routines," their local fan base, and Turton's "wonderfully commercial and identifiable" voice as reasons to give them a second chance (Schroeder 2009, 113).

Their cover of the Shirelles' "I Didn't Mean to Hurt You" (August 1964) had just charted when they rush-released "He's in Town" (October 1964). Drummer Terry Bond remembered American Kim Fowley playing the Tokens' original (July 1964) for them (Woodhouse 2016), while Schroeder believed that someone from publisher Campbell Connelly brought him the disc (Schroeder 2009, 113). Either way, although Fontana released the American recording in the UK, Piccadilly had the Rockin' Berries' disc in shops a week later, and with the advantages of domestic advertising and audiences, it reached *Record Retailer*'s top five. They followed these two releases with covers of the Dovells' "What in the World's Come Over You" (January 1965) and the Reflections' "Poor Man's Son" (April 1965), all four discs featuring Turton and vocal harmonies. However, while their versions blocked the American originals from UK charts, they were reciprocally unable to get airplay in the United States.

When Maurice King merged his artist portfolio with that of Philip and Dorothy Solomon in the fall of 1965, the agency's strategy shifted: the Rockin' Berries now toured cabarets with the Solomon-managed Irish pop-folk trio the Bachelors (Hutchins 1965). In London, where many pop groups were advocating for artistic integrity, sophistication, and experimentation, the Berries (as they would eventually call themselves) continued to mix Lea's impressions (e.g., Harold Wilson) and Turton's covers of sentimental ballads, with diminishing relevance.

Troubles

Birmingham grammar-school friends Rod Allen and Barry Pritchard formed a vocal-harmonies trio with Glen Dale that manager Reg Calvert hired to back his singers in 1961. By 1963, however, he saw their potential as a separate act, called them the Fortunes, and contracted with Shel Talmy to record them. Pritchard provides the falsetto in their attempted resurrection of the Jamies' 1958 hit "Summertime, Summertime" (August 1963), which failed to chart as beat groups flooded the UK adolescent market.

---

[15] Set up by Cadbury, the chocolate company, for its employees.

Responding to trends, Allen took up the bass, Dale rhythm guitar, and Pritchard lead guitar, and they added Dave Carr (keyboards) and Andy Brown (drums). Their "Caroline" (January 1964), written by future Ivy Leaguer Perry Ford with Tony Hiller (Laing 17 January 2008), briefly went onto Radio Caroline's playlist, but when it and two more releases also failed to chart, Talmy ended their contract.

Liverpudlian producer Noel Walker,[16] however, heard potential and convinced Decca to give the Fortunes another chance. "You've Got Your Troubles" (June 1965)—written by British songwriters Roger Greenaway and Roger Cook—features a Les Reed arrangement that concludes with Allen overdubbing a countermelody. The disc reached the top five in the UK and the top 10 in the United States, and their next release, Les Reed and Barry Mason's "Here It Comes Again" (October 1965), did similarly well.

The Fortunes fit the model of "pleasant good-humoured boys" and described themselves as "average, good natured, and clean cut." However, Keith Altham in *New Musical Express* thought otherwise and described them as "undistinguished" (6 August 1965). And when they admitted that session guitarists Vic Flick and Jimmy Page played on their recordings, some questioned their musical competence and authenticity (Altham 29 October 1965).

Tours in the United States and Europe built a media presence, but audiences were identifying with musical styles and segregating into separate markets. In this environment, the falsetto-infused vocal harmonies of groups like the Ivy League, the Rockin' Berries, and the Fortunes offered a parent-friendly alternative to the convention-defying behaviors of some R&B groups. All, however, seemed to be developing hybrids of British-American pop culture.

Man Pop

British producers, record companies, publishers and their ilk—and creators—responded to American consumer demand for British content by continuing to mine the American catalogue. By 1965, however, the search for undiscovered gems was growing intense as producers, managers, and musicians scoured record bins. In Manchester, miles from the publishers on Denmark Street, most musicians worked the same repertoire, relying on contacts in London who could deliver material that would distinguish them from other acts. The group remained the most successful sociomusical performance configuration, while producers and record companies still watched for photogenic singers to sell discs.

---

[16] Both Talmy and Walker had also produced recordings by the Bachelors.

At the Oasis

Looking for Manchester talent, John Burgess had secured Freddie and the Dreamers for Columbia, and Ron Richards had signed the Hollies for Parlophone. With a smaller budget at Fontana, Jack Baverstock arrived in "Cottonopolis"[17] to audition the propitiously named Wayne Fontana and the Jets at the Oasis Club.[18] One of the city's best known singers, Fontana, however, grew nervous when only the Jets' bass player, Bob Lang had arrived. Desperate, they recruited two musicians who were lounging in the club's coffee bar.

Guitarist Eric Stewart remembers that he and drummer Ric Rothwell auditioned for Baverstock with Fontana and Lang after only a "quick rehearsal in the dressing room" made smoother because they "were all more or less playing the same stage set" (Stewart n.d.). Despite the circumstances, Baverstock liked what he heard and made the recording agreement contingent on the new personnel and a change: Wayne Fontana would now be backed by the Mindbenders, named after a recent low-budget horror film.[19]

The Game. As with so many groups in this era, American rhythm-and-blues formed the core of their repertoire, and their first release was a reworking of Fats Domino's "My Girl Josephine" as "Hello! Josephine" (June 1963). The disc edged into *Record Retailer*'s top 50, which was better than their next two releases.[20] Baverstock, however, had confidence in them. After "Stop, Look, and Listen" (May 1964) made it into the UK's top 40, Wayne Fontana and the Mindbenders' cover of Major Lance's "Um, Um, Um, Um, Um, Um" (September 1964) made #5 in *Record Retailer*; both discs were helped by appearances on *Thank Your Lucky Stars* (9 May 1964 and 31 October 1964).

With British bands routinely covering American artists, London publishers proved valuable conduits for new material. In the summer of 1964, Liverpool's Swinging Blue Jeans had scored a British top-five hit with "You're No Good" (May 1964), written by Clint Ballard, Jr. Thus, when Skidmore Music secured the rights to his song "The Game of Love" (February 1965), Baverstock moved quickly (Kirby 2016).

Like the sixties culture that created it, this performance juxtaposes different structural models from different cultural contexts. The verse sections present the "La Bamba" chord sequence to a slow-rock groove, which alternates with a refrain built on Bo Diddley's signature rhythm and concludes with a double-time

---

[17] "Cottonopolis" was a slang name for Manchester reflecting the importance of the textile trade in the city's history.
[18] Fontana (aka Glyn Ellis) had chosen a stage name referencing Elvis Presley's drummer D. J. Fontana.
[19] *The Mind Benders* (1963).
[20] "For You, For You" (October 1963) and a resurrection of the Gladiolas' "Little Darlin'" (January 1964).

reference to the "praise breaks" of gospel music. Apropos of the English context, the Fontana version offers a restrained double-tracked performance, where he carefully duplicates even his exhortations. The song found a pop sweet spot and pervaded British and American radios that spring, leading to an invitation to tour the United States with another Manchester group: Herman's Hermits.

Up to Bolton

The popular British daily TV drama *Coronation Street* taped in Manchester, where in late 1961 the show booked local 13-year-old grammar-school and drama student Peter Noone (as Peter Novak) for a recurring role. Two years later, this son of an accountant confidently stepped in and stayed when a neighborhood band needed a singer. The Heartbeats featured comedy in their act (like fellow Mancunians Freddie and the Dreamers), including having Noone dress in drag as Millie Small, "with balloons for the boobs," to sing "My Boy Lollipop." Reflecting the urban-suburban inside-outside exchange, they "learned all the new jokes" in Manchester before repeating them "in our home of Bolton" (Noone in Bronson 1973).

The Heartbeats were playing a church-hall dance when accountant and aspiring manager Harvey Lisberg came looking for clients (Joynson 1995, 250; Rogan 1988, 172). Eager to promote and book the band, Lisberg contracted with Charles Silverman of Danny Betesh's Kennedy Street Enterprises, who saw the group as a younger version of the Beatles. In developing a promotional package, however, they wanted a new name.[21] Members of the band had joked that Noone reminded them of the cartoon character Sherman,[22] which morphed into Herman and His Hermits before settling on Herman's Hermits (Joynson 1995, 250).[23]

Reviewing the promotional materials in London, Mickie Most thought Noone "looked like a young Kennedy," which made him "saleable, especially in the United States" (Leigh 1 June 2003). Heading "up to Bolton," he heard them already "doing all of the pop R&B stuff such as 'Mother in Law,' 'Poison Ivy,' and so on" but recommended that Lisberg and Silverman replace some of the band

---

[21] Noone and the others drew inspiration from the Beatles' decision to "make a career out of it," and the singer admits that the model of the Liverpudlians "rubbed off on a lot of bands, including us" (Leigh 2004b, 126).
[22] In the cartoon, Sherman was the inquisitive orphan adopted by the genius beagle Mr. Peabody on *The Bullwinkle Show*.
[23] Noone remembers the band sitting in a pub and trying to come up with a name when the *The Bullwinkle Show* came on and they briefly considered calling themselves the Bullwinkles (Joe Smith 1988, 211).

(Most in Buskin 2003). Meanwhile, he went about finding "cute songs" for Noone that would sell discs (Leigh 2004b, 126).[24]

England Commodified. Their first release covered the Earl-Jean's "I'm into Something Good" (August 1964) with Noone letting an English accent creep into his delivery. The success of that Goffin and King song (UK #1 and US #13) led the same writers to offer "Show Me Girl" (November 1964). MGM in the United States, however, wanted something more identifiably English and were rewarded when Carter and Lewis's "Can't You Hear My Heart Beat" (January 1965) also made *Billboard*'s top five. Although covers of the Rays' "Silhouettes" (February–March 1965) and Sam Cooke's "Wonderful World" (April–May 1965) were also hits, the American pop market was developing an insatiable hunger for all things English.

Playing with his Telefunken tape machine, Noone had recorded the audio feed for the ITV Television Playhouse production *The Lads* (15 August 1963), which included an imitation music-hall ditty by Jack Good protégé, screenwriter, and actor Treavor Peacock.[25] Noone and the band had initially learned "Mrs. Brown You've Got a Lovely Daughter" for "weddings and bar mitzvahs" to appeal to the "older people" (Mendelsohn 1980). In the studio, with Noone exaggerating a working-class accent, Most thought it good enough as album filler. However, MGM again thought differently and selected the recording for single release in the United States (April 1965), where it topped *Billboard*, as did their cover of a real music-hall number, "I'm Henry VIII, I Am" (June 1965).[26]

MGM, taking advantage of its parallel media platforms, arranged for Herman's Hermits to make a cameo appearance in *When the Boys Meet the Girls* (1965) and then to star in *Hold On!* (1966) and *Mrs. Brown You've Got a Lovely Daughter* (1968). Noone's background as an actor helped in these films and in television appearances, which also sold records. Mickie Most, however, admitted that all of this was made "for the States, not for England . . . [and] I was involved with feeding the machine" (Joe Smith 1988, 210).

My Masculine Thing

Sixties pop culture thrived on the objectification, commodification, and recontextualization of cultural memes. Curators, creators, and consumers appropriated

---

[24] Both Most and Noone have mentioned session musicians, including a pianist (probably Reg Guest), at least one other instrumentalist (e.g., Vic Flick), and backing singers (John Carter and Ken Lewis) (Buskin 2003; Thompson 2008, 258).

[25] Peacock had hosted Good's first music television shows.

[26] Notably, neither of these recordings appeared as singles in the UK, although Columbia would the EP, *Mrs. Brown You've Got a Lovely Daughter* (June 1965) in the UK. Joe Brown, however, had recorded "I'm Henery the Eighth I Am" (June 1961) for British consumption.

and adapted the plethora of images and sounds that flooded cinema and television screens; magazines, newspapers, and posters; and radios and turntables. Ideas migrated freely from one medium to another, including from film to music.

In the summer of 1963, a ponytailed Albert Finney in tight velvet breeches and an open, loose-fitting shirt featured in the multi-award-winning movie *Tom Jones*. Based on Henry Fielding's comic novel *The History of Tom Jones, a Foundling* (1749), the film reflected the sexual awakening of youth culture that underscored pop culture. The next spring, when Jack Good applied his ideas about pop-music television to the special *Around the Beatles*, he included an American wearing Albert Finney's ponytail and a loose-fitting shirt. P. J. Proby soon added tight velvet breeches to his hybridized version of James Brown channeling Albert Finney to sing Rufus Thomas's "Walkin' the Dog."

LA Baritones. That fall, Good brought his music-and-television concept to America with *Shindig!*, a show that was taped in ABC's Los Angeles studios for national broadcast and often featured the Righteous Brothers, purveyors of Southern California's blue-eyed soul. Phil Spector's production of the duo performing "You've Lost That Loving Feeling" (November 1964) was an international hit, with Bill Medley's distinctive bass-baritone contrasting not only with that of his partner Bobby Hatfield, but also with the high-pitched boy-like voices that dominated male pop. That success helped reestablish the commercial viability of the bass-baritone male voice in the pop market, a sound that also came to be at the center of another group of Los Angelinos.

Scott Engel (Scott Walker), John Maus (John Walker), and drummer Gary Leeds (Gary Walker) had adopted the look of British pop stars, formed the semblance of a band, and called themselves the Walker Brothers. When their cover of Eugene Church's "Pretty Girls Everywhere" (December 1964) failed in the United States, however, their producer, Nick Venet, sent them to London with introductions, suggesting that that environment might better suit them.

They arrived in February 1965 with high hopes and their cover of the Everly Brothers' "Love Her" in hand, but only summer clothes and barely enough money to pay the rent on a Kensington bedsit. Maurice King (who also managed Them) had agreed to look after the Walkers but held back until Philips finally released "Love Her" (April 1965) and Radio Caroline put it into rotation. That exposure led to a booking on *Top of the Pops* (27 May 1965) as Britain warmed to the Californians (Reynolds 25 August 2009).

To begin their British makeover, Johnny Franz and Ivor Raymonde (the team behind Dusty Springfield's initial successes) took over production as the group covered Jerry Butler's "Make It Easy on Yourself" (August 1965), followed by Jimmy Radcliffe's "My Ship Is Coming In" (November 1965) and Frankie Valli's "The Sun Ain't Gonna Shine Any More" (March 1966). All three discs performed well on both British and American charts, and all featured Scott Walker's baritone voice. That tessitura of masculinity that had been at the center of Elvis Presley's voice was back in vogue with youth culture.

Pontypridd Male

In the coal-mining town of Pontypridd, Wales, Jerry Lee Lewis had inspired Tom Woodward to become a singer, but Elvis Presley had given the working-class Welshman a prototype. Hearing the American's rich baritone, Woodward realized: "my God, I can sing like that! We have exactly the same range" (Graham 2015).

Although Welsh and English youth found common ground in their love of American pop music, domestic stereotypes continued to inform attitudes. In 1963, 18-year-old Woodward was performing under the stage name Tommy Scott when Joe Meek became the first to record him. The singer's discomfort with the producer's homosexuality, however, and their inability to secure a record lease, ended that relationship (Graham 2015). After other failed attempts, Scott wondered whether all of London's music industry was gay, an impression reinforced by the way the crowd at the club Beat City responded to another singer, Mick Jagger.

Scott saw Jagger as "sort of camping it up," and even though the two bands were doing the "same kind of material, bloody Chuck Berry stuff," the "kids were screaming" for the Stones. Woodward rationalized that his own appearance "wasn't pretty enough. I wasn't a boyish-looking person. I wasn't effeminate... I had to do my masculine thing and hope that it would work" (Hibbert 1991). This focus on masculinity would define him.

It's His Song. Although Woodward's dark curly hair defied sixties British pop-star stereotypes, Gordon Mills (who had also grown up in Wales) saw a market for the singer's stage persona (Rogan 1988, 154). With a management contract, Mills tied the singer's hair back with a ribbon and renamed him and the band Tom Jones and the Squires.[27] Their first single, "Chills and Fever" (August 1964) failed to chart, even with a television appearance on BBC2's *The Beat Room* (5 October 1964). Mills, nevertheless, used them to record demos of his songs, including one intended for Sandie Shaw.

Mills and Les Reed had written "It's Not Unusual" to echo Sandie Shaw's "(There's) Always Something There to Remind Me" (September 1964), with an arrangement that featured a similar rhythmic groove, instrumentation, and key. Mills and Reed coached Jones in his delivery, which sounded so convincing that,

---

[27] Mills had first renamed the band the Playboys, but in the film *Tom Jones*, Squire Allworthy is the protagonist's benefactor.

when Shaw heard it, she demurred: "whoever sang on this demo, it's his song" (Sharp 2016). Reed remembered playing "It's Not Unusual" (January 1965) on a "beautiful sunny afternoon" at Denmark Street where "all the windows were open." Soon "every publisher in the street was out of the window . . . saying, 'What's that gonna cost?' 'I want that record!' Where do I get that song? Who's that artist? Who did the arrangement?'" (interview 1 May 2001).

Working Man. After Radio Caroline put the disc into rotation, it climbed to the top of *Record Retailer*'s chart in March and later made *Billboard*'s top 10 (Petridis 2020). Jones's growing popularity, especially after several appearances on *Top of the Pops*, however, led P. J. Proby to complain about imitation. Jones, defiant and invoking conservative tropes about adolescent males with long straight hair being effeminate, doubled down on his working-class Welsh roots for the confrontation. "Take a look at these sideburns and the curly hair—brushed back. Do you see any sign of the idol a la fringe and velvet pants?" he rebuffed the American (Altham 12 March 1965a).[28]

In the interplay between media, Jones's alpha-male persona gained invitations to record film title songs, including for *What's New Pussycat* (August 1965) and for the next James Bond installment, *Thunderball* (November 1965). This ubermasculine role, however, led to a confrontation on the set of *Thank Your Lucky Stars* (3 April 1965). During a soundcheck, John Lennon greeted Jones with "How ya doing you Welsh poof?" to which Jones angrily responded, "You come over here you Scouse bastard and I'll show you!" (Sharp 2016).[29]

For both Lennon and Jones, questions about their sexuality and the legitimacy of one's parentage, along with invocations of ethnic stereotypes (Welsh and Scouse) and threatened violence, echoed working-class masculine tropes. Mick Jagger, in contrast, found ways to musically articulate toxic masculinity with a middle-class twist.

---

[28] Jones references colloquial British English in his describing Proby, not as wearing trousers but velvet "pants," which can refer to underwear, as in "underpants."
[29] "Poof" in British slang most commonly means "gay."

278 TRANSITIONS, 1964–1965

Fig. 17.1 Steve Winwood with the Spencer Davis Group, on *Beat-Club*, 1966.

Fig. 17.2 Moody Blues, in "Go Now" (promotional film), 1965.

Fig. 17.3 The Applejacks, in "Tell Me When" (promotional film), 1964.

Fig. 17.4 The Ivy League (Perry Ford, Ken Lewis, John Carter, at New Musical Express Winners Concert, 1965.

Fig. 17.5 The Rockin' Berries, in *Pop Gear*, 1965.

Fig. 17.6 The Fortunes, 1965.

Fig. 17.7 Wayne Fontana and the Mindbenders, on *Hullabaloo*, 1965.

Fig. 17.8 Herman's Hermits, on *The Ed Sullivan Show*, 1965.

Fig. 17.9 Tom Jones, on *The Ed Sullivan Show*, 1965.

18
Meet the Rolling Stones

The Rolling Stones did not come of age playing for sailors, businessmen, prostitutes, and art students in Hamburg's red-light district, or for gangsters entertaining their molls while bouncers trounced knife-wielding thugs in Newcastle. Instead, they had had the relative comfort and advantage of playing for London blues afficionados before Mods and suburban teens discovered them. Moreover, Mick Jagger and Brian Jones possessed an advantage: their social status.

With the familial financial resources to be idealistic about both repertoire and appearance, the notion of "professional amateur" allowed them to challenge conventions. Manager Andrew Oldham had tried to dress the Stones in matching suits, but middle-class privilege intervened: uniforms were what the working-class wore. Real bluesmen did not dress like interchangeable hotel staff members. For a while they compromised. As one concert reviewer noted, "onstage they wear high-heel boots, tight pants, black leather waistcoats and even ties, except for Mick, who wears his shirt with collar detached. . . . None of the slick suits sported by Billy J [Kramer] or Gerry and the Pacemakers" (Wyman with Havers 2002, 90). Soon, however, the ties and vests were also gone.

Oldham surrendered and embraced their sartorial and hirsute defiance and applied it in his marketing. As the band's hair grew longer (albeit no longer than many other bands), he promoted it with a Christmas greeting ad that suggested barbers might be starving because the Rolling Stones did not cut their hair (Wyman with Havers 2002, 92). Repertoire, however, remained the prerogative of Jagger, Jones, and Richard.

"I Wanna Be Your Man" had briefly elevated them from being a covers band, but with Lennon and McCartney material. Jagger and company wanted success, but not if it meant depending on the Beatles. With winter drawing near, they shared tours with Gerry and the Pacemakers (December 1963), with the Ronettes ("Group Scene '64," January 1964), and with Johnny Leyton ("All Stars '64," February 1964). With each provincial stop, Oldham found ways to attract press attention to how the London band threatened English behavioral norms. The Rolling Stones, however needed more than marketing. They needed songs that would convey their authenticity.

British Blokes' Faces

Kate Fox includes modesty as a prevalent English behavioral trait, with the qualification that it disguises arrogance (2014, 284). Boasting represents bad form, which may be why Andrew Oldham and Mick Jagger engaged in it in a *Melody Maker* opinion piece that taunted media critics while belittling those whom the band copied.

Jagger proclaimed his authority on American blues and rhythm-and-blues by asserting that he knew "more about the 'real thing'" than any of the "shout-up merchants." Moreover, with several tours by Black American performers planned for the UK that year, he takes partial credit: "these legendary characters wouldn't mean a light, commercially" if the Stones and others were not playing their music.

LSE student Mick Jagger takes credit for attracting audiences to performances by Black Americans, not my British musicianship, but because of prejudice. As Jagger explained, "girl fans, particularly, would rather have a copy by a British group than the original American version—mainly I suppose because they like the British blokes' faces, and they feel nearer them" (Jagger 1964).

The Stones' fixation with American blues, rhythm-and-blues, and rock 'n' roll had matured in Ealing where devotees celebrated the masters and knew their sources. Context matters, however, and now they played for teens. These audiences, while interested in the music, came to concerts as something they associated with sexuality and defying adult culture. The contexts allowed them to disregard conventions and to express their independence even as their generation found work and/or went to college. What the Stones needed to do was produce recordings that articulated that defiance.

Not Fade Away

While the Rolling Stones toured and in the absence of an album, Decca released an eponymous EP of previously recorded material (January 1964). That decision rested with their manager, who controlled the leasing. They recorded their first album sessions in Regent Sound Studios' modest space in Denmark Street, which even owner James Baring described as having a "pretty dodgy" sound. Oldham, however, liked the freedom of the venue and the absence of oversight, which both gave him substantial control over the recording process and made it relatively cheap. Oldham rationalized the lo-fi audio, telling the owner: "sounds nutty, James. That's what I want!" (Baring interview 28 July 2005).

As per their reputation for blurring the lines between rock 'n' roll and R&B, the Stones brought versions of Bobby Troup's "Route 66,"[1] Chuck Berry's "Carol," and Bo Diddley's "Mona,"[2] along with Motown covers and material from their shows to the album sessions. They also, however, needed a single, and they hybridized elements of Sonny Boy Williamson and Bo Diddley for their cover of Buddy Holly's "Not Fade Away."[3] Holly's original version abstracts Bo Diddley's signature groove with a single electric guitar, string bass, and drums,[4] over which the singer gently hiccups his love plea with polite backing vocals. The Stones' version features a Brian Jones bluesy harmonica and, rather than Holly's halting staggered beat, generates a deep Bo Diddley groove with maracas, drums, and guitar. And they had help.

In the small room, sounds seeped into every microphone as Americans Phil Spector and singer Gene Pitney joined the percussive juggernaut,[5] with Graham Nash, Allan Clarke, and Tony Hicks from the Hollies (Elliott 2012, 27).[6] Jagger delivered the text, moreover, not with Holly's playful entreaty but as an assertive machismo command. Released on 21 February 1964, the disc rose to #3 on *Record Retailer*'s chart just as Oldham launched another publicity ploy.

Your Sister

Kate Fox (2014, 451) observes that the English like to pretend that sex is unimportant, but just as modesty disguises their inclination for arrogance, they often invoke humor to cover their carnal preoccupations.[7] The English Establishment[8] has long attempted to censor sexual content if it is not cleverly couched in humor or some other disguise. Andrew Oldham and Mick Jagger, however, exploited this hypocrisy by making the Rolling Stones performances about sex, its importance to youth culture, and how powerful a wedge it could be between generations. Moreover, they built this campaign on a fundamental cultural belief: men control women.

---

[1] Derived largely from Chuck Berry's 1961 version.
[2] Also known as "I Need You Baby."
[3] Holly recorded "Not Fade Away" (May 1957) only a month after the release of Diddley's "Mona" (April 1957).
[4] Jerry Allison may be playing either heavily damped drums or on some other object like a box.
[5] Bill Wyman refutes this claim saying, "It is often said that we recorded "Not Fade Away" at this session, with Phil Spector playing maracas, but Andrew used this as publicity" (Wyman with Havers 2002, 99).
[6] Clarke plays maracas with Nash, Hicks, and Pitney clapping on the off-beats, while a tambourine (Spector perhaps) plays on the second beat of every other measure.
[7] Films like *Carry On Cabby* (1963) offer examples of the English sexual innuendo.
[8] Described in 1955 as the "matrix of official and social relations by which power is exercised" (see Sandbrook 2005, 560).

In this game, Oldham (2000, 297) crafted the question "Would you let your sister go with a Rolling Stone?" and planted it with Ray Coleman, who used it as the title of a *Melody Maker* article (14 March 1964). The journalist compliantly quotes Jagger emphasizing the way the band's "scruffy" appearance had the intention of alienating parents and endearing them to teens, which led to other publications eagerly looking to prove him right. By the end of May, the *Daily Mirror* described them as the "ugliest group in Britain" (Wyman with Havers 2002, 115). Instead of devotees and proponents of the blues, Oldham positioned them as the bad boys of beat. Consequently, through the spring of 1964, as they played in a different British town almost every day for two and a half months, they adjusted their program to provoke ever-stronger responses from their audiences.

A Disaster. In June, Oldham advanced his most audacious plan yet: an American tour. London Records (an American subsidiary of Decca) had released "Not Fade Away" in March to very little response, a fate similarly shared by their next release, an early Jagger and Richards writing attempt, "Tell Me (You're Coming Back)."[9] Some American disc jockeys, however, did put this disc into their playlists as local venues prepared for the band to arrive.[10] Still, a concert in Detroit barely drew 1,000 to the 15,000-capacity Olympia Stadium, a pattern repeated throughout the tour. In Wyman's words, "the first American tour . . . was a disaster. When we arrived, we didn't have a hit record or anything going for us" (Wyman with Havers 2002, 127).

One of the most telling moments came not in a concert venue but in a television studio. Shortly before the tour was to begin, the Rolling Stones taped an appearance for ABC's variety show *The Hollywood Palace*. A different celebrity hosted each week, with Dean Martin slated for the episode on which the Rolling Stones would make their American debut (13 June 1964). Dressed in nonmatching suits, they played two tunes, opening with "Not Fade Away" followed by "I Just Want to Make Love to You" live before an audience of mostly adults and a few responsive teens. Martin made little attempt to disguise his contempt, rolling his eyes and joking about the length of their hair and the imagined shame of their parents. The Stones were furious when they saw it, but the die had been cast in the United States.

2120 South Michigan Avenue

In the middle of their American tour, Oldham arranged for publicity photos and recording sessions at Chess Records in Chicago. These studios above the label's

---

[9] The band had recorded the song as a demo, but Oldham had allowed it to be issued to coincide with the beginning of their tour.
[10] For example, in advance of their show in Detroit in mid-June, the most powerful station in the region, Windsor, Ontario's CKLW, put "Tell Me" into their rotation.

2120 South Michigan Avenue offices represented a pilgrimage, especially when the Stones met several of their heroes, including Chuck Berry and Muddy Waters (Norman 2012, 150).[11] Moreover, working with engineer Ron Malo, the Stones found a sound that had evaded them in London.

When they had landed in New York, local disc jockey, promoter, and pop gadabout "Murray the K" Kaufman, in addition to showing them about town, had introduced them to a recording by the Valentinos (managed by Allen Klein). Bobby and Shirley Womack had written "It's All Over Now" for the Valentinos, but the disc had failed to achieve national success. Their performance had something of Chuck Berry's "Memphis, Tennessee" to its groove and feel, with a prominent bass line that drove the recording along as Bobby Womack delivered the lyrics with a touch of humor.

The Stones' sped-up version of "It's All Over Now" begins with Jones's guitar chords echoing through Chess Records' hallways before crisply coming into focus. Jagger adopts the role of angry victim who seeks vindication and expands on "Not Fade Away" by appropriating the song to declare his contempt for female independence. "It's All Over Now" (June 1964) topped British charts, replacing the Animals' "The House of the Rising Sun," and in the United States broke into *Billboard*'s top 30. Even better, their cover of "Time Is on My Side" (September 1964), originally recorded by Irma Thomas (June 1964), made the American top 10.

The Rooster. In the late summer of 1964, they began working on their next single and chose something decidedly purist. Howlin' Wolf's "Little Red Rooster" draws on the country-blues metaphor of barnyard fertility and allows Jagger to expand on his lecherous persona. At Regent Sound Studios, Brian Jones overdubbed his electric guitar (Elliott 2012, 46), negotiating the asymmetries of the performance with convincingly salacious slides on the guitar neck, which in live performance underscored the phallic implications of the song.

Released in mid-November 1964, the disc briefly topped British charts, demonstrating how popular electric blues was becoming with a subsection of the record-buying public. Oldham, nevertheless, continued to coerce Jagger and Richards into writing songs, and in the process they learned how to write for themselves. London Records did not release "Little Red Rooster" as a single in the United States. Instead, the Jagger-Richards song "Heart of Stone" (December 1964) broke into *Billboard*'s top 20, establishing their reputation as musicians who wrote their own music.

---

[11] As important for the Blues Incorporated network of musicians and patrons back in the UK, the venue gave the band credibility.

Rolling Roles

Oldham and the Stones tapped into a need of the Bulge Generation to define themselves: neither children nor adults, adolescents sought rituals that symbolically declared their independence. The anthropologist Victor Turner described the role of ritual as enabling "communitas," a "state of equality, comradeship, and common humanity" (Olaveson 2001, 93). Emile Durkheim had gone further, suggesting that attending a ceremony could prove an "exceptionally powerful stimulant" generating a "sort of electricity" and leading to an "extraordinary height of exaltation" (99). Rolling Stones concerts served as such rituals, unleashing waves of emotional energy pent up in adolescents confronting a world in transition.

Portraying the Stones as anticonventional leaders of a youth subculture, however, could complicate life. Bill Wyman complained that shopkeepers sometimes refused to sell them cigarettes nor publicans a pint (Levy 2002, 169). In March 1965 on their way back into London and needing a place to use a toilet, they stopped at a filling station where the attendant recognized them and denied them access. Members of the band resolved their problem by relieving themselves against a wall and saluting as they departed. When brought to court, a judge exacted punishment on the miscreants: a reprimand and a fine of £5 each. The publicity, however, proved priceless.

Black Sheep. The British press understood Oldham's marketing scheme for what it was and happily propagated his stories because they too benefited. When Oldham's clients or their audiences misbehaved, the press sold copy because both fans and detractors could read what they wanted into statements by the manager, the band, and their critics. Adults heard evidence of youth culture's descent into depravity. Adolescents heard rebellion in stories emphasizing the band's appearance and/or defiance of social convention.

Oldham openly declared that popular music culture had "always [had] a black sheep, someone the Establishment can knock" (Altham 12 March 1965b). He offered the example of Billy Fury as an alternative to the wholesome image of Cliff Richard. The Rolling Stones, he argued, stood in the same relationship to the Beatles. In the course of events, some of the Stones embraced this role and exceeded their manager's expectations as their concerts grew into youth-culture loci proclaiming an anti-Establishment world of quasi anarchy. Musicians taunted audiences, fans stormed the stage, men cried, women shrieked, the police struggled to maintain order, and the press loved it.

Ironically, behind these acts of rebellion lay a more complicated story, as Mick Jagger explored his new-found social capital. His significant other, Chrissie Shrimpton, her sister, Jean (one of the most prominent models of the era), and their friends represented his entrée into an extended network that included the

Chelsea Set. A studied mimic, he shifted accents among his stage imitations of Black Americans, himself as a college student, London Cockneys, and a version of the patter of public-school toffs he heard at Knightsbridge parties. Keith Richards later referred to Jagger as a "nice bunch of blokes" (Eggar 1995).

The idea of a stage persona hardly represented a new idea in British popular music, with examples ranging from George Formby's bumbling everyman to Screaming Lord Sutch. Jagger developed a hybrid of Huddie Ledbetter, James Brown,[12] and Oscar Wilde with a dash of Bill Sikes while adapting Black American stage rituals rooted partly in the church and partly in clubs and dance halls. White adolescent audiences reacted ecstatically to hypnotic raves like the Stones' version of Solomon Burke's gospel-inspired "Everybody Needs Somebody to Love" (July 1964) with which the Stones began closing their shows in 1965. That tune, with its guitar-bass-drums ostinato, allowed Jagger to work theater audiences into a frenzy, a role he relished.

Not the Last Time

By the end of 1964, the Rolling Stones only recorded in London when necessary. RCA in Los Angeles and occasionally Chess in Chicago became the band's preferred studios, with tours planned to allow time in those cities. In preparation for those visits, not only did they focus their musical efforts on covering American material but also Jagger and Richards began writing their own songs, something they had been developing since 1963's "Little by Little" for their first LP. Their next UK LP, *The Rolling Stones, No. 2* (January 1965) features renditions of Chuck Berry's "You Can't Catch Me" and "Down the Road a Piece," Muddy Waters's "I Can't Be Satisfied," and other covers. From these and other musical models, Jagger and Richards were appropriating ideas for their own songs, such as the album's "What a Shame," "Grown Up Wrong," and "Off the Hook." With each attempt, the guitarist roughs out a musical framework over which the singer can deliver his stage identity. In the process, they began developing their own brand of R&B.

A second American tour in the fall of 1964 proved cathartic, even if they sometimes performed without an ailing Brian Jones (a sign of things to come). Significantly, they had not yet established a musical identity that distinguished them in the American mind, but that was changing. North American fans were interested in these records but had only a hint of the notoriety the band enjoyed in the UK. Trips to the United States helped some discs to register on *Billboard*'s

---

[12] The Rolling Stones had appeared on *The T.A.M.I. Show* with Brown in Santa Monica, California, October 1964.

charts, but none of these had come near the success of some other British artists. They needed a song and a recording to break through this impasse.

The First Time. Jagger and Richards had heard a disc by the Staple Singers that featured a haunting refrain sung over a tremolo guitar. In "This May Be the Last Time" (1960) the Chicago gospel singers wail about the fragility of life and the need to reconcile with one's maker. In Jagger and Richards's hands, however, the refrain takes on a menacing air. Richards rethinks the accompaniment, speeding it up, deriving a guitar riff from Pops Staple's strumming, and projecting it over a three-chord ostinato for verses they added to the refrain. For his part, Jagger simplifies and transforms the gospel moan into "The Last Time," an angry dismissal of a lover for not obeying him: "I told you once and I told you twice, but you never listen to my advice," he snarls, as though they had a choice.

The Rolling Stones had started rehearsing the song in London, but, returning to Hollywood in January 1965, they developed a performance and a recording that Oldham felt represented the "first Rolling Stones totality" (2003, 180). More significant, he hoped that "The Last Time" (UK February 1965, US March 1965) would be the "big American hit" that would take them to the top of *Billboard*'s charts. When they had mixed the tape, he called Phil Spector to the studio to confirm his belief, only to hear the tycoon of teen disappointingly (and fairly accurately) proclaim "number ten, guys, number ten" (180).

"The Last Time" did, however, top British charts and crystallized the Stones' Anglicization of American blues: a distinctive riff, a layer of guitars, a relentless groove, and Jagger demanding dominion over women. Others were also working with these musical memes, but Jagger's agitated vocals—sometimes shouting if not screaming (perhaps inspired by Van Morrison and Them's performance of "Baby Please Don't Go")—presents the Rolling Stones as an updated version of Britain's angry young men.[13]

The Other World. Popular music in 1965 on both sides of the Atlantic increasingly engaged topics other than romance, reflecting the growing importance of political folk music and a postwar generation preoccupied with contemporary global and local issues. The Bulge and Baby Boom generations discussed the travesty of apartheid in South Africa and Rhodesia, the civil rights movement in the United States, and, increasingly, wars in Africa and in Western and Southeast Asia. Bob Dylan's music encouraged songwriters to write metaphorically, and when the Byrds reimagined his "Mr. Tambourine Man" (April 1965) with an electric 12-stringed guitar, a merger of the Beatles and American folk (with perhaps a nod to Jackie DeShannon and the Searchers) produced a vibrant new option for songwriters and musicians.

---

[13] The British press used "angry young men" of 1950s to describe a generation of mostly middle and working-class writers who advocated for social change.

The Rolling Stones articulated their own version of this cultural trend.

6363 Sunset Boulevard

"The Last Time" reinforced in Oldham, Jagger, and Richards the belief that they had found the Rolling Stones. Where Mick Jagger had once passively waited for the knock on the door that never came in "Tell Me," he was now irate, finished, and seeking revenge.

In the spring of 1965, the Stones began another North American tour with studio time booked at Chess and RCA. Along the way, as they passed through cities like Albany, New York, and Statesboro, Georgia, they prepared material for the recordings they intended to make in Los Angeles. Absorbing Americana as they went, they probably cringed seeing Freddie and the Dreamers' "I'm Telling You Now" and Herman's Hermits' "Mrs. Brown You've Got a Lovely Daughter" topping *Billboard* while "The Last Time" stalled in at the #9 slot.[14] They needed a song and a recording that would take them to the tipping point.

They continued to find inspiration in American music in an era when Motown figured prominently in international charts. Detroit had long been on the Stone's setlist, with covers of Marvin Gaye's "Hitch Hike" and "Can I Get a Witness" appearing on their albums. In that context they heard Martha and the Vandellas' "Dancing in the Street" (July 1964), which had been a huge hit the previous fall. Like much of the music that came out of the "snake pit" at Hitsville U.S.A. on Detroit's West Grand Boulevard, the groove for "Dancing in the Street" trapped you, its heavy downbeat balanced by a ska-like guitar skank on the offbeat. As Martha Reeves described dance uniting America city after city (even as economic riots began erupting in city after city), the Vandellas sang an eerie vocalise that caught Keith Richards's ear. That melodic motif found even bolder articulation in the Vandellas' follow-up recording "Nowhere to Run" (February 1965) with trumpets blasting an inverted variation on that three-note theme.

Satisfaction at Last

Keith Richards has related different versions of this story. In his autobiography, he claims that he began their signature song while at home in London, spitballing ideas late at night onto a cassette. He dozed off, however, filling the the tape with snoring, except for a bit at the beginning (2010, 176). He had found a simple riff while playing with a blues cliché heard on recent Vandellas' recordings and in the

---

[14] The week of 1 May 1965 saw eight of *Billboard*'s top 10 slots occupied by British artists.

Ad Libs' "The Boy from New York City" (December 1964). To that, he added lyrics for a refrain: "I can't get no satisfaction; I've tried, and I've tried, but I can't get no satisfaction." Chuck Berry's "Thirty Days" (October 1955) may have inspired him with its double negative of "If I don't get no satisfaction from the judge . . ." Nevertheless, this snippet provided a platform on which Mick Jagger could build a verse.

As the singer lounged by a Florida swimming pool, palm trees waving over his head, he settled into Richards's rant. Where Bob Dylan and others critiqued racism and violence, Jagger's attention settled on consumerism. Radio ads for detergent and cigarettes (never heard on the BBC but a feature of pirate radio) caught his ear, and his first two verses ridicule America's business of selling mundane objects. In keeping with his sexual predator persona, however, he adds a third verse about the frustrations of a failed seduction.

Arriving at Chess in Chicago, Richards gave his riff to Brian Jones to play on harmonica. This country blues interpretation, however, never gelled, and Jagger and Richards prepared to relegate the recording to album filler (Oldham 2003, 198). Nevertheless, they took it up again a couple of days later when they arrived in Los Angeles. While the RCA studios in Hollywood lacked the same history, edge, and atmosphere of Chess, engineer Dave Hassinger presided over some of the world's best equipment.

Richards and drummer Charlie Watts kicked out a new groove for the song, building on the 4 x 4 meter that had propelled hits the previous year like "Bits and Pieces," "A Hard Day's Night," and "Have I the Right." As the recording and performance evolved, the song's potential emerged. Richards now wanted a horn section for his theme like that on the Vandellas' "Nowhere to Run," but lacking that, he settled for a distortion pedal that road manager Ian Stewart fetched from a local music store.[15]

Monster Band. The new guitar toy of 1965, the "fuzz tone" pedal had originally been intended to allow a guitar to electronically sound like a saxophone.[16] The Stones' recording, unsurprisingly, reveals Richards to be unfamiliar with the device, noisily and sloppily clicking it on at the beginnings of refrains. Still, the take held excitement. When Jagger dubbed his part over the backing track, Oldham, perhaps concerned about censors, had Hassinger bury the vocals in the mix, rendering them ever so slightly difficult to discern.

Neither Jagger nor Richards thought the recording was ready for prime time, even if they sensed its possibilities; however, Oldham heard adrenaline (if not sex) that he feared would be lost if they recorded it again. When put to a vote, the band and producer, overruling Jagger and Richards, chose to release it as a single. Jagger later acknowledged that "(I Can't Get No) Satisfaction" was the recording

---

[15] Probably Wallichs Music City at Sunset and Vine, Hollywood.
[16] The earliest distortion device was probably custom built for Nashville guitarist Chet Atkins in the 1950s; the Maestro Fuzz-Tone commercially arrived in 1963 (Cleveland 2000).

that transformed the Rolling Stones from just another British group into a "huge, monster band." "You always needed one song. We weren't American, and America was a big thing, and we always wanted to make it here" (Jagger in Wenner 14 December 1995). When London Records released the disc in the United States in early June 1965, they saw it top *Billboard*'s charts, followed by similar success in the UK. Satisfaction had been obtained, at least for the time being.

Get Off of My Cloud

During the first days of September 1965, Andrew Oldham had Peter Whitehead train his camera on the Rolling Stones as they made a quick concert trip, to Dublin first and then Belfast. The footage for *Charlie Is My Darling* captures some of the fan ecstasy erupting at these concerts: women and men storming the stage while adult voyeurs feign disinterest. Jagger and Brian Jones play the audience as much as they play music, taunting them sonically and sexually, while Richards, Wyman, and Watts get on with the business at hand. Whitehead, however, also shows them offstage, wrestling with the question of authenticity. As the camera rolls, Jagger describes his stage performances as acting, while Brian Jones relegates almost all of life to theater.

With "Satisfaction," they had captured a way to make American music British, but what would be their next move? After the Irish concerts, they flew directly to Los Angeles with the sole purpose of recording their next single plus material for an album. Jetlagged and under pressure, they labored over a follow-up that could lyrically and musically link them to their current success.

Richards later complained that they had rushed "Get Off of My Cloud" and that although the responsorial refrain held promise, they had "rocked" something that should have been taken at a much slower tempo (Greenfield 1971). For musical continuity, they transpose a variation on the three-note "Satisfaction" theme to a different chord tone, sonically aligning the two recordings but leaving them distinct. Jagger the lyricist has described it as a "stop-bugging-me, post-teenage-alienation song" in which he continues his complaints about advertising (again, detergent), neighbors, and parking tickets (Wenner 1995).

Although Richards describes the recording as Oldham's worst production (Greenfield 1971), when the recording was released in September it also topped international charts, despite a complaint from the BBC's *Juke Box Jury* critic David Jacobs that they had (again) buried the vocals in the mix (Altham 29 October 1965 "Stones"). Nevertheless, the success of "Satisfaction" and "Get Off of My Cloud" proved that the Stones were indeed a huge, monster band.

294 TRANSITIONS, 1964–1965

Fig. 18.1 The Rolling Stones, on *Hollywood Palace*, 1964.

Fig. 18.2 The Rolling Stones, on *The Ed Sullivan Show*, 1965.

Fig. 18.3 Mick Jagger, in *Charlie Is My Darling: Ireland 1965*, 1966/2012.

19
Modifications

While most British adolescents in the 1960s uncritically accepted the social confines into which they had been born (see Donnelly 2005; Levy 2002; Sandbrook 2006), one scene revolted with style. A heterogeneous group, Mods influenced music and fashion through their embrace of modernism. Their emergence in London during the late 1950s and early 1960s offers stories of how urban and suburban English youth hybridized their love of continental fashion with an objectification of urban Black American music culture. Their reaction to the gray of postwar Britain produced a unique British phenomenon.

Tom Wolfe (1968) describes Mods as cultural subversives: members of a "Noonday Underground" spending their lunchtimes in dance clubs and money on clothes. Nik Cohn (1989) presents them as largely a male phenomenon fixated on music, dancing, and clothes and fueled by "purple hearts" (Drinamyl).[1] Shawn Levy (2002, 105) also stereotypes them as young men dressed in Italian or French styled suits cut from lightweight fabrics and, in inclement weather, protected by long coats from military surplus. Not to be outdone, Nicholls (2014) suggests that women Mods were just as music savvy and addicted to dance and amphetamines as their male counterparts.

Richard Weight's study of Mods has them wearing a complex range of clothing designs in a continual state of alteration as their wearers adapted their identities to rapidly evolving social contexts. He contends that "the 1960s was the first decade when the young working classes were seen to be in the vanguard of creating this more democratic culture, not merely as consumers but also as producers" (2015, 120). Notably, Mod men felt liberated and able to dance by themselves without women, burning off the amphetamines by immersing themselves in the music (Hodgkinson 2011). In addition to clubs like The Scene, they congregated in the city-center late-night coffee bars where this often-suburban movement came to listen to records and to chatter. And when London's transportation system shut down late at night, a Vespa motor scooter, often festooned with mirrors, allowed them to negotiate Soho's narrow streets while heading back to the suburbs (Weight 2015, 66).

---

[1] Drinamyl, an amphetamine, was developed for military use during World War II to keep soldiers awake while diminishing their sex drive.

Predominantly English, they too articulated social hierarchy. "Faces"—the most influential Mods—set the constantly changing rules for clothing, hair, and dance styles, leading by example. Peter Townshend describes a "face" as generally older, someone who wore suits and "was a man. He'd got a job. He'd got a car, not a scooter. He knew how to sleep with women" (Hodgkinson 2011). "Tickets" or "numbers"— Mods who could not afford substantial clothing purchases but who made a go of it, often by customizing their clothes by hand—nevertheless had their own influence on this scene.

Mod Worlds

Raised in environments where food, health, petrol, and clothes were rationed, the threat of nuclear annihilation was ever present, democracy was in continual confrontation with dictatorship, and the United States was flooding the world with its pop culture, Mods looked outward to find themselves. In Western Europe— unified against Soviet-backed communist regimes—the economy recovered, and the arts flourished. Moreover, modernist Italian, French, and West German fashion, film, and design appealed to a generation eager to distance themselves from the world of their parents.

Music reinforced the social bonds of Mod culture, beginning in the fifties with the modern jazz of American expatriates who had fled to cities like Paris to escape the racism at home. As the demographic breadth of Modism spread, so did its playlist. In the early sixties, parts of this youth culture danced to instrumentals such as Booker T and the MG's' "Green Onions" (May 1962) and James Brown's "Night Train" (March 1962). Recordings like John Lee Hooker's "Dimples" (September 1956/May 1964) and Ray Charles's "What'd I Say" (July 1959) offered escapes from the stodginess of Britain's postwar malaise. And by the midsixties, deejays were playing Martha and the Vandellas' "Dancing in the Street" (July 1964) and the Skatalites' "Guns of Navarone" (March 1965).

Ready, Steady, Go! declared: "the weekend starts here," launching many a Mod into the free time that bookended their day jobs as they headed to their local dance halls or to Soho and the club scene. The television show and its host Cathy McGowan commodified the Mod scene, spreading current trends in appearance and music to every household tuned to ITV on most Friday evenings. The dance steps, the clothing, as well as the performers seen on the show informed many Mods who later stood around their scooters smoking, popping pills, and waiting to get into clubs.

Art Students. Behind the emergence of Mod cultures, the interwoven forces of economics and education continued to produce unanticipated results. Although Sandbrook (2006, 270) suggests that the idea of a classless meritocracy served only as the "latest aristocratic fad," mid-1960s British popular culture (e.g., Halasz 1966) believed in the emergence of just such a world. Working-class musicians like Billy Fury and middle-class entrepreneurs like Larry Parnes had already framed the rock 'n' roll myth in the fifties. The protagonists of midsixties stories, such as photographer David Bailey and actor Terence Stamp, updated the story of working-class grit, particularly in the arts. Underlying these fables of resourceful diamonds in the rough, however, dwelt a capitalist and colonialist belief in the exploration and exploitation of untapped resources. And a national institution, the British educational system contributed to this monomyth.

This system planned grammar schools as paths to economic respectability for working-class and lower-middle-class adolescents whose families believed in the system. Academic success could land a man an office position or perhaps admission to a postsecondary institution. Prime Minister Harold Wilson, for one, had attended Royds Hall Grammar School in West Yorkshire before gaining admission to Jesus College, Oxford. Grammar-school women who failed to impress "'Cantab,' 'Lond,' and 'Oxon'"[2] trained for the "mind-numbing tedium of taking dictation" and "typing it out with multiple sheets of inky carbon paper" (Nicholson 2019, 283). Some women looked for work in the shops while a select few found their way into publishing, fashion, and entertainment.

For other adolescents, institutions of "further education," most often an arts school or eventually one of the emerging polytechnics, offered another route. Many young men and women in the 1960s found themselves learning to draw, to type, or to master any number of other practical skills the government hoped would benefit the economy or otherwise keep juveniles distracted. Meanwhile, music proved a portal for many students seeking to escape and/or to tolerate these fates, even if only for a lunch hour. In this context, Acton County Grammar School and Ealing Art College (less than 10 miles west of Soho) birthed some of the most intellectually and artistically creative ideas to emerge in 1960s British pop.

Acton Dreams

Pete Townshend remembers very little music around the home: no piano and never a "decent record player." Nevertheless, with music professionals as parents, he learned about being a musician. His father, Cliff, played saxophone in the Royal Air Force Squadronaires, and his mother, Betty, had sung with the Sydney Torch Orchestra, both ensembles well known in Britain. Thus, when the

---

[2] "Cantab" is a Latin abbreviation of Cantabrigian and stands for Cambridge University. "Oxon" similarly abbreviates Oxoniensis and refers to Oxford. "Lond" is the University of London.

Squadronaires played their summer season on the Isle of Man, that was where the 11-year-old Pete saw the film *Rock around the Clock* (1956) and found his calling. His maternal grandmother responded to his interests by buying him his first guitar, albeit a decrepit instrument that was replaced by a decent banjo until he could afford something better (Grundy and Tobler 1983).

Many other students attending Acton County Grammar School also caught the music bug, including Townshend's classmate John Entwistle, whose amateur musician parents had encouraged his interests in piano, trumpet, French horn, saxophone, and guitar. With Townshend (on banjo) and Entwistle (on trumpet), they played together in a school trad band until 1958, when Cliff Richards and the Drifters released "Move It!" Under the influence of American Duane Eddy's twangy and bottom-heavy guitar solos (e.g., "Rebel-'Rouser"), Entwistle added electric bass to his portfolio, building his own instrument (Sweeting 2002). They found that Roger Daltrey—a sheet-metal worker who had also been a student at Acton County (until expelled for smoking)—shared their interests. As the leader, lead guitarist, trombonist, and singer of the Detours, Daltrey recruited first Entwistle to play bass and then Townshend to play rhythm guitar.

Groundcourse. In 1961, 16-year-old Townshend enrolled at nearby Ealing Art College, where he encountered minds such as Ron Kitaj and philosopher Gustav Metzger, the latter sharing ideas about autodestruction that would prove influential. A student's first experience at Ealing, however, was director Roy Ascott's "Groundcourse," an innovative educational approach that challenged assumptions about art.

Ascott believed that creativity was a "behavioural problem" in which "art, science, and personality" were involved in one's "total relationship to a work of art." Notably, he proposed a semiotic theory in which the "relationships of parts" should "not be fixed and may be changed by the intervention of a spectator" (1964, 37). By observing the ways dancers and listeners reacted to his performances, Townshend operationalized Ascott's notion that an "artist always needs to develop an inquisitive interest in the world" (Crippa 2011).

In 1962–1963, the Detours—consisting of Daltrey, Entwistle, and Townshend plus a singer and a drummer—performed around London through an agent arranged by Townshend's mother. They sometimes found themselves opening for well-known bands, such as Johnny Kidd and the Pirates, whose vocal, guitar, bass, and drums setup led the Detours to strip down to a quartet with Daltrey as the singer (McMichael and Lyons 1997, 9). They had abandoned covers of the Beatles and focused their setlists on the blues and rhythm-and-blues when Townshend made another observation. In December 1963, on a show with the Rolling Stones, the guitarist noticed Keith Richards backstage warming up by swinging his arm in an arc. Townshend soon operationalized it as his signature move (Townshend 2012, 59).

In February 1964, when another band called the Detours appeared on *Thank Your Lucky Stars,* they brainstormed for a new name and became "the Who" (Townshend 2012, 60).[3] They still struggled, however, to find a suitable drummer until a youngster asked to audition. North Londoner Keith Moon had taken lessons with Cyril Davies/Lord Sutch veteran Carlo Little and was eager to join. His aggressive drumming complemented the band's sparse guitar-bass sound, and they asked him if he was available that weekend (Fletcher 2000, 78).[4]

High Numbers under Difficult Circumstances

The Detours/Who had worked under several different agent and management arrangements before Pete Meaden came into their lives. A devotee of Modism, which he described as a "euphemism for clean living, under difficult circumstances," Meaden had worked for Andrew Oldham promoting the Rolling Stones and now looked for his own band.

In 1964, he sensed that the moment to commercialize Mod culture had arrived. He could capitalize on the convergence of demographics and economics if he had the "timing just right," because, he believed, "timing is where it's at" (Meaden in Turner 1979). He was already a habitué of clubs like The Scene, knew the audiences, and was deeply invested in Mod culture. He noted, however, that, while Mods followed the Animals, the Kinks, and the Stones, none of these performers explicitly identified with their audiences. Why wasn't there a Mod band?

When Meaden first encountered the Who, they were "wearing Pierre Cardin leather jackets" and Beatle-like haircuts (Turner 1979),[5] but their new focus on rhythm-and-blues, their growing Mod clientele, and a recent mention of them by Bob Dawbarn in *Melody Maker* (18 April 1964) put the band on his radar. In the late spring of 1964, he proposed his management scheme for success: a Mod remake of their image involving clothes, hair, and attitude. He also wanted a new name: the High Numbers, referencing a social subset of Mods (Townshend 2012, 70). Townshend, who was already Mod savvy, has observed that Meaden had a "very deep influence on the band." As manager, he made them "very conscious of the audience" and instilled the "idea of reflecting their feelings rather than

---

[3] They appeared for the last time as the Detours on Valentine's Day in 1964, opening for Carter-Lewis and the Southerners. That spring, Bob Dawbarn (*Melody Maker* 18 April 1964) mentioned the Who among the growing number of London rhythm-and-blues bands.

[4] Fletcher (2000, 78) debunks the story of Moon sitting in at the Oldfield Hotel and instead has the drummer auditioning at a rehearsal.

[5] Mod men wore their hair in a shorter "French cut" style.

just ramming music down their throat," even if some of the "image-grooming" struck the guitarist as "trite" (Grundy and Tobler 1983).

Zoot Suit. The manager knew the myth by heart of how entertainment entrepreneurs discovered diamonds in the rough, polished the products, obtained recording contracts, and reaped the benefits. As a working-class intruder into the music business, however, he lacked the social credentials to get very far in the door. His accent and manners betrayed his background, and he faced challenges with gaining acceptance by London's pop-music industry.

Fontana Records' director, Jack Baverstock, was keen on new talent but had already auditioned the band; nevertheless, he was willing to listen to them again, especially with a new drummer and management. In addition to the covers of R&B tunes that the High Numbers offered, Meaden rewrote existing songs as part of their new Mod orientation. For "Zoot Suit," he reworded "Misery" (a 1963 American hit by the Dynamics) to have Roger Daltrey brag about his skinny tie and his jacket's five-inch vents. "I'm the Face," on the obverse side (derived from Slim Harpo's "Got Love If You Want It"), focuses on "Ivy League jackets" and "white buckskin shoes." When released in early July 1964, however, the disc met an indifferent audience and a disappointed Baverstock.

Although Meaden had studied Mod culture, he had little experience of promoting a record. Under the difficult circumstances of insufficient resources to mount an extended campaign promoting the High Numbers, he ultimately proved receptive to an offer to sell his contract to two other managerial novices.

Railway Accident

Meaden encouraged the High Numbers to articulate the excitement of Mod culture in their performances, especially after seeing the way Mick Jagger worked audiences. In Meaden's Mod quest, however, Townshend also recognized elements of Roy Ascott's ideas about the interrelationships between art and society. The guitarist, thus, began exploring his impressions of this culture during their Tuesday "Bluesday Club" gigs in the basement of the suburban Railway Tavern near the Harrow and Wealdstone station (Neill and Kent 2002, 36).

One way they interpreted Mod culture included playing this small suburban club with amplifiers cranked, which bothered adults and delighted teens. The loudness, however, also inevitably meant feedback from microphones and guitars. One night in July 1964, Townshend "had a whistle on the guitar" and "couldn't shake it off." In the process of attempting to control the sound, he hit the head of the guitar on the low ceiling, flexing the instrument's neck and bending all the notes, not to mention creating a visual show. Later in the evening, he tried it again, but this time the guitar neck broke, leaving "the neck dangling straight up at the ceiling" (Marsh 1983, 124).

The crowd paused over the moment, giggled at the guitarist's misfortune, and expected remonstrations for foolish showmanship. Townshend, however, felt he "had no recourse but to completely look as though I meant to do it, so I smashed the guitar and jumped all over the bits. It gave me a fantastic buzz" (Marsh 1983, 124). The destruction and the sheer expense of destroying a guitar appealed to a culture familiar with everyday violence and liberation through consumerism.

Satanic. Watching from the back, cameraman Kit Lambert had formed a plan with Chris Stamp (the brother of film actor Terence Stamp) to make a documentary about London's burgeoning Mod culture (Townshend 2012, 72). Walking into the working-class Railway Tavern presented little in the way of danger for the Oxford-educated Lambert, who had survived a near fatal encounter with a tribe in South America. The world of pop music, as it had for Brian Epstein and others, promised Lambert an environment in which a gay middle-class man could flourish and find fitful acceptance. What he witnessed that night, however, struck him as "satanic" (72).

For his part, Stamp knew firsthand the successes that other East End working-class lads like his brother might achieve. When Lambert brought him to see a High Numbers' performance, the two absolute beginners converted their plans for cinematic careers into a management scheme. The failure of "Zoot Suit" led Meaden to sell his contract for £150, and in August 1964 the new partnership began by changing the band's name back to the Who (Sweeting 28 November 2012).

The Talmy Touch

As the son of English composer Constant Lambert, Kit Lambert valued not only the importance of music-making but also the art of songwriting. The Who had mostly performed covers of American blues and rhythm-and-blues artists, but the success of Ray Davies's "You Really Got Me" showed a way to adapt American models to British contexts. Townshend and Lambert, moreover, would have realized that bringing original material to the table could enhance their chances of securing another recording contract.

Bob Dylan's songs abandoned the sentimental topic of love. The blues and rhythm-and-blues catalogue that the Who had been exploring celebrated lust. From these models, Townshend began writing music for Mod life, facilitated by Lambert, who purchased two Revox tape decks on which the budding songwriter could record, playback, and superimpose performances to create demos. While the band rehearsed Townshend's songs in October, the manager arranged an audition at EMI with John Burgess, who found the band too loud but encouraged them to call again when they had new material (Neill and Kent 2002, 40).

Everyone in the business had seen how edgy bands could be successful with independent producers, as the Animals had been with Mickie Most and as the Kinks had been with Shel Talmy. Talmy's sound particularly appealed to the Who and their management, but they needed a way to catch the American producer's attention. The connection came through women: Lambert's secretary had made friends with Talmy's wife and passed a tape to her. Despite his success, Talmy continued to be underwhelmed by most British records and bands, considering them "incredibly wimpy." Encountering the Who sometime in the fall of 1964, however, he heard a band with "balls" (Oldham 2003, 267).

I Can't Explain

In late November 1964, the Who commenced a regular Tuesday night residency at the Marquee Club, which helped them to build their London reputation and Mod credibility. Lambert, Stamp, and the band began to call their shows "Maximum R&B," advertising the phrase with a stark black-and-white flyer featuring Townshend with a Rickenbacker guitar in his left hand and an outstretched right arm poised over his head for arced descent.

Bringing that sound into a traditional recording context, however, had already proven to be a problem at Fontana and had contributed to the failed audition at EMI. Talmy, however, dismissed the standard British approach to recording music as "polite" and booked the studio at Pye where he had recorded the Kinks. There, the Who could play at a volume consistent with the kind of sound he and they wanted, a place where they could be sonically rude.

Townshend brought a song inspired by Ray Davies, building the core of "I Can't Explain" on conventional musical materials to deliver lyrics that convey a Mod's amphetamine-addled inarticulateness. One of the most striking aspects of the disc, however, is the recording quality. With Townshend's Rickenbacker electric 12-string guitar at a substantial volume, Talmy compresses and limits the sound such that each acrid chord juts into an arid audio space. He also places 12 microphones (most British studios used two) around Moon's drumkit to capture the sonic assault. "I Can't Explain" would sound like nothing else on the radio.

Process. Talmy paid for the session and, to maximize the tape deck's three channels as well as the studio rental time and engineer Glyn Johns' fee, the independent producer carefully planned out the performance and the way to distribute the instruments. Thus, to save studio time, he also paid for John Carter,

Ken Lewis, and Perry Ford to sing backing vocals.[6] He remembers that his "only concern" was to get the "record right" and "went with anybody who could do it." Townshend insists that Lambert had already rehearsed the band and that Talmy simply taped the performance before mastering the disc (Oldham 2003, 261). Unsurprisingly, Talmy disagrees, describing himself as a "hands-on producer" overseeing "the entire session starting with the sound all the way ... [from] vocals [and] mixes ... to mastering."[7] The American not only brought order to the session, but, as important, he worked out a deal with Decca in the United States.[8]

The Who were one of the first British groups to have their initial disc released in the United States (December 1964) before the UK (January 1965), with a *Billboard* ad in December 1964. Nevertheless, although "I Can't Explain" received airplay in isolated pockets (e.g., Detroit), the American market was unprepared for this new sound. In the UK, Brunswick (American Decca's British label) released the disc in mid-January 1965 only to have Pye counterrelease the Kinks' "Tired of Waiting" the same day.

The Who watched the Talmy-produced Kinks' disc rise while theirs struggled for attention in a chart saturated with outstanding recordings. At the end of the month, however, Lambert and Stamp managed to secure an appearance by the Who on *Ready, Steady, Go!* and an audience packed with Mods. The 29 January 1965 installment proved decisive, with the crowd swamping the set, creating the kind of visual excitement the band generated at its shows. A month after its release, "I Can't Explain" entered *Record Retailer*'s charts and would peak at #8.

Anyway, Anyhow, Anywhere

Controlled chaos emerged as a signature quality of Who performances, with Townshend exploring quasi-controlled feedback from his guitars and amplifiers. Long before other artists began playing with electronic sound in their performances and recordings, Townshend stood on stage, arms spread, guitar dangling from his neck while his amplifier howled. And when he tired of this pose, he slid the neck of the guitar against a microphone stand or dashed his instrument into the face of his amp. For some listeners, Who performances were cacophonous. Others heard a revolution.

---

[6] He maintains that the "Who were incapable [of performing the vocals that well] at that point in time ... but it certainly spurred them into action because they went out and learned after that" (interview 14 February 2001).

[7] See Thompson 2008, 92, for an introduction to Talmy's production approach.

[8] Decca had been broken up under an antitrust agreement. Thus, "Decca Records" refers both to an American and a British company. In the US, British Decca released discs as "London Records"; the American Decca released discs in the UK as "Brunswick Records."

As distinctive as the production for "I Can't Explain" had sounded, the band, their management, and their producer wanted more from the next disc. The inspiration would indirectly reference one of the distinctive features of Mods: their scooters. If you had a Vespa or a Lambretta, you could go anyway, anyhow, and anywhere you chose.

Townshend began "Anyway, Anyhow, Anywhere" after listening to a solo by saxophonist Charlie Parker: "I just scribbled those three words on a piece of paper because I thought that was how he sounded, so free and liberated" (Grundy and Tobler 1983). For him, the song was initially "just a brag . . . nothing more," and he created lyrics with Roger Daltrey that boasted about the freedoms Mods had begun to enjoy in London's urban-suburban landscape (Wenner 1968). Daltrey contributed because "he wanted it to be more about the street" (Townshend in Grundy and Tobler 1983). Thus, in the middle section, the singer proclaims that locked doors cannot stop him, nor social barriers bind him.

Distortion. While the verse serves as the commercial hook, the song's minimalist structure facilitates an extended improvisation over a drone. To fill the sonic and musical space, Entwistle's bass anchors the enterprise, its brassy tone quality serving both to provide a harmonic bottom and a melodic counterpresence to Townshend's electronic explorations. Talmy also brought in pianist Nicky Hopkins, and with that nucleus, they engaged in the collective task of capturing the violence and chaos of a live Who performance in a recording that lasted less than three minutes.

Talmy believes that his production of "Anyway, Anyhow, Anywhere" represents "the first major rock and roll record with distortion." His technique involved pulling "up an instrument on two channels . . . distorting the shit out of one with the limiter" and then mixing it "level-wise under the one that wasn't." He also mastered "very hot records level wise," such that when Townshend strums the chords that open the song, the recording demands attention (interview 14 February 2001). Again, Lambert and Stamp booked the Who for a *Ready, Steady, Go!* appearance, this time simultaneously with the Brunswick release.

As with their first disc, the Who again found themselves in direct competition with another Talmy-produced Kinks disc. Pye may have accidentally released "Tired of Waiting" on the same day that Brunswick released "I Can't Explain"; but having the Kinks' "Set Me Free" appear against "Anyway, Anyhow, Anywhere" (21 May 1965) suggests that Pye's chair, Louis Benjamin, hoped to intimidate Talmy.

Both the Kinks and the Who, however, saw their discs chart a week later, peaking at #9 and #10, respectively, on *Record Retailer*'s charts. Nevertheless, in the United States, where the Who were still relatively unknown, deejays, retailers, and consumers wondered what was happening in London.

My Generation

In early August 1965, the Who secured an appearance at the National Jazz and Blues Festival in Richmond and opened the weekend with the Yardbirds and the Moody Blues on a program that featured some of Britain's most prominent R&B groups, including the Spencer Davis Group, Manfred Mann, Georgie Fame and the Blue Flames, the Graham Bond Organisation, the Animals, the Steampacket, and others. All were aggressively looking for recognition in a crowded market and so were the Who.

Townshend imagined a musical and visual identity for the band that began to move beyond covers of American originals. Referencing ideas about integrating the arts, Townshend insisted that the band lived pop art, which represented to him "something the public is familiar with" but "in a different form. Like clothes. Union Jacks are supposed to be flown. We have a jacket made of one" (Nick Jones 1965).

With "I Can't Explain" and "Anyway, Anyhow, Anywhere," the Who had established an identity and, as a songwriter, Townshend was learning how to use call-and-response patterns around strong hooks in a format they could exploit in live performances. As a group, the Who had also grown more comfortable in the studio, even if Talmy's control over the process and the product sometimes annoyed them. And in the Who, Talmy had found a band willing to take musical risks. Their next single would consolidate these factors.

Townshend explained in *Melody Maker* that the sixties' "big social revolution" had made "youth, and not age . . . important" (Nick Jones 1965). To that end, their next single would both reflect his interests in pop art and be "anti middle-age, anti boss-class, and anti young marrieds" (Nick Jones 1965). "My Generation" may have originated with Jimmy Reed's "Big Boss Man," hybridized with the talking blues and folk protest (Hill 2014), but where the original model worked within a traditional three-chord, 12-bar format, Townshend used only two chords and, to avoid being too repetitive, abruptly raised the pitch several times.[9] The song's most distinguishing feature, however, played on a speech impediment.

Very Big Social Comment. Townshend explained to Barry Miles that "the stutter . . . turned it over." In his demos, the songwriter plays with this device, sometimes heard in blues recordings where the singer stammers to express excitement.[10] Townshend, however, had a different explanation that he believed was a "very big social comment." The lyrics voice "some pilled-up Mod dancing around, trying to explain to you why he's such a groovy guy, but he can't because

---

[9] Townshend: "It was repetitive, there were lots of effective key changes in it so it didn't bore you too much" (Miles 1970).
[10] For example, John Lee Hooker's "Stuttering Blues" from *Don't Turn Me from Your Door* (1963).

he's so stoned he can hardly talk" (Townshend in Miles 1970). The stuttering also emphasizes the song's underlying aggression, especially with the line "Why don't you all f-f-fade away" and its implied expletive.

For musicians unimpressed by the stuttering, "My Generation" also features an impressive bass solo,[11] and the performance ends with feedback and a continuous drumroll around the kit while Entwistle holds down the musical fort. When released in early October 1965, the disc reached *Record Retailer*'s #2 slot, broke into *Billboard*'s charts at #74, and provided the title for their album.

Townshend may be exaggerating when he says that the band "recorded the entire first album in six hours." They had, however, prepared with a "week of rehearsing" during which Lambert got "rid of lousy verses" and coached them (Neill and Kent 2002, 64). *My Generation* (December 1965) includes covers (e.g., James Brown's "Please, Please, Please") but reveals Townshend abandoning a model he disparaged as "fucking Italian love songs" (Townshend in Oldham 2003, 261). In "The Kids Are Alright," "A Legal Matter," "It's Not True," and "Out in the Street" he instead describes personal problems and social relationships by drawing on models that include the folk musicians who were also challenging the idiom in which they worked.

Fig. 19.1 The High Numbers, at Railway Hotel, 1964.

---

[11] Townshend had outlined ideas in his demos encouraging Entwistle to elaborate on the vocal line. Entwistle broke several sets of strings on his Danelectro basses in these sessions, finally settling on a "Fender Jazz Bass and a set of La Bella strings" for the recording. (See Cunningham 1998, 110.)

Fig. 19.2 The Who, on *Ready, Steady, Go!*, 1965.

20
Uncommon Folk

In a December 1965 *New Musical Express* supplement surveying the year's most important musical trends, Keith Altham noted the rise of folk music in the popular-music marketplace. After crowning Bob Dylan and Joan Baez the king and queen of folk, Altham asks Donovan Leitch for his input about the movement. The Scottish singer-songwriter mocks the era when managers renamed male clients to evoke emotion (e.g., Billy Fury) or strength (e.g., Tommy Steele) and declared that the "days of Fred Storm and Jim Iron have gone. Now we are getting real songs and real people in the charts" (Altham December 1965).

Midcentury scholar-performers like Alan Lomax had been deeply concerned about "cultural gray out" (the loss of autochthonous and distinct musical styles) and traveled widely to record and archive music they perceived as endangered by modern technology (Nettl 2015, 174). Meanwhile, the public and record stores broadly applied a notion of "folk music" to everything from ballads collected by the American Francis James Child in the nineteenth century to Indian classical music. For audiences in search of authenticity, the apparent absence of production (double tracking, reverberation, etc.) associated with folk music offered an alternative to the confections of commercial pop and rock recordings.

For many in the Bulge and Boomer generations, attending colleges and universities and learning to question the world they were inheriting, folk offered a vehicle for testing the authority of the Establishment. Here was music with history and truth that could challenge the status quo by exploring issues like racism, classism, and poverty. Identifying what folk music was, in a cosmopolitan setting like London, and who the folk were, however, could prove contentious.

In Search of the British

Globally, many musicians, scholars, and scholar-musicians had searched for musics they believed reflected preindustrial national cultures. At the beginning of the twentieth century, Cecil Sharp collected songs in the UK, the United States, and Australia that he thought captured the essence of British culture, before educational reforms that mandated school for all children destroyed local oral traditions (Nettl 2015, 106). Although his research proved groundbreaking, Sharp managed his sources so as to focus on performers whose songs (and dances) he projected as unsullied by modern urban cultural pollution;[1] and they conveniently had no ownership until discovered, curated, transcribed, and published.

In the generation following Sharp, the notion of folk music continued to be important for British musicians. Their backgrounds, while changing the ideology of the research, nevertheless perpetuated some of Sharp's prerogatives. Music had helped Londoner A. L. ("Bert") Lloyd survive when he was orphaned at 15 and relocated by a veterans' organization in 1924 to work for sheep farmers in Australia. The songs and stories of British immigrants that he heard and learned in the Outback intrigued him, and on his return to the UK in 1935, he continued collecting and singing songs, including while working on a whaling ship (Gregory 1970; Harker 1985, 232).

Lloyd's self-directed studies in British history and folklore (if not his personal story) inspired others.[2] Activist, actor, and playwright Ewan MacColl, looking to establish his authenticity, had been born James Miller but changed his name in 1945 to emphasize his Scottish roots and working-class background. In addition to writing and performing songs that championed labor rights,[3] he and Lloyd collected Child and broadside ballads to sing in concerts and on radio programs, positioning themselves as interpreters of a bucolic agrarian Britain for nostalgic urban audiences.[4] Among the performers they met as they toured the country was Anne Briggs, who sang traditional material that defied commercialization and whose lifestyle proved to be influential on a generation of British folk artists eager for authenticity in a changing world (Harper March 1998).

Urban Nostalgia. In the mid-twentieth century, many in the UK lamented the disappearance of the local pub, where communities had gathered to drink and sometimes sing. Between 1939 and 1962, 30,000 pubs closed; their patrons abandoned their evening or weekend pints to watch television at home (Sandbrook 2005, 130). The shift left publicans looking for new customers at a time when music audiences were growing. In this context, MacColl first established The Ballad and Blues Club (1953) above the Princess Louise (Holborn) before relocating it to rooms at another venue, the Scots Hoose (Cambridge Circus) as folk clubs popped up in cities and towns across the nation. Like proponents of country cricket who would rather see their sport "driven back to the village green" than "yield a jot to the petulant demands of the spectator" (Sandbrook

---

[1] For example, Sharp was against women's suffrage.
[2] Eighteenth-century politicians had originally promoted the notion of being British as a strategy to create unity among the nations of the United Kingdom (Herman 2001, 64).
[3] MacColl nevertheless composed the ballad "The First Time Ever I Saw Your Face" (which he had written for Peggy Seeger) for a play and received royalties.
[4] Both Lloyd and MacColl eventually came under the influence of Alan Lomax during his 1950s McCarthy-era London exile and began recording performances they believed reflected a preindustrial Britain.

2006, 307), MacColl vetted performances, repertoire, and playing styles so as to reject any semblance of commercialism.

Among the targets of MacColl's disdain were acoustic artists who performed songs that record companies marketed as folk. Often not English, these musicians nevertheless found audiences listening for catchy melodies with memorable lyrics evoking nostalgia.

Folk Pop

Connections between the American and British folk revivals were cemented through the emergence of the vinyl long-play (LP) album, a format that signaled "adult" because adolescents primarily purchased cheaper 45-rpm discs. The Clancy Brothers and Tommy Makem were among the first to enjoy transatlantic success, appearing on *The Ed Sullivan Show* (March 1961) and in numerous concert dates in the United States and their native Ireland. Dressed in Aran sweaters, they sang about sailing, drinking, and fighting the English and released albums that had American adults and college students as their intended customers. English consumers, unsurprisingly, proved less receptive, instead preferring acoustic renditions of Tin Pan Alley ballads by a Dublin trio, the Bachelors.

This group—Declan Cluskey, Conleth Cluskey, and John Stokes—scored British hits with remakes of "Charmaine" (December 1962, originally published in 1927), "Whispering" (August 1963, originally published in 1920), and "Diane" (January 1964, originally published in 1927). Shel Talmy produced their first two UK hits shortly after arriving in London, but it was Brit Michael Barclay's production of "Diane" that broke them into *Billboard*'s top 10.[5]

From London but also with Irish roots, the Springfields—Tom and Dusty Springfield (née O'Brien) with Tom Feild—responded to folk revivals under way on both sides of the Atlantic by mixing British and American elements. Their first disc, "Dear John" (May 1961) applies George Formby's ukulele with Lonnie Donegan's music-hall humor to a country song delivered with accents that awkwardly approximate an Appalachian twang. Other recordings (some written by Tom Springfield) sold better but with similar American or vaguely foreign accents, including the now embarrassing "Swahili Papa" (August 1962).

Their biggest recording came with the country-flavored "Silver Threads and Golden Needles" (April 1962), which, although failing to chart in the UK, made *Billboard*'s top 30. "Island of Dreams" (November 1962) and "Say I Won't Be

---

[5] The Bachelors went on to work with producers Marvin Holtzman (another American) and Noel Walker and music directors Reg Guest, Arthur Greenslade, and Ivor Raymonde to score a quick succession of top five hits in 1964, including "I Believe" (March), "Ramona" (May, originally published 1928), and "I Wouldn't Trade You for the World" (August).

There" (March 1963)—again sung with American accents—would bring them into the UK's top five, and readers of both the *New Musical Express* and *Melody Maker* ranked the Springfields as the best British vocal group of 1962. Ambition, however, led Dusty Springfield to launch a solo career, while her brother Tom pursued production.

Another World

London attracted musicians, not only from other parts of the British Isles but also from other parts of the Commonwealth, and included a group of Australians who arrived in May 1964 at Southampton on the SS *Fairsky* (McCarthy 2005). In 1962, former school friends Bruce Woodley, Keith Potger, and Athol Guy had formed the Seekers, a vocal-harmony folk group in Melbourne. With Guy and Woodley working for rival advertising agencies and Potger producing programs for the Australian Broadcasting Corporation, they already had ideas about audiences and how to market themselves. What they lacked was a distinctive sound and identity, a problem that was resolved when Judy Durham introduced herself.

Durham's voice and stage presence reinforced the Seekers' image as a wholesome mass-market version of folk music, and when their Australian albums met with modest national success, Guy booked them as the entertainment on the *Fairsky*. In advance of their London arrival, agent Eddie Jarrett at the Lew Grade Agency listened to their recordings and arranged several important media appearances, including the family variety program *Val Parnell's Sunday Night at the London Palladium* (21 June 1964; Lazarevic 2013). Their short-term stopover in London soon turned into a summer residency and more, including a show in Blackpool, where they met headliner Dusty Springfield. An introduction to her brother followed (Altham 5 February 1965).

A World of Our Own. In his new role as an independent producer, Tom Springfield found in the Seekers a vehicle for ideas he had explored with his sister and Tom Feild. He had written "I'll Never Find Another You" with the same male-and-female vocal mix in mind as Peter, Paul, and Mary, the Rooftop Singers, and the Springfields. Hearing a trend, his arrangement begins with an acoustic 12-string guitar riff reminiscent of the Rooftop Singers' "Walk Right In" (November 1962). After rehearsing the quartet and booking a session rental at EMI, he leased the recording to the company's Columbia label.

When the recording was released in December 1964, Australian expatriate pirate-radio deejays off the UK coast put the disc onto their playlists, helping it to chart. Appearances on *Top of the Pops* put it at the top of *Record Retailer*'s and

New Musical Express's charts by the third week of February 1965 (Michael Smith 2015). Success in London also put the disc on American pop radar, and by spring "I'll Never Find Another You" had also scored a spot in *Billboard*'s top five.

In April 1965 when the *New Musical Express* invited the Seekers to perform on their annual Poll Winner's Concert, the appearance served as an opportunity to launch their next Tom Springfield composition and production. A clear follow-up to their first release, "A World of Our Own" (April 1965) retreats from the sentiment of Tony Hatch and Petula Clark's "Downtown" to a safe domestic space. Instead of heading to clubs to forget one's troubles and cares, Durham brings her lover home with the instruction to "close the door, light the light; we're stayin' home tonight."

The Seekers offered folk pop for a middle-of-the-road audience: clean-cut colonials singing sentimental love songs in harmony with acoustic instruments and no political agenda. The group rejected what they called members of London's "Folk Cult" who played only for "a very restricted audience." Instead, they wanted the "whole world" to hear their recordings (Altham 5 February 1965). The success of this mainstream folk pop foreshadows a trend of the second half of the decade. Meanwhile, an edgier folk scene was emerging from Scotland.

Folk Baroque

In the contexts of a cosmopolitan interest in traditional music, some British musicians explored intercultural exchange. English guitarist Julian Bream and British-American violinist Yehudi Menuhin, for example, collaborated with Indian sarodist Ali Akbar Khan and sitarist Ravi Shankar, respectively, on several musical projects around 1963. This interest in sharing musical ideas illustrates the emerging notion that many cultures have ideas worth hearing, if not emulating.

The originator of the term "folk baroque" may have been *Melody Maker* critic Karl Dallas, who was seeking to describe the inventive acoustic guitar styles emerging in mid-1960s Britain by referencing a musical era perhaps best known for Bach and Handel (Harper 2000). Julian Bream's recordings, especially of music from the Renaissance and Baroque periods, familiarized many guitarists with musical styles while introducing them to new playing techniques. In the world of folk music, Alexis Korner's liner notes for a 1962 EP liberally apply the term "baroque" to describe the finger-picked steel-stringed acoustic guitar style of a young musician with broad musical interests and an eclectic background.

A Taste of Tangier

Perhaps fittingly, a pivotal figure in the transformation of the 1960s British folk music scene may never have felt entirely part of it. Born into a multilingual, multiethnic family—the son of a Scottish father who taught Gaelic in London and a Guyanese mother—Davey Graham grew up in the ethnically diverse neighborhoods around London's Notting Hill Gate.[6] Strongly believing in the power of learning languages, his parents enrolled him at the Lycée Français, which unfortunately was where a playground accident cost him most of the sight in his right eye. (See Denselow 2008; McMullen 1991; Pilgrim 2008.)

He began learning classical guitar at 12, studying with Oliver Hunt (later of the London College of Music), and quickly learned to apply those techniques to playing along with modern jazz (e.g., Thelonious Monk) and blues records (notably Big Bill Broonzy; Graham 1963). After leaving school, he joined the wave of youth traveling to Greece, North Africa, and Paris, busking, listening to local musics, and picking up languages. Back in London, his amalgam of skill and eclectic repertoire impressed guitarists (including Ray Davies), particularly his ability to play a melody and a bass line with internal harmony parts. Equally important, he experimented with altered guitar tunings that emulated the Arabic 'ūd.[7] By age 18, his reputation in select London music circles led director Ken Russell to include a clip of Graham playing in *From Spain to Streatham* (1959), a documentary about the popularity of the guitar in Britain.

His virtuosity attracted the attention of the ever-enthusiastic Alexis Korner, with whom he recorded a Topic Records EP (April 1962).[8] Three items on the disc offer early examples of Graham's polyphonic solo guitar arrangements, heard especially well in his "Angi," a future benchmark for young folk guitarists eager to demonstrate their technical proficiency. Although he played briefly with both Blues Incorporated and with electric blues proponent John Mayall, Graham preferred performing as an acoustic soloist or accompanist, and it was in these roles that his reputation spread.

Eastern Flavour. In May 1963, Decca's Hugh Mendl recorded a concert headlined by the Thamesiders that included Graham's performances of "She Moved through the Fair" and "Mustapha," which foreshadow both the urban Celtic music movement and the incorporation of non-Western musical ideas into Western musical contexts. Expanding on that premise, Graham and singer Shirley Collins performed a program promising an "Eastern flavour" at Notting Hill's Mercury Theatre (July 1964), a small space with a distinguished theatrical

---

[6] Sometimes spelled as "Davy" Graham.
[7] Graham is perhaps best known for popularizing the tuning DADGAD.
[8] A. L. Lloyd served as artistic director for Topic Records.

history. Impressed, Mendl encouraged his colleague Ray Horricks to produce Collins and Graham's *Folk Roots, New Routes* (1964), an album that intermixes traditional European folk songs (e.g., "Lord Gregory") with jazz (e.g., the instrumental "Blue Monk").

Horricks followed this record with a solo project for Graham, *Folk Blues and Beyond* (January 1965), which includes covers of contemporary favorites like Bob Dylan's "Don't Think Twice, It's Alright" along with material from the folk repertoire like "Black Is the Colour of My True Love's Hair" and Big Bill Broonzy's "Rock Me Baby." Also included on the album, Graham's instrumental "Maajun (a Taste of Tangier)" influenced a number of musicians, including Dave Davies, who attempted to apply some of its ideas when working on the Kinks' "See My Friends" (Davies 1996, 75).

Graham should have been one of the best-known performers in the wave of folk and folk-inspired British musicians to emerge in 1965; however, he lacked the midsixties British pop-star image in its most ethnically narrow white-male stereotypes. His close-cropped hair, mixed ethnicity, and elongated moustache challenged photographers, who endeavored to hide his damaged right eye. Moreover, as dexterous as his guitar playing was, his singing voice lacked the range, agility, and expressiveness of more successful performers.

At a more dysfunctional level, as a devotee of cool jazz, Graham purposely addicted himself to cocaine and heroin in imitation of his musical heroes. As his ability to show up for gigs and to perform suffered, promoters shied away from booking him, and musicians such as Shirley Collins refused to perform with him, not knowing which Davey Graham would show up. He continued his trips to North Africa and took lessons on the Indian sarod and sitar, but his career proved one of unfulfilled promise.

Imagining the Casbah

Davey Graham may have been an innovator, but his demeanor and technique proved intimidating. Scottish musician Danny Kyle remembered that while "you could go and sit in total awe of the man," he preferred the slightly younger Bert Jansch. "You would go and listen [to Jansch] and you would say to yourself, 'Here, perhaps I could do some of that' because he made it seem attainable" (Harper 2000).

By the time Bert Jansch left school at 15, he had already tried building his own guitar and had taken work in a garden nursery, in part in order to buy a proper instrument (Irwin 2011). Although some purist folk aficionados had rejected the guitar as a modern intrusion into traditional music, young musicians like Jansch embraced it in the age of skiffle. His love of music also found him seeking like-minded associates and a place to congregate, which led him in the late 1950s to Edinburgh's premier folk club, The Howff.[9]

In addition to traditional Scottish fare, Jansch (like Graham) took a particular interest in the recordings of Big Bill Broonzy: "I found a little EP in an Edinburgh store and for the next year that was all I listened to [but] couldn't understand how you could pick out more than one melody at the same time" (Jansch in Barnes 2007). By trial and error, observation, and lessons from Davey Graham's sister, Jill Doyle Lindsay, Jansch gradually developed his own ways of reproducing the sounds he heard and in the process created his own stylistic amalgam. Perhaps most strategically, among the performers he heard and met at The Howff, Martin Carthy and Anne Briggs showed him a way to escape Edinburgh (Harper 2000). The key to his passage came in the form of "Angi," which he learned from a tape belonging to Graham's sister and which he made a centerpiece of his shows.[10]

Needle of Death. Like Graham and others, Jansch busked around Europe, overcoming his shyness and building confidence as a performer. When he returned, he and Robin Williamson traveled to London to perform at the Troubadour in Earl's Court (Harper 2000). Toward the end of 1964, Anne Briggs was impressed enough to encourage Bill Leader (who had produced Davey Graham's disc with Alexis Korner) to produce an album by Jansch. Major British record companies, however, hesitated to lease the eponymous disc (April 1965), and Leader eventually sold the rights to Transatlantic Records for £100. Although Jansch's version of "Angie" and his Arabic-influenced instrumental "Casbah" were popular, his "Needle of Death" perhaps became the best-known track on the LP. Its story of heroin addiction set as a Scottish border ballad sung with a tremulous voice over delicate fingerpicking fused the aesthetics of London's folk aficionados with evidence of the drug dependency spreading through the community.

Although the folk movement in this era may have been split into camps, we can easily find individuals straddling the divides. The heterogeneity of this cultural scene increased with the opening in mid-April 1965 of the Soho club Les Cousins, a space where musicians from different backgrounds came to trade ideas. Its roster of performers included Bob Dylan, Graham, Jansch, and artists-in-waiting such as John Renbourn, all of whom were ready to push folk music into new stylistic territory.

---

[9] Named for a burial ground in Dundee.
[10] Not having seen Graham and Korner's record, Jansch spelled his version "Angie."

A More Progressive Element

Bob Dylan's early career benefited from the cultural network linking New York and London. Having created a buzz in Greenwich Village clubs and appearing on the cover of the influential folk magazine *Sing Out!* (October–November 1962), he attracted the attention of British director Philip Saville, who invited him to London to appear as a folksinger in a teledrama based on the Evan Jones play *The Madhouse on Castle Street*.[11] The Minnesotan wasted little time making both friends and enemies at clubs like Bunjies Coffee House & Folk Cellar, The Establishment, The Troubadour, The Singers Club, The Roundhouse, and other stops on the London folk scene. In a politically and aesthetically charged atmosphere that pitted folk "purists" against a "more progressive element," Dylan proved a "flashpoint" (Caspar Smith, 2005).

Often in the company of Martin Carthy, the American absorbed ideas that he incorporated into his writing. According to Carthy, Dylan's "time in England was actually crucial to his development" and, after his visit, one could hear "an enormous difference in the way he's singing, in the sort of tunes he's singing, [and] the way he's putting words together" (Caspar Smith 2005). Notably, Carthy claims that Dylan adapted songs he heard performed in London clubs. For example, he suggests that "Girl from the North Country" (May 1963)[12] derives from Carthy's version of "Scarborough Fair," and "With God on Our Side" (January 1964) from Dominic Behan's song "The Patriot Game" (Caspar Smith 2005).[13]

Mainstream Folk. The broad influence of folk music at this point in the sixties percolated into pop music, where musicians who normally relied on electric guitars and drums temporarily went acoustic. For example, "Play with Fire" (February 1965) illustrates how Jagger and Richards took ideas from the folk scene to provide a vehicle for Jagger's misogyny and geosocial commentary. Over an acoustic guitar, its strings plucked rather than strummed, and a harpsichord, Jagger drops London place names like social bombs: the mother owns property in Saint John's Wood, but the "old man" controls her wealth, leaving her to slum and to use drugs in Stepney (working-class east London) rather than posh Knightsbridge.

John Lennon took inspiration from some of the same sources as Dylan (if not the American himself) with "You've Got to Hide Your Love Away," which shares musical similarities with "The Times They Are a Changin." The Beatle used an acoustic 12-string guitar to sonically connect his performance to the folk world for the recording that appeared on their 1965 film soundtrack album *Help!*

---

[11] Rehearsals began in December 1962 and taping lasted until January 1963.
[12] On the LP *The Freewheelin' Bob Dylan*.
[13] On the LP *The Times They Are a-Changin'*.

Sensing that the song had potential as a single, Lennon separately produced a recording of the university folk music group the Silkie singing it.[14] This new production of "You've Got to Hide Your Love Away" (September 1965) features Paul McCartney on guitar and the unusual folk treatment of double-tracked vocals.

Not to be outdone, McCartney arrived at a Beatles session with his own acoustic number, his guitar detuned in a way that hampered anyone accompanying him, until George Martin convinced him that a string quartet would work well. The Beatles and Martin would include "Yesterday" on the *Help!* soundtrack, even though McCartney recorded the song too late to be included in the film. Capitol heard the recording's potential and had substantial success with it as a single in the United States. Meanwhile, in the UK, Marianne Faithfull recorded the British release of the song in the fall of 1965, albeit with an overpowering and unfolklike chorus.

In March 1965, as the ever-changing Dylan prepared to return to the UK for a tour, British CBS released singles of his songs "The Times They Are a-Changin'" and "Subterranean Homesick Blues," both of which reached *Record Retailer*'s top 10. Venues sold out as soon as tickets went on sale, and Britain prepared for that year's version of the American chameleon. Until then, they survived with a Scottish bard.

Catch the Wind

If the battle lines between folk "purists" and "progressives" shifted as individual performers trespassed artistic boundaries, then Donovan Leitch wandered over more than one map. Born in Glasgow and surviving polio as a child (resulting in a limp), Leitch grew up playing in streets still "ripped up with open sewers" from wartime bombing (Monti 2015). In this environment, his father, a tool setter at a Rolls-Royce engine factory, instilled a love of poetry in his son by reading to him every night (Leitch 2005, 7–8).

When the family relocated to Hatfield, near Saint Albans just north of London, rock 'n' roll (and Buddy Holly in particular) captivated the 10-year-old, who took up the drums to play with friends in a short-lived band (Leitch 2005, 13). Soon, however, the Beatles' "Love Me Do"—with its mix of acoustic guitars, harmonica, drums, bass, and harmonies—led him to think, "I want to do that" (89).

In the spring of 1963, after graduating from seconday modern school and briefly attending college, he headed to Cornwall to join a small community of mostly British "Beats" or "beachnics" who were panhandling on the sandy shores of Saint Ives. Between that and working in a café, he began to learn guitar. Returning to Hatfield for the winter of 1964, his focus turned to technique and the basics of

---

[14] This university quartet (three males and a female managed by Brian Epstein) had initially recorded the traditional tune "Blood Red River" (April 1965) but with little recognition.

finger picking, which he learned from local musician Keith "Mac" MacLeod (Emery 1965, 36).

Southern Music. Building a repertoire of covers and originals, he was playing an intermission set at a club in the coastal town of Southend-on-Sea in late 1964 when Peter Eden and songwriter Geoff Stephens saw him. Stephens, although having written a couple of hits, had begun to worry whether songwriting royalties were enough to sustain his young family. When Eden encouraged him to go to The Studio Club that evening, they heard potential in a handful of promising songs and in the young Scots musician.

They proposed a management contract and brought the 18-year-old to Denmark Street to demo some of his material. Southern Music's building had a showroom on the ground floor and offices and studios above, but the rudimentary basement recording studio allowed songwriters to cut demos. Upstairs to the managing director, the tape of the teenaged singer exuded just the right blend of naïveté and worldliness to warrant Bob Kingston offering him a publishing contract. The press and the public soon perceived Donovan (now going only by his first name) as a British response to Bob Dylan.

Stephens and Kingston managed to secure 12 appearances on *Ready Steady Go!*, a remarkable ascent for someone who only a year before had still been learning guitar and had yet to release a record. Donovan debuted on the same show as the Who at the end of January 1965. His unconventional status situated him as an innovator, if for no other reason than that he had largely escaped the normalizing gauntlet of London folk clubs. Of course, appearing on *Ready Steady Go!* also gained him the immediate disdain of folk purists.

By early March 1965, when *New Musical Express* ran an announcement of Dylan's April–May British tour, Donovan had his first disc ready for release. Stephens and Eden had negotiated a Pye recording contract, with Southern Music alum Terry Kennedy producing the singer's "Catch the Wind" (March 1965). For this reworking of ideas from Dylan's "Chimes of Freedom" and "Blowin' in the Wind," Kennedy brought in ex-Shadow Brian Locking to play acoustic bass and a small string section to complement the delicate paean to unrequited love.

Colours. In the UK, Donovan's single outsold Dylan's "The Times They Are a-Changin,'" but Dylan remained the cultural focal point, as his Savoy Hotel rooms saw the Beatles, Donovan, and other musicians arriving to pay their respects.[15] For Donovan's second single, "Colours" (May 1965), released around the time that Dylan departed for the United States, Donovan added banjo and harmonica chording to supplement his guitar playing, perhaps in response to those critics who thought the strings on his first release overly sentimental. "Colours" reached

---

[15] Some of these activities can be seen in D. A. Pennebaker's *Bob Dylan: Don't Look Back* (1967).

Record Retailer's top five in the summer of 1965, along with his first album, *What's Bin Did and What's Bin Hid*.[16]

Through 1965, Donovan continued to cultivate his persona of a Scottish Woody Guthrie, with his cloth cap, harmonica in a brace, and a guitar that bore the first three words of Guthrie's adage "This Machine Kills Fascists." The singer also engaged in political protest, joining Joan Baez on a march, and releasing a version of Buffy Sainte-Marie's "Universal Soldier" (August 1965). By the end of the year, however, his song "Turquoise" (October 1965) responded to changes percolating in pop music and marked the end of his relationship with his management because, as Stephens remembered, "we fell out because he was all sort of LSD and I wasn't" (interview 2 March 2001).

Nowhere Men

When the Byrds arrived from Los Angeles in August 1965, London audiences and critics were eager to hear the band billed as "America's answer to the Beatles" (Altham 20 August 1965). Former Brian Epstein associate Derek Taylor (17 July 1965) had reported from Los Angeles that audiences there had lined up in West Hollywood to hear them at Ciro's, a "large, unfashionable night club on Sunset Strip." The electric 12-string guitar that featured on their recordings realized a merger of the Beatles and American folk (with perhaps a nod to Jackie DeShannon and the Searchers). Some performers and audiences rejected this hybrid of folk and rock, but this particularly successful merger came to play a powerful role in sixties pop-music culture.

In July, "Mr. Tambourine Man" (April 1965) topped charts on both sides of the Atlantic, leading to a grueling tour that eventually landed the Byrds in the UK. True to their serious folk roots, when they appeared at the Flamingo Club, they dispensed with any crowd banter or showmanship, played a half-hour set dominated by Roger McGuinn's electric 12-string, and then left the stage. The combination of the Flamingo's R&B history with folk-rock's aesthetics did not go down well in a city where musicians were expected to put on a show. An attendee complained that the band was "a drag. Absolutely no stage presentation and all their numbers sound like 'Mr. Tambourine Man.' They are not bad, just very, very dull" (Welch 14 August 1965).

Dylan's music, however, encouraged some songwriters to explore the abstract language and metaphors that peppered his lyrics. The Beatles were particularly

---

[16] In the second week of July 1965, four of the top five albums on the *New Musical Express*'s charts were by Bob Dylan, Joan Baez, the Seekers, and Donovan. The soundtrack to *The Sound of Music* occupied the second spot after Dylan.

impressed. On their album *Rubber Soul* (December 1965) Dylan's influence was expanded in John Lennon's "Norwegian Wood (This Bird Has Flown)" and "Nowhere Man," and in George Harrison's "If I Needed Someone." But many other musical and microcultural forces were undulating beneath the surface of the increasingly integrated transatlantic world of popular music.

Fig. 20.1 The Springfields, in *Just for Fun*, 1963.

Fig. 20.2 The Seekers, in "I'll Never Find Another You" (promotional film), 1964.

Fig. 20.3 Davey Graham, on *Hullabaloo*, 1963.

Fig. 20.4 Donovan Leitch, at Newport Folk Festival, 1965.

Epilogue

The first phase of sixties British pop launched with thousands imitating what they heard resonating both from across the Atlantic and domestically: English grafts onto American roots. Through a combination of serendipity, enthusiasm, and determination, they created musical hybrids that drew international attention and changed cosmopolitan culture.

The creators and the curators—the artists, songwriters, publishers, producers, music directors, and engineers whose ideas formed the core of this world—began by adapting existing musical, lyrical, performative, and sonic forms to develop their own versions of postwar cosmopolitan pop culture. Along the way, the places they called home and the spaces where they created music and recordings shaped these ideas.

The consumers of pop culture—the audiences in pubs, clubs, church halls, cinemas, and concert halls—also helped to define the music every time they danced, shouted, screamed, or even just stood and listened, the degree of their attention informative as to what worked and what did not. And among those dancers and gawkers, managers and agents mingled, on the hunt for the faces, voices, and sounds that could sell tickets and maybe discs.

Trends

In the beginning of the modern pop era (1956–1961), Americans topped *Record Retailer*'s charts two weeks for every one by Brits. In 1962, however, that pattern reversed, with domestic artists capturing 64 percent of the top spots, a trend that exploded in 1963 (98 percent),[1] 1964 (91 percent), and 1965 (97 percent).[2] In the first six years of the decade (1960–1965), British artists came to dominate these charts (70 percent), driven significantly by the rise of "beat" groups.

Between 1956 and 1961, the top records had been by vocal soloists (85 percent). In 1963, however, that trend was upended in favor of groups (93 percent), especially those with northern accents. Cliff Richard and the Shadows enjoyed

---

[1] Recordings that carry over from year to the next are included in the previous year's totals, as when the Beatles' "I Want to Hold Your Hand" carried over from 1963 into 1964.

[2] If the Australian Seekers, produced in London by Tom Springfield, are included as domestic artists, then British artists in 1965 occupied the number-one spot for 43 weeks.

#1 discs for 11 weeks in the first months of that year, with Brian Poole and the Tremeloes adding another 3 weeks in the fall for London-based bands. Beginning in April, however, Merseyside groups Gerry and the Pacemakers, the Searchers, Billy J. Kramer with the Dakotas, and of course the Beatles ruled British charts for 34 weeks. Northerners continued to prevail through 1964, with performers from other cities and parts of the country (Manchester, Birmingham, and Wales) joining them at the top of the charts over the next year.[3] In the process, transatlantic pop music simply began to sound different, with British artists playing a major role.

Dynamics. The shift from solo singers backed by orchestras to bands featuring electric guitars and keyboards reflected four important factors. First, electromagnetic technology allowed small groups to be heard by large audiences. Second, these electric bands needed only limited stage space, which allowed promoters more room for patrons. Third, touring big bands characterized by trumpets and saxophones proved financially unfeasible as petroleum prices rose. In comparison, a singing four-piece guitar-bass-and-drums outfit who split their fee into fewer parts represented a more economical alternative. And fourth, the Bulge Generation's preference for blues, rhythm-and-blues, and rock 'n' roll pushed jazz forms—often patronized by an older and smaller audience—to the corners of pop culture.

Electric pop groups also had adaptive advantages. Their eclectic mixes of aesthetics, skill, and commitment levels, and their relatively short existences, meant that they continually dissolved and recombined to maximize survival. Self-reliant, they could quickly appropriate and adapt music to fit their needs and resources, and—in the process of recreating what patrons had heard on discs—they sometimes inadvertently created something new, something British. Groups, however, were also overwhelmingly male, which reflected deep-seated cultural biases about sex, the use of tools (instruments), and leadership.

During the first six years of the decade, men (British and American) topped *Record Retailer*'s charts 85 percent of the time, with British men (soloists and groups) responsible for 61 percent of those hits. Consumers, in comparison, put British women in the same spot only 7 percent of the time, with peaks in 1961—when Petula Clark (1 week), Shirley Bassey (1 week), and Helen Shapiro (6 weeks) combined for eight weeks (15 percent of the year)—and in 1964, when Cilla Black (7 weeks) and Sandie Shaw (3 weeks) had the best-selling records for 10 weeks (21 percent of the year). The next year, 1965, Jackie Trent and Sandie

---

[3] The shift from soloists to groups in the last half of the first six years of the decade (1963–1965) brought those two performance models into rough balance: 49 percent for soloists, 51 percent for groups.

Shaw's back-to-back singles combined for four weeks, but in 1960, 1962, and 1963, no woman (British or American) had a disc in the top spot.

Being English

Kate Fox (2014) describes social dis-ease as the core motivator of English behavior. This communal awkwardness has led governments, churches, clubs, and other organizations to take great interest in laws and rules about how sexes, genders, ethnicities, generations, and classes interact. The sixties, however, brought some of these conventions into question.

Adolescents entering adulthood in this era held numerical superiority and, resenting their lack of legal and political power, discovered that they could defy adults in theaters, dance halls, and clubs. The ritual excitement of performances—the loud music, the feeling of social membership, the rush of hormones—prompted them to challenge established behaviors. In this heady environment, popular culture allowed youth to collectively define themselves, with music providing the contexts for defiance.

Class. "Class consciousness" ranks among the most persistent aspects of English behavior, and London's music and recording industries reflected this "outlook" (Fox 2014, 554). Middle-class managers and producers discovering and exploiting the talents of working-class musicians proved the norm, but some creators of pop culture in the sixties learned to leverage their financial value. This contestation of class privilege was already evident in George Formby's career, recordings, and films, but sixties British pop accelerated this trend.

One symbol of status, enrollment in Britain's elite schools, confirmed class privilege through markers such as classical knowledge (e.g., Latin and Greco-Roman mythology) and behavioral norms (language and manners).[4] Incremental changes in the educational system over the previous decades, however, had begun to allow broader access to grammar schools and universities. The admission of working-class and lower-middle-class students continued to change both those who enrolled and the system intended to normalize them.

One important outcome of education, accent, has served as a traditional signifier of class and ethnicity. Popular culture in the fifties and sixties, however, empowered people in the working class to embrace and to celebrate their identities. Joe Brown, for example, championed his Cockney background, and by the midsixties, Merseyside groups had given Scouse cadence cultural capital. Jazz, blues, and rock 'n' roll musicians, moreover, adopted American pronunciations

---

[4] Music education similarly supported the hegemony of harmonic and formal concepts associated with Europe's aristocratic and colonial past.

from the recordings they imitated. Nevertheless, although some parts of pop culture elevated both English and American proletarian behaviors, social hierarchy persisted in interpersonal relations.

Authenticity. Before a single sound is uttered on stage, musicians and their audiences have already commenced interpreting the experience. What is the performance space like? Who are the audience members? Who are the musicians? Are the clothing, instruments, and movements of the participants appropriate for the setting? And, once the performance begins, does the sound meet expectations? Like actors in a play, musicians and their audiences have roles.

Fox notes that the English make a show of modesty, often to disguise arrogance (2014, 557). Sixties British pop musicians routinely named their influences, with a modesty that acknowledged sometimes obscure performers and recordings. The gesture, however, also implied authority. The holy grail of British pop, authenticity—that intangible quality of originality and/or faithfulness to a source—appealed to musicians, audiences, and critics. Musicians dedicated to this knowledge (particularly of blues culture) were seldom shy about demanding authenticity (e.g., Eric Clapton). Not all musicians, however, aspired to this role.

English culture has long embraced theatre. Pop culture creates environments in which performers and audiences can temporarily escape normative conventions. For example, the transparent sexism and racism, and the sendup of class privilege delivered as slapstick comedy in the *Carry On* film franchise, expressed ideas normally buried in proper English social discourse. In pop music, the Temperance Seven, Screaming Lord Sutch and the Savages, Freddie and the Dreamers, and others invoked humor to mock arrogance, authenticity, and sometimes the very contexts in which they performed.

Location, Location, Location

Sixties British pop arose in a multitude of environments. A legion of neighborhood musicians practiced in bedrooms and front rooms before debuting in local school auditoriums and church halls, and then climbing onto the stages of low-rent former fruit cellars and upper-floor storage rooms. Musicians and their audiences came seeking community in these spaces, where acoustics and architecture shaped both performance and perception. The relatively low ceilings and dense walls of subterranean clubs like The Scene in London made the act of listening a visceral experience. Above ground, theaters like The Palladium brought more fans together, but communal frenzy overpowered the music, orchestra pits separated performers and audiences, and reverberation muddied the sounds of amplified instruments. Larger indoor venues like the Empire Pool in Wembley and outdoor events like the annual National Jazz and Blues Festival lacked proper amplification to project sound into spaces designed for sporting events.

The culture of each village, town, and city informed performer and audience aesthetics, but London determined what entered the national consciousness. Along the way, domestic interurban transportation—the postwar byways and motorways, the railways, and the airways—brought live music to cities and to their suburban and interurban satellites. Internationally, air and ocean routes connected global metropolitan centers, while radio and television broadcasting allowed everyone to believe that they were witnessing a cultural revolution.

The Sixties, Britain, Pop Culture, and Music

As the decade reached its midpoint, the global success of British pop fed national confidence and encouraged experimentation. Apropos of how their families had survived the economic hardships of the war and postwar years, musicians repurposed the materials of pop. They inverted and modified the harmonic and melodic materials of American originals to form the basis of a British style.

Just as in America, where White songwriters, performers, and producers reinterpreted music created by and for Black America, the British took this repertoire and re-spun it. Often they were mediating music that tweens would not have heard, both because their tastes were still maturing and because the recording industry understood the inherent racism of the market. British artists covering Black American music, however, gave it not only a White face but also a transatlantic accent.

A Brave New World

Demographics and technology underlay much of the cultural change in sixties Britain. In addition to the rise of the Bulge Generation, emigration and immigration shifted the ethnic makeup of cities, as Whites fled for Canada and Australia and Brown and Black people arrived from South Asia, Africa, and the Caribbean. The decolonization of the British Empire also brought home bureaucrats, businesspeople, and their families to a country that many of them had never known. And with Europe recovering from the devastation of its cities in World War II, a wave of immigrants crossed the Channel, bringing their aesthetics of food, clothing, and transportation. Already preoccupied with atomic power plants, modern housing projects, and the Cold War, the nation experienced ethnic, class, and generational tensions as Britannia sought to redefine itself in this new world.

Postwar Technology. During World War II, governments had developed drugs to treat injured servicemen on the battlefield and to extend their physical abilities. At the benevolent end of the pharmacological spectrum, antibiotics saved and improved lives that previously had been lost to infections. At the other end, amphetamines pushed the physical and psychological limits of soldiers, pilots, and factory workers. Antibiotics improved life quality and expectancy; amphetamines could prove lethal. Both entered everyday life in postwar Britain.

Pop culture, too, reflected and influenced technological change. Broadcast media saw the expansion of radio (both official and offshore) and television (the BBC and ITV) with programming introducing new musics, clothing styles, and cultural practices to a nation hungry for variety. Publishing, especially with the introduction of color printing, launched an armada of magazines that brought images of pop stars, clothing, and automobiles into the imaginations of a public eager to join the modern world. Meanwhile, electric guitars and keyboards, amplifiers, recording equipment, and home playback systems were transforming music creation and consumption. Some things, however, remained the same.

Plus Ça Change...

Music performances symbolically and functionally reflect both their immediate context and overarching cultural environment. The prevalence of White male musicians in this era was consistent with a culture in which only White men occupied positions of power. Many in Britain and the Western world, however, began to recognize systemic White supremacy, male chauvinism, and the structures sustaining them. For example, the importance of Black American music in Western pop culture, while evidence of appropriation, speaks to the growing cultural integration under way. Women, their abilities less recognized, still found themselves relegated to supportive roles.

Just as working-class men demanded equitable treatment, women too began to question the roles to which Western culture had relegated them. Although change was slow, the testosterone of rock, blues, and rhythm-and-blues came to be challenged by music that embraced intellectual sophistication. With every advance, however, came dangers and pushback. Many aspects of Western and particularly British and English culture remained steadfastly conservative and resistant to social liberalization; but the era did challenge conventions.

The Tide. Change can be described as both perceptual and measurable. That is, individuals in a culture experience change differently depending on their age, gender, sex, class, ethnicity, location, and social network. Access to technology, moreover, can have a measurable impact on lives. The expansion of international air travel and the introduction of television brought the world closer. But one area of development had a particularly important role in placing music at the heart of pop culture: electromagnetic technology.

The electromagnetic revolution fundamentally reshaped how music was created, curated, and consumed. Electric guitars, keyboards, and amplifiers transformed performance spaces, allowing young men (with a few women) to displace both a previous generation and the music that had defined them. In the studio, magnetic tape allowed producers and engineers to play with a physical recording to create a performance that had not existed in real time, while limiters, compressors, direct input, and other technological strategies altered the very nature of the sound. And more was to come.

For the consumer, the primary medium for hearing recorded music had not fundamentally changed in decades: a mechanical device still spun a physical disc with grooves down which a needle careened. Records and the ways people heard them, however, did evolve. Now vinyl discs with microgrooves turned at slower speeds, which quieted the sound of the needle and played stereo tracks that playback electronics enhanced.

In this tidal shift, British pop musicians and production crews positioned themselves to compete with Americans. In some cases, they superseded those whom they had once imitated.

Volume 1 Discography

Abbreviations: *RR* (*Record Retailer and Music Industry News*); *MM* (*Melody Maker*); *NME* (*New Musical Express*); and *BB* (*Billboard*). *New Musical Express* began publishing charts 14 November 1952. *Record Retailer*'s charts begin 10 March 1960.

The Ad Libs. "The Boy from New York City" (George Davis and John T. Taylor). Mary Ann Thomas, Hugh Harris, Danny Austin, Dave Watt, and Norman Donegan with studio musicians. Production: Jerry Leiber and Mike Stoller with Artie Butler (arranger). Recorded: New York, 1964. US release: Blue Cat BC-102, December 1964; *BB* #8 (February 1965). UK release: Red Bird RB 10 102, 5 February 1965.

Allison, Mose. "Parchman Farm" (Mose Allison). Mose Allison (piano and vocal), Addison Farmer (bass) and Nick Stabulas (drums). Production: Bob Weinstock. Recorded: Van Gelder Studio, Hackensack, New Jersey, 8 November 1957. US release: Prestige 45-130, 1958. UK release on *Parchman Farm* [EP], as Esquire EP 214, 1959.

Andrews, Julie. See *My Fair Lady* and *The Sound of Music*.

The Animals. "Baby Let Me Take You Home" (Bert Berns [Russell] and Wes Farrell). Eric Burdon (vocal), Alan Price (organ), Chas Chandler (bass), Hilton Valentine (guitar), and John Steel (drums). Production: Mickie Most with Dave Siddle (engineer). Recorded: De Lane Lea Studios, London, February 1964. UK release: Columbia DB 7247, 19 March 1964; charts 16 April 1964, *RR* #21. US release: MGM K 13242, May 1964. B: "Send You Back to Walker" (Johnnie Mae Matthews).

The Animals. "The House of the Rising Sun" (traditional). Personnel and production as above, 18 May 1964. UK release: Columbia DB 7301, 19 June 1964; charts 25 June 1964, *RR* #1. US release: MGM K 13264, July 1964; *BB* #1 (September 1964).

The Animals. "I'm Crying" (Alan Price and Eric Burdon). Personnel and production as above, August 1964. UK release: Columbia DB 7354, 11 September 1964; charts 17 September 1964, *RR* #8. US release: MGM 13274, September 1964; *BB* #19 (November 1964).

The Animals. *The Animals*. Personnel and production as above. US release: MGM E4264, September 1964. A: "The House of the Rising Sun," "The Girl Can't Help It," "Blue Feeling," "Baby Let Me Take You Home,"

"The Right Time," and "Talkin' 'bout You." B: "Around and Around," "I'm in Love Again," "Gonna Send You Back to Walker," "Memphis, Tennessee," "I'm Mad Again," and "I've Been Around."

The Animals. *The Animals.* Personnel and production as above. UK release: Columbia 33SX 1669, October 1964. A: "Story of Bo Diddley," "Bury My Body," "Dimples," "I've Been Around," "I'm in Love Again," and "The Girl Can't Help It." B: "I'm Mad Again," "She Said Yeh," "The Right Time," "Memphis," "Boom Boom," and "Around and Around."

The Animals. *The Animals on Tour.* Personnel and production as above. US release: MGM E-4281, February 1965. A: "Boom, Boom," "How You've Changed," "Mess Around," "Bright Lights, Big City," "I Believe to My Soul," and "Worried Life Blues." B: "Let the Good Times Roll," "Ain't Got You," "Hallelujah, I Lover Her So," "I'm Crying," "Dimples," and "She Said Yeah."

The Animals. "Don't Let Me Be Misunderstood" (Bennie Benjamin, Sol Marcus, and Gloria Caldwell). Personnel and production as above, December 1964. UK release: Columbia DB 7445, 29 January 1965; charts 4 February 1964, *RR* #3. US release: MGM K 13311; *BB* #15 (April 1965).

The Animals. "We Gotta Get Out of This Place" (Barry Mann and Cynthia Weil). Eric Burdon (vocal), Dave Rowberry (organ), Chas Chandler (bass), Hilton Valentine (guitar), and John Steel (drums). Production as above. UK release: Columbia DB 7639, 8 July 1965; charts 15 July 1965, *RR* #2. US release: MGM K 13382, August 1965; *BB* #13 (September 1965).

The Animals. *Animal Tracks.* Personnel and production as above. UK release: Columbia 33SX 1708, May 1965. A: "Mess Around," "How You've Changed," "Hallelujah I Love Her So," "I Believe to My Soul," "Worried Life Blues," and "Roberta." B: "I Ain't Got You," "Bright Lights Big City," "Let the Good Times Roll," "For Miss Caulker," and "Roadrunner."

The Animals. *Animal Tracks.* Personnel and production as above. US release: MGM E 4305, September 1965. A: "We Gotta Get Out of This Place," "Take It Easy Baby," "Bring It on Home to Me," and "The Story of Bo Diddley." B: "Don't Let Me Be Misunderstood," "I Can't Believe It," "Club A-Go-Go," "Roberta," "Bury My Body," and "For Miss Caulker."

The Applejacks. "Tell Me When" (Les Reed and Geoff Stephens). Al Jackson (vocal), Martin Baggott (guitar), Don Gould (organ), Phil Cash (guitar), Gerry Freeman (drums), and Megan Davies (bass) with Mike Leander (piano). Production: Mike Smith with Mike Leander (music director). Recorded: Decca Studios, West Hampstead, London. UK release: Decca F 11833, 14 February 1964; charts 5 March 1964, *RR* #7.

The Applejacks. "Like Dreamers Do" (John Lennon and Paul McCartney). Personnel and production as above. UK release: Decca F 11916, 5 June 1964; charts 11 June 1964, RR #20.

Arnold, Billy Boy. "I Wish You Would" (Billy Arnold). Billy Boy Arnold (harmonica and vocal) with Henry Gray (piano), Jody Williams (guitar), Milton Rector (bass), and Earl Phillips (drums). Recorded: Universal Recording Studios, Chicago, 5 May 1955. US release: Vee-Jay VJ-146, June 1955.

Arnold, Billy Boy. "I Ain't Got You" (Calvin Carter). Billy Boy Arnold (harmonica and vocal) with Henry Gray (piano), Jody Williams (guitar), Quinn Wilson (bass), and Earl Phillips (drums). Recorded: Universal Recording Studios, Chicago, October 1955. Released as Vee Jay VJ-171, 1956.

Atkins, Chet. "Boo Boo Stick Beat" (Buddy Harman and John D. Loudermilk). Chet Atkins (guitar) with studio musicians. Production: Chet Atkins. US release: RCA Victor 47-7589, August 1959. UK release: RCA 1153, October 1959.

Atwell, Winifred. "Britannia Rag" (Winifred Atwell and Monty Warlock). Production: Hugh Mendl. UK release: Decca F.100015 [78], December 1952; charts 12 December 1962 and 9 January 1953, *NME* #5.

Atwell, Winifred. "Coronation Rag" (Winfred Atwell). Personnel and production as above. UK release: Decca F.10110 [78], May 1953; charts 15 May 1953 and 29 May 1953, *NME* #5.

Atwell, Winifred. "Let's Have Another Party" (arr. Atwell). Winifred Atwell (piano) with guitar and drums. Production: Johnny Franz. Recorded: Philips Studios, London. UK release: P.B.268 [78], November 1954; charts 26 November 1954, *NME* #1 (December 1954–January 1955). A: "Somebody Stole My Gal," "I Wonder Where My Baby Is Tonight," "When the Red, Red Robin," "Bye, Bye blackbird," "The Sheik of Araby," and "Another Little Drink." B: "Lily of Laguna," "Honesuckle and the Bee," "Broken Doll," and "Nellie Dean."

Atwell, Winifred. "Let's Have a Ding-Dong" (arr. Atwell). Personnel and production as above. UK release: Decca DFE 6370, November 1956; charts 4 November 1956, *NME* #3. A: "Ain't She Sweet," "Oh! Johnny, Oh!," "Oh, You Beautiful Doll," "Yes, We Have No Bananas," "Happy Days Are Here Again," "I'm Forever Blowing Bubbles," "I'll Be Your Sweetheart," "If Those Lips Could Only Speak," and "Who's Taking You Home Tonight?"

Atwell, Winifred. "Poor People of Paris" (Garguerite Monnot). Personnel: Winfred Atwell (piano). Production: as above. UK release: Decca 45-F 10681 [45], November 1956, charts 26 November 1956, *NME* #1.

Bacharach, Burt, and His Orchestra and Chorus. "Trains and Boats and Planes" (Burt Bacharach and Hal David). Burt Bacharach with studio orchestra and the Breakaways (backing vocals). Production: Burt Bacharach. Recorded: London. US release: Kapp K-657, April 1965. UK release: London HLR 9968, 7 May 1965; charts 20 May 1965, *RR* #4.

The Bachelors. "Charmaine" (Erno Rapee and Lew Pollack). Conleth Cluskey, Declan Cluskey, and John Stokes with studio musicians. Production: Shel Talmy and Mike Stone with Earl Guest (music director). UK release: Decca F 11559, December 1962; charts 24 January 1963, *RR* #6. US release: London 45-9584, February 1963.

The Bachelors. "Whispering" (John Schonberger, Richard Coburn, and Vincent Rose). Personnel and production as above. UK release: Decca F 11712, August 1963; charts 29 August 1963, *RR* #18. US release: London 45-LON 9623, October 1963.

The Bachelors. "Diane" (Erno Rapee and Lew Pollack). Personnel as above. Production: Michael Barclay with Johnny Keating (arranger). Recorded: London, 1963. UK release: Decca F 11799, 3 January 1964; charts 23 January 1964, *RR* #1 (February 1964); *NME* #2. US release: London 45-9639, February 1964; *BB* #10 (June 1964).

The Bachelors. "I Believe" (Erwin Drake, Jimmy Shirl, Irvin Graham, and Al Stillman). Personnel as above. Production: Marvin Holtzman with Arthur Greenslade (music director). UK release: Decca F 11857, March 1964; charts 19 March 1964, *RR* #2. [US release: B-side to "Diane"; *BB* #33 (August 1964).]

The Bachelors. "Ramona" (Wayne and Gilbert). Personnel as above. Production: Noel Walker with Ivor Raymonde (music director). UK release: F 11910, 4 May 1964; charts 4 June 1964, *RR* #4.

The Bachelors. "I Wouldn't Trade You for the World" (Taylor, Smith, Kirk). Personnel as above. Production: Noel Walker. UK release: Decca F 11949, 7 August 1964; charts 13 August 1964, *RR* #4. US release: London 45-9693, August 1964; BB #69 (October 1964).

Ball, Kenny. "Midnight in Moscow" ["Podmoskovnie Vechera"] (Vasily Solovyov-Sedoi and Mikhail Matusovsky). Kenny Ball and His Jazzmen: Kenny Ball (trumpet), John Bennett (trombone), Dave Jones (clarinet), Ron Weatherburn (piano), Paddy Lightfoot (banjo), Ron Bowden (drums), and Vic Pitt (bass). Released as Pye Jazz 7NJ 2049, October 1961; charts 9 November 1961, *RR* #2. US release: Kapp K-442x, January 1962; *BB* #2 (March 1962).

Banks, Bessie. "Go Now" (Milton Bennett and Larry Banks). Bessie Banks with session musicians. Production: Mike Lieber and Jerry Stoller with Garry Sherman (arranger). Recorded: New York. US release: Tiger TI 102, January 1964, *BB* #40 (7 March 1964).

Chris Barber's Jazz Band and Lonnie Donegan's Skiffle Group. *New Orleans Joys*. Chris Barber (trombone), Pat Halcox (cornet), Monty Sunshine (clarinet), Lonnie Donegan (banjo), Ron Bowden (drums), and Jim Bray (bass).

Production: Hugh Mendl with Arthur Lilly (engineer). Recorded: Decca Recording Studios, West Hampstead, London, 13 July 1954. A: "Bobby Shaftoe," Chimes Blues," "Rock Island Line, and "The Martinique." B: "New Orleans Blues," "John Henry," "Merrydown Rag," and "Stevedore Stomp." UK release: LF 1198, December 1954.

Chris Barber's Jazz Band and Lonnie Donegan's Skiffle Group. "Petite Fleur" (Sidney Bechet). Chris Barber's Jazz Band with Monty Sunshine (clarinet) and unidentified amplified guitar, bass, and drums. UK release: Pye Nixa JN.2026; charts 13 February 1959, *NME* #3. US release: Laurie 3022, December 1958; *BB* #5 (March 1959).

Barrett, Richie. "Some Other Guy" (Jerry Leiber, Mike Stoller, and Richard Barrett). Richie Barrett (vocal). Production: Jerry Leiber and Mike Stoller. Recorded: New York. US release: Atlantic 45-2142, 14 April 1962.

Bassey, Shirley. "The Banana Boat Song" (Erik Darling, Bob Carey, and Alan Arkin). Personnel: Shirley Bassey with Wally Stott and His Orchestra and Chorus. Production: Wally Stott (music director). UK release: Philips JK 1006, February 1957; charts 21 February 1957, *NME* #8.

Bassey, Shirley. "Kiss Me, Honey Honey, Kiss Me" (Al Timothy and Michael Julien). Shirley Bassey with Wally Stott and His Orchestra. Production: Johnny Franz with Wally Stott (arranger). UK release: Philips BF 1782, December 1958; charts 26 December 1958, *NME* #3.

Bassey, Shirley. "As I Love You" (Jay Livingston and Ray Evans). Personnel and production as above. UK release: Philips PB 845, 1958; charts 19 December 1958, recharts 9 January 1959, *NME* #1 (February–March 1959).

Bassey, Shirley. "Reach for the Stars" (Udo Jürgens and David West [aka Norman Newell]). Personnel: Shirley Bassey with Geoff Love and His Orchestra. Production: Norman Newell. UK release: Columbia DB 4685, 21 July 1961; charts 27 July 1961, *RR* #1 (September 1961).

Bassey, Shirley. "Goldfinger" (Leslie Bricusse, Anthony Newley, and John Barry). Shirley Bassey with studio musicians. Production: George Martin with John Barry (music director). Recorded: EMI Recording Studios, London, 20 August 1964. UK release: Columbia DB 7360, 18 September 1964; charts 15 October 1964, *RR* #21. US release: United Artists UA 790, November 1964; *BB* #8 (March 1965).

The Beatles. "Love Me Do" (John Lennon and Paul McCartney). John Lennon (vocal and harmonica), Paul McCartney (vocal and bass), George Harrison (guitar), and Pete Best (drums). Production: George Martin with Norman Smith (engineer). Recorded: EMI Recording Studios, London, 6 June 1962. Unreleased.

The Beatles. "Love Me Do" (John Lennon and Paul McCartney). John Lennon (vocal and harmonica), Paul McCartney (vocal and bass), George Harrison (guitar), and Ringo Starr (drums). Production: George Martin with Norman Smith (engineer). Recorded: EMI Recording Studios, London, 4 September 1962. UK release: Parlophone 45-R 4949, 5 October 1962; charts 11 October 1962, *RR* #17. B: "P.S. I Love You" (John Lennon and Paul McCartney).

The Beatles. "Love Me Do" (John Lennon and Paul McCartney). John Lennon (vocal and harmonica), Paul McCartney (vocal and bass), George Harrison (guitar), Andy White (drums), and Ringo Starr (tambourine). Production: Ron Richards with Norman Smith (engineer). Recorded: EMI Recording Studios, London, 11 September 1962. UK release on *Please Please Me*, Parlophone LP PMC 1202, 22 March 1963. US release: Tollie T-9008, 27 April 1964; BB #1 (May 1964).

The Beatles. "Please Please Me" (John Lennon and Paul McCartney). John Lennon (vocal, guitar, and harmonica), Paul McCartney (vocal and bass), George Harrison (guitar), and Ringo Starr (drums). Production: George Martin with Norman Smith (engineer). Recorded: EMI Recording Studios, London, 26 November 1962. UK release: Parlophone R 4983, 11 January 1963; charts 17 January 1963, *RR* #2, *NME* #1. US release: Vee Jay Records VJ 498, 25 February 1963; rereleased 27 January 1964; BB #1 (March 1964).

The Beatles. *Please Please Me*. Personnel and production as above. UK release: Parlophone LP PMC 1202, 22 March 1963. A: "I Saw Her Standing There," "Misery," "Anna (Go to Him)," "Chains," "Boys," "Ask Me Why," and "Please Please Me." B: "Love Me Do," "P.S., I Love You," "Baby It's You," "Do You Want to Know a Secret," "Taste of Honey," "There's a Place," and "Twist and Shout."

The Beatles. "From Me to You" (John Lennon and Paul McCartney). Personnel and production as above. Recorded: EMI Recording Studios, London, 5 March 1963. UK release: Parlophone R 5015, 11 April 1963; charts 18 April 1963, *RR* #1 (May–June 1963). US release: Vee Jay Records, VJ 522, 6 May 1963; *BB* #41 (April 1964).

The Beatles. *Twist and Shout* [EP]. Personnel and production as above. UK release: Parlophone GEP 8882, 12 July 1963. A: "Twist and Shout" and "A Taste of Honey." B: "Do You Want to Know a Secret" and "There's a Place."

The Beatles. "She Loves You" (John Lennon and Paul McCartney). Personnel and production as above. Recorded: EMI Recording Studios, London, 1 and 4 July 1963. UK release: Parlophone R 5055, 23 August 1963; charts 29 August 1963, *RR* #1; *NME* #1. US release: Swan 4152, 16 September 1963; rereleased 25 January 1964; *BB* #1 (March 1964).

The Beatles. *With the Beatles*. Personnel and production as above. UK release: Parlophone LP PMC 1206, 22 November 1963. A: "It Won't Be Long," "All I've Got to Do," "All My Loving," "Don't Bother Me," "Little Child," "Till There Was You," and "Please Mr. Postman." B: "Roll Over Beethoven," "Hold Me Tight," "You Really Got a Hold on Me," "I Wanna Be Your Man," "Devil in Her Heart," "Not a Second Time," and "Money (That's What I Want)."

The Beatles. "I Want to Hold Your Hand" (John Lennon and Paul McCartney). Personnel and production as above. Recorded: EMI Recording Studios, London, 17 October 1963. UK release: Parlophone R5084, 29 November 1963l charts 5 December 1963, *RR* #1 (December 1963–January 1964). US release: Capitol 5112 (26 December 1963); *BB* #1 (February 1964). B: "This Boy" (John Lennon and Paul McCartney). Studio at EMI Recording Studios, London 17 October 1963.

The Beatles. *Introducing the Beatles*. Personnel and production as above. US release: Vee Jay VJ LP (s) 1062, 10 January 1964. A: "I Want to Hold Your Hand," "I Saw Her Standing There," "This Boy," "It Won't Be Long," "All I've Got to Do," and "All My Loving." B: "Please Please Me," "Baby It's You," "Do You Want to Know a Secret," "A Taste of Honey," "There's a Place," and "Twist and Shout."

The Beatles. *Meet the Beatles*. Personnel and production as above. US release: Capitol LP (s) T 2047, 20 January 1964; BB #1 (February 1964). A: "I Want to Hold Your Hand," "I Saw Her Standing There," "This Boy," "It Won't Be Long," "All I've Got to Do," and "All My Loving." B: "Don't Bother Me," "Little Child," "Till There Was You," "Hold Me Tight," "I Wanna Be Your Man," and "Not a Second Time."

The Beatles. "Can't Buy Me Love" (John Lennon and Paul McCartney). Personnel and production as above. Recording: EMI Pathé Marconi Studios, Paris, France, 29 January 1964, and EMI Recording Studios, London, 25 February 1964. UK release: Parlophone 5114, 20 March 1964; charts 26 March 1964, *RR* #1 (April 1964). US release: Capitol 5150, 16 March 1964; *BB* #1 (April 1964).

The Beatles. "Komm, Gib Mir Deine Hand" and "Sie Liebt Dich." Personnel and production as above. Recorded: EMI Pathé Marconi Studios, Paris, France, 29 January 1964. West German release: Odeon O 22 671, March 1964.

The Beatles. *The Beatles' Second Album*. Personnel and production as above. Recorded: EMI Recording Studios, London, 5 March 1963–1 March 1964. US release: Capitol T-2080, 10 April 1964. A: "Roll Over Beethoven," "Thank You Girl," "You Really Got a Hold on Me," "Devil in Her Heart," "Money (That's What I Want)," and "You Can't Do That." B: "Long Tall

Sally," "I Call Your Name," "Please Mr. Postman," "I'll Get You," and "She Loves You."

The Beatles. *Long Tall Sally* [EP]. Personnel and production as above. UK release: Parlophone GEP 8913, 9 June 1964. A: "Long Tall Sally" and "I Call Your Name." B: "Slow Down" and "Match Box."

The Beatles. "A Hard Day's Night" (John Lennon and Paul McCartney). Personnel as above with George Martin (piano) and Norman Smith (bongos). Production as above. Recorded: EMI Recording Studios, 16 April 1964. UK release: Parlophone R 5160, 10 July 1964; charts 10 July 1964, *RR* #1 (July–August 1964). US release: Capitol 5222, 13 July 1964; *BB* #1 (August 1964).

The Beatles. *A Hard Day's Night*. Personnel and production as above. UK release: Parlophone PMC 1230/PCS 3058, 10 July 1964. A: "A Hard Day's Night," "I Should Have Known Better," "If I Fell," "I'm Happy Just to Dance with You," "And I Love Her," "Tell Me Why," and "Can't Buy Me Love." B: "Any Time at All," "I'll Cry Instead," "Things We Said Today," "When I Get Home," "You Can't Do That," and "I'll Be Back."

The Beatles. *A Hard Day's Night*. Personnel as above with Vic Flick (guitar on "Ringo's Theme"). Production: as above. US release: United Artists UAL 3366/ UAS 6366 13 June 1964; *BB* #1 (July 1964). A: "A Hard Day's Night," "Tell Me Why," "I'll Cry Instead," "I should Have Known Better" (instrumental), "I'm Happy Just to Dance with You," and "And I Love Her" (instrumental). B: "I Should Have Known Better," "If I Fell," "And I Love Her," "Ringo's Theme (This Boy)" (instrumental), "Can't Buy Me Love," and "A Hard Day's Night" (instrumental).

The Beatles. "I'll Cry Instead" (John Lennon and Paul McCartney). Personnel and production as above. Recorded: EMI Recording Studios, London, 1 June 1964. US release: Capitol 5234, 20 July 1964; *BB* #25. B: "I'm Happy Just to Dance with You" (John Lennon and Paul McCartney)

The Beatles. "And I Love Her" (John Lennon and Paul McCartney). Personnel and production as above. Recorded: EMI Recording Studios, London, 27 February 1964. US release: Capitol 5235, 20 July 1964; *BB* #12 (September 1964). B: "If I Fell" (John Lennon and Paul McCartney). Personnel and production as above. Recorded: EMI, London, 27 February 1964.

The Beatles. *Something New*. Personnel and production as above. US release: Capitol LP (s) T 2108, 20 July 1964. A: "I'll Cry Instead," "Things We Said Today," "Any Time at All," "When I Get Home," "Slow Down," and "Matchbox." B: "Tell Me Why," "And I Love Her," "I'm Happy Just to Dance with You," "If I Fell," and "Komm, Gib Mir Deine Hand."

The Beatles. "I Feel Fine" (John Lennon and Paul McCartney). Personnel and production as above. Recorded: EMI Recording Studios, London,

18 October 1964. UK release: Parlophone R5200, 27 November 1964; charts 27 November 1964, *RR* #1 (December 1964–January 1965). US release: Capitol 5327, 23 November 1964; *BB* #1 (December 1965). B: "She's a Woman" (John Lennon and Paul McCartney). Personnel and production as above. Recorded: 8 October 1964. US release: *BB* #4 (December 1964).

The Beatles. *Beatles for Sale*. Personnel and production as above. UK release: Parlophone LP, PMC 1240/PCS 3062, 4 December 1964. A: "No Reply," "I'm a Loser," "Baby's in Black," "Rock and Roll Music," "I'll Follow the Sun," "Mr. Moonlight," and "Kansas City"/"Hey, Hey, Hey, Hey." B: "Eight Days a Week," "Words of Love," "Honey Don't," "Every Little Thing," "I Don't Want to Spoil the Party," "What You're Doing," and "Everybody's Trying to Be My Baby."

The Beatles. "Eight Days a Week" (John Lennon and Paul McCartney). Personnel and production as above. Recorded: EMI Recording Studios, London, 6 and 18 October 1964. US release: Capitol 5371, 15 February 1965; *BB* #1 (March 1965). B: "I Don't Want to Spoil the Party" (John Lennon and Paul McCartney). Personnel and production as above. 29 September 1964. US; *BB* #39 (March 1965).

The Beatles. "Ticket to Ride" (John Lennon and Paul McCartney). Personnel and production as above. Recorded: EMI Recording Studios, London, 15 February 1965. Released as Parlophone R 5265, 9 April 1965; charts 15 April 1965, *RR* #1 (April 1965). US release: Capitol 5407, 19 April 1965; *BB* #1 (May 1965). B: "Yes It Is" (John Lennon and Paul McCartney). EMI Recording Studios, London, 16 February 1965. *BB* #46 (May 1965).

The Beatles. "Help!" (John Lennon and Paul McCartney). Personnel and production as above. Recorded: EMI Recording Studios, London, 13 April 1965. UK release: Parlophone R5305, 23 July 1965; charts 29 July 1965, *RR* #1 (August 1965). US release: Capitol 5476, 19 July 1965; *BB* #1 (September 1965).

The Beatles. *Help!* UK release: Parlophone LP, PMC 1255/PCS 3071, 6 August 1965. A: "Help!," "The Night Before," "You've Got to Hide Your Love Away," "I Need You," "Another Girl," "You're Gonna Lose that Girl," and "Ticket to Ride." B: "Act Naturally," "It's Only Love," "You Like Me Too Much," "Tell Me What You See," "I've Just Seen a Face," "Yesterday," and "Dizzy Miss Lizzy."

The Beatles. *Help!*. US release: Capitol LP, MAS-2386, 13 August 1965; BB #1 (September 1965). A: "Help!," "The Night Before," "You've Got to Hide Your Love Away," and "I Need You" (additional orchestral tracks). B: "Another Girl," "Ticket to Ride," and "You're Going to Lose That Girl" (additional orchestral tracks).

The Beatles. "Yesterday" (John Lennon and Paul McCartney). Paul McCartney (vocal and guitar) with Anthony Gilbert (1st violin), Sidney Sax (2nd violin), Francisco Gabarro (cello) and Kenneth Essex (viola). Production: George Martin (arranger) with Norman Smith (engineer). Recorded: EMI Recording Studios, London, 14 and 17 June 1965. Released as Capitol 5498, 13 September 1965; *BB* #1 (October 1965).

The Beatles. *Rubber Soul*. UK release: Parlophone LP PMC 1267/PCS 3075, 3 December 1965. A: "Drive My Car," "Norwegian Wood," "You Won't See Me," "Nowhere Man," "Think for Yourself," "The Word," and "Michelle." B: "What Goes On," "Girl," "I'm Looking through You," "In My Life," "Wait," "If I Needed Someone," and "Run for Your Life."

The Beatles. *Rubber Soul*. US release: Capitol T-2442, 6 December 1965; BB #1 (January 1966). A: "I've Just Seen a Face," "Norwegian Wood," "You Won't See Me," "Think for Yourself," "The Word," and "Michele." B: "It's Only Love," "Girl," "I'm Looking through You," "In My Life," "Wait," and "Run for Your Life."

Bechet, Sidney. "Petite Fleur" (Sidney Bechet). Sidney Bechet and His All Stars: Sidney Bechet (soprano sax), Guy Longnon and Claude Rabanite (trumpets), Bernard Zacharias (tuba), Claude Luter (clarinet), Christian Azzi (piano), Roland Bianchini (bass), and "Moustache" (drums). French release as Vogue V. 45-06, 1954.

Behan, Dominic. "The Patriot Game" (Dominic Behan). UK release: Topic Records STOP 115, 1964.

Bell, Freddie, and the Bell Boys. "Teach You to Rock" (Freddie Bell and Pep Lattanzi). Freddie Bell and the Bellboys: Frankie Brent (guitar), Jack Kane (saxophone), Russ Conti (piano), Chick Keeney (drums), and Jerry Mayo (trumpet). UK release: Mercury MT 146 [78 rpm], May 1957.

Berry, Chuck. "Thirty Days (to Come Back Home)" (Chuck Berry). Chuck Berry and His Combo: Chuck Berry (guitar and vocal) with Johnnie Johnson (piano), Willie Dixon (bass), and Fred Below (drums). Production: Leonard Chess and Phil Chess with Jack Wiener or Malcolm Chisholm (engineer). Recorded: Chess Studios, Chicago. US release: Chess 1610, October 1955. UK release on *Rhythm and Blues with Chuck Berry* [EP] as London REU 1053, June 1956.

Berry, Chuck. "You Can't Catch Me" (Chuck Berry). Personnel and production as above. US release: Chess 1645, November 1956. UK release: London HLN 8375, February 1957.

Berry, Chuck. "Carol" (Chuck Berry). Recorded: Chess, Chicago, 12 June 1958. US release: Chess 1700, August 1958.

Berry, Chuck. "Back in the U.S.A." (Chuck Berry). Personnel and production as above with Etta James and the Marquees (backing vocals). US release: Chess 1729, May 1959, *BB* #37 (July 1959). UK release: London HLM 8921, July 1959.

Berry, Chuck. *Rockin' at the Hops*. Chuck Berry (vocal and guitar), Matt Murphy (guitar), Johnnie Johnson (piano), L. C. Davis (saxophone), Willie Dixon (bass), Fred Below and Eddie Hardy (drums), and the Ecuadors (backing vocals). Recorded Chess, Chicago, 27 July 1959, 15 February 1960, 29 March 1960, and 12 April 1960). US release: Chess, July 1960. A: "Bye Bye Johnny," "Worried Life Blues," "Down the Road a Piece," "Confessin' the Blues," "Too Pooped to Pop," and "Mad Lad." B: "I Got to Find My Baby," "Betty Jean," "Childhood Sweetheart," "Broken Arrow," "Driftin' Blues," "Let It Rock."

Berry, Chuck. *New Juke Box Hits*. Chuck Berry (vocals and guitar), Jonnie Johnson (piano), L. C. Davis (saxophone), Matt Murphy (guitar), Willie Dixon (bass), and Eddie Hardy (drums). UK release: Pye International NPL.28019, 1960. US release: Chess LP 1456, 1961. A: "I'm Talking about You," "Diploma for Two," "Thirteen Question Method," "Away from You," "Don't You Lie to Me," and "The Way It Was before." B: "Little Star," "Route 66," "Sweet Sixteen," "Run Around," "Stop and Listen," and "Rip It Up."

Berry, Chuck. "Memphis, Tennessee" (Chuck Berry). Chuck Berry (vocal, guitars, and bass) and Jasper Thomas (drums). Recorded: Berry home, Saint Louis, 26 September 1958. US release: Chess 1729, May 1959. UK release: London HLM 8921, July 1959. UK rerelease as Pye International 7N 25218, September 1963, charts 10 October 1963, *RR* #6.

Berry, Chuck. "Come On" (Chuck Berry). Chuck Berry (vocal and guitar) with Johnnie Johnson (piano), Ebby Harding (drums), L. C. Davis (tenor saxophone), and Martha Berry (backing vocal). Production as above, 1961. US release: Chess 1799, October 1961. A: "Go-Go-Go" (Chuck Berry).

Berry, Chuck. *Chuck Berry*. UK release: Pye International NPL.28024, 1963. A: "Come Back Maybelline," "Down the Road a Piece," "Mad Lad," "School Day (Ring! Ring! Goes the Bell)," "Sweet Little Sixteen," "Confessin' the Blues," and "Back in the U.S.A." B: "Johnny B. Goode," "Oh, Baby Doll," "Come On," "I Got to Find My Baby," "Betty Jean," "Round and Round," and "Almost Grown."

Berry, Dave. "Memphis, Tennessee" (Chuck Berry). Dave Berry and The Cruisers: Dave Berry (vocal) with session musicians, including Jim Sullivan (guitar). Production: Mike Smith with Mike Leander (music director). Recorded: Decca Studios, London, 1963. UK release: Decca F 11734, 6 September 1963; charts 19 September 1963, *RR* #19. US release: London 45-9666, April 964.

Berry, Dave. "My Baby Left Me" (Arthur Crudup). Dave Berry with Jimmy Page (lead guitar), Jim Sullivan (rhythm guitar), Earl Guest (piano), and unidentified bass and drums. Production: Mike Smith with Earl (Reg)

Guest (music director). Recorded: Decca Studios, London, 1963. UK release: Decca F 11803, 3 January 1964; charts 9 January 1964, *RR* #37.

Berry, Dave. "Baby, It's You" (Hal David, Burt Bacharach, and Barney Williams). Dave Berry with studio musicians. Production as above. UK release: Decca F 11876, 3 April 1964; charts 30 April 1964, *RR* #24.

Berry, Dave. "The Crying Game" (Geoff Stephens). Dave Berry (vocal) with Jim Sullivan (lead guitar), Vic Flick (rhythm guitar), Earl Guest (piano), Allan Weighell (bass), drums, percussion, and backing vocals. Production as above. UK release: Decca F 11937, 10 July 1964; charts 6 August 1964, *RR* #5. [B-side: "Don't Gimme No Lip, Child" (Barry Richards, Don Thomas, and Jean Thomas).] US release: London 45-LON 9698, September 1964.

The Big Three. "Some Other Guy" (Jerry Leiber, Mike Stoller, and Richard Barrett). Brian Griffiths (guitar and vocal), John Hutchinson (drums and vocal), and John Gustafson (bass and vocal). Production: Noel Walker. Recorded: Decca Studios, London. UK release: Decca F 11614, March 1963; charts 11 April 1963, *RR* #37.

The Big Three. "By the Way" (Mitch Murray). Personnel and production as above, Decca Studios, London. Released as Decca F 11689, June 1963; charts 11 July 1963, *RR* #22.

Bilk, Acker. "Sister Kate" (Armand Piron). Mr. Acker Bilk's Paramount Jazz Band: Ken Sims (trumpet), Acker Bilk (clarinet), John Mortimer (trombone), Roy James (banjo), Ernie Price (bass), and Ron Mackay (drums and vocals). Broadcast on "BBC Jazz Club," 9 or 16 April 1960.

Bilk, Acker. "Stranger on the Shore" (Acker Bilk). Acker Bilk and The Leon Young String Chorale. Production: Denis Preston with Adrian Kerridge (engineer). Recorded: Lansdowne Studios, London. UK release: Columbia DB 4750, November 1961; charts 30 November 1961, *RR* #2. US release: ATCO 45-6217, February 1962; *BB* #1 (May 1962).

Bindi, Umberto. "Il Mio Mondo" (Umberto Bindi and Gino Paoli). Umberto Bindi with Luis Enriquez e La Sua Orchestra and 4 + 4 di Nora Orlandi. Orchestrated and conducted by Luis Enriquez. Italian release: RCA Italiana PM45 3235, 1963.

Black, Cilla. "Love of the Loved" (John Lennon and Paul McCartney). Cilla Black with session musicians, including Les Reed (piano). Produced and arranged by George Martin with Norman Smith (engineer). Recorded: EMI Recording Studios, London, 28 August 1963. UK release: Parlophone R 5065, 27 September 1963; charts 17 October 1963, *RR* #35.

Black, Cilla. "Anyone Who Had a Heart" (Hal David and Burt Bacharach). Cilla Black (vocal) with Kenny Clare (drums), Peter McGurk and Joe Modell (basses), Dennis Newey and Judd Proctor (guitars), Eric Cook (organ), the Breakaways [Vicki Haseman-Brown, Margo Quantrell, and Barbara Moore] (backing vocals), and orchestra led by Anthony Gilbert (violin). Production: George Martin with Johnny Pearson (arranger and conductor) and Norman Smith (engineer). Recorded: EMI Recording Studios, London. UK release: Parlophone 5101, 31 January 1964; charts 6 February 1964, *RR* #1 (February–March 1964), *NME* #1 (February–March 1964).

Black, Cilla. "You're My World" ["Il Mio Mondo"] (Umberto Bindi and Gino Paoli; English lyrics by Carl Sigman). Cilla Black (vocal) with session musicians including Judd Proctor (guitar) and Eric Allen (percussion) and the Breakaways. George Martin (artist-and-repertoire manager) with John Pearson (music director) and Norman Smith (engineer). Recorded: EMI Recording Studios, London, 3 April 1964. UK release: Parlophone R 5133, 1 May 1964; charts 7 May 1964, *RR* #1 (May–June 1964), *NME* #1. US release: Capitol 5196, 1 June 1964; *BB* #26 (August 1964).

Black, Cilla. "It's for You" (John Lennon and Paul McCartney). Personnel and production as above with George Martin (arranger). UK release: Parlophone R 5162, 31 July 1964; charts 6 August 1964, *RR* #7.

Black, Cilla. "You've Lost That Loving Feeling" (Phil Spector, Barry Mann, and Cynthia Weil). Cilla Black with session musicians. Production: George Martin with Johnny Scott (music director) and Norman Smith (engineer). Recorded: EMI Recording Studios, London. UK release: Parlophone R 5225, 8 January 1965; charts 14 January 1965, *RR* #2, *NME* #5.

Blues Incorporated. *R & B from The Marquee*. Alexis Korner's Blues Incorporated: Alexis Korner (guitar), Charlie Watts (drums), Jack Bruce (bass), Dick Heckstall-Smith (tenor saxophone), Cyril Davies (harmonica), and John Baldry (vocals). Production: Jack Good with Jack Clegg (engineer). Recorded: Decca Studios, London, 8 June 1962. UK release: Decca, Ace of Clubs ACL 1130, November 1962. A: "Gotta Move," "Rain Is Such a Lonesome Sound," "I Got My Brand on You," "Spooky but Nice," "Keep Your Hands Off," and "I Wanna Put a Tiger in Your Tank." B: "I Got My Mojo Working," "Finkle's Café," "Hoochie Cooche," "Down Town," "How Long, How Long Blues," and "I Thought I Heard That Train Whistle Blow."

Bo Diddley. "Pretty Thing" (Willie Dixon). Bo Diddley (vocal and guitar), Lester Davenport (harmonica), Clifton James (drums), and Jerome Green (maracas). Production: Leonard and Phil Chess with Bo Diddley. Recorded: Chess Records, Chicago, 14 July 1955. US release: Checker 827, November 1955.

Bo Diddley. "Mona" (Ellas McDaniel). Bo Diddley (vocal and guitar) with Jerome Greene (maracas), Clifton James (drums). Production: Phil Chess.

Recorded: Chess Records, Chicago, 8 February 1957. US release: Checker Records 860, April 1957. A: "Hey, Bo Diddley."

Bo Diddley. "Road Runner" (Ellas McDaniel). Bob Diddley (guitar and vocal), Jerome Green (maracas and vocal), Clifton James (drums), Otis Spann (piano), Peggy Jones (guitar and vocal), and Bobby Baskerville (vocal). Production: Leonard Chess, Phil Chess, and Bo Diddley. Recorded: Chess Records, Chicago, September 1959. US release: Checker 942, January 1960.

Booker T and the MG's. "Green Onions" (Booker T. Jones, Steve Cropper, Lewie Steinberg, and Al Jackson). Booker T. Jones (organ), Steve Cropper (guitar), Lewie Steinberg (bass), and Al Jackson, Jr. (drums). Production: Jim Stewart. Recorded: Stax Records, Memphis, Tennessee, 1962. US release: Volt 102, May 1962; *BB* #3 (September 1962).

Brewer, Teresa. "Bell Bottom Blues" (Hal David and Leon Carr). Recorded: 19 February 1953. US release: Coral Records 61066, charts 13 February 1954, *BB* #17.

Brown, James. "Please, Please, Please" (James Brown and Johnny Terry). James Brown and the Famous Flames: James Brown (vocal), Bobby Byrd, Johnny Terry, Sylvester Keels, and Nash Knox (backing vocals), Nafloyd Scott (guitar), Wilbert Smith (tenor sax), Lucas Gonder (piano), Clarence Mack (bass), and Edison Gore (drums). Production: Ralph Bass. Recorded: King Studios, Cincinnati, Ohio, 4 February 1956. US release: Federal 45-12258, 4 March 1956.

Brown, James. "I'll Go Crazy" (James Brown). James Brown with the Famous Flames (Bobby Byrd, Bobby Bennett, Lloyd Stallworth, Johnny Terry, and Willie Johnson), J. C. Davis (tenor sax), James McGary (alto sax), Bobby Roach (guitar), Bernard Odum (bass), and Nat Kendrick (drums). Recorded: King Studios, Cincinnati, Ohio, 11 November 1959. Release: Federal 45-12369, January 1960.

Brown, James. "Night Train" (Oscar Washington, Lewis P. Simpkins, and Jimmy Forrest). Personnel and production as above. Recorded: King Studios, Cincinnati, Ohio, 9 February 1961. US release: King 45-5614, March 1962.

Brown, Joe. "Jellied Eels" (Lionel Bart). Joe Brown and the Bruvvers. UK release: Decca F 11246, June 1960.

Brown, Joe. "I'm Henery the Eighth I Am" (R. P. Weston and F. Murray). UK release: Piccadilly 7N 35005, June 1961.

Brown, Joe. "A Picture of You" (Peter Oakman and John Beveridge). Joe Brown and His Bruvvers: Joe Brown (vocal and guitar), Pete Oakman (bass), Tony Oakman (guitar), Bohn Beveridge (guitar), and Bobby Graham (drums), with the Breakaways (Vicki Haseman, Margot Quantrell, and Jean Ryder). Production: Ray Horricks with Les Reed (music director). Recorded: Pye

Studios 1962. UK release: Piccadilly 7N 35047, May 1962; charts 17 May 1962, *RR* #2.
Brown, Joe. "It Only Took a Minute" (Mort Garson and Hal David). Personnel and production as above. UK release: Piccadilly 7N 35058, November 1962; charts 15 November 1962, *RR* #6.
Brown, Joe. "That's What Love Will Do" (Trevor Peacock). Personnel and production as above. UK release: Piccadilly 7N 35106, 7 February 1963, *RR* #3 (charts 7 February 1963).
Brown, Joe. "Little Ukulele" (Jack Cottrell). Joe Brown with studio musicians. UK release: Piccadilly 7N 35150, October 1964: *MM* #50 (charts November 1964).
Burke, Solomon. "Everybody Needs Somebody to Love" (Jerry Wexler, Bert Berns, and Solomon Burke). Solomon Burke and band. Production: Bert Berns with Phil Medley (arranger and conductor). Recorded: New York, 28 May 1964. US release: Atlantic 45-2241, July 1964; *BB* #58 (August 1964).
Butler, Jerry. "Make It Easy on Yourself" (Burt Bacharach and Hal David). Jerry Butler with studio orchestra. Production: Calvin Carter with Burt Bacharach (music director). Recorded: New York, 1962. US release: Vee Jay VJ 451, June 1962; *BB* #20 (September 1962).
The Byrds. "Mr. Tambourine Man" (Bob Dylan). Jim McGuinn (electric 12-string guitar), David Crosby (vocal), and Gene Clark (vocal) with members of the Wrecking Crew such as Hal Blaine (drums). Production: Terry Melcher. Recorded: Columbia Studios, Los Angeles, 15 January 1965. US release: Columbia 4-43271, 12 April 1965; *BB* #1 (June 1965). UK release: CBS 201765, May 1965; charts 17 June 1965, *RR* #1.
The Byrds. "Eight Miles High" (Gene Clark, Jim McGuinn, and David Crosby). Personnel and production as above. Recorded: Columbia Studios, Los Angeles, 24–25 January 1966. US release: Columbia 4-43578, 14 March 1966; charts 9 April 1966, *BB* #14 (May 1966). UK release: CBS 202067, 29 April 1966; charts 5 May 1966, *RR* #24.
Carter-Lewis and the Southerners. "Sweet and Tender Romance" (Ken Hawker, John Shakespear, and Powell). John Carter (vocal and guitar), Ken Lewis (vocal and keyboard), Jimmy Page (guitar), Viv Prince (drums), and Rod Clark (bass). Production: Terry Kennedy. UK release: Oriole CB 1835, June 1963.
Carter-Lewis and the Southerners. "Your Momma's Out of Town" (Mitch Murray). John Carter and Ken Lewis with session musicians. Production as above. UK release: Oriole CB 1868, 24 October 1963.
Carter-Lewis and the Southerners. "Skinny Minnie" (Rusty Keefer, Catherine Cafra, Bill Haley, and Milt Gabler). John Carter (guitar and vocal), Ken

Lewis (vocal), Jimmy Page (guitar), Micky Keen (guitar), Rupert Ross (bass), and Viv Prince (drums). Production: Terry Kennedy. UK release: Oriole CB 1919, 27 March 1964.

Carthy, Martin. *Martin Carthy*. Martin Carthy (vocal and guitar) with Dave Swarbrick (violin). UK release: Fontana STL 5269, 1965. A: "High Germany," "The Trees They Do Grow High," "Sovay," "Ye Mariners All," "The Queen of Hearts," "Broomfield Hill," and "Springhill Mine Disaster." B: "Scarborough Fair," "Lovely Joan," "The Barley and the Rye," "The Wind That Shakes the Barley," "The Two Magicians," "The Handsome Cabin Boy," and "And a Begging I Will Go."

Chad and Jeremy (see Stuart, Chad, and Jeremy Clyde).

Channel, Bruce. "Hey! Baby" (Margaret Cobb and Bruce Channel). Bruce Channel (vocals) with Delbert McClinton (harmonica), Ray Torres (drums), Bob Jones and Billy Sanders (guitars), and Jim Rogers (bass). Production: Bill Smith, Marvin Montgomery, and Bruce Channel. US release: Le Cam 953, 1961; Smash S-1731, December 1961, *BB* #1 (March 1962). UK release: Mercury AMT 1171, March 1962; charts 22 March 1962, *RR* #2.

Charles, Ray. "What'd I Say, Pts. 1 and 2" (Ray Charles). Ray Charles (pianos and vocal) with band and The Rayettes. Production: Jerry Wexler with Tom Dowd (recording engineer). Recorded: Atlantic Studios, New York City, 18 February 1959. US release: Atlantic 45-2031, July 1959. UK release: London HLE 8917, July 1959.

Charles, Ray. "Georgia on My Mind" (Hoagy Carmichael and Stuart Gorrell). Ray Charles (vocal and piano) with chorus and strings. Production: Sid Feller with Ralph Burns (arranger and conductor). Recorded: New York City, 25 March 1960. US release: ABC-Paramount 45-10135, August 1960; *BB* #1 (November 1960). UK release: HMV POP 792, October 1960; charts 1 December 1960, *RR* #24.

Church, Eugene, and the Fellows. "Pretty Girls Everywhere" (Eugene Church and Thomas Williams). Eugene Church, Jesse Belvin, Gaynel Hodge, and Tommy Williams with session musicians including Earl Palmer. US release: Class 235, August 1958.

The Clancy Brothers and Tommy Makem. *Come Fill Your Glass with Us*. The Clancy Brothers with Tommy Maken: Tommy Makem, Tom Clancy, Liam Clancy, and Patrick Clancy (voices) with Jack Keenan (guitar and banjo). Studio by David Hancock. US release: Tradition Records TLP 1032, 1959. A: "Whiskey You're the Devil," "The Maid of the Sweet Brown Knowe," "The Moonshiner," "Bold Thady Quill," "Rosin the Bow," "Finnigan's Wake," and "The Real Old Mountain Dew." B: "Courting in the Kitchen," "Mick McGuire," "A Jug of Punch," "Johnny McEldoo," "Cruiscin Lan," "Portlairge," and "The Parting Glass."

The Clancy Brothers and Tommy Makem. *The Clancy Brothers and Tommy Makem*. Patrick Clancy (voice and harmonica), Tom Clancy (voice), Liam Clancy (voice and guitar), and Tommy Makem (voice and tin whistle), with Bruce Langhorne (guitar) and Erick Darling (banjo). Production: Patrick Clancy and Studio by Daniel Hancock. US release: Tradition Records TLP 1042, 1961. A: "Brennan on the Moor," "The Work of the Weavers," "The Stuttering Lovers," "Paddy Doyle's Boots," "The Maid of Fife-E-O," "The Bard of Armagh," "The Jug of Punch," and "Roddy McCorley." B: "The Barnyards of Delgaty," "The Castle of Dromore," "The Bold Tenant Farmer," "Ballinderry," "Bungle Rye," "Eileen Aroon," and Johnny I Hardly Knew You."

The Dave Clark Five. "That's What I Said" (Dave Clark and Ron Ryan). The Dave Clark Five featuring Mike Smith: Mike Smith (organ and vocals), Dave Clark (drums and vocals), Lenny Davidson (guitar and vocals), Rick Huxley (bass guitar and vocals), and Denis Payton (tenor saxophone). Production unidentified. Released as Piccadilly 7N 35500, 28 June 1962. B: "I Knew It All the Time" (Mitch Murray).

The Dave Clark Five. "Do You Love Me" (Berry Gordy). Mike Smith (organ and lead vocals), Lenny Davidson (guitar and vocals), Dave Clark (drums and vocals), Rick Huxley (bass guitar and vocals), and Denis Payton (tenor saxophone). Session musicians probably include Bobby Graham (drums) and Eric Ford (bass). Production: Dave Clark with Adrian Kerridge (engineer). Recorded: Lansdowne Studios, London. UK release: Columbia DB 7112, 5 September 1963; charts 3 October 1963, *RR* #30. US release: Epic 26185, 17 April 1964; *BB* #11 (June 1964).

The Dave Clark Five. "Glad All Over" (Dave Clark and Mike Smith). Personnel and production as above. Recorded: Lansdowne Studios, London, October 1963. UK release: Columbia DB 7154, 15 November 1963; charts 21 November 1963, *RR* #1 (January 1964). US release: Epic 5-9656, 27 December 1963; *BB* #6 (April 1964).

The Dave Clark Five. "Bits and Pieces" (Dave Clark and Mike Smith). Personnel as above. Production: Dave Clark with Les Reed (music director) and Adrian Kerridge (engineer). Recorded: Lansdowne Studios, London. UK release: Columbia DB 7210, 7 February 1964; charts 20 February 1964, *RR* #2. US release: Epic 5-9671, 20 March 1964; *BB* #4 (May 1964).

The Dave Clark Five. "Can't You See That She's Mine" (Mike Smith and Dave Clark). Personnel and production as above. UK release: Columbia DB 7291, 22 May 1964; charts 28 May 1964, *RR* #10. US release: Epic 5-9692, 29 May 1964; *BB* #4 (July 1964).

Clark, Petula. "The Little Shoemaker" (Geoffrey Parsons, John Turner, and Rudi Revil). Petula Clark with Malcolm Lockyer and His Orchestra.

Production: Alan Freeman. UK release: Polygon P 1117, May 1954; charts 11 and 25 June 1954, *NME* #7.

Clark, Petula. "Prends Mon Coeur" (Ferdinand Bonifay and Bill Trader). Petula Clark with studio orchestra and singers. Production: Claude Wolff with Peter Knight (music director, conductor, and arranger). Recorded: London. French release: Vogue 45-PV.15077, 1959.

Clark, Petula. "Sailor" (Werner Scharfenberger, Fini Busch, and David West). Petula Clark with the Peter Knight Orchestra and Chorus. Production: Alan Freeman with Tony Hatch. Recorded: Pye Studios, London. UK release: Pye 7N 15324, January 1961; charts 26 January 1961, *RR* #1.

Clark, Petula. "Downtown" (Tony Hatch). Petula Clark (vocal) with Tony Hatch (piano), the Breakaways (Margot Quantrell, Jean Ryder, and Vicki Brown) and studio musicians including Jim Sullivan (guitar), Vic Flick (guitar), Jimmy Page (guitar), and Ronnie Verrell (drums). Production: Tony Hatch with Bob Leaper (arranger) and Ray Prickett (engineer). Recorded: Pye Studios, London, 16 October 1964. UK release: Pye 7N 15722, November 1964; charts 12 November 1964, *RR* #2. US release: Warner Bros. Records 5494, December 1964; *BB* #1 (January 1965).

Clark, Petula. "I Know a Place" (Tony Hatch). UK release: Pye 7N 15772, February 1965; charts 11 March 1965, *RR* #17. US release: Warner Bros. Records 5612; *BB* #3 (May 1965). Personnel and production as above.

The Clovers. "Love Potion No. 9" (Jerry Leiber and Mike Stoller). Billy Mitchell (lead vocal), Buddy Baily, Matthew McQuater, Harold Winley, and Bill Harris (guitar). Production: Jerry Leiber and Mike Stoller. US release: United Artists UA 180, August 1959; *BB* #23 (November 1959).

The Coasters. "Searchin'" (Jerry Leiber and Mike Stoller). Carl Gardner, Billy Guy, Bobby Nunn, Leon Hughes, and Adolph Jacob with studio musicians. Production: Jerry Leiber and Mike Stoller. Recorded: Atlantic Records, New York, 15 February 1957. US release: ATCO 45-6087, March 1957; BB #5. UK release: London HLE 8450, June 1957; charts 27 September 1957, *RR* #30.

The Coasters. "(Ain't That) Just Like Me" (Billy Guy and Earl Carroll). Cornell Gunter (lead vocal) with studio musicians. Production: Jerry Leiber and Mike Stoller. Recorded: New York, 25 September 1961. US release: ATCO 45-6210, November 1961. UK release: London HLK 9493, January 1962.

Cochrane, Eddie. "C'mon Everybody" (Eddie Cochran and Jerry Capehart). Eddie Cochran (vocals and guitar), Ray Johnson (piano), Connie Smith (bass), Earl Palmer (drums), and Jerry Capehart (tambourine). US release: Liberty F-55166, October 1958. UK release: London HLU 8759, January 1959.

Cogan, Alma. "To Be Worthy of You" (Walter Gross and Raymond Klages). Alma Cogan with Jimmy Watson (trumpet). Production: Wally Ridley with Frank Cordell (conductor). UK release: His Master's Voice B.10280, June 1952.

Cogan, Alma. "Bell Bottom Blues" (Hal David and Leon Carr). Alma Cogan with studio orchestra. Production: Wally Ridley with Frank Cordell (conductor). UK release: HMV 7M188, March 1954; charts 19 March 1954, *NME* #4.

Cogan, Alma. "Dreamboat" (Jack Hoffman). Personnel and production as above. UK release: HMV B 10872 [78], May 1955; charts 27 May 1955, *NME* #1 (July 1955).

Collins, Shirley, and Davy Graham. *Folk Roots, New Routes*. UK release: Decca LK 4652, 1964. Shrley Collins (vocal) and Davy Graham (vocal and guitar). Production: Ray Horricks with Gus Dudgeon. Recorded: Decca Studios, West Hampstead, London. A: Nottamun Town," "Proud Maisrie," "The Cherry Tree Carol," "Blue Monk," "Hares on the Mountain," "Reynardine," "Pretty Saro," and "Rif Mountain." B: "Jane Jane," "Love Is Pleasin,'" Boll Weavil, Holler," "Hori Horo," "Bad Girl," "Lord Gregory," "Grooveyard," and "Dearest Dear."

Colyer, Ken. "The Sheik of Araby." Ken Colyer's Jazzmen with Ken Colyer (trumpet), Monty Sunshine (clarinet), Chris Barber (trombone), Lonnie Donegan (banjo), Jim Bray (bass), and Ron Bowden (drums). Production: D. Maclean. Broadcast: *BBC Jazz Club*, 18 April 1953.

The Contours. "Do You Love Me" (Barry Gordy, Jr.). Joe Billingslea, Billy Gordon, Billy Hoggs, Sylvester Potts, Hubert Johnson, and Hugh Davis (guitar) with the Funk Brothers. Barry Gordon, Jr. (producer). Recorded: Hitsville USA, Detroit. US release: Gordy G 7005, 29 June 1962; *BB* #3 (October 1962).

Cooke, Sam. "Wonderful World" (Lou Adler, Herb Alpert, and Sam Cooke). Sam Cooke with Cliff White (guitar), Adolphus Alsbrook (bass), Ronnie Selico (drums), and backing singers. Recorded: Radio Recorders, Los Angeles, 2 March 1959. US release: Keen 82112, 14 April 1960.

Cordet, Louise. "Don't Let the Sun Catch You Crying" (Marsden, Chadwick, and Maguire). Louise Cordet (vocal) with studio musicians. Produced and arranged by Tony Meehan. Recorded: Decca Studios, London. UK release: Decca F 11824, 7 February 1964.

Cotten, Elizabeth. *Folksongs and Instrumentals with Guitar*. Production: Mike Seeger. US release: Folkways Records, 1958. A: "Wilson Rag," "Freight Train," "Going Down the Road Feeling Bad," "I Don't Love Nobody," "Ain't Got No Honey Baby Now," "Graduation March," and "Honey Babe Your

Papa Cares for You." B: "Vastopol," "Here Old Rattler Here/Sent for My Fiddle Sent for My Bow/George Buck," "Run . . . Run/Mama Your Son Done Gone," "Sweet Bye and Bye/What a Friend We Have in Jesus," "Oh Babe It Ain't No Lie," "Spanish Flang Dang," and "When I Get Home."

Crombie, Tony. "Teach You to Rock" (Freddie Bell and Pep Lattanzi). Tony Crombie and His Rockets [probable personnel]: Tony Crombie (drums), Jim Currie (guitar), Jet Harris (bass), Red Mitchell (piano), Al Cornish (tenor sax), and Cliff Lawrence (voice). Production: Norrie Paramour. UK release: Columbia DB 3822, October 1956; charts 19 October 1956, *NME* #25.

Crombie, Tony. "Brighton Rock" (Lee and Eily). Personnel and production as above. UK release: Columbia DB 3921, 1957.

Crosby, Bing. "Please" (Ralph Rainger and Leo Robin). Bing Crosby with Anson Weeks and His Orchestra with Eddie Lang (guitar). Recorded: Mission Street, San Francisco, 16 September 1932. US release: Brunswick 6394, 1932. UK release: Brunswick 1380, 1932.

The Crystals. "Uptown" (Barry Mann and Cynthia Weil). The Crystals: Dolores Brooks (lead vocal) Barbara Alston, Dolores Kenniebrew, and Patricia Wright with the Wrecking Crew. Produced and arranged by Phil Spector with Larry Levine (engineer). Recorded: Gold Star Studios, Los Angeles. US release: Philles 102, 14 February 1962; charts 2 June 1962, *BB* # 18.

The Crystals. "Da Doo Ron Ron (When He Walked Me Home)" (Phil Spector, Ellie Greenwich, and Jeff Barry). Dolores Brooks (lead vocal) with backing vocals (including Cher) and members of the Wrecking Crew. Production: Phil Spector with Jack Nitzsche (arranger) and Larry Levine (engineer). Recorded: Gold Star Studios, Los Angeles, March 1963. US release: Phillies 112, April 1963; charts 11 May 1963, *BB* #3 (29 June 1963). UK release: London HLU 9732, 31 May 1963; charts 20 June 1963, *RR* #5.

Davies, Cyril. "Country Line Special" (Cyril Davies). Cyril Davies and His Rhythm and Blues All-Stars: Ricky Brown (bass), Cyril Davies (harmonica), Nicky Hopkins (piano), Carlo Little (drums), and Bernie Watson (guitar). Production: Peter Knight, Jr., with Bob Auger (engineer). Recorded: Pye Studios (Marble Arch), 27 February 1963. UK release: Pye 7N 25194, April 1963.

Davis, Billie. "Tell Him" (Bert Russell [aka Bert Burns]). Billie Davis with studio musicians. Production: Robert Stigwood with Charles Blackwell (music director). UK release: Decca F 11572, 18 January 1963; charts 7 February 1963, *RR* #10.

Davis, Billie. "He's the One" (Charles Blackwell). Personnel and production as above. UK release: Decca F 11658, 17 May 1963; charts 30 May 1963, *RR* #40 October 1963).

Davis, Reverend Gary [identified as "Blind Gary Davis"]. *Pure Religion and Bad Company*. Gary Davis (vocal and guitar). Recorded: New York, June 1957. Production: Doug Dobell with Fred Gerlach and Tiny Robinson (engineers). UK release: 77 Records 77 LA 12/14, 1962. A: "Pure Religion," "Mountain Jack," "Right Now," "Buck Dance," "Candy Man," "Devil's Dream," "Moon Goes Down," and "Coco Blues." B: "Runnin' to the Judgement," "Hesitation," "Bad Company," "I Didn't Want to Join the Band," "Evening Sun Goes Down," "Seven Sisters," and "My Heart Is Fixed."

The Spencer Davis Group. "Dimples" (John Lee Hooker). Steve Winwood (vocal and guitar), Spencer Davis (harmonica), Muff Winwood (bass), and Peter York (drums). Production: Chris Blackwell. Recorded: Lansdowne Studios, London. UK release: Fontana TF 471, 22 May 1964.

The Spencer Davis Group. "I Can't Stand It" (Smokey McAllister). Personnel as above. Chris Blackwell for BPR Productions (Chris Blackwell, Harry Robinson, and Chris Peers). Recorded: Lansdowne Studios, London. UK release: Fontana TF 499, 9 October 1964; charts 5 November 1964, *RR* #47.

The Spencer Davis Group. "Every Little Bit Hurts" (Ed Cobb). Personnel as above with Steve Winwood (vocal, piano, and organ). B.P.R Production. Recorded: Lansdowne Studios, London. UK release: Fontana TF 530, 5 February 1965; charts 25 February 1965, *RR* #41.

Day, Doris. "Secret Love" (Sammy Fain and Paul Francis Webster). Personnel: Doris Day with studio orchestra. Production: Ray Heindorf (music director). Recorded: Warner Brothers Studios, Burbank, California, 5 August 1953. US release: Columbia 4-40108, 9 October 1953; *BB* #1. UK release: Philips PB 230, 1954; charts 2 April 1954, *RR* #1.

The DeMarco Sisters. "Dreamboat" (Jack Hoffman). Anne, Arlene, Gina, Gloria, and Terri DeMarco. Production: Neal Hefti (music director). US release: Decca 9-29470, March 1955.

DeShannon, Jackie. "Needles and Pins" (Jack Nitzsche and Sonny Bono). Jackie DeShannon with the Wrecking Crew. Production: Dick Glasser with Jack Nitzsche (arranger). US release: Liberty 55563, 11 April 1963; *BB* #84 (June 1963). UK release: Liberty 55563, May 1963.

DeShannon, Jackie. "When You Walk in the Room" (Jackie DeShannon). Personnel and production as above. US release: Liberty 55645, 8 November 1963; *BB* #99 (January 1964). UK release: Liberty 55645, 29 May 1964.

Dion and the Belmonts. "A Teenager in Love" (Doc Pomus and Mort Shuman). Dion DiMucci, Carlo Mastrangelo, and Fred Milano (vocals) with studio musicians. Production unidentified. US release: Laurie 3027, March 1959; *BB* #5 (May 1959). UK release: London HL 8874, May 1959.

Dixon, Willie. *Willies Blues*. Willie Dixon (vocals and bass), Memphis Slim (piano), Gus Johnson (drums), Wally Richardson (guitar), and Al Ashby and Harold Ashby (tenor sax). Production: Esmond Edwards. Recorded: Van Gelder Studio, Englewood Cliffs, New Jersey, 3 December 1959. US release: Prestige Bluesville BVLP-1003. A: "Nervous," "Good Understanding," "That's My Thing," Slim's Thing," "That's All I Want Baby," and "Don't Tell Nobody." B: "Sittin' and Cryin' the Blues," "Built for Comfort," "I Got a Razor," "Go Easy," and "Move Me."

Domino, Antoine "Fats." "The Sheik of Araby" (Harry Smith, Francis Wheeler, and Ted Snyder). Antoine Domino (vocal and piano) and band. Production: Dave Bartholomew. Recorded: 15 July 1958. US release on *A Lot of Dominos!*, Imperial LP 12066, October 1960.

Domino, Antoine "Fats." "My Girl Josephine" (Antoine Domino and Dave Bartholomew). Fats Domino (vocal and piano) and studio musicians. Production: Dave Bartholomew. Recorded: 18 July 1959. US release: Imperial 5704, 1960; *BB* #14 (December 1960).

Donegan, Lonnie. "Rock Island Line" (traditional). Lonnie Donegan's Skiffle Group: Lonnie Donegan (vocal and guitar), Chris Barber (bass), and Beryl Bryden (washboard). Production: Hugh Mendl with Arthur Lilley (engineer). Recorded: Decca Studios, West Hampstead, London, 13 July 1954. UK release: (1) Decca F 10647, 14 November 1955 and (2) Decca F 10647 [78 rpm], 6 January 1956; charts 6 January 1956 and 13 April 1956, *NME* #8 and #16. [Original release on *New Orleans Joy* (Decca LF 1198), 1954.] US release: London 45-1650, March 1956; *BB* #10 (May 1956).

Donegan, Lonnie. "Don't You Rock Me, Daddy-o" (Bill Varley and Wally Whyton). The Lonnie Donegan Skiffle Group: Lonnie Donegan (vocals and guitar), Micky Ashman (bass), Denny Wright (guitar), and Nick Nichols (drums). Production: Dennis Preston with Joe Meek (engineer). UK release: Pye Nixa N. 15080 [78 rpm], January 1957; charts 18 January 1957, *NME* #4.

Donegan, Lonnie. "Cumberland Gap" (traditional, arrangement by Lonnie Donegan). The Lonnie Donegan Skiffle Group: Lonnie Donegan (vocals and guitar), Micky Ashman (bass), Denny Wright (guitar), and Nick Nichols (drums). Production: Dennis Preston with Joe Meek (engineer). Recorded: Pye Studios, London, 24 February 1957. UK release: Pye N 15087, March 1957, *NME* #1 (charts 5 April 1957). US release: Mercury 71094X45, 5 April 1957.

Donegan, Lonnie. "Puttin' on the Style" (Norman Kazden) [78 rpm disc]. Lonnie Donegan and His Skiffle Group. Lonnie Donegan (lead vocal and banjo) with Les Bennetts (guitar and backing vocal), Pete Huggett (bass), and Nick Nicholls (percussion). Production: Alan Freeman and Michael Barclay. Recorded: London Palladium, 9 May 1957. B: "Gamblin' Man"

(Woody Guthrie with additional verses by Lonnie Donegan). UK release: Pye Nixa N 15093; charts 7 June 1957, *NME* #1 (June 1957).

Donegan, Lonnie. "Does Your Chewing Gum Lose Its Flavour (on the Bedpost Overnight)?" (Marty Bloom, Ernest Breuer, and Billy Rose). Donegan with unidentified personnel. Production unidentified. Recorded: New Theatre, Oxford, 13 December 1958. UK release: Pye Nixa 7N 15181, January 1959; charts 6 February 1959, *NME* #3. US release: Dot 45-15911, 21 July 1961; *BB* #5 (September 1961).

Donegan, Lonnie. "My Old Man's a Dustman (Ballad of a Refuse Disposal Officer)" (Lonnie Donegan and Peter Buchanan). Donegan with unidentified personnel. Recorded: Gaumant Cinema, Doncaster, 20 February 1960. UK release: Pye 7N.15256, 16 March 1960; charts 24 March 1960, *RR* #1 (March–April 1960).

Donegan, Lonnie. "I Wanna Go Home (The Wreck of the John 'B')" (Carl Sandburg, Lee Hayes, and Paddy Roberts). Production: Cromwell. UK release: Pye 7N.15267, May 1960; charts 26 May 1960, *RR* #5).

Donovan. "Catch the Wind" (Donovan Leitch). Donovan (guitar and vocals) with Brian Locking (bass) and unidentified musicians. Production: Terry Kennedy, Peter Eden, and Geoff Stephens. Recorded: Southern Music, London, February 1965. UK release: Pye 7N 15801, 12 March 1965; charts 25 March 1965, *RR* #4. US release: Hickory 45-1309, April 1965; *BB* #23 (July 1965).

Donovan. "Colours" (Donovan Leitch). Donovan Leitch (voice, guitar, banjo, and guitar) with Brian Locking (bass). Production as above, May 1965. UK release: Pye 7N15866, 28 May 1965; charts 3 June 1965, *RR* #4. US release: Hickory 45-1324, July 1965; *BB* #61 (September 1965).

Donovan. What's *Bin Did and What's Bin Hid*. Donovan with session musicians. Donovan Leitch (guitar, harmonica, and voice) with Brian Locking (acoustic bass), and Alan Skipper (drums). Production: Terry Kennedy, Geoff Stephens, and Peter Eden. Recorded: Southern Music, London, February–March 1965. UK release: Pye NPL 18117, 14 May 1965. US release: *Catch the Wind* Hickory DT 90697, June 1965. A: "Josie," "Catch the Wind," "Remember the Alamo," "Cuttin' Out," "Car Car," and "Keep on Truckin'." B: "Gold Watch Blues," "To Sing for You," "You're Gonna Need Somebody on Your Bond," "Tangerine Puppet," "Donna Donna," and "Ramblin' Boy."

Donovan. "Universal Soldier" (Buffy Saint Marie). Personnel and production as above. UK release on *The Universal Soldier* [EP] as Pye NEP 24219, August 1965. US release: Hickory 45-1338, September 1965; *BB* #53 (October 1965).

Donovan. *Fairytale*. Donovan (guitar, harmonica, and vocals) with Shawn Philips (12-string guitar) and unidentified studio musicians. Production: Eden/Stephens and Terry Kennedy. A: "Colours," "To Try for the Sun," "Sunny Goodge Street," "Oh Deed I Do," "Circus of Sour," and "The Summer Day Reflection Song." B: "Candy Man," "Jersey Thursday," "Belated Forgiveness Plea," "Ballad of a Crystal Man," "The Little Tin Soldier," and "Ballad of Geraldine." UK release: Pye NPL 18128, 22 October 1965. US release: Hickory LPM-127, November 1965.

Donovan. "Turquoise" (Donovan Leitch). Personnel and production as above. Recorded: London. Released as Pye 7N 15984, 29 October 1965; charts 11 November 1965, *RR* #30.

The Dovells. "What in the World's Come Over You" (Jimmy Wisner and Billy Jackson). Len Borisoff, Jerry Gross, Arnie Silver, Jim Mealy, and Mike Freda with studio musicians. US release: Parkway P-925, July 1964.

The Drifters [UK]. "Feelin' Fine" (Ian Samwell). Bruce Welch (vocals and rhythm guitar), Hank Marvin (vocals and lead guitar), Jet Harris (vocals and bass guitar), and Tony Meehan (drums). Production: Norrie Paramor (recording manager) and Malcolm Addey (engineer). Recorded: EMI Recording Studios, London. Release: Columbia DB 4263, February 1959. US release: by the Drifters, Capitol F 4220, June 1959. [Withdrawn after protest by Atlantic Records over trademark of the name "The Drifters."]

The Drifters [US]. "Sweets for My Sweet" (Doc Pomus and Mort Shuman). Charlie Thomas (lead vocal) with Jimmy Radcliffe, Cissy Houston, Doris Troy, Dionne Warwick, and Dee Dee Warwick (backing vocals), Mort Shuman (piano), George Barnes and Allan Hanlon (guitar), Abie Baker (bass), Ed Shaughnessy and Gary Chester (drums), with Bobby Rosengarden and Ray Kessler (percussion). Production: Jerry Leiber and Mike Stoller with Stan Applebaum (arranger and conductor). US release: Atlantic 45-2117, 2 July 1961; *BB* #16 (November 1961). UK release: London HLK 9427, September 1961.

Dylan, Bob. *Bob Dylan*. Bob Dylan (vocal, guitar, and harmonica). Production: John H. Hammond. Recorded: Columbia (799 Seventh Avenue), New York City, 20 and 22 November 1961. US release: Columbia CL 1779, 19 March 1962. A: "You're No Good," "Talkin' New York," "In My Time of Dyin'," "Man of Constant Sorrow," "Fixin' to Die," "Pretty Peggy-O," and "Highway 51." B: "Gospel Plow," "Baby, Let Me Follow You Down," "House of the Risin' Sun," "Freight Train Blues," "Song to Woody," and "See that My Grave Is Kept Clean."

Dylan, Bob. "Blowin' in the Wind" (Bob Dylan). Bob Dylan (voice and guitar). Production: John Hammond. Recorded: Columbia Recording Studios, New York, 9 July 1962. US release: Columbia 4-42856, 13 August 1963.

Dylan, Bob. *The Freewheelin' Bob Dylan*. Bob Dylan (vocal, harmonica, guitar, and keyboards) with Leonard Gaskin (bass guitar), Bruce Langhorne (guitar), Herb Lovelle (drums), and Dick Wellstood (piano). Production: John Hammond and Tom Wilson. Recorded: Columbia Recording Studios, New York, 24-2 April, 26 October, 1 and 15 November, and 6 December 1962, and 24 April 1963. US release: Columbia CL 1986, 27 May 1963. A: "Blowin' in the Wind," "Girl from the North Country," "Masters of War," "Down the Highway," "Bob Dylan's Blues," and "A Hard Rain's a-Gonna Fall." B: "Don't Think Twice, It's All Right," "Bob Dylan's Dream," "Oxford Town," "Talkin' World War III Blues," "Corrina, Corrina," "Honey, Just Allow Me One More Chance," and "I Shall Be Free."

Dylan, Bob. *The Times They Are a-Changin'*. Bob Dylan. Production: Tom Wilson. Recorded: Columbia Recording Studios, New York, 6–7 August 1963 and 23, 24, and 31 October 1963. US release: Columbia CL 2105, 13 January 1964. A: "The Times They Are a-Changin'," "Ballad of Hollis Brown," "With God on Our Side," "One Too Many Mornings," and "North Country Blues." B: "Only a Pawn in Their Game," "Boots of Spanish Leather," "When the Ship Comes In," The Lonesome Death of Hattie Carroll," and "Restless Farewell."

Dylan, Bob. *Dylan* [EP]. Production: John Hammond and Tom Wilson. UK release: CBS EP 6051, June 1964. A: "Don't Think Twice, It's Alright" and "Blowin' in the Wind." B: "Corrina, Corrina" and "When the Ship Comes in." Bob Dylan (vocal, guitar, and harmonica).

Dylan, Bob. *Another Side of Bob Dylan*. Bob Dylan. Production: Tom Wilson. Recorded: Columbia Recording Studios, 9 June 1964. US release: Columbia CL 2193, 8 August 1964. A: "All I Really Want to Do," "Black Crow Blues," "Spanish Harlem Incident," "Chimes of Freedom," "I Shall Be Free No. 10," and "To Ramona." B: "Motorpsycho Nitemare," "My Back Pages," "I Don't Believe You (She Acts Like We Never Have Met)," "Ballad in Plain D," and "It Ain't Me Babe."

Dylan, Bob. "The Times They Are a-Changin' " (Bob Dylan). Bob Dylan (vocal, guitar, and harmonica). Production: Tom Wilson. Recorded: Columbia Studios, New York, 24 October 1963. UK release: CBS 201751, March 1965; charts 25 March 1965, *RR* #9.

Dylan, Bob. "Subterranean Homesick Blues" (Bob Dylan). Bob Dylan (vocal and guitar) with Al Gorgoni (guitar), Kenny Rankin (guitar), Bruce Langhorne (guitar), Joseph Macho, Jr. (bass), and Bobby Gregg (drums). Production: Tom Wilson. Recorded: Columbia Recording Studios, New York, 14 January 1965. US release: Columbia 4-43242, 8 March 1965; BB #39 (May 1965). UK release: CBS 201751, March 1965; charts 29 April 1965, *RR* #9.

Dylan, Bob. *Bringing It All Back Home*. Bob Dylan (vocal, harmonica, guitar, and keyboards), Al Gorgoni, John P. Hammond, Bruce Langhorne, and Kenny Rankin (guitars), Paul Griffin and Frank Owens (keyboards), Steve Boone, Bill Lee, and John Sebastian (bass), and Joseph Macho Jr. (drums). Production: Tom Wilson. Recorded: Columbia 7th Ave. and Studio B (New York), 13–15 January 1965. US release: Columbia CL 2328, 22 March 1965. A: "Subterranean Homesick Blues," "She Belongs to Me," "Maggie's Farm," "Love Minus Zero/No Limit," "Outlaw Blues," "On the Road Again," and "Bob Dylan's 115th Dream." B: "Mr. Tambourine Man," "Gates of Eden," "It's Alright, Ma (I'm Only Bleeding)," and "It's All Over Now, Baby Blue."

The Dynamics. "Misery" (G. Stratton and A. Wilson). Isaac Harris, George White, Fred Baker, Samuel Stevenson, and Zerben Hicks (vocals) backed by the Royal Playboys with Mike Hedgi (trumpet), Lou Guido (drums), Stan Petriw (sax), Jim Wyjecka (guitar), Von Dragan (guitar), Hank Rivera (bass guitar), and Stan Topij (organ). US release: Bigtop 45-3161, October 1963.

Earl-Jean. "I'm into Somethin' Good" (Gerry Goffin and Carole King). Earl-Jean [the Cookies]: Earl-Jean McCrea, Dorothy Jones, and Margaret Ross with studio musicians. Production: Gerry Goffin with Carole King (arranger). US release: Colpix CP-729, April 1964. UK release: Colpix PX 729, 1964.

Eddy, Duane. 1958. "Rebel-'Rouser" (Duane Eddy and Lee Hazlewood). Duane Eddy and His "Twangy" Guitar. Production: Lester Sill and Lee Hazlewood. US release: Jamie 1104, 26 May 1958. UK release: London HL 8669, *RR* #19 (charts 5 September 1958).

The Everly Brothers. "Bye Bye Love" (Felice Bryant and Boudleaux Bryant). Don Everly (voice and guitar), Phil Everly (voice and guitar), Chet Atkins (guitar), and Buddy Harmon (drums). Production: Chet Atkins. Recorded: RCA Studios, Nashville, 1 March 1957. US release: Cadence 1315, March 1957. UK release: London HLA 8440, June 1957, *NME* #6 (charts 12 July 1957).

The Everly Brothers. "Cathy's Clown" (Don Everly and Phil Everly). The Everly Brothers with Floyd Cramer (piano), Floyd Chance (bass), and Buddy Harman (drums). Production: Wesley Rose. Recorded: Nashville, 1960. US release: Warner Brothers 515, April 1960; *BB* #1 (May 1960). UK release: Warner Brothers WB 1, 8 April 1960; charts 14 April 1960 *RR* #1 (May–June 1960).

The Everly Brothers. "Nashville Blues" (Felice Bryant and Boudleaux Bryant). US release: *Especially for You* [EP], Warner Brothers EB 1381, 1960. UK release on *Especially for You* [EP] as Warner Brothers WEP 6034, August 1961.

The Everly Brothers. "Love Her" (Barry Mann and Cynthia Weil). US release: Warner Brothers 5389, 18 September 1963. UK release: WB 109, 4 October 1963.

The Exciters. "Tell Him" (Bert Russell). Brenda Reid, Herbert Rooney, Carolyn "Carol" Johnson, and Lillian Walker with studio musicians. Production: Jerry Lieber and Mike Stoller with Techo Wiltshire (music director). US release: United Artists UA 544, 18 October 1962; charts 1 December 1962, *BB* #4 (January 1963).

The Exciters. "Do-Wah-Diddy" (Jeff Barry and Ellie Greenwich). Personnel and production as above. US release: United Artists UA 662, November 1963; *BB* #78 (January 1964). UK release: United Artists UP 1041 ("Do-Wah-Diddy-Diddy"), January 1964.

Faith, Adam. "What Do You Want?" (Les Vandyke) Adam Faith (vocals) with Vic Flick (guitar), Les Reed (piano), and members of the John Barry Seven. Production: John Burgess with John Barry (music director), Les Reed (arranger), and Malcolm Addey (engineer). Recorded: EMI, 25 September 1959. UK release: Parlophone R 4591 on 23 October 1959; charts 20 November 1959, *NME* #1 (December 1959).

Faith, Adam. "Poor Me" (Les Vandyke)/"The Reason" (John Barry). Adam Faith (vocals) with members of The John Barry Seven. Production as above. UK release: Parlophone R 4623, 15 January 1960; charts 22 January 1960, *RR* #1 (March 1960).

Faith, Adam. "Someone Else's Baby" (Les Vandyke and Perry Ford)/"Big Time" (Lionel Bart). Personnel and production. UK release: Parlophone R 4643, 8 April 1960; charts 14 April 1960, *RR* #2.

Faith, Adam. "The First Time" (Chris Andrews). Adam Faith with the Roulettes. Production as above with Johnny Keating (arranger). Released as Parlophone R 5061, 13 September 1963; charts 19 September 1963, *RR* # 5.

Faithfull, Marianne. "As Tears Go By" (Mick Jagger, Keith Richards, Andrew Oldham). Marianne Faithful with studio musicians including Jim Sullivan (guitar). Production: Andrew Loog Oldham with Mike Leander (music director) and Roger Savage (engineer). Recorded: Olympic Sound Studios, Carton Street, London, 28 May 1964. UK release: Decca F 11923, 26 June 1964; charts 13 August 1964, *RR* #9. US release: London 45-9697, October 1964; *BB* #22 (January 1965).

Faithfull, Marianne. "Blowin' in the Wind" (Bob Dylan). Marianne Faithful (vocal) with studio musicians. Production: Andrew Loog Oldham with

David Whitaker (music director). UK release: Decca F 12007, October 1964.

Faithfull, Marianne. "Come and Stay with Me" (Jackie DeShannon). Marianne Faithful (vocal) with studio musicians. Production: Tony Calder with Mike Leander (music director). UK release: Decca F 12075, 5 February 1965; charts 18 February 1965, *RR* #4. US release: London 45-9731, February 1965; *BB* #26 (April 1965).

Faithfull, Marianne. "This Little Bird" (John D. Loudermilk). Marianne Faithful (vocal) with studio musicians. Production: Tony Calder with Mike Leander (music director). UK release: Decca F 12162, 30 April 1965; charts 6 May 1965, *RR* #6. US release: London 45-LON 9759, May 1965; *BB* #32 (July 1965).

Faithfull, Marianne. "Yesterday" (John Lennon and Paul McCartney). Marianne Faithfull with studio musicians and chorus. Production as above. UK release: Decca F 12268, 22 October 1965; charts 4 November 1965, *RR* #36.

Fame, Georgie. "Do the Dog" (Rufus Thomas). Georgie Fame and the Blue Flames: Georgie Fame (vocal and organ), Michael Eve (tenor saxophone), John Marshall (baritone saxophone), Red Reece (drums), Boots Slade (bass), Jim Sullivan (guitar), and Tom Thomas (congas). Production: Ian Samwell with Glyn Johns (engineer). Recorded: The Flamingo, London, 25 September 1963. UK release: Columbia DB 7193, 10 January 1964.

Fame, Georgie. *Rhythm and Blues from the Flamingo*. Personnel, production, and recording as above. UK release: Columbia 33SX 1599, January 1964. A: "Night Train," "Let the Good Times Roll," "Do the Dog," "Eso Beso," and "Work Song." B: "Parchman Farm," "You Can't Sit Down," "Humpty Dumpty," "Shop Around," and "Baby, Please Don't Go."

Fame, Georgie. *Fame at Last*. Personnel as above. Production: Ian Samwell with Earl Guest (music director). UK release: Columbia 33SX 1638, September 1964. A: "Get on the Right Track Baby," "Let the Sunshine In," "The Monkey Time," "All about My Girl," "Point of No Return," and "Gimme That Wine." B: "Pink Champagne," "Monkeying Around," "Pride and Joy," "Green Onions," "I Love the Life, I Live," and "I'm in the Mood for Love."

Fame, Georgie. "Yeh, Yeh" (Rodgers Grant, Pat Henry, and Jon Hendricks). Georgie Fame and the Blue Flames: Georgie Fame (vocals and organ), Bill Eyden (drums), Tex Makins (bass), Speedy Acquaye (congas), Peter Coe (tenor saxophone), Colin Green (guitar). Production: Tony Palmer with Edward Hayes (arranger). Recorded: EMI Recording Studios, London, November 1964. UK release: Columbia DB 7428, December 1964; charts 17 December 1964, *RR* #1 (January 1965); *NME* #1. US release: Imperial 66086, January 1965: *Cashbox* #17 and *BB* #21 (March 1965).

Wayne Fontana and the Mindbenders. "Hello! Josephine" (Antoine Domino and Dave Bartholomew). Wayne Fontana (vocal), Bob Lang (bass guitar), Rick Rothwell (drums), and Eric Stewart (guitar) with unidentified backing vocals. Production: Jack Baverstock. UK release: Fontana TF 404, 21 June 1963; charts 11 July 1963, *RR* #46.

Wayne Fontana and the Mindbenders. "For You, for You" (P. Lee Stirling). Personnel and production as above. UK release: Fontana TF 418, October 1963.

Wayne Fontana and the Mindbenders. "Little Darlin'" (Maurice Williams). Personnel and production as above. UK release: Fontana TF 436, January 1964.

Wayne Fontana and the Mindbenders. "Stop, Look, and Listen" (Jimmy Breedlove and Pat Brown). Personnel and production as above. UK release: Fontana TF 451, 1 May 1964; charts 28 May 1964, *RR* #37. US release: Fontana S-1917, July 1964.

Wayne Fontana and the Mindbenders. "Um, Um, Um, Um, Um, Um" (Curtis Mayfield). Personnel and production as above. UK release: Fontana TF 497, 18 September 1964; charts 8 October 1964, *RR* #5.

Wayne Fontana and the Mindbenders. "Game of Love" (Clint Ballard, Jr.). Personnel and production as above. UK release: TF 535, 22 January 1965; charts 4 February 1965, *RR* #2. US release: Fontana F-1503, February 1965; rereleased as Fontana F-1509, April 1965; *BB* #1 (April 1965).

Formby, George. "With My Little Ukulele in My Hand" (Jack Cottrell). George Formby (vocal and ukulele) with studio orchestra. Prepared as Decca F3615, 1933, but withdrawn. Recorded: Chenil Galleries, London, 1 July 1933. Rerecorded: Decca, Chenil Galleries, London, 12 November 1933. UK release: "My Ukulele" Decca F3752, 1933.

Formby, George. "When I'm Cleaning Windows" (George Formby, Harry Gifford, and Fred E. Cliffe). Personnel and production as above. Recorded: 27 September 1936. UK release: Regal Zonophone MR2199, September 1936.

Formby, George. "When I'm Cleaning Windows" (George Formby, Harry Gifford, and Fred E. Cliffe). George Formby (vocal and ukulele) with Harry Bidgood and His Orchestra. Recorded: Decca Studios, London, 21 January 1950. UK release on *Formby Favourites*, Eclipse 820 609-2, June 1950.

The Fortunes. "Summertime Summertime" (Tom Jameson and Sherman Feller). The Fortunes and the Cliftones: Rod Allen, Glen Dale, and Barry Pritchard (vocals) with studio musicians. Production: Shel Talmy. UK release: Decca F 11718, August 1963.

The Fortunes. "Caroline" (Tony Hiller and Perry Ford). Rod Allen (vocal and bass), Barry Pritchard (vocal and guitar), Glen Dale (vocal and guitar), Dave Carr (piano), and Andy Brown (drums). Production: Shel Talmy. UK release: Decca F 11809, January 1964.

The Fortunes. "Come On Girl" (Barry Pritchard). Production: Shel Talmy with Ivor Raymonde. UK release: Decca F 11912, 29 May 1964.

The Fortunes. "Look Homeward Angel" (Wally Gold). Production: Shel Talmy with Mike Leander (arranger). UK release: Decca F 11985, 18 September 1964.

The Fortunes. 1965. "You've Got Your Troubles" (Roger Greenaway and Roger Cook). Personnel as above with Vic Flick and Jimmy Page (guitars). Production: Noel Walker with Les Reed (arranger). UK release: Decca F 12173, 11 June 1965; charts 8 July 1965, *RR* #2. US release: Press 45-9773, July 1965; *BB* #7 (October 1965).

The Fortunes. "Here It Comes Again" (Les Reed and Barry Mason). Personnel and production as above. UK release: Decca F 12243, 1 October 1965; charts 7 October 1965, *RR* #4. US release: Press 45 PRE 9798, October 1965; *BB* #27 (December 1965).

The Four Seasons. "Sherry" (Bob Gaudio). Frankie Valli (vocals), Bob Gaudio (keyboards and vocals), Tommy DeVito (guitar and vocals), and Nick Massi (bass and vocals). Production: Bob Crewe with Sid Bass (arranger). Recorded: July 1962. US release: Vee-Jay 456, July 1962, *BB* #1 (September 1962). UK release: Stateside 45SS-122, 1962; charts 4 October 1962, *RR* #8.

The Four Tunes. "I Understand Just How You Feel" (Pat Best). Danny Owens (tenor), Pat Best (baritone and guitar), Jimmy Gordon (bass), and Jimmie Nabbie (tenor). Sid Bass (music director). US release: Jubilee 45-5132, May 1954; charts 19 May 1954, *BB* #8.

Freddie and the Dreamers. "If You Gotta Make a Fool of Somebody" (Rudy Clark). Freddie Garrity (vocals), Roy Crewdson (guitar), Derek Quinn (harmonica), Peter Birrell (bass), and Bernie Dwyer (drums). Production: John Burgess with Norman Smith (engineer). Recorded: EMI Recording Studios, London, 21 March 1963. UK release: Columbia DB 7032, 26 April 1963; charts 9 May 1963, *RR* #3.

Freddie and the Dreamers. "I'm Telling You Now" (Freddie Garrity and Mitch Murray). Personnel and production as above. Recorded: London. UK release: Columbia DB 7086, August 1963; charts 8 August 1963, *RR* #2. US release: Capitol 5053, 7 October 1963; rereleased as Tower 125, March 1965; *BB* #1 (April 1965).

Freddie and the Dreamers. "You Were Made for Me" (Mitch Murray). Personnel and production as above. UK release: Columbia DB 7147, 1 November

1963; charts 7 November 1963, *RR* #3. US release: Capitol 5137, 2 March 1964; Tower 127, April 1965, *BB* #21 (June 1965).

Freddie and the Dreamers "I Understand" (Pat Best). Personnel and production as above. UK release: Columbia DB 7381, 23 October 1964; charts 5 November 1964, *RR* #5. US release: Mercury 72377, December 1964; *BB* #36 (May 1965).

Freddie and the Dreamers "Do the Freddie" (Dennis Lambert and Louis Pegues). Personnel and production as above. US release: Mercury 72428, April 1965, *BB* #18 (June 1965).

Fury, Billy. "Maybe Tomorrow" (Billy Fury). Billy Fury (vocals) with Eric Ford and Joe Brown (guitars), Don Storer (drums), Benny Green (soprano saxophone), Ronnie Black (bass), and unidentified female backing vocals [possibly one of the Vernon's Girls]. Production: Frank Lee with Harry Robinson (music director). Recorded: Decca Recording Studios, London, 26 November 1958. UK release: Decca F 11102, 26 January 1959; charts 27 February 1959, *NME* #18.

Fury, Billy. "Margo" (Billy Fury). Recorded: Decca, London, 8 April 1959. Billy Fury (vocals) with Colin Green (guitar) and unidentified session musicians. Production as above. UK release: Decca F 11128, 15 May 1959; charts 26 June 1959, *NME* #28.

Fury, Billy. "Collette" (Billy Fury). Personnel and production as above. Recorded: Decca Recording Studios, London, 8 January 1960. UK release: Decca F 11200, 29 January 1960; charts 10 March 1960, *RR* #9.

Fury, Billy. "That's Love" (Billy Fury). Personnel and production as above. Recorded: Decca Recording Studios, London, 14 April 1960. UK release: Decca 11237, 19 May 1960; charts 26 May 1960, *RR* #19.

Fury, Billy. *The Sound of Fury*. Billy Fury (vocals) with Joe Brown (guitar), Reg Guest (piano), Alan Weighell (electric bass), Bill Stark (acoustic bass), and Andy White (drums) with the Four Jays (backing vocals). Production: Jack Good. Recorded: Decca Recording Studios, London, 14 April 1960. UK release: Decca LF1239, 21 May 1960. A: "That's Love," "My Advice," "Phone Call," "You Don't Know," and "Turn My Back on You." B: "Don't Say It's Over," "Since You've Been Gone," "It's You I Need," "Alright, Goodbye," and "Don't Leave Me This Way."

Fury, Billy. "Halfway to Paradise" (Gerry Goffin and Carole King). Personnel as above. Production: Dick Rowe and Mike Smith with Ivor Raymonde (music director) and Michael Mailes (engineer). Recorded: Decca Recording Studios, London, 9 April 1961. UK release: Decca F 11349, 28 April 1961; charts 11 May 1961, *RR* #3.

Gaye, Barbie. "My Boy Lollypop" (Robert Spencer, Johnny Roberts, and Morris Levy). Barbie Gaye (vocals) with Leroy Kirkland (guitar), Panama Francis (drums), Al Sears (saxophone), and an unidentified piano. Production unidentified. US release: Moonglow 5005, December 1956 and Darl R-1002, January 1957. Jamaican release: Darl R 1002, n.d.

Gaye, Marvin. "Hitch Hike" (Marvin Gaye, William Stevenson, and Clarence Paul). Marvin Gaye with Martha and the Vandellas and members of the Funk Brothers. Production: William Stevenson. Recorded: Hitsville U.S.A., Detroit. US release: Tamla T-54075, 19 December 1962; *BB* #30 (March 1963).

Gaye, Marvin. "Can I Get a Witness" (Brian Holland, Lamont Dozier, and Eddie Holland). Performed by Marvin Gaye with members of the Funk Brothers. Production: Brian Holland and Lamont Dozier. Recorded: Hitsville U.S.A, Detroit, 17 July 1963. US release: Tamla T 54087, 20 September 1963; *BB* #22 (December 1963). UK release: Stateside SS 243, November 1963.

Gerry and the Pacemakers. "How Do You Do It?" (Mitch Murray). Gerry Marsden (lead vocal and guitar), Les Maguire (bass guitar, backing vocals), Les Chadwick (piano), and Freddie Marsden (drums). Production: George Martin and Ron Richards with Peter Bown (engineer). Recorded: EMI Recording Studios, London, January 1963. UK release: Columbia DB 4987, 1 March 1963; charts 14 March 1963, *RR* #1. US release: Laurie 3162, April 1963; rereleased June 1964; *BB* #9 (September 1964). B: "Away with You" (Gerry Marsden and Les Chadwick).

Gerry and the Pacemakers. "I Like It" (Mitch Murray). Performance and production personnel as above, 24 April 1963. UK release: Columbia DB 7041, 24 Mary 1963; charts 30 May 1963, *RR* #1. US release: Laurie 3196, September 1963; rereleased September 1964; *BB* #17 (November 1964). B: "It's Happened to Me" (Gerry Marsden and Les Chadwick).

Gerry and the Pacemakers. "You'll Never Walk Alone" (Richard Rodgers and Oscar Hammerstein II). Gerry Marsden with orchestral accompaniment. Production: Ron Richards with George Martin (arranger) and Peter Bown (engineer). Recorded: EMI Recording Studios, London. UK release: Columbia DB 7126, 4 October 1963; charts 10 October 1963, *RR* #1. US release: Laurie 3218, January 1964; rereleased as Laurie LR-3302, May 1965; *BB* #48 (July 1965). B: "It's All Right" (Gerry Marsden).

Gerry and the Pacemakers. "I'm the One" (Gerry Marsden). Personnel as above. Production: Ron Richards with Peter Bown (engineer). Recorded: EMI Recording Studios, London, December 1963. UK release: Columbia DB 7189, 10 January 1964; charts 16 January 1964, *RR* #2. US release: Laurie 3233, February 1964; *BB* #82 (July 1964).

Gerry and the Pacemakers. "Don't Let the Sun Catch You Crying" (Gerry Marsden). Gerry and the Pacemakers with orchestral accompaniment.

Production: Ron Richards with George Martin (arranger and conductor) and Peter Bown (engineer). Recorded: EMI Recording Studios, 9 December 1963. UK release: Columbia DB 7268, 10 April 1964; charts 16 April 1964, *RR* #6. US release: Laurie LR 3251, May 1964; *BB* #4 (July 1964).

Gerry and the Pacemakers. "It's Gonna Be Alright" (Gerry Marsden). Gerry Marsden et al. Production: Ron Richards. UK release: Columbia DB 7353, 28 August 1964; charts 5 September 1964, *RR* #24. US release: Laurie LR 3293, March 1965, *BB* #23 (May 1965).

Gerry and the Pacemakers. "Ferry Cross the Mersey" ["Ferry across the Mersey" in the American release] (Gerry Marsden). Gerry Marsden et al. with orchestra. Production: as above with Johnny Scott (arranger). UK release: Columbia DB 7437, 11 December 1964; charts 17 December 1964, *RR* #8. US release: Laurie LR 3284, January 1965, *BB* #5 (March 1965).

The Gladiolas. "Little Darlin'" (Maurice Williams). Maurice Williams, Henry Gaston, Wiley Bennett, Charles Thomas, Albert Hill, and Willie Morrow with Willie Jones, William Massey, and Norman Wade. US release: Excello 45-2101, January 1957.

Graham, Davy, and Alexis Korner. *3/4 A.D.* [EP]. Davy Graham (guitar) and Alexis Korner (guitar). Production: Bill Leader. UK release: Topic Records STOP2013, April 1962. A: "Angi" and "Davy's Train Blues." B: "3/4 A.D."

Graham, Davy, and Shirley Collins. *Folk Roots, New Routes*. Davy Graham (guitar) and Shirley Collins (voice and banjo, "Cherry Tree Carol"). Production: Roy Horricks with Gus Dudgeon (engineer). UK release: Decca LK 4652, 1964. A: "Nottamun Town," "Proud Maisrie," "The Cherry Tree Carol," "Blue Monk," "Hares on the Mountain," "Reynardine," "Pretty Saro," and "Rif Mountain." B: "Jane, Jane," "Love Is Pleasin'," "Boll Weavil, Holler," "Hori Horo," "Bad Girl," "Lord Gregory," "Grooveyard," and "Dearest Dear."

Graham, Davy. *The Guitar Player*. Davy Graham (voice and guitar) with Bobby Graham (drums). Production unidentified, 1962. UK release: Pye Golden Guinea Records GGL 0224, 1963. A: "Don't Stop the Carnival," "Sermonette," "Take Five," "How Long, How Long Blues," "Sunset Eyes," and "Cry Me a River." B: "The Ruby and the Pearl," "Buffalo," "Exodus," "Yellow Bird," "Blues for Betty," and "Hallelujah, I Love Her So."

Graham, Davy. *Folk Blues and Beyond*. Davy Graham (guitar and voice) with Tony Reeves (bass) and Barry Morgan (drums). Production: Ray Horricks with Gus Dudgeon (engineer). UK release: Decca LK 4649, January 1965. A: "Leavin' Blues," "Cocaine," "Sally Free and Easy," "Black Is the Colour of My True Love's Hair," "Rock Me Baby," Seven Gypsies," "Ballad of the Sad Young Men," and "Moanin'." B: "Skillet (Good 'n' Greasy)," "Ain't Nobody's Business What I Do," "Maajun (a Taste of Tangier)," "I Can't Keep from

Crying Sometimes," "Don't Think Twice, It's Alright," My Babe," "Goin' Down Slow," and "Better Git in Your Soul."

Graham, Davy, and Shirley Collins. See Shirley Collins and Davy Graham.

Guthrie, Woody, and Cisco Houston. *More Songs by Woody Guthrie and Cisco Houston*. US release: Stinson Records SLP 53, 1952. UK release: Melodisc MLP12-106, 1955. A: "Take a Wiff on Me," "Bad Lee Brown," "The Golden Vanity," "Cumberland Gap," "Sourwood Mountain," "Old Time Religion." B: "Columbus Stockade," "Johnny Hard," Foggy Mountain Top," "Bury Me beneath the Willow," "Skip to My Lou," and "Ezekiel Saw the Wheel."

Haley, Bill, and His Comets. "(We're Gonna) Rock around the Clock" (Max C. Freedman and James E. Myers). Bill Haley (vocal and guitar), Franny Beecher and Danny Cedrone (guitar), Joey D'Ambrosio (tenor sax), John Grande (piano), Billy Williamson (steel guitar), Marshall Lytle (bass), and Bill Gussak (drums). Production: Milt Gabler. Recorded: Pythian Temple, New York City, 12 April 1954. US release: Decca 9-29124, 10 May 1954 and May 1955. UK release: Brunswick 05317, January 1955.

Haley, Bill, and His Comets. "Shake, Rattle, and Roll" (Charles Calhoun [Jesse Stone]). Bill Haley and His Comets with Bill Haley (vocal and guitar), Danny Cedrone (lead guitar), Joey D'Ambrosio (tenor sax), John Grande (piano), Billy Williamson (steel guitar), Marshall Lytle (bass), Bill Gussak (drums), and Don Raymond (backing vocal). Production: Milt Gabler. Recorded: Pythian Temple, New York City, 7 June 1954. US release: Decca 9-29204, 12 July 1954. UK release: Brunswick 05338, October 1954; charts 17 December 1954, *NME* #4.

Harpo, Slim. "I'm a King Bee" (James Moore). Slim Harpo (vocal and harmonica) with Gabriel Perrodin (guitar), John Perrodin (bass), and Clarence Etienne (drums). Production: J. D. Miller. US release: Excello 2131, 1957. B: "Got Love If You Want It" (James Moore).

Harpo, Slim. "Don't Start Crying Now" (James Moore and Jerry West). Personnel and production as above. US release: Excello 45-2194, January 1961. UK release: Pye International 7N 25220, September 1963.

Harris, Jet and Tony Meehan. "Diamonds" (Jerry Lordan). Personnel: Jet Harris (guitar), Tony Meehan (drums), Jimmy Page (guitar), John Paul Jones (bass), Glenn Hughes (saxophones), and. Chris Hughes (piano). Production: Tony Meehan with Malcolm Addey (engineer). Recorded: Decca Studios, London, 23 November 1962. UK release: Decca F 11563, 4 January 1963; charts 10 January 1963, RR #1 (February 1963). US release: London Records 45-LON 9589.

Helms, Bobby. "Schoolboy Crush" (Aaron Schroeder and Sharon Silbert). US release: Decca 9-30682, 1958. UK release: Brunswick 45-05754, 1958.

Herman's Hermits. "I'm into Something Good" (Gerry Goffin and Carole King). Peter Noone (vocal) with session musicians including John Carter, Ken Lewis, and Perry Ford (backing vocals) and Reg Guest (piano). Production: Mickie Most. Recorded: EMI Studios, London, 1 April 1964. UK release: Columbia DB 7338, 7 August 1964; charts 20 August 1964, *RR* #1 (September 1964). US release: MGM K 13280, Septwnber 1964; charts 17 October 1964, *BB* #13 (December 1964).

Herman's Hermits. "Show Me Girl" (Gerry Goffin and Carole King). Personnel and production as above. UK release: Columbia DB 7408, 13 November 1964; charts 19 November 1964, *RR* #19.

Herman's Hermits. *Hermania* [EP]. Personnel and production as above. UK release: Columbia SEG 8380, December 1964. A: "Sea Cruise" and "Mother-in-Law." B: "I Understand" and "Thinkin' of You."

Herman's Hermits. "Can't You Hear My Heartbeat" (John Carter and Ken Lewis). Personnel and production as above. Recorded: De Lane Lea Studios, London, 1 December 1964. US release: MGM K 13310, January 1965; *BB* #2 (March–April 1965).

Herman's Hermits. "Silhouettes" (Frank Slay, Jr., and Bob Crewe). Personnel and production as above. UK release: Columbia DB 7475, 12 February 1965; charts 18 February 1965, *RR* #3. US release: MGM K 13332, March 1965; charts 3 April 1965, *BB* #5 (May 1965).

Herman's Hermits. "Wonderful World" (Barbara Campbell [Herb Alpert, Lou Adler, and Sam Cooke]). Personnel as above. Production: Mickie Most. Recorded: De Lane Lea, London, March 1965. UK release: Columbia DB 7546, 16 April 1965; charts 29 April 1965, *RR* #7. US release: MGM K 13354, May 1965; *BB* #4 (July 1965).

Herman's Hermits. "Mrs. Brown You've Got a Lovely Daughter" (Treavor Peacock). Personnel and production as above. Recorded: De Lane Lea Studios, London, 1 December 1964. US release: MGM K 13341, April 1965; *BB* #1 (May 1965).

Herman's Hermits. *Mrs. Brown You've Got a Lovely Daughter* [EP]. Released as Columbia SEG 8440, June 1965. A: "Mrs. Brown You've Got a Lovely Daughter" and "I Know Why." B: "Show Me Girl" and "Your Hand in Mine."

Herman's Hermits. "I'm Henry VIII, I Am" (Fred Murray and R. P. Weston). Personnel and production as above. Recorded: De Lane Lea Studios, London, 1 February 1965. US release: MGM K 13367, June 1965; *BB* #1 (August 1965).

The High Numbers. "I'm the Face" (Peter Meaden). Roger Daltrey (vocal), Peter Townshend (guitar and backing vocal), John Entwistle (bass and backing vocal), and Keith Moon (drums). Production: Jack Baverstock,

1964. UK release: Fontana TF 480, 3 July 1964. B: "Zoot Suit" (Peter Meaden).

Hill, Alex. *Hometown Skiffle*. Alex Hill (host), Blind Blake, Charlie Spand, Will Ezell, the Hokum Boys, Papa Charlie Jackson, and Blind Lemon Jefferson. US release: Paramount 12886, December 1929.

The Hollies. "(Ain't That) Just Like Me" (Earl Carroll and Billy Guy). Allan Clarke (vocal), Graham Nash (rhythm guitar and vocal), Tony Hicks (guitar and vocal), Eric Haydock (bass), and Don Rathbone (drums). Production: Ron Richards with Peter Bown (engineer). Recorded: EMI Recording Studios, London, 4 April 1963. UK release: Parlophone R 5030, 17 May 1963; charts 30 May 1963, *RR* #25.

The Hollies. "Searchin'" (Jerry Leiber and Mike Stoller). Personnel (with Tommy Sanderson, piano) and production as above. Recorded: EMI Recording Studios, London, 25 July 1963. UK release: Parlophone R 5052, 16 August 1963; charts 29 August 1964, *RR* #12.

The Hollies. "Stay" (Maurice Williams). Personnel and production as above. Recorded: EMI Recording Studios, London, 11 October 1963. UK release: Parlophone R 5077, 15 November 1963; charts 21 November 1964, *RR* #8. US release: Liberty 55674, 31 January 1964.

The Hollies. "Just One Look" (Doris Payne and Gregory Carroll). Personnel as above with Robert Elliot (drums). Production as above. Recorded: EMI Recording Studios, London, 27 January 1964. UK release: Parlophone R 5104, 21 February 1964; charts 27 February 1964, *RR* #2, *NME* #3. US release: Imperial 66026, March 1964.

The Hollies. "Here I Go Again" (Mort Shuman and Clive Westlake). Personnel and production as above. Recorded: EMI Recording Studios, London, 13 April 1964. UK release: Parlophone R 5137, 9 May 1964; charts 21 May 1964, *RR* #4, *NME* #4. US release: Imperial 66044, June 1964.

The Hollies. "We're Through" (L. Ransford [Allan Clarke, Tony Hicks, and Graham Nash]). Personnel and production as above. Recorded: EMI Recording Studios, London, 25 August 1964. UK release: Parlophone R 5178, 11 September 1964; charts 17 September 1964, *RR* #7. US release: Imperial 66070, September 1964.

The Hollies. "I'm Alive" (Clint Ballard, Jr.). Personnel and production as above. Recorded: EMI Recording Studios, London, 5 May 1965. UK release: Parlophone R 5287, 21 May 1965; charts 27 May 1965, *RR* #1. US release: Imperial 66119, June 1965.

Holloway, Brenda. "Every Little Bit Hurts" (Ed Cobb). Brenda Holloway with studio musicians. Production: Hal Davis and Marc Gordon. Recorded: Los Angeles, 1964. US release: Tamla T 54094, 26 March 1964: *BB* #13 (June 1964). UK release: Stateside SS 307, 19 June 1964.

Holly, Buddy. "That'll Be the Day" (Jerry Allison, Buddy Holly, and Norman Petty). The Crickets: Buddy Holly (guitar and vocal), Larry Welbron (bass), and Jerry Allison (drums) with Niki Sullivan, June Clark, Gary Tollett, and Ramona Tollett (backing vocals). [Originally recorded by Buddy Holly and the Three Tunes, 1956.] Production: Norman Petty. Recorded: Norman Petty Recording Studio, Clovis, New Mexico, 25 February 1957. US release: Brunswick 55009, May 1957.

Holly, Buddy. "Peggy Sue" (Buddy Holly, Jerry Allison, and Norman Petty). Buddy Holly and The Crickets: Buddy Holly (guitar and vocal), Joe Mauldin (string bass), and Jerry Allison (drums). Production: Norman Petty. Recorded: Clovis, New Mexico, 29 June and 1 July 1957. US release: Coral 0-61885 on 20 September 1957. UK release: Vogue Coral Q 72293, 15 November 1957; charts 6 December 1957, *NME* #6.

Holly, Buddy. "Not Fade Away" (Charles Hardin [Buddy Holly] and Norman Petty). The Crickets: Buddy Holly (vocal and guitar), Joe Mauldin (bass), and Jerry Allison (drums), with backing vocals. Production as above. Recorded: 27 May 1957. US release: Brunswick 9-55035, 27 October 1957.

Holly, Buddy. "It Doesn't Matter Anymore" (Paul Anka). Buddy Holly with studio musicians. Produced, arranged, and directed by Dick Jacobs. Recorded: Decca Studios, New York, 21 October 1958. US release: Coral Records 9-62074, 5 January 1959; *BB* #13 (April 1959). UK release: Coral Q 72360, February 1959; charts 27 February 1959, *NME* #1.

The Honeycombs. "Have I the Right?" (Ken Howard and Alan Blaikley). Denis D'Ell (vocal), Martin Murray (rhythm guitar), Alan Ward (lead guitar), John Lantree (bass), and Honey Lantree (drums). Production: Joe Meek for RGM Sound Production. Recorded: RGM Sound, London. UK release: Pye 7N 15664, 16 June 1964; charts 23 July 1964, *RR* #1 (August 1964). US release: Interphon IN-7707, September 1964; *BB* #5 (November 1964).

The Honeycombs. "Is It Because?" (Ken Howard and Alan Blaikley). Personnel and production as above. Recorded: RGM Sound, London. UK release: Pye 7N 15705, 9 October 1964; charts 22 October 1964, *RR* #38.

Hooker, John Lee. "Please Don't Go" (Joe Williams). John Lee Hooker (guitar and vocals). Recorded: Detroit, 24 April 1952. US release: Chess LP 1454, 1961, on *John Lee Hooker—Plays and Sings*.

Hooker, John Lee. 1956. "Dimples" (John Lee Hooker and James Bracken). John Lee Hooker (vocal and guitar) with Eddie Taylor (guitar), George Washington (bass), and Tom Whitehead (drums). Recorded: Chicago, March 1956. US release: Vee Jay VJ 205, September 1956. UK release: Stateside SS 297, 29 May 1964; charts 11 June 1964, *NME* #23.

Hooker, John Lee. 1962. "Boom Boom" (John Lee Hooker). John Lee Hooker (vocal and guitar) with Joe Hunter (piano), James Jamerson (bass),

Benny Benjamin (drums), and Larry Veeder (guitar). Recorded: Chicago, 1961. US release: Vee Jay VJ 438, April 1962; *BB* #60, July 1962. UK release: Stateside SS 203, 12 July 1963.

Hooker, John Lee. *Don't Turn Me from Your Door*. John Lee Hooker with Eddie Kirkland and Earl Hooker (guitars). Production: Henry Stone. Recorded: Cincinnati, Ohio, July 1953; Miami, Florida, July 1961. US release: Atco 33-151, February 1963. A: "Stuttering Blues," "Wobbling Baby," "You Lost a Good Man," "Love Me Baby," "Misbelieving Baby," and "Drifting Blues." B: "Don't Turn Me from Your Door," "My Baby Don't Love Me," "I Ain't Got Nobody," "Real Real Gone," "Guitar Lovin' Man," and "Talk about Your Baby."

Howlin' Wolf. "The Little Red Rooster" (Willie Dixon). Howlin' Wolf (vocals), Hubert Sumlin (guitar) Freddie Robinson (guitar), Otis Spann (piano), Willie Dixon (bass), and Fred Below (drums). Production: Leonard Chess, Phil Chess, and Willie Dixon. Recorded: Chess Studios, Chicago, June 1961. US release: Chess 1804, October 1961.

Ifield, Frank. "Wayward Wind" (Stanley Lebowsky and Herb Newman). Frank Ifield with studio musicians. Production: Norrie Paramor. Recorded: EMI Recording Studios, London. UK release: Columbia DB 4960, 17 January 1963; charts 24 January 1963, *RR* #1 (February 1963). US release: Vee Jay VJ 499, February 1963.

Ifield, Frank. "[I'm] Confessin' (That I Love You)" (Doc Daugherty, Ellis Reynolds, and Al Neiburg). Personnel and production as above. UK release: Columbia DB 7062, 21 June 1963; charts 27 June 1963, *RR* #1 (July 1963). US release: Capitol 5032, 2 September 1963; *BB* #16 (October 1963).

The Isley Brothers. "Shout—Part 1" (O'Kelly Isley, Rudolph Isley, and Ronald Isley). Ronald Isley (vocal), O'Kelly Isley, Jr., (vocal), Rudolph Isley (vocal), King Curtis (saxophone), Eric Gale (guitar), Trade Martin (guitar), Cornell Dupree (guitar), Paul Griffin (piano), Chuck Rainey (bass), and Gary Chester (drums). Production: Luigi Creatore and Hugo Peretti. Recorded: RCA, New York, 5 August 1959. US release: RCA 7588, 21 September 1959; *BB* #47 (October 1959).

The Isley Brothers. "Twist and Shout" (Phil Medley and Bert Russell). Personnel as above with variations. Production: Bert Russell. Recorded: New York, 1962. US release: Wand 653, 16 June 1962; *BB* #17 (August 1962).

The Ivy League. "What More Do You Want" (John Carter, Ken Lewis, and Perry Ford). John Carter, Ken Lewis, and Perry Ford (vocals) with Jim Sullivan (guitar), Dave Winter (bass), Mike O'Neill (keyboards), Micky Keen (guitar), and Clem Cattini (drums). Production: Terry Kennedy with

Bill Farley (engineer). Recorded: Regent Sound Studios, London. UK release: Piccadilly 7N 35200, 18 September 1964.

The Ivy League. "Funny How Love Can Be" (John Carter and Ken Lewis). Personnel and production as above. UK release: Piccadilly 7N 35222, January 1965; charts 4 February 1965, *RR* #8. US release: Cameo C-356, March 1965.

The Ivy League. "That's Why I'm Crying" (John Carter and Ken Lewis). Personnel and production as above. UK release: Piccadilly 7N35228, 9 April 1965; charts 6 May 1965, *RR* #22. US release: Cameo C-365, June 1965.

The Ivy League. "Tossing and Turning" (John Carter, Ken Lewis, and Perry Ford). Personnel and production as above. UK release: Piccadilly 7N 35251, June 1965; charts 24 June 1965, *RR* #3. US release: Cameo C0377, September 1965; *BB* #83, October 1965.

James, Dick. "Robin Hood" (Carl Sigman). Dick James (vocal) with orchestra. Production: George Martin. Recorded: EMI Recording Studios, London. UK release: Parlophone 6199, January 1956; charts 20 January 1956, *NME* #14; *MM* #14.

The Jamies. "Summertime, Summertime" (Tom Jameson and Sherman Feller). US release: Epic 5-9281, 14 July 1958, *BB* #26 (September 1958). UK release: Fontana H 153, October 1958.

Jansch, Bert. *Bert Jansch*. Bert Jansch (voice and guitar). Production: Bill Leader. Recorded: 5 North Villas, Camden, London, September 1964–January 1965. Release: Transatlantic Records TRA 125, 16 April 1965. A: "Strolling Down the Highway," "Smokey River," "Oh How Your Love Is Strong," "I Have No Time," "Finches," "Ramblings Going to Be the Death of Me," "Veronica," and "Needle of Death." B: "Do You Hear Me Now?," "Alice's Wonderland," "Running from Home," "Courting Blues," "Casbah," "Dreams of Love," and "Angie."

Jansch, Bert. *It Don't Bother Me*. Bert Jansch (voice, guitar, and banjo) with John Renbourn (guitar) and Roy Harper (voice and guitar). Production: Nathan Joseph and Bill Leader with Ray Pickett (engineer). Recorded: Pye Studios, London, December 1965. Release: Transatlantic TRA 132, December 1965. A: "Oh My Babe," "Ring-a-ding Bird," "Tinker's Blues," "Anti Apartheid," "The Wheel," "A Man I'd Rather Be," and "My Lover." B: "It Don't Bother Me," "Harvest Your Thoughts of Love," "Lucky Thirteen," "As the Day Grows Longer Now," "So Long (Been on the Road So Long)," "Want My Daddy Now," and "900 Miles."

Jansch, Bert. *Jack Orion*. Bert Jansch (guitar and voice) with John Renbourn (guitar). Produced by Bill Leader. UK release: Transatlantic Records TRA 143, September 1966. A: "The Waggoner's Lad," "The First Time Ever I

Saw Your Face," and "Jack Orion." B: "The Gardener," "Nottamun Town," "Henry Martin," "Black Water Side," and "Pretty Polly."

Johnson, Lou. "(There's) Always Something There to Remind Me" (Burt Bacharach and Hal David). Lou Johnson (vocal) with Doris Troy, Dee Dee Warwick, and Cissy Houston (backing vocals) and studio musicians. Produced and arranged by Burt Bacharach. Recorded: Big Hill, New York. US release: Big Hill 552, July 1964, *BB* #49, October 1964. UK release: London HLX 9917, 28 August 1964.

Johnson, Robert. "I Believe I'll Dust My Broom" (Robert Johnson). Robert Johnson (vocal and guitar). Production: Don Law. Recorded: San Antonio, Texas, 23 November 1936. US release: Vocalion 03475, April 1937.

Johnson, Robert. "Cross Road Blues" (Robert Johnson). Robert Johnson (vocals and guitar). Production: Don Law. Recorded: Gunter Hotel, San Antonio, Texas, 27 November 1936). US release: Vocalion, May 1937.

Johnson, Robert. *King of the Delta Blues Singers*. US release: Columbia CL 1654, 1961. UK release: Philips BBL.7539, 1962. A: "Crossroads Blues," "Terraplane Blues," "Come On in My Kitchen," "Walking Blues," "Last Fair Deal Gone Down," "32-20 Blues," "Kindhearted Woman Blues," and "If I Had Possession over Judgement Day." B: "Preaching Blues," "When You Got a Good Friend," "Rambling on My Mind," "Stones in My Passway," "Traveling Riverside Blues," "Milkcow's Calf Blues," "Me and the Devil Blues," and "Hellhound on My Trail."

Jones, Anna. "Sister Kate" (Armand Piron). Anna Jones (vocal) with Fats Waller (piano). Recorded: New York City, July 1923. US release: Paramount 12052, 1923.

Jones, Tom. "Chills and Fever" (Hank Thompson and Billy Gray). Tom Jones and the Squires with studio musicians. Production: Peter Sullivan. UK release: Decca F 11966, 28 August 1964.

Jones, Tom. "It's Not Unusual" (Gordon Mills and Les Reed). Tom Jones with studio musicians including Joe Moretti (guitar), Vic Flick (guitar), Andy White (drums), Stan Barrett (percussion), Kenny Salmon (organ), Eric Ford (bass), John Carter and Ken Lewis (backing vocals), and wind instruments. Production: Peter Sullivan with Les Reed (music director). Recorded: Decca Studios, London, 11 November 1964. UK release: Decca F 12062, 22 January 1965; charts 11 February 1965, *RR* #1. US release: Parrot 45-9737, *BB* #10 (May 1965).

Jones, Tom. "What's New Pussycat?" (Hal David and Burt Bacharach). Personnel as above. Production: Peter Sullivan with Charles Blackwell (music director). Recorded: CTS Studios, London. UK release: Decca F 12203, 6 August 1965; charts 12 August 1965, RR #11. US release: Parrot 45-9765, June 1965, *BB* #3 (July 1965).

Jones, Tom. "Thunderball" (John Barry and Don Black). Personnel as above. Production: Peter Sullivan with John Barry (music director). UK release: Decca F 12292, 26 November 1965; charts 13 January 1966, *RR* #35. US release: Parrot 45-9801, November 1965, *BB* #25 (January 1966).

Kaempfert, Bert. "Wunderland bei Nacht" ["Wonderland by Night"] (Klaus-Günter Neumann). Bert Kaempfert and His Orchestra with Charlie Tabor (trumpet). Production: Bert Kaempfert for Deutsche Grammophon. German release: as Polydor 24 086, 1959 on *Wonderland by Night*. UK release: Polydor NH 66639, November 1960. US release: Decca 31141, August 1960, *BB* #1 (January 1961).

Kidd, Johnny. "Please Don't Touch" (Fred Heath and Guy Robinson). Johnny Kidd and the Pirates: Fred Heath (vocals), Alan Caddy (guitar), John Gordon (bass), Tom Doherty (rhythm guitar), and Don Toy (drums) with Mike West and Tom Brown (backing vocals). Peter Sullivan (recording manager) and Malcolm Addey (engineer). Recorded: EMI Recording Studios, London, 18 April 1959. UK release: His Master's Voice POP 615 on 8 May 1959; charts 12 June 1959, *NME* #25.

Kidd, Johnny. "Shakin' All Over" (Fred Heath). Fred Heath (vocals), Joe Moretti (guitar), Alan Caddy (guitar), Brian Gregg (bass), and Clem Cattini (drums). Production as above. Recorded: EMI Recording Studios, London, 13 May 1960. UK release: His Master's Voice HMV POP 698, 10 June 1960; charts 16 June 1960, *RR* #1.

Kidd, Johnny. "I'll Never Get Over You" (Gordon Mills). Johnny Kidd and the Pirates: Johnny Kidd (vocal), Mick Green (guitar), Frank Farley (drums), and Johnny Spence (bass). Production as above. UK release: HMV POP 1173, 14 June 1963; charts 25 July 1963, *RR* #4.

Kidd, Johnny. "Hungry for Love" (Gordon Mills). Personnel and production as above. UK release: HMV POP 1228, 8 November 1963; charts 28 November 1963, *RR* #20.

Nat King Cole Trio. "(Get Your Kicks on) Route 66" (Bobby Troup). Nat Cole (vocal and piano), Oscar Moore (guitar), and Johnny Miller (bass). Recorded: Radio Recorders, Los Angeles, 1946. US release: Capitol 256, 22 April 1946.

The Kinks. "Long Tall Sally" (Robert Blackwell, Enotris Johnson, and Richard Penniman). Ray Davies (vocal and harmonica), Dave Davies (guitar and backing vocal), Peter Quaife (bass and backing vocal), and Bobby Graham (drums). Production: Shel Talmy with Ray Prickett (engineer). Recorded: Pye Studios, ATV House, London, 20 January 1964. UK release: Pye 7N 15611, 7 February 1964: *MM* #42. US release: Cameo C 308, 27 March 1964.

The Kinks. "You Still Want Me" (Ray Davies). Personnel and production as above. Recorded: Pye Studios, London, 20 January 1964. UK release: Pye 7N 15636, 17 April 1964.

The Kinks. "You Really Got Me" (Ray Davies). The Kinks with Bobby Graham (drums) and Arthur Greenslade (piano). Production: Shel Talmy with Bob Auger (engineer). Recorded: IBC, London, 12 July 1964. UK release: Pye 7N 15673, 4 August 1964; charts 13 August 1964, *RR* #1 (September 1964). US release: Cameo C-0306, 26 August 1964, *BB* #7 (November 1964).

The Kinks. *Kinks*. Personnel as above with Jimmy Page, Jon Lord, and Rasa Davies. Production as above. Recorded: Pye Studios and IBC Studios, London, January-August 1964. UK release: Pye NPL 18096, 2 October 1964. A: "Beautiful Delilah," "So Mystifying," "Just Can't Go to Sleep," "Long Tall Shorty," "I Took My Baby Home," "I'm a Lover Not a Fighter," and "You Really Got Me." B: "Cadillac," "Bald Headed Woman," "Revenge," "Too Much Monkey Business," "I've Been Driving on Bald Mountain," "Stop Your Sobbing," and "Got Love If You Want It."

The Kinks. *You Really Got Me*. Personnel and production as above. US release: Reprise R-6143, October 1964. A: "Beautiful Delilah," "So Mystifying," "Just Can't Go to Sleep," "Long Tall Shorty," and "You Really Got Me." B: "Cadillac," "Bald Headed Woman," "Too Much Monkey Business," "I've Been Driving on Bald Mountain," "Stop Your Sobbing," and "Got Love If You Want It."

The Kinks. "All Day and All of the Night" (Ray Davies). Ray Davies (guitar and lead vocal), Dave Davies (lead guitar and backing vocals), Peter Quaife (bass and backing vocals), Bobby Graham (drums), Mick Avory (tambourine), Perry Ford (piano), and John Goodson (backing vocals). Production as above. Recorded: Pye Studios #2, 23 September 1964. UK release: Pye 7N 15714, 23 October 1964; charts 29 October 1964, *RR* #2. US release: Reprise 0334, 9 December 1964, *BB* #7 (February 1965).

The Kinks. "Tired of Waiting for You" (Ray Davies). The Kinks with Bobby Graham (drums) and Rasa Davies (backing vocals). Production as above. Recorded: Pye Studios, London, 25 August 1964 and IBC Studios, London (guitar overdubs), 29 December 1964. UK release: Pye 7N 15759, 15 January 1965; charts 21 January 1965, *RR* #1 (February 1965). US release: Reprise 0347, *BB* #6 (April 1965).

The Kinks. "Everybody's Gonna Be Happy" (Ray Davies). Ray Davies (piano and vocal), Dave Davies (guitar and backing vocal), Peter Quaife (bass and backing vocal), Bobby Graham (drums), Mick Avory (hand claps), and Rasa Davies and others (backing vocals). Production: Shel Talmy. Recorded: Pye Studios, London, 22–23 December 1964. UK release: Pye 7N 15813, 19 March 1965; charts 25 March 1965, *RR* #20.

The Kinks. "Who'll Be the Next in Line" (Ray Davies). Personnel and production as above. Recorded: Pye Studios, London, 22–23 December 1964. US release: Reprise 0366, 21 July 1965, *BB* #34 (September 1965).

The Kinks. "Set Me Free" (Ray Davies). Personnel and production as above with Alan MacKenzie (engineer). Recorded: Pye Studios, London, 13–14 April 1965. UK release: Pye 7N 15854, 21 May 1965; charts 27 May 1965, *RR* #9. US release: Reprise 0379, 26 May 1965, *BB* #23 (July 1965).

The Kinks. "See My Friends" [also released as "See My Friend"] (Ray Davies). Ray Davies (12-string acoustic and vocal), Dave Davies (electric guitar), Peter Quaife (bass), and Mick Avory (drums). Production: Shel Talmy with Alan MacKenzie and Bob Auger. Recorded: Pye Studios, London, 13-14 April 1965. UK release: Pye 7N 15919, 30 July 1965; charts 5 August 1965, *RR* #10. US release: Reprise 0409, 29 September 1965.

The Kinks. "Till the End of the Day" (Ray Davies). The Kinks with Clem Cattini (drums), Nicky Hopkins (piano), Rasa Davies (backing vocal), and Mick Avory (tambourine). Production as above. Recorded: London, 3–4 November 1965. UK release: Pye 7N 15981, 19 November 1965; charts 2 December 1965, *RR* #8. US release: Reprise 0454, 2 March 1966, *BB* #50 (May 1966).

Kirby, Kathy. "Big Man" (Clive Westlake). Production: Charles Blackwell (producer and arranger) and Malcolm Lockyer (music director). UK release: Decca 45-F 11506, 26 October 1962.

Kirby, Kathy. "Dance On" (Valerie Murtagh, Elaine Murtagh, Ray Adams, and Marcel Stellman). Kathy Kirby with studio orchestra. Production: Peter Sullivan. Recorded: EMI Recording Studios, London. UK release: Decca F 11682, 21 June 1963; charts 15 August 1963, *RR* #11.

Kirby, Kathy. "Secret Love" (Sammy Fain and Paul Francis Webster). Production: Peter Sullivan with Charles Blackwell (music director). UK release: Decca F 11759, October 1963; charts 7 November 1963, *RR* #4.

Kirby, Kathy. "You're the One" ["La Malagueña"/"Malagueña Salerosa"] (Elpidio Ramirez [Alex Quiroz Buelvas] and Marcel Stellman). Production: as above. UK release: Decca F 11892, 1 May 1964.

Kramer, Billy J. "Do You Want to Know a Secret" (John Lennon and Paul McCartney). Billy J. Kramer (voice) with the Dakotas: Mike Maxfield (lead guitar), Ray Jones (bass guitar), Tony Mansfield (drums), and Robin MacDonald (guitar). Production: George Martin. Recorded: EMI Recording Studios, March 1963. UK release: Parlophone 5023 on 26 April 1963; charts 2 May 1963, *RR* #2. US release: Liberty 55586, June 1963.

Kramer, Billy J. "Bad to Me" (John Lennon and Paul McCartney). Personnel and production as above. UK release: Parlophone 5049, 26 July 1963; charts 1 August 1963, *RR* #1. Initial US release: Liberty 55626, September

1963. US rerelease: B-side to "Little Children" as Imperial 66027, May 1964 (charts 30 May 1964), *BB* #9 (June–July 1964).

Kramer, Billy J. "I'll Keep You Satisfied" (John Lennon and Paul McCartney). Personnel and production as above. UK release: Parlophone R 5073, 1 November 1963; charts 7 November 1963, *RR* #4. US release: Liberty 55643, November 1963; US rerelease: Imperial 66048, July 1964; charts 25 July 1964, *BB* #30 (August 1964).

Kramer, Billy J. "Little Children" (Mort Shuman and John Leslie McFarland). Personnel and production as above. UK release: Parlophone 5105, 21 February 1964; charts 23 July 1964, *RR* #1; *NME* #1 (20 March). US release: Liberty 55687, March 1964; re-issued as Imperial Records 66027 [Liberty Records purchased Imperial Records], April 1964; charts 18 April 1964, *BB* #7 (June 1964).

Kramer, Billy J. "From a Window" (John Lennon and Paul McCartney). Personnel and production as above. UK release: Parlophone 5156, 17 July 1964; charts 23 July 1964, *RR* #10. US release: Imperial 66051, August 1964; charts 22 August 1964, *BB* #23 (October 1964).

Kramer, Billy J. "Trains and Boats and Planes" (Burt Bacharach and Hal David). Personnel and production as above. Release: Parlophone R 5285, 14 May 1965; charts 20 May 1965, *RR* #12. US release: Imperial 66115, June 1965; charts 26 June 1965, *BB* #47 (July 1965).

Ladd's Black Aces. "Sister Kate" (Armand Piron) [78 rpm]. Jimmy Lytell (clarinet), Frank Signorelli (piano), Phil Napoleon (trumpet), Miff Mole (trombone), and Jack Roth (drums). Recorded: New York, 21 August 1921. US release: Gennett 49380A, 1922.

Laine, Cleo. "Honeysuckle Rose" (Thomas Waller and Andy Razaf). Personnel: the Johnny Dankworth Seven with vocal by Cleo Laine. UK release: Parlophone: MSP6026, May 1953.

Laine, Cleo. "You'll Answer to Me" (Sherman Edwards and Hal David). Production: Johnny Gregory (music director). UK release: Fontana H 326, July 1961; charts 14 September 1961, *RR* #5.

Laine, Frankie. "To Be Worthy of You" (Walter Gross and Raymond Klages). Frankie Laine with Paul Weston and His Orchestra and Carl Fischer (piano). Recorded: 10 September 1951. US release: Columbia D.B. 3034, December 1951.

Lambert, Hendricks, and Bavan. *At Newport '63*. Performed by Dave Lambert, Jon Hendricks, and Yolande Bavan with Coleman Hawkins (tenor sax), Clark Terry (trumpet), Gildo Mahones (piano), George Tucker (bass), and Jimmie Smith (drums). Production: George Avakian with Mickey Crofford (engineer). US release: RCA Victor, 16 November 1963. A: "One

O'clock Jump," "Watermelon Man," "Sack o' Woe," and "Deedle-le Deedle-lum." B: "Gimmie That Wine," "Yeh-Yeh!," "Walkin'," and "Cloudburst."

The Lana Sisters. "Mister Dee-Jay" (Buddy Kaye and Leon Carr). Riss Chantelle [Iris Long], Lynne Abrams, and Shan [Mary] O'Brien with studio musicians. Production: Jack Baverstock with Johnny Gregory (arranger). UK release: Fontana H 190, April 1959.

The Lana Sisters with Al Saxon. "(Seven Little Girls) Sitting in the Back Seat" (Lee Pockriss and Robert Hilliard). The Lana Sisters with Al Saxon and studio musicians. Production: Jack Baverstock with John Gregory (arranger). UK release: Fontana H 221, October 1959.

Lance, Major. "Um, Um, Um, Um, Um, Um" (Curtis Mayfield). Major Lance (vocal) with studio musicians. Production: Carl Davis with J. Pate (arranger). US release: OKeh 4-7187, 13 December 1964; charts 4 January 1964: *BB* #5 (February 1964).

Ledbetter, Huddie. "Rock Island Line" (traditional). Huddie Ledbetter (vocals and guitar). Moses Ashe (producer). Recorded: New York City, January 1942. US release: Folkways Records FA 2014, 1953.

Lee, Brenda. "Sweet Nothin's" (Ronnie Self). Production: Owen Bradley. Recorded: Nashville, 13 August 1959. US release: Decca 9-30967, 28 September 1959; *BB* #4. UK release (as "Sweet Nuthin's"): Brunswick 05819, January 1960; charts 17 March and 7 April 1960, *RR* #4 (1960).

Lee, Brenda. "I'm Sorry" (Dub Allbritten and Ronnie Self). Personnel and production as above. Recorded: Nashville, 28 March 1960. US release: Decca 9-31093, 16 May 1960; *BB* #1. UK release: Brunswick 05833, 24 June 1960; charts 30 June 1960, *RR* #12.

Leitch, Donovan. See Donovan.

Lewis, Jerry Lee. "Whole Lot of Shakin' Going On" (David Williams and James Hall). Jerry Lee Lewis (piano and vocals) with J. M. Van Eaton (drums) and others. Production: Sam Phillips with Jack Clement (recording engineer). Recorded: Sun Record Company, Memphis, Tennessee. US release: Sun 267 in April 1957; charts 24 June 1957, *BB* #3 (September 1957).

Leyton, John. "Tell Laura I Love Her" (J. Barry and B. Raleigh). John Leyton and studio musicians. Production: Joe Meek. Recorded: RGM Sound, London. UK release: Top Rank JAR 426 in August 1960. A: "Goodbye to Teenage Love" (R. Wakey and B. Evans).

Leyton, John. "The Girl on the Floor Above" (Len Praverman). Johnny Leyton with the Charles Blackwell Orchestra and Chorus. Production: Joe Meek. Recorded: RGM Sound, London. UK release: HMV POP 798 on 14 October 1960.

Leyton, John. "Johnny Remember Me" (Geoffrey Goddard). John Leyton with the Outlaws, including Bobby Graham (drums), Billy Kuy (guitar), Reg

Hawkins (guitar), Chas Hodges (bass), and Charles Blackwell (piano) with Lissa Grey (backing vocals). Production: Joe Meek with Charles Blackwell (music director). Recorded: RGM Sound, London. UK release: Top Rank RAR 577 in July 1961; charts 3 August 1961, *RR* #1.

Leyton, John. "Wild Wind" (Geoffrey Goddard). Personnel and production as above. Recorded: RGM Sound, London. UK release: Top Rank JAR 585, September 1961; charts 5 October 1961, *RR* #2.

Little Richard [Penniman]. "Long Tall Sally" (Enotris Johnson, Robert Blackwell, and Richard Penniman). Little Richard (vocal and piano) with Edgar Blanchard (guitar), Frank Fields (bass), Lee Allen (tenor sax), Alvin Tyler (baritone sax), and Earl Palmer (drums). Production: Robert "Bumps" Blackwell. Recorded: J&M Studios, New Orleans, 10 February 1956. US release: Specialty SP-572, March 1956; charts 7 April 1956, *BB* #13 (May 1956). UK release: London HLO 8366, January 1957; charts 8 February 1957, *NME* #3.

Little Richard [Penniman]. "Lucille" (Richard Penniman and Albert Collins). Personnel and production as above. US release: Specialty 598, February 1957; charts 23 March 1957, *BB* #27 (April 1957). UK release: London HLO 8446, June 1957; charts 28 June 1957, *NME* #10.

Lord Rockingham's XI. "Fried Onions" (Harry Robertson). Lord Rockingham's XI: Harry Robinson (director), Benny Green (baritone saxophone), Cherry Wainer (organ), Don Storer (drums), Reg Weller (percussion), Red Price (tenor sax), Rex Morris (tenor sax), Cyril Reubens (baritone sax), Ronnie Black (double bass), Bernie Taylor (guitar), and Eric Ford (guitar). Production: Jack Good with Harry Robinson (music director). UK release: Decca F 11024, May 1958.

Lord Rockingham's XI. "Hoots Mon" (based on "A Hundred Pipers"). Production: as above. UK release: Decca 45-F 11059, September 1958; charts 24 October 1958, *NME* #1.

Loudermilk, John D. "Tobacco Road" (John D. Loudermilk). John D. Loudermilk (guitar and vocal) with electric guitar, bass, and drums. US release: Columbia 4-41562, 18 January 1960.

Loudermilk, John D. *Twelve Sides of John D. Loudermilk*. US release: RCA Victor LPM-2539, 1962. A: "All of This for Sally," "Angela Jones," "Big Daddy," "The Bully on the Beach," "He's Just a Scientist (That's All)," and "Rhythm and Bluesy." B: "Road Hog," "The Little Bird," "Tobacco Road," "Everybody Knows," "Google Eye," and "Oh How Sad."

Lulu and the Luvvers. "Shout" (O'Kelly Isley, Rudolph Isley, and Ronald Isley). Studio with session musicians including Jim Sullivan (guitar), Vic Flick (guitar) Clem Cattini (drums), the Breakaways (Margot Quantrell, Vicki Haseman, and Jean Hawker), and Earl Guest (piano). Production: Peter

Sullivan with Earl Guest (music director). Recorded: IBC Studios, London. UK release: Decca F 11884, 17 April 1964; charts 14 May 1964, *RR* #7.

Lulu. "Here Comes the Night" (Bert Berns). Personnel as above. Production: Bern Berns with Mike Leander (music director). UK release: Decca F 12017, 6 November 1964.

Lulu. "Leave a Little Love" (Les Reed and Robin Conrad [Peter Callander]). Production: Peter Sullivan with Mike Leander (music director). UK release: Decca F 12169, 28 May 1965; charts 17 June 1965, *RR* #8. US release: Parrot 45-9778, July 1965.

Lulu. "Try to Understand" (Pamela Sawyer and Lori Burton). Personnel and production as above. UK release: Decca F 12214, 20 August 1965; charts 2 September 1965, *RR* #25.

Lynn, Vera. "We'll Meet Again" (Ross Parker and Hughie Charles). Personnel: Vera Lynn with Arthur Young (Novachord). Production: Norman Keen. Recorded: Decca Records, 29 September 1939. UK release: Decca F.7268, 1939.

Lynn, Vera. "(There'll Be Bluebirds Over) The White Cliffs of Dover" (Walter Kent and Nat Burton). Personnel: Vera Lynn accompanied by Montovani and His Orchestra). Production: Norman Keen. UK release: Decca F.8110, 1942.

Lyttelton, Humphrey. "Bad Penny Blues" (Humphrey Lyttelton). Humphrey Lyttelton and His Band: Humphrey Lyttelton (trumpet), John Parker (piano), Jim Bray (bass), and Stan Greig (drums). Denis Preston (recording manager) with Joe Meek (engineer). Recorded: IBC Studios, London, 20 April 1956. UK release: Parlophone ER 4148 in 1956; charts 13 July 1956, *NME* #19.

Manfred Mann. "Why Should We Not" (Mann). Paul Jones (lead vocal), Manfred Mann (keyboard), Mike Hugg (drums), Mike Vickers (saxophone), and Dave Richmond (bass). Production: John Burgess with Norman Smith (engineer). Recorded: EMI Recording Studios, London. UK release: HMV POP 1189, 26 July 1963.

Manfred Mann. "Cock-a-Hoop" (Paul Jones). Paul Jones (lead vocal), Manfred Mann (keyboard), Mike Hugg (drums), Mike Vickers (guitar), and Dave Richmond (bass). Production as above. UK release: HMV POP 1225, 25 October 1963; charts 23 January 1964, *RR* #5.

Manfred Mann. "5-4-3-2-1" (Paul Jones, Mike Hugg, and Manfred Mann). Manfred Mann with Paul Jones (lead vocal and harmonica), Manfred Mann (keyboard), Mike Hugg (drums), Mike Vickers (guitar), and Tom McGuinness (bass). Production as above. UK release: HMV POP 1252, 10 January 1964; charts 23 January 1964, *RR* #5.

Manfred Mann. "Hubble Bubble (Toil and Trouble)" (Mike Hugg, Paul Jones, Manfred Mann, Tom McGuiness, and Mike Vickers). Personnel and production as above. UK release: HMV POP 1282, 10 April 1964; charts 16 April 1964, *RR* #11.

Manfred Mann. "Do Wah Diddy Diddy" (Jeff Barry and Ellie Greenwich). Manfred Mann with Paul Jones (lead vocal and maracas), Manfred Mann (keyboard), Mike Hugg (drums and timpani), Mike Vickers (guitar), and Tom McGuinness (bass). Production as above. Recorded: EMI Recording Studios, London, 11 June 1964. UK release: HMV POP 1320, 10 July 1964; charts 16 July 1964, *RR* #1 (August 1964). US release: Ascot AS 2157, August 1964; charts 5 September 1964; *BB* #1 (October 1964).

Manfred Mann. "Sha-La-La" (Robert Taylor and Robert Moseley). Personnel and production as above. Recorded: EMI Recording Studios, London, 22–23 September 1964. Release: HMV POP 1346, 9 October 1964; charts 15 October 1964, *RR* #3. US release: Ascot AS 2165, November 1964; charts 14 November 1964, *BB* #12 (January 1965).

Marsden, Beryl. "I Know (You Don't Love Me No More)" (Barbara George). Production: Peter Sullivan with Mike Leander (music director). UK release: Decca F.11707, August 1963. B: "I Only Care about You" (Johnny Powell).

Marsden, Beryl. "Who You Gonna Hurt?" (Joy Byers). Production: Ivor Raymond (arranger and conductor). UK release: Columbia DB 7718, 1965.

Martha and the Vandellas. "Dancing in the Street" (Marvin Gaye, William Stevenson, and Joe Hunter). Martha Reeves (vocal) with Lois Ashford, Betty Kelly, Mickiey Stevenson, and Ivy Jo Hunter (backing vocals) and the Funk Brothers, including Marvin Gaye (drums), James Jamerson (bass), Jack Ashford (percussion), Joe Hunter (percussion), Henry Cosby (sax), Thomas Bowles (sax), Russ Conway (trumpet), Herbert Williams (trumpet), Paul Riser (trombone), George Bohannon (trombone), Robert White (guitar), Eddie Willis (guitar), and Joe Messina (guitar). Production: William Stevenson. Recorded: Hitsville U.S.A., Detroit, 19 June 1964. US release: Gordy F-7033, 31 July 1964; charts 22 August 1964, *BB* #2 (October 1964). UK release: Stateside SS 345, 9 October 1964; charts 29 October 1964, *RR* #28.

Martha and the Vandellas "Nowhere to Run" (Brian Holland, Lamont Dozier, and Eddie Holland). Martha and the Vandellas (as above) and the Funk Brothers including Benny Benjamin (drums), James Jamerson (bass), Earl Van Dyke (piano), Jack Ashford (percussion), Joe Hunter (percussion), Robert White (guitar), and Eddie Willis (guitar). Production: Lamont Dozier and Brian Holland. Recorded: Hitsville U.S.A., 21 October 1964.

US release: Gordy G 7039m 10 February 1965, *BB* #8 (April 1965). UK release: Tamla Motown TMG 502; charts 1 April 1965, *RR* #26.
Maurice and the Zodiacs. "Stay" (Maurice Williams). Maurice Williams, Henry Gaston, Charles Thomas, Albert Hill (bass), Little Willie Morrow (drums), and Wiley Bennett (piano). Production: Homer Fesperman. US release: Herald H-552, September 1960; charts 3 October 1960; *BB* #1 (November 1960). UK release: Top Rank JAR 526, December 1960; charts 5 January 1961, *RR* #14.
Chas McDevitt Skiffle Group Featuring Nancy Whiskey. "Freight Train" (Elizabeth Cotten). Nancy Whiskey (lead vocal and guitar), Mas McDevitt (guitar, backing vocal, and whistling), John Paul (bass), Dennis Carter (guitar and backing vocal), Marc Sharratt (washboard), and Jimmie MacGregor (guitar and backing vocals). Production: Jack Baverstock. Recorded: Levy's Sound Studios, New Bond Street, London. UK release: Oriole 1352, December 1956; charts 12 April 1957, *NME* #5. US release: Chic 1008, n.d., *BB* #13 (June 1957).
McShann, Jay. "Confessin' the Blues" (Walter Brown and Jay McShann) [78 rpm]. Walter Brown (vocal) Jay McShann (piano), Gene Ramey (bass), and Gus Johnson (drums). Recorded: Dallas, Texas, 30 April 1941. US release: Decca 8559, June 1941.
Millie. "Don't You Know" (Tony Thomas and Millie Small). Millie Small (vocal) with studio musicians. Production: B.P.R. Productions (Chris Blackwell) with Harry Robinson (music director). Recorded: Olympic Studios, London. UK release: Fontana TF 425, 30 November 1963.
Millie. "Don't You Know" "My Boy Lollipop" (Robert Spencer and Johnny Roberts). Millie Small with Ernest Ranglin (guitar), Pete Peterson (trumpet), Pete Hogman (harmonica), Mike Wells (drums), and unidentified saxophones. Production: Chris Blackwell with Ernest Ranglin (arranger and music director) and Graeme Goodall (engineer). Recorded: Olympic Studios, London. UK release: Fontana TF 449, February 1964; charts 12 March 1964, *RR* #2 and *NME* #2. US release: Smash S-1893, April 1964, *BB* #2 (July 1964).
Millie. "Don't You Know" "Sweet William" (Philip Springer and Buddy Kaye). Millie Small (vocal) with Ernest Ranglin (guitar) and an unidentified studio band. Production as above. UK release: Fontana TF 479, June 1964; charts 25 June 1964, *RR* #30. US release: Smash S-1920, July 1964, *BB* #40 (September 1964).
Mitchell, Guy. "Singing the Blues" (Melvin Endsley). Guy Mitchell with Ray Conniff and His Orchestra. Production: Mitch Miller. Recorded: Columbia 30th Street Studio, New York City. US release: Columbia 4-40769, 1 October

1956; *BB* #1 (December 1956–February 1957). UK release: Philips JK 1001, December 1956; charts 7 December 1956, *NME* #1 (January 1957).

The Moody Blues. "Steal Your Heart Away" (Bobby Parker). Denny Laine (vocal and guitar), Mike Pinder (piano), Ray Thomas (percussion and vocal), Clint Warwick (bass), and Graeme Edge (drums). Production: Alex Murray. Recorded: Olympic Sound Studios, London, 25 July 1964. UK release: Decca F 11971, 4 September 1964. B: "Lose Your Money (But Don't Lose Your Mind)" [based on a recording by Sonny Terry and Brownie McGhee] (Denny Laine and Mike Pinder).

The Moody Blues. "Go Now!" (Milton Bennett and Larry Banks). Personnel and production as above with Phil Woods (recording engineer). Recorded: Marquee Club (studio), London, September 1964. UK release: Decca F 12022, 13 November 1964; charts 10 December 1964, *RR* #1 (January 1965). US release: London 45-LON 9726, December 1964; charts 20 February 1965; *BB* #10 (April 1965).

The Moody Blues. "I Don't Want to Go On without You" (Bert Berns and Jerry Wexler). Personnel as above. Production by AM/PW. UK release: Decca F 12095, 26 February 1965; charts 4 March 1965, *RR* #33.

The Moody Blues. "From the Bottom of My Heart" (Mike Pinder and Denny Laine). Personnel as above. Production: Denny Cordell with Derek Varnals (engineer). Release: Decca 12166, 28 May 1965; charts 10 June 1965, *RR* #22. US release: London 45-LON 9764, May 1965.

The Moody Blues. *The Magnificent Moodies*. A: "I'll Go Crazy," "And My Baby's Gone," "Go Now," "It's Easy Child," "Can't Nobody Love You," and "I've Got a Dream." B: "Let Me Go," "I Don't Want to Go On without You," "True Story," "It's Ain't Necessarily So," "Bye Bye Bird," and "From the Bottom of My Heart." UK release: Decca LK 4711, 28 July 1965.

The Moody Blues. "Everyday" (Denny Laine and Mike Pinder). Personnel and production as above. UK release: Decca F 12266, October 1965; charts 18 November 1965, *RR* #44. US release: "Ev'ry Day," London 45-LON-9799, November 1965.

Muddy Waters. "Rollin' Stone" (McKinley Morganfield). Muddy Waters (vocals and guitar). Production: Leonard Chess and Phil Chess. Recorded: Chess Studios, Chicago, February 1950. US release: Chess 1426, 1950.

Muddy Waters. "I'm Your Hoochie Cooche Man" (Willie Dixon). Muddy Waters (vocal and guitar), Jimmy Rogers (guitar), Little Walter (harmonica), Otis Spann (piano), Willie Dixon (bass), and Elgin Evans (drums). Production: Leonard Chess and Phil Chess. Recorded: Chess Records, 7 January 1954. US release: Chess 1560, 1954.

Muddy Waters. "I Want to Be Loved" (Willie Dixon). Muddy Waters (vocals), Jimmy Rogers and Otis Spann (guitars), Little Walter (harmonica), Willie

Dixon (bass), and Fed Below (drums). US release: Chess 1596, April 1955.

Muddy Waters. *The Best of Muddy Waters*. Muddy Waters (vocals and guitar), Ernest Crawford (bass), Willie Dixon (bass), Little Walter (harmonica), Walter Horton (harmonica), Jimmy Rogers (guitar), Otis Spann piano), Fred Below (drums), Elgin Evans (washboard), and Lenard Chess (bass drum). Production: Leonard and Phil Chess. Recorded: Chess Studios, Chicago. US release: Chess LP 1427, April 1958. A: "I Just Want to Make Love to You," "Long Distance Call," "Louisiana Blues," "Honey Bee," "Rollin' Stone," and "I'm Ready." B: "Hoochie Coochie," "She Moves Me," "I Want You to Love Me," "Standing around Crying," "Still a Fool," and "I Can't Be Satisfied."

My Fair Lady (Frederick Loewe and Alan Jay Lerner). Personnel: Rex Harrison, Julie Andrews, and Stanley Holloway with cast and orchestra. Production Goddard Lieberson with Franz Allers (music director), Trude Rittman (arranger), and Phil Lang and Robert Russell Bennett (orchestrators). US release: Columbia OL 5090, 2 April 1956; *BB* #1 (1956). UK release: Philips RBL 1000 and B 07245 L, 1958.

The Nashville Teens. "Tobacco Road" (John D. Loudermilk). Arthur Sharp (vocal), Ray Phillips (vocal), John Hawken (piano), John Allen (guitar), Pete Shannon (bass), and Barry Jenkins (drums). Production: Mickie Most. Recorded: De Lane Lea Sound Studios, London. Released Decca F 11930, 26 June 1964; charts 9 July 1964, *RR* #6. US release: London 45-9689, August 1964, *BB* #14 (November 1964).

The Nashville Teens. "Google Eye" (John D. Loudermilk). Personnel and production as above. UK release: Decca F 12000, 9 October 1964; charts 22 October 1964, *RR* #10. US release: London 45-9712, November 1964.

The Nashville Teens. "Parchman Farm" (Mose Allison). Personnel and production as above. UK release on *The Nashville Teens* [EP] as Decca DFE 8600, November 1964. US release: London 45-9736, February 1965.

The Nashville Teens. "Find My Way Back Home" (Dennis Lambert and Lou Courtney [Louis Pegues]). Personnel as above. Production: Dennis Lambert and Lou Courtney. Recorded: New York, January 1964. UK release: Decca F 12089, 26 February 1965; charts 4 March 1965, *RR* #34. US release: London 45-9736, February 1965, *BB* #98 (March 1965).

The Nashville Teens. "This Little Bird" (John Loudermilk). Personnel as above. Production: Andrew Loog Oldham for Andesound. UK release: Decca F 12143, 30 April 1965; charts 20 May 1965, RR #38. US release: MGM K 13357, 1965.

Orbison, Roy. "Only the Lonely (Know the Way I Feel)" (Roy Orbison and Joe Melson). Roy Orbison (vocal) with Harold Bradley (guitar), Hank Garland (guitar), Bob Moore (bass), Floyd Cramer (piano), and Buddy Harman (drums). Production: Fred Foster. US release: Monument 45-421, May 1960, *BB* #2 (July 1960). UK release: London HLU 9149, June 1960; charts 28 July 1960, *RR* #1.

Orbison, Roy. "Candy Man" (Beverly Ross and Fred Neil). Roy Orbison (vocal and harmonica) with Boudleaux Bryant (guitar), Harold Bradley (guitar), Scotty Moore (guitar), Bob Moore (bass), Floyd Cramer (piano), Buddy Harman (drums), and female chorus. Production: Fred Foster. US release: Monument 447, July 1961, *BB* #25 (November 1961). UK release: London HLU 9405, September 1961. A: "Crying."

Orbison, Roy. "Oh, Pretty Woman" (Roy Orbison and Bill Dees). Roy Orbison and the Candy Men: Roy Orbison (vocal and guitar), Billy Sanford (guitar), Jerry Kennedy guitar), Wayne Moss (guitar), Floyd Cramer (piano), Henry Strezelecki (bass), Boots Randolph (saxophone), Charlie McCoy (saxophone), Buddy Harman (drums), and Paul Garrison (percussion). Production: Fred Foster with Bill Porter (engineer). Recorded: Nashville, 1 August 1964. US release: Monument 45-851, 28 August 1964; *BB* #1 (September 1964). UK release: London HLU 9919, 4 September 1964; charts 10 September 1964, *RR* #1 (November 1964).

The Orlons. "Don't Throw Your Love Away" (Bill Jackson and Jim Wisner). Stephen Caldwell, Marlena Davis, Rosetta Hightower, and Shirley Brickley (vocals) with studio musicians. Production: Dave Appell with Bill Jackson and Jim Wisner (arrangers). US release: Cameo C 287, November 1963. UK release: Cameo-Parkway C 287, February 1964.

Page, Patti. "You'll Answer to Me" (Sherman Edwards and Hal David). Patti Page with the Mike Stewart Singers and studio orchestra. Production: Hugo Winterhalter (arranger and conductor). US release: Mercury 71823, May 1961.

Parker, Bobby. 1961. "Watch Your Step" (Bobby Parker). Bobby Parker (vocal and guitar) with Thomas Tribble (drums) and others. Recorded: Edgewood Studio, Washington, DC. US release: V-Tone 223, July 1961, *BB* #51 (July 1961). UK release: London HLU 9393, July 1961. B: "Steal Your Heart Away" (Bobby Parker).

Perkins, Carl. "Glad All Over" (Aaron Schroeder, Sid Tepper, and Roy Bennett). Carl Perkins (guitar and vocal), Jay Perkins (rhythm guitar), Clayton Perkins (bass), and W. W. Holland (drums). Production: Sam Phillips. Recorded: Sun Records, Memphis, Tennessee. US release: Sun 287, 31 December 1957. UK release: London HLS 8527, December 1957.

Peter and Gordon. "A World without Love" (John Lennon and Paul McCartney). Peter Asher (vocal and guitar), Gordon Waller (vocal), with session musicians including Vic Flick (electric 12-string guitar), Harold Smart (organ),

Allan Weighell and Ron Prentiss (bass), Andy White (drums), etc. Production: Norman Newell with Geoff Love (music director) and with Peter Bown and Malcolm Addey (engineers). Recorded: EMI Recording Studios, London, 21 January 1964. UK release: Columbia DB 7225, 22 February 1964, *RR* #1 charts 22 February 1964). US release: Capitol 5175, 27 April 1964, *BB* #1 (June 1964).

Peter and Gordon. "Nobody I Know" (John Lennon and Paul McCartney). Personnel and production as above. UK release: Columbia DB 7292, 29 May 1964; charts 4 June 1964, *RR* #10. US release: Capitol 5211, 15 June 1964, *BB* #12 (August 1964).

Peter and Gordon. "I Don't Want to See You Again" (John Lennon and Paul McCartney). Personnel and production as above. UK release: Columbia DB 7356, 11 September 1964. US release: Capitol 5372, 22 September 1964, *BB* #16 (November 1965).

Peter, Paul, and Mary. "Blowin' in the Wind" (Bob Dylan). Peter Yarrow (guitar and voice), Paul Stookey (guitar and voice), and Mary Travers (voice). Production: Albert Grossman. US release: Warner Brothers 5368, 18 June 1963; *BB* #2 (August 1963). UK release: Warner Brothers WB 104, 12 July 1963; charts 10 October 1963, *RR* #13.

Phillips, Phil, and the Twilights. "Sea of Love" (Phil Phillips and George Khoury). Production: Eddie Shuler. Recorded: Goldband Studio, Lake Charles, Louisiana, 1959. US release: Khoury's Records 711; Mercury Records 71465, 1959; *BB* #2 (August 1959).

Poole, Brian, and the Tremeloes. "Twist Little Sister" (Peter Oakman and John Beveridge). Brian Poole (vocals), Alan Blakely (rhythm guitar), Alan Howard (bass), Dave Munden (drums), and Rick West (lead guitar). Production: Mike Smith. Recorded: Decca, London. UK release: Decca F 11455, 20 April 1962.

Poole, Brian, and the Tremeloes. "Blue" (Ennio Favilla, Tony Renis, Arthur Altman, and Mogol (Giulio Rapetti). Personnel and production as above. UK release: Decca F 11515, 21 September 1962.

Poole, Brian, and the Tremeloes. "A Very Good Year for Girls" (Clint Ballard and Fred Tobias). Personnel and production as above. UK release: Decca F 11567, January 1963.

Poole, Brian, and the Tremeloes. "Keep on Dancing" (Brian Poole, Alan Blakely, and Mike Smith). Personnel and production as above. UK release: Decca F 11616, March 1963.

Poole, Brian, and the Tremeloes. "Twist and Shout" (Bert Russell and Phil Medley). Personnel and production as above. UK release: Decca F 11694, June 1963; charts 4 July 1963, *RR* #4.

Poole, Brian, and the Tremeloes. "Do You Love Me" (Barry Gordy, Jr.). Personnel and production as above. UK release: Decca F 11739, 6 September 1963; charts 12 September 1963, *RR* #1 (October 1963).

Poole, Brian, and the Tremeloes. "Candy Man" (Beverly Ross and Fred Neil). Personnel and production as above. UK release: Decca F 11823, January 1964; charts 30 January 1964, *RR* #6.

Presley, Elvis. "Heartbreak Hotel" (Mae Boren Axton, Thomas Durden, and Elvis Presley). Elvis Presley (vocal) with Scotty Moore (guitar), Chet Atkins (guitar), Bill Black (bass), Floyd Cramer (piano), and D. J. Fontana (drums). Production: Steve Sholes with Bob Farris (engineer). Recorded: RCA Studios, Nashville, 10 January 1956. US release: RCA Victor 47-6420, 27 January 1956, *BB* #1 (April–May–June 1956). UK release: HMV 7M 385, March 1956; charts 11 May 1956, *NME* #2.

Presley, Elvis. "My Baby Left Me" (Arthur Crudup). Elvis Presley (vocal and guitar) with Scotty Moore (guitar), Bill Black (bass), and D. J. Fontana (drums). Production: Steve Sholes. Recorded: RCA, Nashville, 14 April 1956. US release: RCA 47-6540, 4 May 1956. UK release: HMV 7M 424, July 1956. A: "I Want You, I Need You, I Love You."

Presley, Elvis. "All Shook Up" (Otis Blackwell and Elvis Presley). Elvis Presley with the Jordanaires (Gordon Stoker, Hoyt Hawkins, Neal Matthews, and Hugh Jarrett). Personnel and production as above. Recorded: Radio Recorders, Hollywood, California, 12 January 1957. US release: RCA Victor 47-6870, 22 March 1957; *BB* #1 (April–June 1957). UK release: His Master's Voice POP 359, 21 June 1957; charts 28 June 1957, *RR* #1, *NME* #1 (July–August 1957).

Presley, Elvis. "(Now and Then There's) A Fool Such as I" (Bill Trader). Elvis Presley with Hank Garland, Chet Atkins, and Elvis Presley (guitars), Bob Moore (bass), Floyd Cramer (piano), and D. J. Fontana and Buddy Harman (drums), with the Jordanaires. Recorded: RCA Studio B, Nashville, 10 June 1958. US release: RCA 47-7506, 10 March 1959. B: "I Need Your Love Tonight" (Sid Wayne and Bix Reichner). Personnel and production as above. Recorded: RCA Studios, Nashville, 10 June 1958.

Presley, Elvis. "Rock-a-Hula Baby" (Ben Weisman, Fred Wise, and Dolores Fuller). Personnel and production as above. Recorded: Radio Recorders, Los Angeles, 23 March 1961. US release: RCA Victor, 1 October 1961; *BB* #23. UK release: RCA 1270; charts 1 February 1962, *RR* #1.

Presley, Elvis. "Return to Sender" (Winfield Scott and Otis Blackwell). Elvis Presley with the Jordanaires and Barney Kessel and Tiny Timbrell (guitars), Ray Siegel (bass), Boots Randolph (sax), Hal Blaine (drums), and Bernie Mattinson (percussion). Production: Steve Sholes and Chet Atkins. Recorded:

Radio Recorders, Hollywood, California, 27 March 1962. US release: RCA Victor 47-8100, 5 September 1962. UK release: RCA 1320, 1962; charts 29 November 1962, *RR* #1 (December 1962).

Presley, Elvis. "(You're the) Devil in Disguise" (Bill Giant, Bernie Baum, and Florence Kaye). Elvis Presley with Scotty Moore and Grady Martin (guitars), Harold Bradley and Bob Moore (bass), Floyd Cramer (piano), D. J. Fontana and Buddy Harman), the Jordanaires with Millie Kirkham (backing vocals) and Boots Randolph (percussion). Production: Bill Porter (engineer). Recorded: RCA Studios, Nashville, 26 May 1963. US release: RCA Victor 47-8188, 18 June 1963; *BB* #3 (August 1963). UK release: RCA 1355, June 1963; charts 4 July 1963, *RR* #1 (August 1963).

Prieto, Antonio. "La Novia" (Joaquín Prieto). Antonio Prieto with the José Sabre Marroquín Orchestra. Spanish release: RCA 37-2056, 1961.

Radcliffe, Jimmy. "My Ship Is Coming In" (Joey Brooks). US release: Aurora 154, July 1965.

Ray, James. "If You Gotta Make a Fool of Somebody" (Rudy Clark). James Ray (vocals) accompanied by the Hutch Davie Orchestra. Production: Gerry Granahan with Hutch Davie (arranger). US release: Caprice CAP-110 in October 1961, *BB* #22 (January 1962). UK release: Pye 7N 25126 in February 1962.

The Rays. "Silhouettes" (Frank Slay, Jr., and Bob Crewe). Harold Miller, Walter Ford, David Jones, and Harry James with studio musicians. Production: Frank Slay, Jr., and Bob Crewe. Recorded: 1957. US release: XYZ X-102, August 1957: *BB* #3. UK release: London HLU 8505, November 1957.

Reed, Jimmy. "Big Boss Man" (Luther Dixon and Al Smith). Jimmy Reed (vocal, guitar, and harmonica) with Lee Baker (guitar), William Bates (guitar), Willie Dixon (bass), and Earl Phillips (drums). Production: Luther Dixon. Recorded: Vee Jay Records, Chicago, 29 March 1960. US release: Vee Jay VJ 800, 1961.

The Reflections. "Poor Man's Son" (Bob Mahilton, Joanne Bratton, Ronnie Savoy, and Steve Venet). Tony Micale (lead), Phil Castrodale (tenor), Dan Bennie (tenor), Ray Steinberg (baritone), and John Dean (bass). Production: Rob Recco and Steve Venet with Charlie Callelo. US release: Golden World GQ-20, February 1965. UK release: Stateside SS 406, 23 April 1965.

Reynolds, Jody. "Endless Sleep" (Jody Reynolds and Dolores Nance). Jody Reynolds (vocal) with Al Casey (guitar) and session musicians. Recorded: Gold Star Studios, Los Angeles, March 1958. US release: Demon Records FF-1507, March 1958. UK release: London HL 8658, June 1958; *MM* #19.

Richard, Cliff, and the Drifters. "Move It!" (Ian Samwell). Cliff Richard (vocals), Ernie Shear (lead guitar), Ian Samwell (rhythm guitar), Terry Smart (drums), and Frank Clark (bass). Norrie Paramor (recording manager) and Malcolm Addey (engineer). Recorded: EMI Recording Studios, London, 24 July 1958. UK release: Columbia DB 4178, 29 August 1958; charts 12 September 1958, *NME* #2. US release: Capitol F 4096, November 1958. B: "Schoolboy Crush" (Aaron Schroeder and Sharon Gilbert).

Richard, Cliff, and the Drifters. "Living Doll" (Lionel Bart). Cliff Richard with Hank Marvin (lead guitar), Bruce Welch (rhythm guitar), Jet Harris (bass), and Tony Meehan (drums). Production as above. Recorded: EMI Recording Studios, London, 28 April 1959. UK release: Columbia DB 4306 in July 1959; charts 10 July 1959, *NME* #1 (July 1959). US release: ABC-Paramount 45-10,042, August 1959.

Richard, Cliff, and the Shadows. "Travellin' Light" (Sid Tepper and Roy C. Bennett). Cliff Richard with Hank Marvin (lead guitar), Bruce Welch (rhythm guitar), Jet Harris (bass), and Tony Meehan (drums). Production: Norrie Paramor with Malcolm Addey (engineer). Recorded: EMI Recording Studios, London, 25 July 1959. UK release: Columbia DB 4351 in October 1959; charts 9 October 1959, *NME* #1. US release: ABC-Paramount 45-10066, November 1959.

Richard, Cliff, and the Shadows. "A Voice in the Wilderness" (Norrie Paramor and Bunny Lewis). Personnel and production as above. Recorded: EMI Recording Studios, London, 20 December 1959. UK release: Columbia DB 4398, 15 January 1960; charts 22 January 1960, RR#2.

Richard, Cliff, and the Shadows. "Please Don't Tease" (Bruce Welch and Peter Chester). Personnel and production as above. Recorded: EMI Recording Studios, London, 25 March 1960. UK release: Columbia DB 4479, 24 June 1960; 30 June 1960, *RR* #1 (July 1960). US release: ABC-Paramount 45-10136, August 1960.

Richard, Cliff, and the Shadows. "The Young Ones" (Sid Tepper and Roy C. Bennett). Personnel and production as above. Recorded: EMI Recording Studios, 11 August and 5 December 1961. UK release: Columbia DB 4761, 11 January 1962; charts 11 January 1962, *RR* #1 (January–February 1962).

Richard, Cliff, and the Shadows. "The Next Time" (Buddy Kaye and Philip Springer). Personnel and production as above. Recorded: EMI Recording Studios, 10 May and 19 November 1962. UK release: Columbia DB 4950, 30 November 1962; charts 6 December 1962, RR #1 (January 1963). B: "Bachelor Boy" (Cliff Richard and Bruce Welch). Personnel and production as above. Recorded: EMI Recording Studios, 16 November 1962.

Richard, Cliff, and the Shadows. *Summer Holiday.* Personnel and production as above with Grazina Frame, the Associated British Studio Orchestra

(Stanley Black, conductor), the Norrie Paramor Strings, and the Michael Sammes Singers. UK release: Columbia 33SX1472, 18 January 1963. A: "Seven Days to a Holiday," "Summer Holiday," "Let Us Take You for a Ride," "Les Girls," "Round and Round," "Foot Tapper," "Stranger in Town," and "Orlando's Mine." B: "Bachelor Boy," "A Swinging Affair," "Really Waltzing," "All at Once," "Dancing Shoes," "Yugoslav Wedding," "The Next Time," and "Big News."

Richard, Cliff, and the Shadows. "Summer Holiday" (Bruce Welch and Brian Bennett). Cliff Richard with Bruce Welch (rhythm guitar, backing vocal), Hank Marvin (lead guitar), Brian Bennett (drums), Brian Locking (bass), and the Norrie Paramor Strings. Production as above. Recorded: EMI Recording Studios, London, 9 May and 19 November 1962. UK release: Columbia DB 4977, 8 February 1963; charts 21 February 1963, *RR* #1 (March 1963).

Richard, Cliff, and the Shadows. "It's All in the Game" (Charles Dawes and Carl Sigman). Cliff Richard with studio orchestra. Production as above. Recorded: EMI Recording Studios, London. Release: Columbia DB 7089, August 1963; charts 22 August 1963, *RR* #2. US release: Epic 5-9633, 25 October 1963, *BB* #25 (February 1964).

Richard, Cliff, and the Shadows. "Don't Talk to Him" (Cliff Richard and Bruce Welch). Cliff Richard with Bruce Welch (rhythm guitar, backing vocal), Hank Marvin (lead guitar), Brian Bennett (drums), and John Rostill (bass). Production as above. Recorded: EMI Recording Studios, London, 11 October 1963. UK release: Columbia DB 7150, 1 November 1963; charts 7 November 1963, *RR* #2.

Richard, Cliff, and the Shadows. "I'm the Lonely One" (Gordon Mills). Cliff Richard with the Shadows. Production as above. UK release: Columbia DB 7203, 31 January 1964; charts 6 February 1964, *RR* #8.

The Righteous Brothers. "You've Lost That Lovin' Feelin'" (Phil Spector, Barry Mann, and Cynthia Weil). Bill Medley (vocal), Bobby Hatfield (vocal) with Los Angeles session musicians including Don Randi (piano), Tommy Tedesco (guitar), Carol Kaye (electric bass), Ray Pohlman (acoustic bass), Steve Doublas (sax), and Earl Palmer (drums). Production: Phil Spector with Gene Page (arranger) and Larry Levine (engineer). Recorded: Gold Star Studios, Los Angeles, October 1964. US release: Philles Records 124, November 1964, *BB* #1 (February 1965). UK release: London HLU 9943, January 1965; charts 14 January 1965, *RR* #1 (February 1965).

The Rockin' Berries. "I Didn't Mean to Hurt You" (Ellie Greenwich and Tony Powers). Clive Lea (vocal), Geoff Turton (lead vocal and guitar), Chuck Botfield (guitar), Roy Austin (bass), and Terry Bond (drums). Production:

John Schroeder. Release: Piccadilly 7N 35197, 28 August 1964; charts 1 October 1964, *RR* #43.

The Rockin' Berries. "He's in Town" (Gerry Goffin and Carole King). Personnel and production as above. Release: Piccadilly 7N 35203, 2 October 1964; charts 15 October 1964, *RR* #3. US release: Reprise 0329, November 1964.

The Rockin' Berries. "What in the World's Come Over You" (Jim Wisner and Bill Jackson). Personnel and production as above. UK release: Piccadilly 7N 35217, 6 January 1965; charts 21 January 1965, *RR* #23. US release: Reprise 0355, March 1965.

The Rockin' Berries. "Poor Man's Son" (Bob Mahilton, Joanne Bratton, Ronnie Savoy, and Steve Venet). Personnel and production as above. Release: Piccadilly 7N 35236, 23 April 1965; charts 13 May 1965, *RR* #5. US release: Reprise 0377, May 1965.

Roe, Tommy. "Sheila" (Tommy Roe). Production: Felton Jarvis. US release: ABC-Paramount 45-10329 in August 1962. UK release: HMV POP 1060, 24 August 1962.

Rodgers, Jimmie (F.). "Honeycomb" (Robert Merrill). Jimmy Rodgers with Hugo Peretti and His Orchestra. Release: Roulette R-4015, July 1957, *BB* #1 (September–October 1957). UK release: Columbia DB 3986, August 1957.

Rogers, Julie. "The Wedding (La Novia)" (Joaquín Prieto and Fred Jay). Julie Rogers with Johnny Arthy and His Orchestra and Chorus. Production: Johnny Franz. UK release: Mercury MF 820, 3 July 1964. US release: Mercury 72332, October 1964, *BB* [Easy Listening] #1 (January 1965).

The Rolling Stones. "Come On" (Chuck Berry). Mick Jagger (vocals), Brian Jones (harmonica, vocals), Keith Richards (guitar, vocals), Bill Wyman (bass), and Charlie Watts (drums). Production: Andrew Loog Oldham for Impact Sound with Roger Savage (engineer). Recorded: Olympic Studios, London, 10 May 1963. UK release: Decca F 11675, 7 June 1963; charts 25 July 1963, *RR* #21.

The Rolling Stones. "Poison Ivy" (Jerry Leiber and Mike Stoller). Production: Andrew Oldham and Michael Barclay. Recorded: Decca Studios, London, 15 July 1963. Released on *The Rolling Stones* [EP] (see below).

The Rolling Stones. "I Wanna Be Your Man" (John Lennon and Paul McCartney). Mick Jagger (vocal), Brian Jones (slide guitar), Keith Richards (guitar), Bill Wyman (bass), and Charlie Watts (drums). Production: Andrew Oldham and Eric Easton. Recorded: De Lane Lea Studios, London, 7 October 1963. Release: Decca F 11764, 1 November 1963; charts 14 November 1963, *RR* #12.

The Rolling Stones. *The Rolling Stones* [EP]. Production: Andrew Loog Oldham for Impact Sound. Release: Decca DFE 8560, 10 January 1964.

A: "Bye Bye Johnny" and "Money." B: "You Better Move On" and "Poison Ivy."

The Rolling Stones. "Not Fade Away" (Norman Petty and Charles Hardin [Buddy Holly]). Mick Jagger (vocals), Brian Jones (harmonica), Keith Richards (guitars), Allan Clarke (maracas), Bill Wyman (bass), and Charlie Watts (drums) with Phil Spector (tambourine) and Gene Pitney, Graham Nash, and Tony Hicks (hand claps). Production: Andrew Loog Oldham with Bill Farley (engineer). Recorded: Regent Sound Studios, London, 28 January and 4 February 1964. UK release: Decca F 11485, 21 February 1964; charts 27 February 1964, *RR* #3. US release: London 45-LON 9657, 6 March 1964, *BB* #48 (July 1964).

The Rolling Stones. *The Rolling Stones*. Production: Andrew Oldham and Eric Easton with Bill Farley. UK release: Decca LK 4605, 17 April 1964. A: "Route 66," "I Just Wanna Make Love to You," "Honest I Do," "I Need You Baby," "Now I've Got a Witness (Like Uncle Gene and Uncle Phil)," and "Little by Little." B: "I'm a King Bee," "Carol," "Tell Me," "Can I Get a Witness," "You Can Make It If You Try," and "Walking the Dog."

The Rolling Stones. "Tell Me (You're Coming Back)" (Mick Jagger and Keith Richards). Personnel and production as above. US release: London 45-LON 9682, 12 June 1964, *BB* #24 (August 1964).

The Rolling Stones. "It's All Over Now" (Bobby Womack and Shirley Womack). Personnel as above. Production: Andrew Loog Oldham (Impact Sound) with Ron Malo (recording engineer). Recorded: Chess Studios, Chicago, 10 June 1964. Release: Decca F 11764 on 26 June 1964; charts 2 July 1964, *RR* #1 (July 1964). US release: 45-LON 9687, 24 July 1964, *BB* #26 (September 1964).

The Rolling Stones. "Time Is on My Side" (Jerry Ragovoy and Jim Norman). Personnel as above. Production: Andrew Loog Oldham for Impact Sound with Bill Farley (recording engineer). Recorded: Regent Sound and IBC, London, 24–26 June 1964. US release: London 45-LON 9708, 25 September 1964, *BB* #6 (December 1964).

The Rolling Stones. "Time Is on My Side" (Jerry Ragovoy and Jim Norman). Production: Andrew Loog Oldham with Ron Malo (recording engineer). Recorded: Chess Studios, Chicago, 10 June and 8 November 1964. UK release on *The Rolling Stones No. 2*, Decca LK 4661, 15 January 1965.

The Rolling Stones. "Little Red Rooster" (Willie Dixon). Personnel as above. Production: Impact Sound (Andrew Oldham). Recorded: Regent Sound, London, 2–3 September 1964. UK release: Decca F12014, 13 November 1964; charts 19 November 1964, *RR* #1 (December 1964); *NME* #1 (3 December).

The Rolling Stones. "Heart of Stone" (Keith Richards and Mick Jagger). The Rolling Stones with Ian Stewart (piano) and Jack Nitzsche (tambourine). Production: Andrew Oldham for Impact Sound with Dave Hassinger (engineer). Recorded: RCA Studios, Hollywood, 2 November 1964. US release: London 45 LON 9725, 19 December 1964, *BB* #19 (February 1965).

The Rolling Stones. *The Rolling Stones, No. 2*. Personnel as above. Produced for Impact Sound by Andrew Oldham with various personnel. UK release: Decca LK 4661, 15 January 1965. A: "Everybody Needs Somebody to Love," "Down Home Girl," "You Can't Catch Me," "Time Is on My Side," "What a Shame," and "Grown Up Wrong." B: "Down the Road a Piece," "Under the Boardwalk," "I Can't Be Satisfied," "Pain in My Heart," "Off the Hook," and "Susie Q."

The Rolling Stones. "The Last Time" (Mick Jagger and Keith Richards). Personnel as above with Jack Nitzsche (tambourine). Production as above. Recorded: De Lane Lea Studios, London, 11–12 January 1965 and RCA Studios, Hollywood, California, 17–18 January and 18 February 1965. UK release: Decca F 12104, 26 February 1965; charts 4 March 1965, *RR* #1 (March 1965). US release: London 45 LON 9741, 13 March 1965, *BB* #9 (May 1965). B: "Play with Fire" (Nanker Phelge). Mick Jagger (vocals and tambourine) and Keith Richards (acoustic guitar) with Phil Spector (guitar) and Jack Nitzsche (harpsichord). Production as above at RCA Studios, Hollywood, California, January–February 1965. *BB* #96 (May 1965).

The Rolling Stones. "(I Can't Get No) Satisfaction" (Mick Jagger and Keith Richards). Personnel and production as above with Ron Malo (engineer, Chicago). Recorded: Chess Studios, Chicago, 10–11 May 1965 and with Dave Hassinger (engineer), RCA Studios, Hollywood, California, 12 May 1965. UK release: Decca F 12220, 20 August 1965; charts 26 August 1965, *RR* #1 (September 1965). US release: London 45 LON 9766, 5 June 1965, *BB* #1 (July 1965).

The Rolling Stones. *Out of Our Heads*. [A different version of the album appeared in the US.] Mick Jagger (vocals and harmonica), Keith Richards (vocals and guitar), Brian Jones (guitar, harmonica, and keyboards), Jack Nitzsche (keyboards and percussion), Ian Stewart (keyboards), Bill Wyman and Phil Spector (bass) and Charlie Watts (drums). Production as above. Recorded: Chess Studios, May 1965; RCA Studios, Los Angeles, October–November 1964, January 1965, and May 1965; UK tour, March 1965. UK release: Decca LK 4733, 24 September 1965. A: "She Said Yeah," "Mercy, Mercy," "Hitch Hike," "That's How Strong My Love Is," "Good Times," and "Gotta Get Away." B: "Talkin' bout You," "Cry to Me," "Oh, Baby (We Got a

Good Thing Going)," "Heart of Stone," "The Under Assistant West Coast Promotion Man," and "I'm Free."
The Rolling Stones. "Get Off of My Cloud" (Mick Jagger and Keith Richards). Personnel and production as above. Recorded: RCA Studios, Hollywood 6–7 September 1965. UK release: Decca F 12263, 22 October 1965; charts 28 October 1965, *RR* #1 (November 1965). US release: London 45-9792, 24 September 1965, *BB* #1 (November 1965).
The Rooftop Singers. "Walk Right In" (Gus Cannon and Hosea Woods). Erik Darling (acoustic 12-string guitar), Bill Svanoe (acoustic 12-string guitar), and Lynne Taylor. Production: Erik Darling and Bill Svanoe. US release: Vanguard Records VRS-35017, November 1962, *BB* #1 (January 1963). UK release: Fontana TF 271700, 18 January 1963; charts 31 January 1963, *RR* #10.
Roy and Millie and the City Slickers. "We'll Meet" (Roy Panton). Roy Panton and Millie Small (vocals) with the City Slickers (including Roland Alphonso). Production: Roy Robinson. Recorded: Federal Recording Studios, Jamaica. Jamaican release: Carib-Dis-Co Records, 1962. UK release: Island WI 005, 1962.
Rydell, Bobby. "Forget Him" (Mark Anthony [Tony Hatch]). US release: Cameo C-1070-45, December 1963, *BB* #4 (January 1964). UK release: Cameo-Parkway C 108, April 1963; charts 23 May 1963, *RR* #13.
Sainte-Marrie, Buffy. *It's My Way*. US release: Vanguard VSD-79142, April 1964. A: "Now That the Buffalo's Gone," "The Old Man's Lament," "Anaias," "Mayoo Sto Hoon," "Cod'ine," "Cripple Creek," and "The Universal Soldier." B: "Babe in Arms," "He Lived Alone in Town," "You're Gonna Need Somebody on Your Bond," "The Incest Song," "Eyes of Amber," and "It's My Way."
Sainte-Marrie, Buffy. "The Universal Soldier" (Buffy Sainte-Marie). UK release: Fontana TF 614, September 1965.
Sakamoto, Kyu. "*Ue o Muite Arukō*" ["I Look Up as I Walk"] (Rokusuke Ei [lyrics] and Hachidai Nakamura [music]). Production unidentified. Japanese release: Toshiba JP-5083, 15 October 1961. US release (as "Sukiyaki"): as Capitol 4945, 25 March 1963, *BB* #1 (June 1963). UK release (as "Sukiyaki"): on HMV 1171, June 1963.
Santamaría, Mongo. "Yeh-Yeh!" (Rodgers Grant and Pat Patrick). Mongo Santamaría Orch with Mongo Santamaría (congas), Bobby Capers (saxophone), Marty Sheller (trumpet), Mauricio Smith (flute), Osvaldo Martinez (percussion), Pat Patrick (saxophone), Ray Lucas (drums), Rodgers Grant (piano), and Victor Venegas (bass). Production: Orrin Keepnews and Larry Maxwell with Ray Fowler (engineer) for Bill Grauer Productions, Inc. US release: Battle BF-45917, May 1963.

Sarne, Mike. "Come Outside" (Charles Blackwell). Personnel: Mike Sarne (vocals) with Wendy Richard (spoken responses) and the Charles Blackwell Orchestra. Production: Charles Blackwell (music direction). UK release: Parlophone R 4902, May 1962; charts 10 May 1962, *RR* #1 (June–July 1962).

Sarne, Mike, featuring Billie Davis. "Will I What" (Bill Bates, John Shakespear [John Carter], and Ken Hawker [Ken Lewis]). Personnel: Mike Sarne and Billie Davis with the Charles Blackwell Orchestra. Production: Charles Blackwell. UK release: Parlophone R 4932, August 1962; charts 30 August 1962, *RR* #18.

The Searchers. "Sweets for My Sweet" (Doc Pomus and Mort Shuman). Tony Jackson (bass and lead vocal), Mike Pender (guitar and backing vocal), John McNally (guitar and backing vocal), and Chris Curtis (drums and backing vocal). Production: Tony Hatch. Recorded: Pye, London. UK release: Pye 7N.15533, June 1963; charts 27 June 1963; *RR* #1 (August 1963); *NME* #1 (August 1963); *MM* #1 (charts 6 July 1963).

The Searchers. *Meet the Searchers*. Production: Tony Hatch. UK release: Pye NLP 18086, August 1963. A: "Sweets for My Sweet," "Alright," "Love Potion No. 9," "Farmer John," "Stand by Me," and "Money (That's What I Want)." B: "Da Doo Ron Ron," "Ain't Gonna Kiss Ya," "Since You Broke My Heart," "Tricky Dicky," "Where Have All the Flowers Gone," and "Twist and Shout."

The Searchers. *Ain't Gonna Kiss Ya* [EP]. UK release: Pye NEP 24177, 10 September 1963; *MM* #13 (charts 21 September 1963). A: "Ain't Gonna Kiss Ya" and "Love Potion No. 9"; B: "Alright" and "Farmer John."

The Searchers. *Sugar and Spice*. Personnel and production as above. UK release: Pye NPL 18089, 16 October 1963. A: "Sugar and Spice," "Don't You Know," "Some Other Guy," "One of These Days," "Listen to Me," and "Unhappy Girls." B: "Ain't That Just Like Me," "Oh My Love," "Saints and Searchers," "Cherry Stones," "All My Sorrows," and "Hungry for Love."

The Searchers. "Sugar and Spice" (Fred Nightingale). Personnel and production as above. UK release: Pye 7N.15566, 22 October 1963; charts 24 October 1963, *RR* #2; *NME* #3; *MM* #3 (charts 26 October 1963). US release: Liberty 556464, August 1963, *BB* #44 (June 1964).

The Searchers. *Sweets for My Sweet* [EP]. Personnel and production as above. UK release: Pye NEP 24183 in December 1963. A: "Sweets for My Sweet" and "It's All Been a Dream." B: "Since You Broke My Heart" and "Money."

The Searchers. "Needles and Pins" (Jack Nitzsche and Sonny Bono). Personnel and production as above. UK release: Pye 3 January 1964; charts 16 January 1964, *RR* #1 (February 1964), *NME* #1; *MM* #1 (charts 18 January 1964). US release: Kapp 577, February 1964, *BB* #13 (April 1964).

The Searchers. "Don't Throw Your Love Away" (Bill Jackson and Jim Wisner) Personnel and production as above. Release: Pye 7N 15630, April 1964; charts 16 April 1964, *RR* #1 (May 1964); *MM* #1 (charts 18 April 1964). US release: Kapp 593, May 1964, *BB* #16 (July 1964).

The Searchers. "Some Day We're Gonna Love Again" (Sharon McMahan). Personnel and production as above. UK release: Pye 7N. 5670, 7 July 1964; charts 16 July 1964, *RR* #11. US release: Kapp K-609, July 1964; charts 1 August 1964.

The Searchers. "When You Walk in the Room" (Jackie DeShannon). Mike Pender (guitar and vocal), Frank Allen (bass and vocal), John McNally (guitar and vocal), and Chris Curtis (drums and vocal). Production: Tony Hatch. UK release: Pye 7N 15694 on 11 September 1964; *RR* #3 (charts 17 September 1964); *MM* #5 (charts 19 September 1964). US release: Kapp K-618, September 1964, *BB* #35 (November 1964).

The Searchers. "What Have They Done to the Rain" (Malvina Reynolds). Personnel and production as above. UK release: Pye 7N 15739, November 1964, charts 3 December 1964, *RR* #13; *MM* #4 (charts 2 January 1965). US release: Kapp K-644, January 1965, *BB* #29 (February 1965).

The Searchers. "Love Potion Number Nine" (Jerry Leiber and Mike Stoller). Tony Jackson (bass and vocals), Mike Pender (guitar and vocals), John McNally (guitar and vocals), and Chris Curtis (drums and vocals). Production: Tony Hatch. US release: Kapp Winners Circle Series KJB 27, October 1964, *BB* #3 (January 1965). [Originally released on *Meet the Searchers*, August 1963.]

Seeger, Pete. *The Bitter and the Sweet*. Production: John Hammond. Recorded: The Bitter End, New York. US release: Columbia CL 1916, December 1962. A: "We Shall Overcome," "Living in the Country," "Mr. Tom Hughes's Town," "Where Have All the Flowers Gone," "Barbara Allen," and "Turn! Turn! Turn!" B: "Around the World of Old Joe Clark," "Windy Old Weather," "Ram of Darby," "Juanita," "Andorra," and "The False Knight upon the Road."

The Seekers. "I'll Never Find Another You" (Tom Springfield). Judy Durham (vocals), Athol Guy (vocals, bass), Keith Potger (vocals, 12-stringed guitar), and Bruce Woodley (vocals, guitar) with added percussion. Production: Tom Springfield and Eddie Jarrett. Recorded: EMI Recording Studios, London, 4 November 1964. UK release: Columbia DB 7431, 4 December 1964; charts 7 January 1965, *RR* #1 (February 1965). US release: Capitol 5383, 8 March 1965, *BB* #4 (May 1965).

The Seekers. "A World of Our Own" (Tom Springfield). Personnel as above. Production: F. X. B. Productions (Tom Springfield). UK release: Columbia

DB 7532, 9 April 1965; charts 15 April 1965, *RR* #3. US release: Capitol 5430, 24 May 1965, *BB* #19 (July 1965).

The Seekers. "Chilly Winds" (Keith Potger). Personnel and production as above. Release: Decca F 22167, 4 June 1965. US release: Marvel 1060, April 1965.

The Seekers. "The Carnival Is Over" (Tom Springfield). Personnel as above with orchestra. Production: Tom Springfield with Robert Richards (arranger). UK release: Columbia DB 7711, 15 October 1965; charts 28 October 1965, *RR* #1 (November–December 1965). US release: Capitol 5531, 26 October 1965.

The Shadows. "Feelin' Fine" (Ian Samwell). Bruce Welch (vocals and rhythm guitar), Hank Marvin (vocals and lead guitar), Jet Harris (vocals and bass guitar), and Tony Meehan (drums). Norrie Paramor (recording manager) with Malcolm Addey (engineer). Recorded: EMI Recording Studios, London. Release: Columbia DB 4263, February 1959. US release: by the Drifters, Capitol F 4220, June 1959. Withdrawn after protest by Atlantic Records over trademark of the name "The Drifters."

The Shadows. "Jet Black" (Jet Harris). Personnel and production as above. UK release: Columbia DB 4325, 26 June 1959. US release: by the Four Jets, B-side to "Driftin'," Capitol 4270, September 1959.

The Shadows. "Saturday Dance" (Pete Chester and Hank Marvin). Personnel and production as above. UK release: Columbia DB 4387, December 1959. US release: B-side to "Lonesome Fella," ABC-Paramount 45-100073, February 1960.

The Shadows. "Apache" (Jerry Lordan). Hank Marvin (lead guitar), Bruce Welch (rhythm guitar), Jet Harris (bass), Tony Meehan (drums), and Cliff Richard (tacked drum). Production as above. Recorded: EMI Recording Studios, London, 17 June 1960. UK release: Columbia DB 4484, July 1960; charts 21 July 1960, *RR* #1 (August–September 1960). US release: ABC-Paramount 45-10, 138, August 1960.

The Shadows. "Man of Mystery" (Michael Carr). Personnel and production as above. UK release: Columbia DB 4530, November 1960; charts 10 November 1960, *RR* #5. US release: Atlantic 45-2135, February 1962.

The Shadows. "F.B.I." (Peter Gormley [Hank Marvin, Bruce Welch, and Terrance Harris). Personnel and production as above. UK release: Columbia DB 4580, 2 February 1961; charts 9 February 1961, *RR* #6. US release: Atlantic 45-2111, July 1961.

The Shadows. "Frightened City" (Norrie Paramor). Personnel and production as above. UK release: Columbia DB 4637, 4 May 1961; charts 11 May 1961, *RR* #3. US release: the B-side to "F.B.I."

The Shadows. "Kon Tiki" (Michael Carr). Personnel and production as above. Recorded: EMI Recording Studios, London, August 1961. UK release: Columbia DB 4698, August 1961; charts 7 September and 23 November 1961, *RR* #1. US release: B-side to "Man of Mystery."

The Shadows. "Wonderful Land" (Jerry Lordan). Personnel and production as above. UK release: Columbia DB 4790, February 1962; charts 1 March 1962, *RR* #1 (March–April 1962). US release: Atlantic 45-2146, 7 April 1962.

The Shadows. "Dance On!" (Val Murtagh, Elaine Murtagh, and Ray Adams). Hank Marvin (guitar), Bruce Welch (guitar), Brian Locking (bass), and Brian Bennett (drums). UK release: Columbia DB 4948, 7 December 1962; charts 13 December 1962, RR #1 (January 1963). US release: Atlantic 45-2177, February 1963.

Shannon, Del. "Runaway" (Del Shannon and Max Crook). Del Shannon (guitar and vocals) with Al Caiola, Al Casamenti, and Bucky Pizzarelli (guitar), Moe Wechsler (piano), Milt Hinton (bass), Bill Ramall (baritone sax), and Joe Marshall (drums). Production: Harry Balk with Fred Weinberg (engineer) and Bill Ramall (arranger). Recorded: Bell Sound Studios, New York, 21 January 1961. US release: Bigtop 45-3075, 18 February 1961; *BB* #1 (April 1961). UK release: London HLX 9317, March 1961; charts 27 April 1961, *RR* #1 (July 1961).

Shapiro, Helen. "Don't Treat Me like a Child" (John Schroeder and Mike Hawker). Helen Shapiro with the Mike Sammes Singers and session musicians. Norrie Paramor (artist-and-repertoire manager) with Martin Slavin (music director) and Malcolm Addey (engineer). Recorded: EMI Recording Studios, London. UK release: Columbia DB 4589 on 10 February 1961; charts 23 March 1961, *RR* #3. US release: Capitol 4561, May 1961.

Shapiro, Helen. "You Don't Know" (John Schroeder and Mike Hawker). Personnel and production as above. Recorded: EMI Recording Studios, London. UK release: Columbia DB 4670 on 23 June 1961; charts 29 June 1961, *RR* #1 (August 1961). US release: Capitol 4627, September 1961. B: "Marvelous Lie."

Shapiro, Helen. "Walking Back to Happiness" (John Schroeder and Mike Hawker). Personnel as above. Norrie Paramor (artist-and-repertoire manager and arranger) with Malcolm Addey (engineer). Recorded: EMI Recording Studios, London. UK release: Columbia DB 4715 on 22 September 1961; charts 28 September 1961, *RR* #1 (October 1961). US release: Capitol 4662, October 1961, *BB* #100 (December 1961).

Shapiro, Helen. "Tell Me What He Said" (John Barry). Personnel as above. Norrie Paramor (artist-and-repertoire manager), Martin Slavin (music director), and Malcolm Addey (engineer). Recorded: EMI Recording Studios, London. UK release: Columbia DB 4782, 9 February 1962; charts 15 February 1962, *RR* #2. B: "I Apologise" (John Schroeder, Raymond Dutch, and Jeff Rabin).

Shapiro, Helen. "Let's Talk about Love" (Norrie Paramor and Bunny Lewis). Helen Shapiro with Norrie Paramor and His Orchestra. Production: Norrie Paramor with Malcolm Addey (engineer). UK release: Columbia DB 4824, 27 April 1962; charts 3 May 1962, *RR* #23.

Shapiro, Helen. "Little Miss Lonely" (John Schroeder and Mike Hawker). Personnel and production as above. UK release: DB 4869, 6 July 1962; charts 12 July 1962, *RR* #8.

Shapiro, Helen. "Keep Away from Other Girls" (Bob Hilliard and Burt Bacharach). Helen Shapiro with Martin Slavin and His Orchestra. Production: Norrie Paramor with Martin Slavin (music director) and Malcolm Addey (engineer). UK release: Columbia DB 4908, 12 October 1962; charts 18 October 1962, *RR* #40.

Shapiro, Helen. "Queen for Tonight" (Ben Raleigh and Artie Wayne). Personnel as above. Production: Norrie Paramor with Malcolm Addey (engineer). Recorded: EMI Recording Studios, London, 1962. UK release: Columbia DB 4966, 25 January 1963; charts 7 February 1963, *RR* #33.

Shaw, Sandie. "As Long as You're Happy, Baby" (Chris Andrews). Sandi Shaw with session musicians. Production: Tony Hatch with Chris Andrews (music director). Release: Pye 7N 15671, 10 July 1964. US release: Mercury 72315, August 1964.

Shaw, Sandie. "(There's) Always Something There to Remind Me" (Burt Bacharach and Hal David). Personnel as above. Production: Chris Andrews with Les Williams (music director). Release: Pye 7N 15704, 25 September 1964; charts 8 October 1964, *RR* #1 (October–November 1964). US release: Reprise 0320, November 1964, *BB* #52 (January 1965).

Shaw, Sandie. "Girl Don't Come" (Chris Andrews). Personnel and production as above. UK release: Pye 7N 15743, 27 November 1964; charts 10 December 1964, *RR* #3. US release: Reprise 0342, February 1965, *BB* #42 (April 1965). B: "I'd Be Far Better Off without You" (Chris Andrews).

Shaw, Sandie. "I'll Stop at Nothing" (Chris Andrews). Personnel as above. Production: Chris Andrews with Ken Woodman (music director). UK release: Pye 7N 15783, 12 February 1965; charts 18 February 1965, *RR* #4. US release: Reprise 0394, August 1965.

Shaw, Sandie. "Long Live Love" (Chris Andrews). Personnel and production as above. UK release: Pye 7N 15841, 7 May 1965; charts 13 May 1965, *RR* #1 (May–June 1965). US release: Reprise 0375, May 1965, *BB* #97 (June 1965).

Shelton, Anne. "Lilli Marlene" (Hans Leip and Norbert Schultze, with Tommie Connor) [78 rpm]. Anne Shelton accompanied by Stanley Black and His Orchestra. UK release: Decca F.8434, May 1944.

Shelton, Anne. "Lay Down Your Arms" (Leon Land, Ake Gerhard, and Paddy Roberts). Anne Shelton with Wally Stott and His Orchestra and Chorus. Production: Johnny Franz with Wally Stott (arranger) and Joe Meek (engineer). UK release: Philips 4-40759/PB 616, 1956; charts 24 August 1956, *NME* #1 (September–October 1956).

Shelton, Anne. "Sailor" (David West [Norman Newell], Fini Busch, and Werner Scharfenberger). Anne Shelton with Wally Stott and His Orchestra and Chorus. UK release: Philips PB.1096, 1961; charts 26 January 1961, *RR* #10.

Sheridan, Tony, and the Beat Brothers. "My Bonnie" (trad., Tony Sheridan and Bert Kämpfert). Tony Sheridan (vocals and guitar) with John Lennon (guitar and backing vocal), Paul McCartney (bass and backing vocal), George Harrison (guitar and backing vocal), and Pete Best (drums). Production: Bert Kämpfert. Recorded: Friedrich-Ebert-Halle, 22 June 1961. German release: Polydor 24 673, 23 October 1961. UK release (Tony Sheridan and the Beatles): Polydor NH 66833, 5 January 1962.

The Shirelles. "Will You Love Me Tomorrow" (Carole King and Gerry Goffin). Shirley Owens (vocal), Doris Coley (vocal), Addie Harris (vocal) and Beverly Lee (vocal) with studio musicians. Production: Luther Dixon with Carole King (arranger). US release: Scepter 1211, November 1960; charts 14 November 1960. UK release: Top Rank JAR 540; charts 9 February 1961, *RR* #4. B: "Boys" (Luther Dixon and Wes Farrell). Production: Luther Dixon.

The Shirelles. "Baby It's You" (Burt Bacharach, Luther Dixon, and Mac David). Production: Luther Dixon with Burt Bacharach (arranger). Recorded: Bell Sound Studios, New York, 1960. US release: Scepter 1227, November 1961, *BB* #8 (February 1962).

The Shirelles. "I Didn't Mean to Hurt You" (Ellie Greenwich and Tony Powers). Production: Jerry Leiber and Mike Stoller with Bert Keyes (arranger). US release: Scepter 1255, June 1963. UK release: Stateside SS 213, August 1963. A: "Don't Say Goodnight and Mean Goodbye."

The Shirelles. "Sha-La-La" (Robert Taylor and Robert Moseley). Production: Ludix Productions with Bert Keyes (arranger). US release: Scepter 1967, March 1964; *BB* #69 (April 1964). UK release: Pye International 7N 25240, April 1964.

The Silkie. "Blood Red River" (The Silkie). Sylvie Tatler (voice), Kevyn Cunningham (bass), Mike Ramaden (voice and guitar), and Ivor Aylesbury (voice and guitar). Release: Fontana TF 556, 9 April 1965.

The Silkie. "You've Got to Hide Your Love Away" (John Lennon and Paul McCartney). Personnel as above with Paul McCartney (guitar) and George Harrison (tambourine). Production: John Lennon with Paul McCartney (music director) and Michael Weighel (engineer). Recorded: IBC Studios, London, 9 August 1965. UK release: Fontana TF 603, 10 September 1965; charts 23 September 1965, *RR* #28. US release: Fontana F-1525, September 1965, *BB* #10 (November 1965).

The Skatalites. "Guns of Navarone" (Dimitri Tiomkin). Tommy McCook (saxophone), Rolando Alphonso (saxophone), Lester Sterling (trumpet and saxophone), Lloyd Brevett (bass), Lloyd Knibbs/Winston Grennan (drums), Don Drummond (trombone), Jerry Haynes (guitar), Jackie Mittoo (keyboards), Johnny Moore (trumpet), and Roland Alphonso (spoken commentary). Jamaican release [as Roland Alfonso and the Studio One Orchestra]: Mu-zik City C 10, 1965. UK release: Island WI 168, March 1965; charts 20 April 1967, *RR* #36.

Small, Millie. See Millie.

Snow, Hank. "(Now and Then There's) A Fool Such as I" (Bill Trader). Hank Snow and the Rainbow Ranch Boys. US release: RCA 47-5034, November 1952.

The Soul Sisters. "I Can't Stand It" (Smokey McAlister). Soul Sisters: Thresia Cleveland and Ann Gissendanner (vocal) with studio musicians. Production: Juggy Murray, RMH Productions. Recorded: New York City, 1963. US release: Sue 799, January 1964, *BB* (R & B) #8, (Pop) #46 (April 1964).

The Sound of Music (Richard Rodgers and Oscar Hammerstein II). Personnel: Julie Andrews, Peggy Wood, and Christopher Plummer with cast and orchestra. Production: Neely Plumb with Saul Chaplin (assoc.), Irwin Kostal (arranger and conductor), and Robert Mayer, Douglas Williams, Murray Spivak, and John Norman (engineers and editors). US release: RCA Victor LSOD-2005, 2 March 1965; *BB* #1. UK release: RCA Victor SB-6616, 5 March 1965; *RR* #1.

Springfield, Dusty. "I Only Want to Be with You" (Mike Hawker and Ivor Raymonde). Dusty Springfield with studio singers and musicians including Allan Weighell (bass), Jim Sullivan (guitar), Clem Cattini (drums), and the Breakaways. Production: John Franz with Ivor Raymonde (arranger). Recorded: Philips Studios, Marble Arch, London, 17 October 1963. UK release: Philips BF 1292, November 1963; charts 21 November 1963, *RR* #4. US release: Philips 40162, December 1963, *BB* #12 (March 1964).

Springfield, Dusty. "I Just Don't Know What to Do with Myself" (Burt Bacharach and Hal David). Personnel and production as above. UK release: Philips BF 1348, June 1964; charts 2 July 1964, *RR* #3.

Springfield, Dusty. "In the Middle of Nowhere" (Beatrice Verdi and Buddy Kaye). Dusty Springfield with the Echoes: Vic Briggs (guitar), Jimmy O'Brien and/or Allan Price (keyboards), John Dryden (drums), Doug Reece (bass), Ian Harper (trumpet), Derek Andrews (trumpet), Derek Wadsworth (trombone), and Tony Scott (percussion) with Doris Troy, Madeline Bell, Kiki Dee, and Lesley Duncan (backing vocals). Production: John Franz with Ivor Raymonde (arranger). UK release: Philips BF 1418, June 1965; charts 1 July 1965, *RR* #8. US release: Philips 40303.

Springfield, Dusty. "Some of Your Lovin'" (Gerry Goffin and Carole King). Personnel and production as above. Release: Philips BF 1430, September 1965; charts 16 September 1965, *RR* #8.

The Springfields. "Dear John" (adaptation by Tom Springfield). Tom Springfield (guitar and voice), Dusty Springfield (voice), and Tim Feild (guitar and voice) with ukulele, drums, and bass. Production: John Franz with Ivor Raymonde (arranger). UK release: Philips PB 1145, May 1961.

The Springfields. "Breakaway" (Tom Springfield). Personnel and production as above. UK release: Philips BF 1168, July 1961; charts 31 August 1961, *RR* #31.

The Springfields. "Silver Threads and Golden Needles" (Dick Reynolds and Jack Rhodes). Personnel as above with Judd Proctor (electric guitar), drums, piano, tambourine, and a string section. Production as above. UK release: Philips PB 1241, April 1962. US release: Philips 40038, June 1962, *BB* #20 (September 1962).

The Springfields. "Swahili Papa" (Tom Springfield). Personnel as above with piano, drums, flute, congas, and bass. Production as above. UK release: Philips 326 536 BF, August 1962.

The Springfields. "Island of Dreams" (Tom Springfield). Personnel as above with strings, brass, piano, drums, and bass. Production as above. UK release: Philips 326557 BF, November 1962; charts 13 December 1962, *RR* #5.

The Springfields. "Say I Won't Be There" (Tom Springfield). Personnel as above with piano, electric guitar, drums, strings, and bass. Production as above. UK release: Philips 326577 BF, 14 March 1963; charts 28 March 1963, *RR* #5.

Staple Singers, The. "This May Be the Last Time" (traditional, arranged by Shirley Joiner). Roebuck Staples (vocal and guitar), Cleotha Staples (vocal), Mavis Staples (vocal), and Pervis Staples (vocal). Production unidentified. Release: Sharp 45-603, 1960.

Steele, Tommy. "Rock with the Caveman" (Tommy Steele, Lionel Bart, and Mike Pratt). Tommy Steele (vocals and guitar) with Ronnie Scott (tenor sax), Major Holley (bass), Dave Lee (piano), Kirk Dunning (drums), and unidentified electric guitarist. Production: Hugh Mendl with Roland Shaw (music director) and Arthur Lilley (engineer). Recorded: Decca Studios, London, 24 September 1956. UK release: Decca F10795, October 1956, *NME* #13 (charts 26 October 1956).

Steele, Tommy. "Singing the Blues" (Melvin Eadsley). Tommy Steele (vocals and guitar) with Leo Pollini (drums), Alan Stuart (sax), Dennis Price (piano), Allan Weighell (bass), and unidentified studio musicians, singers, and whistler. Production as above. UK release: Decca F 10819, November 1956; charts 14 December 1956, *NME* #1 (January 1957).

Stuart, Chad, and Jeremy Clyde. "Yesterday's Gone" (Chad Stuart and Wendy Kidd). Chad Stuart and Jeremy Clyde with studio musicians. Production: John Barry. Recorded: EMI Recording Studios, London, 31 July 1963. UK release: Ember EMBS 180, 27 September 1963; *RR* #37. US release: World Artists 1021, April 1964; *BB* #21 (July 1964).

Stuart, Chad, and Jeremy Clyde (as Chad and Jeremy). "A Summer Song" (Clive Metcalfe, Keith Noble, and Chad Stuart). Chad and Jeremy with session musicians. Production: Shel Talmy with Johnnie Spence (arranger and conductor). Recorded: CTS Studios, London, June 1964. UK release: United Artists UP-1062, 31 July 1964. US release: World Artists 1027, July 1964; *BB* #7 (September 1964).

Stuart, Chad, and Jeremy Clyde. *Yesterday's Gone*. Personnel as above. Production: Shel Talmy (with John Barry). US release: World Artists WAM 2002, 24 July 1964. A: "A Summer Song," "Now and Forever," "Dirty Old Town," "Like I Love You Today," "September in the Rain," and "Yesterday's Gone." B: "If She Was Mine," "Willow Weep for Me," "Only for the Young," "Too Soon My Love," "The Truth Often Hurts the Heart," and "No Tears for Johnnie."

Stuart, Chad, and Jeremy Clyde. "Willow Weep for Me" (Ann Ronell). Personnel and production as above. Recorded: EMI Recording Studios, London. UK release: United Artists UP 1070, November 1964. US release: the A-side of World Artists 1034, November 1964; *BB* #15 (January 1965). A: "If She Was Mine" (Buie and Goldsboro).

Stuart, Chad, and Jeremy Clyde. *Chad & Jeremy Sing for You*. Personnel and production as above. UK release: Ember ZB 8091, n.d. A: "Yesterday's Gone," "If She Was Mine," "Willow Weep for Me," "No Tears for Johnny," "The Truth Often Hurts the Heart," and "If I Loved You." B: "September in the Rain," "Like I Love You Today," "Donna Donna," "A Summer Song," "Dirty Old Town," and "From a Window."

Stuart, Chad, and Jeremy Clyde. *Chad & Jeremy Sing for You*. Personnel as above with session musicians. Production: Jimmy Haskell with George Tipton and Ian Freebairn-Smith (arrangers). Recorded: Los Angeles. US release: World Artists Records, WAM2005, January 1965. A: "My Coloring Book," "What Do You Want with Me," "From a Window," "If You've Got a Heart," "No Other Baby," and "Donna Donna." B: "The Girl from Ipanema," "Four Strong Winds," "Only Those in Love," "You Know What," "Sleep Little Boy," and "My How the Time Goes By."

Sutch, Screaming Lord, and the Savages. "'Til the Following Night" (David Sutch). David Sutch (vocals), Carlo Little (drums), Andy Wren (piano), Ken Payne (bass), and Roger Mingay (guitar) with Pete Newman on tenor saxophone. Production: Joe Meek. Recorded: R.G.M. Sound Recording. UK release: HMV POP 953, December 1961.

The Swinging Blue Jeans. "You're No Good" (Clint Ballard, Jr.). Ray Ennis (vocal and guitar), Les Braid (bass and keyboard), Ralph Ellis (guitar), and Norman Kuhlke (drums). Production: Walter Ridley. UK release: His Master's Voice POP 1304, 29 May 1964; charts 4 June 1964, *RR* #3.

Taylor, Vince, and His Playboys. "Brand New Cadillac" (Vince Taylor). Vince Taylor (vocals) with Joe Moretti (guitar), Lou Brian (piano), Brian Locking (bass), and Brian Bennett (drums). UK release: Parlophone R 4505, 3 April 1959.

The Thamesiders with Davy Graham. *From a London Hootenanny* [EP]. The Thamesiders: Martin Carthy (voice and guitar), Marian Gray (voice and guitar), and Pete Maynard (voice and bass) with Davy Graham (guitar). Production: Hugh Mendl with Wally Whyton (music director) and Mike Savage and Gus Dudgeon (engineers). Recorded: London, May 1963. UK release: Decca DFE 8538, 1963. A [Thamesiders]: "Wimoweh" and "Who Rolled the Stone Away?" B [Davy Graham]: "She Moves through the Fair" and "Mustapha."

Them. "Don't Start Crying Now" (James Moore and Jerry West). Van Morrison (vocal), Billy Harrison (guitar), Ronnie Millings (drums), Alan Henderson (bass), and Jackie McAuley (keyboard). Production: Dick Rowe with Arthur Greenslade (music director). Recorded: Decca Studios, London, June 1964. UK release: Decca F 11973, 4 September 1964. US release: Parrot 45 PAR 9702, October 1964.

Them. "Baby Please Don't Go" (Joe Williams). Van Morrison (vocal and harmonica), Billy Harrison (guitar), Alan Henderson (bass), Pat McAuley, Jackie McAuley (keyboard), and Pat McAuley (drums and tambourine) with Jimmy Page (guitar). Production: Bert Berns. Recorded: Decca Studios, London. UK release: Decca F 12018, 6 November 1964; charts 7 January 1965, *RR* #10. US release: Parrot 45-9727, January 1965. B: "Gloria" (Van Morrison). Van Morrison (vocal and harmonica), Billy Harrison (guitar), Alan Henderson (bass), Pat McAuley, Jackie McAuley (keyboard), and Pat McAuley (drums and tambourine) with Bobby Graham (drums). Production: Dick Rowe and Bert Berns with Arthur Greenslade (music director). Recorded: Decca Studios, London, June 1964. *BB* #71 (May 1966).

Them. *Them* [EP]. Release: Decca DFE 8612, February 1965. A: "Don't Start Crying Now" and "Philosophy." B: "Baby Please Don't Go" and "One Two Brown Eyes."

Them. "Here Comes the Night" (Bert Berns). Personnel and production as above. UK release: Decca F 12094, 5 March 1965; charts 25 March 1965, *RR* #2. US release: Parrot 45-9749, April 1965, *BB* #24 (July 1965).

Them. *Them*. A: "Here Comes the Night," "Mystic Eyes," "Don't Look Back," "Little Girl," "One Two Brown Eyes," and "Gloria." B: "One More Time," "If You and I Could Be as Two," "I Like It Like That," "I'm Gonna Dress in Black," "Route 66," and "Go on Home Baby." US release: Parrot PA-61005, June 1965.

Them. *Them*. Personnel as above. Production: Tommy Scott, Bert Berns, and Dick Rowe. A: "Mystic Eyes," "If You and I Could Be as Two," "Little Girl," "Just a Little Bit," "I Gave My Love a Diamond," "Gloria," and "You Just Can't Win." B: "Go on Home Baby," "Don't Look Back," "I Like It Like That," "I'm Gonna Dress in Black," "Bright Lights Big City," "My Little Baby," and "(Get Your Kicks on) Route 66." UK release: Decca LK 4700, July 1965.

Thomas, Irma. "Anyone Who Knows What Love Is (Will Understand). Production: Eddie Ray with H. B. Barnum (arranger). US release: Imperial 66041, June 1964. B: "Time Is on My Side" (Jerry Ragovoy and Jim Norman).

Thomas, Rufus. "The Dog" (Rufus Thomas). Recorded: Stax Records, Memphis, Tennessee. US release: Stax S-130, December 1962, *BB* #87 (March 1963).

Thomas, Rufus. "Walking the Dog" (Rufus Thomas). Recorded: Stax Records, Memphis, Tennessee. US release: Stax S-140, September 1963, *BB* #10 (December 1963).

The Tokens. "He's in Town" (Gerry Goffin and Carole King). Hank Medress, Jay Siegel, Mitch Margo, and Phil Margo. Production: Big Time Productions with Brooks Arthur (engineer). US release: B. T. Puppy Records 502, July 1964, *BB* #43 (September 1964). UK release: Fontana TF 500, 25 September 1964.

The Tornados. "Telstar" (Joe Meek; Ivy Music). George Bellamy (guitar), Heinz Burt (bass guitar), Alan Caddy (lead guitar), Clem Cattini (drums), and Roger Lavern (keyboards) with Geoff Goddard (Clavioline and vocal). Production: Joe Meek. Recorded: RGM Sound, 16–17 July 1962. UK release: Decca F 11494, August 1962; charts 30 August 1962, *RR* #1 (October–November 1962). US release: Decca F 11494, August 1962, *BB* #1 (December 1962).

The Tornados. "Globetrotter" ["Globetrottin'"] (Joe Meek): Personnel and production as above. UK release: Decca F 11562, January 1962; charts 10 January 1963, *RR* #5. US release: London 45-9579, January 1963.

Trent, Jackie. "Where Are You Now" (Tony Hatch and Jackie Trent). Jackie Trent (vocal) with studio accompaniment. Recorded: Pye Studios, London, December 1964. Produced and arranged by Tony Hatch. UK release: Pye 7N.15776, 28 April 1965; charts 22 April 1965, *RR* #1 (May 1965). US release: Parkway P-955, May 1965.

Troy, Doris. "Just One Look" (Gregor Carroll and Doris Troy). Doris Troy with Ernie Hayes (piano), Wally Richardson (guitar), Bob Bushnell (bass), Bernard Purdie (drums) and others. Production: Arti Ripp for Award Music Production. Recorded: 1963. US release: Atlantic 45-2188, May 1963; BB #10. UK release: London HLK 9749, 5 July 1963.

Valens, Ritchie. "Donna" (Richie Valens). Ritchie Valens (guitar and vocal) with Buddy Clark (bass), Carol Kaye and Irving Ashby (guitar), Ernie Freeman (piano), and Earl Palmer (drums). Production: Bob Keene. Recorded: Gold Star Studios, Los Angeles, 16 December 1958. US release: Del-Fi 4110, 18 October 1958; *BB* #2. B: "La Bamba" (traditional adapted by Ritchie Valens). Production and personnel as above with Rene Hall (baritone guitar). US release: *BB* #22 (February 1959). UK release: London HL 8803, February 1959.

The Valentinos. "It's All over Now" (Bobby Womack and Shirley Womack). Friendly Womack, Jr., Curtis Womack, Bobby Womack, Harry Womack, and Cecil Womack. Production: Sam Cooke. US release: SAR Records SAR 152, May 1964, BB #94 (July 1964). UK release: Soul City SC 106, August 1968.

Valli, Frankie. *Frankie Valli—Solo*. Philips PHS 600-247. A: "My Funny Valentine," "(You're Gonna) Hurt Yourself," "Ivy," "Secret Love," and "Can't Take My Eyes Off You." B: "My Mother's Eyes," "The Sun Ain't Gonna Shine Any More," "The Trouble with Me," "The Proud One," and "You're Ready Now."

The Walker Brothers. "Pretty Girls Everywhere" (Eugene Church and Thomas Williams). Scott Walker, John Walker, and Gary Walker (vocals) with studio musicians. Production: Ben-Ven Productions, with Shorty Rogers (arranger) and Nick Venet (music director). Recorded: Los Angeles. US release: Smash S-1952, December 1964. UK release: Philips BF 1401, 26 February 1965.

The Walker Brothers. "Love Her" (Barry Mann and Cynthia Weil). Personnel as above. Production: Nick Venet with Jack Nitzsche (arranger). Recorded: Los Angeles. UK release: Philips BF 1409, 9 April 1965; charts 29 April 1965, *RR* #20. US release: Smash S-1976, April 1965.

The Walker Brothers. "Make It Easy on Yourself" (Burt Bacharach and Hal David). Personnel as above with London session musicians including Jim Sullivan and Alan Parker (guitars). Production: Johnny Franz with Ivor Raymond (music director). Recorded: Philips Studios, London. UK release: Philips BF 1428, August 1965; charts 19 August 1965, RR #1 (23 September 1965). US release: Smash S-2000, September 1965, and as Smash S-2009, October 1965, BB #16 (December 1965).

The Walker Brothers. "My Ship Is Coming in" (Joey Brooks). Personnel and production as above. UK release: Philips 26 November 1965; charts 2 December 1965, RR #3. US release: Smash S-2016, January 1966, BB #63 (1965).

The Walker Brothers. "The Sun Ain't Gonna Shine Any More" (Bob Crew and Bob Gaudio). Personnel and production as above. UK release: Philips BF 1473, 15 February 1966; charts 3 March 1966, RR #1 (17 March 1966). US release: Smash S-2032, March 1966, BB #13 (May 1966).

Waller, Thomas "Fats." "The Sheik of Araby" (Harry Smith, Francis Wheeler, and Ted Snyder). Fats Waller and His Rhythm: Fats Waller (piano and vocals), Herman Autrey (trumpet), Gene Sedric (tenor saxophone), Al Casey (guitar), Cedric Wallace (bass), and Wilmore "Slick" Jones (drums). Recorded: RCA Victor, New York, 12 April 1938. US release: His Master's Voice E.A. 2167, 1938.

Warwick, Dionne. "Anyone Who Had a Heart" (Burt Bacharach and Hal David). Dionne Warwick with studio musicians. Production: Burt Bacharach and Hall David with Ed Smith (engineer). Recorded: Bell Sound Studios, New York, November 1963. US release: Scepter 1262, November 1963, BB #8 (February 1964). UK release: Pye International 7N 25234, February 1964; charts 13 February 1964, RR #42.

Waters, Muddy (see Muddy Waters)

Weedon, Bert. "Apache" (Jerry Lordan). Bert Weedon (guitar) with studio musicians. UK release: Top Rank JAR 415, July 1960.

The Who. "I Can't Explain" (Peter Townshend). Roger Daltrey (lead vocal), John Entwistle (bass guitar), Keith Moon (drums), and Pete Townshend (guitar) with John Carter, Ken Lewis, and Perry Ford (backing vocals). Production: Shel Talmy with Glyn Johns (engineer). Recorded: Pye Studios, London, November 1964. UK release: Brunswick 05926, 15 January 1965; charts 18 February 1965, RR #8. US release: Decca 31725, 8 December 1964, BB #93 (April 1965). B: "Bald Headed Woman" (Shel Talmy).

The Who. "Anyway, Anyhow, Anywhere" (Peter Townshend and Roger Daltrey). Roger Daltry (lead vocals), John Entwistle (bass guitar and backing vocal), Keith Moon (drums), and Pete Townshend (guitar and backing vocal) with

Nicky Hopkins (piano). Production as above. Recorded: 13–14 April 1965. UK release: Brunswick 05935, 21 May 1965: charts 27 May 1965, *RR* #10. US release: Decca 31801, 5 June 1965.

The Who. "My Generation" (Peter Townshend). Roger Daltrey (lead vocals), John Entwistle (bass guitar and backing vocal), Keith Moon (drums), and Pete Townshend (guitar and backing vocal). Production as above. Recorded: 13 October 1965. UK release: Brunswick 05944, 29 October 1965; charts 4 November 1965, RR #2. US release: Decca 31877, 20 November 1965, *BB* #74 (12 February 1966).

The Who. *My Generation*. The Who with Nicky Hopkins (piano). Production as above, April and 11–15 October 1965. UK release: Brunswick LAT 8616, 3 December 1965; charts 25 December 1965, *RR* #5. US release: Decca DL 4664, 25 April 1966. A: "Out in the Street," "I Don't Mind," "The Good's Gone," "La-La-La-Lies," "Much Too Much," and "My Generation"; B: "The Kids Are Alright," "Please, Please, Please," "It's Not True," "I'm a Man," "A Legal Matter," and "The Ox."

Wilde, Marty. "Endless Sleep" (Jody Reynolds, 1958). Marty Wilde (vocals) with session musicians. Production: John Franz. Recorded: Philips Studios, London. UK release: Philips PB 835, June 1958; charts 11 July 1958, *NME* #4.

Wilde, Marty. "My Lucky Love" (Joe Tanner). Personnel and production as above. UK release: Philips PB 850, August 1958.

Wilde, Marty. "Donna" (Ritchie Valens). Marty Wilde with session musicians. Production as above. UK release: Philips PB 902 in February 1959; charts 6 March 1959, *NME* #3.

Wilde, Marty. "Teenager in Love" (Doc Pomus and Mort Shuman). Personnel and production as above. UK release: Philips PB 926, May 1959; charts 5 June 1959, *NME* #2.

Wilde, Marty. *Wilde about Marty*. Production: as above. UK release: Philips BL.7342, August 1959. A: "Down the Line," "Love of My Life," "Put Me Down," "Blue Moon of Kentucky," "Dream Love," "You've Got Love," and "I Flipped." B: "All American Boy," "Mean Woman Blues," "Are You Sincere?," "High School Confidential," "Don't Pity Me," "Splish Slash," and "So Glad You're Mine."

Wilde, Marty. "Sea of Love" (George Khoury and John Phillip Baptiste). Production as above. Release: Philips 959, September 1959; charts 25 September 1959, *NME* #3.

Wilde, Marty. "It's Been Nice" (Mort Shuman and Doc Pomus). Production as above. UK release: Philips PB.972, December 1959; charts 11 December 1959, *NME* #3. B: "Bad Boy" (Marty Wilde).

Williams', Joe, Washboard Blues Singers. "Baby, Please Don't Go" (Joe Williams). Joe Williams (vocal and guitar), Dad Tracy (violin), and Chasey Collins (washboard). Production: Lester Melrose. Recorded: Chicago, 31 October 1935. US release: Bluebird B-6200-A, 1935.

Williams, Maurice. See Maurice and the Zodiacs.

The Yardbirds. "I Wish You Would" (Billy Boy Arnold). Keith Relf (vocals), Eric Clapton (guitar and vocals), Paul Samwell-Smith (bass guitar), Chris Dreja (guitar), and Jim McCarty (drums). Production: Giorgio Gomelsky. Recorded: R. G. Jones Studios, New Malden, UK, February 1964. [Some sources suggest the Studio at Olympic Sound Studios.] UK release: Columbia DB 7283, 1 May 1964. US release: Epic 5-9709, 7 August 1964. B: "A Certain Girl" (Naomi Neville [Allen Toussaint]).

The Yardbirds. "Good Morning Little Schoolgirl" (H. G. Demarais). Personnel as above with Eric Clapton (harmonizing vocals on "Good Morning Little Schoolgirl"). Production and Recording: as above. UK release: Columbia DB 7391, 30 October 1964; charts 12 November 1964, *RR* #43. B: "I Ain't Got You" (Calvin Carter).

The Yardbirds. "For Your Love" (Graham Gouldman). Personnel as above with Brian Auger (harpsichord), Ron Prentice (acoustic bass), and Denny Piercy (bongos). Production: Giorgio Gomelsky with Paul Samwell-Smith (arranger). Recorded: Olympic Sound Studios, 1 February 1965. UK release: Columbia DB 7499, 5 March 1965; charts 18 March 1965, *RR* #3. US release: Epic 5-9790, 9 April 1965, *BB* #6 (July 1965). B: "Got to Hurry" (Giorgio Gomelsky).

The Zombies. "She's Not There" (Rod Argent). Colin Blunstone (vocals), Paul Atkinson (guitar), Rod Argent (keyboards, vocals), Hugh Grundy (drums), and Chris White (bass). Ken Jones (artist-and-repertoire manager) with Terry Johnson and Gus Dudgeon (engineers). Recorded: Decca Studios, London, 12 June 1964. UK release: Decca F 11940, 24 July 1964; charts 13 August 1964, *RR* #12. US release: Parrot 45-9695, 7 September 1964, *BB* #2 (December 1964).

The Zombies. "Leave Me Be" (Chris White). Personnel and production as above. Recorded: 31 August and 5 September 1964. UK release: Decca F 12004, 16 October 1964.

The Zombies. "Tell Her No" (Rod Argent). Personnel and production as above. Recorded: Decca Studios, London, 25 November 1964. UK release: Decca F 12072, 29 January 1965; charts 11 February 1965, *RR* #42. Released in Parrot 45-9723, 28 December 1964, *BB* #6 (February 1965).

The Zombies. "She's Coming Home" (Rod Argent). Personnel and production as above. UK release: Decca F 12125, 9 April 1965. US release: Parrot 45-9747, 27 March 1965.

The Zombies. "Whenever You're Ready" (Rod Argent). Personnel and production as above. Recorded: 24 June 1965. UK release: F 12225, 3 September 1965. US release: Parrot 45-9786, 16 August 1965.

Volume 1 Media Sources

The 6.5 Special. See *The Six-Five Special.*

The Adventures of Robin Hood. Direction: Terry Bishop, Bernard Knowles, Ralph Smart, etc. Production: Sidney Cole, Hannah Weinstein (executive), and Thelma Connell (associate) for Incorporated Television Company, Sapphire Films, and Yeoman Films Ltd. Writers: Ring Lardner, Jr., Ian McLellan Hunter, John Dyson, etc. Cast: Richard Greene, Archie Duncan, Alexander Gauge, Alan Wheatley, Bernadette O'Farrell, etc. Broadcast: Incorporated Television Company (UK), 1955–1960.

Alma Cogan. Cast: Alma Cogan with Stan Foster and His Music. Broadcast: BBC Television, February–March 1956.

The Alma Cogan Show. Production: Douglas Moodie with Douglas Squires (choreography), Stan Foster (music director), and Alan Reeve-Jones and Edwin Braden (songs). Cast: Alma Cogan with Michael Miller, Terry Skelton, John Prescott, and Roderick Joyce (dancers) and guests. Broadcast: BBC Television, April–May 1957.

Anne to You. Production: Alick Hayes (1944–45). Cast: Anne Shelton, Hubert Gregg, Neal Arden, Nat Allen and His Combined Dance and Concert Orchestra, etc. Broadcast: General Forces Programme, September 1944–March 1945.

The Archers. Production: Tony Shryane. Writers: Geoffrey Webb, Edward Mason, etc. with Godfrey Baseley (editor). Music: Arthur Wood, Kenneth Pakeman, David Turner, etc. Cast: Harry Oakes, Gwen Berryman, June Spencer, Lesley Saweard, Tamsin Grieg, Felicity Jones, Charlotte Connor, etc. Broadcast: BBC Home Service (1950) and BBC Light Programme (1951–1967).

Around the Beatles. Direction: Rita Gillespie. Production: Jack Good with Brian Epstein (associate producer) and Harry Robinson (music director). Writers: Barry Cawtheray. Music: IBC Studios, 19 April 1964. Film: Wembley Park Studios, 28 April 1964. Cast: Beatles, Long John Baldry, Cilla Black, P. J. Proby, Millie Small, Sounds Incorporated, the Vernons Girls, etc. UK broadcast: ITV/Rediffusion London, 6 May 1964. US broadcast: ABC, 15 November 1964. [46:14]

The Beat Room. Direction: James Moir. Production: James Gilbert (executive producer) with Barry Langford and James Moir. Cast: Patrick Campbell (host) with guests. Broadcast: BBC2, 6 July 1964 –29 January 1965.

The Beat Show. Production: Geoff Lawrence. Music: Bernard Herrmann and the National Dance Orchestra, etc. Cast: Clinton Ford, the Beatles, etc. Broadcast: BBC Radio, Light Programme, Playhouse Theatre, Manchester, 1962.

The Beatles at Shea Stadium. Direction: Robert Precht. Production: Robert Precht with Vince Calandra and Tony Jordan for Sullivan Productions with NEMS Enterprises and Subafilms. Cinematography: Andrew Laszlo with Arline Carson and Sidney Katz. Music: the Beatles. Cast: the Beatles. Broadcast: BBC, 1 May 1966.

The Big Broadcast. Direction: Frank Tuttle. Production: Benjamin Glazer. Writers: William Ford Manley (play) and George Marion Jr. (screenplay). Cinematography: George J. Folsey. Music: John Leipold and Ralph Rainger. Cast: Bing Crosby, Stuart Erwin, Leila Hyams, etc. Distribution: Paramount Pictures, 14 October 1932.

Biggles. Direction: Chris McMaster, Stuart Latham, Douglas Hurn, etc. Production: Harry Elton and Kitty Black for Granada Television. Writers: Thomas Clarke, Alick Hayes, W. E. Johns, etc. Cast: Neville Whiting, David Drummond, John Leyton, etc. Broadcast: ITV, 1961.

The Billy Cotton Band Show. Direction: Michael Hurll and Terry Hughes (1968). Production: Leslie Roberts, Bill Cotton, Michael Hurll, Johnny Stewart, Duncan Wood, etc. Writers: Eddie Gurney, Arthur Pastor, Jimmy Grafton, Robert Gray, and Eric Davidson. Music: Harry Rabinowitz, Fred Tomlinson, Ronnie Hazlehurst, etc. Cast: Bill Cotton (host), Kathie Kay, the Billy Cotton Band, etc. UK broadcast (168 episodes): BBC TV, 29 March 1956–20 July 1968.

The Black and White Minstrel Show. Direction: George Inns, Alan Field, Peter Robinson, etc. Production: George Inns, Ernest Maxin, Brian Whitehouse, etc. Writers: George Inns, Alan Field, Peter Robinson, etc. Cast: the Television Toppers, the Mitchell Minstrels, and guests. UK broadcast: BBC, 1958–1978.

Blackboard Jungle. Direction: Richard Brooks. Production: Pandro S. Berman. Writers: Evan Hunter (book) and Richard Brooks (screenplay). Cinematography: Russell Harlan with Ferris Webster (editing). Music: Max C. Freedman, Jimmy DeKnight, Willis Holman, and Jenny Lou Carson. Cast: Glen Ford, Sidney Poitier, Vic Morrow, etc. Distribution: Metro-Goldwyn-Mayer, March 1955.

Blues and Gospel Train. Direction: Philip Casson. Production: John Hamp, Granada Television. Cast: Muddy Waters, Sonny Terry, Brownie McGhee,

Sister Rosetta Tharpe, Rev. Gary Davis, Otis Spann, and Cousin Joe Pleasant. Broadcast: ITV, 19 August 1964.

Bob Dylan: Don't Look Back. Direction: D. A. Pennebaker. Production: John Court and Albert Grossman for Leacock-Pennebaker. Writers: D. A. Pennebaker. Cinematography: Howard Alk, Jones Alk, Ed Eshwiller, and D. A. Pennebaker. Music: Robert Van Dyke (recordist). Cast: Bob Dylan, Albert Grossman, Joan Baez, etc. Distribution: 17 May 1967.

Bonanza. Direction: Lewis Allen, Robert Altman, James Neilson, etc. Production: David Dortort, James W. Lanae, Thomas Thompson, etc. Writers: David Dortort, Anthony Lawrence, David Lang, etc. Cinematography: Haskell Boggs, William P. Whitley, etc. with Marvin Coil, Ellsworth Hoagland, etc. (editors). Music: Ray Evans (theme), David Rose, Walter Scharf, etc. Cast: Lorne Greene, Pernell Roberts, Dan Blocker, etc. Broadcast: National Broadcasting Company (NBC), 12 September 1959.

Boy Meets Girls. Direction: Rita Gillespie. Production: Jack Good. Writers: Trevor Peacock. Music: Bill Shepherd. Cast: Marty Wilde, Jack Good's Firing Squad, Billy Fury, etc. Broadcast: ABC Weekend Television, September 1959–February 1960.

The Bullwinkle Show/Rocky and His Friends/The Adventures of Rocky and Bullwinkle and Friends. Direction: William T. Hurtz, Gerald Baldwin, Ted Parmelee, Peter Burness, etc. Production: Bill Scott, Jay Ward, Bud Gourley, Ponsonby Britt, and Peter Reich for Bullwinkle Studios, Jay Ward Productions, and Producers Associates for Television. Writers: Chris Jenkyns, George Atkins, Chris Hayward, Bill Scott, Jay Ward, etc. Cinematography: Barbara Baldwin, Sam Clayberger, Adrienne Diamond, etc. Music: Frank Comstock, Dennis Farnon, Fred Steiner, and George Steiner. Cast: June Foray, Paul Frees, etc. Broadcast: American Broadcasting Company (1959–1961) and National Broadcasting Company (1961–1964).

Carousel. Direction: Henry King. Production: Henry Ephron and Darryl Zanuck. Writers: Ference Molnár (book) and Richard Rodgers and Oscar Hammerstein II (musical), with Phoebe Ephron and Henry Ephron (screenplay). Cinematography: Charles G. Clarke with William H. Reynolds (editor). Music: Richard Rodgers. Cast: Gordon MacRae, Shirley Jones, etc. Distribution: 20th Century Fox, 16 February 1956.

Carry On Cabby. Direction: Gerald Thomas. Production: Peter Rogers with Fran Bevis (associate producer) for Peter Rogers Productions. Writers: Sidney Green and Richard Hills (story) with Talbot Rothwell (screenplay). Cinematography: Alan Hume with Archie Ludski (editor). Music: Eric Rogers. Cast: Sidney James, Hattie Jacques, Charles Hawtrey, etc. Distribution: Anglo-Amalgamated Film Distributors, 7 November 1963.

Charlie Girl [stage production]. Direction: Wallace Douglas. Writers: Hugh Williams, Margaret Vyner (Williams), and Ray Cooney. Music: David Heneker and John Taylor with orchestrations by Arthur Wilkinson and dirction by Kenneth Alwyn. Cast: Joe Brown, Christine Holmes, Anna Neagle, etc. Debut: Adelphi Theatre, 15 December 1965.

Charlie Is My Darling. Direction: Peter Whitehead. Production: Andrew Loog Oldham. Cinematography: Peter Whitehead. Music: Rolling Stones. Cast: Rolling Stones. Debut: Mannheim Film Festival, October 1966.

The Cliff Richard Show. Production: Albert Locke. Writers: Jackie Rae. Cast: Cliff Richard, Peter Elliott, Pat Laurence, etc. Broadcast: ATV, 30 July 1960.

Coronation Street. Direction: Derek Bennett, Michael Scott, Eric Price, etc. Production: Stuart Latham (1960–1964). Writers: Tony Warren etc. Music: Eric Spear. Cast: William Roache, Doris Speed, Patricia Phoenix, etc. Broadcast: Granada Television, 1960–1990.

Don't Knock the Rock. Direction: Fred F. Sears. Production: Sam Katzman for Clover Productions. Writers: Robert E. Kent. Cinematography: Benjamin H. Kline with Paul Borofsky and Edwin H. Bryant (editors). Music: Ross DiMaggio and Fred Karger (supervisors). Cast: Bill Haley and the Comets, Ala Freed, the Treniers, Little Richard, etc. Distribution: Columbia Pictures, 14 December 1956.

Dr. No. Direction: Terence Young. Production: Albert R. Broccoli and Harry Saltzman with Stanley Sopel (associate). Cinematography: Ted Moore with Peter Hunt (editor). Music: Monty Norman and John Barry (music). Writers: Ian Fleming (author) with Richard Maibaum, Johanna Harwood, and Berkely Mather (screenplay). Cast: Sean Connery, Ursula Andress, Joseph Wiseman, Jack Lord, etc. Released by United Artists, 7 October 1962 (UK) and 29 May 1963 (US).

Drumbeat. Direction: Stewart Morris. Production: Stewart Morris. Cinematography: Ron Green. Music: John Barry. Cast: Gus Goodwin and Trevor Peacock (hosts) with Marty Wilde, Vince Eager, Cliff Richard, etc. Broadcast: BBC, beginning April 1959 (22 episodes).

Easybeat. Writers: Brian Matthew, Keith Fordyce, and David Symonds. Music: various. Broadcast: BBC Light Programme, Sunday mornings, 1960–1967.

The Ed Sullivan Show. Direction: Robert Bleyer, John Moffitt, Tim Kiley, John Wray, etc. Production: Robert Precht, Ed Sullivan, and Marlo Lewis (executive), Jack McGeehan and Robert Tamplin (associate), and Chester Feldman for CBS and Sullivan Productions. Writers: Buddy Arnold, Robert Mott, Robert Precht, etc. Cast: Ed Sullivan (host) and guests. Distribution: CBS, 1948–1971.

Exodus. Direction: Otto Preminger. Production: Otto Preminger Films. Writers: Leon Uris (novel) with Dalton Trumbo (screenplay). Cinematography: Sam Leavitt with Louis R. Loeffler (editor). Music: Ernest Gold. Cast: Paul Newman, Eva Marie Saint, Peter Lawford, Sal Mineo, etc. Distribution: United Artists, 15 December 1960.

Expresso Bongo. Direction: Val Guest. Production: Conquest [Val Guest Productions] and Jon Penington (Britannia Films). Cinematography: John Wilcox with Bill Lenny (editor). Music: Robert Farmon, Norrie Paramor, Monty Norman, and David Henneker. Writers: Wolf Mankowitz (author) with Julian More (screenplay). Cast: Laurence Harvey, Cliff Richard, Sylvia Sims, Yolande Donlan, Eric Pohlmann, etc. Distribution: British Lion Films, 11 December 1959 (UK) and 12 April 1960 (US).

Ferry Cross the Mersey. Direction: Jeremy Summers. Production: Brian Epstein and Michael Holden. Writers: David Franden (screenplay) and Tony Warren (story). Cinematography: Gilbert Taylor. Music: Gerry Marsden, George Martin, etc. Cast: Gerry and the Pacemakers, Cilla Black, etc. Distribution: United Artists, January 1965.

Find the Singer. Direction: Bimbi Harris and Christopher Hodson. Production: Associated-Rediffusion Television. Music: Bernard Herrmann. Cast: Lou Preager (host) with Maurice Burman, Kenneth MacLeod, Alma Cogan, etc. Broadcast: ITV, 1959 (18 episodes).

The Friday Spectacular. Direction: Muriel Young. Production: EMI, Manchester Square, London. Cast: the Beatles, Gerry and the Pacemakers, etc. Broadcast: Radio Luxembourg.

From Russia with Love. Direction: Terence Young. Production: Albert R. Broccoli and Harry Saltzman with Stanley Sopel (associate). Cinematography: Ted Moore (cinematographer) with Peter R. Hunt (editor). Music: John Barry. Writers: Ian Fleming (author) with Richard Maibaum, Johanna Harwood, and Berkley Mather (screenplay). Cast: Sean Connery, Daniela Bianchi, Robert Shaw, Pedro Armendáriz, etc. Distribution: United Artists, 11 October 1963 (UK) and 8 April 1964 (US).

From Spain to Streatham [aka *The Guitar Craze* or *Hound Dogs and Bach Addicts*]. Direction: Ken Russell. Production: Peter Newington with Nancy Thomas, BBC Television. Writers: Frank Duncan. Cinematography: Ken Russell with Allan Tyrer (editor). Music: various. Cast: John Williams, Mr. Skinner, Mrs. M. Griffiths, Laurie Griffiths, Davina Dundas, Teresa Power, Dave Graham, Len Williams, Evelyn Wilding, Avro Boys. Broadcast: Monitor, BBC, 7 June 1959.

Gentlemen Prefer Blondes. Direction: Howard Hawks. Production: Sol C. Siegel. Writers: Anita Loos and Joseph Fields (story) with Charles Lederer (screenplay). Cinematography: Harry J. Wild with Hugh S. Fowler (editor). Music: Hoagy Carmichael, Jule Styne, Eliot Daniel, and Lionel Newman. Cast: Marilyn Monroe, Jane Russell, Charles Coburn, etc. Distribution: 20th Century Fox, July 1953.

The Girl Can't Help It. Direction: Frank Tashlin. Production: Frank Tashlin. Writers: Garson Kanin (novel) with Frank Tashlin and Herbert Baker (screenplay). Cinematography: Leon Shamroy with James B. Clark (edotor). Music: Lionel Newman (supervisor). Cast: Tom Ewell, Jayne Mansfield, Edmond O'Brien, Juie London, etc. Distribution: Twentieth Century Fox, 1 December 1956 (US) and 11 March 1957 (UK).

Goldfinger. Direction: Guy Hamilton. Production: Albert R. Broccoli and Harry Salzman with Stanley Sopel and Terence Young (associates). Cinematography: Ted Moore with Peter Hunt (editor). Music: John Barry. Writers Ian Fleming (author) with Richard Maibaum and Paul Dehn (screenplay). Cast: Sean Connery, Gert Fröbe, Honor Blackman, Shirley Eaton, etc. Distribution: United Artists, 20 September 1964 (UK) and 25 December 1964 (US).

The Great Escape. Direction: John Sturges. Production: John Sturges. Writers: Paul Brickhill with James Clavell and W. R. Burnett (screenplay). Cinematography: Daniel L. Fapp. Music: Elmer Bernstein. Cast: Steve McQueen, James Garner, Richard Attenborough, etc. Distribution: United Artists 20 June 1963.

Guns at Batasi. Direction: John Guillermin. Production: George H. Brown. Writers: Rober Holles with Leo Marks, Marshall Pugh, and C. M. Pennington-Richards (adaptation) and Rober Holles (screenplay). Cinematography: Douglas Slocombe. Music: John Addison. Cast: Richard Attenborough, Jack Hawkings, Flora Robson, etc. Distribution: 20th Century Fox, September 1964 (UK) and 16 November 1964 (US).

A Hard Day's Night. Direction: Richard Lester. Production: Walter Shenson with Denis O'Dell (assistant) and David V. Picker (executive). Cinematograph: Gilbert Taylor with John Jympson (editor). Writers: Alun Owen. Music: the Beatles. Cast: John Lennon, Paul McCartney, George Harrison, Ringo Starr, etc. Distribution: United Artists, 6 July 1964 (UK) and 11 August 1964 (US).

Harpers West One. Direction: Wilfred Eades. Production: Hugh Rennie, Rex Firkin, Royston Morley. Writers: Georffey Bellman, Derrick De Marney, Richard Harris, Diana Noel, and John Whitney. Cast: Graham Crowden, Trestram Jellinek, Arthur Hewlett, etc. Broadcast: Associated Television, 24 July 1961.

Help! Direction: Richard Lester. Production: Walter Shenson. Cinematography: David Watkin with John Victor-Smith (editor). Music: the Beatles and Ken Thorne (director). Writers: Marc Behm with Charles Wood (screenplay). Cast: the Beatles, Leo McKern, Eleanor Bron, Victor Spinetti, Roy Kinnear, etc. Distribution: United Artists, 29 July 1965 (UK) and 25 August 1965 (US).

Here Come the Huggetts. Direction: Ken Annakin. Production: Betty E. Box for Gainsborough Pictures. Writers: Mabel Constanduros, Denis Constanduros, Peter Rogers (screenplay). Cinematography: Reginald H. Wyer with Gordon Hales (editor). Music: Antony Hopkins. Cast: Jack Warner, Kathleen Harrison, Petula Clark, etc. Distribution: General Film Distributors, 24 November 1948.

Hold On! Direction: Arthur Lubin. Production: Sam Katzman (Sam Katzman Productions). Writers: Robert Kent. Cinematography: Paul Vogel with Ben Lewis (editor). Music: Fred Karger. Cast: Peter Noone, Shelley Fabrares, etc. Distribution: Metro-Goldwyn-Mayer, 22 June 1966 (US) and 12 August 1966 (UK).

The Hollywood Palace. Direction: Grey Lockwood. Production: William O Harbach with Nick Vanoff for Zodiac Enterprises, American Broadcasting Company, and United Artists Television. Writers Joe Bigelow and Jay Burton. Cinematography: Nick Giordano. Cast: various. Broadcast: American Broadcasting Company, 1964–1970.

Hullabaloo. Direction: Ben Churchill. Production: ABC Television. Cast: Rory McEwen (presenter), Cyril Davies and His Rhythm and Blues All Stars, Davy Graham, etc. Broadcast: ITV, 28 September 1963—4 January 1964.

Hullabaloo. Direction: Steve Binder and Bill Davis. Production: Gary Smith and James S. Stanley, the Gary Smith Company and Hullabaloo Enterprises. Writers: John Aylesworth. Music: Peter Matz (music director). Cast: Sammy Davis, Jr., Petula Clark, etc. Broadcast: NBC, January 1965–April 1966.

It's Dark Outside. Direction: Derek Bennett and Gerard Dynevor. Production: Derek Bennett and Granada Television. Writers: Marc Brandel, Reed De Rouen, Paul Erickson, etc. Music: Derek Hilton (theme). Cast: William Mervyn, Keith Barron, Alice Brand, etc. Broadcast: ITV, 3 January 1964–23 April 1965.

It's Trad, Dad! Direction: Richard Lester. Production: Max Rosenberg and Milton Subotsky. Cinematography: Gilbert Taylor with Bill Lenny (editor). Music: Ken Thorne (director). Writers: Milton Subotsky. Cast: Helen Shapiro, Craig Douglas, Johnny Leyton, Chubby Checker, etc.: Columbia Pictures, 30 March 1962.

Jazz Club. Production: Jimmy Grant, Terry Henebery, etc. Cast: George Melly, David Jacobs, Kenny Ball, Monty Sunshine, etc. Broadcast: BBC Light Programme, BBC Radio, 1950–1969.

The Jazz Singer. Direction: Alan Crosland. Production: Darryl F. Zanuck. Writers: Samson Raphaelson with Alfred A. Cohn (screenplay). Cinematography: Hal Mohr. Music: Louis Silvers. Cast: Al Jolson, May McAvoy, etc. Distribution: Warner Brothers Pictures. 6 October 1927.

Juke Box Jury. Production: David Bell and the British Broadcasting Corporation. Writers: Peter Potter. Music: John Barry (theme). Featuring: David Jacobs (host) with guests. BBC TV Theatre, Shepherd's Bush Green, London Distribution: British Broadcasting Corporation, 1959–1990.

Keeping in Step. Direction: Rollo Gamble. Production: Daniel Farson. Writers: Daniel Farson, Elkan Allan, Stanley Craig, Geoffrey Golden, and Nichola Sterne. Cinematography: Ted Wooldridge with David Gill (editor). Cast: Daniel Farson, Adam Faith, etc. Broadcast: Associated Rediffusion Television, 1958 (9 episodes).

Keep Your Seats, Please! Direction: Monty Banks. Production: Basil Dean for Associated Talking Pictures. Writers: Ilya Ilf and Yevgeni Petrov (novel) with Thomas Geraghty, Anthony Kimmins, and Ian Hay (screenplay). Cinematography: John Boyle. Music: Ernest Irving. Cast: George Formby, Florence Desmond, Gus McNaughton, etc. Distribution: Associated British Film Distributors, 26 August 1936.

The Lads (ITV Television Playhouse). Direction: Casper Wrede. Production: Cecil Clark for Associated-Rediffusion Television. Writers: Ronald Harwood. Music: Trevor Peacock. UK Broadcast: ITV, 15 August 1963.

Look at Life. Direction: various. Production: Rank Organization. Writers: various. Cinematography: various. Music: various. Cast: various. Distribution: The Rank Organization, 1959–1969.

The Madhouse on Castle Street. Direction: Philip Saville. Production: Philip Saville. Writers: Evan Jones. Music: Bob Dylan. Cast: David Warner, Bob Dylan, Maureen Pryor, etc. Broadcast: BBC-Television, 13 January 1963.

Marty. Direction: Delbert Mann. Production: Harold Hecht and Burt Lancaster. Writers: Paddy Chayefsky. Cinematography: Joseph LaShelle. Music: Roy Webb. Cast: Ernest Borgnine, Betsy Blair, etc. Distribution: United Artists, 11 April 1955.

Medal for the General. Direction: Maurice Elvey. Production: Louis H. Jackson with Maurice Elvey and Wallace Orton, British National Films. Writers: James Ronald (novel) and Elizabeth Baron (screenplay). Cinematography: James Wilson with Grace Garland (editor). Music: William Alwyn. Cast: Godfrey Tearle, Jeanne de Casalis, Petula Clarke, etc. Distribution: Anglo-American Film Corporation, 6 November 1944.

The Mind Benders. Direction: Basil Dearden. Production: Michael Relph for Novus. Writers: James Kennaway (screenplay). Cinematography: Denys N. Coop with John Guthridge (editor). Music: Georges Auric. Cast:

Dirk Bogarde, Mary Ure, etc. Distribution: Anglo-Amalgamated Film Distributors, 21 February 1963 (UK).

The Mouse on the Moon. Direction: Richard Lester. Production: Walter Shenson. Writers: Michael Pertwee. Cinematography: Milkie Cooper. Music: Ron Grainer. Cast: Margaret Rutherford, Bernard Cribbins, Terry-Thomas, etc. Distribution: United Artists, 1963.

Mrs. Brown, You've Got a Lovely Daughter. Direction: Saul Swimmer. Production: Allen Klein. Cinematography: Jack Hildyard with Tristam Cones (editing). Music: Mickie Most, Ron Goodwin, and John Paul Jones. Writers: Norman Thaddeus Vane. Cast: Peter Noone, Herman's Hermits, Stanley Holloway, etc. Distribution: Metro-Goldwyn-Mayer, January 1968.

Murray the K's Christmas Show/Xmas Show/Big Holiday Show, Brooklyn Fox, New York.

My Fair Lady. Direction: George Cukor. Production: Jack L. Warner for Warner Bros. Writers: George Bernard Shaw (play), Alan Jay Lerner (book and screenplay). Cinematography: Harry Stradling, Sr. with William Ziegler (ed.). Music: Frederick Loewe, André Previn, etc. Cast: Audrey Hepburn, Rex Harrison, Stanley Holiday, etc. Distribution: Warner Bros., New York, 21 October 1964.

No Trams to Lime Street. Direction: Ted Kotcheff. Production: Sydney Newman for ABC Weekend Television. Writers: Alun Owen. Cinematography: n.a. Music: Robert Farnon. Cast: Tom Bell, J. G. Devlin, etc. Broadcast: ITV, 18 October 1959.

Oh Boy! Direction: Rita Gillespie. Production: Jack Good. Writers: Trevor Peacock. Cinematography: Jim Boyers. Music: Harry Robinson. Cast: Cliff Richard, Marty Wilde, etc. Broadcast: 1958–1959. Distribution: ITV, September 1958 to May 1959.

Oliver! [stage production]. Direction: Peter Coe with Malcolm Clare (choreography). Music and lyrics: Lionel Bart. Cast: Ron Moody, Georgia Brown, Martin Horsey, etc. Production: The New Theatre, 30 June 1960.

The Patty Duke Show. "Patty Pits Wits, Two Brits Hits." Direction: Bill Colleran. Production: Stanley Prager with John Ross for Crislaw Productions, United Artists Television. Writers: Arnold Horwitt, Sidney Sheldon, and William Asher. Cinematography: George Stoetzel with Bernard Leslie (editor). Music: Sid Ramin. Cast: Patty Duke, Jeremy Clyde, Chad Stuart, etc. Broadcast: American Broadcasting Company, 17 February 1965.

People and Places. Production: Johnnie Hamp, Granada Television. Cast: Elaine Grundy, Peter Jones, Bill Grundy, Chris Howland, Gay Byrne, and Muriel Young (presenters). First broadcast: Granada Television, Manchester, 9 July 1957.

Pet's Parlour. Cast: Petula Clark and Joe Henderson with guests. Broadcast: BBC Television, November–December 1950, December 1951, February–March 1952, and July 1953.

The Petula Clark Show. Production: Russell Turner. Music: George Clouston (conductor) with Peter Knight (orchestrations). Cast: Petula Clark, the Dallas Boys, Tommy Steele, etc. Broadcast: BBC, January–February 1956 and December 1956–January 1957.

Please. Direction: Arvid E. Gillstrom. Production: Mack Sennett for Mack Sennett Comedies. Writers: Dean Ward and Vernon Dent. Cinematography: Gus Peterson with John English (editor). Cast: Bing Crosby, Vernon Dent, Mary Kornman, etc. Distribution: Paramount Pictures, 15 December 1933.

Pop Go the Beatles. Production: Terry Henebery. Cast: the Beatles and guests. BBC Radio, Light Programme, 1963.

Pops and Lenny. Direction: Robert Gray. Production: Peter Whitmore. Cast: Terry Hall, etc. Broadcast: 1962–1963.

Rashōmon. Direction: Akira Kurosawa. Production: Minoru Jingo for Daiei Film. Writers: Ryūnosuke Akutagawa with Akira Kurosawa and Shinobu Hashimoto (screenplay). Cinamatography: Kazuo Miyagawa with Akira Kurosawa (editor). Music: Fumio Hayasaka. Cast: Toshiro Mifune, Machio Kyō, Masayuki Mori, etc. Distribution: Daiei Film, 25 August 1950.

Ready Steady Go! Direction: Robert Fleming, Rollo Gamble, Michael Lindsay-Hogg, Daphne Shadwell, etc. Production: Francis Hitching, Elkan Allan, and Vicki Wickham. Writers: Barry Cawtheray. Cinematography: Mike Rhodes with Francis Hitching, Vicki Wickham, and John Zambardi (editors). Music: Les Reed and Johnny Pearson. Cast: Cathy McGowan, Keith Fordyce, and David Gell (presenters). Broadcast: 1963–1966. Distribution: Associated-Rediffusion Television.

Rock around the Clock. Direction: Fred F. Sears. Production: Sam Katzman. Writers: Robert E. Kent and James B. Gordon (story and screenplay). Cinematography: Benjamin H. Kline. Music supervisor: Fred Karger. Cast: Bill Haley and the Comets, the Platters, Ernie Freeman Combo, etc. Distribution: Columbia Pictures, 21 March 1956 (US).

Rock You Sinners. Direction: Denis Kavanagh. Production: B. C. Fancey and Jeffrey Kruger. Writers: B. C. Fancy. Cinematography: Hal Morey with Monica Kimick and Roy Smith (editors). Music: Jeffrey Kruger (supervisor). Cast: Philip Gilbert, Adrienne Scott, etc. Distribution: Small Film Distributors, 1957.

The Running Jumping and Standing Still Film. Direction: Richard Lester and Peter Sellers. Production: Peter Sellers. Writers: Spike Milligan, Peter Sellers, Mario Fabrizi, and Richard Lester. Cinematography: Richard Lester. Music:

Richard Lester. Cast: Peter Sellers and Spike Milligan. Distribution: British Lion Films, November 1959.

Saturday Club. Production: Jimmy Grant, Brian Willey, Bernie Andrews, etc. Cast: Brian Matthew, Ray Orchard, Keith Skues, and performers. Broadcast: BBC Light Programme, BBC Radio, June 1957–January 1969.

Sea Fury. Direction: Cy Endfield. Production: Benjamin Fisz and Earl Saint John for The Rank Organisation, Aqua Film Productions, and S. Benjamin Fisz Productions. Writers: John Kruse and Cy Endfield (story and screenplay). Cinematography: Reginald Wyer with Arthur Stevens (editor). Music: Philip Green. Cast: Stanley Baker, Victor McLaglen, Luciana Paluzzi, etc. Distribution: Rank Film Distributors, 26 August 1958.

The Searchers. Direction: John Ford. Production: Merian C. Cooper and Patrick Ford. Writers: Alan LeMay with Frank Nugent (screenplay). Cinematography: Winton C. Hoch with Jack Murray (editor). Music: Max Steiner. Cast: John Wayne, Jeffrey Hunter, Vera Miles, etc. Distribution: Warner Brothers, 16 May 1956.

The Sheik. Direction: George Melford. Production: George Melford for Paramount Pictures. Writers: Edith Maude Hull (novel) with Monte M. Katterjon (adaptation). Cinematography: William Marshall. Music: Roger Bellon. Cast: Rudolph Valentino, Agnes Ayres, Ruth Miller, etc. Distribution: Paramount Pictures, Los Angeles, 31 October 1921.

Serious Charge. Direction: Terence Young. Production: Mickey Delamar for Alva Films. Writers: Philip King (play); Mickey Delemar and Guy Elmes (screenplay). Cinematography: Georges Périnal with Allan Harris (editor). Music: Leighton Lucas and Lionel Bart. Cast: Anthony Quayle. Distribution: Eros Films, 1959.

Shindig! Direction: Richard Dunlap, Selwyn Touber, Dean Whitmore, Rita Gillespie, Mel Ferber, and Jørn Winther. Production: Selig Seligman and Leon Mirell (executive producers) and Jack Good, Louis Heyward, Howard Lipstone, Phillip Browning (producers) with David Mallet, Marilyn Moore, and Arthur Stolnitz (associate producers) for American Broadcasting Company, Selmur Productions, and Circle Seven Productions. Writers: Jimmy O'Neill. Cinematography: John Shouse, Milt Kleinberg, and Victor Lewis. Music: Ray Pohlman, Don Ralke, and Harry Robertson. Cast: Jimmy O'Neill, Sam Cooke, the Everly Brothers, the Beatles, etc. Broadcast: ABC, September 1964–Fall 1965.

Sincerely Yours—Vera Lynn. Cast: Vera Lynn, Howard Thomas, and Fred Hartley and His Music. Broadcast: BBC Forces Programme, November 1941–March 1942.

Six-Five Special. Direction: Ray Lakeland etc. Production: Jack Good, Russell Turner, Josephine Douglas, etc. Writers: Jeremy Lloyd and Trevor Peacock.

Music: Harry Robinson and Andre Gersh. Cast: Josephine Douglas, Pete Murray, Don Lang, Jim Dale, etc. Broadcast: BBC, 1957–1958.

Snow White and the Seven Dwarfs. Direction: David Hand, William Cottrell, Wilfred Jackson, Larry Morey, Perce Pearce, and Ben Sharpsteen. Production: Walt Disney for Walt Disney Productions. Writers: Ted Sears, Richard Creedon, Otto Englander, Dick Rickard, Earl Hurd, Merrill de Maris, Dorothy Ann Blank, and Webb Smith. Cinematography: Mickey Batchelder, Ken Moore, and Max Morgan. Music: Frank Churchill, Paul Smith, and Leigh Harline. Cast: Adriana Caseolotti, Lucille La Verne, etc. Distribution: RKO Radio Pictures, 21 December 1937.

The Sound of Music. Direction: Robert Wise. Production: Robert Wise with Saul Chaplin (associate) and Peter Levathes and Richard D. Zanuck (executives) for Argyle Enterprises and Robert Wise Productions. Writers: Maria von Trapp (author) with Howard Lindsay and Russel Crouse (stage adaptation), and Ernst Lehman (screenplay). Cinematography: Ted D. McCord with William H. Reynolds (editor). Music: Richard Rodgers and Oscar Hammerstein II with Irwin Kostal (score). Cast: Julie Andrews, Christopher Plummer, Richard Haydn, Peggy Wood, etc. US release: Twentieth Century Fox, 2 March 1965. UK release: Twentieth Century Fox Film, 29 March 1965.

Stranger on the Shore. Direction: Kevin Sheldon. Production: Kevin Sheldon. Writers: Sheila Hodgson. Cinematography: Douglas Wolfe with Larry Toft (editor). Music: Acker Bilk. Cast: Richard Vernon, Beatrix Mackey, Amanda Grinling, etc. Broadcast: BBC TV, September 1961.

Strictly for the Sparrows. Direction: John Llewelln. Production: John Moxey for Associated-Rediffusion, Television Playhouse. Writers: Ted Willis. Cast: Kenneth Cope, Philip Locke, Naomi Moir, Bernice Swanson, and Billy Fury. Broadcast: ITV, 31 October 1958.

Sullivan, Ed. See *The Ed Sullivan Show*.

Sunday Night at the London Palladium (1955–1965) / *The London Palladium Show* (1966–1969). Production: ATV, London. Broadcast: ITV. (See *Val Parnell's Sunday Night at the London Palladium*).

Take It from Here. Production: Charles Maxwell. Writers: Frank Muir and Denis Norden. Music: Wilfred Babbage and the Keynotes and the Augmented BBC Revue Orchestra, Frank Cantell (conductor). Cast: Jimmy Edwards, Dick Bentley, and Joy Nichols (1948–1953); June Whitfield and Alma Cogan (1953–1960). Broadcast: BBC Light Programme, March 1948–March 1960.

The Talent Spot. Production: Brian Willey. Cast: Gary Marshall (host). Broadcast: BBC Light Programme, 17 April–18 December 1962.

The T.A.M.I. Show. Direction: Steve Binder. Production: William Sargent, Jr., Lee Savin, and Al Ham for Screen Entertainment Co., Screencraft

International, and Theatrofilm. Cinematography: Jim Kilgore with Kent Mackenzie and Bruce B. Pierce (editors). Music: Jack Nitzsche (arranger and conductor). Cast: the Beach Boys, James Brown, the Supremes, the Rolling Stones, etc. Distribution: American International Pictures, December 1964–January 1965.

Thank Your Lucky Stars. Production: ABC Weekend Television. Production: Philip Jones. Cast: Brian Matthew and Pete Murray (hosts) with guests. Broadcast: Independent Television, 1961–1966.

Them. Direction: Gordon Douglas. Production: David Weisbart for Warner Brothers. Writers: George Worthing Yates (story), Russell S. Hughes (adaptation), and Ted Sherdeman (screenplay). Cinematography: Sidney Hickox with Thomas Reilly (editor). Music: Bronislau Kaper. Cast: James Whitmore, Edmund Gwenn, etc. Distribution: Warner Brothers, June 1954 (US) and July 1954 (UK).

This Is Life: For the Record. Production: Rank Organisation. Music: John Schroeder. Cast: Helen Shapiro, Norrie Paramor, John Schroeder, Malcolm Addey, etc. Distribution: Rank Organisation, 1961.

Three Hats for Lisa. Direction: Sidney Hayers. Production: Jack Hanbury for Seven Hills Productions. Writers: Leslie Bricusse (story); Leslie Briscusse and Talbot Rothwell (screenplay). Cinematography: Alan Hume with Tristam Cones (editor). Music: Leslie Bricusse with Eric Rogers. Cast: Joe Brown, Sophie Hardy, Sidney James, etc. Distribution: Anglo-Amalgamated Film Distributors, 30 May 1965.

Thunderball. Direction: Terence Young. Production: Kevin McClory. Production: Kevin McClory with executive producers Albert Broccoli and Harry Saltzman. Writers: Ian Fleming (novel), Kevin McClory and Jack Whittingham (story), and Jack Whittington (screenplay). Cinematography: Ted Moore with Peter Hunt and Ernest Hosler (editors). Music: John Barry. Cast: Sean Connery, Claudine Auger, Adolfo Celi, etc. Distribution: United Artists, 29 December 1965 (UK).

Tom Jones. Direction: Tony Richardson. Production: Michael Balcon (executive producer), Tony Richardson (producer) and Michael Holen and Oscar Lewenstein (associate producers). Cinematography: Walter Lassaly with Antony Gibbs (editor). Writers: Henry Fielding (novel) and John Osborne (screenplay). Music: John Addison. Cast: Albert Finney, George Devine, Susannah York, David Warner, etc. Distribution: United Artists, London, 26 June 1963.

Top of the Pops. Direction: Melvyn Cornish, James Moir, Stanley Dorfman. Production: Johnnie Stewart, Stanley Dorfman, Melvyn Cornish, Colin Charman, and Neville Wortman. Music: Vince Clarke and George Kajanus with Johnny Pearson and Arthur Greenslade. Cast: Jimmy Savile,

Peter Murray, Cliff Richard, etc. First broadcast: British Broadcasting Corporation, January 1964.

Tuesday Rendezvous. Production: John Rhodes, Associated-Rediffusion Television. Writers: Bert Weedon, Muriel Young, etc. Music: Bert Weedon, etc. Cast: Muriel Young, Bert Weedon, Wally Whyton, etc. Broadcast: ITV, 1961–1963.

Upstairs, Downstairs. Direction, Joan Kemp-Welch, Derek Bennett, Raymond Menmuir, Bill Bain, Christopher Hodson, et al. Production: Rex Firkin and John Hawkesworth for London Weekend Television. Writers: Charlotte Bingham, Julian Bond, Raymond Bowers, Terence Brady, Maureen Duffy, et al. Editing: Geoff Beames. Music: Alexander Faris. Cast: Gordon Jackson, David Langton, Jean Marsh, Angela Baddeley, et al. Broadcast: ITV and London Weekend Television, 1971.

Val Parnell's Sunday Night at the London Palladium. Direction: Bill Lyon-Shaw, Albert Locke, Brian Tesler, Francis Essex, and Jon Scoffield. Production: Val Parnell, Bill Ward, Albert Locke, Colin Clews, and Brian Tesler for Associated Television. Writers: Sidney Green, Richard Hills, Eric Merriman, Eric Sykes, and Basil Thomas. Music: Jack Parnell, Cast: Bruce Forsyth, Tommy Trinder, Norman Vaughan, Dickie Henderson, and Don Arroll (hosts) with guests. Broadcast: Independent Television, 1955–1967.

Variety. Producer: Harry Pringle. Cast: Vickers Twins, Petula Clark, Henri Vadden Clifford Stanton, Jackie Hunter, Jack Payne's Orchestra conducted by Stanley Andrews. Broadcast: BBC Television, 24 June 1946–13 April 1951.

Vera Lynn Sings. Direction: Freddie Robertson. Production: Albert Stevenson with Leslie Roberts. Music: David McCallum, Sr. Cast: Vera Lynn, etc. Broadcast (42 episodes): 1956–1959.

Von Ryan's Express. Direction: Mark Robson. Production: Saul David. Writers: David Westheimer with Wendell Mayes and Joseph Landon (screenplay). Cinematography: William H. Daniels. Music: Jerry Goldsmith. Cast: Frank Sinatra, Trevor Howard, John Leyton, etc. Distribution: 20th Century Fox, 23 June 1965.

Wham!! Direction: Ben Churchill. Production: Jack Good. Music: Syd Dale. Cast: Joe Brown, Billy Fury, Vernons Girls, etc. Broadcast: ABC Weekend Television, ITV, April–June 1960.

What a Crazy World. Direction and production: Michael Carreras. Cinematography: Otto Heller with Max Benedict (editor). Writers: Alan Klein and Michael Carreras. Music: Stanley Black (director). Cast: Joe Brown, Susan Maughan, Marty Wilde, etc. Distribution: Warner-Pathé, 5 December 1963.

What's New Pussycat. Direction: Clive Donner. Production: Charles K. Feldman for Famartists Productions. Writers: Woody Allen. Cinematography: Jean Badal with Fergus McDonnell (editor). Music: Burt Bacharach and Hal David. Cast: Peter Sellers, Peter O'Toole, Ursula Andress, etc. Distribution: United Artists, 22 June 1965.

When the Boys Meet the Girls. Direction: Alvin Ganzer. Production: Sam Katzman (Sam Katzman Productions). Writers: Robert E. Kent. Cinematography: Paul Vogel with Ben Lewis (editor). Music: Fred Karger. Cast: Connie Francis, Harve Presnell, Peter Noone, etc. Distribution: Metro-Goldwyn-Mayer, 10 October 1965 (US) and 2 February 1966 (UK).

Youngest Sweetheart—Petula Clark. Cast: Petula Clark and Miriam Reed. Release: British Pathé, 14 May 1945.

The Young Ones. Direction: Sidney J. Furie. Production: Kenneth Harper and Andrew Mitchell. Writers: Peter Myers and Ronald Cas. Cinematography: Douglas Slocombe with Jack Slade (editor). Music: Stanley Black and Ronald Cass. Cast: Cliff Richard, Robert Morley, etc. Distribution: Paramount Pictures, December 1961.

Z Cars. Direction: Michael Leeston-Smith, Eric Hills, John McGrath, Christopher Moorahan, David Rose, Eric Tayler, Herbert Wise, John Llewellyn Moxey, James Mactaggart, etc. Production: David Rose etc. Writers: Allan Prior, Robert Barr, etc. Cinematography: Ian Stone etc. with Ian Callaway etc. (editors). Music: Bridget Fry with Fritz Spiegl. Cast: James Ellis, Brian Blessed, Robert Keegan, etc. First broadcast: BBC TV, 2 January 1962.

Volume 1 References

Interviews

See volume 2.

Publications[1]

Adams, Douglas. *Life, the Universe, and Everything*. London: Pocket Books, 1982.
Altham, Keith. "12345678910: The Top 2 with Their Top 10—Peter & Gordon." *Fabulous* (26 September 1964)..
Altham, Keith. "Marianne Faithful: Yours Faithfully." *Fabulous* (3 October 1964).
Altham, Keith. "The Seekers: Seekers Are Goon Fans." *New Musical Express* (5 February 1965): 13.
Altham, Keith. "Tom Jones." *New Musical Express* (12 March 1965a): 4.
Altham, Keith. "Startling Stones Discovery!" *New Musical Express* (12 March 1965b): 3.
Altham, Keith. "Sandie Shaw: Unsure Sandie." *New Musical Express* (19 March 1965): 4.
Altham, Keith. "Marianne Never Does What a Pop Star Should." *New Musical Express* (9 April 1965): 9.
Altham, Keith. "Hollies Get into No. 1 Hit Mood." *New Musical Express* (2 July 1965): 3.
Altham, Keith. "Eve Taylor: Queen Bee of Show Business." *New Musical Express* (16 July 1965): 9.
Altham, Keith. "Fortunes Have Got Their Own Troubles." *New Musical Express* (6 August 1965): 9.
Altham, Keith. "Byrds Weak Stage Act." *New Musical Express* (20 August 1965): 10.
Altham, Keith. "Fortunes Admit It: They Use Session Boys!" *New Musical Express* (29 October 1965a): 10.
Altham, Keith. "The Rolling Stones: Stones Hit Back." *New Musical Express* (29 October 1965b).: 3.
Altham, Keith. "New Sounding Kinks." *New Musical Express* (24 December 1965): 10.
Altham, Keith. "The Year the Folk Moved in." *New Musical Express Annual* (December 1965).
Altham, Keith. "Spotlight on the Spencers: Steve Winwood—Modest Wonder Boy." *New Musical Express* (11 February 1966): 4.
American Anthropological Association. "Statement on Ethnography and Institutional Review Boards" (4 June 2004): americananthro.org/ParticipateAndAdvocate/Content.aspx?ItemNumber=1652 (accessed December 2021).
"The American Invasion Is On! And Now It's Mitchell Torok." *New Musical Express* (15 February 1957): 10.

---

[1] Many period articles obtained at rocksbackpages.com.

Apolloni, Alexandra M. *Freedom Girls: Voicing Femininity in 1960s British Pop*. New York: Oxford University Press, 2021.
Appiah, Kwame Anthony. "The Case for Capitalizing the B in Black." *Atlantic* (18 June 2020): theatlantic.com/ideas/archive/2020/06/time-to-capitalize-blackand-white/613159/ (accessed January 2022).
Ascott, Roy. "The Construction of Change." *Cambridge Opinion* 41 (*Modern Art in Britain*) (1964): 37–42.
Aston, Martin. "Child Stars: We Blame the Parents!" *Q* (August 1994).
Auld, Tim. "Interview with 1960s Icon Sandie Shaw." *Telegraph* (13 September 2010): telegraph.co.uk/culture/7995004/Interview-with-1960s-icon-Sandie-Shaw.html (accessed September 2016).
Babiuk, Andy. *Beatles Gear: All the Fab Four's Instruments from Stage to Studio*. San Francisco: Backbeat Books, 2015.
Babiuk, Andy, and Greg Prevost. *Rolling Stones Gear: All the Stones' Instruments from Stage to Studio*. San Francisco: Backbeat Books, 2013.
Badman, Keith. *The Beatles Off the Record*. London: Book Sales Limited, 2000.
Barnard, Jason. "Allan Clark—Would You Believe?" *The Strange Brew* (2014): thestrangebrew.co.uk/allan-clarke-hollies-microsite/would-you-believe (accessed March 2016).
Barnard, Jason. "Mike Pender—Origins of the Searchers and the Search for Myself." *The Strange Brew* (2015): thestrangebrew.co.uk/articles/mike-pender-origins-of-the-searchers-and-the-search-for-myself (accessed January 2016).
Barnes, Mike. "Bert Jansch: Invisible Jukebox." *The Wire* (February 2007).
Barratt, Nick. "Family Detective, an Investigation into Our Hidden Histories. This Week: Mick Jagger." *Telegraph* (London): (5 November 2005).
Barrett, Adie. *Johnny Kidd & the Pirates: Kidd's Story* (2006). adiebarrett.co.uk/johnnykidd/story/story-index.htm (accessed November 2015).
Barrow, Tony. *John, Paul, George, Ringo, & Me: The Real Beatles Story*. New York: Thunder's Mouth Press, 2005.
BBC. "Sunday for the Forces." *Radio Times* (27 February 1941): 7.
BBC. "Sunday for the Forces." *Radio Times* (21 November 1942): 7.
BBC. "Weekly News" (12 December 1942): petulaclark.net/radio/radio40.html (accessed February 2022).
BBC. *The BBC Story: 1920s*. (n.d.): downloads.bbc.co.uk/historyofthebbc/1920s.pdf (accessed August 2022).
The Beatles. *The Beatles Anthology* (Brian Roylance, Julian Quance, Oliver Craske, and Roman Milisic, eds.). San Francisco: Chronicle Books, 2000.
"Beatles' New LP—Advance over 250,000." *Record Retailer and Music Industry News* (7 November 1963): 6.
"Beatles' Next: Half Million Already." *Record Retailer and Music Industry News* (5 March 1964): 31.
"Beatles Reaction Puzzles Even Psychologists." *Science News Letter* (29 February 1964): 141.
"Beatles Single—865,000." *Record Retailer and Music Industry News* (12 March 1964): 1.
Beauvoir, Simone de. *The Second Sex* (H. M. Parshley, ed. and trans.). New York: Knopf, 1953.
Black, Cilla. *What's It All About?* Croydon, UK: Ebury Press, 2003.
Black, Johnny. "Steve Winwood." *Mojo* (May 1997).

Black, Johnny. "Cliff Richard: Cliffstory." *Music Week* (September 2008).
Black, Roy. "The Woman Who Started It All." *The Gleaner* (13 October 2013): jamaica-gleaner.com/gleaner/20131013/ent/ent4.html (accessed April 2016).
Bob, Bulls Head. "Alex Wharton—The Making of Go Now." *Brumbeat.net* (2009): brumbeat.net/wharton.htm (accessed June 2016).
Bourdieu, Pierre. *Outline of a Theory of Practice* (Richard Nice, trans.). Cambridge: Cambridge University Press, 1977.
Bradley, Dick. *Understanding Rock 'n' Roll: Popular Music in Britain 1955–1964*. Buckingham, UK: Open University Press, 1992.
Bragg, Billy. "Go Lonnie Go." *Guardian* (21 June 2004): theguardian.com/music/2004/jun/21/popandrock (accessed October 2015).
Bramwell, Tony, with Rosemary Kingsland. *Magical Mystery Tours: My Life with the Beatles*. New York: Saint Martin's Press, 2005.
Bret, David. *Brit Girls of the Sixties*. Vol. 3. *Cilla Black, Sandie Shaw, & Lulu*. Author, 2014.
Briggs, Asa. *History of Broadcasting in the United Kingdom: The Birth of Broadcasting*. Oxford: Oxford University Press, 1961.
Bronson, Harold. "So What's Wrong with Herman's Hermits." *Zoo World* (27 September 1973).
Brown, Tony. "He Plays Jazzed-up Waltzes, Uses Saxophones, Guitars—Chris Barber—Is He Playing a Dangerous Game?" *Melody Maker* (2 December 1961): 2–3.
Burdon, Eric, with J. Marshall Craig. *Don't Let Me Be Misunderstood*. New York: Thunder's Mouth Press, 2001.
Buskin, Richard. "Mickie Most: Record Producer." *Sound on Sound* (August 2003): soundonsound. com/sos/aug03/articles/mickie-most.htm (accessed April 2016).
Campbell, Joseph. *The Hero with a Thousand Faces*. New York: Pantheon Books, 1949.
Cane-Honeysett, Laurence. "Millie Small, the Lollipop Girl." *Record Collector* (2010): recordcollectormag.com/articles/millie-small-the-lollipop-girl (accessed March 2020).
Cawley, Laurence. "Radio Caroline 50 Years On: The Man Who Pressed the 'On' Button." *BBC News* (28 March 2014). bbc.com/news/uk-england-essex-26769631 (accessed May 2016).
Chapman, Robert. "The 1960s Pirates: A Comparative Analysis of Radio London and Radio Caroline." *Popular Music* 9.2 (1990): 165–178.
Chapman, Robert. *Selling the Sixties: The Pirates and Pop Music Radio*. London: Routledge, 1992.
"Chart Error on Elvis Disc: 'Ridiculous Situation' Says Decca Official." *Record Retailer and Music Industry News* (25 January 1962): 28.
Church, Michael. "Caribbean Cleo—The Amazing Cleo Laine." *Caribbean Beat* 13 (Spring 1995): caribbean-beat.com/issue-13/caribbean-cleo-amazing-cleo-laine#axzz7KEjdtVyW (accessed February 2022).
Churchill, Winston S. *The Second World War*. Vol. 1. *The Gathering Storm*. London: Cassell, 1948.
Clapton, Eric. *Clapton: The Autobiography*. New York: Broadway Books, 2007.
Clayson, Alan. *Hamburg: The Cradle of British Rock*. Sanctuary, 1997.
Clayson, Alan. *The Yardbirds*. San Francisco: Backbeat Books, 2002.
Clayson, Alan. "Phil Solomon: Pop Impresario Who Handled Them and the Bachelors and Rescued Radio Caroline." *Independent* (20 June 2011): independent.co.uk/news/obituaries/phil-solomon-pop-impresario-who-handled-them-and-the-bachelors-and-rescued-radio-caroline-2300235.html (accessed June 2016).

Cleave, Maureen. "Why the Beatles Create All That Frenzy." *Evening Standard* (2 February 1963).

Cleave, Maureen. "Kathy Kirby: But the Smile Does Have to Go on and on . . ." *Evening Standard* (7 September 1963).

Cleave, Maureen. "In This Business Where You're Old at 20, Millie and Lulu Are the Younger Fry." *Evening Standard* (4 July 1964).

Cleveland, Barry. "Reexamining Vintage Analog Effects." *Electronic Musician* (1 January 2000): emusician.com/gear/1332/reexamining-vintage-analog-effects/31535 (accessed September 2016).

"Club, Disc Boom as Rock-and-Roll Craze Spreads: Rock-and-Roll Clubs Are Opening Throughout the Country and Record Sales Are Soaring." *Melody Maker* (14 July 1956): 2.

Coates, Norma. "(R)evolution Now? Rock and the Political Potential of Gender." *Sexing the Groove: Popular Music and Gender* (Sheila Whitely, ed.): 50-64. Abingdon: Routledge, 1997.

Cobb, David. "Interview: Cleo Laine, John Dankworth." *Macleans* (5 September 1977): archive.macleans.ca/article/1977/9/5/interview (accessed January 2022).

Cohn, Nik. *Ball the Wall: Nik Cohn in the Age of Rock*. London: Picador, 1989.

Coleman, Ray. "Vive Les Beat-tles! In French That Means 'They're Fab!'—and That's What All Paris Is Saying Right Now." *Melody Maker* (25 January 1964): 8-9.

Coleman, Ray. "Would You Let Your Sister Go with a Rolling Stone?" *Melody Maker* (14 March 1964): 8-9.

Coleman, Ray. "Just What Is R & B? For Weeks, *MM* Readers Have Been Asking This Question." *Melody Maker* (9 May 1964): 7.

Coleman, Ray. "Bang! Beatles Are Back! New Hit Shoots Way over Half Million Mark." *Melody Maker* (18 July 1964): 1.

Collis, John. *Van Morrison: Inarticulate Speech of the Heart*. New York: Da Capo Press, 1997.

Cooper, Charlie. "My Secret Life: Sandie Shaw, 66, Singer." *Independent* (30 March 2013): independent.co.uk/news/people/profiles/my-secret-life-sandie-shaw-66-singer-8551806.html (accessed September 2016).

Crippa, Elena. "Roy Ascott: Teaching Change." *Tate* (15 June 2011): tate.org.uk/context-comment/blogs/roy-ascott-teaching-change (accessed November 2016).

"Crombie Forms Rock-and-Roll Unit." *Melody Maker* (4 August 1956): 1, 4.

"Crombie Rocks." *Melody Maker* (15 September 1956): 9.

Cunningham, Mark. *Good Vibrations: A History of Record Production*. London: Sanctuary, 1998.

Cushman, Marc. *Long Distance Voyagers: The Story of the Moody Blues*. Vol. 1. *1964–1979*. San Diego, CA: Jacobs/Brown Press, 2017.

Cusick, Suzanne G. "On Musical Performances of Gender and Sex." *Audible Traces: Gender, Identity, and* Music (Elaine Barkin and Lydia Hamessley, eds.): 25–48. Los Angeles: Carciofoli, 1999.

David, Hubert W. "Songsheet." *Melody Maker* (26 May 1956): 10.

Davies, Dave. *Kink: An Autobiography*. New York: Hyperion, 1996.

Davies, Hunter. *The Beatles*. New York: Norton, 2006.

Davies, Ray. "What a Kink Thinks." *Melody Maker* (3 October 1964).

Davies, Ray. *X-Ray: The Unauthorized Autobiography*. London: Penguin Books, 1994.

Dawbarn, Bob. "Rock-'n'-Roll Pays Off." *Melody Maker* (8 December 1956): 3.
Dawbarn, Bob. "The Searchers' Secret? Guitars Stuck Together with Tape." *Melody Maker* (10 August 1963): 6.
Dawbarn, Bob. "What Now for the Searchers? This Hit May Open Up Fresh Horizons." *Melody Maker* (1 February 1964): 9.
Dawbarn, Bob. "Three Weeks after Being Voted Jazz Star Why I'm Going Pop!" *Melody Maker* (22 February 1964): 12.
Dawbarn, Bob. "Massive Swing to R & B: 'In Beat, the Audience Screams at the Group . . . In R & B, the Group Screams at the Audience.'" *Melody Maker* (18 April 1964): 8-9.
Dawbarn, Bob. "'Suddenly We're Popping,' Say the Animals." *Melody Maker* (16 May 1964): 6.
Dawbarn, Bob. "Watch Out for the Ivy League." *Melody Maker* (6 February 1965): 9.
Denselow, Robin. "Davey Graham." *Guardian* (16 December 2008). theguardian.com/music/2008/dec/17/folk-blues-music (accessed January 2017).
Devoy, Adrian. "Lulu: 'I've Had the Most Unbelievable Life." *Event Magazine* (28 February 2015).
Doncaster, Patrick. "On the Record: Popland Goes British . . ." *Daily Mirror* (24 January 1963): 15.
Donnelly, Mark. *Sixties Britain: Culture, Society, and Politics*. Harlow, UK: Pearson, 2005.
Dopson, Roger. *Tommy Steele and the Steelmen: The Rock 'n' Roll Years* Maidenhead, Berkshire, UK: See for Miles Records, 1990.
Dowlding, William J. *Beatlesongs*. New York: Simon & Schuster, 1989.
Eggar, Robin. "Mick Jagger." *Esquire* (1995).
Elliott, Martin. *The Rolling Stones Compete Recording Sessions 1962–2912*. London: Cherry Red Books, 2012.
Emerick, Geoff, and Howard Massey. *Here, There, and Everywhere: My Life Recording the Music of the Beatles*. New York: Gotham Books, 2006.
Emery, John. "Donovan's Big Influence? It's Not Dylan!" *Beat Instrumental* (May 1965): 36.
Epstein, Brian. *Cellarful of Noise*. London: Souvenir Press, 1998.
"Epstein Opens Press Office in New York." *Record Retailer and Music Industry News* (11 June 1964): 4.
Everett, Walter. *The Beatles as Musicians: Quarry Men through Revolver*. New York: Oxford University Press, 2001.
Ewbank, Tim, and Stafford Hildred. *Cliff: An Intimate Portrait of a Living Legend*. Virgin Digital, 2010.
Faist, Rudy. "Interview with Dr. Paul Arnold." (21 March 2007): geocities.ws/mikegriffiths6/Dr_Paul_Arnold_Zombies_first_bass_player_interviewed.html (accessed March 2024).
Faithfull, Marianne, with David Dalton. *Faithfull: An Autobiography*. New York: Cooper Square Press, 2000.
Fanelli, Damian. "The Kinks' Dave Davies Talks Reunion, His Kinks-Era Guitars, Meeting Jimi Hendrix, and More." *Guitar World* (22 December 2015).
Fielding, Henry. *The History of Tom Jones, a Foundling*. London: Andrew Millar, 1749.
"Fifty Years of Fame! The Georgie Fame Interview" *Soul and Jazz and Funk* (2 October 2015): soulandjazzandfunk.com/interviews/3644-fifty-years-of-fame-the-georgie-fame-interview.html (accessed June 2016).
Fletcher, Tony. *Moon (the Life and Death of a Rock Legend)*. New York: HarperCollins, 2000.
Fong-Torres, Ben. "Dusty Springfield: 'That Noise Is the Joy.'" AllMusic.com (1999).

"Force's Other Sweetheart, Anne Shelton Dies at 64." *The Herald* (31 July 1994): heraldscotland.com/news/12735697.forces-other-sweetheart-anne-shelton-dies-at-64/ (accessed February 2022).

Fordham, John. "Tito Burns Obituary: Jazz Bandleader Turned Pop Manager and Booking Agent." *Guardian* (2 September 2010): theguardian.com/music/2010/sep/02/tito-burns-obituary (accessed September 2015).

Fordyce, Keith. "Tips All the Hit Singles." *New Musical Express* (11 January 1963): 4.

Foster, Mo. *17 Watts? The Birth of British Rock Guitar*. London: Sanctuary, 2000.

Foucault, Michel. "Panopticism." *The People, Place, and Space Reader* (Jen Jack Gieseking and William Mangold, eds.): 327–329. New York: Routledge, 2014.

Fox, Kate. *Watching the English: The Hidden Rules of English Behavior*. 2nd ed. London: Nicholas Brealey, 2014.

Frame, Peter. *The Complete Rock Family Trees: The Development and History of Rock Performers Including Eric Clapton, Crosby Stills Nash & Young, Led Zeppelin, Rolling Stones, Fleetwood Mac, Genesis, Madness, T. Rex, Police . . .* London: Omnibus Press, 1993.

Frame, Peter. *The Beatles and Some Other Guys: Rock Family Trees of the Early Sixties*. London: Omnibus Press, 1997.

Frame, Peter. *Rockin' around Britain: Rock 'n' Roll Landmarks of the UK and Ireland*. London: Omnibus Press, 1999.

Frame, Peter. *The Restless Generation: How Rock Music Changed the Face of 1950s Britain*. London: Rogan House, 2007.

Freedman, Jean R. *Whistling in the Dark: Memory and Culture in Wartime London*. Lexington: University Press of Kentucky, 1998.

Freeman, Paul. "Dame Cleo Laine: Music Royalty." *Pop Culture Classics* (October 2010): popcultureclassics.com/cleo_laine.html (accessed January 2022).

Friedan, Betty. *The Feminine Mystique*. New York: Norton, 1963'

Frith, Simon. "Billie Davis: Woman in Pop." *Let It Be Rock* (September 1973).

Frontani, Michael R. *The Beatles: Image and the Media*. Jackson: University Press of Mississippi, 2007.

Geddes, George. "Jerry Lordan Story." Rock 'n' Roll—Schallplatten (1999): n.a.

Geller, Debbie. *In My Life: The Brian Epstein Story*. Edited by Anthony Wall. New York: Thomas Dunne Books, 2000.

Gillett, Charlie. *The Sound of the City: The Rise of Rock and Roll*. New York: Pantheon Books, 1983.

Graham, Davy. *The Guitar Player* [liner notes]. Pye Golden Guinea Records GGL 0224, 1963.

Graham, Jane. "Tom Jones Interview: "The Women, the Sex . . . I Don't Regret Anything." *The Big Issue* (23 October 2015).

Graves, Tom. "An Interview with Millie Small." *Goldmine* (August 2016).

Green, Matthew. "Coffee in a Coffin: The Fascinating Story of Le Macabre—and Soho's 1950s Espresso Revolution." *Telegraph* (9 March 2017): telegraph.co.uk/travel/destinations/europe/united-kingdom/england/london/articles/the-amazing-story-of-soho-1950s-espresso-revolution/ (accessed October 2019).

Greenfield, Robert. "Keith Richard: The Rolling Stone Interview." *Rolling Stone* (19 August 1971). rollingstone.com/music/news/keith-richards-the-rolling-stone-interview-19710819 (accessed February 2016).

Greer, Germaine. *The Female Eunuch*. London: Paladin, 1970.

Gregory, Mark. "A. L. Lloyd: Folklore and Australia." *Australian Folk Songs* (1970) : folkstream.com/reviews/lloyd/ (accessed January 2017).
Griffiths, David. "The Dave Clark Five: Do-It-Yourself Dave." In *Record Mirror* (14 December 1963).
Griffiths, David. "Manfred Mann: More of the Manfred Men." *Record Mirror* (9 May 1964).
Griffiths, David. "Marianne Faithfull: The Battle over a Bird." *Record Mirror* (8 April 1965).
Griffiths, David. "Kathy and the Problems of Being a Girl Singer." *Record Mirror* (18 March 1967).
Groom, Brian. "'Manpool': Time to Kiss and Make Up." *Financial Times* (24 February 2014).
Gross, Jesse. "Another British Invasion of B'way: Plays, Actors, and Lotsa Directors." *Variety* (21 October 1959): 2.
Grundy, Stuart, and John Tobler. "Pete Townshend." *Guitar Greats*. BBC Books (1983).
Guerra, Tom. "Hilton Valentine: From Animal to Skiffledog." *Mambo Sons* (n.d.): https://tomguerra.com/tom-guerra-interviews-hilton-valentine/ (accessed April 2016).
Halasz, Piri. "Great Britain: You Can Walk across It on the Grass." *Time* (15 April 1966): 30–34.
Hamilton, Michael. "Newcastle Blues Legend Eric Burdon Talks about His Early Days and the Animals." *NE4ME* (1 July 2010). ne4me.co.uk/celebrities-3/newcastle-legend-burdon-animals-147.html (accessed April 2016).
Hardy, Rebecca. "As the Darling of the Decade, Sandie Shaw Was Immune to the Sordid Behavior Going on around Her. Now It's Time to Lift the Lid on the Swinging Sixties . . ." *Daily Mail* (28 June 2013): dailymail.co.uk/femail/article-2349780/Sandie-Shaw-lifts-lid-swinging-sixties-.html (accessed September 2016).
Harker, Dave. *Fakesong: The Manufacture of British "Folksong" 1700 to the Present Day*. Milton Keynes: Open University Press, 1985.
Harper, Colin. "Anne Briggs: In Search of the Wild Rover." *Mojo* (March 1998).
Harper, Colin. "Bert Jansch and Davey Graham." *Mojo* (July 2000).
Harris, Craig. "Yesterday's Gone, Today's Just Arrived: Chad & Jeremy." *Dirty Linen: Folk and World Music* (May/June 2009): 21–23.
Harris, June. "Winifred Atwell: More Albums from Winnie." *Disc* (28 November 1959).
Harris, June. "Merseyside Beat Pays Off at Last!" *Disc* (23 March 1963).
Hart, Keith. "Popular Anthropology." *Anthropology Today* 22.3 (June 2006): 25.
Haslam, S. Alexander, Stephen D. Richer, and Katherine J. Reynolds. "Identity, Influence, and Change: Rediscovering John Turner's Vision for Social Psychology." *British Journal of Social Psychology* 51 (2012): 201–218.
Hattenstone, Simon. "Bassey Is Back." *Guardian* (23 October 2009): theguardian.com/music/2009/oct/24/shirley-bassey-interview (accessed January 2022).
Hebdige, Dick. *Subculture: The Meaning of Style*. London: Routledge, 1979.
Herman, Arthur. *How the Scots Invented the Modern World*. New York: Three Rivers Press, 2001.
Hibbert, Tom. "Who the Hell Does Tom Jones Think He Is?" *Q* (March 1991).
Hill, Kathryn. "'To F-f-f-ade Away?': The Blues Influence in Pete Townshend's Search for an Authentic Voice in 'My Generation.'" *Popular Music History* 9.2 (2014): 111–135.
Hinman, Doug. *The Kinks: All Day and All of the Night*. San Francisco: Backbeat Books, 2004.
Hodgkinson, Will. "Pete Townshend on Mod: A Conversation." *Subbaculture* (14 June 2011).

Hoffmann, Hank. "Skiffledog Is an Animal: Guitarist Hilton Valentine Rocks His Roots on New CD." *The Arts Paper* (31 March 2011): https://theartspaper.wordpress.com/2011/03/31/skiffledog-is-an-animal-guitarist-hilton-valentine-rocks-his-roots-on-new-cd/ (accessed April 2016).

Holmgren, Jostein, Peder M. Isager, and Thomas W. Schubert. "Evidence for Magnitude Representations of Social Hierarchies: Size and Distance Effects." *Public Library of Science* 13.9 (7 September 2018): 1–19.

Howell, Signe. "Ethnography." *The Open Encyclopedia of Anthropology* (18 February 2018): anthroencyclopedia.com/entry/ethnography (accessed March 2024).

Howells, Andy. "Brian Poole Returns as Tremeloes Frontman." *Entertainment South Wales* (4 April 2014): entertainmentsouthwales.com/2014/04/04/2014-04-brian-poole-returns-as-tremeloes-html/ (accessed March 2024).

Hutchins, Chris. "Music Capitals of the World: London." *Billboard* (9 October 1965): 30.

Hutton, Jack. "Stateside Snub for Stones: They Are Fed Up . . . They Have Talked about Pulling Out . . . about Cutting the Tour Short." *Melody Maker* (13 June 1964): 8–9.

"Introducing . . . the Beatles." *Record Retailer and Music Industry News* (4 October 1962): 29.

Irwin, Colin. "Bert Jansch: On the Road So Long." *Mojo* (December 2011).

Jackson, Stephen. *Britain's Population: Demographic Issues in Contemporary Society*. London: Routledge, 1998.

Jagger, Mick. "The Rolling Stones Write for *Melody Maker*: 'We're Not on the Bandwagon . . . So Will the Shout-up Merchants Just Belt Up?'" *Melody Maker* (21 March 1964): 3.

James, Dawn. "Billy J: 'It Isn't Going to Last Forever.'" *Rave* (March 1965).

James, Gary. "Interview with Dave Clark." *Classic Bands* (1994): classicbands.com/DaveClarkInterview.html (accessed January 2016).

James, Gary. "Interview with Hilton Valentine of the Animals." *Classic Bands* (2005): classicbands.com/AnimalsInterview.html (accessed April 2016).

James, Gary. "Interview with Eric Burdon." *Classic Bands* (2010): classicbands.com/EricBurdonInterview.html (accessed April 2016).

James, Gary. "Interview with Martin Murray and Jim Green of Martin Murray's Honeycombs." *Classic Bands* (n.d.): classicbands.com/HoneycombsInterview.html (accessed March 2016).

James, Gary. "Interview with Spencer Davis." *Classic Bands* (n.d.): classicbands.com/SpencerDavisInterview.html (accessed July 2016).

James, Tony. "Tony Meets Sir Cliff." *BBC* (6 May 2005): bbc.co.uk/cumbria/content/articles/2005/06/03/cliff_preview.shtml (accessed October 2015).

Jean-Marie. "Girl in a Girl's World: To Make Sandie Sure . . ." *Rave* (February 1965).

Johansen, Claes. *The Zombies: Hung Up on a Dream, a Biography—1962–1967*. London: SAF, 2001.

Johnson, Derek. "Singles." *New Musical Express* (8 November 1963): 4.

Jones, Nick. "Well, What Is Pop Art? Who Guitarist Pete Townshend Has a Go at a Definition." *Melody Maker* (3 July 1965): 11.

Jones, Peter. "Millie: A Blue Beat Bombshell!" *Record Mirror* (4 April 1964).

Jones, Peter. "Peter and Gordon: Jane Asher Speaks . . ." *Record Mirror* (11 April 1964).

Jopling, Norman. "Beat Group Names from America and Liverpool." *Record Mirror* (4 August 1962).

Jopling, Norman. "Manfred Mann: Meet the Manfreds." *Record Mirror* (2 May 1964).

Jopling, Norman. "Manfred Mann: The Paul Jones Mann." *Record Mirror* (16 May 1964).

Joynson, Vernon. *The Tapestry of Delights: The Comprehensive Guide to British Music of the Beat, R & B, Psychedelic, and Progressive Eras, 1963–1976*. Telford, UK: Borderline Productions, 1995.

Judd, Deany. "My Mentor: Lulu Recalls the Manager Who Kept Her Singing Career on the Rails." *Guardian* (1 August 2008): theguardian.com/money/2008/aug/02/workandcareers1 (accessed March 2016).

Judge, Timothy A., and Daniel M. Cable. "The Effect of Physical Height on Workplace Success and Income: Preliminary Test of a Theoretical Model." *Journal of Applied Psychology* 89.3 (June 2004): 428–441.

Kamp, David. "The British Invasion." *Vanity Fair* (November 2002): vanityfair.com/culture/features/2002/11/british-invasion-oral-history (accessed January 2003). Republished 10 February 2014.

Killelea, Amanda. "'People Say I Should Have Made It Like Cilla': Singers Could Have Been as Big as the Star." *Daily Record* (18 September 2014): dailyrecord.co.uk/entertainment/celebrity-interviews/people-say-should-made-like-4277447 (accessed March 2022).

Kirby, Michael Jack. "Wayne Fontana and the Mindbenders: Game of Love." *Way Back Attack* (2016): waybackattack.com/fontanawayne.html (accessed June 2016).

Kynaston, David. *Modernity Britain: Opening the Box, 1957–1959*. London: Bloomsbury, 2013.

Laing, Dave. "Rod Allen." *Guardian* (17 January 2008): theguardian.com/news/2008/jan/17/mainsection.obituaries1 (accessed July 2016).

Laing, Dave. "Jet Harris." *Guardian* (21 March 2011): theguardian.com/music/2011/mar/18/jet-harris-obituary (accessed September 2015).

Laing, Dave. "Kathy Kirby Obituary." *Guardian* (20 May 2011): theguardian.com/music/2011/may/20/kathy-kirby-obituary (accessed February 2022).

Laing, Dave. "Cilla Black Obituary." *Guardian* (2 August 2015): theguardian.com/tv-and-radio/2015/aug/02/cilla-black (accessed March 2016).

Laing, Dave. "Vera Lynn Obituary: Singer Had a Lifelong Connection with British Wartime Spirit." *Irish Times* (18 June 2020): irishtimes.com/culture/music/vera-lynn-obituary-singer-had-a-lifelong-connection-with-british-wartime-spirit-1.4282594 (accessed February 2022).

Lamb, Andrew. "Music Hall." *Grove Music Online*. Oxford University Press (20 January 2001).

Lazarevic, Jade. "50 Years of the Seekers." *Newcastle Herald* (25 January 2013): theherald.com.au/story/1250433/50-years-of-the-seekers/ (accessed January 2017).

Leigh, Spencer. *Lonnie Donegan: The EP Collection* (liner notes). Maidenhead, Berkshire, UK: See for Miles Records, 1992.

Leigh, Spencer. "Mickie Most: Record Producer Who Scored Hit after Hit." *Independent* (1 June 2003): independent.co.uk/news/obituaries/mickie-most-36586.html (accessed March 2016).

Leigh, Spencer. "Tony Jackson: Singer and Guitarist with the Searchers." *Independent* (18 August 2003): independent.co.uk/news/obituaries/tony-jackson-36958.html (accessed March 2016).

Leigh, Spencer. "Garrity, Frederick." *Oxford Dictionary of National Biography*. New York: Oxford University Press, 2004a.

Leigh, Spencer. *Twist and Shout! Merseybeat, the Cavern, the Star-Club, and the Beatles*. Liverpool: Nirvana Books, 2004b.

Leigh, Spencer. "Mike Smith: Lead Singer with the Sixties Beat Group the Dave Clark Five." *Independent* (29 February 2008): independent.co.uk/news/obituaries/mike-smith-lead-singer-with-the-sixties-beat-group-the-dave-clark-five-790032.html (accessed January 2016).

Leigh, Spencer. "Gordon Waller: Musician Who Enjoyed Success in the US as Part of Peter and Gordon." *Independent* (22 July 2009): independent.co.uk/news/obituaries/gordon-waller-musician-who-enjoyed-success-in-the-us-as-part-of-peter-and-gordon-1757208.html (accessed March 2016).

Leigh, Spencer. "Johnny Pearson: Composer, Pianist and Arranger Who Worked on *Top of the Pops* during Three Decades." *Independent* (22 March 2011): independent.co.uk/news/obituaries/johnny-pearson-composer-pianist-and-arranger-who-worked-on-lsquotop-of-the-popsrsquo-during-three-2249980.html (accessed March 2016).

Leigh, Spencer. "Mike Smith: Record Producer Who Had a String of No 1 Hits but Turned Down the Beatles." *Independent* (31 December 2011): independent.co.uk/news/obituaries/mike-smith-record-producer-who-had-a-string-of-no-1-hits-but-turned-down-the-beatles-6283369.html (accessed September 2017).

Leigh, Spencer. "Rick Huxley: Bassist with The Dave Clark Five." In *Independent* (13 February 2013): independent.co.uk/news/obituaries/rick-huxley-bassist-with-the-dave-clark-five-8493861.html (accessed January 2016).

Leigh, Spencer. "Gerry Marsden: Musician Who Sung Liverpool FC's Iconic 'You'll Never Walk Alone.'" *Independent* (3 January 2021): independent.co.uk/news/obituaries/gerry-marsden-death-musician-liverpool-fc-obituary-b1781757.html.

Leigh, Spencer, and John Firminger. *Halfway to Paradise: Britpop, 1955–1962* (1996). Folkestone, Kent: Finbarr International, 1996.

Leitch, Donovan. *The Autobiography of Donovan: The Hurdy Gurdy Man*. New York: Saint Martin's Press, 2005.

Levy, Shawn. *Ready, Steady, Go! The Smashing Rise and Giddy Fall of Swinging London*. New York: Doubleday, 2002.

Lewisohn, Mark. *The Beatles Recording Sessions*. New York: Harmony Books, 1988.

Lewisohn, Mark. *The Complete Beatles Chronicle*. New York: Harmony Books, 1992.

Lewisohn, Mark. *Tune in the Beatles: All These Years*. Vol. 1. New York: Crown Archetype, 2013.

Lomax, Alan. *Folk Song Style and Culture*. New Brunswick, NJ: Transaction Books, 1968.

Lomax, Alan. *Folk Song Style and Culture*. Washington, D.C.: Colonial Press Inc., American Association for the Advancement of Science, 1968.

Lomax, Alan. "Universals in Song." *The World of Music* 19.1/2 (1977): 117–130.

Low, Setha M. (ed.). *Theorizing the City: The New Urban Anthropology Reader*. New Brunswick, NJ: Rutgers University Press, 1999.

Low, Setha M. "Spatializing Culture: An Engaged Anthropological Approach to Space and Place." The People, Place, and Space Reader (Jen Jack Gieseking, William Mangold, Cinci Katz, Setha Low, and Susan Saegert, eds.): 34-38. New York, Routledge, 2014.

Lowe, Melanie. "'Tween' Scene: Resistance within the Mainstream." *Music Scenes: Local, Translocal, and Virtual* (Richard Peterson and Andy Bennett, eds.): 80–95. Nashville: Vanderbilt University Press, 2004.

Lowman, Robbie. "Alley-gations." *Record Retailer and Music Industry News* (11 October 1962).

Lowman, Robbie. "Spatialities: The Rebirth of Urban Anthropology through Studies of Urban Space." *A Companion to Urban Anthropology* (Donald M. Nonini, ed.): 15–27. Chichester, UK: Wiley, 2014.

Lulu. *Lulu: I Don't Want to Fight*. London: Little, Brown Book Group, 2002.
Lundberg, Ferdinand, and Marynia E. Farnham. *Modern Woman: The Lost Sex*. New York: Harper & Brothers, 1947.
MacDonald, Ian. *Revolution in the Head: The Beatles' Records and the Sixties*. London: Pimlico, 1998.
Maguire, Kevin. "Sixties Icon Sandie Shaw: 'I Suffered Unwanted Advances but It Was Very Different Then.'" *Mirror* (21 June 2013): mirror.co.uk/3am/celebrity-news/sandie-shaw-i-suffered-unwanted-1972986 (accessed September 2016).
Majd, Hooman. "Chris Blackwell." *Interview Magazine* (24 March 2009): interviewmagazine.com/music/chris-blackwell/ (accessed March 2016).
Mann, William. "What Songs the Beatles Sang . . ." *Times* (27 December 1963): 9.
"Marked Rise in October Sales." *Record Retailer and Music Industry News* (10 January 1963): 5.
Marsden, Beryl. "Beryl Marsden." *Mersey Beat* (n.d.): triumphpc.com/mersey-beat/a-z/berylmarsden.shtml (accessed March 2022).
Marsh, Dave. *Before I Get Old: The Story of the Who*. London: Plexus, 1983.
Martin, George, with Jeremy Hornsby. *All You Need Is Ears*. New York: Saint Martin's Press, 1979.
Martland, Peter. *Since Records Began: EMI, the First 100 Years* (Ruth Edge, consultant ed.). Portland, OR: Amadeus Press, 1997.
Martoccio, Angie. "Spencer Davis, Founder of the Spencer Davis Group, Dead at 81." *Rolling Stone* (20 October 2020): rollingstone.com/music/music-news/spencer-davis-group-obituary-1078226/ (accessed June 2021).
Marwick, Arthur. *The Sixties: Cultural Revolution in Britain, France, Italy, and the United States, c. 1958–1974*. Oxford: Oxford University Press, 1998.
Marwick, Arthur. *British Society since 1945*. London: Penguin Books, 2003.
Massey, Howard. *The Great British Recording Studios*. Milwaukee: Hal Leonard Books, 2015.
McCarthy, Dennis. *The Judith Story*. Judithdurham.org (2005): judithdurham.org.uk/ (accessed January 2017).
McCormick, Neil. "Dave Clark: Inscrutable Pop Mastermind." *Telegraph* (24 February 2015). telegraph.co.uk/culture/music/rockandpopfeatures/11401510/Dave-Clark-Five-Bigger-than-Beatles.html (accessed January 2016).
McLuhan, Marshall. *Understanding Media: The Extensions of Man*. Toronto: McGraw-Hill, 1964.
McMichael, Joe, and Jack Lyons. *The Who Concert File* (edited by Chris Chralesworth). New York: Omnibus Press, 1997.
McMullen, Phil. "Davey Graham: A Terrascopic Interview." *Ptolemaic Terrascope* (1991).
Melly, George. *Revolt into Style: The Pop Arts in Britain*. London: Penguin Books, 1970.
Mendelsohn, John. "The Zombies: *Early Days* (London)." *Rolling Stone* (15 November 1969).
Mendelsohn, John. "The Hermit Trembles: Peter Noone Looks Back." *Creem* (December 1980).
Midgley, Dominic. "Pirate That Ruled the Airwaves: Radio Caroline Was the Boat That Rocked the Music Business." *Express* (22 March 2014): express.co.uk/news/uk/466222/Pirate-that-ruled-the-airwaves-Radio-Caroline-was-the-boat-that-rocked-the-music-business (accessed May 2016).
Miles, Barry. "From the Marquee to the Met: Watching the Who." *Crawdaddy* (September 1970).

Miles, Barry. *Many Years from Now*. New York: Holt, 1997.
Miles, Barry. *The Beatles: A Diary*. London: Omnibus Press, 1998.
Millard, André. *Beatlemania: Technology, Business, and Teen Culture in Cold War America*. Baltimore: Johns Hopkins University Press, 2012.
Mills, David. "Trust Me, I'm an Anthropologist." *Anthropology Today* 22.2 (April 2006): 1–2.
Mitchell, Adrian. "Pops: Crawling Up—The Beatles with a Fierce New Noise." *Daily Mail* (1 February 1963): 10.
Monti, Adrian. "Folk Singer Donovan Leitch: Having Polio as a Child Made Me the Man I Am Today." *Express* (1 August 2016). express.co.uk/life-style/health/695432/Dovovan-Leitch-folk-singer-childhood-polio-musician (accessed February 2017).
"Music Has to Progress, Otherwise We'd All Still Be Doing, 'Rock around the Clock': Bennett? Williams? I Could Outsing Them Put Together." *Melody Maker* (21 August 1965): 14–15.
Myers, Marc. "Going Back Downtown." *Wall Street Journal* (12 June 2013): wsj.com/articles/SB10001424127887324866904578513153605764288 (accessed March 2022).
Myers, Marc. "How the Kinks Roughed Up Their Sound." *Wall Street Journal* (29 October 2014): wsj.com/articles/how-the-kinks-roughed-up-their-sound-1414596698 (accessed April 2021).
Nash, Graham. *Wild Tales: A Rock & Roll Life*. New York: Crown Archetype, 2013.
Neill, Andy, and Matt Kent. *Anyway Anyhow Anywhere: The Complete Chronicle of the Who 1958–1978*. London: Virgin Books, 2002.
Nettl, Bruno. *The Study of Ethnomusicology: Thirty-Three Issues and Concepts*. Urbana: University of Illinois Press, 2015.
"New Rockin' Horses Band Gets Rolling: Don Sollash Leads." *Melody Maker* (13 October 1956): 2.
"New to You: The Beatles." *Disc* (6 October 1962): 8.
Nicol, Colin. "Allan Crawford in Conversation with Colin Nicol." The Pirate Radio Hall of Fame (1999): offshoreradio.co.uk/odds37.htm (accessed May 2016).
Nicholls, Robert Wndham. "'What Would They Know about Green Onions': Musical Lifestyles of 1960s London Mods." *Popular Music History* 9.2 (2014): 155–172.
Nicholson, Virginia. *How Was It for You? Women, Sex, Love and Power in the 1960s*. London: Viking Press, 2019.
Nonini, Donald M. (ed.). *A Companion to Urban Anthropology*. Chichester, UK: Wiley-Blackwell, 2014.
Norman, Philip. *The Beatles in Their Generation*. New York: Simon & Schuster, 2003.
Norman, Philip. *Mick Jagger*. New York: HarperCollins, 2012.
Norris, Ray. "John McNally—The Quiet Searcher." The Searchers Official Website.
Nott, James. *Going to the Palais: A Social and Cultural History of Dancing and Dance*. Oxford: Oxford University Press, 2015.
Olaveson, Tim. "Collective Effervescence and Communitas: Processual Models of Ritual and Society in Emile Durkheim and Victor Turner." *Dialectical Anthropology* 26 (2001): 89–124.
Olden, Mark. "White Riot: The Week Notting Hill Exploded." *Independent* (29 August 2008). independent.co.uk/news/uk/home-news/white-riot-the-week-notting-hill-exploded-912105.html (accessed August 2015).
Oldham, Andrew Loog. *Stoned: A Memoir of London in the Sixties*. New York: Saint Martin's Press, 2000.

Oldham, Andrew Loog. *2Stoned*. London: Vintage, 2003.
Osborne, John. *The Entertainer*. London: Faber and Faber, 1957.
Palao, Alec. *Zombie Heaven*. London: Big Beat Records, 1997.
Parker, David. "Breakfast with Marty Wilde." *The Beat* (February 2014): beat-magazine.co.uk/2014/breafast-with-marty-wilde (accessed October 2015).
Parker, Melissa. "Petula Clark Interview: So Much More Than 'Downtown,' International Entertainment Legend Gets In-Depth and Intimate." *Smashing Interviews Magazine* (13 January 2014): smashinginterviews.com/interviews/musicians/petula-clark-interview-so-much-more-than-downtown-international-entertainment-legend-gets-in-depth-and-intimate (accessed September 2016).
Payne, Jack. "Showtalk." *Melody Maker* (19 January 1957): 5.
Paytress, Mark. *The Rolling Stones Off the Record*. London: Omnibus Press, 2003.
Peterson, Richard A., and Andy Bennett. "Introducing Music Scenes." *Music Scenes: Local, Translocal, and Virtual* (Andy Bennett and Richard Peterson, eds.): 1–15. Nashville: Vanderbilt Universty Press, 2004.
Petridis, Alexis. "Ronan O'Rahilly: Pirate Radio's Godfather Made a Sea Change in British Pop." *Guardian* (21 April 2020): theguardian.com/music/2020/apr/21/ronan-orahilly-pirate-radio-godfather-made-a-sea-change-in-british-pop (accessed April 2020).
Pidgeon, John. A Conversation with Alexis Korner (unpublished, 15 November 1971).
Pidgeon, John. "Blues Incorporated: How British R & B Trashed Trad." *Rock's Backpages* (24 September 2009).
Pilgrim, John. "Davy Graham: Virtuoso Guitarist at the Heart of the British Folk Revival Whose Playing Influenced a Generation." *The Independent* (16 December 2008): independent.co.uk/news/obituaries/davy-graham-virtuoso-guitarist-at-the-heart-of-the-british-folk-revival-whose-playing-influenced-a-1192738.html (accessed January 2017).
Pressly, Linda. "The 'Forgotten' Race Riot." BBC News (21 May 2007). news.bbc.co.uk/2/hi/uk_news/6675793.stm (accessed August 2015).
Repsch, John. *The Legendary Joe Meek: The Telstar Man*. London: Cherry Red Books, 2000.
Reynolds, Anthony. "The Monster Who Made Scott Walker a Superstar." The Express (25 August 2009): express.co.uk/entertainment/music/122669/The-monster-who-made-Scott-Walker-a-superstar (accessed July 2016).
Rice, Timothy. "Reflections on Music and Identity in Ethnomusicology." *Serbian Journal of Ethnomusicology* (2007): 17–38.
Richards, Keith, with James Fox. *Life*. New York: Little, Brown, 2010.
Roberts, Chris. "It's All Happening Beatlewise." *Melody Maker* (9 February 1963): 9.
Roberts, Chris. "Lennon and McCartney Tell You . . . How to Write a Hit!" Melody Maker (1 February 1964): 11.
Robertson, Peter. "Girl with the Giggle in Her Voice." *Daily Express* (21 October 2016): express.co.uk/life-style/life/723571/Alma-Cogan-singer-overtaken-rock-roll-life (accessed February 2022).
"Rock and Roll Has Got the Debs Too." *The People* (16 September 1954).
"Rock 'n' Roll (or Was It Skiffle) Comes to Town: Mr. Donegan and Mr. Steele." *Melody Maker* (8 December 1956): 8.
Rogan, Johnny. *Starmakers & Svengalis: The History of British Pop Management*. London: Queen Anne Press, 1988.
Rogan, Johnny. *Ray Davies: A Complicated Life*. London: Bodley Head, 2015.

Sandbrook, Dominic. *Never Had It So Good: A History of Britain from Suez to the Beatles.* London: Little, Brown Book Group, 2005.

Sandbrook, Dominic. *White Heat: A History of Britain in the Swinging Sixties.* London: Little, Brown Book Group, 2006.

Saunders, Metal Mike. "The Zombies: Everything You Wanted to Know!" *Fusion* (November 1972).

Savage, Jon. "The Magazine Explosion." *Guardian* (5 September 2009): theguardian.com/music/2009/sep/06/sixties-60s-pop-magazines-beatles (accessed December 2020).

Savage, Jon. "The Blackheath Jungle." Mojo (February 1995a).

Savage, Jon. "The Great Pretender." *Mojo* (February 1995b).

Schaffner, Nicholas. "The Kinks." *The British Invasion: From the First Wave to the New Wave* (Nicholas Schaffner, ed.): 94–111. New York: McGraw-Hill, 1982a.

Schaffner, Nicholas. "Billy J. Kramer." *The British Invasion: From the First Wave to the New Wave* (Nicholas Schaffner, ed.): 237. New York: McGraw-Hill, 1982b.

Schreuders, Piet, Mark Lewisohn, and Adam Smith. *The Beatles London.* New York: Saint Martin's Press, 1994.

Schroeder, John. *Sex & Violins: My Affair with Life, Love, and Music.* Brighton, UK: Pan Press, 2009.

Schroeder, John. *All for the Love of Music.* Kibworth Beauchamp, UK: Matador, 2016. (Reprint of Schroeder, *Sex & Violins*, in new layout)

Schwartz, Roberta Freund. *How Britain Got the Blues: The Transmission and Reception of American Blues Style in the United Kingdom.* Aldershot, UK: Ashgate Publishing Limited, 2007.

Scott, Keith. "Impressions of Cyril from the Piano Stool." Cyril Davies . . . British Blues Harp Pioneer (2012): cyrildavies.com/Scott1.html (accessed February 2016).

Shapiro, Harry. *Alexis Korner: The Biography.* London: Bloomsbury, 1996.

Sharp, Ken. "Tom Jones: The Interview." *Rockcellar Magazine* (20 December 2016): rockcellarmagazine.com/2016/01/08/tom-jones-the-interview-long-lost-suitcase/#sthash.AUOFJH3c.dpbs (accessed December 2016).

Shaw, Sandie. "Interview: Sandie Shaw." *M Magazine* (22 June 2015): m-magazine.co.uk/features/interviews/interview-sandie-shaw/ (accessed May 2016).

Sheff, David. *The Playboy Interviews with John Lennon and Yoko Ono.* New York: Playboy Press, 1981.

"The Short, Busy Life of Cliff Richard." *Melody Maker* (12 November 1960): 15.

Sigman, Michael. "Lost in Translation: Cilla Black, Carl Sigman, and the 'Translational Fallacy' in Lyric Writing." *ASCAP* (2 September 2015): ascap.com/playback/2015/09/action/lost-in-translation.aspx (accessed March 2022).

Simon, Scott. "War Stories from Petula Clark." *Weekend Edition Saturday* (21 December 2013): npr.org/2013/12/21/255568247/war-stories-from-petula-clark (accessed May 2016).

Simpson, Dave. "Petula Clark: How We Made Downtown." *Guardian* (11 October 2016): theguardian.com/music/2016/oct/11/petula-clark-tony-hatch-how-we-made-downtown (accessed October 2016).

Small, Christopher. *Musicking: The Meanings of Performing and Listening.* Middletown, CT: Wesleyan University Press, 1998.

Smith, Alan. "Winifred Atwell: Win Gets in Trim for Hit!" *New Musical Express* (18 May 1962): 9.

Smith, Alan. "Newcomers to the Charts: Liverpool's Beatles Wrote Their Own Hit." In *New Musical Express* (26 October 1962): 2.

Smith, Caspar Llewellyn. "Flash-back." *Guardian* (17 September 2005): guardian.co.uk/music/2005/sep/18/folk.popandrock (accessed February 2017).

Smith, Joe. *Off the Record: An Oral History of Popular Music*. Edited by Mitchell Fink. New York: Warner Books, 1988.

Smith, Michael. "No Major Label Would Sign the Seekers even though They'd Overtaken UK TV." *The Music* (6 November 2015): themusic.com.au/interviews/all/2015/11/06/the-seekers-athol-guy-music-victoria-hall-of-fame-2015-michael-smith/ (accessed February 2017).

Smith, Roger. "Club a'Gogo." *Ready Steady Gone: Gigging in the North East, 1965–1972* (2011): readysteadygone.co.uk/club-agogo-newcastle-2/ (accessed April 2016).

Smith, Roger. "Mike Jeffrey, Part 1." *Ready Steady Gone* (2012): readysteadygone.co.uk/mike-jeffery-part-1/ (accessed April 2016).

Southall, Brian, with Rupert Perry. *Northern Songs: The True Story of the Beatles' Song Publishing Empire*. London: Omnibus Press, 2006.

Spizer, Bruce. *The Beatles Are Coming! The Birth of Beatlemania in America*. New Orleans: 498 Productions, 2003.

Stabile, Carol A. *The Broadcast 41: Women and the Anti-Communist Blacklist*. Goldsmiths Press, London, 2018.

Stafford, Caroline, and David Stafford. *Fings Ain't Wot They Used t' Be: The Lionel Bart Story*. Omnibus Press, 2011.

Stanley, Bob. "The Legacy of Dusty Springfield." *Times* (London) (3 April 2009).

Stephens, Sylvia. "Cathy McGowan, Sandie Shaw, Cilla Black, Lulu: Screening the Girls." *Fabulous* (21 February 1964).

Stephens, Sylvia. "Teledate with Marianne Faithfull." *Fabulous* (12 December 1964).

Stewart, Eric. "Wayne Fontana and the Mindbenders: Memories." *Manchester Beat* (n.d.): manchesterbeat.com/groups/waynefontanaminders/waynefontanamindbenders.php (accessed June 2016).

"Storm over USAF Men in 'No Fee' Band, 'Matter of Principle,' Say MU Members." *Melody Maker* (29 September 1956): 2.

Stratton, Jon. "Chris Blackwell and 'My Boy Lollipop': Ska, Race, and British Popular Music." *Journal of Popular Music Studies* 22.4 (2010): 436–465.

Sutch, David, with Peter Chippindale. *Life as Sutch: The Official Autobiography of a Monster Raving Loony*. London: HarperCollins, 1991.

Swanson, Dave. "51 Years Ago: Manfred Mann Record of the No. 1 Hit 'Do Wah Diddy Diddy.'" *Ultimate Classic Rock* (11 June 2015): ultimateclassicrock.com/manfred-mann-do-wah-diddy-diddy/ (accessed March 2016).

Sweeting, Adam. "John Entwistle: Brilliant Rock Guitarist Who Gave Stability and Polish to the Who." *Guardian* (29 June 2002): theguardian.com/news/2002/jun/29/guardian obituaries.arts (accessed November 2016).

Sweeting, Adam. "Chris Stamp Obituary." *Guardian* (28 November 2012): theguardian.com/music/2012/nov/28/chris-stamp (accessed November 2016).

Taylor, Charles. *A Secular Age*. Cambridge, MA: Harvard University Press, 2007.

Taylor, Derek. "The Byrds: Strictly for the Byrds!" *Melody Maker* (17 July 1965).

Thompson, Dave. "The Chad and Jeremy Story." *Goldmine* (2000).

Thompson, Gordon R. "'Georgia on My Mind': The History of an American Popular Song." master's thesis, University of Illinois, Champaign-Urbana, 1978.

Thompson, Gordon R. "Music and Values in Gujarati-Speaking Western India." Ph.D. diss, University of California, Los Angeles, 1987.

Thompson, Gordon R. *Please Please Me: Sixties British Pop, Inside Out*. New York: Oxford University Press, 2008.
Tims, Hilton. "Mr Success." *Daily Mail* (17 September 1964): 4, 16.
Tobler, John, and Stuart Grundy. *The Record Producers*. New York: Saint Martin's Press, 1982.
Townshend, Pete. *Who Am I: A Memoir*. New York: Harper Perennial, 2012.
Travis, Alan. "After 44 Years Secret Papers Reveal Truth about Five Nights of Violence in Notting Hill." *Guardian* (24 August 2002): theguardian.com/uk/2002/aug/24/artsandhumanities.nottinghillcarnival2002 (accessed August 2015).
Turner, Steve. "The Ace Face's Forgotten Story: Pete Meaden." *New Musical Express* (17 November 1979).
"UK Settles WWII Debts to Allies." *One-Minute World News* (29 December 2006). news.bbc.co.uk/2/hi/6215847.stm (accessed January 2011).
United Kingdom. Education Act 1944 (3 August 1944).
United Kingdom. British Nationality Act 1948 (30 July 1948).
United Kingdom. The Commonwealth Immigrants Act 1962 (18 April 1962).
Unterberger, Ritchie. *Urban Spacemen and Wayfaring Strangers: Overlooked Innovators and Eccentric Visionaries of '60s Rock*. San Francisco: Miller Freeman Books, 2000.
Vallance, Tom. "Obituary: Lionel Bart." *Independent* (5 April 1999): independent.co.uk/arts-entertainment/obituary-lionel-bart-1085282.html (accessed October 2015).
Warwick, Jacqueline, and Allison Adrian. Introduction to *Voicing Girlhood in Popular Music: Performance, Authority, Authenticity* (Jacqueline Warwick and Allison Adrian, eds.): 1–11. New York: Routledge, 2016.
Watts, Michael. "Shirley Bassey: The Soul of Showbiz." *Melody Maker* (18 September 1971).
Watts, Michael. "Tom Wilson: The Man Who Put Electricity into Dylan." *Melody Maker* (31 January 1976).
Webber, Richard. "Whatever Happened to . . . Manfred Mann?" *Express* (18 October 2014): express.co.uk/life-style/life/523496/Manfred-Mann-singer-Manfred-Lubowitz (accessed March 2016).
Weight, Richard. *Mod! From Bebop to Britpop, Britain's Biggest Youth Movement*. London: Vintage Books, 2015.
Welch, Chris. "The Byrds: Flamingo Club, London." *Melody Maker* (14 August 1965).
Welch, Chris. "Alan Price: Price Cuts." *Melody Maker* (23 March 1974).
Welch, Chris. "Georgie Fame: Fanning the Flames." *Melody Maker* (3 August 1974).
Welch, Chris. "Obituary: Dusty Springfield." *Independent* (3 March 1999): independent.co.uk/arts-entertainment/obituary-dusty-springfield-1078196.html (accessed January 2016).
Wells, John. "The Battle of the Girls Is Really Hotting Up." *Disc* (14 April 1962): 12.
Wenner, Jann. "Pete Townshend Settles Down." *Rolling Stone* (28 September 1968): rollingstone.com/music/news/pete-townshend-the-rolling-stone-interview-part-two-19680928 (accessed October 2016).
Wenner, Jann. "Lennon Remembers, Part One." *Rolling Stone* (21 January 1971): rollingstone.com/music/music-news/lennon-remembers-part-one-186693/ (accessed December 2019).
Wenner, Jann. "Lennon Remembers, Part Two." *Rolling Stone* (4 February 1971): rollingstone.com/music/music-news/lennon-remembers-part-two-187100/ (accessed December 2019).

Wenner, Jann. "Mick Jagger Remembers." *Rolling Stone* (14 December 1995): rollingstone.com/music/news/mick-jagger-remembers-19951214 (accessed September 2016).
White, Alan. "Early Blues Interview: John Steel, Drummer." *EarlyBlues.com* (2011): earlyblues.com/Interview%20-%20John%20Steel.htm (accessed April 2016).
Williams, Paul. "City Songs." *Crawdaddy* (March 1966).
Wilson, John S. "Din Overpowers Dave Clark Five." *New York Times* (30 May 1964): 9.
Witts, Richard. "Needle Time: The BBC, the Musicians' Union, Popular Music, and the Reform of Radio in the 1960s." *Popular Music History* 7.3 (2012): 241–262.
Witts, Richard. "Manpool, the Musical: Harmony and Counterpoint on the Lancashire Plain." *Popular Music History* 10.1 (2015): 10–29.
Wolfe, Tom. "The Noonday Underground." *The Pump House Gang*. New York: Farrar, Straus, and Giroux, 1968: 97-112.
Womack, Kenneth. *Maximum Volume: The Life of Beatles Producer George Martin, the Early Years, 1926–1966*. Chicago: Chicago Review Press, 2017.
Woodhouse, John R. "The Moody Blues." *Brumbeat* (2015): brumbeat.net/moody.htm (accessed June 2016).
Woodhouse, John R. "The Rockin' Berries." *Brumbeat* (2016): brumbeat.net/berries.htm (accessed June 2016).
Wyman, Bill, with Richard Havers. *Rolling with the Stones*. London: Dorling Kindersley, 2002.
Young, Graham. "Sinatra, McQueen, and Me." *Sunday Mercury* (Birmingham, UK) (29 December 2013): go-gale-com (accessed November 2019).
"Your Review Guide to the New Discs." *Record Retailer and Music Industry News* (4 October 1962): 4, 6, 32.
Yule, Andrew. *The Man Who "Framed" the Beatles: A Biography of Richard Lester*. New York: Donald I. Fine, 1994.
Zekas, Rita. "Downtown Sunday Night." *Toronto Star* (5 November 2000): petulaclark.net/live/2000/torontostar05.html (accessed September 2016).

Song Index

"'Til the Following Night," 64, 401
"(Ain't That) Just Like Me," 112, 348
"(I Can't Get No) Satisfaction," 291–93, 390
"(There's) Always Something There to Remind Me," 276–77, 370, 396
"(You're the) Devil in Disguise," 115, 385

"5-4-3-2-1," 377

"A Hard Day's Night," 150–51
"A Hundred Pipers," 66, 376
"A Legal Matter," 307, 405
"A Picture of You," 50
"A Summer Song," 174, 400
"A Teenager in Love," 46–47, 351, 405
"A World without Love," 159, 382–83
"A World of Our Own," 313, 393–94
"Ain't Got You," 258, 332, 333, 406
"All Day and All of the Night," 253, 372
"All I've Got to Do," 99–100, 337
"All My Loving," 99–100, 337
"All Shook Up," 27, 384
"And I Love Her," 151, 338
"Angi," 314, 316, 363
"Angie," 369
"Anyone Who Had a Heart," 342–43, 404
"Anyway, Anyhow, Anywhere," 305, 306, 404–5
"Apache," 67, 173, 394, 404
"As Long as You're Happy, Baby," 234, 396
"As Tears Go By," 236, 357
"As Time Goes By," 236

"Baby It's You," 163, 336, 337, 342, 397
"Baby Let Me Follow You Down," 167, 354
"Baby Let Me Take You Home," 167, 331
"Baby Please Don't Go," 256–57, 290, 358, 402, 406
"Baby's in Black," 153, 339
"Bachelor Boy," 92, 386
"Back in the USA," 133
"Bad Boy," 47, 405
"Bad Penny Blues," 53, 377
"Bad to Me," 107, 111, 159, 373–74
"Big Man," 208, 373
"Bits and Pieces," 187–189, 292, 347

"Black Is the Colour of My True Love's Hair," 315, 363–64
"Blowin' in the Wind," 167, 236, 319, 354, 355, 357–58, 383
"Blue Monk," 315, 349, 363
"Boo Boo Stick Beat," 164, 333
"The Boy from New York City," 291–92, 331
"Brand New Cadillac," 62, 401
"Brighton Rock," 33, 350
"Built for Comfort," 124, 351–52
"By the Way," 157, 342
"Bye Bye Johnny," 139, 341, 388–89

"Can I Get a Witness," 291, 362, 389
"Can't Buy Me Love," 147–48, 150, 153, 337, 338
"Can't You Hear My Heart Beat," 269, 274, 365
"Can't You See That She's Mine," 188, 347
"Candy Man" (1) 118, 382, 384
"Candy Man" (2) 351, 354
"Carol," 285, 340, 389
"Caroline," 271, 360
"Casbah," 316, 369
"Catch the Wind," 319, 353
"Cathy's Clown," 91, 356
"Champagne Charlie," 18
"Charmaine," 311, 334
"Chimes of Freedom," 319, 355
"Cock-A-Hoop," 178, 377
"Collette," 49, 361
"Colours," 319, 353
"Come and Stay with Me," 236, 358
"Come On," 136, 137, 138, 341, 388
"Come Outside," 202, 392
"Confessin' (That I Love You),"
"Confessin' the Blues," 133, 341, 379
"Country Line Special," 125, 127, 350
"The Crying Game," 163—164, 342
"Cumberland Gap," 26–27, 53, 352, 364

"Dance On!" / "Dance On," 67, 92, 208, 395
"Dancing in the Street," 211, 291, 297, 378
"Dear John," 213, 311, 399
"Devil in Disguise," 96, 115, 385
"Devil in Her Heart," 99, 337–38
"Diamonds," 92, 364

"Diane," 311, 334
"Dimples," 265–66, 297, 332, 351, 367
"Do the Dog," 127, 248, 358
"Do the Freddie," 162, 361
"Do Wah Diddy," 179, 357
"Do You Love Me," 118, 119–20, 187, 347, 349, 384
"Do You Want to Know a Secret," 107, 159, 336, 337, 373
"Does Your Chewing Gum Lose Its Flavour (on the Bedpost Overnight)?," 28, 353
"The Dog," 127, 402
"Don't Bother Me," 99–100, 337
"Don't Let Me Be Misunderstood," 250, 332
"Don't Let the Sun Catch You Crying," 158, 349, 362–63
"Don't Start Crying Now," 255–56, 364, 401
"Don't Talk to Him," 115, 148, 175–76, 387
"Don't Think Twice, It's Alright," 315, 355, 363–64
"Don't Throw Your Love Away," 161, 382, 393
"Don't Treat Me Like a Child," 55, 395
"Don't You Know" (1), 54, 55, 395
"Don't You Know" (2), 230, 379
"Don't You Rock Me, Daddy-o," 26–27, 352
"Donna," 33, 403, 405
"Doo Wah Diddy Diddy," 179, 357, 378
"Down Town," 124
"Downtown," 211–212, 313, 348

"Eight Days a Week," 152–53, 339
"Eight Miles High," 161, 345
"Endless Sleep," 46–47, 385, 405
"Every Little Bit Hurts," 265–66, 351, 366
"Everybody Needs Somebody to Love," 289, 345, 390
"Everybody's Gonna Be Happy," 253, 372
"Everyday," 267, 380

"F.B.I.," 67, 394
"Feelin' Fine," 67, 354, 394
"Ferry Cross the Mersey," 158, 363
"Find My Way Back Home," 191, 381
"The First Time," 53, 357
"The Flying Trapeze," 18
"For You, for You," 272, 359
"For Your Love," 258, 406
"Forget Him," 96, 391
"Freight Train," 28, 349–50, 379
"Fried Onions," 66, 376
"Frightened City," 67, 394
"From a Window," 159, 374, 400
"From Me to You," 94–95, 100, 134, 336

"From the Bottom of My Heart," 267, 380
"Funeral March" (*Sonata No. 2 in Bb Minor*), 63, 64

"Gamblin' Man," 27, 352–53
"Game of Love," 272, 359
"Georgia on My Mind," 265, 346
"Get Off of My Cloud," 293, 391
"Girl Don't Come," 234–35, 396
"Girl from the North Country," 317, 355
"The Girl on the Floor Above," 53, 375
"Glad All Over" (1), 120, 382
"Glad All Over" (2), 120, 187–88, 347
"Globetrotter," 92, 403
"Gloria," 256, 401–2
"Go Now," 267, 278f, 334, 380
"God Save the Queen," 172
"Goldfinger," 206, 335
"Good Morning Little Schoolgirl," 258, 406
"Google Eye," 191, 376, 381
"Got to Hurry," 258, 406
"Green Onions," 250, 297, 344, 358

"Halfway to Paradise," 49, 82, 361
"Have I the Right?," 188–89, 367
"He's in Town," 270, 387–88, 402
"Heart of Stone," 287, 390–91
"Heartbreak Hotel," 119, 130, 384
"Hello! Josephine" (aka, "My Girl Josephine"), 272, 359
"Here Comes the Night," 229, 377, 402
"Here I Go Again," 162–63, 366
"Here It Comes Again," 271, 360
"Hey! Baby," 82, 346
"Hold Me Tight," 99–100, 337
"Honeycomb," 189, 388
"Hoochie Cooche" / "Hoochie Coochie," 124, 343
"Hoots Mon," 66, 376
"House of the Rising Sun," 168, 192, 250, 287, 331–32
"How Do You Do It?," 83, 105, 110, 362
"Hubble Bubble (Toil and Trouble)," 179, 378
"Hungry for Love," 115, 371, 392

"I Believe," 311, 334
"I Believe I'll Dust My Broom," 133, 370
"I Can't Explain," 303–304, 305, 306, 404
"I Can't Stand It," 265–66, 351, 398
"(I Can't Get No) Satisfaction" (see "Satisfaction")
"I'd Be Far Better Off without You," 234–35, 396
"I Didn't Mean to Hurt You," 270, 387–88, 397

SONG INDEX

"I Don't Want to Go On without You," 267, 380
"I Don't Know How (to Tell You)," 236
"I Don't Want to See You Again," 176, 383
"I Don't Want to Spoil the Party," 153, 339
"I Feel Fine," 153–54
"If I Fell," 151, 338
"If I Needed Someone," 320–21, 340
"If You Gotta Make a Fool of Somebody," 110, 138, 360, 385
"I Just Don't Know What to Do with Myself," 215, 398
"I Just Want to/Wanna Make Love to You," 286, 381, 389
"I Know a Place," 212, 348
"I'll Cry Instead," 151, 338
"I'll Keep You Satisfied," 107, 159, 374
"I'll Never Find Another You," 312, 321*f*, 393
"I'll Never Get Over You," 115, 371
"I'll Stop at Nothing," 234–35, 396
"I'm a Loser," 153, 339
"I'm Alive," 163, 366
"I'm Crying," 250, 331, 332
"I'm Happy Just to Dance with You," 151, 338
"I'm Henery the Eighth, I Am" / "I'm Henry the VIII, I Am," 50, 274, 344, 365
"I'm into Something Good," 274, 356, 365
"I'm Telling You Now," 110, 111, 162, 291, 360
"I'm the Lonely One," 115, 387
"I'm the One," 158, 362
"I'm Your Hoochie Cooche Man," 124, 380
"I Need You Baby" (aka "Mona"), 285, 389
"I Only Want to Be with You," 214, 215, 398
"I Understand" / "I Understand Just How You Feel," 161–62, 360, 361, 365
"I Wanna Be Your Man," 99–100, 138, 167, 283, 337, 388
"I Want to Be Loved," 136, 380–81
"I Want to Hold Your Hand," 100, 101
"I Want You to Love Me," 133, 381
"I Wish You Would," 258, 333, 406
"I Wouldn't Trade You for the World," 311, 334
"Il Mio Mondo" (see "You're My World")
"In Spite of All the Danger," 75
"In the Middle of Nowhere," 215, 399
"Is It Because?," 189, 367
"Island of Dreams," 311–12, 399
"It Doesn't Matter Anymore," 52, 367
"It Only Took a Minute," 50, 345
"It Won't Be Long," 99–100, 337
"It's All in the Game," 115, 387
"It's All Over Now," 287–118, 389, 403
"It's Been Nice," 47, 405
"It's for You," 227, 343

"It's Gonna Be Alright," 158, 363
"It's Not True," 307, 405
"It's Not Unusual," 276–77, 370

"Jellied Eels," 50, 344
"Jenny," 23
"John Henry," 25, 334–35
"Johnny Remember Me," 54, 375–76
"Just One Look," 162, 366

"The Kids Are Alright," 307, 405
"Kon Tiki," 67, 395

"The Last Time," 290, 291, 390
"Leave a Little Love," 229, 377
"Leave Me Be," 180–81, 406
"Like Dreamers Do," 80, 267–68, 332
"Little by Little," 289, 389
"Little Child," 99–100, 159, 337
"Little Children," 159, 373–74
"Little Darlin'," 272, 359, 363
"Little Red Rooster," 287, 368, 389
"The Little Shoemaker," 211, 347–48
"Living Doll," 40, 41, 386
"Long Live Love," 234–35, 396
"Long Tall Sally," 130, 151, 194, 195, 338, 371, 376
"Loose Your Money (but Don't Loose Your Mind)" / "Lose Your Money (but Don't Lose Your Mind)," 266–67
"Lord Gregory," 315, 349, 363
"The Lost Chord," 18
"Love Her," 275, 357, 403
"Love Me Do," 69, 82–83, 84, 85, 91, 94, 95, 101, 104, 318–19, 335–36
"Love of the Loved," 226, 342
"Love Potion No. 9" / "Love Potion Number Nine," 136, 161, 348, 392
"Lucille," 63, 64, 190, 194, 376

"Maajun (a Taste of Tangier)," 315, 363–64
"Make It Easy on Yourself," 275–76, 345, 404
"La Malagueña" (see "You're the One")
"Man of Mystery," 67, 394, 395
"Margo," 49, 361
"Maybe Tomorrow," 49, 75, 361
"Memphis, Tennessee," 163, 287, 331–32, 341
"Midnight in Moscow," 21, 334
"Misery" (1), 93, 336
"Misery" (2), 301, 356
"Mona" (aka, "I Need You Baby"), 285, 343–44
"Money" / "Money (That's What I Want)," 80, 337, 388–89, 392
"Mother in Law," 273–74, 365

"Move It," 38–39, 40, 41, 62, 299, 386
"Mr. Tambourine Man," 290, 320, 345, 356
"Mrs. Brown You've Got a Lovely Daughter," 274, 291, 365
"Mustapha," 314, 401
"My Baby Left Me," 163, 341–42, 384
"My Bonnie," 78, 397
"My Boy Lollipop/Lollypop," 231, 273, 361–62, 379
"My Generation," 306–7, 405
"My Girl Josephine," 272, 352
"My Old Man's a Dustman (Ballad of a Refuse Disposal Officer)," 28, 353
"My Ship Is Coming In," 275–76, 385, 404

"Nashville Blues," 190, 356–57
"Needle of Death," 316, 369
"Needles and Pins," 160, 351, 392
"The Next Time," 92, 386
"Night Train," 297, 344, 358
"Nobody I Know," 176, 383
"Not a Second Time," 99–100, 337
"Not Fade Away," 285, 286, 287, 367, 389
"Norwegian Wood (This Bird Has Flown)," 320–21, 340
"(Now and Then There's) A Fool Such as I" (aka "Prends Mon Coeur"), 211, 384, 398
"Nowhere Man," 320–21, 340
"Nowhere to Run," 291, 292, 378–79

"Only the Lonely," 91, 381–82
"Out in the Street," 307, 405

"P.S. I Love You," 83, 94–95, 336
"Parchman Farm," 190, 331, 358, 381
"The Patriot Game," 317, 340
"Peggy Sue," 109, 367
"Petite Fleur," 20–21, 335, 340
"Play with Fire," 317, 390
"Please Don't Tease," 67, 386
"Please Don't Touch," 61–62, 371
"Please Please Me," 83, 91, 92, 93–94, 95, 336, 337
"Please, Please, Please," 307, 344, 405
"Please," 91, 350
"Poison Ivy," 138, 273–74, 388
"Poor Man's Son," 270, 385, 388
"Poor Me," 53, 357
"Pretty Girls Everywhere," 275, 346
"Pretty Thing," 136, 343
"Puttin' on the Style," 27, 352–53

"Ramona," 311, 334
"Rebel-'Rouser," 299, 356
"Return to Sender," 92, 384–85
"Rock around the Clock" (aka "(We're Gonna) Rock around the Clock"), 4, 26, 364
"Rock Island Line," 25–27, 334–35, 352, 375
"Rock with the Caveman," 34, 35–36, 399–400
"Roll Over Beethoven," 99, 337–38
"Route 66," 285, 341, 371, 389, 402
"Rule Britannia," 172
"Runaway," 68, 395

"Sailor," 211, 348, 397
"Satisfaction," ("(I Can't Get No) Satisfaction") 291–93, 390
"Saturday Dance," 67, 394
"Say I Won't Be There," 311–12, 399
"Scarborough Fair," 317, 346
"Schoolboy Crush," 38, 39, 364, 386
"Sea of Love," 46–47, 383, 405
"Searchin'," 112, 348, 366
"Secret Love," 208, 337, 351, 373
"See My Friends," 315, 373
"Set Me Free," 253, 305, 373
"Sha-La-La," 179, 378, 397
"Shakin' All Over," 62, 208, 371
"She Loves You," 96–97, 100, 111, 138, 147–48, 336, 337–38
"She Moved through the Fair," 314
"She's a Woman," 153, 338–39
"She's Coming Home," 181, 407
"She's Not There," 180–81, 406
"The Sheik of Araby," 22, 80, 333, 349, 352, 404
"Sheila," 109, 388
"Sherry," 84, 360
"Shout," 228–29, 368, 376–77
"Show Me Girl," 274, 365
"Silhouettes," 274, 365, 385
"Silver Threads and Golden Needles," 311–12, 399
"Singing the Blues," 36, 379–80, 400
"Sister Kate," 23, 342, 370, 374
"Some Day We're Gonna Love Again," 161, 393
"Some of Your Lovin'," 215, 399
"Some Other Guy," 157, 335, 342, 392
"Stay," 112, 366, 379
"Stop, Look, and Listen," 272, 359
"Stranger on the Shore," 23, 342
"Subterranean Homesick Blues," 318, 355, 356
"Sugar and Spice," 109, 160, 392
"Sukiyaki" (aka "Ue o Muite Arukō"), 5, 391

SONG INDEX   447

"Summer Holiday," 115, 386–87
"Summertime," 181, 225
"Summertime, Summertime," 270, 359, 369
"The Sun Ain't Gonna Shine Any More," 275–76, 379, 403
"Swahili Papa," 311, 399
"Sweet William," 231, 379
"Sweets for My Sweet," 108–9, 354, 392

"Teach You to Rock," 33, 38–39, 340, 350
"Tell Her No," 180–81, 406
"Tell Laura I Love Her," 53, 54, 375
"Tell Me What He Said," 56, 395
"Tell Me (You're Coming Back)," 286, 389
"Tell Me When," 267–68, 279f, 332
"Telstar," 68–69, 402
"That's What Love Will Do," 50, 345
"That'll Be the Day," 60, 75, 367
"That's Love," 49, 361
"That's What I Said," 119, 347
"That's Why I'm Crying," 269, 369
"Thirty Days" (aka "Thirty Days (to Come Back Home)," 291–92, 340
"This Little Bird," 236, 358, 376, 381
"This May Be the Last Time," 290, 399
"Till the End of the Day," 253, 373
"Till There Was You," 80, 99, 337
"The Times They Are a Changin'," 317–18, 319, 355
"Tired of Waiting for You," 253, 304, 372
"Tobacco Road," 190–191, 376, 381
"Tossing and Turning," 269, 369
"Trains and Boats and Planes," 159, 333, 374
"Travellin' Light," 40, 386
"Try to Understand," 229, 377
"Turquoise," 320, 354
"Twist and Shout," 93, 95, 118, 121, 203, 229, 336, 337, 368, 383, 392
"Twist Little Sister," 117, 383

"Ue o Muite Arukō," ("I Look Up as I Walk") (see "Sukiyaki")
"Um, Um, Um, Um, Um, Um," 272, 359, 375
"Universal Soldier," 320, 353, 391

"Walk Right In," 312, 391
"Walking Back to Happiness," 56, 214, 395
"Watch Your Step," 153, 382
"Wayward Wind," 115, 368

"We Gotta Get Out of This Place," 251, 332
"The Wedding" (aka "La Novia"), 232, 385, 388
"We'll Meet," 229, 230, 391
"We'll Meet Again," 203–4, 377
"We're Through," 163, 366
"(We're Gonna) Rock around the Clock" (see "Rock around the Clock")
"What Do You Want," 52, 357
"What Have They Done to the Rain," 161, 393
"What More Do You Want," 269, 368–69
"What'd I Say," 153, 297, 346
"When I'm Cleaning Windows," 19, 359
"When You Walk in the Room," 161, 351, 393
"Whenever You're Ready," 181, 407
"Where Are You Now," 232, 403
"Who'll Be the Next in Line," 253, 373
"Why Should We Not," 178, 377
"Whispering," 311, 334
"Wild Wind," 54, 376
"Willow Weep for Me," 174, 400
"Wishing Well," 107
"With God on Our Side," 317, 355
"With My Little Ukulele in My Hand," 19, 50, 359
"Wonderful Land," 67, 395
"Wonderful World," 274, 349, 365
"Wonderland by Night," (aka "Wunderland bei Nacht"), 5, 371

"Yeh Yeh," 252, 358, 374–75, 391
"Yesterday," 318, 339, 340, 358
"Yesterday's Gone," 173, 174, 400
"The Young Ones," 41, 386
"You Can't Catch Me," 289, 340, 390
"You Don't Know," 54, 55, 395
"You Really Got Me," 195–96, 197, 253, 254, 302, 372
"You Still Want Me," 194, 195, 372
"You Were Made for Me," 111, 162, 360–61
"You'll Never Walk Alone," 105–6, 111, 158, 362
"You're My World" (aka, "Il Mio Mundo"), 227, 342, 343
"You're No Good," 272, 401
"You're the One," 208, 373
"You've Got to Hide Your Love Away," 317–18, 339, 398
"You've Got Your Troubles," 271, 360
"You've Lost That Lovin' Feeling," 227, 343

"Zoot Suit," 301, 302, 365–66

Subject Index

The 2i's Coffee Bar, 59 Old Compton Street, Soho, London, 31, 34, 35, 37–38, 39, 41, 45, 46, 51, 63, 64–65, 76–77, 167

The 6.5 Special (see *The Six-Five Special*)

Abbey Road Studios (see EMI Recording Studios)

ABC, ABC Television Center, 4151 Prospect Avenue, Los Angeles, 156, 162, 275, 286

Acquaye, Speedy (b. Nii Moi Acquaye, 1931): Ghanaian-British musician (percussion: Georgie Fame and the Blue Flames), 127, 252, 358

Acton County Grammar School, Acton, 298, 299

The Ad Libs (Bayonne, New Jersey): Hugh Harris, Danny Austin, Dave Watt, Norman Donegan, and Mary Ann Thomas, 291–92, 331

Adams, Douglas (b. 1952): English author, 171

Addey, Malcolm (b. 1933): English recording engineer, xi–xii, 39, 52, 61, 354, 357, 371, 382–83, 386, 394, 395

The Adventures of Robin Hood, 92, 174–75, 409

Albert Hall (see Royal Albert Hall)

Alexandra Palace, Alexandra Palace Way, London, 192

All Stars '64, 283

Allan, Elkan (b. Elkan Cohen, 1922): English television producer, 98, 416, 418

Allen, Frank (b. Francis McNeice, 1943): English musician (bass and vocals: Searchers), 161, 393

Allen, Rod (b. Rodney Bainbridge, 1943): English musician (singer and bass: Fortunes), 270–71, 359–60

Allison, Jerry (b. 1939): American musician (drums: Crickets) and songwriter, 285, 367

Allison, Mose (b. 1927): American musician (piano and vocal) and songwriter, 190, 331, 381

Altham, Keith: English journalist, xii, 235, 236–37, 271, 309

Ambrose, Bert (b. Benjamin Ambrose, aka Albert Ambrose, Warsaw, Poland, Russian Empire, 1896): British bandleader and manager, 203, 204, 207, 208

American Federation of Musicians (AFM), 25, 26, 181, 188, 189, 191

American Forces Network (AFN), 126, 247

Andrews, Chris (b. 1942): Musician (singer), music director, and songwriter, 234, 357, 396

Andrews, Julie (b. Julia Elizabeth Wells, 1935): English musician (singer) and actress, 204, 420, 210, 331, 381, 398

The Animals (Newcastle): (1) Eric Burdon, Chas Chandler, Alan Price, John Steel, and Hilton Valentine; (2) Dave Rowberry replaces Price, 166, 170f, 191, 246–47, 249, 250–51, 255–56, 266, 287, 300, 303, 306, 331–32

The Applejacks (Birmingham): Al Jackson, Martin Baggott, Don Gould, Phil Cash, Gerry Freeman, and Megan Davies, 267–68, 279f, 332

Arden, Don (b. Harry Levy, 1926): English manager and agent; office: 52-55 Carnaby Street, Soho, London (1965), 135, 191

Ardmore and Beechwood, 363 Oxford Street, London, 80, 84, 92, 93

Argent, Rod (b. 1945): English musician (keyboards: Zombies) and songwriter, 179–181, 406–7

Armstrong, Louis (b. 1901): American musician (trumpet), 20, 23, 130, 265

Arne, Thomas (b. 1710): English composer, 172

Arnold, Billy Boy (b. William Arnold, 1935): American musician (singer, harmonica, and guitar), 258, 333, 406

Arnold, Paul (b. ca, 1945): English musician (bass: Zombies), 179–80

Ascot Records, 729 7th Avenue, New York, NY, United States, 179

Ascott, Roy (b. 1934): English artist and educator, 299, 301

Asher Family (home), 57 Wimpole Street, Marylebone, London, 100, 175

Asher, Jane (b. 1946): English actress, 100, 175, 176

Asher, Margaret (b. Margaret Eliot, 1914): English musician (oboe) and teacher, 100

Asher, Peter (b. 1944): English musician (guitar and singer), 156, 174—175, 382
Ashton, Bill (see Billy J, Kramer)
Associated-Rediffusion/Rediffusion, 128 Wembley Park Drive, Wembley, London, 413, 416, 418, 420, 422
Associated Television (ATV), Eldon Avenue, Elstree/Borehamwood, Hertfordshire, 413, 414, 416, 418, 420, 422
Atkins, Chet (b. Chester Atkins, 1924): American musician (guitar) and songwriter, 164, 292, 333, 356, 384
Atkinson, Paul (b. 1946): English musician (guitar: Zombies), 171, 179, 406-7
Attlee, Clement (b. 1883): English Labour politician, UK PM (1945-1951), 3
Atwell, Winifred (b. 1914): Trinidadian musician (piano), 205, 207, 213, 333
Auger, Brian (b. 1939): English musician (keyboards: Steampacket), 249, 406
Austin, Roy (b. 1943): English musician (bass: Rockin' Berries), 269
Authenticity, 22, 33, 96, 121, 129, 205, 257, 271, 283, 293, 309, 310, 326
Avory, Mick (b. 1944): English musician (drums: Kinks), 133, 194-95, 198*f*, 372-73
Ayres, Agnes (b. 1898): American actor, 22

Bach, Johann Sebastian (b. 1685): German composer, 313
Bacharach, Burt (b. 1928): American songwriter, 159, 226-227, 333, 234, 342, 345, 370, 374, 396, 397, 398, 404, 423
The Bachelors (Dublin): Con Cluskey, Dec Cluskey, and John Stokes, 173, 256, 270, 271, 311, 334
Baez, Joan (b. 1941): American voice and songwriter, 309, 320, 411
Bailey, David (b. 1938): Fashion photographer, 298
Baker, Ginger (b. Peter Baker, 1939): English musician (drums: Cream), 249
Baldry, John (aka "Long" John Baldry, b. 1941): English musician (singer: Blues Incorporated), 124, 128*f*, 266, 343, 409
Baldwin, Stanley (b. 1867): English politician, 21
Ball, Kenny (b. 1930): English musician (trumpet), 21, 334, 415
Ballad and Blues Club (1) The Round House, 83 Wardour Street, London and (2) Scots Hoose, 6 Moor Street, Cambridge Circus, London, 310
Ballard, Clint, Jr, (b. 1931): American songwriter, 163, 272, 359, 366, 383, 401

Banks, Bessie (b. Bessie White, 1938): American musician (singer), 266-67, 268, 334
Barber, Chris (b. Donald Christopher Barber, 1930): English musician (trombone) and band leader, 20, 24, 25, 28, 122, 123, 125, 349, 352
  Chris Barber's Jazz Band (London): Chris Barber, Pat Halcox, Monty Sunshine, Lonnie Donegan, Ron Bowden, and Jim Bray among others, 21, 25, 123, 334-35
Barclay, Michael: British record producer and songwriter, 311, 334, 352-53, 388
Bardot, Brigitte (b. 1934): French actress, 235
Baring, James (aka James Cecil Baring, 6th Baron Revelstoke): English peer and studio owner, xi-xii, 284
Barrett, Richard (aka, Richie Barrett, b. 1933): American musician (singer) and songwriter, 157, 335, 342
Barrow, Tony (b. 1936): English journalist and publicist, 84, 85, 98, 146, 152
Barry, John (b. John Barry Prendergast, 1933): English musician (trumpet), arranger, and songwriter, 51, 52, 56, 173, 335, 357, 371, 412, 413, 414, 416, 421
  The John Barry Seven (London): John Barry, Vic Flick, Mike Peters, Jimmy Stead, Dennis King, Dougie Wright, Keith Kelly, 52, 65-66, 175-76, 357
Bart, Lionel (b. Lionel Begleiter, 1930): British songwriter, 34, 35-36, 40, 46, 236, 344, 357, 386, 399-400, 417, 419
Bascobel Productions, 22 Kingly Street, Soho, London, 193
Bassey, Shirley (b. 1937): Welsh musician (singer), 206-207, 215, 239*f*, 324-25, 227, 335
Bavan, Yolande (b. 1942): Sri Lankan musician (singer: Lambert, Hendricks, and Bavan), 252, 374-75
Baverstock, Jack: English record producer (Wayne Fontana and the Mindbenders) and label manager, 272, 301, 359, 365-66, 375, 379
Baxter, Art (b. 1926): English musician (singer) Art Baxter and His Rock and Roll Sinners (London), 33-34
BBC, Broadcast House, Portland Place, Marylebone, London, 17, 19, 21-22, 23, 25, 32, 33-34, 36, 39, 44, 45-46, 47, 49, 50, 51, 52, 55, 61-62, 65, 72-73, 90-91, 95-96, 112, 117, 124, 130, 132-33, 172, 189, 192, 197, 203, 204, 208-9, 210-11, 212, 213, 214, 227, 247, 248, 268, 276, 292, 293, 328, 342, 349

The Beach Boys (Hawthorne, California): Brian Wilson, Mike Love, Al Jardine, Dennis Wilson, and Carl Wilson, 60, 145, 269, 420–21
Beat City, 79 Oxford Street, Soho, London, 276
The Beat Room (BBC2), 276, 410
The Beatles (Liverpool): John Lennon, Paul McCartney, George Harrison, Pete Best, Stu Sutcliffe, and Ringo Starr, ix, 2, 4, 13, 34, 69, 72–85, 89–101, 104, 105–6, 107, 111, 112, 117, 118, 120, 134, 135, 136, 137, 138, 139, 143–54, 156, 157, 159, 162–63, 174, 175, 176, 180–81, 187, 188, 194, 197, 214, 225, 226, 266, 273, 283, 288, 299, 318, 320, 323–24, 335–40, 397, 409, 410, 413, 414–15, 418, 419
  Around the Beatles, 275, 409
  The Beatles Book, 98
  Pop Go the Beatles, 95–96, 97, 418
Beauvoir, Simone de (b. 1908): French philosopher and author, 235
Bechet, Sidney (b. 1897): American musician (saxophone and clarinet), 20, 335, 340
Beck, Jeff (b. Geoffrey Beck, 1944): English musician (guitar: the Yardbirds), 154
Beecham, Sir Thomas (b. 1879): English conductor, 11–12
Beecher, Fanny (b. Frank Beecher, 1921): American musician (guitar), 26–27, 364
Behan Dominic (b. 1928): Irish singer and songwriter, 317, 340
Bell, Freddie (b. Ferdinando Bello, 1931), American musician (singer), 350
  Freddie Bell and the Bellboys (New Jersey): Jack Kane, Frankie Brent, Russ Conti, Chick Keeney, and Jerry Mayo, 33, 66–67, 340
Bellamy, George (b. 1940): English musician (guitar: Tornados), 68, 402
Benjamin, Louis (b. 1922): English entrepreneur, 189, 194, 196, 305
Bennett, Andy: English sociologist, xi–xii
Bennett, Cliff (b. 1940): English musician (singer),
  Cliff Bennett and the Rebel Rousers (London): Cliff Bennett, Chas Hodges, Mick Burt, Nicky Hopkins, Maurice Groves, etc., 160
Bennetts, Les (b. 1940), English musician (guitar and vocals), 27, 352–53
Bentham, Jeremy (b. 1748): English philosopher, 12–13
Berns, Bert (b. 1929; aka Bert Russell): American songwriter and record producer, 229, 256, 331, 345, 377, 380, 401–2

Berry, Chuck (b. 1926): American musician (singer and guitar) and songwriter, 38–39, 125, 130, 132–33, 136–37, 139, 163, 168, 204, 236–37, 276, 181, 285, 286–87, 289, 291–92, 340–41, 388
Berry, Dave (b. David Grundy, 1941): English musician (singer), xi–xii, 163–64, 197, 341–42
  Dave Berry and the Cruisers (Sheffield): Dave Berry, Roy Barber, John Fleet, Frank Miles, and Kenny Slade, 163, 341
Best, Mona (b. Alice Mona Shaw, 1924): mother of Pete Best and entrepreneur, 75, 77
Best, Pete (b. 1941): English musician (drums: the Beatles), 77, 78, 80, 82, 83, 335, 397
Betesh, Danny (b. 193?): English manager (Freddie and the Dreamers), agent (Dave Berry), and promoter, 110, 161–62, 163, 273
Beveridge, John: English musician (guitar: Joe Brown and His Bruvvers), 50, 117, 344–45, 383
The Big Broadcast, 91, 410
The Big Three (Liverpool): Brian Griffiths, John Hutchinson, and John Gustafson, 104, 157, 342
Biggles, 53, 410
Bilk, Acker (b. Bernard Bilk, 1929): English musician (clarinet), 22–23, 29*f*, 123, 420
  Mr. Acker Bilk and His Paramount Jazz Band (London): Acker Bilk, Ken Sims, John Mortimer, Roy James, Ernie Price, and Ron Mackay, 22–23, 342
Billboard, 26, 36, 148–49, 153, 158, 159, 160, 162, 174, 176, 179, 180–81, 187, 189, 204, 212, 214, 231, 232, 258, 269, 274, 277, 287, 289–90, 291, 304, 307, 311–13, 331
Bindi, Umberto (b. 1932): Italian musician (singer) and songwriter, 227, 342, 343
Birmingham Town Hall, Victoria Square, Birmingham, 265
Birth control/contraception, 5, 89, 143, 223
Black, Cilla (b. Priscilla White, 1943): English musician (singer), 104, 157, 225–27, 231–32, 233, 235, 237*f*, 240*f*, 324–25, 342–43, 409, 413
The Black and White Minstrel Show, 17, 410
Blackboard Jungle, 46, 410
Blacksmiths Arms, 56 Saint Peter's Street, Saint Albans, 179–80
Blackwell, Charles (b. 1940): English music director and songwriter, xi–xii, 54, 202, 208, 232–233, 350, 351, 370, 373, 375–76, 392
Blackwell, Chris (b. 1937): Jamaican music entrepreneur and record producer, 229, 230–31, 265–66, 351, 379

452 SUBJECT INDEX

Blaikley, Alan (b. 1940): English manager and songwriter, 188–89, 367
Blaikley, Howard: Pseudonym for English songwriters Ken Howard and Alan Blaikley, 189
Blakley, Alan (b. 1942): English musician (guitar: Tremeloes), 117
The Blue Angel, 14 Berkeley Street, Mayfair, London, 46
The Blue Flames (see Georgie Fame)
Blues and Gospel Train, 249, 259f, 410–11
Blues Incorporated (London): Alexis Korner, Cyril Davies, Charlie Watts, Long John Baldry, Jack Bruce, Dick Heckstall-Smith, and others, 123–125, 127, 132–33, 134, 178, 193, 194–95, 248, 249, 257, 278, 286–87, 343
Blunstone, Colin (b. 1945): Musician (singer: Zombies), 179–80, 182, 406–7
Bo Diddley (b. Ellas McDaniel, 1928): American musician (guitar and singer) and songwriter, 131, 133–134, 136, 138, 167, 272–73, 285, 332
The Boll-Weevils (see the Kinks)
Boltwood, Derek: British music journalist, xii
Bonds, Gary U, S, (b. Gary Anderson, 1939): American musician (singer), 118
Bond, Graham (b. 1937): English musician (vocal, saxophone, and organ: Graham Bond Organisation), 249, 265–66
The Graham Bond Organisation (London): Graham Bond, Jack Bruce, Ginger Baker, and Dick Heckstall-Smith, 166, 249, 306
Bond, Terry (b. 1943): English musician (drums: Rockin' Berries), 269, 270
Bono, Sonny (b. Salvatore Bono, 1935): American musician (singer) and songwriter, 160, 351, 392
Booker T and the MG's (Memphis, TN): Booker T, Jones, Steve Cropper, Donald Dunn, and Al Jackson, 250, 297, 344
Booth, George (See Formby, George), 19
Bonanza, 67, 411
Botfield, Chuck (b. Bryan Botfield, 1943): English musician (guitar: Rockin' Berries), 269
Boult, Sir Adrian (b. 1889): English musician and conductor, 10–12
Bowie, David (b. David Jones, 1947): English musician and songwriter, 164
Boy Meets Girls, 45–46, 47, 49, 53, 411
Boyd, Franklyn (b. William Price, 1925), English publisher and manager, 39, 41

Boyfriend (magazine), 90–91
Bradford Mecca Locarno, Manningham Lane, Bradford, 252
The Breakaways (London): Margo Quantrell, Vicki Haseman, and Jean Ryder, 214, 333, 342–43, 344–45, 348, 376–77, 398
Bream, Julian (b. 1933): English musician (classical guitar), 313
Brewer, Teresa (b. Theresa Breuer, 1931): American musician (singer), 210, 344
Bricklayers Arms, 7 Broadwick Street, Soho, London, 132, 133
Briggs, Anne (b. 1944): Scottish musician (singer), 310, 316
Brill Building, 1619 Broadway, New York City, 211
British Establishment, 37, 89, 98, 130, 186, 208–9, 231, 248, 251, 288, 309
The British Museum, Great Russell Street, London, 34
The Brook Brothers (Winchester, Hampshire): Geoff Brooks and Richard Brooks, 117
Broonzy, Big Bill (b. Lee Bradley, 1893/1903): American musician (guitar and singer), 24, 25, 121–22, 130, 314, 315, 316
Brown, Andy (b. 1944): English musician (drums: Fortunes), 271, 360
Brown, James (b. 1933): American musician (singer), songwriter, bandleader and producer, 266–67, 275, 289, 297, 307, 344, 420–21
Brown, Joe (b. 1941): English musician (singer, guitar, ukulele), xi–xii, 49–50, 58f, 187, 228, 274, 325–26, 344–45
Joe Brown and His Bruvvers (London): Joe Brown, Pete Oakman, Tony Oakman, Bohn Beveridge, and Bobby Graham, 117–118, 60
Brown, Rick/Ricky (see Ricky Fenson)
Bruce, Jack (b. John Bruce, 1943): Scottish musician (bass and singer: Blues Incorporated, Graham Bond Organisation, and Cream) and songwriter, 124, 249, 343
Brunswick Records (see Decca Records), 304, 305
Bryden, Beryl (b. 1920), English musician (singer), 25, 352
The Bulge Generation, 5–6, 37, 75–76, 84, 89, 96, 115, 129, 134, 144, 162, 204, 206–7, 209, 212, 226, 231, 232, 245, 284, 288, 290, 309, 314, 324, 327

Bullock, Clementine (see Cleo Laine)
The Bullwinkle Show, 273, 411
Bunjies Coffee House and Folk Cellar, 27 Litchfield Street, London, 317
Burbidge, Graham (b. 1933): English musician (drums: Blues Incorporated), 124
Burdon, Eric (b. 1941): English musician (singer: Animals) and songwriter, 132, 165–68, 250–51, 266, 331–32
Burgess, John: English record producer and entrepreneur, 110, 52, 178, 179, 272, 302–3, 357, 360, 377
Burke, Solomon (b. 1940): American musician (singer), 289, 345
Burman, Maurice: English musician (drums and piano) and teacher, 54, 59f, 209, 413
  The Maurice Burman School of Modern Pop Singing, 137 Bickenhall Mansions, Baker Street, London, 54, 55
Burnette, Johnny (b. 1934): American musician (singer and guitar), 118
  Johnny Burnette and the Rock 'n Roll Trio (Memphis, Tennessee): Johnny Burnette, Paul Burlison, Dorsey Burnette, and Tony Austin, 26
Burns, Tito (b. Nathan Bernstein, 1921): English manager and agent, 41, 181
Burns Guitars (aka Ormston Burns Ltd), Chesham Close, Cedar Road, Romford, Essex, 17, 115, 148
Burt, Heinz (b. 1942): German-English musician (bass: Tornados; and singer), 68, 402
Burton, James (b. 1939): American musician (guitar), 47
Butler, Jerry (b. Jerry Butler, Jr, 1939): American musician (singer) and songwriter, 275–76, 345
Butlins Camps, 117
Bye Bye Birdie, 47–48
The Byrds (Los Angeles): Jim McGuinn, David Crosby, Gene Clark, Chris Hillman, and Michael Clarke, 161, 290, 320, 345
Byrne, Nicky (b. Douglas Anthony Nicholas Byrne, b. ca, 1926): English entrepreneur, 149, 266

Cadbury Club, Bournville Lane, Bournville, Birmingham, 23
Caddy, Alan (b. 1940): English musician (guitar: Tornados), 62–63, 68, 371, 402
Calder, Tony (b. 1943): English manager and record producer, 236, 358

Calvert, Eddie (b. Albert Calvert, 1922): English musician (trumpet), 185
Calvert, Reg (b. 1928): English manager and broadcast entrepreneur, 270
Camden Head, 2 Camden Walk, Islington, London, 194–95
Campbell, Joseph (b. 1904): American author and educator, 77, 191–92
Campbell Connelly, 10-11 Denmark Street, Saint Giles, London, 270
Canterbury Arms/Music Hall, 143 Westminster Bridge Road, Lambeth, London, 18
Capable Management, 185 Bickenhall Mansions, Marylebone, London, 269–70
Carnegie Hall, 881 7th Avenue, New York, New York, 156, 188
Carousel, 106
Carr, Dave (b. 1943): English musician (keyboards: Fortunes), 271, 360
Carry On Cabby, 285
Carter, John (b. John Shakespeare, 1942): English musician (singer: Ivy League) and songwriter, xi–xii, 268, 274, 279f, 303–304, 345–46, 365, 368–69, 370, 392, 404
Carter, Hal (b. Harold Burrows, 1935): English road manager (Fury), 195–96
Carter-Lewis and the Southerners (London): John Carter, Ken Lewis, Jimmy Page, Viv Prince, and Rod Clark, 268, 345
Carthy, Martin (b. 1941): English musician (guitar and vocal), 316, 317, 346, 401
Carulli, Ferdinando (b. 1770: Italian composer, 192
The Casbah Coffee Club, 8 Hayman's Green, West Derby, Liverpool, England, 75
Cashbox, 252
Cattini, Clem (b. 1937): English musician (drummer: Tornados; sessions), xi–xii, 62–63, 68, 368–69, 371, 373, 376–77, 398, 402
The Cavemen (London): Tommy Hicks, Lionel Bart, and Mike Pratt, 34
The Cavern Club, 10 Mathew Street, Liverpool, 78–79, 85f, 94, 103, 105, 108, 112, 157, 195, 225, 227
CBS Studio 50, 1697 Broadway, New York, New York, 145, 187, 188
Cedrone, Danny (b. 1920): American musician (guitar: Bill Haley and His Comets), 26–27, 364
Central School of Speech and Drama, 62-64 Eton Avenue, Swiss Cottage, London, 173

Chad and Jeremy (London): David Chadwick (Chad Stuart) and Jeremy Clyde, 173–74, 176, 181, 182, 183f, 400–1, 417
Chadwick, David (see Chad Stuart), 173–74
Chadwick, Les (b. 1943): English musician (bass: Gerry and the Pacemakers), 104–5, 158, 349, 362–63
Chandler, Chas (b. Bryan Chandler, 1938): English musician (bass: Animals), 165, 251, 331, 332
Channel, Bruce (b. Bruce McMeans, 1940): American musician (singer) and songwriter, 82, 346
Chappell and Co., Chappell Studios, (a) 50 New Bond Street, Mayfair, London (1950s); (b) 52 Maddox Street, Mayfair, London (1967), 267
Charles, Ray (b. 1930): American musician (piano and singer) and songwriter, 126–27, 153, 250, 264–65, 268, 297, 346
Charlie Is My Darling, 293, 295f, 412
Charlie Girl, 50
Chelsea Set, 149, 245–47, 288–89
Chess Records, 2120 South Michigan Avenue, Chicago, 132, 286–87, 289
Child, Francis James (b. 1825): American folklorist, 309
Chopin, Frédéric (b. 1810): Polish musician (piano) and composer, 63, 190, 205
Church, Eugene (b. 1938): American musician (singer) and songwriter, 275
    Eugene Church and the Fellows (Los Angeles): Jesse Belvin, Gaynel Hodge, and Tommy Williams, 346
Churchill, Sir Winston (b. 1874): English politician; UK PM 1940-1945, 1951-1955, 21, 201
Ciro's, 8433 Sunset Boulevard, West Hollywood, Los Angeles, 320
The Clancy Brothers and Tommy Makem (Dublin): Liam Clancy, Paddy Clancy, Tom Clancy, and Tommy Makem, 311, 346–47
Clapton, Eric (b. 1945): Musician (guitar: Yardbirds) and songwriter, 125–26, 246–47, 257, 258, 326, 406
Clark, Dave (b. 1942): Musician (drums: Dave Clark Five) and songwriter, 118–20
    The Dave Clark Five (London): Dave Clark, Mike Smith, Lenny Davidson, Rick Huxley, and Denis Payton, 119–20, 128f, 162, 187–89, 194, 195, 347
Clark, Petula (b. Sally Clark, 1932): Musician (voice), 202, 210–12, 214, 223–24, 313, 324–25, 234, 347–48
    Pet's Parlour, 210–11

    The Petula Clark Show, 36, 211
    Youngest Sweetheart–Petula Clark, 212
Clarke, Allan (b. 1942): Musician (singer: Hollies) and songwriter, 111, 162–63, 285, 366, 389
Clarke, Frank (b. 1924?): English musician (bass), 39
Cleave, Maureen (b. 1941): English journalist, xii, 92–93, 207–8, 229
Clouston, George (b. 1913): English studio owner, 136, 340
The Clovers (Washington, DC): Billy Mitchell (lead vocal), Buddy Baily, Matthew McQuater, Harold Winley, and Bill Harris, 136, 348
Club A'Gogo, Handyside Buildings, Percy Saint Newcastle, 165, 166, 167
Cluskey, Con (b. Conleth Cluskey, 1941): Irish musician (voice and guitarist: Bachelors), 311, 334
Cluskey, Dec (b. Declan Cluskey, 1942): Irish musician (voice and guitarist: Bachelors), 311, 334
Clyde, Jeremy (b. 1941): English musician (guitar and singer: Chad and Jeremy), 173–74, 400–1, 417
The Coal Hole, 91-92 Strand, Covent Garden, London, 18
Cochran, Eddie (b. 1938): American musician and songwriter, 50, 31, 38–39, 126, 348
Coe, Peter (b. 1930): musician (tenor saxophone: Georgie Fame and the Blue Flames), 252, 358
Cogan, Alma (b. Alma Angela Cohen, 1932): English musician (singer), 55, 202, 209, 213–14, 349, 413, 420
    Alma Cogan, 210, 409
    The Alma Cogan Show, 210, 409
Cohn, Nik (b. 1946): British music journalist, 296
Coleman, Ray (b. 1937): English journalist, xii, 160, 146, 286
The Coliseum, 1132-1146 3rd Street NE, Washington, District of Columbia, 156
Collins, Grenville: English manager, 193
Collins, Shirley (b. 1935): English folk singer, 314, 315, 349, 363
Colman, Sid: British music publisher, 80, 81, 91–92
Columbia Records, 38, 39, 54, 56, 127, 167, 168, 225, 258, 272, 312
Colyer, Ken (b. 1928): English musician (trumpet), 22
    Ken Colyer's Jazzmen (London): (a) Ken Colyer, Monty Sunshine, Ron Bowden,

Lonnie Donegan, and Jim Bray and (b) Ken Colyer, Mac Duncan, Ian Wheeler, Johnny Bastable, Ron Ward, and Colin Bowden, 22–23, 24, 349
Ken Colyer's Studio 51, 10-11 Great Newport Street, Covent Garden, London, 138
Commodore Theatre, 395 King Street, London, 233
El Condor Club, 17 Wardour Street, Soho, London, 46
The Contours (Detroit): Joe Billingslea, Billy Gordon, Billy Hoggs, Sylvester Potts, Hubert Johnson, and Huey Davis, 118, 349
Cook, Roger (b. 1940): English songwriter and musician (singer: Kestrels), 271, 360
Cooke, Sam (b. Samuel Cook, 1931): American musician (singer) and songwriter, 365, 403
Cordell, Frank (b. 1918): English arranger and conductor, 209, 349
Cordet, Louise (b. Louise Boisot, 1945): English musician (singer), 158, 349
Coronation Street, 45–46, 273, 412
Cotten, Elizabeth (b. 1893), American musician (vocals and guitar) and songwriter, 28, 349–50, 379
Cotton, Billy (b. 1899), English band leader, 48
The Billy Cotton Band Show, 50, 410
Les Cousins, 49 Greek Street, Soho, London, 316
Courtney, Lou (b. Louis Pegues, 1943): American musician (singer) and songwriter, 191, 381
Coward, Noël (b. 1899): English playwright and songwriter, 193
Cramer, Floyd (b. 1933): American musician (piano, Elvis), 106, 356, 381–82, 384
The Crawdaddy Club, 1 Kew Road, Richmond upon Thames, Surrey, 134, 135, 136, 137, 166, 249, 257, 265, 266
Crawford, Allan (b. 1921?): Australian-British publisher and broadcaster, 247–48
The Crickets (Lubbock, Texas): Buddy Holly, Niki Sullivan, Jerry Allison, and Joe B. Mauldin, 60, 76, 367
Cripps, Bruce (see Bruce Welch)
Criscione, Louise: American music journalist, xii
Criterion Theatre, 218-223 Piccadilly, Saint James's, London, 210
Crombie, Tony (b. Anthony Kronenberg, 1925): English musician (drums) and bandleader, 38, 55
Tony Crombie and His Rockets (London): Tony Crombie, Jim Currie, Jet Harris, Red Mitchell, Al Cornish, and Cliff Lawrence, 33–34, 350
Cronkite, Walter (b. 1916): American broadcast journalist, 145
Crosby, Bing (b. Harry Crosby, Jr, , 1903): American singer and actor, 91, 350, 410, 418
Croydon Civic Hall, Katharine Street, Croydon, London, 123
Croydon College of Art, College road, Croydon, 194
Cumberland Hotel, 6 Bryanston Street, Marylebone, London, 209
The Crystals (New York): (1) Barbara Alston, Dolores Kenniebrew, Myrna Giraud, Mary Thomas, and Patricia Wright; (2) Barbara Alston, Mary Thomas, Dolores Brooks, Delores Kenniebrew, and Patricia Wright, 211, 213, 350
Curtis, Chris (b. Chris Crummey, 1941): English musician (drums and singer: Searchers) and songwriter, 107–9, 160–61, 392
Curtis, Lee (b. Peter Flannery, 1939): English musician (singer and guitar, Lee Curtis and the All-Stars), 104, 224–25, 392–93
Lee Curtis and the All-Stars: Lee Curtis, Frank Bowen, Tony Waddington, Wayne Bickerton, and Bernie Rogers, 224

The Daily Express, 173–74
Daily Mail, 92–93
Daily Mirror, 90
The Dakotas (see Billy J, Kramer)
Dale, Glen (b. Richard Garforth, 1943): English musician (voice and guitar: Fortunes), 270, 359–60
Dallas, Karl, (b. 1931): English music journalist, 313
Daltrey, Roger (b. 1944): English musician (singer: Who), 299, 301, 305, 365–66, 404–5
Dankworth, John (b. 20 September 1927 – 6 February 2010): English musician (saxophone), 206
Johnny Dankworth Seven: John Dankworth (alto saxophone), Keith Christie (trombone), Alan Ganley (drums), and others, 206, 374
Datebook, 156
David, Hal (b. Harold David, 1921): American lyricist, 159, 226, 333, 234, 342, 344, 345, 349, 370, 374, 382, 396, 398, 404
David, Hubert W, (b. 1904): English songwriter and journalist, 103

Davies, Cyril (b. 1932): English musician (harmonica, guitar: Blues Incorporated, Cyril Davies Rhythm and Blues All-Stars), 122, 124–26, 127, 129, 131–33, 300, 343
Cyril Davies Rhythm and Blues All-stars (London): Cyril Davies, Carlo Little, Ricky Fenson, Nicky Hopkins, and others, 128*f*, 125–26, 129, 350
Davies, Dave (b. 1947): English musician (guitar and singer: Kinks), 192, 194–95, 253, 315, 371–73
Davies, Megan (, 1944): English musician (bass: Applejacks), 267–68, 332
Davies, Kathleen "Peggy" (b. 1932): sister of Ray and Dave Davies, 192
Davies, Rasa (b. Rasa Dicpetris, 1946): Lithuanian-English musician (backing vocals: Kinks), 372
Davies, Ray (b. 1944): English musician (guitar and singer: Kinks) and songwriter ("Well Respected Man"), 192–97, 198*f*, 253–54, 314, 371–73
Ray Davies Quartet (see the Kinks), 192
Davies, Rene (b. 1926): sister of Ray and Dave Davies, 192
Davies (family home), 6 Denmark Terrace, Fortis Green, London, 192
Davis, Billie (b. Carol Hedges, 1945): musician (singer), 232–233, 350, 392
Davis, Gary, Reverend (b. 1896): American musician (guitar and singer) and songwriter,
Davis, Miles (b. 1926): American jazz musician (trumpet), 179, 246
Davis, Spencer (b. Spencer Davies, 1939): English musician (guitar and vocal, Spencer Davis Group), 264–66
The Spencer Davis Rhythm and Blues Quartet: 264–65
The Spencer Davis Group (Birmingham, England): Spencer Davis, Muff Winwood, Steve Winwood, and Peter York, 265, 278*f*, 306, 351
Davison, Harold (b. 1922): English agent (Dave Clark Five), 187
Harold Davison Agency, Regent House, 235-241 Regent Street, London, 119
Dawbarn, Bob (b. 1928): English music journalist, xii, 33–34, 250, 269, 300–1
De Gaulle, Charles (b. 1890): French President, 98
De Hems, 11 Macclesfield Street, Soho, London, 135
De Lane Lea Studios/Kingsway, 129 Kingsway, Holborn, London, 112, 167, 168, 190, 331, 365, 381, 388

D'Ell, Dennis (b. Dennis Dalziel, 1943): English musician (singer: Honeycombs), 188, 367
Dean, James (b. 1931): American actor, 51–52, 76
Decca Records (offices), 9 Albert Embankment, Lambeth, London, 25, 26–27, 35, 48–49, 50, 53, 79, 80, 82, 84, 117, 118, 137, 157, 158, 163–164, 185, 189, 208, 228–29, 233–34, 247, 255–56, 266–68, 269–70, 271, 284, 286, 314
Decca Studios, 165 Broadhurst Gardens, West Hampstead, London, 12, 13, 80, 82, 117, 124, 127, 138, 180, 225, 332, 334–35, 341–42, 343, 349, 352, 361, 370, 377, 383–84, 388, 399–400, 401–2, 406–7
The DeMarco Sisters (Rome, New York), Anne DeMarco, Arlene DeMarco, Gina DeMarco, Gloria DeMarco, and Terri DeMarco 210, 351
Dene, Terry (b. Terence Williams, 1938), English musician (singer), 45, 193
Terry Dene and the Dene Aces/Terry Dene's Dene Aces (London), 193
Denmark Productions, Denmark Street, Saint Giles, London, 194
Denmark Street, Saint Giles, London, 54, 91–92, 103, 105, 119, 148–49, 193, 268, 271, 276–77, 284, 319
DeShannon, Jackie (b. 1941): American musician and songwriter, 160, 161, 236, 290, 320, 351, 358, 393
The Detours (see the Who)
Dietrich, Marlene (b. Marie Dietrich, 1901): German-American actress and musician (singer), 201
Dion and the Belmonts (New York): Dion DiMucci, Carlo Mastrangelo, Angelo D'Aleo, and Fred Milano, 46–47, 351
Disc / *Disc and Music Echo*, 1661 Fleet Street, London, ix, 85
Disques Vogue, 211
Dixon, Willie (b. 1915): American musician (bass), songwriter, and record producer, 124, 249, 340, 341, 343, 345, 368, 380, 385, 389
Dodd, Clement "Coxsone" (b. 1932): Jamaican producer, 229
Dominion Theatre, 268-269 Tottenham Court Road, London, 18
Doncaster, Patrick (b. 1917): English music journalist, 92–93
Donegan, Lonnie (b. Anthony Donegan, 1931), Scottish-English musician (guitar and vocals) and songwriter, 25–28, 30*f*, 32, 35–36, 53, 61, 311, 334–35, 349, 352–53
Lonnie Donegan's Skiffle Group (London): (a) Lonnie Donegan, Chris

Barber, and Beryl Bryden; (b) Lonnie Donegan, Micky Ashman, Denny Wright, and Nick Nichols; and (c) Lonnie Donegan, Les Bennetts, Pete Huggett, and Nick Nicholls, 334–35, 352–53
Donnelly, Mark: British historian, 143
Donovan (see Leitch, Donovan)
Don't Knock the Rock, 66–67, 412
Douglas-Home, Sir Alec (b. 1903): English Conservative politician; UK PM 1963-1964, 98, 145
The Dovells (Philadelphia): Len Borisoff, Jerry Gross, Arnie Silver, Jim Mealy, and Mike Freda, 270, 354
Dover Castle, 43 Weymouth Mews, Marylebone, London, 196
Dreja, Chris (b. 1945): Musician (guitar/bass: Yardbirds), 257, 406
The Drifters (New York): Clyde McPhatter, Ben E, King, and others,
The Drifters (London) (see Cliff Richard and the Drifters.)
Driscoll, Julie (b. 1947): English musician (singer: Brian Auger and the Trinity), 266
Dr. No, 69, 152, 230, 412
Drumbeat, 49, 52, 213, 412
Dudgeon, Gus (b. Angus Boyd Dudgeon, 1942): Recording engineer, 180, 349, 363–64, 401, 406–7
Dunbar, John (b. 1943): English artist, 235, 237
Durham, Judith (b. Judith Cock, 1943): Australian musician (singer: Seekers), 312, 313, 393
Durham Cathedral, Durham, County Durham, England, 173
Durkheim, Emile (b. 1858): French sociologist, 288
Dylan, Bob (b. Robert Zimmerman, 1941): American songwriter and musician, 121, 153, 167, 168, 236, 290, 292, 302–3, 309, 315, 316, 317, 318, 319, 320–21, 345, 354–56, 357–58, 383, 411, 416
Bob Dylan: Don't Look Back, 319
Dynamics, the (Detroit): Isaac Harris, George White, Fred Baker, and Samuel Stevenson, 301, 356

Eager, Vince (b. Roy Taylor, 1940), English musician (singer), 45, 412
Ealing Art College, 32 Saint Mary's Road, Ealing, London, 298, 299
Groundcourse, 299
Ealing Rhythm and Blues Club, 42a The Broadway, Ealing, London, 123, 131–132, 139–40

Earl-Jean (b. Earl-Jean McCrea, 1942): American musician (singer), 274, 356
Easton, Eric (b. 1927): English manager, 135, 388, 389
Easybeat, 268, 412
Eddy, Duane (b. 1938): American musician (guitar), 62, 299, 356
Eden, Peter (b. 193?): English manager, 319, 353
Edge, Graeme (b. 1941): English musician (drums: Moody Blues), 266, 380
Edgecombe, Johnny (b. 1932): Antigua and Barbuda-born promoter, 126
Education, 5, 21, 31, 44, 81, 89, 131, 171, 173, 176, 297–98, 299, 309–10, 325–26
  Education Act of 1944, 89
  Grammar schools, 5, 74, 80, 89, 131, 165, 171, 179, 180, 264, 270, 273, 298, 299, 325
  Secondary Modern schools, 171, 192, 5, 89
Eisenhower, Dwight (b. 1890): American president, 34
Elgar, Sir Edward (b. 1857): English composer, 10–12
Elizabeth II, Queen (b. 1926): British monarch, 19–20, 44, 205
Elliott, Bobby (b. 1941): English musician (drums: Hollies), 112
Elliott, Jack ("Ramblin' ") (b. Elliot Adnopoz, 1931): American musician and songwriter, 25
Elstree Studios, Shenley Road, Borehamwood, Hertfordshire, 118–19
Ember Records, 12 Great Newport Street, London, 173–74
Emerick, Geoff (b. 1945): English recording engineer, 13
EMI (Electric and Musical Industries), EMI House, 20 Manchester Square, Marylebone, London, 33, 38, 40, 53, 54–55, 61, 79, 80–81, 82, 84, 85, 100, 105, 110, 119, 145, 148, 151, 159, 175, 176, 178, 179, 185, 189, 228, 233–34, 247, 265–66, 269–70, 302–3, 312
EMI Pathé Marconi Studios, 62 Rue de Sevres, Paris, 147–48, 337
EMI Recording Studios, 3 Abbey Road, Saint John's Wood, London, 6, 10–13, 52, 56, 59f, 91, 93, 94, 95, 96, 97, 99, 107, 152, 303, 335–40, 342–43, 354, 357, 358, 360–61, 362–63, 365, 366, 368, 369, 371, 373–74, 377–78, 382–83, 386–87, 393–96, 400–1
Empire Pool (aka Wembley Pool), Engineers Way, Wembley Park, Wembley, 247, 326–27
Entwistle, John (b. 1944): English musician (bass, vocals, and French horn: Who), 299, 305, 307, 365–66, 404–5

Epic Records, 550 Madison Ave, New York, New York, 187
Epstein, Brian (b. 1934): English artist manager, 78–79, 80–81, 91–92, 93, 95, 104, 105, 106–7, 108, 134, 135–36, 139, 145, 146, 149–50, 152–53, 157, 159, 166, 185, 224, 225, 226–27, 228, 302, 317–18, 320, 409, 413
Erisso, Baroness (b. Eva von Sacher-Masoch, 1912): Austrian aristocrat and mother of Marianne Faithfull, 236–37
Essoldo Theatre, Claughton Road, Birkenhead, 48
The Establishment, 18 Greek Street, Soho, London, 317
Estes, Sleepy John (b. John Estes, 1899): American musician (guitar and singer) and songwriter, 249
Eton College, Eton, Berkshire, England, 5, 173
Evans, Bill (b 1929): American musician (piano) and composer, 179
The Evening Standard, 92–93, 229
The Everly Brothers (Iowa, US): Don Everly and Phil Everly, 28, 31, 84, 91, 111, 117, 138, 166, 167, 173, 190, 268, 275, 356–57
The Exciters (Queens, New York City): Brenda Reid, Carolyn Johnson, Lillian Walker, and Herb Rooney, 179, 233, 357
Exodus, 55, 413
Expresso Bongo, 41, 413
Ezell, Will (b. 1892): American musician (piano and singer), 24, 366

Fairsky, SS, 312
Faith, Adam (aka Terry Denver, b. Terence Nelhams-Wright, 1940): Musician (singer and actor), 51–53, 57*f*, 81, 83, 178, 213, 233–11, 241*f*, 357, 416
Faithfull, Marianne (b. 1946): English musician (singer), 12–13, 235–37, 242*f*, 245–46, 318, 357–58
Fallon, Jack (b. 1915): Canadian musician (bass) and promoter, 34
Fame, Georgie (b. Clive Powell, 1943): English musician (keyboards, singer, guitar), 126–27, 248, 251–52, 260*f*, 358
  Georgie Fame and the Blue Flames (London): Georgie Fame, Neeomi Acquaye, Tex Makins, Peter Coe, Glen Hughes, Colin Green, etc, 126–27, 251–52, 306, 358
Fats Domino (b. Antoine Domino, 1928): American musician and songwriter, 4, 36, 105, 126, 130, 272, 352

Feild, Tim (b. Richard Timothy Feild, aka Reshad Field, 1934): English musician (guitar and singer), 213, 311, 312, 399
The Feminine Mystique, 199, 201
Fenson, Ricky (aka Rick Brown, b. 1945): English musician (bass: Screaming Lord Sutch, Georgie Fame, and others), 125–26, 128*f*, 133, 350
Ferry Cross the Mersey, 158, 413
Fielding, Henry (b. 1707): English author, 275, 421
Fields, Gracie (b. Grace Stansfield, 1898): English actress and singer, 18–19
Find the Singer, 54, 413
Finney, Albert (b. 1936): English actor, 275, 421
Finsbury Park Empire Theatre, 2 Saint Thomas's Road, Finsbury Park, London, 36
Fisher, Matthew (b. 1946): English musician (organ: Procol Harum) and songwriter, xi–xii
Fitzgerald, Ella (b. 1917): American musician (singer), 130
The Flamingo Club (1) Mapleton Hotel, Leicester Square, London and (2) 33-37 Wardour Street, Soho, London, 33–34, 126, 127, 134, 135, 173, 235, 249, 251, 320, 358
Flannery, Joe (b. 1931): English manager and agent, 224–25
Flick, Vic (b. 1937): English musician (guitar), xi–xii, 13, 119, 175–76, 228–29, 271, 273–74, 338, 342, 348, 357, 360, 370, 376–77, 382–83
Flynn, Errol (b. 1909): Australian-American actor, 62–63
Folkways Records, 17 West 60th Street, New York, New York, 26
Fontana, D, J, (b. Dominic Joseph Fontana, 1931): American musician (drums, Elvis Presley), 272
Fontana, Wayne (b. Glyn Ellis, 1945): English musician (singer: Wayne Fontana and the Mindbenders), 272–73
  Wayne Fontana and the Mindbenders (Manchester, England): Wayne Fontana, Bob Lang, Ric Rothwell, and Eric Stewart, 272, 281*f*
Fontana Records (see Philips Records), 231, 265–66, 270, 272, 301, 303
Ford, Eric: English musician (guitar and bass), 119, 347, 361, 370, 376
Ford, Perry (b. Bryan Pugh, 1940): English songwriter and musician (singer: Ivy

League), 268, 271, 279f, 304, 357, 360, 365, 368–69, 372, 404
Fordyce, Keith (b. 1928): English disc jockey, television presenter, and critic, 92, 412, 418
Formby, George (b. George Hoy Booth, 1904): English musician: actor, songwriter, 105, 18–20, 27, 29f, 50, 289, 311, 325, 359, 416
Formby, George Sr, (b. James Lawler Booth, 1875): English comedian and singer, 19
Keep Your Seats, Please!, 19, 416
The Formby Sniffle Gloup (Liverpool), Ronald Wycherley [Billy Fury] and others, 48
The Fortunes (Birmingham): Rod Allen, Glen Dale, Barry Pritchard, Dave Carr, and Andy Brown, 270–71, 280f, 359–60
Foster, John (b. 1939?): English manager, 37–38, 41
Foster, Stephen (b. 1826): American songwriter and musician, 17
Foucault, Michel (b. Paul-Michel Foucault, 1926): French philosopher, 12–13
The Four Seasons (Newark, New Jersey): Frankie Valli, Bob Gaudio, Tommy DeVito, and Dick Massi, 84, 360
The Four Tunes (New York City): Danny Owens, Pat Best, Jimmy Gordon, and Jimmie Nabbie, 161–62, 360
Fowley, Kim (b. 1939): American record producer and publicist, 270
Fox, Kate: English anthropologist, xii, 8, 26, 72, 110, 111, 120, 164, 171–72, 203, 284, 285, 325, 326
Fox Theater, 2211 Woodward Avenue, Detroit, Michigan, 26
Fox Theatre, 20 Flatbush Avenue, Brooklyn, New York, 181, 417
Frame, Peter (b. 1942): English journalist and historian, xii, 127, 264
Franz, Johnny (b. 1922): English record producer, 46–47, 48–49, 206, 213, 214, 232, 275–76, 333, 335, 388, 397, 398–99, 404, 405
Freddie and the Dreamers (Manchester): Freddie Garrity, Pete Birrell, Roy Crewsdon, Bernie Dwyer, and Derek Quinn, 110–11, 114f, 161–62, 178, 272, 273, 291, 326, 360–61
Free Trade Hall, Peter Street, Manchester, 111
Freeman, Alan A, (b. 1920): English record producer, 125, 347–48, 352–53
Freeman, Robert (b. 1936): English photographer, 100

The Freight Train, Berwick Street, Soho, London, 62
The Friday Spectacular, 85, 413
From Russia with Love, 97, 152, 173, 413
From Spain to Streatham, 314, 413
Fury, Billy (b. Ronald Wycherley, 1940): English musician and songwriter, 48–49, 50, 56f, 61, 68, 69, 75, 76, 81, 82, 83, 84, 104–5, 106–7, 126–27, 195–96, 288, 309, 361, 411, 420, 422

Gaitskell, Hugh (b. 1906): English politician, 92, 98
Gallup, Cliff (b. 1930): American musician (guitar: Gene Vincent), 47
Ganjou, George, Russian-Polish-British manager, 38
Garland, Judy (b. 1922): American singer and actor, 206
Garrity, Freddie (b. 1936): English musician (singer: Freddie and the Dreamers), 110–11, 114f, 161–62, 360–61
Gateways Club, 239 Kings Road, Chelsea, London, 215
Gaumont Theatre, 58 Shepherd's Bush Green, Shepherd's Bush, London, 38
Gaye, Barbie (b. 1942): American musician (singer), 230, 361–62
Gaye, Marvin (b. Marvin Gay, Jr, 1939): American musician (singer), songwriter, and producer, 291, 362, 378
Gentle, Johnny (b. John Askew, 1936), English musician (singer), 45, 76
Gentlemen Prefer Blondes, 207, 413–14
George VI (b. 1895): British monarch, 19–20
Gerry and the Pacemakers (see Gerry Marsden)
Gillett, Charlie (b. 1942): English music scholar and disc jockey, 8, 84
The Girl Can't Help It, 31, 414
The Gladiolas (South Carolina): Maurice Williams, Henry Gaston, Wiley Bennett, Charles Thomas, Albert Hill, and Willie Morrow with Willie Jones, William Massey, and Norman Wade, 363
Glasser, Dick (b. 1933): American record producer, 160, 161
The Gleneagles (see Lulu and the Luvvers)
Goddard, Geoff (b. 1937): English songwriter, 54, 68, 375–76, 402
Goffin, Gerry (b. 1939): American songwriter, 49, 274, 356, 361, 364, 388, 397, 399, 402
Golden Eagle, Hill Street, Birmingham, 264, 265
Goldfinger, 152

Gomelsky, Giorgio (b. 1934): Georgian-Swiss-British manager, record producer, and promoter, 134, 136, 166, 193, 257, 258, 265, 406

Gonella, Nat (b. 1908): English musician (trumpet and voice), 265

Good, Jack (b. 1931): English record and television producer, 36, 39, 40, 41, 45–47, 48–49, 51–52, 53, 54, 62, 65, 66, 78, 83, 90, 98, 124, 134, 135, 161–62, 175–76, 230, 274, 275, 343, 361, 376, 409, 411, 417, 419–20, 422

    Jack Good's Firing Squad (London): Eric Ford, Bryan Daley, Allan Weighell, and Andy White, 83, 411

Goodman, Shirley (b. 1936): American R and B singer, 229

Gordon, Aloysius "Lucky" (b. 1931): Jamaican musician (singer: Blue Flames), 126

Gordon, Tony: English agent, 228

Gouldman, Graham (b. 1946): English songwriter and musician (bass: Mockingbirds), xi–xii, 258, 406

Grade, Lew (b. Lev Winogradsky, 1906): British agent and media executive, Lew Grade Agency, 312

Graham, Bobby (b. Robert Neate, 1940): Musician (drums: Joe Brown and sessions) and record producer (Pretty Things), xi–xii, 60, 119, 187, 194–95, 196, 256, 344–45, 347, 371–72, 375–76

Graham, "Davey"/"Davy" (b. David Michael Gordon Graham, 1940): British musician (guitar) and composer, 314–15, 316, 322*f*, 349, 363–64, 401, 413

Gramophone Company (see EMI), 10–11

Granada Cinema, 5-9 Saint Peters Street, Bedford, 135

Granada Television, Salford, Manchester, 84, 109, 410–11, 415, 417, 412

Grant, Jimmy: English radio producer, 117, 415, 419

Gray, Lissa (aka Lissa Grey), British actor and musician (singer), 54

Gray, Owen (b. 1939): Jamaican musician (singer), 229

The Great Escape, 54, 414

Green, Colin: English musician (guitar: Georgie Fame and the Blue Flames), 50, 127, 358, 361

Green, Richard: English music journalist, xii

Greenaway, Roger (b. 1938): Songwriter and musician (singer: Kestrels), 271, 360

Greenslade, Arthur (b. 1923): Musician (piano: sessions), music director, arranger, conductor, and songwriter, xi–xii, 196, 311, 334, 372, 401, 421–22

Greer, Germaine (b. 1939): Australian writer (*The Female Eunuch*), 224

Gregg, Brian (b. 1939): English musician (bass: Tornados), 62–63, 371

Grenoble University, 173

Griffiths, David: British music journalist, xii, 120

Group Scene '64, 283

Grundy, David (see Dave Berry)

Grundy, Hugh (b. 1945): English musician (drummer: Zombies), 179, 180, 406–7

Guest, Reg (aka Earl Guest, b. 1930): English musician (piano: Billy Fury and sessions), music director, and arranger, 164, 228, 273–74, 311, 341–42, 361, 365, 376–77

Guildhall School of Music and Drama, John Carpenter Street, London, 81, 100, 174–75

Guns at Batasi, 54

Gunnell, Rik (b. 1931): Entrepreneur, manager, and record producer, 127

Guthrie, Woody (b. Woodrow Wilson Guthrie, 1912): American musician and songwriter, 24, 26–27, 320, 352–53, 364

Guy, Athol (b. 1940): Australian musician (bass: Seekers), 312, 393–94

Hackney Empire, Mare Street, Hackney Central, London, 65–66

Haley, Bill (b. 1925): American musician (guitar and vocal), 4, 26, 31, 33

    Bill Haley and His Comets (Chester, Pennsylvania): Bill Haley, Franny Beecher, Johnny Grande, Ralph Jones, Rudy Pomlilli, Al Rex, and Billy Williamson, 18, 27, 36, 37–38, 111, 345–46, 364, 412, 418

Hammerstein II, Oscar (b. 1895): American lyricist, 106, 362, 398, 411, 420

Handel, Georg Friedrich (b. 1726): German composer and musician, 313

A Hard Day's Night, 149–51, 155*f*, 338, 414

Harpers West One, 53, 414

Harpo, Slim (b. James Moore, 1924): American musician (harmonica, guitar, and singer), 255–56, 301, 364

Harris, Jet (b. Terence Harris, 1939): English musician (bass: Shadows), 33, 39–40, 43*f*, 66, 67, 92, 115, 233, 350, 354, 386–87, 394–95

Harris, June: English journalist, xii

Harrison, Billy (b. 1942): Northern Irish musician (guitar: Them), 255, 256, 401–2

Harrison, George (b. 1943): English musician (guitar and singer: Beatles) and songwriter, 74–76, 80, 99–100, 102*f*, 107, 115, 137, 146, 148, 151, 152, 180–81, 320–21, 335–40, 397, 398, 414

Harrison, Harold (b. 1909): father of George Harrison, 74–75

Harrison, Louise (b. Louise French, 1911): mother of George Harrison, 74–75

Harrow School, 5 High Street, Harrow, England, 230

Harry, Bill (b. 1938): English journalist and editor/publisher (*Mersey Beat*) and publicist (Kinks), xi–xii, 90, 104

Harvey, Lawrence (b. Laruschka Skikne, 1928): Lithuania-British actor, 41

Hassinger, Dave (b. 1927): American recording engineer (Rolling Stones), 292, 390

Hatch, Tony (b. 1939, a, k, a, Fred Nightingale and Mark Anthony): English record producer, arranger, and songwriter, 96, 108, 109, 160, 211, 212, 232, 233–34, 313, 348, 391, 392–93, 396, 403

Hatfield, Bobby (b. 1940): American musician (singer), 275, 387

Hawken, John (b 1940): English musician (piano: Nashville Teens), xi–xii, 190, 191, 198*f*, 381

Hawker, Jean (b. Jean Ryder, 1938): English musician (singer), 214, 376–77

Hawker, Mike (b. 1936): English songwriter, 55, 56, 214, 395, 396, 398

Hawkins, Screaming Jay (b. Jalacy Hawkins, 1929): American musician (piano and singer) and songwriter, 63

Haydock, Eric (b. 1943): English musician (bass: Hollies), 112, 366

The Heartbeats (see Herman's Hermits)

Heatley, Spike (b. 1933): English musician (bass: Blues Incorporated), 124

Heath Fred (see Johnny Kidd)
 Freddie Heath and His Rock n' Roll Combo (Johnny Kidd and the Pirates), 61

Heckstall-Smith, Dick (b. 1934): English musician (saxophone: Blues Incorporated), 124, 249, 343

Helms, Bobby (b. 1933): American musician (singer and guitar), 38, 364

Help! 152–53, 317–18, 339, 414–15

Henderson, Alan (b. 1944): Northern Irish musician (bass: Them), 255, 256, 401–2

Hendricks, Jon (b. 1921): American lyricist and musician (singer: Lambert, Hendricks, and Bavan), 252, 358, 374–75

Here Come the Huggetts, 210, 415

Herman's Hermits (Manchester, England): Peter Noone, Karl Green, Keith Hopwood, Derek Leckenby, and Barry Whitman, 269, 272–74, 281*f*, 291, 365, 417

Hibbert, Tom (b. 1952): English music journalist, xii

Hicks, Tony (b. 1945): English musician (guitar: Hollies) and songwriter, 112, 163, 285, 366, 389

The High Numbers (see the Who)

Hill, Alex (b. 1906): American musician (piano), 24, 366

Hiller, Tony (b. Toby Hiller, 1927): English songwriter, 271, 360

Hindemith, Paul (b. 1995): German composer, 264–65

Hitsville U, S, A, (See Motown)

The HMV Shop, 363 Oxford Street, Mayfair, London, 38

Les Hobeaux (London): Les Bennetts, Alan Jones, David Russell, Winky Wimbledon, Keith Larner, and Roger Smith, 27

Hoffmann, Dezo (b. 1912): Czechoslovakian photographer, 84

The Hokum Boys (Chicago, Il): Tampa Red and Thomas A, Dorsey, 24

Hold On!, 274, 415

The Hollies (Manchester, England): Allan Clarke, Graham Nash, Eric Haydock, Bobby Elliott, and Tony Hicks, 111–12, 162–63, 169*f*, 195, 272, 285, 366

Holloway, Brenda (b. 1946): American musician (singer) and songwriter, 265–66, 366

Holloway, Stanley (b. 1890): English comedian and singer, 18–19, 381, 417

Holly, Buddy (b. Charles Holley, 1936): American musician (guitar and singer) and songwriter, 31, 48, 49, 52, 54, 60, 66, 75, 76, 107–8, 109, 117, 130, 131, 181, 192, 193, 204, 285, 318, 367, 389

The Hollywood Palace, 174, 286, 294*f*, 415

Holtzman, Marvin: American producer, 311, 334

The Honeycombs (London): Denis D'Ell, Martin Murray, Alan Ward, John Lantree, and Honey Lantree, 188–89, 367

Hooker, John Lee (b. 1912): American musician (guitar and singer) and songwriter, 131, 166, 250, 256, 265–66, 297, 306, 351, 367–68

Hopkins, Lightnin' (b. Samuel Hopkins, 1912): American musician (guitar and singer) and songwriter, 249

Hopkins, Nicky (b. 1944): English musician (piano: Screaming Lord Sutch, Rhythm and Blues All Stars), 70*f*, 125–26, 305, 350, 373, 404–5

Horne, Lena (b. 1917): American singer and actor, 206

Hornsey College of Arts and Crafts, Crouch End, Haringey, London, 193

Horricks, Ray (b. 1933): English record producer, 50, 314, 344–45, 349, 363

Houston, Cisco (b. Gilbert Houston, 1918): American musician and songwriter, 26–27, 354, 364

Howard, Alan (b. 1941): English musician (bass: Tremeloes), 117, 383–84

Howard, Ken (b. 1939): English songwriter and manager, 188–89, 367

Howes, Arthur: English promoter, 194, 195–96

The Howff, 369 High Street, Edinburgh, 315–16

Howlin' Wolf (b. Chester Arthur Burnett, 1910): American musician, 46, 131, 132, 249, 287, 368

Hugg, Mike (b. Michael Hug, 1942): English musician (drums: Manfred Mann), 177, 178, 377–78

Hullabaloo (UK), 322*f*

Hullabaloo, 156, 162, 181, 242*f*, 281*f*, 415

Hunt, Dave: British musician (trombone), 193
 Dave Hunt's Rhythm and Blues Band (London): Dave Hunt (trombone), Ray Davies (guitar), and others, 195

Hunt, Oliver (b. 1934): English musician (classical guitar) and teacher, 314

The Hutchinson Family (New Hampshire, USA): Judson Hutchinson, John Hutchinson, Asa Hutchinson, and Abby Hutchinson, 17

IBC Recording Studios, 35 Portland Place, Marylebone, London, 12–13, 53, 136, 196, 372–73, 376–77, 389, 398, 409

Ifield, Frank (b. 1937): Australian-English musician (singer), 115, 368

Ilford Palais de Danse, 246-250 High Road, Ilford, 207, 233

Immediate Records, 69 New Oxford Street, London, 236

Independent Television (see Associated-Rediffusion)

Indra Club, 64 Große Freiheit, Hamburg, West Germany,

Ingham, Beryl (aka, Beryl Formby, b. 1941): English manager, The Irani Brothers (Fred and Sam), Coffee bar owners, Iron Door Club.13 Temple Street, Liverpool (1960–1964), 77

Island Records, 8 Basing Street, Notting Hill, London, 225, 230

The Isley Brothers (Cincinnati, Ohio): O'Kelly Isley, Jr, Rudolph Isley, and Ronald Isley, 95, 96, 121, 228, 368

Italia Conti Academy, 23 Goswell Road, Barbican, London, 230

It's Dark Outside, 232, 415

It's Trad, Dad!, 150, 415

ITV / Independent Television, 128 Wembley Park Drive, Wembley, London, 33–34, 36, 39, 44, 45–46, 47, 53, 54, 55, 90–91, 92, 95–96, 118, 232, 274, 297, 328

The Ivy League (Birmingham/London): John Carter, Ken Lewis, and Perry Ford, 269, 271, 279*f*, 368–69

The Jacaranda, 21-23 Slater Street, Liverpool, 76

Jackson, Bill: Australian songwriter, 160–61, 354, 382, 388

Jackson, Papa Charlie (b. 1887): American musician (banjo and singer), 24, 366

Jackson, Tony (b. 1938): English musician (bass and singer: Searchers), 108, 107–8, 109, 160, 161, 392–93

Jacobs, David (b. 1912): English lawyer, 149

Jacobs, David (b. 1926): English broadcaster, 293, 415, 416

Jagger, Eva (b. Eva Schutts, 1913): English mother of Mick Jagger, 130

Jagger, Joe (b. Basil Fanshawe Jagger, 1913): English father of Mick Jagger, 130

Jagger, Mick (b. 1943): English musician (singer: Rolling Stones) and songwriter, 122–23, 124, 129, 130–40, 236, 237, 276, 277, 283–93, 295*f*, 301, 317, 357, 388–91

Jairazbhoy, Nazir (b. 1928): Indo-English-American musician (sitar) and ethnomusicologist, xi–xii

James, Clifton (b. 1936): American musician (drums), 249, 343–44

James, Dick (b. Leon Vapnick, 1920): English music publisher, 83, 92, 93–94, 96
 Dick James Music, (1) 132 Charing Cross Road, Soho, London and (2) 71-75 New Oxford Street, Bloomsbury, London, 93–94, 148–49

The Jamies (New York City): Tom Jameson, Serena Jameson, Jeannie Roy, and Arthur Blair, 270, 369

Jansch, Bert (b. 1943): Scottish musician (guitar, voice) and songwriter, 315–16, 369–70
Jarrett, Eddie: Australian agent, 312, 393
Jay, Fred (b. Friedrich Jacobson, 1914): Austrian-American lyricist, 232, 388
The Jazz Cellar (aka The Cellar), High Street, Kingston upon Thames, 190, 249, 257
Jazz Club, 22, 23, 124, 133, 342, 349, 415
Jazz News, 125, 132, 133, 177
The Jazz Singer, 111, 416
Jefferson, "Blind" Lemon (b. 1893): American musician (guitar and voice), 24, 121–22, 366
Jeffery, Mike (b. 1933): English manager, 166, 250–51
Johnny and the Moondogs (see the Beatles)
Johns, Glyn (b. 1942): English recording engineer, 136, 303, 358, 404
Johnson, Lonnie (b. Alonzo Johnson, 1899): American musician and songwriter, 25
Johnson, Lou (b. 1941): American musician, 234, 370
Johnson, Robert (b. 1911): American musician (guitar and singer) and songwriter, 24, 121–22, 133, 370
Jolson, Al (b. Asa Yoelson, 1886): American musician (singer) and actor, 111, 416
Jones, Anna: American musician (singer), 23, 370
Jones, Brian (aka Elmo Lewis, b. 1942): English musician (guitar and harmonica: Rolling Stones), 132, 133–34, 136, 137, 138, 139, 283, 285, 287, 289–90, 292, 293, 388–91
Jones, Evan (b. 1927): Jamaican playwright, 317
Jones, John Paul (b. John Baldwin, 1946): English musician (bass and organ: Jet Harris) and music director, 90, 246–47, 251
Jones, Ken (b. 1927): English manager and record producer (Zombies), 180, 406–7
Jones, Paul (b. Paul Pond, 1942): English musician (voice and harmonica, Manfred Mann), 132, 178, 377–78
Jones, Peter (b. 1930): English music journalist, 135
Jones, Philip (b. Philip Mervyn-Jones, 1944): English television executive, 92, 421
R. G. Jones (b. Ronald Godfrey Jones): English recording engineer, R, G, Jones Studios, Morden Manor, London Road, Morden, London, 258, 406

Jones, Tom (aka, Tommy Scott; b. Thomas Jones Woodward, 1940): Welsh musician (singer), 182, 276–77, 282f, 370–71
Tom Jones and the Squires (Wales): Tom Jones, Mickey Gee, Vernon Hopkins, Chris Slade, and Dave Cooper, 276
Jopling, Norman (b. 1948): English music journalist, xii, 104, 135, 136, 137
Juke Box Jury, 55, 96, 175, 180–81, 226, 293, 416

Kämpfert/Kaempfert, Bert (b. Berthold Kämpfert, 1923): German record producer and band leader, 78, 397
Kaiserkeller, 36 Große Freiheit, Hamburg, West Germany, 77
Kapp Records, 161
Kassner, Edward (b. 1920): Anglo-Austrian publisher, record-company executive, and record producer, 194, 196
Katz, Charlie: English musician (violin) and contractor, 196
Kaufman, Murray "the K" (b. 1922): American disc jockey and impresario, 287
Keeler, Christine (b. 1942): English model, 97, 110, 126, 251
Keeping in Step, 52, 416
Kennedy, John: New Zealander photographer and manager, 34
Kennedy, John F, (b. 1917): American president, 7, 145, 146, 273–74
  John F, Kennedy International Airport, Queens, New York,
Kennedy Street Enterprises, Kennedy House, 14 Piccadilly, Manchester, 110, 273
Kennedy, Terry (b. Terry Rowe): English musician (guitar: Dene Aces), record producer, and publisher, 193, 268, 319, 345–46, 353–54, 368–69
Kerridge, Adrian: English recording engineer and record producer, 119–20, 187, 342, 347
Khan, Ali Akbar (b. 1922): Indian musician (sarod), 313
Kidd, Johnny (b. Frederick Heath, 1935): English musician and songwriter, 52, 61–63, 115, 208, 299, 371
  Johnny Kidd and the Pirates (London): (1) Fred Heath, Alan Caddy, John Gordon, Tom Doherty, and Don Toy; (2) Fred Heath, Alan Caddy, Brian Gregg, and Clem Cattini; and (3) Johnny Kidd, Mick Green, Frank Farley, and Johnny Spence, 61
King, Maurice (b. ca, 1925): English manager (Walker Brothers), 270

King Pleasure (b. Clarence Beeks, 1922): American musician (singer), 126–27
Kingston, Bob: British publisher (Southern Music), 319
Kingston School of Art, River House, 53-57 Hight Street, Kingston upon Thames, Surrey, 257
The Kingston Trio (Palo Alto, California): Dave Guard, Bob Shane, and Nick Reynolds, 213
The Kinks (London): Ray Davies, Dave Davies, Peter Quaife, and Mick Avory, 192–97, 198*f*, 253–54, 257, 261*f*, 268, 300, 303, 304, 305, 315, 371–73
Kirby, Kathy (b. Kathleen O'Rourke, 1938): English musician (singer), 207–8, 212, 213, 219*f*, 235, 373
Kirchherr, Astrid (b. 1938): West German photographer, 77–78, 100
Kitaj, Ronald (b. 1932): American artist and educator, 299
Knight, Jr., Peter (b. 1941): English record producer (Amen Corner), xi–xii, 125, 350
Klein, Allen (b. 1931): American publisher, record company owner, and manager, 251, 287, 417
Klein, Jody: American music executive, xi–xii
Korner, Alexis (b. 1928): English musician (guitar and singer: Blues Incorporated), 132, 316, 122–25, 127, 129, 132–33, 193, 313, 314, 343, 363
Koschmider, Bruno (b. 1926): West German club owner, 76–77
Kramer, Billy J, (b. William Ashton, 1943): English musician (singer), 106–7, 111, 157, 159, 283
  Billy J, Kramer with the Dakotas (Liverpool-Manchester): Billy J, Kramer, Tony Mansfield, Robin MacDonald, Ray Jones, and Mike Maxfield, 104, 107, 159, 323–24, 373–74
Kruger, Jeff (b. Jeffrey Krugerkoff, 1931): English agent, club owner, and entrepreneur, 33–34, 173, 418
Khrushchev, Nikita (b. 1894): Soviet First Secretary, 34
Kyle, Danny (b. 1939): Scottish folk singer and songwriter, 315

The Lads, 274, 416
Ladd's Black Aces (New York): Jimmy Lytell, Frank Signorelli, Phil Napoleon, Miff Mole, and Jack Roth, 23, 374

Laine, Cleo (b. 1927): English musician (singer), 205–206, 374
Laine, Denny (b. Brian Hines, 1944): English musician (guitar and vocal, Moody Blues), 266–67, 268, 380
Laine, Frankie (b. Francesco LoVecchio, 1913): American musician (singer), 206, 209, 374
Lambert, Constant (b. 1905): English composer and conductor, 302
Lambert, Dave (b. 1917): American musician (singer: Lambert, Hendricks, and Bavan) and lyricist,
Lamber, Hendricks, and Bavan (New York): Dave Lambert, Jon Hendricks, and Yolande Bavan, 252, 374–75
Lambert, Dennis (b. 1947): American songwriter, 191, 361, 381
Lambert, Kit (b. Christopher Lambert, 1935): English manager, record producer, and entrepreneur, 302, 304, 305, 307
The Lana Sisters (London): Iris Long, Lynne Abrams, and Mary O'Brien (Dusty Springfield), 213, 375
Lance, Major (b. 1939): American musician (singer), 272, 375
Lang, Bob (b. 1946): English musician (bass: Wayne Fontana and the Mindbenders), 272, 359
Lansdowne Studios, Lansdowne House, 1 Lansdowne Road, Notting Hill, London, 12–13, 53, 119–20, 187, 188–89, 342, 347, 351
Lantree, Honey (b. Ann Lantree, 1943): English musician (drums: Honeycombs), 188, 189, 367
Lantree, John (b. 1940): English musician (bass: Honeycombs), 188, 367
LaVern, Roger (b. Roger Jackson, 1937): English musician (keyboards), 68, 402–3
Lawrence, Cliff, British musician (singer), 33
Lea, Clive (b. 1942): English musician (singer: Rockin' Berries), 269, 387–88
Leader, Bill (b. 1929): English recording engineer and record producer, 316, 363, 369
Leander, Mike (b. Michael Farr, 1941): English arranger, 236, 267–68, 332, 341, 357–58, 360, 377, 378
Ledbetter, Huddie (b. 1888): American musician (singer and guitar), 24, 26, 121, 123, 289, 375
Lee, Brenda (b. Brenda Mae Tarpley, 1944): American musician (singer), 54–55, 224, 227–28, 375

SUBJECT INDEX 465

Lee, Frank, British record producer, 48–49, 361
Lefebvre, Henri (b. 1901): French philosopher and sociologist, 10
Leiber, Jerry (b. 1933): American songwriter and record producer, 138, 161, 331, 335, 342, 348, 354, 366, 388, 393, 397
Leitch, Donovan (b. 1946): Scottish musician and songwriter, 309–10, 318–20, 353–54
Lennon, Alfred (b. 1912), Father of John Lennon, 73–74
Lennon, John (b. 1940): English musician (guitar and vocals: Beatles) and songwriter, 6, 72, 73–76, 77–78, 80, 81, \82, 83, 91, 93–94, 96, 99–100, 101, 102*f*, 105–6, 107, 109, 111, 115, 138, 148, 150, 151, 153–54, 158, 159, 167, 175, 203, 226, 227, 228–29, 267–68, 277, 283, 317–18, 320–21, 332, 335–40, 342, 343, 358, 373–74, 382–83, 388, 397, 398, 414
Lennon, Julia (b. Julia Stanley, 1914), Mother of John Lennon, 73–74
Leo's Jazz Club, British Legion Hall, Windsor, Berskshire, 129
Leslie, Peter, English publicist, 22–23
Lester, Richard (b. Richard Liebman, 1932): American film director, 150–51, 414–15, 417, 418–19
Lewis, Jerry Lee (b. 1935): American musician and songwriter, 130, 31, 38, 61–62, 66–67, 105, 126, 165-66, 186, 190, 276, 375
Lewis, Ken (b. Kenneth Hawker, 1940): English musician (singer: Ivy League) and songwriter, 268–69, 274, 279*f*, 304, 345–46, 365, 368–69, 370, 392, 404
Lewisohn, Mark (b. 1958): English biographer, ix, 72, 81, 82
Levis, Carroll (b. 1910): Canadian broadcaster, 75–76
Levy, Shawn (b. 1961): American author, 296
Leybourne, George (b. Joseph Saunders, 1842): English songwriter and musician, 18
Leyton, John (b. 1936): English singer and actor, 53–54, 57*f*
Life, 156
Lilley, Arthur (b. 1916): English recording engineer, 35–36, 352, 399–400
The Lindella Club / Lindella Dance Club, 54 Union Street, Glasgow, Scotland, 228
Lindsay, Jill Doyle (b. Jill Graham): Scottish musician (guitar), 316
Lisberg, Harvey (b. 1940): English manager, 273–74

Litherland Town Hall, Hatton Hill Road, Litherland, Merseyside, 78
Little, Carlo (b. Carl O'Neil Little, 1938): English musician (drums: Savages), xi–xii, 31, 63, 70*f*, 125–26, 128*f*, 133, 300, 350, 401
Little Richard (b. Richard Penniman, 1932): American musician (singer and piano) and songwriter, 4, 31, 63, 126, 130, 135, 138, 190, 194, 376, 412
Livingston, Alan (b. 1917): American record executive, 145, 146–47
Lloyd, A. L. (b. Albert "Bert" Lancaster Lloyd, 1908): English musician and song collector, 310, 314
Lloyd, Freddy: English musician (guitar: Teddy and Freddy), 51–52
Locking, Brian "Licorice" (b. 1938): English musician (bass guitar: Shadows), 319, 353, 387, 395, 401
Lockwood, Joseph (b. 1904): English record executive, 185
Lomax, Alan (b. 1915): American musician, folklorist, ethnomusicologist, and song collector, 121, 172, 309, 310
Lomax, John (b. 1867): American folklorist, 121
London Blues and Barrelhouse Club, 83 Wardour, Soho, London, 123
London College of Music, 47-48 Great Marlborough Street, London, 314
London Records, 539 West 25th Street, New York, New York, 286, 287, 292–93, 304
London School of Economics, Houghton Saint Holborn, London, 131
London Skiffle Club (a.k.a., London Skiffle Centre), Roundhouse Pub, Soho, 123
Look at Life, 55, 416
Lord Rockingham's XI (London): Harry Robinson, Benny Green, Cherry Wainer, Don Storer, Reg Weller, Red Price, Rex Morris, Cyril Reubens, Ronnie Black, Bernie Taylor, and Eric Ford, 48–49, 65–66, 376
Lordan, Jerry (b. 1934), English songwriter, 67, 394, 395, 404
Loudermilk, John D, (b. 1943): American musician (voice and guitarist) and songwriter, 190, 191, 236, 358, 376, 381
Love, Geoff (b. 1917): English music director, conductor, and arranger, 175–76, 335, 382
Lowman, Robbie (b. Robina): British journalist, 84

Lulu (b. Marie Lawrie, 1948; aka Lulu Kennedy-Cairns): Scottish musician (singer), 227–29, 231–32, 377
  Lulu and the Luvvers (a.k.a. Gleneagles, Glasgow): Lulu, Alex Bell, Ross Neilson, James Dewar, Tommy Tierney, and David Mullin, 228, 376–77
Lycée Français de Londres, Queensberry Mews, South Kensington, London,
Lynn, Vera (b. 1917): English musician (singer), 203–4, 206, 207, 209, 212, 216f, 377
  Sincerely Yours–Vera Lynn, 209, 419
  Vera Lynn Sings, 209, 422
Lyttelton, Humphrey (b. 1921): English musician (trumpet), 53, 377

MacColl, Ewan (b. James Miller, 1915): English musician, collector, and songwriter, 310–11
MacDonald, Ian "Mac" (b. Ian MacCormick, 1948): English journalist and author, 143
MacLeod, Keith "Mac" (b. 1941): English musician (guitar), 318–19
Macmillan, Harold (b. 1894): English Conservative politician; UK PM 1957-1963, 3–4, 97, 98
The Madhouse on Castle Street, 317, 416
Maguire, Les (b. 1941): English musician (piano: Gerry and the Pacemakers), 104–5, 209, 349, 362
Makem, Tommy (b. 1932): Irish musician (singer, banjo, and harmonica: the Clancy Brothers and Tommy Makem), 311, 346–47
Malo, Ron (b. 1935): American recording engineer, 286–87, 389, 390
Mann, Barry (b. Barry Imberman, 1939): American songwriter, 211, 251, 332, 343, 350, 357, 387, 403
Mann, Manfred (b. Manfred Lubowitz, 1940): South African musician (keyboards: Manfred Mann), 177, 180
  Manfred Mann (London, aka the Mann-Hugg Blues Brothers): Mike Hugg, Mike Vickers, Dave Richmond, Paul Jones, Tom McGuinness, and Manfred Mann, 178, 182, 266, 306, 377–78
Mann, William (b. 1924): English music critic, xii, 101
Manne, Shelly (b. 1920): American musician (drums), 177
Manny's Music, 156 West 48th Street, New York City, New York, 164

The Maritime Blues Club Maritime Hotel, College Square North, Belfast, Northern Ireland, 255–56
Marty, 46, 416
The Marquee Club (1) [1958] 165 Oxford Street, Soho, London; (2) [1964] 90 Wardour, Soho, London, 134, 123, 124, 125, 127, 133, 178, 197, 235, 249, 266, 267, 303, 343, 380
Marquis Enterprises, 37 Soho Square, London, 180
Marsden, Freddie (b. 1940): English musician (drummer: Gerry and the Pacemakers), 104–5, 349
Marsden, Gerry (b. 1942): English musician (singer and guitar: Gerry and the Pacemakers) and songwriter, 104–6, 111, 113f, 157–58, 349, 362–63, 413
  Gerry and the Pacemakers (Liverpool): Gerry Marsden, Freddie Marsden, Les Chadwick, and Les Maguire, 104–6, 362–63, 413
Marsden, Beryl (b. Beryl Hogg, 1947), English musician (singer), 224–25, 226, 378
Martha and the Vandellas (Detroit): Martha Reeves, Lois Reeves, and Delphine Reeves, 211, 213, 291–92, 297, 362, 378–79
Martin, Dean (b. Dino Crocetti, 1917): American actor and musician (singer), 286
Martin, George (b. 1926): English record producer, 6, 13, 80–81, 82–83, 91, 93, 95, 96, 100, 101, 104, 105, 106, 107, 110, 145, 147–48, 150–51, 152, 158, 159, 174–75, 225, 226, 318, 335–40, 342–43, 362–63, 369, 373–74, 413
Martin, John: British editor and manager, 125
The Marvelettes (Detroit): Katherine Anderson, Gladys Horton, Georgeanna Tillman, and Wanda Young, 99
Marvin, Hank (b. Brian Rankin, 1941): English musician (guitar: Shadows), 39–40, 43f, 66–67, 115, 254, 354, 386–87, 394–95
Marwick, Arthur (b. 1936): Scottish historian, 2
Mason, Barry (b. 1935): English musician (singer) and songwriter, 271, 360
Massey, Marion (b. Marion Gordon, ca, 1933): English manager, 228–29
Maurice and the Zodiacs (Nashville, Tennessee): Maurice Williams, Henry Gaston, Wiley Bennett, Charles Thomas, Willie Morrow, and Albert Hill, 112, 379
Mayall, John (b. 1933): English musician (keyboards and harmonica), 314
McAuley, Jackie (b. John McAuley, 1946): Irish musician (keyboards: Them), 256, 402

McAuley, Pat (b. 1944): Northern Irish musician (keyboard and drums: Them), 256, 401–2
McCartney, James (b. 1902), father of Paul and Mike McCartney, 74
McCartney, Mary (b. Mary Mohin, 1909): mother of Paul and Mike McCartney, 74
McCartney, Paul (b. 1942): English musician (bass, Beatles) and songwriter, 13, 73, 74–76, 77–78, 79–80, 81, 82, 83, 91, 92–93, 94, 95, 96, 98, 99–101, 102*f*, 111, 138, 147–48, 151, 152–53, 154, 158, 159, 167, 175, 176, 226, 227, 267–68, 283, 317–18, 332, 335–40, 342, 343, 358, 373, 374, 382–83, 388, 397, 398, 414
McCarty, Jim (b. 1943): English musician (drums, Yardbirds), 257, 406
McDevitt, Chas (b. 1934), British musician (guitar and vocals, Chas McDevitt Skiffle Group)
Chas McDevitt Skiffle Group (London): Chas McDevitt, John Paul, Dennis Carter, Marc Sharratt, and Jimmie MacGregor, 28, 379
McFarland, John (b. 1926): American songwriter, 159, 374
McGhee, Brownie (b. Walter McGhee, 1915): American musician (guitar and singer) and songwriter, 25, 249, 380, 410–11
McGowan, Cathy (b. 1943): British television presenter, 226, 228–29, 231–32, 297, 418
McGriff, Jimmy (b. 1936): American musician (organ), 249
McGuinn, Roger (b. James Roger McGuinn, 1942): American musician (guitar and singer) and songwriter, 320, 345
McKay, Ron (b. 1929): English musician (drums and vocal: Acker Bilk), 23
McLaughlin, John (b. 1942): English musician (guitar: Graham Bond Organisation), 127, 249
McLuhan, Marshall (b. 1911): Canadian philosopher, 203
McNally, John (b. 1941): English musician (guitar and singer: Searchers), 107–8, 109, 392–93
McPhatter Clyde (b. 1932), American musician (singer: Drifters), 40
McShann, Jay (b. 1916): American musician (piano), 133, 379
Meaden, Pete (b. 1941): English publicist and manager, 135, 300–1, 302, 365–66
Mecca Dance Ltd, (Mecca Agency Limited), Dean Street, London, 116, 120, 252

Medal for the General, 210, 416
Medley, Bill (b. 1940): American musician (vocals: Righteous Brothers), 275, 387
Meehan, Tony (b. 1943): English musician (drummer: Shadows) and record producer, 39–40, 43*f*, 66, 67, 92, 115, 158, 349, 354, 386–87, 394–95
Meek, Joe (b. Robert Meek, 1929): English songwriter, record producer, and label manager, 26–27, 53–54, 64, 68, 119–20, 136, 188–89, 208, 276, 352, 367, 375–76, 377, 397, 401, 402, 403
Melody Maker, 19 Denmark Street, London, ix, 32, 33–34, 35–36, 85, 90, 100, 103, 105, 107, 118–19, 131, 160, 163, 197, 206–7, 250, 284, 286, 300–1, 306, 309, 311–12, 313
Mendelsohn, John (b. 1947): American music critic, 181
Mendl, Hugh (b. 1919): English record producer, 25, 35–36, 48–49, 314, 333, 334–35, 352, 399, 401
Menuhin, Yehudi (b. 1916): American-British musician (violin), 313
Mercury Theatre, 2 Ladbroke Road, Notting Hill Gate, London, 314
Mersey Beat, 81a Renshaw Street, Liverpool, 79, 90, 104, 106–7
Metzger, Gustav (b. 1926): German-British artist, 299
MGM, 274
Mildmay Tavern, 130 Balls Pond Road, Islington, London, 188
Miles, Barry (b. 1943): English author, xii, 306
Miller, Rice (see Sonny Boy Williamson)
Millie (see Millie Small)
Milligan, Spike (b. Terence Milligan, 1918): English actor and writer, 150, 418–19
Milling, Ronnie (b. 1937): Northern Irish musician (drummer: Them), 256, 255, 401–2
Mills, Gordon (b. 1935): English manager and songwriter, 115, 276, 370, 371
The Miracles (Detroit, Michigan): Smokey Robinson, Bobby Rogers, Claudette Robinson, Ronald White, Peter Moore, and Marv Tarplin, 99
Mitchell, Adrian (b. 1932): English journalist and poet, 92–93
Mitchell, Guy (b. Albert Cernik, 1927): American musician (singer), 4, 36, 379–80
Mitham, Norman (b. 1941), English musician (guitar: Drifters), 37, 39

Mods, 246–47, 251, 256, 283, 296–97, 300–1, 304, 305
The Moka Bar, 29 Frith Street, Soho, London, 31
Monk, Thelonious (b. 1917): American musician (piano) and composer, 314
Monroe, Marilyn (b. Norma Mortenson, 1926): American actress, 201, 207, 208, 413–14
Montez, Chris (b Ezekiel Christopher Montanez, 1943): American musician (singer and guitarist), 95
The Moody Blues (Birmingham): Graeme Edge, Denny Laine, Mike Pinder, Ray Thomas, and Clint Warwick, 266–67, 278f, 306, 380
Moon, Keith (b. 1947): English musician (drummer: Who), 300, 365–66, 404–5
Moorehouse, Geoffrey (b. Geoffrey Heald,1931): English journalist, 263–64
Monty Python (London): Graham Chapman, John Cleese, Terry Gilliam, Eric Idle, Terry Jones, and Michael Palin, 34
Moretti, Joe (b. 1938): English musician (guitar: Vince Taylor and sessions), xi–xii, 62, 127, 370, 371, 401
Morrison, Van (b. George Ivan Morrison, 1945): Northern Irish musician (singer: Them) and songwriter, 255–56, 261f, 290, 401–2
Morton, Charles (b. 1819): English concert promoter, 18
Mosley, Oswald (b. 1929): English fascist politician, 3–4
Most, Mickie (b. Michael Peter Hayes, 1938): English record producer, 139, 167, 190–191, 251, 266, 269, 273–74, 303, 331–32, 365, 381, 417
  The Most Brothers (London): Michael Hayes and Alex Wharton, 167
  Mickie Most and the Gear (London): Mickie Most, Micky Dallon, and Alan Cartwright, 167
Motown, 2648 West Grand Boulevard, Detroit, Michigan, 80, 99, 127, 214, 285, 291
The Mound City Blue Blowers (Saint Louis, Mo,): Red McKenzie, Dick Slevin, Jack Bland, and Frank Billings, 24
The Mouse on the Moon, 150, 417
Mrs. Brown, You've Got a Lovely Daughter, 274, 417
Muddy Waters (b. McKinley Morganfield, 1913): American musician (guitar and singer) and songwriter, 28, 46, 64, 121, 122, 123, 124, 131, 132, 133, 136, 249, 255, 256, 286–87, 289, 380–81, 410

Munden, Dave (b. 1943): English musician (drums and singer: Tremeloes), 117, 383
Murray, Alex (b. Alex Wharton, 1939): English manager and record producer, 266–67, 380
Murray, Martin (b. 1941): English musician (guitar, Honeycombs), 188, 367
Murray, Mitch (b. Lionel Stitcher, 1940): English songwriter, xi–xii, 83, 91, 105, 110, 111, 119, 157–58, 189, 342, 345, 347, 360–61, 362
Murray the K (b. Murray Kaufman, 1922): American disc jockey and concert promoter, 287
Murray the K's Christmas Show, Fox Theatre, 20 Flatbush Avenue, Brooklyn, 181, 191, 417
Musicians' Union, 20, 21, 25, 32, 35, 181
My Fair Lady, 204, 381, 417

Nash, Graham (b. 1942): English musician (guitar and singer: Hollies) and songwriter, 111, 162–63, 195, 285, 366, 389
The Nashville Teens (Webridge, London): Arthur Sharp, Ray Phillips, John Hawken, John Allen, Barry Jenkins, and Pete Shannon, 189–91, 198f, 236, 381
National Jazz and Blues Festival, 327
  Richmond Athletic Association Grounds, Kew Foot Road, Richmond, Surrey, (26-27 August 1961; 28-29 July 1962; 10-11 August 1963; 7-9 August 1964; 6-8 August 1965), 266, 306
Nelhams, Terry (see Adam Faith)
NEMS Enterprises Ltd, Sutherland House, 5/6 Argyll Street, London, 93, 135, 410
Nero and the Gladiators (London): Mike O'Neill, Rod Slade, Joe Moretti, and Laurie Jay, 61
New Musical Express, 5 Denmark Street, London, ix, 22, 36, 40, 74, 84, 90, 92, 94–95, 105, 107, 162–63, 195, 204, 205, 208, 210, 211, 261f, 271, 279f, 309, 311–13, 319, 331
New Theatre Oxford, 24-26 George Street, Oxford, 28, 353
News of the World, 188 Strand, London, 110
Newell, Norman (b. 1919): English record producer and songwriter, 175–76, 335, 382–83, 397
Newport Jazz Festival, 252
Nicholls, Nick: English musician (drums, Lonnie Donegan), 26–27, 352–53
Nicholson, Virginia (b. 1955): English historian, 2, 202

Nicol, Jimmy (b. 1939): English musician (drums: Beatles), 152

Nitzsche, Jack (b. 1937): American songwriter, arranger, session musician, and record producer, 160, 161, 350, 351, 390, 392, 403, 420–21

No Trams to Lime Street, 150, 417

Noone, Peter (b. 1947): English musician (singer: Herman's Hermits), 273–74, 365, 415, 417, 423

Norden, Denis (b. 1922): English comedy writer, 209, 420

North End Music Stores [NEMS], (1) 50/52 Great Charlotte Street, Liverpool; (2) 12/14 Whitechapel, Liverpool, 79

Northern Songs, 132 Charing Cross Road, Saint Giles, London, 93

O'Brien, Dion (see Tom Springfield)

O'Rahilly, Ronan (b. 1940): Irish entrepreneur, manager (Blues Incorporated), club owner (Scene), and broadcaster (Radio Caroline), 166, 246–47, 248, 251, 257

Oakman, Peter (b. 1943): English musician (bass: Joe Brown and His Bruvvers), 50, 117, 344–45, 383

The Oasis Club.45-47 Lloyd Street, Manchester, 103, 272

Odeon Cinema, Oxford Street, Manchester, 111

Official Monster Raving Loony Party, 63

Oh Boy!, 39, 40, 41, 45–46, 47, 48–49, 51–52, 65, 78, 135, 175–76, 417

Oldfield Hotel, 1089 Greenford Road, Greenford, Ealing, London, 300

Oldham, Andrew Loog (b. 1944): English manager (Rolling Stones), record producer (Rolling Stones), and entrepreneur (Immediate Records), 135–36, 137–38, 139, 140, 143, 152, 235–37, 245–46, 257, 283–84, 285, 286–87, 288, 290, 292, 291, 293, 300, 357–58, 388–90

Oliver!, 152, 417

Oliver, Paul (b. 1927): English historian, 121

Olympia Stadium, 5920 Grand River Avenue, Detroit, 286

The Olympia Theatre, 28 Boulevard des Capucines, Paris, 146

Olympic Studios (1958), Carton Street, Marylebone, London, 10, 12–13, 136, 137, 236, 266–67, 357, 379, 380, 388, 406

Orbison, Roy (b. 1936): American musician (singer and guitar) and songwriter, 91, 118, 153, 381–82

The Orlons (Philadelphia): Rosetta Hightower, Shirley Brickley, Marlena Davis, Stephen Caldwell, 160, 382

Ornstein, George "Bud" (b. 1918): American film executive, 149–50, 152–53

Osborne, John (b. 1929), English playwright, 20, 421

The Entertainer (1957), 20

Owen and Millie (Kingston, Jamaica): Owen Gray and Millie Small, 229

Owen, Alun (b. 1925): Welsh screenwriter, 92–93, 150, 151, 414, 417

The Oxford, Oxford Street and Tottenham Court Road, London, 18

The Pacemakers (see Gerry and the Pacemakers)

Page, Jimmy (b. 1944): English musician (guitar: Carter-Lewis and the Southerners), songwriter, and record producer, 256, 268, 271, 341, 345–46, 348, 360, 372, 401–2

Page, Larry (b. Leonard Davies, 1938): British singer, manager, record producer, and entrepreneur, 194, 196, 197

Page, Patti (b. Clara Fowler, 1927): American singer and actor, 206, 382

The Palladium, 8 Argyll Street, Soho, Westminster, London, W1, 27, 36, 98–99, 206–7, 312, 326–27, 352–53, 420, 422

Palmer, Tony (b. 1941): American record producer, 252, 358

Panton, Roy (b. 1941): Jamaican musician (singer), 229, 391

Paolozzi, Eduardo (, 1924): Scottish artist, 77–78

Paramor, Norrie (b. 1914): English record producer, arranger, and songwriter, 33, 38, 39, 40, 41, 54–56, 59f, 67, 203, 354, 368, 386–87, 394–96, 413, 421

Parker, Bobby (b. 1937): American musician (voice and guitar) and songwriter, 153, 266–67, 382

Parker, Charlie (b. 1920), American musician (saxophone), 20, 305, 380

Parlophone (see EMI)

Parnell, Val (b. 1892): English television presenter,

Val Parnell's Sunday Night at the London Palladium, 36, 98–99, 206–7, 312, 420

Parnes, Larry (b. 1929): English manager, 35, 37, 45–46, 48–50, 54, 55, 69, 75, 76, 106–7, 126, 133–34, 228, 298

Pathé Marconi Studios (see EMI Pathé Marconi Studios)

The Patty Duke Show, 174, 417
Pavey, Ken (b. 1932): English musician (guitar: Drifters), 39
Payne, Jack (b. 1899): English musician (piano) and critic, 28, 422
Peacock, Trevor (b. 1931): English television presenter, writer, and songwriter, 274, 345, 365, 411, 412, 416, 417, 419–20
Pearson, John (b. 1925): English musician (piano), arranger, and band leader, 227, 342–43, 418, 421–22
Pender, Mike (b. Michael Prendergast, 1941): English musician (guitar and singer: Searchers), 107–8, 160–61, 392, 393
Pendleton, Harold (b. 1924): English promoter, publisher, and manager, 125, 133
People and Places, 85, 417
Performing Right Society (PRS), 93, 268
Perkins, Carl (b. 1932): American musician (guitar and singer) and songwriter, 120, 156, 168, 186, 190, 382
Peter, Paul, and Mary (New York, 1961): Peter Yarrow, Paul Stookey, and Mary Travers, 167, 312, 383
Peter and Gordon (London): Peter Asher and Gordon Waller, 174, 176, 182, 183*f*, 382–83
Philby, Kim (b. Harold Philby, 1912): British intelligence officer, 97
Philharmonic Hall, Hope Street, Liverpool, 107–8, 137
Philips Records and Philips Studios, 2-4 Stanhope Place, Saint George's Fields, London, 46–47, 53, 214, 247, 275, 333, 398
Phillips, Percy (b. 1896), English recordist, 75
Phil Phillips and the Twilights (Lake Charles, Louisiana), 47, 383
Phillips, Ray (b. 1939): English musician (singer: Nashville Teens), 183*f*, 190, 381
Phillips, Sam (b. 1923): American record producer, 186, 382
Phonographic Performance Ltd, 93
Piccadilly Records (see Pye Records)
The Piccadilly Jazz Club, Ham Yard, Great Windmill Street, Soho, London, 246
Picker, Mike: Irish brother-in-law to Ray Davies, 192
Picker, Peg: sister of Ray and Dave Davies, 192
Pickwick Club, 15-16 Great Newport Street, Covent Garden, London, 175
Pidgeon, John (b. 1947): English music journalist, 129, 139
Pinder, Mike (b. 1941): English musician (keyboard: Moody Blues), 266–67, 380

Pirate radio, 247–48, 312–13
Piron, Armand (b. 1888): American musician (violin) and bandleader, 23, 342, 370, 374
Pitney, Gene (b. 1940): American musician (singer), 285, 389
Pitt, Kenneth (b. 1922): English manager (Manfred Mann), 178
The Platters (Los Angeles): Tony Williams, Paul Robi, Zola Taylor, David Lynch, and Herb Reed, 4, 36, 418
Pleasant, Cousin Joe (b. Pleasant Joseph, 1907): American musician (singer), 249, 410–11
Please, 91
Pollini, Leo, British musician (drums), 36, 400
Pomus, Doc (b. Jerome Felder, 1925): American songwriter, 47, 351, 354, 392, 405
Pond, Paul (see Jones, Paul)
Poole, Brian (b. 1941): English musician (singer: Brian Pool and the Tremeloes), 117
Brian Poole and the Tremeloes (Barking, England): Brain Poole, Rick Westwood, Dave Munden, Alan Howard, and Alan Blakley, 80, 117
Pops and Lenny, 58*f*, 95, 418
Potger, Keith (b. 1941): Australian musician (guitar: Seekers), 312, 393–94
Polydor Records, 78
Powell, Enoch (b. 1912): English politician, 223
Power, Duffy (b. Raymond Howard, 1941): English musician (singer), 45
Pratt, Mike (b. 1931): English songwriter, 34, 399–400
Presley, Elvis (b. 1935): American musician (singer), 4, 27, 33, 47–48, 49, 64, 84, 92, 96, 106, 115, 119, 130, 149, 186, 211, 272, 275–76, 384–85
Preston, Denis (b. Sydney Denis Preston, 1916): English entrepreneur and record producer, 26–27, 53, 342, 352, 377
Price, Alan (b. 1942): English musician (keyboards: Animals) and songwriter, 165, 166, 168, 250, 331–32, 399
The Alan Price Trio and the Alan Price Rhythm and Blues Combo (see also the Animals), 165, 166
Prince of Wales Theatre, 1 Oxendon Street, Westminster, London, 99
Princess Louise, 208 High Holborn, Holborn, London, 310
Pride, Dickie (b. Richard Kneller, 1941), English musician (singer), 45, 133–34

Prieto, Antonio (b. 1926), Chilean singer and actor, 232, 385, 388
Prima, Louis (b. 1910): American musician (singer and trumpet) and bandleader, 126–27
Prince, Viv (b. 1941): English musician (drums: Pretty Things), 268, 345–46
Pritchard, Barry (b. 1944): English musician (singer and guitar: Fortunes), 270, 271, 359–60
Proby, P. J. (b. James Smith, 1938): American musician (singer), 275, 277, 409
Profumo, John (b. 1915): English politician, 97, 110
Pye Records and PYE Studios (aka Pye Studios Marble Arch), ATV House, Great Cumberland Place (40 Bryanston Street), Marylebone, London, 26–27, 53, 56, 108, 125, 160, 189, 194, 195, 196, 197, 204–5, 208, 233–34, 247, 253, 269–70, 303, 304, 305, 319

Quaife, Peter (b. 1943): English musician (bass: Kinks), 192, 193, 194 , –95, 198*f*, 371–73
Quant, Mary (b. 1934): English fashion designer, 135, 223–24, 234, 245–46
Quantrell, Margo (b. 1942): English musician (singer), xi–xii, 108, 342–43, 344–45, 348, 376–77
The Quarry Men (Liverpool): (a) John Lennon, Eric Griffiths, Pete Shotton, Bill Smith/Nigel Walley/Ivan Vaughan/Len Garry, Colin Hanton, and Rod Davis; (b) John Lennon, Paul McCartney, George Harrison, and Colin Hanton, 74, 75
Queen (London): Freddie Mercury, Brian May, Roger Taylor, John Deacon, 267
Queen Mother (Elizabeth, Queen), 99
Quickly, Tommy (b. Thomas Quigley, 1945): English musician (singer), 152
Quinn, Derek (b. 1942): English musician (guitar: Freddie and the Dreamers), 114*f*

Rachman, Peter (b. Perec Rachman, 1962): Ukrainian-British landlord, 3
Radcliffe, Jimmy (b. 1936): American musician, songwriter, and producer, 275–76, 354, 385
Radio Atlanta, 248
Radio Caroline, 248
Radio London, 248
Radio Luxembourg (studios), 38 Hertfort Street, Mayfair, London,

Radio Nord, 247, 248
Radio Times, 175
Railway Tavern, High Street, Wealdstone, Harrow, London, 301, 302
Ranglin, Ernest (b 1932): Anglo-Jamaican musician (guitar), record producer, and songwriter, 231, 379
Rank Organisation, 55, 419, 421
Rankin, Brian (see Marvin, Hank)
Rashōmon, x, 418
Rathbone, Don: English musician (drums: Hollies), 112, 366
The Ravens (see the Kinks)
Ray, James (b. James Jay Raymond, 1941): American musician (singer), 110, 385
Ray, Johnny (b. 1927), American musician (singer and piano) and songwriter, 4, 36
Raymonde, Ivor (b. Ivor Pomerance, 1926): English record producer, arranger, and songwriter, 213, 214, 225, 275–76, 311, 334, 360, 361, 398, 399
The Rays (New York): Harold Miller, Walter Ford, David Jones, and Harry James, 274, 385
RCA Studios, 6363 Sunset Boulevard, Hollywood, Los Angeles, California, 289, 291, 292, 390
RCA Studios, 30 Music Square, Nashville, Tennessee, 356, 384
RCA Studios, New York, 368, 404
Ready Steady Go! Associated Rediffusion/Rediffusion London, (1) Television House, Kingsway, London; (2) Wembley TV Studios, 128 Wembley Park Drive, Wembley, London, 39–40, 46, 98, 112, 113*f*, 118, 139, 157, 162, 178, 179, 188, 195, 197, 214, 222*f*, 226, 227, 228–29, 231–32, 234, 237*f*, 238*f*, 251, 256–57, 260*f*, 267, 297, 304, 305, 308*f*, 418
Record Mirror (aka *New Record Mirror*): 116 Shaftesbury Ave, London, 120, 135, 231
Record Retailer and Music Industry News [aka, *Record Retailer*], 29 Villiers Street, London, ix, 84, 92, 100, 105, 112, 115, 120, 138, 251, 153, 157, 159, 163, 164, 168, 178, 180–81, 187, 197, 202, 211, 212, 226, 236, 256–57, 258, 270, 272, 277, 285, 304, 305, 307, 312–13, 318, 320, 323, 324–25, 331
Reed, Jimmy (b. Mathis James Reed, 1925): American musician (guitar and singer) and songwriter, 131, 306, 385

SUBJECT INDEX

Reed, Les (b. 1935): English songwriter, music director, arranger, and musician (piano), xi–xii, 52, 187, 267–68, 271, 276–77, 332, 342, 344–45, 347, 357, 360, 370, 377, 418

Reeves, Martha (b. 1941): American musician (singer), 291, 378–79

Martha and the Vandellas (Detroit): Martha Reeves, Rosaland Ashford, and Betty Kelley, 291, 378–79

The Reflections (Detroit): Tony Micale, Phil Castrodale, Dan Bennie, Ray Steinberg, John Dean, and Frank Amodeo, 270, 385

Regent Sound Studios, (1) 4 Denmark Street, Saint Giles, London (1962); (2) 164-66 Tottenham Court Road, Camden, London (1966), 119, 193, 195, 269, 284, 287, 369, 389

Reith, Sir John (b. 1889): Scottish broadcasting executive, 21–22

Relf, Keith (b. 1943): Musician (singer and harmonica: Yardbirds) and songwriter, 257, 406

Renbourn, John (b. 1944): English musician (guitar) and songwriter, xi–xii, 316, 369–70

Reprise Records, 253

Reynolds, Jody (b. Ralph Reynolds, 1932), American musician (singers and guitar), 46–47, 385, 405

Reynolds, Malvina (b. 1900): American musician and songwriter, 161, 393

RGM Sound Ltd, 304 Holloway Road, Islington, London, 53, 68, 188–89, 364, 367, 375–76, 402

Rhythm and Blues Festival, Birmingham Town Hall, Birmingham (28 February 1964), 265

Rickenbacker Guitars, 115, 148, 303

Richard, Cliff (b. Harry Webb.1940): Indo-English musician (singer), 31, 37–41, 43*f*, 47–48, 60, 61, 66–67, 89, 90, 92 , –110, 115, 148, 152, 162–63, 175–76, 181, 193, 213, 254, 288, 299, 323–24, 386–87, 394, 412, 413, 417, 421–22, 423

The Cliff Richard Show, 412

Cliff Richard and the Drifters (London): Cliff Richard, Ian Samwell, Jet Harris, Hank Marvin, and Bruce Welch, 37–40, 60, 67, 299, 386

Cliff Richard and the Shadows (London): Cliff Richard, Jet Harris, Hank Marvin, and Bruce Welch, Richards, Keith (b. 1943): English musician (guitar, Rolling Stones) and songwriter, 130–34, 136, 139, 140, 236, 237, 286, 287, 289, 290, 291, 292–93, 299, 317, 357, 388–91

Richards, Ron (b. 1929): English record producer, 82, 83, 105, 110, 112, 228, 272, 336, 362–63, 366

Richard, Wendy (b. 1943): English actress, 202, 232-33, 392

The Ricky-Tick Club, Peascod Street, Windsor, Berkshire, 129, 139

Ridgepride, 79A Warwick Square, Pimlico, London, 266

Ridley, Wally (b. 1913): English record producer and songwriter, 209, 349, 401

The Righteous Brothers (Los Angeles): Bobby Hatfield and Bill Medley, 227, 275, 387

Robinson, Guy (b. Guy Tynegate-Smith): English artist manager, 61, 62

Robinson, Harry (b. Henry Robertson, 1932): Scottish arranger and musician (piano), 48–49, 65–66, 230, 351, 361, 376, 377, 379, 409, 417, 419–20

Rock around the Clock, 4, 26–27, 33, 66–67, 74, 298–99, 418

Rock You Sinners, 33, 418

Rockers, 246

The Rockin' Berries (Birmingham): Roy Austin, and Terry Bond, Chuck Botfield, Clive Lea, and Geoff Turton, 269–70, 271, 280*f*, 387–88

The Rockin' Horses (London): 33–34

Rodgers, Jimmie (b. 1897): American musician (guitar and singer) and songwriter, 189, 388

Rodgers, Richard (b. 1902) and Oscar Hammerstein (b. 1895): American composers, 106, 157–58, 362, 398, 411, 420

Roe, Tommy (b. 1942): American musician (singer), 95, 109, 388

Rogan, Johnny (b. 1953): British journalist and author, xii

Rogers, Julie (b. Julie Rolls, 1943): English musician (singer), 232, 388

Rolling Stone, 72, 181

The Rolling Stones/Rollin' Stones (London): Mick Jagger, Brian Jones, Keith Richards, Charlie Watts, and Bill Wyman, 98, 99–100, 129–40, 152, 160, 167, 194–95, 235, 236, 246–47, 255–56, 257, 283–93, 294*f*–95*f*, 299, 300, 388–91, 412, 420–21

The Ronettes (New York City): Veronica Bennett, Estelle Bennett, and Nedra Talley, 213, 283

The Rooftop Singers (New York): Erik Darling, Bill Svanoe, and Lynne Taylor, 312, 391

Rothwell, Ric (b. Eric Rothwell, 1944): English musician (drummer, Wayne Fontana and the Mindbenders), 272, 359

The Roundhouse (pub), 83 Wardour Street, Soho, London, 123, 317

Rowberry, Dave (b. 1940): English musician (keyboards: Animals; sessions), 251, 332

Rowe, Dick (b. 1921): English record producer, 48–49, 80, 117, 137, 180, 185, 255–56, 361, 401–2

Roy and Millie and the City Slickers: Roy Panton, Millie Small, Herman Sang, and others, 229, 391

Royal Albert Hall, Kensington Gore, Kensington, London, 134, 175

Royal Academy of Dramatic Arts, 62-64 Gower Street, London, 79

The Royal Academy of Music, Marylebone Road, London, 205

Royds Hall Grammar School, Huddersfield, West Yorkshire, 298

Russell, Henry (b. 1812): English songwriter and musician, 17, 18

Russell, Ken (b. Henry Kenneth Russell, 1927): English film director, 314

Rydell, Bobby (b. Robert Ridarelli, 1942): American musician (singer), 52, 96, 391

Saint Albans School, Abbey Mill Ln, Saint Albans, Hertfordshire, 179–80

Saint Albans Grammar School for Boys, Brampton Road, Saint Albans, Hertfordshire, 179, 180

Saint Pancras Town Hall, Lancing Street, Camden, London, 122

Sainte-Marie, Buffy (b. Beverly Sainte-Marie, 1941): Canadian musician (singer) and songwriter, 320, 391

Sakamoto, Kyu (b. Sakamoto Hisashi, aka Hisashi Ōshima, 1941): Japanese musician (singer), 5, 391

Salford Lads Club, Coronation Street, Ordsall, Manchester, 111

Samwell, Ian (b. 1937): English musician (guitar: Cliff Richard and the Drifters), songwriter, and record producer, 37–40, 47, 67, 127, 251, 354, 358, 386, 394

Samwell-Smith, Paul (b. 1943): English musician (bass: Yardbirds), songwriter, and record producer (Yardbirds), 257, 258, 406

Sandbrook, Dominic (b. 1974): English historian, 2, 297–98

Santamaría, Mongo (b. Ramón Santamaría Rodríguez): Cuban musician (percussion) and bandleader, 252, 391

Sargent, Sir Malcolm (b. 1895): English conductor, 11–12

Sarne, Mike (b. Michael Scheuer, 1940): English singer and actor, 202, 232–33, 392

Sassoon, Vidal (b. 1928): English hair designer, 223–24, 228–29, 234

Saturday Club, 90, 95–96, 117, 268, 419

Saturday Evening Post, 156

Saunders, Mike (b. 1952): American music critic, 182

Savage, Roger: English engineer, 137, 357, 388

The Savages (see Screaming Lord Sutch and the Savages)

Saville, Philip (b. Philip Savile, 1930): English director, 317, 416

Savoy Hotel, Strand, London, 319

Savoy-Plaza Hotel, 767 Fifth Avenue, New York, 148

Saxon, Al (b. Allen Fowler, 1932): English singer, actor, and songwriter, 213, 375

The Scene, Ham Yard, 41 Great Windmill Street, Soho, London, 166, 246–47, 250, 251, 254, 296, 326–27

Schroeder, John (b. 1935): English songwriter, record producer, and label manager, xi–xii, 45, 54–56, 203, 204–5, 214, 270, 387–88, 395–96, 421

The Scots Hoose, Cambridge Circus, 6 Moor Street, Soho, London, 310

Scott, Keith: British musician (piano: Blues Incorporated), 124

Scott, Ken (b. 1947): English recording engineer, xi–xii

Scott, Ronnie [1] (b. Ronald Schatt, 1927): English musician (saxophone) and club owner, 20, 35–36, 55, 399–400

Sea Fury, 48, 419

The Searchers, 107–8, 419

The Searchers (Liverpool): (1) John McNally, Tony Jackson, Mike Pender, Chris Curtis; (2) John McNally, Frank Allen, Mike Pender, Chris Curtis, 104, 107–9, 157, 160–61, 169f, 176, 211, 290, 320, 323–24, 392–93

The Second Sex, 235

Secombe, Harry (b. 1921): Welsh comedian and writer, 175

Secunda, Tony (b. 1940): English artist manager (Moody Blues), 266

Seeger, Peggy (b. Margaret Seeger, 1935): American musician (voice, guitar, banjo, and concertina), 310

Seeger, Pete (b. 1919): American musician (voice and banjo) and songwriter, 109, 393

The Seekers (Melbourne): Judy Durham, Athol Guy, Keith Potger, and Bruce Woodley, 312–13, 321f, 323, 393–94

Sellers, Peter (b. Richard Sellers, 1925): English actor, 150, 418–19, 423

Seltaeb, Fifth Avenue, New York, 149, 266

Serious Charge, 40–419

The Shadows (London): Ian Samwell, Hank Marvin, Bruch Welch, Jet Harris, Tony Meehan, Brian Locking, Brian Bennett, and others, 40, 41, 43f, 66–67, 68, 70f, 92, 115, 208, 233, 394–95

Shankar, Ravi (b. 1920): Indian musician (sitar), 313

Shannon, Del (b. Charles Westover, 1934), American musician (singer and guitar) and songwriter, 68, 395

Shapiro, Helen (b. 1946): English musician (singer), 54–56, 59f, 89, 92–93, 94, 135, 150, 203, 204–5, 209, 214, 227, 229, 324–25, 395–96, 415, 421

Sharp, Arthur (b. 1940): English musician (singer: Nashville Teens), xi–xii, 190, 198f, 381

Sharp, Cecil (b. 1859): English folksong collector, 309–10

Shaw, George Bernard (b. 1856): Irish playwright, 5, 10–11, 171, 417

Shaw, Sandie (b. Sandra Ann Goodrich, 1947): English musician (singer), 223–24, 231–32, 233–35, 241f, 276–77, 324–25, 396

Shear, Ernie: Scottish musician (guitar), 39, 386

The Sheik, 22, 419

Shelley, Percy Bysshe (b. 1972): English poet, 180

Shelton, Anne (b. Patricia Sibley, 1923): English musician (singer), 55, 204, 207, 209, 211, 213, 397

Anne to You, 209, 409

Shenson, Walter (b. 1919): American film producer, 149–50, 153, 414–15, 417

The Sheratons, the (aka Sheritons and Sherabons; see the Honeycombs)

Sheridan, Tony (b. Anthony McGinnity, 1940): English musician (guitar and singer), 39, 78, 106, 397

Shindig!, 156, 162, 184f, 261f, 262f, 275, 419

The Shirelles (Passaic, New Jersey, US): Addie Harris, Shirley Owens, Beverly Lee, and Doris Coley, 163, 179, 214, 224, 270, 397

Shirley and Lee (New Orleans): Shirley Goodman and Leonard Lee, 229

Shrimpton, Christine "Chrissie" (b. 1945): English model and actor, 288–89

Shrimpton, Jean (b. 1942): English model and actor, 288–89

Shuman, Mort (b. 1938): American songwriter, 47, 159, 162–63, 351, 354, 366, 374, 392, 405

Sidcup Art College, Grassington Road, Sidcup, Greater London, 131

Sigman, Carl, (b. 1909): American lyricist, 227, 343, 369, 387

The Silkie (Hull): Sylvia Tatler, Mike Ramsden, Ivor Aylesbury, and Kevin Cunningham, 317–18, 397, 398

Silver, Charles: English publisher, 93–94

Silverman, Charles: English artist manager (Herman's Hermits) and songwriter, 273–74

Simone, Nina (b. Eunice Waymon, 1933): American musician (singer and songwriter), 250

Sinatra, Frank (b. 1915): American musician (singer), 182, 185, 422

Sing Out!, 317

Six-Five Special, 36, 39, 45–46, 47, 49, 51, 65, 115, 206, 419–20

The Skatalites (Jamaica): Doreen Shaffer, Tommy McCook, Rolando Alphonso, Lester Sterling, Lloyd Brevett, etc., 297, 398

Skidmore Music Ltd, Warwick House, 38 Soho Square, London, 272

The Skiffle Cellar, 49 Greek Street, Soho, London, 25

The Skiffle Center (see the Roundhouse)

Small, Millie (b. 1946): Jamaican-British musician (singer), 229–31, 241f, 273, 379, 391, 409

Smart, Harold (b. 1921): British musician (organ), 175–76, 382–83

Smart, Terry (b. 1942), English musician (drummer: Drifters), 37–38, 39, 386

Smash Records, 230, 231

Smith, Alan: British music journalist, xii, 84, 205

Smith, Jimmy (b. 1925): American musician (organ)

Smith, Mike (b. 1943): English musician (singer and keyboards: Dave Clark Five) and songwriter, 119–20, 187, 188, 347

Smith, Mike (b. 1935): English record producer, 79, 117, 263–64, 267–68, 332, 341–42, 361, 383–84

Smith, Norman (b. 1923): English engineer, record producer, and songwriter, xi–xii, 81, 101, 335–40, 342–43
Smith, Reg (see Marty Wilde)
Snow, Hank (b. Clarence Snow, 1914): Canadian-American musician and songwriter, 211, 398
Snow White and the Seven Dwarfs, 107, 420
Solomon, Dorothy (b. ca, 1924): British music entrepreneur, 270
Solomon, Philip (b. 1924): British artist manager and entrepreneur, 256
Sommerville, Brian (b. 1932): English journalist and publicist, 146, 197
Sons of the Saddle (London): Tommy Hicks and Jack Fallon, 34
The Soul Sisters (Jamaica): Nora Dean, Cecile Campbell, and Rita Marley, 265–66, 398
The Sound of Music, 204, 320, 398, 420
Southern Music Publishing, 8 Denmark Street, Saint, Giles, London, 54, 247, 268, 319
Spand, Charlie (b. 1893): American musician (piano and singer), 24, 366
Spann, Otis (b. 1924): American musician, 122, 123, 249, 344, 368, 380–81, 411
Spector, Phil (b. 1939): American record producer and songwriter, 136, 185, 211, 275, 285, 290, 343, 350, 387, 389, 390
Springfield, Dusty (b. Mary Isobel Catherine Bernadette O'Brien, 1939): English musician (singer), 208, 212–15, 222*f*, 234, 275–76, 312, 398–99
Springfield, Tom (b. Dionysius O'Brien, 1934): English musician (guitarist and singer: Springfields), songwriter, and record producer, 311, 312, 313, 393–94, 399
The Springfields (London): Tom Springfield, Dusty Springfield, and Tim Field/Mike Hurst, 213, 311–12, 321*f*, 323
The Squadronaires [aka, The Royal Air Force Dance Orchestra] (London): Jimmy Miller, Tommy McQuater, Archie Craig, Clinton French, George Chisholm, Eric Breeze, Tommy Bradbury, Harry Lewist, Jimmy Durrant, Andy McDevitt, Cliff Townshend, Ronnie Aldrich, Sic Colin, Arthur Maden, and Jock Cummings with various singers, 203, 298–99
Stamp, Chris (b. 1942): English artist manager and entrepreneur, 302, 303, 304, 305
Stamp, Terence (b. 1938): English actor, 298, 302

Stanley, Mimi (aka Mimi Smith, b. Mary Stanley, 1906): English aunt of John Lennon, 73–74
The Staple Singers (Chicago): Roebuck "Pops" Staples (vocal and guitar), Cleotha Staples (vocal), Mavis Staples (vocal), and Pervis Staples (vocal), 290, 399
Staples, Pops (b. Roebuck Staples, 1914): American musician (guitar and singer) and songwriter, 290, 399
The Star-Club, 39 Große Freiheit, Saint Pauli, Hamburg, 107, 108
Starr, Ringo (b. Richard Starkey, 1940): English musician (drummer: Beatles), 81, 82, 83, 102*f*, 104–5, 138, 150, 151, 152, 154, 336–40, 414
The Steampacket (London): John Baldry, Julie Driscoll, Rod Stewart, Brian Auger, Vic Briggs, Rick Fenson/Brown, and Micky Waller, 266, 306
Steel, John (b. 1941): English musician (drums: Animals), 165, 166, 167, 250, 331–32
Steele, Tommy (b. Thomas Hicks, 1936), English musician (guitar and vocals), 34–37, 42*f*, 44, 45, 46–47, 50, 61, 105, 118, 213, 309, 399–400, 418
The Steelmen (London): Leo Pollini, Allan Weighell, Alan Stuart, and Dennis Price, 36
Stephen, John (b. 1934): Scottish clothier, 197
Stephen, Sylvia (n.a.): British music journalist, 231–32
Stephens, Geoff (b. 1934): English songwriter and manager, xi–xii, 52, 164, 231, 267–68, 319, 332, 342, 353–54
Stevens, Dave: British musician (piano), 124
Stewart, Eric (b. 1945): English musician (guitar: Wayne Fontana and the Mindbenders), 272, 359
Stewart, Ian (b. 1938): English musician (keyboards: Rolling Stones) and road manager, 132, 137, 292, 390
Stewart, Rod (b. 1945): English-Scottish musician (singer, Jeff Beck) and songwriter, 193, 266
Stigwood, Robert (b. 1934): Australian record producer and manager, 53, 54, 232, 350
Stoller, Mike (b. 1933): American songwriter and record producer, 138, 161, 331, 334, 335, 342, 348, 354, 357, 366, 388, 393, 397
Stokes, John (b. Sean Stokes, 1940): Irish musician (voice and bass: Bachelors), 311, 334

476 SUBJECT INDEX

The Stork Club, Swallow Street, Mayfair, London, 35
Stramsact Limited, 19a Warwick Square, London, 149
Strictly for the Sparrows, 49, 420
Strong, Barrett (b. 1941): American musician (vocal and piano) and songwriter, 99
Stuart, Chad (b. David Stuart Chadwick, 1941): English musician (singer and guitar: Chad and Jeremy) and songwriter, 173–74, 400–1, 417
The Studio Club, Station Road, Westcliff-on-Sea, Southend-on-Sea, 319
Sullivan, Sir Arthur (b. 1842): English composer, 18
Sullivan, Ed (b. 1901): American television impresario, 145, 147, 152, 157, 159, 187, 188, 226
  The Ed Sullivan Show, 28, 41, 89, 114f, 145, 156, 158, 159, 160, 162, 168, 169f, 170f, 214, 281f, 282f, 294f, 311, 368–69, 412
Sullivan, "Big Jim" (b. James Tomkins, 1941): English musician (guitar: Wildcats and sessions), xi–xii, 25, 46, 47, 50, 124, 127, 164, 341–42, 348, 357, 358, 376–77, 398, 403
Sullivan, Peter (b. 1933), British record producer, 61, 62, 115, 208, 225, 228, 229, 370–71, 373, 377, 378
Sumlin, Hubert (bl 1931): American musician (guitar), 249, 368
Sunday Night at the London Palladium (see Val Parnell)
Sunnyland Slim (b. Albert Luandrew, 1906): American musician (piano), 249
Sunshine, Monty (b. 1928): English musician (clarinet), 21, 334–35, 349, 415
The Surrey Music Hall, Westminster Bridge Road, London, 18
Sutch, David (b. 1940): English musician (singer), 63–64, 69f, 90, 289
  Screaming Lord Sutch and the Savages (aka, Raving Savages): David Sutch, Carlo Little, Andy Wren, Ken Payne, Roger Mingay (guitar), Pete Newman, Bernie Watson, Rickiy Fenson, Nicky Hopkins, and others, 63–64, 70f, 125, 133, 300, 326, 401
Sutcliffe, Stu (b. 1940): British artist and musician (bass: the Beatles), 76, 77–78, 81, 100
The Swinging Blue Jeans (Liverpool): Ray Ennis, Les Braid, Norman Kulke, and Terry Sylvester, 272, 401

The T.A.M.I. Show, 289, 420
Take It from Here, 209, 420
The Talent Spot, 90–91, 420

Tallis, Thomas (b. 1505): English composer, 172
Talmy, Shel (b. 1937): American record producer, xi–xii, 173–74, 194–95, 196, 253, 270, 271, 302–7, 311, 334, 359–60, 371–73, 400, 404–5
Tamla Records, 99
Taylor, Derek (b. 1932): English journalist and publicist, 320
Taylor, Dick (b. 1943): English musician (guitar), 131, 132, 133
Taylor, Eve (b. Evelyn Henshall, 1915): English artist manager (Sandie Shaw), 51–52, 202, 213, 233–34, 235
Taylor, Neville, and the Cutters (London): 65–66
Taylor, Vince (b. Brian Holden, 1939): Anglo-American musician (singer), 62, 401
Technology, xi, 1, 6–7, 10, 19–20, 60, 152–53, 212, 263, 309, 324, 327–29
The Temperance Seven (London): Clifford Bevan, Joe Clark, Colin Bowles, Alan Swainston Cooper, John Cavies, martin Fry, John Gieves-Watson, Philip Harrison, Cephas Howard, Brian Innes, and Paul McDowell, 22–23, 326
Terry, Sonny (b. Saunders Teddell/Terrell, 1911): American musician (harmonica and singer), 25, 249, 380
The Thamesiders (London): Martin Carthy, Marian Gray, and Peter Maynard, 314, 401
Thank Your Lucky Stars, 55, 92, 95–96, 104, 110, 112, 118, 135, 137, 139, 162, 164, 265, 168, 174, 176, 179, 189, 226, 227, 234, 272, 277, 300, 421
Tharpe, "Sister" Rosetta (b. Rosetta Nubin, 1915): American musician (guitar and singer) and songwriter, 122, 249, 259f, 410–11
Thatcher, Margaret (b. 1925): Conservative Member of Parliament, 224
Them, 255, 421
Them (Belfast, Northern Ireland): (1) Billy Harrison, Alan Henderson, Ronnie Milling, Van Morrison, and Eric Wrixon; (2) Van Morrison, Pat McAuley, Jackie McAuley, Peter Bardens, and others, 255–57, 261f, 290, 401–2
This Is Life: For the Record, 421
Thomas, Irma (b. Irma Lee, 1941): American musician (singer), 287, 402
Thomas, Ray (b. 1941): English musician (singer, harmonica, and percussion: Moody Blues), 266, 267
Thomas, Rufus (b. 1917): American musician (singer) and songwriter, 127, 275, 358, 380, 402

SUBJECT INDEX 477

Thornton, Willie Mae (b. 1926), American musician (singer), 46
Three Hats for Lisa, 50, 421
Thunderball, 277, 421
Tiger Beat, 156
The Times, 1 London Bridge Street, London, 101
Tina's, Albemarle Street, Mayfair, London, 173
The Tokens (Brooklyn, NY): Hank Medress, Jay Siegel, Mitch Margo, and Phi Margo, 270, 402
Tom Jones/The History of Tom Jones, a Foundling (film and book), 275, 276, 421
Top of the Pops, 112, 162, 164, 169*f*, 176, 179, 189, 197, 214, 227, 236–37, 275, 277, 312–13, 421–22
Top Rank Records, 67
Top Ten Club, 136 Reeperbahn, Saint Pauli District, Hamburg, 78
Topic Records, 314
Torch, Sidney (b. 1908): English musician (piano), arranger, and bandleader, Sidney Torch Orchestra, 298–99
The Tornados (London): Alan Caddy, Clem Cattini, George Bellamy, Heinz Butt, and Roger LaVern, 68–69, 71*f*, 92, 126–27, 188–89, 402, 403
Tottenham Royal (Mecca Dance Hall Tottenham), 415-419 High Road, Tottenham, London, 119
Townshend, Betty (b. Elizabeth Dennis): English musician (singer: Squadronaires) and mother of Peter Townshend, 298–99
Townshend, Cliff (b. 1916): English musician (saxophone: Squadronaires) and father of Peter Townshend, 298–99
Townshend, Peter (b. 1945): English musician (guitar: Who) and songwriter, 147, 297, 298–302, 303, 304, 305, 306–7, 307*f*, 365–66, 404–5
Transatlantic Records, 316
The Tremeloes (see Brian Poole and the Tremeloes)
The Treniers (Alabama): Clifton Trenier, Claude Trenier, Buddy Trenier, Skip Trenier, Gene Gilbeaux, Don Hill, Jimmy Johnson, and Henry Green, 67, 412
Trent, Jackie (b. Yvonne Burgess, 1940): English musician (singer) and songwriter, 232, 233, 324–25, 403
Trident Studios, 17 Saint Anne's Court, Soho, London, 12–13
The Troubadour, 275 Old Brompton Road, Earl's Court, London, 316, 317

Troup, Bobby (b. Robert Troup, Jr, 1918): American songwriter, 285, 371
Troy, Doris (b. Doris Higginsen, 1937): American musician (singer) and songwriter, 162, 354, 370, 399, 403
Tuesday Rendezvous, 90–91, 422
Turing, Alan (b. 1912): English mathematician, 109
Turner, John (b. 1947): English social psychologist, 44
Turner, Victor (b. 1920): British anthropologist, 288
Turton, Geoff (b. 1944): English musician (guitar and singer: Rockin' Berries), 269–70, 387–88
The Twisted Wheel (1) Brazennose Street (off Albert Square), Manchester (1963), 103
The Two Ronnies (London): Ronnie Barker and Ronnie Corbett, 34

The Undertakers (Liverpool): Geoff Nugent, Chris Huston, Bob Evans, Jimmy McManus, Mushy Cooper, Les Maguire, Jackie Lomax, and others, 224
United Artists, 55, 149–50, 151, 152
University College School, Frognal, Hampstead, London, 188
University of Birmingham, 264
University of London, 80, 174–75
Upstairs, Downstairs, 9

Valens, Ritchie (b. Richard Valenzuela, 1941): American musician and songwriter, 46–47, 204, 403, 405
Valentine, Dickie (b. Richard Maxwell, 1929), English musician (singer), 34–35
Valentine, Hilton (b. 1943): English musician (guitar: Animals), 166, 167, 168, 250, 331–32
Valentine, Penny (b. 1943): English music journalist, xii, 202
Valentino, Rudolph (b. Rodolfo Guglielmi di Valentina d'Antonguella): Italian actor, 22, 419
The Valentinos [aka, the Womack Brothers] (Cleveland, Ohio): Friendly Womack, Jr, Curtis Womack, Bobby Womack, Harry Womack, and Cecil Womack, 287, 403
Valli, Frankie (b. 1934): American musician (vocalist: Four Seasons), 275–76, 360, 403
Vaughn, Sarah (b. 1924): American musician (singer), 130
Vee-Jay Records, 147
Venet, Nick (b. Nikolas Venetoulis, 1936): American record producer, 275, 403

The Vernons Girls (Liverpool), Lyn Cornell, Vicky Haseman, Joyce Baker, Jean Owen, Margo Quantrell, Jean Ryder, and others, 65–66, 92–93, 104, 409, 422
Vickers, Mike (b. 1940): English musician (guitar and saxophone: Manfred Mann), 178, 377–78
Vincent, Gene (b. Vincent Craddock, 1935): American musician and songwriter, 31, 62–63, 126, 164
The Vipers Skiffle Group [aka, the Vipers] (London): Wally Whyton, John Martyn, Freddy Lloyd, Tony Tolhurst, and John Pilgrim, 34, 39–40, 81
Von Ryan's Express, 54, 422
Voormann, Klaus (b. 1938): West German musician and artist, 77

WABC, New York, 174
Wace, Robert: English artist manager, 193, 194, 196, 197
Wadmore, Teddy: British musician (electric bass), 335
Wainer, Cherry (b. 1935), South African musician (organ: Lord Rockingham's IX), 65, 376
Walker, Noel: English record producer, 271, 311, 334, 342, 360
The Walker Brothers (Los Angeles and London): Scott Walker, John Walker, and Gary Walker, 181, 275–76, 403–4
  Walker, Gary (b. Gary Leeds, 1942): American musician (voice and drummer: Walker Brothers), 275
  Walker, John (b. John Maus, 1943): American musician (voice and guitarist, Walker Brothers), 275
  Walker, Scott (b. Noel Scott Engel, 1943): American musician (voice and bass: Walker Brothers), 275–76
Waller, Fats (b. Thomas Waller, 1904): American musician (piano), 22, 23, 206, 370, 374, 404
Waller, Gordon (b. 1945): Scottish musician (singer and guitar), 174–76, 382–83
Walsh, Alan: English media reporter, xii
Walsh, Peter: English manager, 117
Ward, Alan (b. 1945): English musician (guitar: Honeycombs), 188, 367
Ward, Stephen (b. 1912): English osteopath, 97
Warwick, Clint (b. Albert Eccles, 1940): English musician (bass, Moody Blues), 266, 267, 380
Warwick, Dionne (b. Marie Dionne Warrick, 1940): American musician (singer), 226, 354

Washington, Baby (b. Justine Washington, 1940): American musician (singer), 214
Watford Town Hall, Rickmansworth Road, Watford, England, 180
Watson, Bernie (b. 1962): British musician (guitar: Screaming Lord Sutch), 70*f*, 125–26, 128*f*, 350
Watts, Charlie (b. 1941): English musician (drums: Rolling Stones), 124, 134, 140, 292, 293, 343, 388–91
Watts, Michael: British music journalist, 206–7
Webb, Dorothy (b. Dorothy Dazely, 1920): mother of Cliff Richard, 37
Webb, Harry (see Cliff Richard)
Webb, Rodger (b. 1904): father of Cliff Richard, 37
Weedon, Bert (b. 1920), English musician (guitar), 67, 404, 422
Weighell, Allan (b. 1922): English musician (bass), xi–xii, 36, 342, 361, 382–83, 398, 400
Weight, Richard: English author, 296
Weil, Cynthia (b. 1940): American songwriter, 211, 251, 332, 343, 350, 357, 387, 403
Welch, Bruce (b. Bruce Cripps, 1941): English musician (guitar: Shadows), 39–40, 43*f*, 66, 67, 92, 148, 354, 386–87, 394–95
Wellesley, Gerald, 7th Duke of Wellington (b. 1885): Anglo-Irish diplomat, 173
Wembley Pool (aka, Empire Pool), Arena Square, Engineers Way, Wembley Park, Wembley, London, 162–63, 326–27
West, Rick (b. Richard Westwood, 1953): English musician (guitar: Tremeloes), 117, 383–84
Westlake, Clive (b. 1932): Welsh songwriter, 162–63, 208, 366, 373
Westminster Palace, 174
Westminster Abbey, 174
Westminster School for Boys, 174–75
Wham!!, 45–46, 62, 422
What a Crazy World, 50, 422
What's New Pussycat, 277, 423
When the Boys Meet the Girls, 274, 423
Whiskey, Nancy (b. Anne Wilson, 1935), Scottish musician (singer and guitarist), 28, 379
White, Andy (b. 1930): Scottish musician (drums), xi–xii, 83, 336, 361, 370, 382–83
White, Chris (b. 1943): English musician (bass: Zombies) and songwriter, 180–81, 406–7
White, Priscilla (see Cilla Black)
Whitehead, Peter (b. 1937): English cinematographer, 293

The Who (West London): Peter Townshend, Roger Daltry, John Entwistle, and Keith Moon, 298–307, 308*f*, 404–5
Wickham, Andrew (b. 1947): English publicist, 236–37
Wickham, Vicki (b. 1939): English television producer and artist manager, 202, 214, 418
Wilde, Marty (b. Reginald Smith, 1939; aka Frere Manston): English musician (singer) and songwriter, 39, 46–48, 49, 60, 61, 405, 411, 412, 417, 422
　The Wildcats (London): Jim Sullivan, Tony Belcher, Bobby Graham, Brian Locking, and others, 46, 47, 60
Wilde, Oscar (b. 1854): Irish poet and playwright, 289
Williams, Allan (b. 1930): English music entrepreneur, 76–77, 79
Williams, Hank (b. 1923): American musician (guitar and singer) and songwriter, 34, 74, 192
Williams, "Big" Joe (b. 1903): American musician (singer and guitar) and songwriter, 367, 401–2
　Joe Williams' Washboard Blues Singers (Chicago, USA): Joe Williams, Dad Tracy, and Chasey Collins, 256, 406
Williams, Les (b. Leslie Williams): English music director and arranger, 234
Williams, Paul (b. 19 May 1948): American music journalist (*Crawdaddy*), 211
Williamson, Sonny Boy, II (b. Alex/Alek "Rice" Miller, 1912): American musician (vocal and harmonica), 166, 249, 257, 265, 285
Willis, Bobby (b. 1942): English songwriter and road manager (Cilla Black), 225–26
Wilson, Brian (b. 1942): American musician (bass and vocals: Beach Boys), songwriter, and record producer, 269
Wilson, Harold (b. 1916): British Labour politician; UK PM 1964-1970, 98, 270, 298
Winwood, Muff (b. Mervyn Winwood, 1943): English musician (bass, Spencer Davis Group) and record producer, 264–65, 351
Winwood, Steve (aka, Steve Anglo, b. 1948): English musician (keyboards, piano, and voice: Spencer Davis Group, Traffic, and Blind Faith) and songwriter, 264–66, 268, 278*f*, 351
Wisner, Jim (b. 1931): American songwriter, 160–61, 354, 382, 388, 393
Wolfe, Tom (b. 1930): American author, 296

Womack, Bobby (b. 1944): American musician (singer and guitar), songwriter, and record producer, 287, 389, 403
Womack, Shirley: American musician (singer) and songwriter, 287, 389, 403
Wood, Art (b. 1937): English musician (singer: Blues Incorporated), 124
Wood, L. G. (b. Leonard George Wood): English record executive, 81
Woodley, Bruce (b. 1942): Australian musician (guitar and singer: Seekers), 312, 393
Woodman, Ken (b. 1928): English musician (trumpet) and arranger, 234–35, 396
Woodward, Tom (see Tom Jones)
World Artists Records, 174
The Worried Men (London): Terry Nelhams-Wright, Freddy Lloyd, Dennis Nelhams, Chas Beaumont, Pete Darby, and Roger Van Engel, 51
Worth, Johnny (aka Les Vandyke, b. John Worsley, 1931): English songwriter, 52, 53, 357
Wright, Denny (b. Denys Wright, 1924): English musician (guitar), 26–27, 352
Wrixon, Eric (b. 1947): Northern Irish musician (keyboards: Them), 255, 256
WWDC, Washington, DC, 145–46
Wyman, Bill (b. William Perks, 1936): English musician (bass: Rolling Stones), 133–34, 140, 285, 286, 288, 293, 388–91
Wynter, Mark (b. Terence Lewis, 1943): English musician (singer), 135

The Yardbirds (London): (1) Chris Dreja, Jim McCarty, Keith Relf, and Paul Samwell-Smith and Anthony "Top" Topham, (2) with Eric Clapton, 246–47, 257–58, 262*f*, 265, 306, 406
York, Peter (b. 1942): English musician (drummer: Spencer Davis Group), 264–65, 351
Young, Muriel (b. 1923): English radio and television presenter, 85, 413, 417, 422
Young, Roy (b. 1934): English musician (singer and piano), 52
Young, Terence (b. 1915), British film director, 40, 412, 414, 419, 421
The Young Ones, 43*f*, 423

Z Cars, 72–73, 92–93, 423
The Zombies (Saint Albans, Hertfordshire): Rod Argent, Paul Atkinson, Colin Blunstone, Hugh Grundy, and Chris White, 171, 179–82, 184*f*, 406–7